Frommer's®

P9-BII-141

Hong Kong

9th Edition

by Beth Reiber

Here's what the critics say about Frommer's:

"Amazingly easy to use. Very portable, very complete."

—*Booklist*

"Detailed, accurate, and easy-to-read information for all price ranges."
—*Glamour Magazine*

"Hotel information is close to encyclopedic."

—*Des Moines Sunday Register*

"Frommer's Guides have a way of giving you a real feel for a place."
—*Knight Ridder Newspapers*

Wiley Publishing, Inc.

About the Author

Long before she could read, **Beth Reiber** spent hours pouring over her grandparents' latest *National Geographic* magazines. After several years in Germany as a freelance travel writer for major U.S. newspapers and in Tokyo as the editor of *Far East Traveler*, she wrote several Frommer's guides, including *Frommer's Japan* and *Frommer's Tokyo*. She also contributes to several Frommer's guides, including *Frommer's Europe by Rail*, *Frommer's USA*, and *Frommer's China*. When not on the road, she resides in Lawrence, Kansas, with her two sons, a dog, and a cat in an 1890 Victorian home.

Published by:

Wiley Publishing, Inc.

111 River St.
Hoboken, NJ 07030-5774

ISBN: 978-0-470-07833-4

Editor: mcd editorial.
Production Editor: Eric T. Schroeder
Cartographer: Roberta Stockwell
Photo Editor: Richard Fox
Production by Wiley Indianapolis Composition Services

Front cover photo: The streets of Hong Kong
Back cover photo: Dragon-boat races in Aberdeen harbor

For information on our other products and services or to obtain technical support, please contact our Customer Care Department within the U.S. at 800/762-2974, outside the U.S. at 317/572-3993 or fax 317/572-4002.

Wiley also publishes its books in a variety of electronic formats. Some content that appears in print may not be available in electronic formats.

Manufactured in the United States of America

5 4 3 2 1

Contents

List of Maps

Acknowledgments

I would like to thank some fine and very special people who graciously extended their help in the preparation of this book: Lillibeth Bishop, Eliza Cheng, and Claire Lau of the Hong Kong Tourist Board; and João H. Rodrigues, Teresa Costa Gomes, and Christina Lau of the Macau Government Tourist Office. A special thanks goes to my sons, Matthias and Johannes, for putting up with my long absences ever since they can remember.

An Invitation to the Reader

In researching this book, we discovered many wonderful places—hotels, restaurants, shops, and more. We're sure you'll find others. Please tell us about them, so we can share the information with your fellow travelers in upcoming editions. If you were disappointed with a recommendation, we'd love to know that, too. Please write to:

Frommer's Hong Kong, 9th Edition
Wiley Publishing, Inc. • 111 River St. • Hoboken, NJ 07030-5774

An Additional Note

Please be advised that travel information is subject to change at any time—and this is especially true of prices. We therefore suggest that you write or call ahead for confirmation when making your travel plans. The authors, editors, and publisher cannot be held responsible for the experiences of readers while traveling. Your safety is important to us, however, so we encourage you to stay alert and be aware of your surroundings. Keep a close eye on cameras, purses, and wallets, all favorite targets of thieves and pickpockets.

Other Great Guides for Your Trip:

Frommer's Beijing

Frommer's China

Frommer's Shanghai

Frommer's Southeast Asia

Suzy Gershman's Born to Shop Hong Kong, Shanghai & Beijing

Frommer's Star Ratings, Icons & Abbreviations

Every hotel, restaurant, and attraction listing in this guide has been ranked for quality, value, service, amenities, and special features using a **star-rating system.** In country, state, and regional guides, we also rate towns and regions to help you narrow down your choices and budget your time accordingly. Hotels and restaurants are rated on a scale of zero (recommended) to three stars (exceptional). Attractions, shopping, nightlife, towns, and regions are rated according to the following scale: zero stars (recommended), one star (highly recommended), two stars (very highly recommended), and three stars (must-see).

In addition to the star-rating system, we also use **seven feature icons** that point you to the great deals, in-the-know advice, and unique experiences that separate travelers from tourists. Throughout the book, look for:

Finds	Special finds—those places only insiders know about
Fun Fact	Fun facts—details that make travelers more informed and their trips more fun
Kids	Best bets for kids and advice for the whole family
Moments	Special moments—those experiences that memories are made of
Overrated	Places or experiences not worth your time or money
Tips	Insider tips—great ways to save time and money
Value	Great values—where to get the best deals

The following **abbreviations** are used for credit cards:

AE	American Express	DISC	Discover	V	Visa
DC	Diners Club	MC	MasterCard		

Frommers.com

Now that you have the guidebook to a great trip, visit our website at **www.frommers.com** for additional travel information on more than 3,500 destinations. We update features regularly to give you instant access to the most current trip-planning information available. At Frommers.com, you'll find scoops on the best airfares, lodging rates, and car rental bargains. You can even book your travel online through our travel booking partners. Other popular features include:

- Online updates of our most popular guidebooks
- Vacation sweepstakes and contest giveaways
- Newsletter highlighting the hottest travel trends
- Online travel message boards with featured travel discussions

What's New in Hong Kong

Here are the latest openings, offerings, changes, and events in Hong Kong.

PLANNING YOUR TRIP Oasis Hong Kong (© **0844/482-2323** in the U.K.; www.oasishongkong.com), a low-fare, long-haul airline with inexpensive seats even for business class, made its inaugural flight from London Gatwick to Hong Kong in October 2006. Future plans call for extending service from Hong Kong to Oakland, California, and Chicago.

GETTING TO KNOW HONG KONG The location of the **Star Ferry** in the Central District has moved from its pier next to City Hall to the Central Ferry Piers. While the new location is convenient for transfers to ferries heading to the islands, it's a hike from Central's business core.

For complete information on getting to know Hong Kong, see chapter 4.

WHERE TO STAY The **Mandarin Oriental**, 5 Connaught Rd., Central (© **800/526-6566** in the U.S. and Canada), which closed for a top-to-bottom renovation, now offers larger, more contemporary rooms. To fend off public outcry, however, it retained many of its beloved institutions—like the Captain's Bar—with faithful remakes.

Meanwhile, competition in Central has heated up with the addition of two new luxury hotels. The gorgeous **Four Seasons Hotel Hong Kong,** 8 Finance St. (© **800/819-5053** in the U.S. and Canada), boasts the best location money can buy, right between the Central Ferry

Piers and Hong Kong Station. Also capturing the well-heeled travel market is **Landmark Mandarin Oriental,** 15 Queen's Rd. Central (© **800/526-6566** in the U.S. and Canada), a boutique version of its sister hotel with 113 contemporary rooms most notable for huge bathrooms and round tubs.

For new, cheaper alternatives, Causeway Bay is the place to be. Most noteworthy are **Express by Holiday Inn,** 33 Sharp St. East (© **888/465-4329** in the U.S. and Canada), a no-frills chain with decent-size rooms, and **Lanson Place Boutique Hotel & Residences,** 133 Leighton Rd. (© **852/3477 6888**), which offers stylish rooms complete with kitchenettes and home theater systems, great for longer stays.

Unable to compete (and pay the high price of rent), the **Hyatt Regency Hong Kong** has closed, to be replaced by an office building.

For complete information on Hong Kong's hotels, see chapter 5.

WHERE TO DINE The hottest restaurant of the moment—for those who can afford its prices and are savvy enough to book well in advance—is **Caprice,** in the Four Seasons (© **852/ 3196 8888**). Serving the French creations of chef Vincent Thiery, it boasts a dramatic setting, great views, an impressive wine list, and—a growing trend in the dining experience—a Chef's Table with an up-close view of kitchen activity.

For fun, relaxed dining, the best newcomer is **Top Deck, at the Jumbo**

(© 852/2553 3331), an open-air restaurant atop the Jumbo Kingdom floating restaurant in Aberdeen. Seafood is its main draw, but the impressive Sunday seafood brunch, children's menu and play corner, afternoon tea buffet, and live jazz Wednesday evenings make this a great destination for any occasion.

Vegetarians rejoice! Hong Kong, which is woefully short on meatless options aside from a few common dishes served at Chinese and Indian restaurants, finally has **Life,** 10 Shelley St. in SoHo (© 852/2810 9777), serving vegetarian and vegan dishes in a laid-back, bohemian atmosphere.

Partyers who want their breakfast at 4am—or 4pm for that matter—should hit **The Flying Pan,** with two locations at 9 Old Bailey St., Central (© 852/2140 6333), and 81–85 Lockhart Rd., Wan Chai (© 852/2528 9997), both open 24 hours and offering huge American and British breakfasts with bottomless cups of coffee.

For complete information on Hong Kong's restaurants, see chapter 6.

EXPLORING HONG KONG Symphony of Lights, an 18-minute multimedia light and laser extravaganza shown nightly at 8pm, has now expanded to both sides of the harbor and is projected from more than 30 buildings. In addition to the Tsim Sha Tsui waterfront, another favorite viewing spot is Bauhinia Square on the Wan Chai waterfront.

Peak Tower, Victoria Peak (© 852/2849 7654), has been totally renovated and now features a rooftop observation deck with 360-degree views, an expanded Madame Tussauds Hong Kong, and more options in dining and shopping. **Chi Lin Buddhist Nunnery,** Chi Lin Road, Diamond Hill (© 852/2354 1604), constructed in the 1990s using ancient techniques, now has a garden, styled after famous gardens in Suzhou.

For complete information on exploring Hong Kong, see chapters 7 and 8.

SIDE TRIPS FROM HONG KONG There are new attractions in the hinterlands as well. The ferry and bus ride to the Giant Tian Tan Buddha on Lantau is a must, but the new **Skyrail cable car** between the Buddha and Tung Chung (terminus of a subway line) makes for a great 25-minute scenic return trip. Also new near the Buddha are **Wisdom Path,** a pathway designed in a figure eight and marked by 38 pillars bearing an old Sutra; and **Ngong Ping Village** (© 852/2109 9898), with a museum devoted to the life of Siddhartha Gautama (the man who became Buddha), an animation theater that tells a tale of greed and friendship, restaurants, and shops.

In the New Territories, there's the new **Hong Kong Wetland Park,** Tin Shui Wai (© 852/3152 2666), with a visitor center that explains the importance of wetlands for our planet, along with marshes, mudflats, mangroves, and other habitats, viewable from boardwalks.

For more information on exploring outlying areas in Hong Kong, see chapter 11.

MACAU What isn't new in Macau, the Las Vegas of Asia? The Hyatt has closed, but new hotels that have signed on to make their debut over the next few years include a Sheraton, Hilton, Four Seasons, Shangri-La, Conrad, and a whole new Hyatt. A number of U.S.-owned casino/hotel properties will also open over the next year, including Venetian-Macao-Resort Hotel, MGM Grand Macau, and Wynn Macau. Luckily, for those more interested in this former Portuguese enclave's past than its high-dollar developments, Macau's historic center has recently been declared a UNESCO World Heritage Site.

For complete information on what's developing in Macau, see chapter 12.

The Best of Hong Kong

Every time I come to Hong Kong, I feel as though I've wandered onto a movie set. Maybe I'm an incurable romantic, but when I stand at the railing of the famous Star Ferry as it glides across the harbor, ride a rickety old tram as it winds its way across Hong Kong Island, or marvel anew at the stunning views afforded from atop Victoria Peak, I can't help but think I must have somehow landed in the middle of an epic drama where the past has melted into the present. So many images float by—wooden boats bobbing up and down in the harbor beside huge ocean liners; crumbling tenements next to ultra-modern high-rises; squalid alleys behind luxury hotels; old Chinese people pushing wheelbarrows as Rolls-Royces glide by; market vendors selling chicken feet and dried squid while talking on cellular phones.

In fact, one of the most striking characteristics of Hong Kong is this interweaving of seeming contradictions and the interplay of the exotic and the technically advanced. There are as many skyscrapers here as you're likely to see anywhere, but they're built with bamboo scaffolding. Historic trams rumble through Central, while below ground is one of the most efficient subways in the world, complete with the world's first "contactless" tickets, cards that can be waved over a scanner without even taking them out of your purse or wallet. The city has what are arguably some of the best and most sophisticated restaurants in the world, but it also has *dai pai dong,* street-side food stalls. Hong Kong is home to one of the world's largest shopping malls, but there are also lively street markets virtually everywhere.

Because of these dazzling contrasts, Hong Kong offers visitors something unique—the chance to experience a vibrant Chinese city without sacrificing the comforts of home. To be sure, much of Hong Kong's Western fabric comes from the legacy left by the British, who ruled the colony until 1997, when it was handed back to China as a Special Administrative Region (thus the SAR abbreviation you'll see there and throughout this book). British influence is still evident everywhere, from Hong Kong's school system to its free-market economy, from its rugby teams to its double-decker buses, and from English pubs and tea in the afternoon to (my favorite) orderly queues. But though the city was molded by the British, it has always been, at heart, Chinese, with Chinese medicine shops, street vendors, lively dim sum restaurants, old men taking their caged birds for walks, and colorful festivals. Indeed, for the casual visitor, Hong Kong seems little changed since the 1997 handover. No doubt some visitors remain oblivious to even the most visible sign of that change: the replacement of the Union Jack and old flag of the Crown Colony of Hong Kong with the red, starred flag of China and the new red Hong Kong flag with its emblem of the bauhinia flower.

Hong Kong was founded as a place to conduct business and to trade, and it continues to serve that purpose both aggressively and successfully. Hong Kong is the "Wall Street of Asia," with banking, international insurance, advertising, and

Hong Kong Region

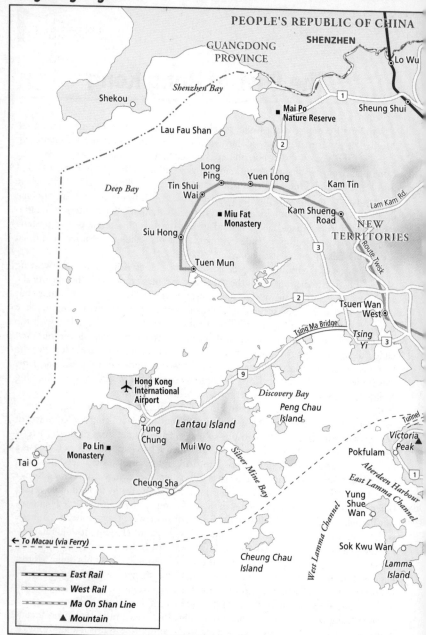

PEOPLE'S REPUBLIC OF CHINA

GUANGDONG PROVINCE

SHENZHEN

⊙ Lo Wu

Shenzhen Bay

Shekou ○

(1)

■ Mai Po Nature Reserve

Sheung Shui

Lau Fau Shan ○

(2)

Long Ping ⊙

Tin Shui Wai ⊙

Yuen Long ⊙

Kam Tin

Deep Bay

■ Miu Fat Monastery

Kam Shueng Road ⊙

Lam Kam Rd.

NEW TERRITORIES

Siu Hong ⊙

Route Twisk

Tuen Mun ⊙

(3)

(2)

Tsuen Wan West ⊙

Tsing Ma Bridge

Tsing Yi

(3)

(9)

✈ Hong Kong International Airport

Discovery Bay

Peng Chau Island

Tung Chung ○

Lantau Island

Mui Wo ○

Tunnel

Victoria Peak ▲

Pokfulam

Aberdeen Harbour

East Lamma Channel

Po Lin Monastery ■

Tai O ○

Silver Mine Bay

(1)

Cheung Sha ○

Yung Shue Wan ○

← To Macau (via Ferry)

West Lamma Channel

Sok Kwu Wan ○

Lamma Island

Cheung Chau Island

▬▬▬▬	**East Rail**
▬▬▬▬	**West Rail**
▬▬▬▬	**Ma On Shan Line**
▲	**Mountain**

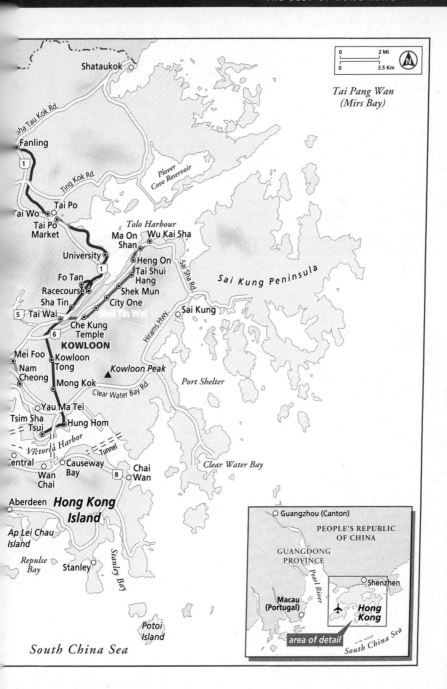

Shataukok

Tai Pang Wan
(Mirs Bay)

0   2 Mi
0   3.5 Km

Sha Tau Kok Rd.

Fanling

1

Ting Kok Rd.

Plover
Cove Reservoir

Tai Wo

Tai Po

Tai Po
Market

Tolo Harbour

Ma On   Wu Kai Sha
Shan

University

1

Heng On
Tai Shui
Hang

Sai Sha Rd.

Sai Kung Peninsula

Fo Tan

Racecourse

Shek Mun

City One

Sha Tin

Tai Wai

Sai Kung

5

Sai Tin Wai

Che Kung
Temple

6

Hirams Hwy.

KOWLOON

Mei Foo

Kowloon
Tong

Nam
Cheong

Kowloon Peak

Port Shelter

Mong Kok

Clear Water Bay Rd.

Yau Ma Tei

Tsim Sha
Tsui

Hung Hom

Victoria Harbor

Tunnel

Central

Causeway
Bay

Chai
Wan

Clear Water Bay

Wan
Chai

8

Aberdeen   **Hong Kong
Island**

Ap Lei Chau
Island

Repulse
Bay

Stanley

Stanley Bay

Potoi
Island

South China Sea

Guangzhou (Canton)

PEOPLE'S REPUBLIC
OF CHINA

GUANGDONG
PROVINCE

Pearl River

Shenzhen

Macau
(Portugal)

*Hong
Kong*

area of detail

South China Sea

publishing among its biggest industries. Hong Kong also boasts the world's eighth-largest trading economy and is one of the world's leading exporters of toys, garments, and watches.

Little wonder, then, that as a duty-free port, Hong Kong attracts approximately 21 million visitors a year, making tourism one of its leading industries. Shopping is one of the main reasons people come here, and at first glance, the city does seem rather like one huge department store. But there's much more to Hong Kong than shopping. There's also wining, dining, and sightseeing, as well as isolated places to get away from it all.

For those who wish to journey farther afield, Macau, a former Portuguese enclave handed back to China in 1999, is just an hour's boat ride away; and vast China itself lies just beyond Hong Kong's border, making it the perfect gateway for trips to Guangzhou, Shanghai, Beijing, and beyond.

The more you search for in Hong Kong, the more you'll find. Before long, you, too, may find yourself swept up in the drama.

1 The Most Unforgettable Travel Experiences

• **Observing a Chinese Festival:** Hong Kong has lots of colorful festivals, featuring everything from dragon boat races to celebrations honoring Tin Hau, goddess of the sea. Cantonese opera, performed on temporary stages, is also common at Chinese festivals. See "Hong Kong Calendar of Events" in chapter 2.

• **Riding the Star Ferry:** To reacquaint myself with the city, one of the first things I do on each return trip is to hop aboard the Star Ferry for one of the most dramatic—and cheapest—5-minute boat rides in the world. Hong Kong's harbor is one of the world's busiest, and beyond it rises one of earth's most breathtaking skylines. See p. 59.

• **Gazing upon Hong Kong from Victoria Peak:** You don't know Hong Kong until you've seen it from here. Take the funicular to Victoria Peak, famous for its views of Central, Victoria Harbour, South China Sea, Kowloon, and undulating hills beyond, followed by a 1-hour circular hike and a meal with a view. Don't miss the nighttime view, one of the most spectacular and romantic in the world. See p. 164.

• **Listening to the World's Largest Professional Chinese Orchestra:** Established 30 years ago, the 80-member Hong Kong Chinese Orchestra is the world's largest, playing traditional and modern Chinese instruments in orchestrations that combine Chinese and Western musical elements. See p. 224.

• **Celebrating Sundown with a Cocktail:** Many hotel lounges offer spectacular views of the city as well as live music. As the sun disappears, watch the city explode in neon. See "The Bar, Pub & Lounge Scene" section of chapter 10, beginning on p. 228, for venues with especially good views.

• **Partying until Dawn at Lan Kwai Fong:** It's standing room only at bars and pubs in Central's most famous nightlife district, where the action spills out onto the street and continues until dawn. Other burgeoning nightlife districts include SoHo, Knutsford Terrace, and Wan Chai. See chapter 10.

• **Paying Respects at the Big Buddha:** Laze on the open aft deck during the 50-minute ferry ride to Lantau island (and enjoy great views of the harbor and skyline along the way), followed by a hair-raising bus ride over lush hills to see the world's largest, seated, outdoor bronze Buddha, located at the Po Lin Monastery. Complete your pilgrimage with a vegetarian meal at the monastery and a visit to Ngong Ping Village with its Walking with Buddha museum, and then make your return trip via a new cable car offering more great views. See the "Lantau" section of chapter 11, beginning on p. 245.

- **Zipping Over to Macau:** Macau, a Portuguese outpost until it was handed back to the Chinese in 1999, is just an hour away by jetfoil and offers a fascinating blend of Chinese and Mediterranean lifestyles, evident in its spicy cuisine, colorful architecture, temples, churches, and handful of special-interest museums. It's also famous for its Las Vegas–style casinos. Although you can "do" Macau in a day, I strongly urge you to spend at least a couple days here. You'll save money doing so, too: Macau's hotels and restaurants cost a fraction of their Hong Kong counterparts. See chapter 12.

2 The Best Splurge Hotels

- **Hotel InterContinental Hong Kong** (18 Salisbury Rd., Tsim Sha Tsui; ✆ **800/327-0200** in the U.S., or 852/2721 1211): No hotel lobby boasts a better view of Victoria Harbour and Hong Kong Island than the light-infused lobby of this standout property, right at water's edge in Tsim Sha Tsui. State-of-the-art rooms (most with harbor views), a spa renowned for its anti-jet-lag and healing treatments, restaurants that are as fun as they are excellent, and free tai chi and yoga classes make this one of the city's top choices. See p. 79.

- **Four Seasons Hotel Hong Kong** (8 Finance St., Central; ✆ **800/819-5053** in the U.S., or 852/3196 8888): A strategic location near the Central Ferry Piers, Hong Kong Station (with direct access to the airport), MTR subway, and Central's financial district make this contemporary property number one for convenience. Yet it cocoons guests from the mad whirl of central Hong Kong with the best money can buy, including a luxury spa, outdoor pools and Jacuzzis with great harbor views, top-notch restaurants, and rooms to die for. See p. 80.

- **The Peninsula** (Salisbury Rd., Tsim Sha Tsui; ✆ **800/462-7899** in the U.S., or 852/2920 2888): The grand old dame of Hong Kong, this historic hotel, built in 1928, exudes elegance and colonial splendor, with one of the most famous, ornate lobbies in town, a must for afternoon tea. A tower, added in 1993, gave the Peninsula an edge over newer competitors by adding well-equipped, spacious rooms and a top-floor restaurant designed by Philippe Starck. A newly added spa, classes ranging from cooking to tai chi, Hong Kong's most venerable restaurants, and outstanding service assure this historic hotel a top rating despite newer and more glamorous competitors. See p. 86.

- **Island Shangri-La Hong Kong** (Pacific Place, Central; ✆ **866/565-5050** in the U.S., or 852/2877 3838): There's no mistaking you're anywhere but Asia in Hong Kong Island's tallest hotel, adorned with lush Tai Ping carpets, artistic flower arrangements, and more than 500 paintings and artwork, including the world's largest Chinese landscape painting. Spacious rooms combine

Asian touches (like Chinese lacquerware TV cabinets) with up-to-date technology (like LCD TVs and DVD players), but the top-floor French restaurant opts for old-world charm as it wows with one of the best dining views in Hong Kong. See p. 88.

3 The Best Moderately Priced Hotels

- **Eaton Hotel** (380 Nathan Rd., Yau Ma Tei; ℂ **800/223-5652** in the U.S., or 852/2782 1818): This efficient hotel goes the extra mile, with free daily guided tours of the nearby Temple Street Night Market, a four-story glass-enclosed atrium lobby overlooking a garden terrace, a rooftop pool, and free Internet service in its cybercafe. See p. 91.
- **Bishop Lei International House** (4 Robinson Rd., Mid-Levels; ℂ **852/ 2868 0828**): There's nothing fancy about this hotel, but I love its location near the Central–Mid-Levels Escalator in a residential neighborhood, its outstanding views from otherwise standard rooms, its coffee shop with an outdoor terrace, and its outdoor pool. A great choice for expat wannabes. See p. 94.
- **Jia** (1–5 Irving St., Causeway Bay; ℂ **852/3196 9000**): Designed by Philippe Starck, this boutique hotel is Hong Kong's hippest, with 54 stylish rooms complete with kitchenettes and entertainment centers. Guests also enjoy a host of freebies, including free local calls, free Internet access, free breakfast and cocktail hour, free access to a nearby gym, and—for long-staying guests—a free massage. See p. 95.
- **Lanson Place Boutique Hotel & Residences** (133 Leighton Rd., Causeway Bay; ℂ **852/3477 6888**): This Jia competitor offers much of the same at slightly lower prices, including upbeat, contemporary rooms with kitchenettes (and a welcoming basket of goodies, large LCD TVs, and DVD players (there's a free DVD library). Breakfast and wireless connections are also free. See p. 96.

4 The Most Unforgettable Dining Experiences

- **Eating Your Way through China:** There's no better place in the world to sample regional Chinese cuisine than Hong Kong, where you can eat everything from the ubiquitous Cantonese food to Sichuan, Shanghainese, Hunanese, Beijing, Chiu Chow, and Pekingese dishes. See chapter 6.
- **Stuffing Yourself at a Buffet Spread:** If you have a big appetite or like variety in your meals, the best Hong Kong bargain is the all-you-can-eat buffet spread. Almost all hotels offer buffet lunches and dinners; other restaurants may feature buffets for lunch. Most offer an assortment of international fare, from Japanese sushi and Chinese dishes to pasta and carveries. See chapter 6.
- **Dining with a View:** Enjoy Chinese or Western cuisine at one of Hong Kong's many restaurants that offer spectacular views of either Kowloon (with its glowing neon lights) or Hong Kong Island (with its skyscrapers and Victoria Peak). In fact, Hong Kong boasts so many restaurants with views, the dilemma will be in the choosing. The absolute winners? Those atop Victoria Peak. See

"Around Hong Kong Island" in chapter 6, beginning on p. 152.

- **Dining on Dim Sum:** Nothing conveys a sense of Chinese life more vividly than a visit to a crowded, lively Cantonese restaurant for breakfast or lunch, when you can feast on spring rolls, steamed dumplings, and other goodies served in bamboo steamers. See the "Dim Sum" section in chapter 6, beginning on p. 155, for more on Hong Kong's dim sum restaurants.

- **Taking High Tea at a Posh Hotel:** The British rulers may be gone, but their legacy lives on in the afternoon tea. Virtually all upper-class hotels offer afternoon tea, but my favorites are those offered by The Peninsula and Hotel InterContinental. Come for afternoon tea, nibble on finger sandwiches, and gaze away. See p. 159.

- **Relaxing at an Open-Air Seafood Restaurant:** Get rid of stress by relaxing over a meal of fresh seafood at one of Hong Kong's rural waterfront seafood restaurants. My favorite place is Lamma island. See p. 253.

5 The Best Things to Do for Free (or Almost)

- **Expand Your Horizons at Hong Kong's Museums:** A Museum Pass allowing entry to five major museums, covering everything from Chinese art and Hong Kong's history to space, science, and cultural life in the New Territories, costs just HK$30 (US$3.90/£2.10). Or, go on Wednesday, when these same museums are absolutely free. For more information on Hong Kong's museums, see chapter 7.

- **Explore Hong Kong's Parks:** Hong Kong's parks are destinations in themselves, offering a wide range of free activities and attractions. Among the most unique are Kowloon Walled City Park, once a no-man's land of slums and now a Chinese garden, and Hong Kong Park, with a huge aviary and the Flagstaff House Museum of Tea Ware. For descriptions of Hong Kong's many parks, see chapter 7.

- **Meet the People:** Learn about pearls, jade, feng shui (geomancy), Cantonese opera, and other cultural traditions on free, 1-hour tours and lectures given by local experts. There are even free harbor cruises aboard an authentic junk. To learn more about the Hong Kong Tourism Board's "Meet the People" program, stop by a HKTB Visitor Information & Services Centre for the *Cultural Kaleidoscope* brochure, which outlines the current free offerings. See p. 178.

- **Get Up Early to Watch Tai Chi:** Before breakfast, head to one of Hong Kong's many parks to watch people going through the slow, graceful motions of tai chi, or shadow boxing. For the best viewing, go to Kowloon Park, Hong Kong Park, Victoria Park, or the Zoological and Botanical Gardens (see section 4 of chapter 7, beginning on p. 172, for more on these parks and gardens). You can even participate in free practice sessions, held 4 mornings a week on the Tsim Sha Tsui waterfront promenade. See p. 181.

- **Explore the Western District:** Produce, bolts of cloth, live snakes, ginseng, dried seafood, Chinese herbs and medicines, a historic temple, a museum dedicated to Chinese and Western medicine, and antiques and collectibles are just some of the things you'll see while strolling through one of Hong Kong's most fascinating neighborhoods. See p. 188.

- **Stroll Tsim Sha Tsui's Waterfront:** There's a pedestrian promenade that stretches from the Star Ferry eastward along the Sha Tsui and Tsim Sha Tsui East waterfront, providing close-up views of the harbor and Hong Kong Island with its skyscrapers. After dark, this is a wonderful romantic stroll, with the lights of Hong Kong Island shimmering across the water. A bonus: Every evening at 8pm, Hong Kong puts on a spectacular laser-and-light show projected from skyscrapers on both sides of the harbor. The best place to see this colorful extravaganza? On the Tsim Sha Tsui waterfront. See p. 199.

- **Imbibe at Happy Hour at a British Pub:** To save money engaged in our favorite sport (we are talking darts here, aren't we?), end a busy day of sightseeing and shopping by rubbing elbows with Hong Kong's working population as they take advantage of happy-hour prices in British pubs throughout the city. Most pubs and bars offer a happy hour that can stretch on for hours, with two drinks for the price of one or drinks at reduced prices. See "The Bar, Pub & Lounge Scene" section of chapter 10, beginning on p. 228, for more on Hong Kong's pubs and bars.

6 The Best Shopping Experiences

- **Looking for Chinese Souvenirs:** Hong Kong has some great Chinese emporiums, selling vases, vase stands, porcelain figurines, chinaware, calligraphy brushes, bird cages, jade, jewelry, silk jackets, furniture, teas, and various Chinese crafts and products. See chapter 9.

- **Browsing Antiques Shops on Hollywood Road:** Whether you have thousands of dollars to spend on Ming dynasty heirlooms or just a couple of bucks for a snuff bottle, there's something for everyone in the dozens of antiques shops lining this famous Hong Kong Island road and from outdoor vendor stalls on nearby Cat Street. A sightseeing bonus is Man Mo Temple (p. 171), Hong Kong's oldest temple, on Hollywood Road. See p. 194 and the "Antiques & Collectibles" section of chapter 9, beginning on p. 208.

- **Window-Shopping on Nathan Road:** Open-fronted clothing boutiques, jewelry stores, camera shops, tailors, tourists from around the world, international cuisine, huge neon signs, and whirling traffic combine to make this boulevard Hong Kong's most famous shopping street. See p. 199.

- **Feeling Groovy at Shanghai Tang:** This 1930s-style Chinese department store is oh-so-chic, with lime-green- or fuchsia-colored jackets, 1930s reproduction home decor, and more. The shopping bag that comes with your purchase is a bonus—just way too cool—and the shop's free postcards are also pretty fab. See p. 212.

- **Bargaining at a Street Market:** Hong Kong has more street markets than you can shake a stick at, located on both sides of the harbor and in operation from morning to night. Most famous is Temple Street Night Market, where you can shop for casual clothing, music, toys, and accessories; enjoy a meal at a *dai pai dong* (roadside food stall); watch amateur street musicians; and have your fortune told. See p. 217.

- **Bargain-Hunting in Stanley:** Stall after stall of casual wear, silk clothing, tennis shoes, accessories, and souvenirs and crafts imported from China make this a shopper's paradise.

And after a day of bargaining, I like to recuperate in one of Stanley's trendy yet casual restaurants. See p. 218.

- **Shopping for Everything at a Mall:** Hong Kong is famous for its shopping malls, and with good reason. Ranging from humongous affairs like Harbour City to chic, high-end complexes like ifc mall, shopping malls are great escapes on humid or rainy days and offer everything from clothing and toys to electronics and antiques. See "Megamalls & Shopping Centers" in chapter 9, beginning on p. 219.

- **Visiting a Tailor:** Nothing beats the thrill of having something custom-made to fit you perfectly. If this is your dream, make a trek to a tailor one of your first priorities so that you'll have time for several fittings. See p. 220.

7 The Best Activities for Families

- **Running Free in Hong Kong's City Parks:** Hong Kong's parks are great destinations for families. Children can go swimming or explore playgrounds at Kowloon Park (including one with restored fortifications and cannon emplacements), see jaguars and monkeys at the Zoological and Botanical Gardens, and walk through an aviary at Hong Kong Park. See p. 172.

- **Cavorting with Mickey at Hong Kong Disneyland:** The smallest of the world's Disney properties, Hong Kong Disneyland nevertheless has the usual attractions, high-powered shows, and fireworks extravaganza, as well as the world's only Fantasy Gardens, where kids can meet famous Disney characters. A must for families crossing all Disney properties off their to-do list. See p. 174.

- **Regressing to Childhood at Ocean Park:** Southeast Asia's largest oceanarium and fun park boasts one of the world's longest and fastest roller coasters among its many thrill rides; a great cable-car ride with breathtaking views of the South China Sea; playgrounds just for kids; and a theater with seats that move with the action on the screen. If it's wildlife you're wild about, you'll find the world's largest reef aquarium, a shark tank with an underwater pedestrian tunnel, a fascinating collection of weird and wonderful goldfish, an aviary and butterfly dome, pandas, and a dolphin and killer-whale show. A must for kids of all ages. See p. 175.

- **Heading for the Beach:** Life's a beach at a number of Hong Kong Island destinations, but to make an excursion out of it, take a ferry (kids love that!) to one of the outlying islands like Cheung Chau or Lamma, where there are beaches with lifeguards, changing rooms, and showers. See p. 180, 247, and 250.

8 The Best Offbeat Experiences

- **Taking a Tram:** Take a double-decker tram ride from one end of Hong Kong Island to the other for an unparalleled view of life in the crowded city as you pass skyscrapers, street markets, traditional Chinese shops, and department stores. See p. 58.

- **Hopping Aboard the Central–Mid-Levels Escalator:** Hop aboard the world's longest covered people mover as it snakes its way uphill in a series of escalators. You can hop off at one of 29 exits to enjoy a drink or meal at one of the many establishments along its link, or take it to the top for a 20-minute ride. See p. 61.

• **Having Your Fortune Told:** Want to know about your future love life, marriage, family, or career? Consult one of Hong Kong's many fortunetellers; those who speak English can be found at Man Mo Temple in the Western District, Wong Tai Sin temple, and the Tin Hau Temple near the Temple Street Night Market. See p. 171 and 202, respectively.

• **Hearing the Birds Sing at Yuen Po Street Bird Garden:** See pampered birds at this unusual garden, brought by their owners so they can sing and communicate with other birds on their daily outing. Vendors sell exotic birds, wooden bird cages, porcelain bird dishes, and other paraphernalia. See p. 173 and 202.

• **Escaping to the New Territories:** The New Territories are a vast area stretching from the densely populated area of Kowloon to the Chinese border. Almost half of Hong Kong's population is housed here in huge satellite towns, but pockets of rural life and preserved country parks remain. One of the best things to do is follow a self-guided hike that will take you past traditional Chinese homes, temples, and other buildings in a small village. See p. 237.

• **Hiking across Lamma:** An excursion to this outlying island will do your soul good. Start with the 35-minute ferry trip, followed by a 90-minute hike across the island, perhaps some swimming at a beach, and finally a meal of fresh seafood at an open-air waterfront restaurant. See the "Lamma" section of chapter 11, beginning on p. 250.

2

Planning Your Trip to Hong Kong

Much of the anxiety associated with travel comes from a fear of the unknown—not knowing what to expect can give even seasoned travelers butterflies. This chapter will help you prepare for your trip to Hong Kong—but don't stop here. Reading through the other chapters before leaving will also help you in your planning. Just learning that Hong Kong has hiking trails and beaches, for example, may prompt you to pack your hiking boots or swimsuit. However, keep in mind that information given here may change during the lifetime of this book.

1 Visitor Information

The **Hong Kong Tourism Board (HKTB)** offers a wealth of free information for travelers. See "Orientation" in chapter 4 for a complete listing of tourist offices in Hong Kong itself and a rundown of available booklets and brochures.

HKTB ONLINE

You can have a virtual visit to Hong Kong by visiting HKTB's home page at **www.discoverhongkong.com**. The site provides a comprehensive overview of Hong Kong—maps of the region, major attractions, a detailed weekly calendar of performing arts and festivals, listings for hotels and restaurants, and guided tours. It even provides e-ticketing service so you can book shows, events, and concerts online before your arrival. And if you're traveling to Hong Kong with your PDA (Palm or Pocket PC), there's a free download from www.discoverhongkong.com of the *Hong Kong Leisure Guide for Business Travellers,* which includes maps (you can even pinpoint your location in Hong Kong if your PDA is equipped with a GPS device), information on sightseeing, shopping, and dining, and voice readings of useful Cantonese phrases. A similar program called **Mobile Host** is available for travelers with mobile phones; see "Visitor Information" in chapter 4.

OVERSEAS

Although the information stocked by HKTB offices abroad is sometimes not as up-to-date or as thorough as that available in Hong Kong itself or through the Internet (see above), it's worth contacting a local HKTB office before leaving home for general information and a map.

In the **United States:** General information can be obtained by calling © **800/282-4582.** HKTB offices are located at 115 E. 54th St., 2nd Floor, New York, NY 10022-4512 (© **212/421-3382;** fax 212/421-8428; nycwwo@hktb.com); and 10940 Wilshire Blvd., Suite 2050, Los Angeles, CA 90024-3915 (© **310/208-4582;** fax 310/208-1869; laxwwo@hktb.com).

In **Canada:** Hong Kong Trade Centre, 9 Temperance St., Toronto, ON, Canada M5H 1Y6 (© **800/563-4582** or 416/366-2389; fax 416/366-1098; yyzwwo@hktb.com).

In the **United Kingdom:** 6 Grafton St., London W1S 4EQ, England (© **20/7533-7100;** fax 20/7533-7111; lonwwo@hktb.com).

In **Australia:** Hong Kong House, Level 4, 80 Druitt St., Sydney, NSW 2000, Australia (© **02/9283-3083;** fax 02/9283-3383; sydwwo@hktb.com).

2 Entry Requirements & Customs

ENTRY REQUIREMENTS

The only document most tourists need to enter the Hong Kong Special Administrative Region (SAR) is a passport, valid for at least 6 months beyond the planned departure date from Hong Kong. Americans, Australians, New Zealanders, Canadians, and other British Commonwealth citizens can stay for 90 days without a visa, while citizens of the United Kingdom can stay for 180 days without a visa. Immigration officers may also ask arriving visitors for proof of onward travel or a return ticket (unless they are in transit to mainland China or Macau) and proof that they have adequate funds for their stay in Hong Kong (generally, a confirmed hotel reservation and a credit card will suffice).

Once in Hong Kong, visitors must carry photo identification at all times, such as a passport or driver's license. Safeguard your passport in an inconspicuous, inaccessible place like a money belt. If you lose it, visit the nearest consulate of your native country as soon as possible for a replacement. As an extra safety precaution, it's a good idea to photocopy your passport.

If you plan to make an excursion to mainland China, you'll need a visa, which can easily be obtained in Hong Kong. Applications require one photo and generally take 3 working days to process (see section 3 of chapter 11, beginning on p. 254, for information on obtaining a visa to China).

PASSPORTS

For information on how to get a passport, go to "Passports" in the "Fast Facts: Hong Kong" section of chapter 4; the websites listed provide downloadable passport applications as well as the current fees for processing passport applications. For an up-to-date, country-by-country listing of passport requirements around the world, go to the "Foreign Entry Requirement" Web page of the U.S. State Department at **http://travel.state.gov**.

CUSTOMS

ENTERING HONG KONG   Visitors 18 and older are allowed to bring into the SAR duty-free a 1-liter (34-oz.) bottle of alcohol and 200 cigarettes (or 50 cigars or 250 grams of tobacco). For more information, go to www.info.gov.hk/customs.

WHAT YOU CAN TAKE HOME FROM HONG KONG
U.S. Citizens

For specifics on what you can bring back and the corresponding fees, download the invaluable free pamphlet *Know Before You Go* online at **www.cbp.gov**. (Click on "Travel," and then click on "Know Before You Go! Online Brochure") Or contact the **U.S. Customs & Border Protection (CBP),** 1300 Pennsylvania Ave., NW, Washington, DC 20229 (© **877/287-8667**) and request the pamphlet.

Canadian Citizens

For a clear summary of Canadian rules, write for the booklet *I Declare,* issued by the **Canada Border Services Agency** (© **800/461-9999** in Canada, or 204/983-3500; **www.cbsa-asfc.gc.ca**).

U.K. Citizens

For information, contact **HM Customs & Excise** at © **0845/010-9000** (from outside the U.K., 020/8929-0152), or consult their website at **www.hmce.gov.uk**.

Australian Citizens

A helpful brochure available from Australian consulates or Customs offices is *Know Before You Go.* For more information, call the **Australian Customs Service** at ℗ **1300/363-263,** or log on to **www.customs.gov.au.**

New Zealand Citizens

Most questions are answered in a free pamphlet available at New Zealand consulates and Customs offices: *New Zealand Customs Guide for Travellers, Notice no. 4.* For more information, contact **New Zealand Customs,** The Customhouse, 17–21 Whitmore St., Box 2218, Wellington (℗ **04/473-6099** or 0800/428-786; **www.customs.govt.nz**).

3 Money

According to figures released by the Hong Kong Tourism Board, the average per capita spending of overnight visitors to Hong Kong is HK$4,663 (US$606/£333) per day on hotels, meals, shopping, and entertainment (frugal travelers, of course, can experience Hong Kong on much less). While Hong Kong may seem expensive compared to many other Asian cities, bargains abound, especially when it comes to off-season hotel rates, meals at local Chinese restaurants, public transportation, and museum admissions. With a long history of tourism—and shopping—Hong Kong is well equipped to meet visitors' money demands.

CURRENCY

The basic unit of currency is the **Hong Kong dollar (HK$),** which is divided into 100 cents. Since 1983, when negotiations between Britain and China concerning Hong Kong's future sent public confidence and the value of the Hong Kong dollar into a nose dive, the Hong Kong dollar has been officially pegged to the U.S. dollar at a rate of 7.8 (which means that US$1 equals HK$7.80), giving the Hong Kong currency greater stability.

Three banks, the Hongkong and Shanghai Banking Corporation (HSBC), the Bank of China, and the Standard Chartered Bank, all issue their own colorful notes, in denominations of HK$10, HK$20, HK$50, HK$100, HK$500, and HK$1,000. The government also issues a $10 note. As for coins, they're issued by the government in bronze for HK10¢, HK20¢, and HK50¢ pieces; in silver for HK$1, HK$2, and HK$5; and in nickel and bronze for HK$10.

At any rate, throughout the SAR, you'll see the dollar sign ("$"), which of course refers to Hong Kong dollars, not U.S. dollars. To prevent confusion, this guide identifies Hong Kong dollars with the symbol "HK$" (followed in parentheses by the U.S. dollar conversion). Although the official conversion rate is pegged at 7.8, you'll receive slightly less at banks, hotels, and currency exchange offices. During my last trip, I encountered exchange rates ranging from 7.72 (at a Wing Lung Bank) to 7.07 (at a currency exchange office).

For the matter of convenience, all conversions in this book are based on HK$7.70 to US$1 and HK$14 to £1. If the exchange rate changes drastically—that is, it is no longer pegged to the U.S. dollar—plan your budget accordingly.

When exchanging money in Hong Kong, you'll get the best rate at banks. The exchange rate can vary among banks, however, so it may pay to shop around if you're exchanging a large amount. In addition, most banks also charge commission; a check during my last visit revealed commissions ranging from HK$40 (US$5.20/£2.85) at a Wing Lung Bank to HK$100 (US$13/£7.14) at a Hongkong and Shanghai Bank. Others many not charge commission but have lower rates. Most charge a commission on traveler's checks (unless, of course, you're cashing American Express checks at an American Express office), but the exchange rate is usually better for traveler's checks than cash. Ask your hotel where the closest **Hang Seng Bank** or

The Hong Kong Dollar, the British Pound & the U.S. Dollar

For American Readers   Although the official conversion rate is pegged at HK$7.80 for 1 U.S. dollar, the average rate of exchange at banks and exchange offices is closer to HK$7.70 (or HK$1 = US13¢) so this is the rate of exchange used to calculate the U.S. dollar values given in this book (rounded off to the nearest nickel for prices less than US$10 and to the nearest dollar for prices more than US$10). While stable since it was pegged to the U.S. dollar, this exchange rate may not be the same when you travel to Hong Kong. Therefore, the following table should be used only as a guide.

For British Readers   At this writing, £1 equals approximately HK$14 (or HK$1= 7 pence), and this was the rate of exchange used to calculate the pound values in the table below.

HK$	US$	UK£	HK$	US$	UK£
0.25	0.03	0.02	150	19.48	10.71
0.50	0.06	0.04	200	25.97	14.29
1.00	0.13	0.07	250	32.47	17.86
2.00	0.26	0.14	300	38.96	21.43
3.00	0.39	0.21	350	45.45	25.00
4.00	0.52	0.29	400	51.95	28.57
5.00	0.65	0.36	450	58.44	32.14
6.00	0.78	0.43	500	64.94	35.71
7.00	0.91	0.50	550	71.43	39.29
8.00	1.04	0.57	600	77.92	42.86
9.00	1.17	0.64	650	84.42	46.43
10.00	1.30	0.71	700	90.91	50.00
15.00	1.95	1.07	750	97.40	53.57
20.00	2.60	1.43	800	103.90	57.14
25.00	3.25	1.79	850	110.39	60.71
30.00	3.90	2.14	900	116.88	64.29
35.00	4.55	2.50	1,000	129.87	71.43
40.00	5.19	2.86	1,250	162.34	89.29
45.00	5.84	3.21	1,500	194.80	107.14
50.00	6.49	3.57	1,750	227.27	125.00
75.00	9.74	5.36	2,000	259.74	142.86
100.00	12.99	7.14	2,250	292.21	160.71

Wing Lung Bank is, since I find these generally have favorable rates and low commission. The main bank of Wing Lung is at 45 Des Voeux Road Central in the Central District (© **852/2826 8333**), while Hang Seng has a convenient location next to Kowloon Hotel at 4 Hankow Rd., Tsim Sha Tsui (© **852/2198 0575**).

Hotels give a slightly less favorable exchange rate but are convenient because they're open at night and on weekends. Money changers are found in the tourist areas, especially along Nathan Road in Tsim Sha Tsui. Avoid them if you can. They often charge a commission or a "changing fee," or give a much lower rate. Check exactly how much you'll get in return before handing over your money. If you exchange money at Hong Kong International Airport, change only what you need to get into town—US$50 or £28 should be enough—because the exchange rate here is lower than what you'll get at banks in town.

ATMs

The easiest and best way to get cash away from home is from an ATM (automated teller machine), sometimes referred to as a "cash machine." There are ATMs throughout Hong Kong, making a credit or debit card the most convenient way to obtain cash since it eliminates the hassle of exchanging money only during banking hours. The **Cirrus** (℃ **800/424-7787;** www.mastercard.com) and **PLUS** (℃ **800/843-7587;** www.visa.com) networks span the globe; look at the back of your bank card to see which network you're on. Be sure you know your 4-digit personal identification number (PIN) and daily withdrawal limit before you depart. *Note:* Remember that many banks impose a fee every time you use a card at another bank's ATM, and that fee can be higher for international transactions (up to $5 or more) than for domestic ones (where they're rarely more than $2). In addition, the bank from which you withdraw cash may charge its own fee. For international withdrawal fees, ask your bank.

Holders of MasterCard and Visa can use ATMs at the airport and various convenient locations around the city, including the Star Ferry concourses in Kowloon and Central, all major MTR (subway) stations, and major banks such as the Hongkong and Shanghai Banking Corporation and Hang Seng Bank (which have 24-hr. machines). American Express cardholders have access to Jetco ATMs around town and can also withdraw local currency or traveler's checks at the Express Cash machines at both American Express offices (see "Fast Facts: Hong Kong" in chapter 4).

CREDIT CARDS

Credit cards are a safe way to carry money, provide a convenient record of all your expenses, and generally offer relatively good exchange rates. You can withdraw cash advances from your credit cards at banks or ATMs, provided you know your PIN. Keep in mind that you'll pay interest from the moment of your withdrawal, even if you pay your monthly bills on time. Also, note that many banks now assess a 1% to 3% "transaction fee" on *all* charges you incur abroad (whether you're using the local currency or your native currency).

Although many of the smaller shops in Hong Kong will give better prices if you pay in cash with local currency, most shops accept international credit cards, although some of the smaller ones do not. Look for credit card signs displayed on the front door or near the cash register. Readily accepted credit cards include American Express, Visa, and MasterCard. Note, however, that shops have to pay an extra fee for transactions that take place with a credit card—and they will try to pass on that expense to you. Keep this in mind if you're bargaining (see section 1 in chapter 9, "Shopping"), and make sure the shopkeeper knows whether you're going to pay with cash or plastic. All major hotels and better restaurants accept credit cards, but budget restaurants often don't. If you do pay with a credit card, check to make sure that "HK" appears before the dollar sign given for the total amount.

TRAVELER'S CHECKS

You can buy traveler's checks at most banks. They are offered in denominations of $20, $50, $100, $500, and sometimes $1,000. Generally, you'll pay a service charge ranging from 1% to 4%.

The most popular traveler's checks are offered by **American Express** (© 800/ 807-6233 or 800/221-7282 for card holders—this number accepts collect calls, offers service in several foreign languages, and exempts Amex gold and platinum cardholders from the 1% fee); **Visa** (© 800/732-1322)—AAA members can obtain Visa checks for a $9.95 fee (for checks up to $1,500) at most AAA offices or by calling © 866/339-3378; and **MasterCard** (© 800/223-9920).

If you carry traveler's checks, keep a record of their serial numbers separate from your checks in the event that they are stolen or lost. You'll get a refund faster if you know the numbers.

You'll need your passport to exchange traveler's checks. Traveler's checks can be readily exchanged for Hong Kong dollars at banks, hotels, and currency-exchange offices (banks provide the most favorable rates). Traveler's checks also command a slightly better exchange rate than cash. Although Thomas Cook and other agencies can issue traveler's checks in Hong Kong currency, I don't think this offers any advantage, since Hong Kong shops, restaurants, and hotels are not as willing as their U.S. counterparts to accept traveler's checks for payment.

4 When to Go

Hong Kong's peak tourist season used to be in spring and fall, but now tourists come to Hong Kong virtually year-round, especially from neighboring mainland China. It's best, therefore, to make hotel reservations in advance, particularly if you're arriving during the Chinese New Year, one of the festivals described below, or the two peak vacation periods for mainland Chinese (the so-called "Golden Weeks" beginning May 1 and Oct 1). In addition, major conventions and trade fairs can also tie up the city's best hotels, particularly in spring (Mar–Apr) and autumn (Oct–Nov); check www.discover hongkong.com for an updated calendar. If you're on a budget, keep in mind that many Hong Kong hotels offer package deals and cheaper rates in summer and winter.

CLIMATE

Because of its subtropical location, Hong Kong's weather is generally mild in winter and uncomfortably hot and humid in summer, with an average annual rainfall of 89 inches. The most pleasant time of year is late September through early December, when skies are clear and sunny, temperatures are in the 70s (21°C–26°C), and the humidity drops to 70%. January and February are the coldest months, when temperatures can drop to 50°F (10°C) but are usually in the upper 50s and 60s (14°C–20°C). You'll want a jacket during this time. In spring (Mar–May), the temperature can range between 64°F and 81°F (18°C–27°C) and the humidity rises to about 82%, with fog and rain fairly common. That means you'll need a raincoat and there may not be much of a view from the cloud-enveloped Victoria Peak. By May, it can also be quite hot and muggy.

By summer (late May to mid-Sept), temperatures are often in the 90s (32°C–37°C), humidity can be 90% or more, and there's little or no relief, even at night. If you're visiting the SAR this time of year, you'd be prudent to carry a hat, sunblock, sunglasses, and plenty of bottled water with you wherever you go.

You'll also want a light jacket for air-conditioned rooms and an umbrella. This is when Hong Kong receives the most rain; it's also typhoon season. However, Hong Kong has a very good warning system, so there's no need to worry about the dangers of a tropical storm.

Hong Kong's Average Monthly Temperatures & Days of Rain

	Jan	Feb	Mar	Apr	May	June	July	Aug	Sept	Oct	Nov	Dec
Temp. (F°)	61	61	64	72	77	80	84	84	80	77	70	64
Temp. (C°)	16	16	18	22	25	28	29	29	28	25	21	18
Days of Rain	5.6	8.9	10.1	11.1	14.9	14.2	17.5	17.3	14.4	8.6	5.9	3.9

HOLIDAYS

Hong Kong has 17 public holidays a year, including some of the festivals described below. The majority are Chinese and are therefore celebrated according to the lunar calendar, with different dates each year (for a rundown of Hong Kong's 2007 holidays, see "Fast Facts: Hong Kong" in chapter 4; for 2008 lunar holidays, which had not yet been determined when we went to press, go to www.info.gov.hk/info/holiday_e. htm). Since most shops, restaurants, and attractions remain open except during the Chinese New Year, the holidays should not cause any inconvenience to visitors. Banks, however, are closed.

HONG KONG CALENDAR OF EVENTS

If you're lucky, your trip might coincide with one of Hong Kong's colorful festivals. The only time shops and offices close at festival time is during the Chinese New Year, though some in Tsim Sha Tsui remain open to cater to tourists.

Below are the most popular events, including Chinese festivals and festivals of the arts. Your best source for additional information on all of these events is the **Hong Kong Tourism Board** (② **852/2508 1234** in Hong Kong; www. discoverhongkong.com), which can provide detailed information on where events are being staged and how to get there. For several of the festivals, HKTB even offers organized tours, which are one of the best ways to secure front-row seats without battling the crowds.

January/February

Chinese New Year. The most important Chinese holiday, this is a 3-day affair, a time for visiting friends and relatives, settling debts, doing a thorough housecleaning, consulting fortunetellers, and worshipping ancestors. Strips of red paper with greetings of wealth, good fortune, and longevity are pasted on doors, and families visit temples. Most shops (except those in tourist areas) close down for at least 2 or 3 days; streets and building facades are decorated with elaborate light displays; flower markets sell peach trees, chrysanthemums, and other good-luck flowers; a colorful parade winds its way along the waterfront, usually on the first day; and a dazzling display of fireworks lights up the harbor, usually on the second day of the holiday. Since this festival is largely a family affair (much like the Christian Christmas), it holds little interest for the tourist. In fact, if you're planning a side trip into China, this would be the worst time to go, since all routes to the mainland are clogged with Hong Kong Chinese returning home to visit relatives. Late January or early February (Feb 17–20, 2007).

February/March

Hong Kong Arts Festival. This is a 3-week-long celebration with performances by world-renowned orchestras, pop and jazz ensembles, and opera, dance, and theater companies (including experimental theater and Chinese operas); and with ethnic music and art exhibitions. For a schedule of events, venues, and ticket information, call (C) 852/2824 2430 or HKTB at (C) 852/2508 1234, or visit the website www.hk.artsfestival.org. February/March.

March

Hong Kong Sevens Rugby Tournament, Hong Kong Stadium. Known as "The Sevens," this is one of Hong Kong's most popular, and one of Asia's largest, sporting events, with more than 20 teams from around the world competing for the Cup Championship. Tickets (priced at HK$880/US$114/£63 for a 3-day pass), are often sold out. For more information, contact the Hong Kong Rugby Football Union at (C) 852/2504 8311 or check the websites www.hkrugby.com or www.hksevens.com.hk. Fourth weekend in March.

March/April

Ching Ming Festival, all Chinese cemeteries (especially in Aberdeen, Happy Valley, Chai Wan, and Cheung Chau island). A Confucian festival to honor the dead, observed by sweeping ancestral graves, burning incense, offering food and flowers, and picnicking among the graves. Contact HKTB at (C) 852/2508 1234. Fourth or fifth day of the Third Moon, March/April (Apr 5, 2007; Apr 5, 2008).

April

Tin Hau Festival, all Tin Hau temples, especially in Joss House Bay and Yuen Long. This colorful festival celebrates the birth of Tin Hau, goddess of the sea and Hong Kong's most popular deity among fishing folk. The celebration stems from a legendary fisherman's daughter who could supposedly calm stormy seas and protect fishermen. To pay her tribute, fishing boats are decorated with colorful flags, there are parades and lion dances, and family shrines are carried to shore to be blessed by Taoist priests. A similar festival is held at A-Ma Temple in Macau. Contact HKTB, which organizes special tours of the events, at (C) 852/2508 1234. Twenty-third day of the Third Moon, usually in April (May 9, 2007).

Hong Kong International Film Festival, Hong Kong Arts Centre, Hong Kong Cultural Centre, City Hall, and other venues around town. More than 300 films from more than 40 countries are featured at this 2-week event, including new releases, documentaries, and archival films. Tickets for most events cost HK$55 (US$7.15/£3.90). For more information, call (C) 852/2970 3300, or check www.hkiff.org.hk. Two weeks in April.

April/May

Cheung Chau Bun Festival, Pak Tai Temple, Cheung Chau island. Unique to Hong Kong, this weeklong affair is thought to appease restless ghosts and spirits. Originally held to placate the unfortunate souls of those murdered by pirates, it features a street parade of lions and dragons and Chinese opera, as well as floats with children seemingly suspended in the air, held up by cleverly concealed wires. The end of the festival is heralded by three bun-covered scaffolds erected in front of the Pak Tai Temple, with selected contestants scrambling up them to retrieve the buns. These buns supposedly bring good luck to those who receive them. HKTB organizes tours of the parade; call (C) 852/2508 1234. Usually late April or early May (May 24, 2007).

Buddha's Birthday, Buddhist temples throughout Hong Kong. Worshippers flock to pay respect to Siddhartha, founder of Buddhism, and to bathe Buddha statues. The Po Lin Monastery on Lantau island is one of the most popular destinations on this day.

Contact the HKTB at ℃ **852/2508 1234.** Ninth day of the Fourth Moon, usually either in April or May (May 24, 2007).

June

Dragon Boat Races (Tuen Ng Festival). Races of long, narrow boats, gaily painted and powered by 20 to 22 oarsmen who row to the beat of drums. It originated in ancient China, where legend held that an imperial adviser drowned himself in a Hunan river to protest government corruption. His faithful followers, wishing to recover his body, supposedly raced out into the river in boats, beating their paddles on the surface of the water and throwing rice to distract sea creatures from his body. Qualifying heats are held in Aberdeen, Sai Kung, Cheung Chau, and Lantau, with final races on the main day best seen from Stanley Beach. For a front-row seat, contact HKTB at ℃ **852/2508 1234** for special race-day tours. Fifth day of the Fifth Moon (June 19, 2007).

August

Yue Lan Festival (Festival of the Hungry Ghosts). Released from the underworld, ghosts are believed to roam the earth for 1 lunar month each year. Religious ceremonies and offerings of food and paper replicas of life's necessities are burned to appease the spirits of discontented ghosts (those who were murdered, died without proper funeral rites, or are without descendants to care for them), in an attempt to prevent the unhappy souls from seeking vengeance on humans. Popular venues are King George V Memorial Park in Kowloon and Moreton Terrace Playground in Causeway Bay. Contact HKTB at ℃ **852/2508 1234** for more information. Fourteenth day of the Seventh Moon (Aug 26, 2007).

September/October

Mid-Autumn Festival, Victoria Park, Kowloon Park, and Victoria Peak. Held in early autumn, this major festival (sometimes referred to as the Moon Festival) celebrates the harvest and the brightest moon of the year. In honor of the event, local people light lanterns in the shapes of fish, flowers, and even ships and planes, gaze at the moon, and eat mooncakes (sweet rolls with sesame seeds, duck eggs, and ground lotus seeds). The mooncakes commemorate the 14th-century uprising against the Mongols, when written messages calling for the revolt were concealed in cakes smuggled to the rebels. Today the Urban Council organizes lantern carnivals in parks on both Hong Kong Island and Kowloon, where you can join the Chinese for strolls among hundreds of lanterns, making this one of Hong Kong's most charming and picturesque festivals. In addition, don't miss the dragon fire dance in Causeway Bay's Tai Hang district. Contact HKTB at ℃ **852/2807 1234.** Fifteenth day of the Eighth Moon, either in September or October (Sept 25, 2007).

October

Chung Yueng Festival, all Chinese cemeteries. The second time of year when ancestral graves are swept and offerings are made. It's also a popular hiking day. Ninth day of the Ninth Moon (Oct 19, 2007).

5 Travel Insurance

The cost of travel insurance varies widely, depending on the cost and length of your trip, your age and health, and the type of trip you're taking, but expect to pay between 5% and 8% of the vacation itself. You can get estimates from various

Travel in the Age of Bankruptcy

Airlines go bankrupt, so protect yourself by **buying your tickets with a credit card.** The Fair Credit Billing Act guarantees that you can get your money back from the credit card company if a travel supplier goes under (and if you request the refund within 60 days of the bankruptcy). **Travel insurance** can also help, but make sure it covers against "carrier default" for your specific travel provider. And be aware that if a U.S. airline goes bust mid-trip, a 2001 federal law requires other carriers to take you to your destination (albeit on a space-available basis) for a fee of no more than $25, provided you rebook within 60 days of the cancellation.

providers through **InsureMyTrip.com.** Enter your trip cost and dates, your age, and other information, for prices from more than a dozen companies.

TRIP-CANCELLATION INSURANCE

Trip-cancellation insurance will help retrieve your money if you have to back out of a trip or depart early, or if your travel supplier goes bankrupt. Permissible reasons for trip cancellation can range from sickness to natural disasters to the State Department declaring a destination unsafe for travel.

For more information, contact one of the following recommended insurers: Access America (✆ 866/807-3982; www. accessamerica.com); Travel Guard International (✆ 800/826-4919; www.travel guard.com); Travel Insured International (✆ 800/243-3174; www.travelinsured. com); and Travelex Insurance Services (✆ 888/457-4602; www.travelex-insurance. com).

MEDICAL INSURANCE

For travel overseas, most U.S. health plans (including Medicare and Medicaid) do not provide coverage, and the ones that do often require you to pay for services upfront and reimburse you only after you return home. As a safety net, you may want to buy travel medical insurance, particularly if you're traveling to a high-risk area where emergency evacuation might be necessary. If you require additional medical insurance, try **MEDEX Assistance** (✆ 410/453-6300; www. medexassist.com) or **Travel Assistance International** (✆ 800/821-2828; www. travelassistance.com; for general information on services, call the company's Worldwide Assistance Services, Inc., at ✆ 800/777-8710).

LOST-LUGGAGE INSURANCE

On international flights (including U.S. portions of international trips), baggage coverage is limited to approximately $9.07 per pound, up to approximately $635 per checked bag. If you plan to check items more valuable than what's covered by the standard liability, see if your homeowner's policy covers your valuables, get baggage insurance as part of your comprehensive travel-insurance package, or buy Travel Guard's "BagTrak" product.

If your luggage is lost, immediately file a lost-luggage claim at the airport, detailing the luggage contents. Most airlines require that you report delayed, damaged, or lost baggage within 4 hours of arrival. The airlines are required to deliver luggage, once found, directly to your house or destination free of charge.

6 Health & Safety

STAYING HEALTHY

The two major health concerns for travelers to Hong Kong the past few years have been **SARS** and **avian flu.** At press time, neither poses a threat for those going to the SAR (yes, its name is an unfortunate coincidence). Hong Kong culled its entire poultry population several times after the first reported bird flu outbreak in 1997 (the last reported human case of avian flu in Hong Kong was in 2003), and importation of poultry from mainland China is immediately halted whenever any outbreaks occur there. As for SARS, there have been no major occurrences since the 2003 outbreak that sickened 1,755 people in Hong Kong and killed 299 of them. However, Hong Kong monitors all passengers arriving by air, boat, and train by taking their temperatures. Passengers with pneumonia or fever, as well as those arriving from infected areas, are kept under close monitoring or isolation. To avoid being unnecessarily detained, don't travel with a fever.

As an extra precaution, you might wish to have a flu shot before departing for Hong Kong. Once in Hong Kong, you'll notice dispensers for hand sanitizers virtually everywhere, including restrooms, shops, hotels, and other public places; since good hygiene is the best defense against infectious disease, wash your hands as often as you can. You might also want to avoid markets with live poultry.

Otherwise, no shots or inoculations are required for entry to the SAR, but you will need proof of a vaccination against cholera if you have been in an infected area during the 14 days preceding your arrival. The United States **Centers for Disease Control and Prevention** (© **800/311-3435;** www.cdc.gov) provides up-to-date information on health hazards by region or country—including the latest outbreaks of avian flu—and offers tips on food safety. Health issues, including avian flu, are also monitored by Hong Kong's **Department of Health** (© **852/2833 0111;** www.dh.gov.hk).

Prescriptions can be filled at Hong Kong pharmacies only if they're issued by a local doctor. To avoid the hassle, be sure to bring more prescriptions than you think you'll need, clearly labeled in their original packages; pack prescription medications in your carry-on luggage. It's also a good idea to carry copies of your prescriptions in case you run out, including generic names in case a local pharmacist is unfamiliar with the brand name. Over-the-counter items are easy to obtain, though name brands may be different from those back home, and some ingredients allowed elsewhere may be forbidden in Hong Kong (and vice versa).

If you're traveling during the hot and humid summer months, limit your exposure to the sun, especially during the first few days of your trip and particularly from 11am to 2pm. Use a sunscreen with a high protection factor. To avoid dehydration, you should also carry a water bottle, especially when hiking. Another

Healthy Travels to You

The following government websites offer up-to-date health-related travel advice.

- **Australia:** www.dfat.gov.au/travel
- **Canada:** www.hc-sc.gc.ca/index_e.html
- **U.K.:** www.dh.gov.uk/PolicyAndGuidance/HealthAdviceForTravellers/fs/en
- **U.S.:** www.cdc.gov/travel

concern when hiking in the New Territories or the islands is snakes. I've never seen one, but of Hong Kong's 49 native species, 9 are venomous.

Generally, you're safe eating anywhere in Hong Kong, even at roadside food stalls. Stay clear of local oysters and shellfish, however, and remember that many restaurants outside the major hotels and tourist areas use MSG in their dishes as a matter of course, especially fast-food restaurants and Chinese kitchens that import products from the mainland. Water is safe to drink except in rural areas, where you should drink bottled water.

WHAT TO DO IF YOU GET SICK AWAY FROM HOME

There are many Western-trained physicians in Hong Kong. If you get sick, you may want to contact the concierge at your hotel—some upper-range hotels have in-house doctors or clinics. Otherwise, your embassy in Hong Kong can provide a list of area doctors who speak English. You can also contact the **International Association for Medical Assistance to Travellers** (© 716/754-4883, or 416/652-0137 in Canada; www.iamat. org), an organization that lists many local English-speaking doctors and also posts the latest developments in global SARS and avian flu outbreaks. Otherwise, if you can't find a doctor who can help you right away, try the emergency room at the local hospital. Many emergency rooms have walk-in-clinics for cases that are not

life-threatening. See "Fast Facts: Hong Kong" in chapter 4 for a list of hospitals and emergency numbers.

Doctors and hospitals generally do not accept credit cards and require immediate cash payment for health services. See "Medical Insurance," under "Travel Insurance," above.

STAYING SAFE

Hong Kong is relatively safe for the visitor, especially if you use common sense and stick to such well-traveled nighttime areas as Tsim Sha Tsui, Lan Kwai Fong, or Causeway Bay. On the other hand, the main thing you must guard against is pickpockets. They often work in groups to pick men's pockets or slit open a woman's purse, quickly taking the valuables and then relaying them on to accomplices who disappear in the crowd. Favored places are Tsim Sha Tsui, Causeway Bay, and Wan Chai. You should also be on guard on crowded public conveyances such as the MTR and public markets.

There have also been isolated cases of hikers being robbed in country parks and Victoria Peak. It's best, therefore, to hike in groups of two or more.

To be on the safe side, keep your valuables, including your passport, in your in-room safe or hotel's safe-deposit box. If you need to carry your passport or large amounts of money, conceal everything in a money belt.

7 Specialized Travel Resources

TRAVELERS WITH DISABILITIES

Hong Kong can be a nightmare for travelers with disabilities. City sidewalks—especially in Central and Kowloon—can be so jampacked that getting around on crutches or in a wheelchair is exceedingly difficult. Moreover, to cross busy thoroughfares it's often necessary to climb stairs to a pedestrian bridge or use an

underground tunnel. Also, most shops are a step or two up from the street, due to flooding during rainstorms.

As for transportation, taxis are probably the most convenient mode of transportation, especially since they can load and unload passengers with disabilities in restricted zones under certain conditions and do not charge extra for carrying wheelchairs and crutches. Otherwise, the MTR (subway) has wheelchair access (elevators, ramps, or other aids) at major stations, as well as tactile pathways leading to platforms and exits for the visually impaired. Ferries are accessible to wheelchair users on the lower deck, and approximately 41% of buses are wheelchair accessible. More information is available from the **Transport Department,** Floor 41, Immigration Tower, 7 Gloucester Road, Wan Chai (© **852/ 2804 2660;** www.td.gov.hk), which publishes a booklet called *A Guide to Public Transport for People with Disabilities,* which can also be downloaded online. Another good source is the **Joint Council for the Physically and Mentally Disabled/Hong Kong Council of Social Services,** which published the *Hong Kong Guide for Disabled Visitors* in 1998. Though dated, it provides wheelchair accessibility for hotels, consulates, museums, restaurants, shopping malls, performing venues and more and is available online at www.hkcss.org.hk/rh/access guide or at offices of the Hong Kong Tourism Board (see "Visitor Information" at the beginning of chapter 4).

U.S. organizations that offer assistance to travelers with disabilities include **MossRehab** (www.mossresourcenet.org); the **American Foundation for the Blind** (© **800/232-5463;** www.afb.org); and **SATH** (Society for Accessible Travel & Hospitality; © **212/447-7284;** www. sath.org). **AirAmbulanceCard.com** is now partnered with SATH and allows you to preselect top-notch hospitals in case of an emergency.

GAY & LESBIAN TRAVELERS

There are only a handful of openly gay establishments in Hong Kong, concentrated mostly in the Lan Kwai Fong/ SoHo nightlife districts (see chapter 10 for club listings), but several clubs have gay or lesbian nights. *Gmagazine,* a monthly for gays distributed free to clubs, bars, and other venues, has an events calendar.

Otherwise, **The International Gay and Lesbian Travel Association** (© **800/ 448-8550** or 954/776-2626; www.iglta. org) is the trade association for the gay and lesbian travel industry, and offers an online directory of gay- and lesbian-friendly travel businesses; go to their website and click on "Members."

The following travel guides are available at many bookstores, or you can order them from any online bookseller: *Spartacus International Gay Guide* (Bruno Gmünder Verlag; www.spartacusworld. com/gayguide) and *Odysseus: The International Gay Travel Planner* (Odysseus Enterprises Ltd.); and the *Damron* guides (www.damron.com), with separate, annual books for gay men and lesbians.

SENIOR TRAVEL

Seniors receive half-price or free admission to most museums in Hong Kong. In addition, seniors can ride the cross-harbor ferry free of charge and receive reduced fares for ferries to the outlying islands, the trams (including the Peak Tram), and the subway system. Some discounts are available to seniors older than 60; others for seniors older than 65. In any case, seniors should carry identification for proof of age and should keep in mind that there are many stairs to climb in Hong Kong, including overhead pedestrian bridges and in subway stations. In addition, remember that it is *very* hot and humid in summer.

Before leaving home, consider becoming a member of the **AARP** (formerly known as the American Association of Retired Persons), 601 E St. NW, Washington, DC 20049 (© **888/687-2277;** www.aarp.org), which brings such benefits as *AARP: The Magazine* and a monthly newsletter. Anyone 50 and older can join.

Many reliable agencies and organizations target the 50-plus market. **Elderhostel** (© 877/426-8056; www.elder hostel.org) arranges study programs for those aged 55 and over. **ElderTreks** (© 800/741-7956; www.eldertreks.com) offers small-group tours to off-the-beaten-path or adventure-travel locations, restricted to travelers 50 and older. **INTRAV** (© 800/456-8100; www. intrav.com) is a high-end tour operator that caters to the mature, discerning traveler (not specifically seniors), with trips around the world.

FAMILY TRAVEL

Hong Kong is a great place for older kids, since many of the attractions are geared toward them and even offer discounts for children, sometimes as much as 50%. In addition, public transportation is half price for children. As for very young children, keep in mind that there are many stairs to climb, particularly in Central with its elevated walkways, and in subway stations, making child backpack carriers easier than strollers. Also, young children may not be welcome at finer restaurants.

As for hotels, many allow children under a certain age (usually 12 but occasionally up to 18) to stay free of charge in their parent's room. Generally, only one child is allowed, or there's a maximum limit of three persons per room, and there's no extra charge *only* when no extra bed is required. Baby cots are usually available free of charge, and most hotels also offer babysitting.

To locate those accommodations, restaurants, and attractions that are particularly kid-friendly, refer to the "Kids" icon throughout this guide. For lists of kid-friendly hotels and restaurants, see p. 83 and 135 respectively. "Especially for Kids" on p. 176 describes attractions and activities geared toward children.

Recommended family travel websites include **Family Travel Forum** (www. familytravelforum.com); **Family Travel** **Network** (www.familytravelnetwork. com); **Traveling Internationally with Your Kids** (www.travelwithyourkids. com); and **Family Travel Files** (www.the familytravelfiles.com).

FOR STUDENTS

Students receive a slight discount to most museums in Hong Kong, but major attractions like Ocean Park do not offer discounts.

Before you leave home, you'd be wise to arm yourself with an **International Student Identity Card (ISIC),** which offers substantial savings on plane tickets and entrance fees. It also provides you with basic health and life insurance and a 24-hour help line. The card is available from **STA Travel** (© 800/781-4040 in North America; www.sta.com or www. statravel.com; or www.statravel.co.uk in the U.K.), the biggest student travel agency in the world. **Travel CUTS** (© 800/667-2887 or 416/614-2887; www.travelcuts.com) offers similar services for both Canadians and U.S. residents. Irish students may prefer to turn to **USIT** (© 01/602-1600; www.usitnow. ie), an Ireland-based specialist in student, youth, and independent travel.

In Hong Kong, **Sincerity Travel,** 1703 Silvercord Rd., Tsim Sha Tsui (© 852/ 2736 1618), can issue an ISIC to bona fide students and can help with cheap flights, accommodations, cruises, and rail passes to other destinations for travelers of all ages. It's open Monday through Friday from 9:30am to 6pm and Saturday from 9:30am to 1pm.

FOR SINGLES

You shouldn't have any problems as a single traveler to Hong Kong. Almost every time I've come here, I've traveled alone. The biggest problem is one of expense, since many hotels charge the same for both double and single occupancy. The other problem is Chinese food—it's best when enjoyed with a group. Try fixed-price meals or all-you-can-eat buffets when dining alone, or join one of the organized tours where meals are often included.

Female travelers may also want to check out the website **Journeywoman** (www.journeywoman.com), a "real life" women's travel information network where you can sign up for a free e-mail newsletter and get advice on everything from etiquette and dress to safety. They have a special section called "GirlTalk Hong Kong," which carries tips on accommodations, restaurants, shopping, things to do, what to wear, and details of venues where solo female travelers will feel at home, submitted by women who have traveled to Hong Kong.

8 Planning Your Trip Online

SURFING FOR AIRFARES

The most popular online travel agencies are **Travelocity** (**www.travelocity.com**, or www.travelocity.co.uk); **Expedia** (**www.expedia.com**, www.expedia.co.uk, or www.expedia.ca); and **Orbitz** (**www.orbitz.com**).

In addition, most airlines now offer online-only fares that even their phone agents know nothing about. For the websites of airlines that fly to and from Hong Kong, go to "Getting There," p. 30.

Other helpful websites for booking airline tickets online include:

- www.cheapflights.com
- www.kayak.com
- www.opodo.co.uk
- www.priceline.com
- www.sidestep.com

SURFING FOR HOTELS

In addition to **Travelocity, Expedia, Orbitz,** and **Priceline** (see above), the following websites will help you with booking hotel rooms online:

- www.hotels.com
- www.quickbook.com
- www.travelaxe.net
- www.tripadvisor.com
- www.asiatravel.com
- www.asiahotels.com
- www.planetholiday.com

Be sure to compare online rates with those of individual hotel websites to make sure you're getting a good deal. It's also a good idea to **get a confirmation number** and **make a printout** of any online booking transaction.

9 The 21st-Century Traveler

INTERNET ACCESS AWAY FROM HOME
WITHOUT YOUR OWN COMPUTER

Most hotels have business centers with computers for Internet access, but they can be expensive (some, however, are available free for hotel guests). Otherwise, cybercafes are growing in number, though they are still few and far between. In addition to the suggestions below, check **www.cybercaptive.com** and **www.cybercafe.com**. The Hong Kong Tourist Board also maintains a list of current cybercafes in their offices.

Shadowman, 21A Ashley Rd., Tsim Sha Tsui (© **852/2366 5262**), is a small cybercafe with a handful of computers, providing free Internet access for 20 minutes with the purchase of a drink or food and charging HK$10 (US$1.30/70p) per 15 minutes beyond that. It also offers wireless access. It's open Monday through Thursday from 8am to midnight, Friday and Saturday from 8am to 1am, and Sunday from 10am to midnight.

Pacific Coffee (www.pacificcoffee.com) is Hong Kong's largest chain of coffee shops, most with two or more computers that customers can access for free (you'll probably have to wait in line and use is restricted to 15 min. per visit). Locations include shop 1022 in the International Finance Center (IFC), above Hong Kong Station in Central (© **852/ 2868 5100**), open Sunday through Thursday from 7am to 11pm and Friday and Saturday from 7am to midnight.

WITH YOUR OWN COMPUTER

More and more hotels, cafes, and retailers are signing on as Wi-Fi (wireless fidelity) "hotspots." In Hong Kong, accessibility begins at its airport, where passengers with laptops equipped with PC-LAN cards can access the Internet from almost anywhere in the terminal, using technology developed by Pacific Century Cyber Works (PCCW). There are also 170 PowerPhones at the airport, where travelers with laptops can connect with the Internet by plugging into the phone's dataport. In the city, PowerPhones at major MTR stations and other locations also provide Internet access.

All upper-range and most medium-priced hotels in Hong Kong are equipped with high-speed dataports that allow guests to use laptop computers. More and more are also offering wireless access (check individual hotel listings in chapter 5 for dataport information or call your hotel in advance to see what your options are). In some hotels, Internet access is available upon purchase of an Internet access card for about HK$100 (US$13/ £7.15), valid for anywhere from 100 minutes to unlimited use for 5 days, depending on the hotel (in general, the more expensive the hotel, the more expensive its Internet rates). Other hotels charge a flat rate per day, with HK$120 (US$16/£8.55) for 24 hours the prevailing rate. A small percentage of hotels offer it for free.

Although Hong Kong's electricity uses 220 volts and 50 cycles (compared to the U.S. 110 volts and 60 cycles), most laptop computers nowadays are equipped to deal with both. However, you'll need a prong adapter. Upper-end hotels have built-in adapters that accept foreign (including U.S.) prongs; otherwise, housekeeping can probably lend you one for free. For moderate and budget hotels, you'll probably need a **connection kit** of the right power and phone adapters, a spare phone cord, and a spare Ethernet network cable—or find out whether your hotel supplies them to guests.

Lots of cafes, bars, and restaurants offer wireless, including Starbucks, Pacific Coffee, Delifrance, KFC, and Häagen-Dazs, with locations throughout Hong Kong. Ask your hotel concierge for the nearest location.

Major Internet Service Providers (ISPs) have **local access numbers** around the world, allowing you to go online by placing a local call. The **iPass** network also has dial-up numbers around the world. You'll have to sign up with an iPass provider, who will then tell you how to set up your computer for your destination(s). For a list of iPass providers, go to www.ipass.com and click on "Individuals Buy Now." One solid provider is **i2roam** (www.i2roam.com; © **866/811-6209** or 920/235-0475).

USING A CELLPHONE

The three letters that define much of the world's wireless capabilities are GSM (Global System for Mobiles), a big, seamless network that makes for easy cross-border cellphone use throughout Europe and dozens of other countries worldwide. In the U.S., T-Mobile, AT&T Wireless, and Cingular use this quasi-universal system; in Canada, Microcell and some Rogers customers are GSM, and all Europeans and most Australians use GSM.

Using your own mobile phone in Hong Kong is easy, as most of the telephone systems used around the world (such as GSM 900, PCS 1800, and CDMA) are operational in Hong Kong. If your cellphone is on a GSM system,

Online Traveler's Toolbox

Veteran travelers usually carry some essential items to make their trips easier. Following is a selection of handy online tools to bookmark and use:

- **Airplane Food** (www.airlinemeals.net)
- **Airplane Seating** (www.seatguru.com and www.airlinequality.com)
- **E-ticketing** (www.discoverhongkong.com)
- **Hong Kong Calendar of Events** (www.discoverhongkong.com)
- **Foreign Languages for Travelers** (www.travlang.com)
- **Maps** (www.mapquest.com)
- **Hong Kong Subway Navigator** (www.mtr.com.hk)
- **Time and Date** (www.timeanddate.com)
- **Travel Warnings** (http://travel.state.gov, www.fco.gov.uk/travel, www.voyage.gc.ca, or www.dfat.gov.au/consular/advice)
- **Universal Currency Converter** (www.xe.com/ucc)
- **Visa ATM Locator** (www.visa.com), **MasterCard ATM Locator** (www.mastercard.com)
- **Weather** (www.intellicast.com and www.weather.com)

and you have a world-capable multiband phone such as many Sony Ericsson, Motorola, or Samsung models, you can make and receive calls in Hong Kong. Mobile operators in Hong Kong have roaming agreements with most overseas operators, enabling visitors to use their own phone in Hong Kong. Just call your wireless operator and ask for "international roaming" to be activated on your account. Unfortunately, per-minute charges can be high, so be sure to ask about pricing before you leave.

It is more economical to buy a removable computer memory phone chip (called a **SIM card**), which allows you to make calls at local rates. Cheap, prepaid SIM cards are sold at retailers throughout Hong Kong. **CSL** is a well-known local company that offers a variety of phone services, including a prepaid SIM card (✆ **852/179 179**; http://prepaid.hkcsl.com) that costs as low as HK$88 (US$11/£6.30) and allows up to 293 minutes of local calls, with local calls costing HK30¢ (US4¢/2p) a minute, as well as international calls. It's sold at **1010 Centres**

throughout Hong Kong, including Century Square, 1–13 D'Aguilar St., Central (✆ **852/2918 1010**), open daily from 8:30am to 11pm; and Canton Plaza, 82–84 Canton Rd., Tsim Sha Tsui (✆ **852/2910 1010**), open daily from 8:30am to 10pm, as well as 7-Eleven convenience stores. CSL also offers a Hong Kong Special Edition SIM card aimed at tourists that costs HK$48 (US$6.25/£3.40) that includes 96 minutes of local calls. In any case, you'll get a local phone number and lower calling rates.

Be aware, however, that not all phones work on all networks, so show your phone to the salesperson. In addition, you need to have an "unlocked" phone that allows you to install a prepaid SIM. Many cellphone operators sell "locked" phones that restrict you from using a SIM card other than the one they supply with your phone. Getting an already locked phone unlocked can be a complicated process, but it can be done; call your cellular operator and say you'll be going abroad for several months and want to use the phone with a local provider.

Renting a mobile phone is also an option. Most upper- and medium-range hotels offer rental phones at their business centers, though it's an expensive convenience (at the Peninsula, you'll pay as much as HK$400/US$52/£30 per day, plus HK$5/US65¢/35p per minute). A better option is to rent from a local company. CSL (© **852/2883 3938;** http:// roam.hkcsl.com/eng/rent/rent.htm) offers phones for HK$35 (US$4.55/£2.50) a day, plus a refundable deposit of HK$200 to HK$500 (US$26–US$65/£14–£36) depending on the model. In addition, you must still buy a SIM card as outlined above. Handsets can be rented at one of several CSL 1010 or One2Free retail shops, including those at the airport, located at Level 7 of the departure hall; 1–13 D'Aguilar St. in Central; and 82–84 Canton Rd., Tsim Sha Tsui.

North Americans can rent one before leaving home from **InTouch USA** (© 800/ 872-7626; www.intouchglobal.com) or **RoadPost** (© 888/290-1606 or 905/272-5665; www.roadpost.com). InTouch will also, for free, advise you on whether your existing phone will work overseas; simply call © **703/222-7161** between 9am and 4pm EST, or go to **http://intouchglobal. com/travel.htm**.

10 Getting There

With dozens of airlines and half a dozen cruise lines serving Hong Kong from around the world, it's certainly not difficult to get there. Your itinerary, the amount of time you have, and your pocketbook will probably dictate how you travel. Below are some pointers to get you headed in the right direction.

BY PLANE
Because the flight to Hong Kong is such a long one (almost 16 hr. from Chicago, 12 hr. from London, and 9 hr. from Sydney), you may wish to splurge for a roomier seat and upgraded service, including special counters for check-in, private lounges at the airport, and better meals, as well as a higher ticket price when choosing your carrier. You should also consider a mileage program, since this round-trip flight will earn you a lot of miles.

THE MAJOR AIRLINES Airlines that fly nonstop between North America and Hong Kong include **Air Canada** (© **888/247-2262;** www.aircanada. com), with daily flights from Vancouver and Toronto; **Cathay Pacific Airways** (© **800/233-2742;** www.cathaypacific. com), Hong Kong's own airline with daily service from Los Angeles, San Francisco, New York, Toronto, and Vancouver; **Continental Airlines** (© **800/231-0856;** www.continental.com), with flights most days of the week from Newark; **Singapore Airlines** (© **800/ 742-3333;** www.singaporeair.com), with daily service from San Francisco; and **United Airlines** (© **800/538-2929;** www.united.com), with daily service from San Francisco and Chicago. Other airlines flying between North America and Hong Kong with stops en route include **Northwest Airlines** (© **800/ 447-4747;** www.nwa.com), **Japan Airlines** (© **800/525-3663;** www.japanair. com), **Korean Air** (© **800/438-5000;** www.koreanair.com), and **Philippine Airlines** (© **800/435-9725;** www. philippineairlines.com).

From the United Kingdom, **Cathay Pacific** (© **020/8834-8888**), **British Airways** (© **0870/850-9850;** www. britishairways.com), **Qantas** (© **08457/ 747-767;** www.qantas.com.au) and **Virgin Atlantic Airways** (© **08705/747-747;** www.virgin-atlantic.com) offer daily nonstop service from London to Hong

Kong. **Oasis Hong Kong** (© 0844/482-2323 in the U.K.; www.oasishongkong.com), a low-fare, long-haul airline with inexpensive seats even for business class, made its inaugural flight from London Gatwick to Hong Kong in October 2006. Future plans call for extending service from Hong Kong to Oakland, California, and Chicago.

From Australia, Cathay Pacific (© 131747) offers service from Sydney, Auckland, Melbourne, Brisbane, Cairns, Adelaide, and Perth; Virgin Atlantic (© 1300-727-340) offers daily service from Sydney; and **Qantas** (© 131313) offers daily service from Sydney, Melbourne, Brisbane, Cairns, and Perth. From New Zealand, **Cathay Pacific** (© 0800/800454) offers daily nonstop service from Auckland.

FLYING FOR LESS: TIPS FOR GETTING THE BEST AIRFARE

- Passengers who can book their ticket either **long in advance or at the last minute,** or who **fly midweek** or **at less-trafficked hours** may pay a fraction of the full fare. If your schedule is flexible, say so, and ask if you can secure a cheaper fare by changing your flight plans.
- Search **the Internet** for cheap fares (see "Planning Your Trip Online," above).
- Keep an eye on local newspapers for **promotional specials** or **fare wars,** when airlines lower prices on their most popular routes. You rarely see fare wars offered for peak travel times, but if you can travel in the off-months, you may snag a bargain.
- **Consolidators,** also known as bucket shops, are great sources for international tickets, although they usually can't beat Internet fares within North America. Start by looking in Sunday newspaper travel sections; U.S. travelers should focus on the *New York Times, Los Angeles Times,* and *Miami Herald.* U.K. travelers should search in the *Independent, The Guardian, or The Observer.* For less-developed destinations, small travel agents who cater to immigrant communities in large cities often have the best deals. *Beware:* Bucket shop tickets are usually nonrefundable or rigged with stiff cancellation penalties, often as high as 50% to 75% of the ticket price, and some put you on charter airlines, which may leave at inconvenient times and experience delays. Several reliable consolidators are worldwide and available online. **STA Travel** has been the world's lead consolidator for students since purchasing Council Travel, but their fares are competitive for travelers of all ages. **ELTExpress** (Flights.com; © 800/TRAV-800; www.eltexpress.com) has excellent fares worldwide, particularly to Europe. They also have "local" websites in 12 countries. **FlyCheap** (© 800/FLY-CHEAP; www.1800flycheap.com), owned by package-holiday megalith MyTravel, has especially good fares to sunny destinations. **Air Tickets Direct** (© 800/778-3447; www.airticketsdirect.com) is based in Montreal and leverages the currently weak Canadian dollar for low fares; they also book trips to places that U.S. travel agents won't touch, such as Cuba.
- Join **frequent-flier clubs.** Frequent-flier membership doesn't cost a cent, but it does entitle you to better seats, faster response to phone inquiries, and prompter service if your luggage is stolen or your flight is canceled or delayed, or if you want to change your seat. And you don't have to fly to earn points; **frequent-flier credit cards** can earn you thousands of miles for doing your everyday shopping. With more than 70 mileage

Tips Coping with Jet Lag

A major consideration for visitors flying to Hong Kong, especially on long flights from North America, is jet lag. Traveling east, however, is more difficult on your internal clock than traveling west, because most peoples' bodies are more inclined to stay up late than fall asleep early.

To minimize jet lag, follow these tips:

- Reset your watch to your destination time before you board the plane.
- Drink lots of water before, during, and after your flight. Avoid alcohol.
- Exercise and sleep well for a few days before your trip.
- Exercise during the flight by walking around the cabin and flexing your arms, hands, legs, and feet.
- If you have trouble sleeping on planes, fly eastward on morning flights.
- Daylight is the key to resetting your body clock. At the website for Outside In (www.bodyclock.com), you can get a customized plan of when to seek and avoid light.
- Once you reach Hong Kong, schedule your day according to local time.

awards programs on the market, consumers have never had more options. Investigate the program details of your favorite airlines before you sink points into any one. Consider which airlines have hubs in the airport nearest you, and, of those carriers, which have the most advantageous alliances, given your most common routes. To play the frequent-flier game to your best advantage, consult Randy Petersen's **Inside Flyer** (www.insideflyer.com). Petersen and friends review all the programs in detail and post regular updates on changes in policies and trends.

LONG-HAUL FLIGHTS: HOW TO STAY COMFORTABLE

- Your choice of airline and airplane will definitely affect your leg room. Find more details about U.S. airlines at **www.seatguru.com**. For international airlines, the research firm Skytrax has posted a list of average seat pitches at **www.airlinequality.com**.
- Emergency exit seats and bulkhead seats typically have the most legroom. Emergency exit seats are usually left unassigned until the day of a flight

(to ensure that someone able-bodied fills the seats); it's worth getting to the ticket counter early to snag one of these spots for a long flight. Many passengers find that bulkhead seating (the row facing the wall at the front of the cabin) offers more legroom, but keep in mind that bulkheads are where airlines often put baby bassinets, so you may be sitting next to an infant.

- To have two seats for yourself in a three-seat row, try for an aisle seat in a center section toward the back of coach. If you're traveling with a companion, book an aisle and a window seat. Middle seats are usually booked last, so chances are good you'll end up with three seats to yourselves.
- Ask about entertainment options. Many airlines offer seatback video systems where you get to choose your movies or play video games—but only on some of their planes. (Boeing 777s are your best bet.)
- To sleep, avoid the last row of any section or the row in front of an emergency exit, as these seats are the least likely to recline. Avoid seats near

highly trafficked toilet areas. Avoid seats in the back of many jets—these can be narrower than those in the rest of coach. You also may want to reserve a window seat so you can rest your head and avoid being bumped in the aisle.

- Get up, walk around, and stretch every 60 to 90 minutes to keep your blood flowing.
- Drink water before, during, and after your flight to combat the lack of humidity in airplane cabins. Avoid alcohol, which will dehydrate you.
- If you're flying with kids, don't forget to carry on toys, books, pacifiers, and chewing gum to help them relieve ear pressure buildup during ascent and descent.

ARRIVING AT HONG KONG INTERNATIONAL AIRPORT

No one who ever flew into Hong Kong's former Kai Tak Airport could quite forget the experience of landing in one of the world's most densely populated cities. The runway extended out into the bay, past apartments so close you could almost reach out and touch the laundry fluttering from the bamboo poles.

But Kai Tak, which ranked as the world's third-busiest airport in 1996, was retired in 1998. Taking its place is the **Hong Kong International Airport** (© 852/2181 8888; www.hongkong airport.com), four times the size of Kai Tak. Situated just north of Lantau island on Chek Lap Kok island and reclaimed land, about 32km (20 miles) from Hong Kong's central business district, the state-of-the-art airport is one of the world's most user-friendly.

After Customs, you'll find yourself in the arrivals hall. One of the first things you should do is stop by one of three **Hong Kong Tourism Board (HKTB)** counters, where you can pick up a map of the city, sightseeing brochures, and a wealth of other information, as well as get directions to your hotel. They're open daily from 7am to 11pm. iCyberLink computers provide access to Discover-hongkong.com 24 hours a day.

Also in the arrivals hall is the counter of the **Hong Kong Hotel Association** (© **852/2383 8380** or 852/2769 8822; ww.hkha.com.hk), where you can book a room in one of its 90-some member hotels without paying a service fee; open daily from 6am to midnight. Note that while they do not have information on rock-bottom establishments, they can book rooms in several low-priced lodgings and the YMCAs.

If you plan on traveling to Macau sometime during your stay in Hong Kong, stop by the **Macau tourist information counter,** also in the arrivals lobby, at AO6; it's open daily from 9am to 1pm, 1:30 to 6pm, and 6:30 to 10pm. However, if you are traveling directly to Macau from Hong Kong International Airport via the new Ferry Transfer service, *do not pass through immigration.* Rather, follow signs to the Ferry Transfer desk where you can purchase ferry tickets and proceed directly to the ferry pier (see chapter 12, "Macau," for more information).

You can **exchange money** at the arrivals hall, but since the rate here is rather unfavorable, it's best to exchange only what you need to get into town—about US$50 should do it.

If you need to leave luggage at the airport, there is a **luggage-storage counter** on the departure floor.

GETTING INTO TOWN FROM THE AIRPORT

The quickest way to get to downtown Hong Kong is via the sleek **Airport Express Line** (© 852/2881 8888; www. mtr.com.hk), which is straight ahead after passing Customs and entering the arrivals hall. Trains run every 12 minutes between 6am and 1am and take 20 minutes to reach Kowloon Station (off Jordan Rd. and accessible to hotels in Tsim Sha Tsui and Yau Ma Tei) and 24 minutes to reach Hong Kong Station, on Hong Kong Island in the Central District. From both Kowloon and Hong Kong stations, free shuttle bus service transfers passengers to most major hotels, departing every 12 to 24 minutes between 6:18am and 11:10pm (see www.mtr.com.hk for a list of hotels served). Fares for the Airport Express are HK$90 (US$12/£6.40) to Kowloon and HK$100 (US$13/£7.15) to Central; round-trip tickets are HK$160 (US$21/£11) and HK$180 (US$23/£13), respectively. Or, if you're in Hong Kong only 3 days, consider purchasing the Tourist Transport Pass for HK$300 (US$39/£21), which allows unlimited travel by public transportation for 3 days and includes the trip from and to the airport. If you're in Hong Kong longer than 3 days, a Tourist Transport Pass for HK$220 (US$29/£16) includes a single journey to or from the airport plus 3 days of public transportation (see "Getting Around" in chapter 4 for more information and other ticket options).

In addition to the Airport Express train, there are also dedicated airport buses that connect the airport with major downtown Hong Kong areas. Easiest if you have lots of luggage—but most expensive—is the **Airport Shuttle** (© **852/2735 7823**), which provides door-to-door service between the airport and major hotels. Tickets, available at a counter in the airport arrivals hall, cost HK$150 (US$19/£11), with buses departing every 30 minutes. It takes about 30 to 40 minutes to reach Tsim Sha Tsui, depending on the traffic.

Slower, with more stops, are **Cityflyer Airbuses** (© **852/2873 0818;** www.city bus.com.hk), also with ticket counters in the arrivals hall (if you pay onboard, you must have exact fare). Most important for tourists are Airbus A21, which travels through Mong Kok, Yau Ma Tei, Jordan, and down Nathan Road through Tsim

Sha Tsui on its way to the KCR East Rail Hung Hom Station; and Airbus A11, which travels to Hong Kong Island, with stops in Central, Wan Chai, and Causeway Bay. Buses depart every 10 to 30 minutes, with fares costing HK$33 (US$4.30/£2.35) to Kowloon and HK$40 (US$5.20/£2.85) to Central and Causeway Bay.

The easiest way to travel from the airport, of course, is to simply jump in a **taxi,** since taxis are quite cheap in Hong Kong but expensive for the long haul from the airport. Depending on traffic and your final destination, a taxi to Tsim Sha Tsui costs approximately HK$300 (US$39/£21) and takes 30 to 45 minutes, while a taxi to the Central District will cost about HK$365 (US$47/£26) and will take 35 to 50 minutes. There's also an extra luggage charge of HK$5 (US65¢/35p) per piece of baggage.

NOTES ON DEPARTING   Passengers flying Cathay Pacific, Virgin, and a handful of other airlines are offered the extra benefit of being allowed to check in for return flights at one of two satellite stations—at Hong Kong Station in Central and at Kowloon Station, both served by the Airport Express Line (see above). Both allow you advance check-in any time from 24 hours to 90 minutes before your flight: You'll get your boarding pass, and your bags will be transferred to the airport. Note, however, that since the September 11, 2001 terrorist attacks, some U.S.-bound flights do not allow check-in at satellite stations. At the time of going to press, Cathay Pacific and Continental did not allow check in at Hong Kong and Kowloon stations for U.S.-bound flights, while Northwest and United did (call your airline to inquire about its policy). In any case, there is a left-luggage service at both stations, open daily 6am to 1am and useful if your flight is later in the day and you want to do some sightseeing before heading for the airport. Rates per piece of luggage are HK$35 ($4.55/£2.50) for up to 3 hours and HK$50 (US$6.50/£3.55) for 3 to 24 hours.

If you travel directly to the airport and go through check-in there, plan on arriving about 2 hours before departure. Although most tickets now include airport departure tax in their price, you may be required to pay the tax (HK$120/US$16/£8.55) if yours does not. At any rate, passengers waiting for flights can browse at the Hong Kong Sky Mall, with more than 100 outlets offering merchandise and food.

A final note about departing: Travelers may not bring sharp objects (knives, cutters, scissors, razor blades, household cutlery) in their carry-on but may pack them in checked bags. Also, gels, aerosols, and liquids in carry-on baggage must fit into one quart-size clear plastic bag; otherwise, check it or it will be confiscated.

BY TRAIN

It's unlikely you'll arrive in the SAR by train, unless, of course, you're traveling via China. The Beijing-Kowloon Railway provides a direct link between the two cities in approximately 25 hours and costs HK$1,191 (US$155/£85) for a bed in a deluxe, two-bed cabin, HK$934 (US$121/£67) for a "soft bed" in a four-bed cabin, and HK$601 (US$78/£43) for a "hard bed" in a six-bed cabin, one-way. Service is also available from Shanghai in about 26 hours, costing HK$508 to HK$1,039 (US$66–US$135/£36–£74) one-way, and from Guangzhou (formerly

Canton), costing HK$190 to HK$230 (US$25–US$30/£14–£16) and taking less than 2 hours.

In any case, the end terminus for train travel to Hong Kong is East Tsim Sha Tsui Station, with an underground pedestrian passageway linking it to the nearest MTR subway station in Tsim Sha Tsui and its many hotels.

BY BOAT

Some 30 international cruise ships make Hong Kong a port of call each year. The SAR's main docking facility for cruise liners is Ocean Terminal, located in the heart of Tsim Sha Tsui and part of a massive shopping complex which includes 700 shops and 50 restaurants. Just a stone's throw away is the Star Ferry with service to Hong Kong Island.

There is also extensive ferry service from neighboring Guangdong Province, across the border in mainland China, offered by the Chu Kong Passenger Transport Co. (© 852/2852 3876; www.cksp.com.hk). Ferries from Nan Hai (port of call for Guangzhou), Zhu Hai, Shantou, Sanbu, and a dozen other cities arrive at the China HK Ferry Terminal in Tsim Sha Tsui.

TurboJet (© 852/2859 3333; www.turbojet.com.hk) operates jetfoil service from Macau and Shenzhen to the Hong Kong Macau Ferry Terminal on Hong Kong Island, with MTR connection to the rest of the city. A limited number of jetfoils also go to the China HK Ferry Terminal.

11 Packages for the Independent Traveler

Package tours are simply a way to buy the airfare, accommodations, and other elements of your trip (such as airport transfers and sometimes even city tours and other activities) at the same time and often at discounted prices.

One good source of package deals is the Hong Kong Tourism Board's website at Discoverhongkong.com, which lists the latest deals from various tour companies. Another good source is the airlines themselves. From the U.S., **United Airlines** offers the most options with its

> **Tips   Ask Before You Go**
>
> Before you invest in a package deal or an escorted tour:
> - Always ask about the cancellation policy. Can you get your money back? Is there a deposit required?
> - Ask about the accommodations choices and prices for each. Then look up the hotels' reviews in a Frommer's guide and check their rates online for your specific dates of travel. Also find out what types of rooms are offered.
> - Request a complete schedule. (Escorted tours only.)
> - Ask about the size and demographics of the group. (Escorted tours only.)
> - Discuss what is included in the price (transportation, meals, tips, airport transfers, and the like). (Escorted tours only.)
> - Finally, look for hidden expenses. Ask whether airport departure fees and taxes, for example, are included in the total cost—they rarely are.

United Vacations (© 800/917-9246; www.uv-asia.com), with a variety of escorted and independent package deals to Hong Kong and other Asian destinations. In Hong Kong, **Cathay Pacific Holidays** (© 852/2747 4388 in Hong Kong; www.cxholidays.com) offers a long list of Hong Kong hotel options in conjunction with its flights. Several big **online travel agencies**—Expedia, Travelocity, Orbitz, Site59, and Lastminute.com—also do a brisk business in packages.

Of the tour companies offering packages to Asia, three of the largest are

Pacific Delight Tours (© 800/221-7179; www.pacificdelighttours.com); **Pacific Bestour** (© 800/688-3288; www.bestour.com); and **Gate 1 Travel** (© 800/682-3333; www.gate1travel.com).

Travel packages are also listed in the travel section of your local Sunday newspaper. Or check ads in the national travel magazines such as *Budget Travel Magazine, Travel + Leisure, National Geographic Traveler,* and *Condé Nast Traveler.*

12 Escorted General-Interest Tours

Escorted tours are structured group tours, with a group leader. The price usually includes everything from airfare to hotels, meals, tours, admission costs, and local transportation.

Despite the fact that escorted tours require big deposits and predetermine hotels, restaurants, and itineraries, many people derive security and peace of mind from the structure they offer. Escorted tours—whether they're navigated by bus, motorcoach, train, or boat—let travelers sit back and enjoy the trip without having to drive or worry about details. They take

you to the maximum number of sights in the minimum amount of time with the least amount of hassle. They're particularly convenient for people with limited mobility and they can be a great way to make new friends.

On the downside, you'll have little opportunity for serendipitous interactions with locals. The tours can be jam-packed with activities, leaving little room for individual sightseeing, whim, or adventure—plus they often focus on the heavily touristed sites, so you miss out on many a lesser-known gem.

Among the many companies offering group tours are **Pacific Delight Tours** and **Pacific Bestour** (see "Packages for the Independent Traveler," above), which offer trips primarily to China but include stops in Hong Kong; **General Tours** (© **800/221-2216;** www.generaltours. com); and **China Focus Travel** (© **800/ 868-7244;** www.chinafocustravel.com).

Luxury **cruise liners** are also a common sight in Hong Kong's harbor, anchored conveniently right next to the SAR's largest shopping mall at Ocean Terminal on the Kowloon side. Cruise lines with ports of call in Hong Kong include **Cunard** (© **800/7-CUNARD;** www.cunard.com), **Holland America** (© 877/724-5425; www.hollandamerica. com), and **Princess Cruises** (© **800/ PRINCESS;** www.princesscruises.com). More information on package tours and cruises can be obtained from your travel agent.

13 Recommended Reading

If you want to read something about Hong Kong before setting out on your trip, good places to start are *A History of Hong Kong* by Frank Welsh (Harper-Collins, 1997) or *A Modern History of Hong Kong* by Steve Tsang (I.B. Tauris, 2004), both of which give a thorough historical account of the colony's ignoble beginnings to the 1997 handover. Life in the infamous Walled City is the subject of Greg Girard and Ian Lambot's *City of Darkness: Life in Kowloon Walled City* (Watermark Publications, 2003), complete with photographs of a life now vanished. Even though it remains slightly dated, one of my favorite books is Jan Morris's *Hong Kong* (Vintage, 1997), which traces the evolution of the British colony from its birth during the Opium Wars to just before the handover. This book gives a unique perspective on the workings of the former colony and imparts an astonishing wealth of information, making it fascinating armchair reading. Business travelers may want to pick up *Culture Shock! Hong Kong: A Survival Guide to Customs and Etiquette* (Marshall Cavendish, 2005) by Betty Wei and Elizabeth Li.

I love looking at pictures of old Hong Kong, and especially fascinating is Nigel Cameron's *An Illustrated History of Hong Kong* (Oxford University Press, 1991), with photographs that show Hong Kong of yore and vividly illustrate how much the city has changed. An even more thorough pictorial history is presented in *Old Hong Kong* (FormAsia Books Ltd., 2002), edited by Trea Wiltshire and covering Hong Kong from 1860 through the June 1997 handover.

For an intimate view of Hong Kong, a longtime favorite is *Hong Kong: Borrowed Place, Borrowed Time* (Praeger, 1968) by Richard Hughes, a foreign correspondent who lived in Hong Kong for several decades and was said to have been the inspiration for several characters in John Le Carré's novels. Similarly, another exceptional—though hard to find—read is Austin Coates's *Myself a Mandarin* (Heinemann, 1977), which gives a passionate firsthand account of the author's experiences working as a Special Magistrate in Hong Kong's New Territories. A great accompaniment to any guidebook is *Travelers' Tales Hong Kong* (Travelers' Tales Inc., 1996), an anthology edited by James O'Reilly and filled with personal accounts and essays by well-known writers about life in Hong Kong, including those by Jan Morris, Bruce Chatwin, and Paul Theroux. *Hong Kong: Somewhere Between Heaven and Earth* (Oxford University Press, 1996), edited by Barbara-Sue White, is a collection of poems, short stories, novel excerpts, letters, speeches, and diaries with ties to Hong Kong, written by both Chinese and people of other nationalities from all walks of life—soldiers, doctors, politicians, writers, and others, from Queen Victoria to Jules Verne and ranging from historical accounts dating from the Song dynasty to the present day.

Fictional accounts that depict the character of Hong Kong are Richard Mason's *The World of Suzie Wong* (World Pub., 1957) and Han Suyin's *A Many-Splendored Thing* (Little Brown, 1952), an autobiographical account of life in Hong Kong shortly after the Chinese revolution in the late 1940s and early 1950s. James Clavell's *Tai-Pan* (Atheneum, 1966) is a novel about Hong Kong's beginnings; *Noble House* (Delacorte Press, 1981) is its sequel. John Le Carré's *The Honourable Schoolboy* (G. K. Hall, 1977) details the activities of George Smiley, acting head of the British Secret Service in Hong Kong. *The Monkey King,* by Timothy Mo (Faber & Faber, 1988), is a hilarious account of a Macau native who marries into a dysfunctional Cantonese family in 1950s Hong Kong. More recent is Paul Theroux's *Kowloon Tong* (Houghton Mifflin, 1997), the story of a British expatriate born and raised in Hong Kong but who lives as an outsider, never learning Chinese and failing to understand what's at stake when he's offered a large sum of money by a Chinese mainlander for his family business just before the handover. *Fragrant Harbor* (Putnam, 2002) by John Lanchester is a historical novel that brings to life Hong Kong from the 1930s to the present, as seen through the eyes of an Englishman in love with a Chinese woman and spying for the Empire during the Japanese occupation.

Suggested Hong Kong Itineraries

If your time in Hong Kong is limited, my suggested itineraries below will make the most of it by guiding you to the best the city has to offer, coordinating sightseeing with dining and evening plans. Keep in mind that some attractions are closed 1 day of the week, so plan your days accordingly.

1 The Best of Hong Kong in 1 Day

Seeing the top sights of Hong Kong in 1 day requires an early start, discipline, and a bit of stamina. This "greatest hits" tour begins with a stroll along the Tsim Sha Tsui waterfront promenade and a dim sum breakfast, and includes two museum stops, shopping at a swanky Chinese emporium, a ride on the famous Star Ferry, a tram ride to Victoria Peak, and a stroll on Nathan Road to Kong's famous night market. *Start: MTR to Tsim Sha Tsui.*

❶ Tsim Sha Tsui Promenade
If you only have 1 day to spend in Hong Kong, I feel for you. Start the day with an early-morning stroll along the Tsim Sha Tsui Promenade, from which you have a great view of the harbor with its boat traffic and Hong Kong Island. If it's Monday, Wednesday, Thursday, or Friday, you might even want to join a free 1-hour lesson in tai chi, conducted at 8am on the promenade near the Avenue of Stars, where plaques list Hong Kong's most famous celebrities. See p. 181.

> **☕ Take a Break**
> Located in the Hong Kong Cultural Centre, next to the Star Ferry, **Serenade Chinese Restaurant** ⚑ is my top choice for dim sum with a view of Victoria Harbour. It opens at 8am daily. Located on Salisbury Road (⒞ **852/2722 0932**). See p. 156.

❸ Hong Kong Museum of Art ⚑⚑⚑
Beside the Cultural Centre is this impressive museum housing Hong Kong's best collection of Chinese antiquities and fine art, including bronzes, paintings, and ceramics, shown on a rotating basis. Its relatively small size makes it easy to see in an hour or less; I also like the Victoria Harbour views from its windows. Closed Tuesday, opens the rest of the week at 10am. See p. 166.

❹ Chinese Arts and Crafts Ltd
For one-stop shopping, this two-story Chinese emporium in the Star House, across from the Star Ferry, is Hong Kong's best upscale chain for high-quality jade, jewelry, Chinese clothing, embroidered tablecloths, antiques, rosewood furniture, and more. If you're looking for a high-quality gift—or something special for yourself—this is a good place to look. See p. 212.

The Best of Hong Kong in 1 Day

1. Tsim Sha Tsui Promenade
2. Serenade Chinese Restaurant
3. Hong Kong Museum of Art
4. Chinese Arts and Crafts Ltd
5. Star Ferry
6. Victoria Peak
7. The Peak Lookout
8. Nathan Road
9. Hong Kong Museum of History
10. Temple Street Night Market

5 Star Ferry

No visit to Hong Kong would be complete without at least one trip across Victoria Harbour aboard one of the famous Star Ferries, which have been plying the waters between Hong Kong Island and Kowloon since 1898. The 5-minute trip (have your camera ready!) will deposit you at the Central Ferry Piers, where other ferries depart for the outlying islands. See p. 244.

Take the open-top shuttle bus no. 15C from the Star Ferry bus no. 23 to the Peak Tram Station.

6 Victoria Peak

Board the Peak Tram, which began operations in 1888, for its 8-minute climb up Victoria Peak, where you'll be rewarded with fantastic views from Hong Kong Island's tallest hill if the weather is clear. There's an observation platform atop Peak Tower, with 360-degree panoramic views. If you have the time and energy, walk the 1-hour circular stroll around the Peak. See p. 164.

7 TAKE A BREAK
The Peak Lookout 🕮🕮, a former tram station across from Peak Tower, is a delightful setting for American, Chinese, Indian, Japanese, and Southeast Asian fare, especially if the weather is nice and you can sit on its outdoor terrace surrounded by lush greenery. Other good choices abound in Peak Tower and Peak Galleria across the street. Located at 121 Peak Rd. (✆ 852/2849 1000). See p. 152.

Take the Peak Tram back to Central and walk 10 minutes to the Central MTR station, where you should board the subway for Tsim Sha Tsui Station.

8 Nathan Road

Nicknamed the "Golden Mile of Shopping" for its endless string of shops selling electronics, jewelry, clothing, and a million other goods, this is Kowloon's most famous street. See p. 206.

9 Hong Kong Museum of History

For a quick course in Hong Kong's history, from its days as a small fishing village through its years as a British colony, this museum is a must-see. Closed Tuesday. See p. 166.

10 Temple Street Night Market

Hong Kong's most famous night market exudes a festive atmosphere with its outdoor stalls selling everything from Chinese souvenirs to clothing and accessories, fortunetellers, and street opera singers. Open daily from 4pm, but the real action doesn't get underway until 7pm. If you want to dine here, you'll find many open-air casual restaurants near Temple Street. Otherwise, in the basement of the Eaton Hotel, 380 Nathan Rd. (✆ **852/2782 1818**), is a Cantonese spot, **Yat Tung Heen Chinese Restaurant,** good for seafood and regional dishes. See p. 219.

2 The Best of Hong Kong in 2 Days

After a full day following the "The Best of Hong Kong in 1 Day," above, you'll find yourself packing in the activities for Day 2 as well, starting with some shopping at chic Shanghai Tang and a Central street market before heading to the colorful Western District with its traditional Chinese shops, Hong Kong Island's oldest temple, and the city's best antiques district. Next it's on to Aberdeen, famous for its floating junk population, where you'll dine aboard a floating restaurant before heading to Stanley Market, a fun destination for inexpensive clothing and souvenirs. End the day on the Tsim Sha Tsui Promenade for the nightly Symphony of Lights extravaganza. *Start: MTR or Star Ferry to Central.*

1 Shanghai Tang

This classy shop revolutionized traditional Chinese clothing with mod cheongsams, Chinese jackets, and other fashionable wear in eye-popping colors. It also sells home accessories, purses, and funky goods. See p. 212.

2 Li Yuen Street East and Li Yuen Street West

These two parallel pedestrian lanes between Queen's Road Central and Des Voeux Road Central are packed with stalls selling clothing and accessories, both Western and Chinese. See p. 218.

3 Western District

West of Central, this colorful neighborhood features traditional Chinese shops selling ginseng, herbal medicine, preserved foods, and funeral goods, concentrated on Wing Lok Street, Des Voeux Road, and Queen's Road West. For a more thorough tour of this area, see the walking tour starting on p. 188.

The Best of Hong Kong in 2 Days

Transit stops

KOWLOON

TSIM SHA TSUI
TSIM SHA TSUI EAST
Tsim Sha Tsui

Star Ferry to Central

WESTERN DISTRICT
CENTRAL DISTRICT
SOHO
MID-LEVELS
Central
ADMIRALTY
LAN KWAI FONG
Victoria Peak
Mt. Davis
Mt. Gough
Mt. Kellett

Victoria Harbour

CAUSEWAY BAY
WAN CHAI
HAPPY VALLEY

HONG KONG ISLAND

Telegraph Bay

Aberdeen

Ap Lei Chau Island

Deep Water Bay

Repulse Bay
Repulse Bay

East Lamma Channel

Stanley
Stanley Beach

Bluff Head

1 Shanghai Tang
2 Li Yuen Street East and Li Yuen Street West
3 Western District
4 Sammy's Kitchen
5 Hollywood Road
6 Cat Street
7 Man Mo Temple
8 Aberdeen
9 Jumbo Kingdom
10 Stanley Market
11 Symphony of Lights
12 Hutong

TAKE A BREAK

It's nothing fancy, but **Sammy's Kitchen,** a family-owned restaurant and one of the few serving Western food in the Western District, has been dishing out inexpensive Western and Chinese fare since 1970. A throwback to older days in decor and atmosphere, it's also good for breakfast, lunch, or simply a refreshing drink. Located at 204–206 Queen's Road West. ✆ **852/2548 8400.** See p. 155.

5 Hollywood Road

This long street stretching through the Western District to Central is lined with shops selling high-end Chinese antiques and furniture, as well as curio stores selling snuff bottles, old postcards, and bric-a-brac. See p. 208.

6 Cat Street

A pedestrian lane parallel to Hollywood Road, it's lined with street vendors and shops selling antiques, junk, and reproductions. See p. 208.

7 Man Mo Temple

Located on Hollywood Road and dating back to the 1840s, Hong Kong Island's oldest temple makes for a picturesque stop. See p. 171.

Take a taxi to Aberdeen's waterfront promenade, on the south side of Hong Kong Island.

8 Aberdeen

Although now surrounded by high-rises, Aberdeen is still known for its fishing fleet of modern boats and traditional junks, many inhabited by boat people who have lived on the sea for generations. If you wish, you can take a sampan tour for an up-close view. See p. 169.

9️⃣ TAKE A BREAK

Take the free shuttle boat from Aberdeen's waterfront promenade to **Jumbo Kingdom** 🍴 (📞 852/2553 9111), a colorful floating restaurant where you can feast on dim sum and Cantonese fare. Alternatively, on the top deck is the **Top Deck, at the Jumbo** (📞 852/2553 3331), which features alfresco dining and an international menu of seafood. See p. 154.

Catch bus no. 73 or take a taxi to

🔟 Stanley Market

This market is great for both Western and Chinese clothing for the whole family, as well as traditional Chinese souvenirs, making it a fun, laid-back destination. See p. 218.

Take bus no. 6, 6A, 6X, or 260 to Central or bus no. 973 to Kowloon.

⓫ Symphony of Lights

Guinness World Records rates this the world's largest permanent light-and-sound show, where every evening at 8pm more than 30 buildings on both sides of the harbor put on a light-and-laser show. The best vantage point is at Avenue of the Stars on the Tsim Sha Tsui Promenade. See p. 236.

1️⃣2️⃣ WINDING DOWN

Breathtaking views, a dramatic setting, and innovative northern Chinese cuisine make **Hutong** 🍴🍴🍴 one of Hong Kong's most talked-about restaurants. In other words, make reservations as early as possible. Located on the 28th floor at 1 Peking Rd. 📞 852/3428 8342. See p. 156.

---

3 The Best of Hong Kong in 3 Days

While you could spend a third day—and even a fourth and a fifth—visiting more attractions and soaking up Hong Kong's lively street life (see the suggested walking tours in chapter 8), visitors with limited time in Hong Kong should consider an excursion to Lantau, home of a giant outdoor Buddha and adjoining monastery offering vegetarian lunches. ***Start:*** *Central Ferry Piers.*

---

❶ Ferry to Lantau

Though you can now reach Lantau via MTR followed by cable car, I recommend the old-fashioned method of transportation—the ferry—on your outbound journey, where from the outdoor deck in deluxe class you're treated to great views along the way. See p. 245.

❷ Bus to Ngong Ping Plateau

Bus no. 2 from Silvermine Bay (*Mui Wo* in Chinese) hurtles around hair-raising

curves and up and down lush countryside on its 45-minute trip to Ngong Ping. See p. 246.

❸ Giant Buddha

Built in 1993, this is the world's largest seated outdoor bronze Buddha. Climb 260-some steps to the viewing platform for sweeping views from Ngong Ping Plateau, 738m (2,460 ft.) above sea level. See p. 246.

The Best of Hong Kong in 3 Days

1. Ferry to Lantau
2. Bus to Ngong Ping Plateau
3. Giant Buddha
4. Po Lin Monastery
5. Wisdom Path
6. Ngong Ping Village
7. Ngong Ping Skyrail
8. Peninsula Hotel Lobby
9. Lan Kwai Fong

🍴 TAKE A BREAK

Dining at **Po Lin Monastery** 🏯🏯 was a draw long before the Giant Buddha and other attractions came on the scene. There are two fixed-price vegetarian meals to choose from, served daily 11:30am to 4:30pm. Be sure to see the monastery's ornate temple, which houses three bronze statues of Buddha representing the past, present, and future. ✆ **852/2985 5248.** See p. 247.

5 Wisdom Path

Wooden pillars, placed in the form of a figure eight to symbolize infinity, display the Heart Sutra, a centuries-old prayer revered by Confucians, Buddhists, and Taoists alike. See p. 247.

6 Ngong Ping Village

Ngong Ping's newest attraction features "Walking with Buddha," a multimedia experience relating Siddhartha's path to enlightenment; "Monkey's Tale Theatre," which presents the parable of a selfish monkey who learns a powerful lesson about sharing and kindness; Ngong Ping Tea House, offering fine teas and cakes and demonstrations of traditional Chinese tea ceremonies; and restaurants and shops. See p. 247.

7 Ngong Ping Skyrail

This cable car travels 5.7km (3.5 miles) in about 25 minutes, providing panoramic views of Lantau, the South China Sea, and even the airport along the way. See p. 246.

Take the MTR to Tsim Sha Tsui.

TAKE A BREAK
Hong Kong's most famous spot for afternoon tea—and people-watching—is the ornate lobby of the venerable **Peninsula** hotel ★★★, built in 1928. A classical string quartet serenades as you feast on scones, finger sandwiches, pastries, and fine teas, served daily from 2 to 7pm. Located on the corner of Nathan and Salisbury roads. ⓒ 852/2920 2888. See p. 159.

Take the MTR to Central.

❾ Lan Kwai Fong

It's a party scene every night in Lan Kwai Fong, Hong Kong's most famous nightlife district. Bars and restaurants beckon with open facades, and the action invariably spills out onto the streets. See chapters 6 and 10 for recommendations on where to eat and drink.

4

Getting to Know Hong Kong

Hong Kong is an easy city to get to know: It's surprisingly compact, with most streets clearly marked in English and with helpful signs indicating the direction to Hong Kong's major sights. And not only is public transportation well organized and a breeze to use, but the Star Ferry and the trams themselves are also sightseeing attractions. In general, however, walking is the best way to go, particularly in the narrow, fascinating lanes and alleys where vehicles can't go. This chapter describes the layout of the city, explains how best to get around it, gives practical advice, and tells you where to turn for additional information.

1 Orientation

For information on getting to the city from the airport, see "Getting There" in chapter 2.

VISITOR INFORMATION

The **Hong Kong Tourism Board (HKTB)** is an excellent source for travel information. Before your trip, check its website at **www.discoverhongkong.com**.

There are three HKTB counters in the arrivals hall of the Hong Kong International Airport, open daily from 7am to 11pm. In town, there are two HKTB Visitor Information & Services Centres, one on each side of the harbor. On the Kowloon side, there's a convenient office in Tsim Sha Tsui, right in the Star Ferry concourse, open daily from 8am to 8pm. On Hong Kong Island, there's an underground office in the Causeway Bay MTR station (F exit), open daily 8am to 8pm. It's rather inconvenient, however, unless you're in Causeway Bay; look for the F exit on Jardine's Crescent.

If you have a question about Hong Kong, you can call the English-speaking **HKTB Visitor Hotline** (© 852/2508 1234), available daily from 8am to 6pm. After-hours a telephone-answering device will take your call and a member of HKTB will contact you the next day at your hotel.

In addition to HKTB's free map, providing close-ups of Tsim Sha Tsui, the Central District, Wan Chai, and Causeway Bay, HKTB publishes a wealth of free, excellent literature about Hong Kong. *Visitor's Kit* is a booklet that gives a brief rundown of Hong Kong's major tourist attractions and information on shopping and dining, while *Hong Kong Museums & Heritage* is useful for its information on museums and declared historical monuments and how to reach them using public transportation. *Hong Kong Kaleidoscope* outlines HKTB's current free classes and seminars in its "Meet the People" program. *Discover Hong Kong by Rail* is useful for trips to the New Territories, while *Hong Kong Walks* is designed for those who like to explore on foot. Business travelers should pick up *Hong Kong Leisure Guide for Business Travelers* (also available for PDA download at www.discoverhongkong.com), while *Hong Kong Family Fun Guide* highlights children's sights and activities. In addition, invaluable leaflets

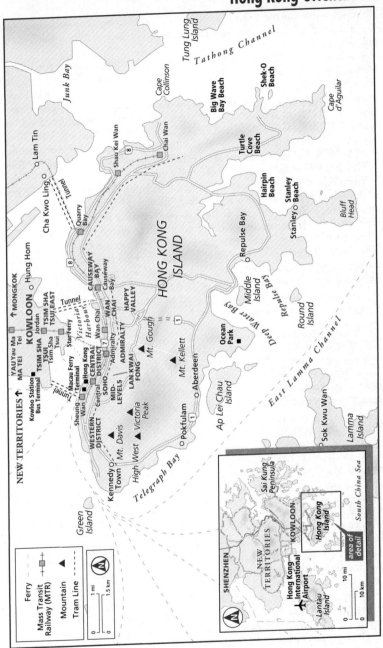

are available showing the major bus routes throughout Hong Kong, including Hong Kong Island, Kowloon, and the New Territories, and for current ferry schedules to the outlying islands.

Travelers with mobile phones can have their own virtual guide by purchasing a **Mobile Host** PIN card for HK$60 (US$7.80/£4.30) at HKTB offices and more than 100 telephone retail shops in Hong Kong. Good for 3 days, the guide provides information on shopping, dining, and sightseeing venues, including how to reach them. It alerts participants to specific shop sales, gives information on seasonal foods and menus, provides a 3-day calendar of events, tells the weather forecasts, gives 30-second or 3-minute spiels on attractions, and links callers to useful telephone numbers and hot lines. You can access the same information without a PIN card by dialing *454, but international roaming charges will apply.

To find out what's going on during your stay in Hong Kong, pick up HKTB's free weekly leaflet *What's On—Hong Kong*, which tells what's happening in theater, music, and the arts, including concerts and special exhibitions in museums. *HK Magazine*, distributed free at restaurants, bars, and other outlets around town (and aimed at a young expat readership), is a weekly that lists what's going on at the city's theaters and other venues, including plays, concerts, exhibitions, the cinema, and events in Hong Kong's alternative scene. *Where Hong Kong, CityLife,* and *bc* are other free magazines published monthly with information on Hong Kong. *Where Hong Kong* and *CityLife* are distributed to rooms in major hotels and are also available at HKTB offices. *bc* is distributed to bookstores and restaurants.

CITY LAYOUT

The Hong Kong Special Administrative Region (SAR), with a population of 6.8 million, is located at the southeastern tip of the People's Republic of China, some 1,996km (1,237 miles) south of Beijing; it lies just south of the Tropic of Cancer at about the same latitude as Mexico City, the Bahamas, and Hawaii. Most people who have never been to Asia probably think of Hong Kong as an island—and they'd be right if it were 1842. But not long after the colony was first established on Hong Kong Island, the British felt the need to expand, which they did by acquiring more land across Victoria Harbour on the Chinese mainland. Today, Hong Kong Island is just a small part of the SAR, which covers 1,100 sq. km (425 sq. miles) and measures 49km (30 miles) north to south and 73km (45 miles) east to west—much of it mountainous.

Hong Kong can be divided into four distinct parts: Hong Kong Island, Kowloon Peninsula, New Territories, and the outlying islands. On **Hong Kong Island** are the Central District (Hong Kong's main financial and business district and usually referred to simply as Central), the Western District, Wan Chai, and Causeway Bay, all on the island's north side. Hong Kong Island is the home to such major attractions as Hong Kong Park, Victoria Peak, Stanley Market, Ocean Park, Aberdeen, the Zoological and Botanical Gardens, and several shopping malls, including Pacific Place, ifc mall, and Times Square.

Across Victoria Harbour, at the tip of **Kowloon Peninsula,** is Tsim Sha Tsui and its many hotels, restaurants, museums, and shops, as well as Tsim Sha Tsui East, and the Yau Ma Tei and Mong Kok districts.

The **New Territories** are by far the largest area, stretching north of Kowloon all the way to the Chinese border. Once a vast area of peaceful little villages, fields, and duck farms, the New Territories in the past few decades have witnessed a remarkable mushrooming of satellite towns with huge public-housing projects. Sha Tin, with a population of around 620,000 and home of one of Hong Kong's two horse-racing tracks, is the largest; in all, the New Territories house approximately half of the SAR's population. And yet, much of the New Territories remains open and uninhabited. Close to 70% of Hong Kong's total landmass is rural, with 23 country parks and 14 nature reserves accounting for more than 40% of Hong Kong's land area. The fact that Hong Kong is more than just a city surprises many first-time visitors.

As for Hong Kong's 260 **outlying islands,** most are barren and uninhabited; those that aren't lend themselves to excellent exploration into Hong Kong's past. Lantau, Lamma, and Cheung Chau are three of the region's best known and most easily accessible islands, where a gentler, slower, and more peaceful life prevails. Lantau, boasting the world's largest seated bronze Buddha (located at a monastery noted for its vegetarian meals), is the most popular destination, accessible by ferry and cable car. Lamma is famous for its open-air waterfront seafood restaurants, beaches, pleasant hiking trail, and expat community, while Cheung Chau makes for a pleasant half-day excursion with its lively traditional village, boat population, and beach.

For the visitor, however, most hotels, restaurants, and points of interest are concentrated in the following areas: **Tsim Sha Tsui, Tsim Sha Tsui East,** and **Yau Ma Tei** on the Kowloon side; and **Central District, Wan Chai,** and **Causeway Bay** on Hong Kong Island. Because these areas are so compact, the city must rank as Asia's most accessible and navigable city. I'd argue that Hong Kong is also the most stunning, given the ferries, cargo ships, fishing boats, and ocean liners bustling in Victoria Harbour, juxtaposed against many peaks that punctuate the cityscape.

MAIN ARTERIES & STREETS   Hong Kong Island's Central District is larger now than it was originally, thanks to massive land reclamation. **Queen's Road,** now several blocks inland, used to mark the waterfront, as did **Des Voeux Road** and **Connaught Road** in subsequent years. Today they serve as busy thoroughfares through Central, since the steep incline up Victoria Peak follows close on their heels. From the Central District, **Hennessy, Lockhart, Jaffe,** and **Gloucester** roads lead east through Wan Chai to Causeway Bay.

It wasn't until 1972 that the first **cross-harbor tunnel** was built, connecting Causeway Bay on Hong Kong Island with Tsim Sha Tsui East in Kowloon. In 1989 a second tunnel was completed under Victoria Harbour; a third tunnel was completed in conjunction with Hong Kong's new International Airport.

On the Kowloon side, the most important artery is **Nathan Road,** which stretches north up the spine of Kowloon Peninsula and is lined with hotels and shops. **Salisbury Road** runs east and west at the tip of Tsim Sha Tsui from the Star Ferry through Tsim Sha Tsui East along the waterfront. Also on the waterfront is the **Tsim Sha Tsui Promenade** affording great nighttime views of neon-lit Hong Kong Island.

FINDING AN ADDRESS   With a good map, you should have no problem finding an address. Streets are labeled in English (though signs are sometimes lacking in more congested areas like the Western District and Yau Ma Tei) and building numbers progress consecutively. For the most part, streets that run east to west (such as Des Voeux Rd. Central, Hennessy Rd., Lockhart Rd., and Salisbury Rd.) all have the even-numbered buildings on the north side of the street and the odd-numbered ones on the south. From Central, roads running through Wan Chai all the way west to Causeway Bay start with the lowest numbers near Central, with the highest-numbered buildings ending at Causeway Bay. On Nathan Road, Kowloon's most important thoroughfare, the lowest-numbered buildings are at the southern tip near the harbor;

the numbers increase consecutively, with the evens on the east and the odds to the west.

Remember that the floors inside buildings follow the British system of numbering. What Americans call the first floor, therefore, is called the ground floor in Hong Kong; the American second floor is numbered the first floor. In addition, if you're trying to find a specific office or factory outlet in a big building, it's useful to know that number 714 means it's on the seventh floor in Room 14, while 2312 means Room 12 on the 23rd floor.

STREET MAPS You can get a free map of the SAR, which shows the major roads and streets of Tsim Sha Tsui, Yau Ma Tei, Mong Kok, the Central District, the Western District, Wan Chai, and Causeway Bay, from the HKTB (see "Visitor Information" above). It should be adequate for locating most hotels, restaurants, sights, shops, and bars mentioned in this book. There are also free giveaway maps available at most hotels. If you want to explore Hong Kong in more detail, you can purchase an entire book with maps of the city region and areas in the New Territories called *Hong Kong Guidebook,* available at bookstores, but you probably won't need this. Online, electronic maps are available at www.ypmap.com and www.centamap.com (click "ENG" or "English" for the English-language versions).

THE NEIGHBORHOODS IN BRIEF

Hong Kong Island

Central District This is where the story of Hong Kong all began, when a small port and community were established on the north end of the island by the British in the 1840s. Named "Victoria" in honor of the British queen, the community quickly grew into one of Asia's most important financial and business districts, with godowns (waterfront warehouses) lining the harbor. Today the area known as the Central District but usually referred to simply as "Central" remains Hong Kong's nerve center for banking, business, and administration. If there is a heart of Hong Kong, it surely lies here, but there are few traces remaining of its colonial past.

The Central District boasts glass and steel high-rises representing some of Hong Kong's most innovative architecture, some of the city's most posh hotels, expensive shopping centers filled with designer shops, office buildings, and restaurants and bars catering to Hong Kong's white-collar workers,

primarily in the nightlife districts known as Lan Kwai Fong and SoHo. Although hotel choices in Central are limited to upper-range hotels, staying here makes you feel like a resident yourself, as you rub elbows with the well-dressed professional crowds who work in Central's office buildings. Banks are so important to the Central District that their impact is highly visible—the Hongkong and Shanghai Bank, designed by British architect Norman Foster, and the Bank of China Tower, designed by I. M. Pei, are just two examples of modern architecture that dramatically transformed the Central District's skyline in the 1980s. Hong Kong's tallest building is the 88-story International Finance Centre, which towers above Hong Kong Station and the ifc mall shopping complex near the Central Ferry Piers.

Yet Central is also packed with traditional Chinese restaurants, outdoor markets, and the neon signs of family-run businesses. Trams—certainly one of Hong Kong's most endearing sights—chug their way straight through Central. There are also oases of greenery at Chater Garden—popular with office workers for a lunchtime break—the Botanical Gardens, and Hong Kong Park with its museum of teaware, housed in Hong Kong's oldest colonial-age building.

Lan Kwai Fong Named after an L-shaped street in Central, this is Hong Kong's premier nightlife and entertainment district, occupying not only Lan Kwai Fong but also neighboring streets like D'Aguilar, Wyndham, and other hillside streets. Filled with restaurants and bars in all price categories but popular mostly with people in their 20s and 30s, it's a fun place to spend an evening.

Victoria Peak Hong Kong's most famous mountaintop, Victoria Peak has long been Hong Kong's most exclusive address. Cooler than the steamy streets of Central below, Victoria Peak, often called simply The Peak, was the exclusive domain of the British and other Europeans—even nannies had to have the governor's permission to go there, and the only way up was by sedan carried by coolies or by hiking. Today, Victoria Peak is much more easily reached by the Peak Tram and affords Hong Kong's best views of Central, Victoria Harbour, and Kowloon. In fact, the view is nothing short of stunning. Also on The Peak are shops, restaurants, and multimillion-dollar mansions, glimpses of which can be had on a circular 1-hour walk around The Peak.

Mid-Levels Located above Central on the slope of Victoria Peak, the Mid-Levels has long been a popular residential area for Hong Kong's yuppies and expatriate community. Though not as posh as the villas on The Peak, its swank apartment buildings, grand sweeping views, lush vegetation, and slightly cooler temperatures make it a much-sought-after address. To serve the army of white-collar workers who commute down to Central every day, the world's longest escalator links the Mid-Levels with Central, an ambitious project with 20-some escalators and moving sidewalks (all free) stretching a half-mile (you can board and exit as you wish).

SoHo This relatively new dining and nightlife district, flanking the Central–Mid-Levels Escalator that connects Central with the Mid-Levels, is popular with area residents and those seeking a quieter, saner alternative to the crowds of Lan Kwai Fong. Dubbed SoHo for the region "south of Hollywood Road," it has since blossomed into an ever-growing neighborhood of cafe-bars and intimate restaurants specializing in ethnic and innovative cuisine, making SoHo one of the most exciting destinations in Hong Kong's culinary and nightlife map. Most establishments center on Elgin, Shelley, and Staunton streets.

Western District Located west of the bustling Central District, the Western District is a fascinating neighborhood of Chinese shops and enterprises and is one of the oldest, most traditional areas on Hong Kong Island. Since it's one of my personal favorites, I've spent days wandering its narrow streets and inspecting shops selling traditional herbs, ginseng, medicines, dried fish, antiques, and other Chinese products. The Western District is also famous for Hollywood Road, long popular for its many antiques and curio shops, and for Man Mo Temple, one of Hong Kong's oldest temples. Unfortunately, modernization has taken its toll, and more of the old Western District seems to have vanished every time I visit, replaced by new high-rises and other projects.

Admiralty Actually part of the Central District, Admiralty is located just below Hong Kong Park, centered around an MTR subway station of the same name. It consists primarily of tall office buildings and Pacific Place, a classy shopping complex flanked by three deluxe hotels.

Wan Chai Located east of Central, few places in Hong Kong have changed as dramatically or noticeably as Wan Chai. It became notorious after World War II for its sleazy bars, easy women, tattoo parlors, and sailors on shore leave looking for a good time. Richard Mason's 1957 novel *The World of Suzie Wong* describes this bygone era of Wan Chai; during the Vietnam War, it also served as a popular destination for American servicemen on R & R. Although a somewhat raunchy nightlife remains along Lockhart, Jaffe, and Luard roads, most of Wan Chai has slowly become respectable (and almost unrecognizable) the past few decades with the addition of mostly business-style hotels, more high-rises, the Hong Kong Arts Centre, the Academy for Performing Arts, and the huge Hong Kong Convention and Exhibition Centre, a familiar sight on the Wan Chai waterfront with its curved roof and glass facade. Near the convention center is Star Ferry service to Tsim Sha Tsui.

Causeway Bay Just east of Wan Chai, Causeway Bay is popular as a shopping destination, since shops stay open late and several department stores have branches here. The whole area was once a bay until land reclamation turned the water into soil several decades ago. Now it's a busy area of Japanese department stores; clothing, shoe, and accessory boutiques; street markets; the Times Square shopping complex; and restaurants. On its eastern perimeter is the large Victoria Park.

Happy Valley Once a swampland, Happy Valley's main claim to fame is its racetrack, built in 1846—the oldest racetrack in Asia outside of China.

Aberdeen On the south side of Hong Kong Island, Aberdeen was once a fishing village but is now studded with high-rises and housing projects. However, it is still known for its hundreds of sampans, junks, boat people, and huge floating restaurant. Just to the east, in Deep Water Bay, is Ocean Park, with its impressive aquarium and amusement rides.

Stanley Once a fishing village, Stanley is now a lively center for discount markets selling everything from silk suits to name-brand shoes, casual wear, and souvenirs. It's located on the quiet south side of Hong Kong Island and boasts a popular public beach, a residential area popular with Chinese and foreigners alike, and, most recently, a growing number of trendy restaurants strung along a waterfront promenade.

Kowloon Peninsula

Kowloon North of Hong Kong Island, across Victoria Harbour, is the Kowloon Peninsula. Kowloon gets its name from *Gau Lung,* which means "nine dragons." Legend has it that about 800 years ago, a boy emperor named Ping counted eight hills here and remarked that there must be eight resident dragons, since dragons were known to inhabit hills. (The ninth "dragon" was the emperor himself.)

Today the hills of Kowloon provide a dramatic backdrop for one of the world's most stunning cityscapes. Kowloon Peninsula is generally considered the area south of these hills, which means it also encompasses a very small part of the New Territories. However, "Kowloon" is most often used to describe its southernmost tip, the 12 sq. km (4⅔ sq. miles) that were ceded to Britain "in perpetuity" in 1860. Its northern border is Boundary Street, which separates it from the New Territories; included in this area are the districts Tsim Sha Tsui, Tsim Sha Tsui East, Yau Ma Tei, and Mong Kok. Once open countryside, Kowloon has practically disappeared under the dense spread of hotels, shops, restaurants, and housing and industrial projects. It has also grown due to relentless land reclamation.

Tsim Sha Tsui At the southern tip of Kowloon Peninsula is Tsim Sha Tsui (also spelled "Tsimshatsui"), which, after Central, rates as Hong Kong's most important area. This is where most tourists stay and spend their money, since it has the greatest concentration of hotels, restaurants, and shops in Hong Kong. In fact, some of my acquaintances living in Hong Kong avoid Tsim Sha Tsui like the plague, calling it the "tourist ghetto." On the other hand, Tsim Sha Tsui does boast the a cultural center for the performing arts, a great art museum, Kowloon Park, one of the world's largest shopping malls, a nice selection of international restaurants, a jumping nightlife, and Nathan Road, appropriately nicknamed the "golden mile of shopping." Although you'd be foolish to spend all your time in Tsim Sha Tsui, you'd also be foolish to miss it.

Tsim Sha Tsui East Not surprisingly, this neighborhood is east of Tsim Sha Tsui. Built entirely on reclaimed land, the area has become increasingly important, home to a rash of expensive hotels, shopping and restaurant complexes, science and history museums, and the KCR East Tsim Sha Tsui Station, providing direct train service to mainland China and connected to the Tsim Sha Tsui MTR station via underground pedestrian passageway. A hover-ferry service also connects Tsim Sha Tsui East with Central.

Yau Ma Tei If you get on the subway in Tsim Sha Tsui and ride two stations to the north (or walk for about 25 min. straight up Nathan Rd.), you'll reach the Yau Ma Tei district (also spelled "Yaumatei"), located on Kowloon Peninsula just north of Tsim Sha Tsui. Like the Western District, Yau Ma Tei is very Chinese, with an interesting produce market, a jade market, and the fascinating Temple Street Night Market. There are also several modestly priced hotels here, making this a good alternative to tourist-oriented Tsim Sha Tsui.

Mong Kok On Kowloon Peninsula north of Yau Ma Tei, Mong Kok is a residential and industrial area, home of the Bird Market, the Ladies' Market on Tung Choi Street, and countless shops catering to Chinese. Its northern border, Boundary Street, marks the beginning of the New Territories.

2 Getting Around

If you've just been to Tokyo or Bangkok, Hong Kong will probably bring a rush of relief. For one thing, English is everywhere—on street signs, on buses, and in the subways. In addition, almost 1,000 red and blue directional signs throughout Hong Kong point to attractions and points of interest. The city of Hong Kong is so compact, and its public transportation system so efficient and extensive, that it's no problem at all zipping from Tsim Sha Tsui to Causeway Bay or vice versa for a meal or some shopping. Even the novice traveler should have no problem getting around. Transportation is also extremely cheap. Just remember that cars drive on the left side of the street, English-style, so be careful when stepping off the curb.

> **Tips**   **Public Transport Tips**
>
> Keep in mind that transportation on buses and trams requires the **exact fare.**
> It's therefore imperative to have lots of loose change with you wherever you
> go. Even though ferries and subways will give change, you'll find it more con-
> venient if you have exact change, especially during rush hours. Alternatively,
> and especially if you're in Hong Kong for more than a couple of days, consider
> purchasing a stored-value **Octopus** card, good for travel on virtually all modes
> of transportation, including subways, the Kowloon-Canton Railway trains, the
> Airport Express Line, trams (including the Peak Tram), buses, ferries, and some
> minibuses, as well as for purchases at specified convenience stores, fast-food
> outlets, and vending machines, and even for some pay phones.

BY PUBLIC TRANSPORTATION

Each mode of transportation in the SAR—bus, ferry, tram, and train/subway—has its
own fare system and thus requires a new ticket each time you transfer from one mode
of transport to another. However, if you're going to be in Hong Kong for a few days,
consider purchasing the **Octopus.** This electronic smart card allows users to hop on
and off trains, trams, subways, buses and ferries without worrying about purchasing
tickets each time or fumbling for exact change. Sold at Customer Service Centres at
all MTR subway stations, train stations, and some ferry piers, the Octopus costs a
minimum of HK$150 (US$19/£11), including a HK$50 (US$6.50/£3.55) refundable deposit (minus a HK$7/90¢/50p handling fee if returned within 3 months), and
can be reloaded in HK$50 (US$6.50/£3.55) and HK$100 (US$13/£7.15) units.
Children and seniors pay HK$70 (US$9.10/£5) for the card, including deposit. Alternatively, you can also buy one of two Airport Express Tourist Octopus cards, good for
3 days of unlimited travel: The HK$300 (US$39/£21) card includes a round-trip
from and to the airport on the Airport Express Line; the HK$220 (US$29/£16) card
includes one trip from or to the airport.

To use the Octopus, simply sweep the card across a special pad at the entry gate
(you'll notice that most commuters don't even bother removing the card from their
wallets or purses); the fare is automatically deducted. The Octopus is valid for all
MTR subways, the Kowloon-Canton Railway trains (which serve the New Territories), the Airport Express Line (which runs between the airport and Kowloon and
Central), all trams (including the Peak Tram), buses, some minibuses, the Star Ferry,
and ferries to outlying islands. In addition, the Octopus can be used for purchases at
all 7-Eleven, Circle K, and Metro Store convenience stores, fast-food chains like KFC,
Starbucks, and McDonald's, some vending machines, and even to make phone calls at
Pacific Century Cyber Works (PCCW) public telephones. At the end of your Hong
Kong stay, be sure to turn in the Octopus card for a refund of your deposit (minus a
HK$7/90¢/50p handling fee) and any unused value stored in the card. For informa-
tion, call the Octopus Hotline at © **852/2266 2222** or check its website at www.
octopuscards.com.

BY SUBWAY   The Star Ferry and trams are so popular and at times so crowded that
it's hard to imagine what they must have been like before Hong Kong's subway system was constructed to relieve the human crunch. Hong Kong's **Mass Transit Railway (MTR)** is modern, efficient, clean, and easy to use, and it's also much faster than

the older modes of transportation (and sometimes even taxis). Take note, however, that there are no public toilets at any of the stations or on the trains, and that smoking, drinking, and eating are prohibited. The MTR operates daily from 6am to 1am. For general inquiries, call the MTR 24-hour Hotline at © **852/2881 8888** or check its website at www.mtr.com.hk.

Built primarily to transport commuters in the New Territories to and from work and running under the harbor to link Kowloon with Hong Kong Island, the MTR serves more than 2.4 million passengers a day. You'll probably want to avoid rush hours, unless you enjoy feeling like a sardine in a can. There are six lines, each color-coded, with the next station displayed above each compartment door and announced in English, so you shouldn't have any problem finding your way around. Stations are named for the areas they serve: Go to Central MTR station if you're looking for an address in the Central District, to Mong Kok MTR station if you're looking for a place in Mong Kok, Kowloon. Probably the most important line for tourists is the **red-coded Tsuen Wan Line,** which starts in Central on Hong Kong Island, goes underneath Victoria Harbour to Tsim Sha Tsui, and then runs north the length of Nathan Road, with stops at Jordan, Yau Ma Tei, and Mong Kok stations before heading northwest to the satellite town of Tsuen Wan in the New Territories. The **blue-coded Island Line,** with 14 stations, operates on the north side of Hong Kong Island from Sheung Wan (where you'll find the Macau Ferry Pier) east to Chai Wan, passing through Central, Wan Chai, and Causeway Bay. Three other lines, used mainly by commuters, are the **Kwun Tong Line,** which arches from Yau Ma Tei eastward to the New Territories; the **Tseung Kwan O Line,** which runs from North Point on Hong Kong Island and then goes under the harbor before connecting with the Kwun Tong Line; and the **Tung Chung Line,** which mirrors the Airport Express Line as it runs from Hong Kong Station in Central to Kowloon Station and onward to Tung Chung on Lantau island. The newest line, **Disney Resort Line,** branches off the Tung Chung Line to Disneyland. Additionally, the **Airport Express Line,** serving airport passengers, runs between Hong Kong Station in Central and Hong Kong International Airport, with a stop at Kowloon Station.

Single-ticket, one-way fares range from HK$4 to HK$26 (US50¢–US$3.40/ 30p–£1.85) depending on the distance, but the most expensive ride is the trip underneath the harbor, which costs HK$9 (US$1.15/65p) from Tsim Sha Tsui to Central (still cheap, but outrageous when compared to the Star Ferry's fare of HK$2.20/US30¢/15p for first class). Fares for seniors 65 and older and children ages 3 to 11 range from HK$3 to HK$13 (US40¢–US$1.70/20p–90p). Fares are indicated by inputting your destination on a touch screen above all vending machines, which accept HK$10, HK$5, HK$2, HK$1, and HK50¢ coins, as well as HK$500 and HK$100 notes, and give back change.

In any case, your ticket is plastic, the size of a credit card, and you feed it into a slot at the turnstile. It disappears and then shoots up at the other end of the turnstile. *Be sure to save your ticket*—at the end of your journey, you will again insert your ticket into the turnstile (only this time you won't get it back). Since these tickets are used again and again and have a magnetized strip, be careful not to bend or damage them.

As mentioned above, if you think you're going to be doing a lot of traveling on public transportation, consider buying the Octopus, which saves you from having to buy another ticket each time you ride. Alternatively, there's a Tourist MTR 1-Day Pass, available at MTR Customer Service Centres and valid for 24 hours, for HK$50 (US$6.50/£3.55).

Understanding the Deluge: Tropical Storm Warnings

It's not likely you'll experience a tropical storm during your stay in Hong Kong, but if you do, consider it part of your Asian experience. Called typhoons in this part of the world (after the Cantonese *dai fung*, which translates as "big wind") and hurricanes in the West, these severe tropical storms generally vent their fury from May to November and are especially prevalent in September. There's no need to worry that a storm may sneak up on you unawares—storms are tracked and monitored and are rated according to their strength. Their approach dominates local news, but even if you don't read the newspapers or listen to the evening news, there are other telltale signs of a coming typhoon—MTR stations, hotel lobbies, and businesses post notices, and shopkeepers cover their windows with storm shutters.

Whenever a severe tropical rainstorm or typhoon is approaching Hong Kong, an alert is broadcast continuously on TV and the radio to keep you informed of the storm's movements. To keep people better informed of the severity of a storm, a system of numbers has been developed that begins at Typhoon Signal No. 1, continues to Typhoon Signal No. 3, and then jumps to Typhoon Signal No. 8 and up. (There used to be numbers in between, but these were dropped when the long range proved too confusing.)

Typhoon Signal No. 1 goes up when a tropical storm that could escalate into a typhoon has moved within an 800km (497-mile) radius of Hong Kong. Although public transportation and organized tours and outdoor activities continue as scheduled, this signal indicates that the public should be on alert. Most locals, however, are rather indifferent to a No. 1, especially since this condition can last for several days, with little physical indication of an approaching storm.

Typhoon Signal No. 3 is given when the winds have escalated, accompanied, perhaps, by heavy rains. By this time, organized guided tours and harbor cruises have generally been suspended. Visitors should check with authorities before venturing on day trips to the outlying islands or Macau. Some businesses may close, as employees head for home while public transportation is still running.

Typhoon Signal No. 8 indicates that the gale has reached Hong Kong. Banks, offices, museums, and most shops and restaurants close, and road, ferry, and air transport are suspended. You should never take a Signal No. 8 lightly, but rather, remain in your hotel and celebrate with a typhoon party, which is pretty much what everyone else does. There's nothing like a tropical storm to set the adrenaline running.

Full details of Hong Kong's typhoon warning system can be found in the local telephone directory. For information during a storm, listen to TV or radio broadcasts or call the Hong Kong Observatory at © **852/2835 1473** or check its website at www.hko.gov.hk.

BY TRAIN   In addition to the MTR and Airport Express Line, there are four other rail lines in Hong Kong, operated by the **Kowloon-Canton Railway (KCR) Corporation** (© **852/2929 3399;** www.kcrc.com.hk), which also operates long-distance through trains to mainland China. If you're curious about the New Territories, their scenery, and satellite towns, KCR is a fast, cheap, and painless way to see it. Most useful for visitors is the **East Rail,** which travels from the KCR East Tsim Sha Tsui Station at the tip of Kowloon up to Sheung Shui in the New Territories. That is, Sheung Shui is where you must get off if you don't have a visa to go onward to China. If you do have a visa, you can continue to the border station of Lo Wu and travel onward all the way through China—and even Russia and Europe if you want to, ending up in London. There are two different kinds of trains on this line: the express through-train to Guangzhou, Shanghai, and Beijing; and the local commuter service for those going to towns in the New Territories.

At any rate, if you're taking the East Rail commuter train, you'll make stops at Hung Hom, Mong Kok, Kowloon Tong, Tai Wai, Sha Tin, Fo Tan, Racecourse (on horse-racing days only), University, Tai Po Market, Tai Wo, and Fanling before reaching Sheung Shui. The whole trip from East Tsim Sha Tsui to Sheung Shui takes only 38 minutes, so it's the easiest and fastest way to see part of the New Territories. It's also convenient, with trains running every 3 to 8 minutes daily from approximately 5:28am (from East Tsim Sha Tsui) to midnight. Finally, it's also cheap, costing HK$12.50 (US$1.60/90p) for ordinary (second) class and HK$25 (US$3.25/£1.80) for first class if you go all the way from East Tsim Sha Tsui to Sheung Shui. Fares to Lo Wu cost HK$36.50 (US$4.75/£2.60) and HK$73 (U$9.50/£5.20), respectively. Seniors 65 and older and children aged 3 through 11 pay half fare; those under 3 travel free. Connecting to East Rail at Tai Wai Station is the new **Ma On Shan Rail,** useful for visiting Che Kung Temple.

Serving the western part of the New Territories is the **West Rail,** which links Sham Shui Po in West Kowloon with Tuen Mun in the northwestern part of the New Territories in 30 minutes, with fares ranging from HK$4.50 to HK$13 (US60¢–US$1.70/30p–90p). Extending from the western end of the West Rail is a feeder **Light Rail** transit system, useful for visiting Hong Kong Wetland Park. Trains run from about 6am to midnight.

If you think you're going to do a lot of traveling by train in 1 day, there's a KCR Tourist Pass Combo for HK$30 (US$3.90/£2.15), which provides unlimited travel on all KCR rail lines (except to the last stop, Lo Wu).

BY BUS   Hong Kong buses are a delight—especially the British-style double-deckers. They're good for traveling to places where other forms of public transport don't go, such as to the southern part of Hong Kong Island like Stanley or up into parts of Kowloon and the New Territories. Bus numbers containing an "X" are for express buses, with limited stops. Depending on the route, buses run from about 6am to midnight, with fares ranging from HK$1.20 to HK$45 (US15¢–US$5.85/10p–£3.20); the fare is halved for children under 12 and seniors over 65. Air-conditioned buses cost more than non-air-conditioned buses. (There aren't many buses that are not air-conditioned nowadays, but they still exist in some rural areas.) *You must have the exact fare,* which you deposit into a box as you get on. Make sure, therefore, that you always carry a lot of spare change, or buy an Octopus card. Drivers often don't speak English, so you may want to have someone at your hotel write down your destination in Chinese, particularly if you're traveling in the New Territories. And with the exception of congested areas like Central or Tsim Sha Tsui, you must flag down a bus to make it stop, especially in the New Territories or on an island.

Hong Kong's buses are operated by three companies: **New World First Bus** (© 852/ **2136 8888;** www.nwfb.com.hk), which operates mainly on Hong Kong Island; **Kowloon Motor Bus** (KMB; © **852/2745 4466;** www.kmb.com.hk), operating in Kowloon and the New Territories; and the common yellow buses run by **Citybus** (© **852/2873 0818;** www.citybus.com.hk), operating on Hong Kong Island, Kowloon, and in the New Territories. There are two major bus terminals, located at or near both ends of the Star Ferry. On Hong Kong Island, most buses depart from Exchange Square in the Central District or from bus stops in front of the Central Ferry Piers. Some buses also depart from Admiralty Station. In Kowloon, buses depart the Star Ferry concourse in Tsim Sha Tsui.

The HKTB has individual leaflets for Hong Kong Island, Kowloon, and the New Territories that show bus routes to most of the major tourist spots, indicating where you can catch buses, their frequency and fares, and where to get off. Keep in mind that buses can get very crowded at rush hours and that some buses look pretty ancient—which can make the winding trip to Stanley in a double-decker bus a bone-rattling and exciting experience.

BY TRAM   Tram lines are found only on Hong Kong Island. Established in 1904 along what used to be the waterfront, these are narrow, double-decker affairs that clank their way 16km (10 miles) in a straight line slowly along the northern edge of the island from Kennedy Town in the west to Shau Kei Wan in the east, with one branch making a detour to Happy Valley. Passing through the Central District, Wan Chai, and Causeway Bay on Des Voeux Road, Queensway Road, and Hennessy Road, they can't be beat for atmosphere and are easy to ride since most of them go only on one line (those branching off to Happy Valley are clearly marked). In the zeal to modernize Central, it's a wonder that these trams have survived at all. Ever since the advent of the subway, there's been talk of getting rid of them, but this has raised a storm of protest. Comprising the largest fleet of double-decker trams in the world, they are easily one of the most nostalgic forms of transportation in Hong Kong.

Enter the trams from the back and go immediately up the winding stairs to the top deck. The best seats in the house are those in the front row, where you have an unparalleled view of Hong Kong: laundry hanging from second-story windows, signs swinging over the street, markets twisting down side alleys, crowded sidewalks, and people darting in front of the tram you'd swear couldn't have made it. Riding the tram is one of the cheapest ways of touring Hong Kong Island's northern side, and the fare is the same no matter how far you go. Once you've had enough, simply go downstairs to the front of the tram and deposit the exact fare of HK$2 (US25¢/15p) into a little tin box next to the bus driver as you exit. If you don't have the exact amount, don't panic—no one will arrest you for overpaying a few cents. Children and seniors pay half fare. You can also use the Octopus card. Trams run daily from about 6am to 1am. More information is available at © **852/2548 7102** or www.hktramways.com.

In addition to the old-fashioned trams, there's also the **Peak Tram** (© **852/2849 7654;** www.thepeak.com.hk), a funicular that transports passengers to one of Hong Kong's star attractions: Victoria Peak and its incomparable views. Its lower terminus is on Garden Road in Central, which you can reach via a HK$3.20 (US40¢/20p) shuttle bus departing from the Central Ferry Piers at 10- to 20-minute intervals daily from 10am to 11:45pm. The tram itself runs every 10 to 15 minutes from 7am to midnight, with round-trip tickets costing HK$30 (US$3.90/£2.15) for adults, HK$9 (US$1.15/65p) for children, and HK$14 (US$1.80/£1) for seniors. You can also use an Octopus card.

BY STAR FERRY   A trip across Victoria Harbour on one of the white-and-green ferries of the **Star Ferry Company** (© **852/2367 7065;** www.starferry.com.hk) is one of the most celebrated rides in the world. Carrying passengers back and forth between Hong Kong Island and Kowloon ever since 1898, these boats have come to symbolize Hong Kong itself and are almost always featured in travel articles on Hong Kong Island. They all incorporate the word "star" in their names, like *Night Star, Twinkling Star,* or *Meridien Star.*

The Star Ferry is very easy to ride. Simply use your Octopus or drop your coins into a slot on the ancient-looking turnstile, follow the crowd in front of you down the ramp, walk over the gangway, and find a seat on one of the polished wooden benches. A whistle will blow, a man in a sailor uniform will haul up the gangway, and you're off, dodging fishing boats, tugboats, and barges as you make your way across the harbor. Businesspeople who live in Hong Kong are easy to spot (they're usually buried behind their newspapers); visitors, on the other hand, tend to crowd around the railing, cameras in hand.

The whole trip is much too short, about 7 minutes total from loading pier to unloading dock, with the ride across the harbor taking about 5 minutes. But that 5-minute ride is one of the best in the world, and it's also one of the cheapest. It costs only HK$1.70 (US20¢/10p) for ordinary (second) class (seniors over 65 can ride ordinary class for free); if you really want to splurge, it's only HK$2.20 (US30¢/15p) for first class. First class is located on the upper deck, and it has its own entryway and gangway (follow the signs in the ferry concourse); if it's raining or cold, first class is preferable because there are glass windows in the bow. Otherwise I find ordinary class much more colorful and entertaining because it's the one the locals use and the view of the harbor is often better.

Star Ferries ply the waters daily from 6:30am to 11:30pm between Hong Kong Island's Central District and the tip of Kowloon's Tsim Sha Tsui. Ferries depart every 4 to 5 minutes, except for early in the morning or late at night, when they leave every 10 minutes.

BY OTHER FERRIES   Besides the Star Ferry, there are also many ferries to other parts of the city. Ferries from the Central District, for example, also go back and forth to Kowloon's Hung Hom from 7am to 7pm for HK$5.30 (US70¢/40p). There's hover-ferry service between Central and Tsim Sha Tsui East (near the Grand Stanford Hotel), running at 20-minute intervals between 7:40am and 8:20pm and costing HK$4.50 (US60¢/30p). From Wan Chai, there's ferry service to Tsim Sha Tsui, running from 7:30am to 11pm and costing HK$2.20 (US30¢/15p), and to Hung Hom, available from about 7am to 7pm and costing HK$5.30 (US70¢/40p).

In addition to ferries crossing the harbor between Kowloon and Hong Kong Island, a large fleet serves the many outlying islands and the northern part of the mainland. If you want to go to one of the outlying islands, you'll find that most of these ferries depart from the Central Ferry Piers (home also to the Star Ferry) in Central. The latest schedules and fares are available from the Hong Kong Tourism Board (HKTB). One thing to keep in mind is that on the weekends the fares are higher and the ferries are unbelievably crowded with locals who want to escape the city, so it's best to travel on a weekday. Even so, the most you'll ever pay for a ferry, even on deluxe class on a weekend, is HK$31 (US$4/£2.20). You can use the Octopus card. See chapter 11, "Side Trips from Hong Kong," for more information on ferries to specific islands.

BY TAXI

REGULAR TAXIS   As a rule, taxi drivers in Hong Kong are strictly controlled and are fairly honest. If they're free to pick up passengers, a red FOR HIRE flag will be raised in the windshield during the day and a lighted TAXI sign will be on the roof at night. You can hail them from the street, though there are some restricted areas, especially in Central. In addition, taxis are not allowed to stop on roads with a single yellow line between 7am and 7pm; they are not allowed to stop at all on roads with a double yellow line. Probably the easiest place to pick up a taxi is on side streets, at a taxi stand (located at all bus terminals), or at a hotel. Taxis are generally abundant anytime except when it's raining, during rush hour (about 5–8pm), during shift change (usually around 4pm), and on horse-racing days from September to May. Since many drivers do not speak English, it's a good idea to have your destination written in Chinese. Passengers are required by law to wear seatbelts.

Taxis on Hong Kong Island and Kowloon are red. Fares start at HK$15 (US$1.95/£1.05) for the first 2km (1¼ miles), then are HK$1.40 (US18¢/10p) for each additional 200m (about 656 ft.). Waiting time, incorporated in the meter, is HK$1.40 (US20¢/10p) per minute, luggage costs an extra HK$5 (US65¢/35p) per piece, and taxis ordered by phone add a HK$5 (US65¢/35p) surcharge. Extra charges to pay for the driver's return trip are also permitted for trips through harbor tunnels and Aberdeen Tunnel. Note, too, that there's an additional charge per bird or animal you might want to bring with you in the taxi! For a tip, simply round off your bill to the nearest HK$1 or add a HK$1. Although taxi drivers can service both sides of Victoria Harbour, they tend to stick to a certain neighborhood and often aren't familiar with anything outside their area.

Taxis in the New Territories are green, with fares starting at HK$12.50 (US$1.60/90p) at flag-fall. They cover only the New Territories and are not allowed to transport you back into Kowloon.

If you have a complaint about a taxi driver, call the taxi complaint hotline at (© **852/2889 9999**), but make sure you have the taxi's license number. The driver's name, photograph, and car number are displayed on the dashboard.

MINIBUSES   These small, 16-passenger buses are the poor person's taxis; although they are quite useful for the locals, they're a bit confusing for tourists. For one thing, although the destination may be written in both Chinese and English, you almost need a magnifying glass to read the English, and by then the vehicle has probably already whizzed by. Even if you can read the English, you may not know the bus's route or where it's going.

There are two types of vehicles, distinguishable by color. The green-and-yellow public "light buses" (though also called minibuses) follow fixed routes, have numbers, and charge fixed rates ranging from HK$2 to HK$20 (US25¢–US$2.60/14p–£1.40), depending on the distance, and require the exact fare as you enter (they also accept Octopus cards). The most useful ones on Hong Kong Island are probably those that depart from the Star Ferry concourse for Bowen Road and Ocean Park, as well as those that travel from Central's Lung Wui Road to Victoria Peak or from Causeway Bay to Stanley.

The red-and-yellow **minibuses** are a lot more confusing, because they have no fixed route and will stop when you hail them from the street (except for some restricted areas in Central). However, they're useful for traveling along Nathan Road or between

Central and Causeway Bay. Fares range from HK$2 to HK$23 (US25¢–US$2.90/14p–£1.65), depending on the distance and demand (higher fares are charged on rainy days, race days, or cross-harbor trips), and you pay as you exit. Just yell when you want to get off.

BY CAR

Rental cars are not advisable in Hong Kong and hardly anyone uses them, even businesspeople. For one thing, nothing is so far away that you can't get there easily, quickly, and cheaply by taxi or public transport. In addition, there probably won't be any place to park once you get to your destination. If you want a chauffeur-driven car, most major hotels have their own private fleet—you can even rent a limousine. If you're still determined to rent a car or plan to take a driving tour of the New Territories (you are not allowed to enter mainland China), self-drive firms—such as Avis and Hertz—have branches here, along with a couple of dozen local firms. Your hotel concierge should be able to make arrangements. A valid driver's license is required, and, remember, traffic flows on the left-hand side of the street.

BY RICKSHAW

Rickshaws hit the streets of Hong Kong in the 1870s and were once the most common form of transport in the colony. Now, however, they are almost a thing of the past—no new licenses are being issued. A couple of ancient-looking men sometimes hang around the Star Ferry terminal in the Central District, but they're usually either snoozing or reading the paper. I've never once seen them hauling a customer. Rather, they make money by charging up to HK$50 (US$6.50/£3.55) for tourists who want to take their pictures.

ON FOOT

One of the great things about Hong Kong is that you can explore virtually the entire city proper on foot, with directional signage posted seemingly everywhere directing you to tourist attractions. You can walk from the Central District all the way through Wan Chai to Causeway Bay in about an hour or so, while the half-hour walk up Nathan Road to Yau Ma Tei is recommended to all visitors. Unfortunately, land reclamation has been carried out so ambitiously, it may even be possible one day to walk from Hong Kong Island to Kowloon.

In the Central District, there are mazes of covered, elevated walkways to separate pedestrians from traffic, connecting office buildings, shopping complexes, and hotels. In fact, some roads have no pedestrians because they're all using overhead passageways. These walkways can be confusing, though signs direct pedestrians to major buildings. Tourists will probably find streets easier to navigate if using a map, but walkways are convenient when it rains and are safer, since the walkways separate pedestrians from traffic.

There's also an interesting "people-mover," the free Central–Mid-Levels Escalator between Central on Des Voeux Road Central and the Mid-Levels on Victoria Peak. It's a series of moving walkways and escalators that snake their way through the Central District up the steep slope of the Peak. Constructed in the hope of alleviating traffic congestion for commuters who live in the Mid-Levels (about halfway up the Peak), the combination escalator/walkway has a total length of just less than .8km (½ mile) and transports approximately 27,000 people a day, moving downward in the morning until 10am and then reversing uphill the rest of the day to accommodate those returning home. There are many entrances/exits, so commuters can get on and off as they like.

FAST FACTS: Hong Kong

Your hotel concierge or guest relations manager is usually a valuable source of information. The Hong Kong Tourism Board (HKTB) is also well equipped and eager to help visitors and answer their questions.

American Express There are two American Express offices, located on both sides of Victoria Harbour. On Hong Kong Island, you'll find American Express on the first floor of the Henley Building, 5 Queen's Rd. Central, in the Central District (© **852/3192 7788**). In Tsim Sha Tsui, it's at 48 Cameron Rd. (© **852/3191 3838**). Both are open Monday through Friday from 9am to 5pm and Saturday from 9am to 12:30pm. American Express cardholders can withdraw local currency and traveler's checks 24 hours a day at automated teller machines (ATMs) at both locations, as well as at Jetco ATMs throughout Hong Kong, as long as you know your personal identification number.

Business Hours Although open hours can vary, banking hours are generally Monday through Friday from 9am to 4:30pm and Saturday from 9am to 12:30pm. Keep in mind, however, that some banks stop their transactions—including foreign currency exchange—an hour before closing time.

Most business offices are open Monday through Friday from 9am to 5pm, with lunch hour from 1 to 2pm; Saturday business hours are generally 9am to 1pm.

Most shops are open 7 days a week. Shops in the Central District are generally open from 10am to 7:30pm; in Causeway Bay and Wan Chai, 10am to 9:30pm; and in Tsim Sha Tsui, 10am to 9 or 10pm (and some even later than that). As for bars, most stay open until at least 2am; some stay open until the crack of dawn.

Currency & Currency Exchange See "Money," p. 15.

Dentists & Doctors Most first-class hotels have medical clinics with registered nurses, as well as doctors, on duty at specified hours or on call 24 hours for emergencies. Otherwise, the concierge can refer you to a doctor or dentist. See chapter 5 for hotels with in-house physicians. The U.S. consulate can also provide information on English-speaking doctors. If it's an emergency, dial © **999** (a free call) or contact one of the recommendations under "Hospitals," below.

Drugstores There are no 24-hour drugstores in Hong Kong, so if you need something urgently in the middle of the night, you should contact one of the hospitals listed below. One of the best-known pharmacies in Hong Kong is **Watson's,** which dates back to the 1880s. Today, there are more than 100 Watson's in Hong Kong, most of them open from 9am to 10pm. Ask the concierge at your hotel for the location of a Watson's or drugstore nearest you (only about half the Watson's dispense medicine; the rest deal only in cosmetics and toiletries).

Electricity The electricity used in Hong Kong is 220 volts, alternating current (AC), 50 cycles (in the U.S. it's 110 volts and 60 cycles). Outlets are the British-style three-pin, rectangular plugs. Most hotels are equipped to fit shavers of different plugs and voltages, and higher-end hotels also have outlets with built-in plug adapters to fit foreign prongs. Most laptop computers nowadays are equipped to deal with both 110 and 220 volts. Otherwise, you'll need a transformer and plug adapter (ask your hotel whether they have a plug adapter you can use—they often do, for free).

Embassies & Consulates If you need to contact a consulate about an application for a visa, a lost passport, tourist information, or an emergency, telephone first to find out the hours of the various sections. The visa section, for example, may be open only during certain hours of the day. In addition, consulates are usually closed for their own national holidays and often for Hong Kong holidays as well.

The **American Consulate,** 26 Garden Rd., Central District (© **852/2523 9011;** 852/2841 2211 for the American Citizens Service; www.hongkong.usconsulate. gov), is open Monday through Friday from 8:30am to 12:30pm and 1:30 to 5:30pm. The **Canadian Consulate,** 11th–14th floor of Tower One, Exchange Square, 8 Connaught Place, Central District (© **852/2867 7348;** www.dfait-maeci. gc.ca/asia/hongkong), is open Monday through Friday from 9am to noon and 2 to 4pm.

The **British Consulate,** at 1 Supreme Court Rd., Central District (© **852/2901 3000,** or 852/2901 3262 for passport inquiries; www.britishconsulate.org.hk), is open Monday through Friday from 8:45am to 3pm.

The **Australian Consulate** is on the 23rd floor of Harbour Centre, 25 Harbour Rd., Wan Chai, on Hong Kong Island (© **852/2827 8881;** www.australia.org.hk), and is open Monday through Friday from 9am to 5pm. The **New Zealand Consulate** is on the 65th floor of Central Plaza, 18 Harbour Rd., Wan Chai (© **852/ 2525 5044;** www.nzembassy.com/hongkong), and is open Monday through Friday from 8:30am to 1pm and 2 to 5pm.

For information on visa applications to mainland **China,** contact a tour operator such as China Travel Service (see "China" in chapter 11).

Emergencies All emergency calls are free—just dial © **999** for police, fire, or ambulance.

Holidays Most Chinese festival holidays are determined by the lunar calendar, which changes each year, while national and Christian religious holidays, such as Labour Day, Easter, or National Day, are the same each year. Note, however, that if a public holiday falls on a Sunday, Monday becomes a holiday. For more detailed information on specific holidays and they way they're celebrated, see "Hong Kong Calendar of Events" in chapter 2.

Public holidays for 2007 are: New Year's Day (Jan 1); Lunar New Year (Feb 17–20); Easter (Good Friday through Easter Monday); Ching Ming Festival (Apr 5); Labour Day (May 1); Buddha's Birthday (May 24); Tuen Ng Festival (Dragon Boat Festival, June 19); Establishment Day of the Special Administrative Region (Hong Kong's return to China, July 2); day following Mid-Autumn Festival (Sept 26); National Day (Oct 1); Chung Yeung Festival (Oct 19); Christmas (Dec 25–26). For 2008 lunar holidays, which had not yet been announced at the time we went to press, go to www.info.gov.hk/info/holiday_e.htm.

Hospitals There are 41 public hospitals in Hong Kong. The following can help you round-the-clock: Mary Hospital, 102 Pokfulam Rd., Hong Kong Island (© **852/ 2855 3838**); and Queen Elizabeth Hospital, 30 Gascoigne Rd., Kowloon © **852/ 2958 8888**).

Internet Access See "The 21st-Century Traveler" in chapter 2.

Languages Before the 1997 handover, English and Cantonese were Hong Kong's two official languages. Now, however, English and "Chinese" are listed as the two official languages. There is no one Chinese language, however. While most Hong Kong Chinese speak Cantonese, that's a foreign language in Beijing, where the official language is Mandarin *(Putonghua)*. In reality, Mandarin has also become the official language of the SAR and is being taught in Hong Kong schools. At any rate, while Mandarin and Cantonese differ widely, they use the same characters for writing. Therefore, while a Hong Kong Chinese and a mainland Chinese may not be able to communicate orally, they can read each other's newspapers. Chinese characters number in the tens of thousands; knowledge of at least 1,500 characters is necessary to read a newspaper. Chinese is difficult to learn primarily because of the tonal variations. Western ears may find these differences in pronunciation almost impossible to detect, but a slight change in tone changes the whole meaning. One thing you'll notice, however, is that Chinese is spoken loudly—whispering does not seem to be part of the language.

Despite the fact that English is an official language and is spoken in hotels and tourist shops, few Chinese outside these areas understand it. Bus drivers, taxi drivers, and waiters in many Chinese restaurants do not speak English and will simply shrug their shoulders to your query. To avoid confusion, have someone in your hotel write out your destination in Chinese so that you can show it to your taxi or bus driver. Most Chinese restaurants in tourist areas—and all those listed in this book—have English menus. If you need assistance, try asking younger Chinese, since it's more likely that they will have studied English in school.

Liquor Laws The drinking (and smoking) age in Hong Kong is 18. The hours for bars vary according to the district, though those around Lan Kwai Fong and Tsim Sha Tsui stay open the longest, often until dawn. Beer is available at convenience stores, including 7-Eleven, while a larger selection of beer, wine, and liquor is available from the basement food emporiums of department stores.

Lost & Found To report stolen or lost property, call the police (© **852/2527 7177**) or go to the nearest police station. If you've lost your passport, make a police report at the nearest station and then contact your embassy or consulate for a replacement. The minute you discover your wallet has been lost or stolen, alert all of your credit card companies and file a report at the nearest police station. Your credit card company or insurer may require a police report number or record of the loss. Most credit card companies have an emergency toll-free number to call if your card is lost or stolen; they may be able to wire you a cash advance immediately or deliver an emergency credit card in a day or two. Visa's Hong Kong emergency number is © **852/800 900 782**. American Express cardholders and traveler's check holders should call © **852/2811 6122**. MasterCard holders should call © **852/800 96 6677**. If you need emergency cash over the weekend when all banks and American Express offices are closed, you can have money wired to you via **Western Union** (© **800/325-6000** from the U.S.; www.westernunion.com). There are many Western Union locations in Hong Kong, including one in the post office at 10 Middle Rd., Tsim Sha Tsui (see "Mail," below).

Luggage Storage & Lockers The best and most convenient place to store luggage is at your hotel, even if you plan on traveling to Macau or China for a couple of days. Otherwise, there are luggage-checking services ("left-luggage") at Hong Kong International Airport, Hong Kong Station, Kowloon Station, the Macau Ferry Terminal on Hong Kong Island, and the China Hong Kong Terminal on Canton Road, Tsim Sha Tsui.

Mail Postal service is cheap and reliable. Most hotels have stamps and can mail your letters for you. Otherwise, there are plenty of post offices throughout the SAR. Most are open Monday through Friday from 9:30am to 5pm and Saturday from 9:30am to 1pm. The main post office is on Hong Kong Island at 2 Connaught Place, in the Central District (© 852/2921 2222), where you'll find stamps sold on the first floor (what those from the U.S. would call the second floor). If you don't know where you'll be staying in Hong Kong, you can have your mail sent here "Poste Restante." The post office will hold mail for 2 months; when you come to collect it, be sure to bring along your passport for identification. On the Kowloon side, the main post office is at 10 Middle Rd., which is 1 block north of Salisbury Road (© 852/2366 4111). Both are open Monday through Saturday from 8am to 6pm and Sunday from 9am to 2pm.

Mailboxes are green in Hong Kong. Airmail letters up to 20 grams and postcards cost HK$3 (US40¢/20p) to the United States or Europe. You can count on airmail letters to take about 5 to 7 days, sometimes longer, to reach the United States.

To mail a package via surface mail to the United States, it costs HK$251 (US$33/£18) for a package weighing 5 kilos (11 lb.) and HK$441 (US$53/£32) for a package weighing 10 kilos (22 lb.). A 5-kilo package sent airmail will cost HK$419 (US$54/£30), a 10-kilo package HK$799 (US$104/£57). Post offices sell boxes called Postpak that are handy for mailing items home; they come in several sizes costing HK$6.50 (US84¢/45p) to HK$35 (US$4.55/£2.50). For general inquiries, call © 852/2921 2222.

Newspapers The *South China Morning Post* and *The Standard* are the two local English-language daily newspapers. The *South China Morning Post* is often delivered to guest rooms free or available at the front desk or hotel kiosk, at newsstands, and bookstores. For a different perspective, you might also want to pick up the *China Daily,* from Beijing. The *Asian Wall Street Journal, Financial Times, International Herald Tribune,* and *USA Today International* are also available.

Passports Allow plenty of time before your trip to apply for a passport; processing normally takes 3 weeks but can take longer during busy periods (especially spring). And keep in mind that if you need a passport in a hurry, you'll pay a higher processing fee.

For Residents of Australia: You can pick up an application from your local post office or any branch of Passports Australia, but you must schedule an interview at the passport office to present your application materials. Call the **Australian Passport Information Service** at © 131-232, or visit the government website at www.passports.gov.au.

For Residents of Canada: Passport applications are available at travel agencies throughout Canada or from the central **Passport Office,** Department of Foreign Affairs and International Trade, Ottawa, ON K1A 0G3 (℃ **800/567-6868;** www.ppt.gc.ca).

For Residents of Ireland: You can apply for a 10-year passport at the **Passport Office,** Setanta Centre, Molesworth Street, Dublin 2 (℃ **01/671-1633;** http://foreign affairs.gov.ie/services/passports). Those under age 18 and over 65 must apply for a €12 3-year passport. You can also apply at 1A South Mall, Cork (℃ **021/ 272-525)** or at most main post offices.

For Residents of New Zealand: You can pick up a passport application at any New Zealand Passports Office or download it from their website. Contact the **Passports Office** at ℃ **0800/225-050** in New Zealand or 04/474-8100, or log on to www.passports.govt.nz.

For Residents of the United Kingdom: To pick up an application for a standard 10-year passport (5-year passport for children under 16), visit your nearest passport office, major post office, or travel agency or contact the **United Kingdom Passport Service** at ℃ **0870/521-0410** or search its website at www. ukpa.gov.uk.

For Residents of the United States: Whether you're applying in person or by mail, you can download passport applications from the U.S. State Department website at **http://travel.state.gov.** To find your regional passport office, either check the U.S. State Department website or call the **National Passport Information Center** toll-free number (℃ **877/487-2778)** for automated information.

Police You can reach the police for an emergency by dialing ℃ **999,** the same number as for a fire or an ambulance. This is a free call. There's also a 24-hour crime hot line (℃ **852/2527 7177).**

Restrooms The best places to track down public facilities in Hong Kong are its many hotels. Fast-food restaurants and shopping malls are other good bets. Attendants on duty nowadays rarely expect tips, but if you encounter one who does, HK$2 (US25¢/14p) is sufficient. Note that there are no public facilities at any of the MTR subway stations. Hotels and tourist sites usually have Western toilets, but you may encounter Chinese toilets on ferries and in rural areas. To use them, squat facing the hood. Since some public facilities may not have toilet paper, be sure to carry tissue.

Smoking Virtually all hotels, except those in the rock-bottom category, have nonsmoking rooms, and many restaurants, especially large ones and those in hotels, have nonsmoking sections (some are even entirely smoke free). Smoking is also prohibited in cinemas, shopping malls, supermarkets, department stores, and banks. Under proposed legislation, the smoking ban will be extended to all indoor spaces (including restaurants and bars) by July 2009.

Taxes Hotels will add a 10% service charge and a 3% government tax to your bill. Restaurants and bars will automatically add a 10% service charge, but there is no tax. There's an airport departure tax of HK$120 (US$16/£8.55) for adults and children older than 12, but this is usually—though not always—included in your ticket price. If you're taking the boat to Macau, you must pay a Hong Kong departure tax of HK$19 (US$2.45/£1.35), which is already included in the price of your boat ticket.

Telephone The international country code for Hong Kong is 852. Therefore, to **call Hong Kong:**

1. Dial the international access code: 011 from the U.S.; 00 from the U.K., Ireland, or New Zealand; or 0011 from Australia.
2. Dial the country code: 852.
3. Then dial the number (there is no city code for Hong Kong). So the whole number you'd dial would be 011-852-0000-0000.

To make international calls: To make international calls from Hong Kong, first dial ⓒ **001** (or **0080** or **009**, depending on which competing telephone services you wish to use) and then the country code (U.S. or Canada 1, U.K. 44, Ireland 353, Australia 61, New Zealand 64). Next dial the area code and number. For example, if you wanted to call the British Embassy in Washington, D.C., you would dial 001-1-202-588-7800.

For directory assistance in English: Dial ⓒ **1081** if you're looking for a number inside Hong Kong; ⓒ **10013** for numbers to all other countries.

For collect calls: To make a collect call from any public or private phone in Hong Kong, dial ⓒ **10010**.

Toll-free numbers: Numbers beginning with **800** within Hong Kong are toll-free. However, calling a 1-800 number in the United States from Hong Kong is not free but rather costs the same as an overseas call.

In Hong Kong, local calls made from homes, offices, shops, restaurants, and some hotel lobbies are free, so don't feel shy about asking to use the phone. Otherwise, local calls from public phones cost HK$1 (US15¢/7p) for each 5 minutes; from hotel rooms, about HK$4 to HK$5 (US50¢–US65¢/30p–35p).

Most hotels in Hong Kong offer direct dialing. Otherwise, long-distance calls can be made from specially marked International Dialing Direct (IDD) public phones. The most convenient method of making international calls is to use an Octopus card (see "Getting Around," earlier in this chapter). Alternatively, a PCCW Hello PhoneCard, which comes in denominations ranging from HK$50 to HK$500 (US$6.50–US$65/£3.55–£36), is available at PCCW shops, 7-Eleven convenience stores, machines located beside telephones, and other locations around Hong Kong. Simply insert the card into the slot and dial. You can also charge your telephone call to a major credit card by using one of about 100 credit card phones in major shopping locations.

You can also make cashless international calls from any telephone in Hong Kong by using Home Direct, which gives you immediate and direct access to an operator in the country you're calling. Calls can then be charged collect or charged to an overseas telephone card, making it cheaper than a regular international call from Hong Kong. Some designated Home Direct telephones in Hong Kong, located at the airport, Ocean Terminal in Tsim Sha Tsui, and other locations, even allow you to talk with an operator in your country with the push of a button. Home Direct numbers from Hong Kong are ⓒ **800 96 0161** for Australia, ⓒ **800 96 1100** for Canada, ⓒ **800 96 0064** for New Zealand, and ⓒ **800 96 0044** for the United Kingdom. For the United States, dial ⓒ **800 96**

1111 or 800 93 2266 for AT&T, © **800 96 1121** for MCI, and © **800 96 1877** for Sprint. For more information on dial access numbers for Home Direct, phone locations, where PhoneCards can be purchased and operated, time zones, or other matters pertaining to international calls, call © **10013**.

Television There are two English-language TV channels, TVB Pearl and ATV World, broadcasting weekday mornings, evenings, and all day weekends and holidays, with a choice of local programs and shows imported from America, Australia, and Britain. In addition, all first-class and most moderate hotels have satellite television (with imported American, Australian, and British programming, a sports channel, BBC and CNN news channels, and MTV) and/or cable TV (BBC). Generally, satellite provides more channels, though services can vary depending on how many programs a hotel is signed up for (in general, the cheaper the hotel, the fewer channels available). Many hotels also offer in-house pay movies and may also subscribe to the Hongkong Channel, which features short, 5-minute features on Hong Kong's history, transportation networks, traditional customs and festivals, cultural events, shopping tips, and other information.

Time Zone Hong Kong is 8 hours ahead of Greenwich Mean Time, 13 hours ahead of New York, 14 hours ahead of Chicago, and 16 hours ahead of Los Angeles. Since Hong Kong does not have a daylight saving time, subtract 1 hour from the above times if you're calling the United States in the summer. Because Hong Kong is on the other side of the International date line, you lose 1 day when traveling from the West to Asia. Don't worry—you gain it back when you return, which means that you arrive back home the same day you left Hong Kong.

Tipping Even though restaurants and bars will automatically add a 10% service charge to your bill, you're still expected to leave small change for the waiter (who may never see any of that automatic 10% service charge). A general rule of thumb is to leave 5%, but in most Chinese restaurants where meals are usually inexpensive, it's acceptable to leave change up to HK$5 (US65¢/35p). In the finest restaurants, you should leave 10%. If you're paying by credit card, pay a cash tip, since a gratuity put on a credit card is likely to go to the restaurant and not the staff.

You're also expected to tip taxi drivers, bellhops, barbers, and beauticians. For taxi drivers, simply round up your bill to the nearest HK$1 or add a HK$1 (US15¢/7p) tip. Tip people who cut your hair 5% or 10%, and give bellhops HK$10 to HK$20 (US$1.30–US$2.60/70p–£1.40), depending on the number of your bags. If you use a public restroom with an attendant, you may be expected to leave a small gratuity—HK$2 (US25¢/14p) should be enough—but this is now a rarity in Hong Kong. In addition, chambermaids and room attendants are usually given about 2% of the room charge.

Useful Phone Numbers The Hong Kong Tourism Board's hot line is © **852/2508 1234**, with service available daily from 8am to 6pm. The Police Crime Hotline is © **852/2527 7177**. Other useful numbers are:

U.S. Dept. of State Travel Advisory © 202/647-5225 (manned 24 hr.)
U.S. Passport Agency © 202/647-0518
U.S. CDC Traveler's Health Hotline © 877/394-8747
Hong Kong's Department of Health © 852/2833 0111.

Water It's considered safe to drink urban tap water, though most people prefer bottled water, which is widely available. In summer it's wise to carry bottled water with you. Some hotels have their own purification systems. I always drink the water and have never gotten ill. If you travel into rural Hong Kong or China, however, drink only bottled water.

Weather If you want to check the day's temperature and humidity level or the 2-day forecast, dial © **187 8200** or 187 8066. Both are in English and both are free. Otherwise, if a storm is brewing and you're worried about a typhoon, tune in to one of the radio or television stations described above.

5

Where to Stay

After years of declining tourism—due to events like the September 2001 terrorist attacks in the United States and the 2003 outbreak of Severe Acute Respiratory Syndrome (SARS)—Hong Kong is once again a hotelier's dream. While long-distance tourism in Hong Kong is increasing at a steady pace, regional tourism accounts for most of the surge in growth—thanks to a huge influx of mainland Chinese who, because of relaxed visa regulations, are filling Hong Kong's hotels in ever-increasing numbers. A never-ending parade of conventions, trade fairs, and other events also contributes to Hong Kong's healthy tourism industry.

Hotel occupancy in Hong Kong now stands at 86%, with increased demand causing room rates to rise. Hotels are not cheap in the SAR, especially when compared with those in many other Asian cities. Rather, prices are similar to what you'd pay in major U.S. and European cities, and while US$175 might get you the best room in town in Topeka, Kansas, in Hong Kong it will get you a small, undistinguished box not unlike a highway motel room. In other words, except for the cost of getting to Hong Kong, your biggest expenditure is going to be for a place to stay.

Still, bargains abound, especially on the Internet (see "Planning Your Trip Online" on p. 27). Additionally, upper-end hotels may offer special packages, including weekend getaways, off-season incentives, and upgrades, while lower-end hotels may offer special promotional rates in the off season.

You should always book rooms well in advance, especially if you have a particular hotel, location, or price category in mind. The SAR's biggest hotel crunches traditionally occur twice a year, during Hong Kong's most clement weather: in March through May and again in October and November. In addition, major trade fairs at Hong Kong's convention center can wreak havoc on travelers who arrive without reservations; on one of my visits, all of Hong Kong's hotels were fully booked. Unsurprisingly, prices are highest during peak season and major trade fairs. While bargains are abundant during the off seasons, many hotels use their published rack rates during peak season and major trade fairs.

As for trends in the hotel industry, Hong Kong's biggest markets nowadays are business travelers and tourists from mainland China. This translates into crowded elevators and lobbies in the moderately priced hotels that Chinese frequent. Hotels catering to executive-level business travelers, meanwhile, have beefed up business services, from state-of-the-art business centers to in-room high-speed or wireless Internet connections.

Hotels have also improved services and in-room amenities, so that even moderately priced rooms nowadays have hair dryers, room safes, minibars or refrigerators you can stock yourself, hot-water kettles with free tea and coffee, and usually cable or satellite TVs with in-house

Where to Stay in Kowloon

Booth Lodge **3**
BP International House **11**
Caritas Bianchi Lodge **2**
Chungking Mansion **27**
Dorset Seaview Hotel **5**
Eaton Hotel **6**
Empire Hotel Kowloon **13**
Guangdong Hotel **18**
Holiday Inn Golden Mile **28**
Hotel InterContinental Hong Kong **30**
Imperial Hotel **26**
InterContinental Grand Stanford **21**
Kimberley Hotel **14**
Kowloon Hotel **29**
Kowloon Shangri-La, Hong Kong **22**
Langham Hotel **33**
Majestic Hotel **8**
The Marco Polo Gateway **34**
The Marco Polo Hongkong Hotel **32**

The Marco Polo Prince **16**
Miramar **15**
Nathan Hotel **7**
New Kings Hotel **4**
New World Renaissance Hotel **23**
The Peninsula **30**
Pruton Prudential Hotel **9**
Ramada Hotel Kowloon **17**
Regal Kowloon Hotel **20**
Royal Garden **19**
The Salisbury YMCA **31**
Shamrock Hotel **10**
Sheraton Hong Kong Hotel & Towers **25**
Stanford Hillview Hotel **12**
YMCA International House **1**

pay movies. Nonsmoking floors are common in virtually all hotels except for some of the inexpensive ones. Most hotels also have tour desks or can book tours for you through the concierge or front desk.

Unless otherwise stated, all hotels in this book have air-conditioning (a must in Hong Kong), private bathroom, and telephones with international direct dialing. Room service (either 24 hr. or until the wee hours of the morning), babysitting, and same-day laundry service are standard features of very expensive to moderate hotels, as are Western and Asian restaurants and business centers. Many also offer health clubs with fitness rooms and swimming pools free for guests (though a few charge extra for their use).

Some hotels even differentiate among their guests, charging health-club fees, for example, for those who book through a travel agent but not for those who pay rack rates (the maximum quoted rates). Guests booking through travel agents may also receive fewer amenities. Note that while many hotels allow children under a specific age (usually under 12) to room free with parents, there are restrictions. Some allow only one child, while others allow a maximum of three people in a room. All charge extra if an extra bed is required.

It's nearly impossible to predict what might happen over the next few decades, let alone the next few years. In 1985, there were 18,180 hotel rooms in Hong Kong. Today that number has swelled to more than 47,000, with more on the way. Only one thing is certain: If the tourists continue to pour into Hong Kong, hotels will continue to happily raise their rates.

1 Best Hotel Bets

Choosing a favorite hotel in Hong Kong can be a bit overwhelming, if not impossible, because the choices are so vast and there are so many competitors. Few cities offer such a large number of first-rate hotels, and few places can compete with the service that has made the Hong Kong hotel industry legendary. With apologies to the rest, here are my personal favorites. For my picks on the best splurge and moderately priced hotels, see chapter 1.

- **Best Historic Hotel:** This category has no competition: **The Peninsula,** Salisbury Road, Tsim Sha Tsui (© 800/462-7899), Hong Kong's oldest hotel, has long been the grand old hotel of Hong Kong. Built in 1928 and boasting the most ornate lobby in Hong Kong, it retains the atmosphere of a colonial past, even down to its restaurants, Gaddi's and The Verandah, both of which have changed little over the decades. Even its new tower, with high-tech rooms and a trendy rooftop restaurant, only adds to the general aura. See p. 86.

- **Best for Business Travelers:** If you can afford it, spring for a room at **The Ritz-Carlton,** 3 Connaught Rd., Central (© 800/241-3333), conveniently located right in the heart of Central's financial district. Small and intimate and filled with art and antiques, it seems more like an expensive apartment complex than a hotel; it offers rooms with sweeping harbor views; excellent service; a state-of-the-art business center; and a health club with a heated outdoor swimming pool. For even more pampering, executive floors offer special privileges, including a private lounge with complimentary snacks and drinks throughout the day. And for busy executives with no time for shopping, the hotel even offers personal shoppers. See p. 81.

- **Best for a Romantic Getaway:** Go to Macau, where the **Westin Resort Macau,** Estrada de Hac Sa on Colôane Island (© 800/228-3000), has the perfect and most idyllic setting for those who want to get away from it all, with large rooms

Where to Stay in the Central District

Bishop Lei International House **1**
Conrad International Hong Kong **8**
Four Seasons Hong Kong **3**
Island Shangri-La Hong Kong **6**
JW Marriott Hotel **7**
Landmark Mandarin Oriental **2**
Mandarin Oriental **4**
The Ritz-Carlton **5**

Tramway
Post Office

(each with private terrace) overlooking the sea, landscaped grounds, indoor and outdoor pools, and a nearby beach for moonlit walks. See p. 271.

- **Best Trendy Hotel:** Design guru Philippe Starck is the mastermind behind **Jia,** 1–5 Irving St., Causeway Bay (ⓒ **852/3196 9000**), a 57-room boutique hotel featuring whimsical furniture in its lobby but minimalist, high-tech decor and gadgets in its rooms. A slew of freebies (such as broadband access, continental breakfast, and evening cocktails), rooms that are divided into distinct living, dining, and working areas, and access to a couple of Hong Kong's hottest clubs make this a shoo-in for fashion-conscious travelers ready to burrow in. See p. 95.
- **Best Budget Hotel:** The overwhelming number-one choice has long been **The Salisbury YMCA,** Salisbury Road, Tsim Sha Tsui (ⓒ **800/537-8483**), with a fantastic location right next to the prestigious (and very expensive) Peninsula and just a short walk from the Star Ferry. Rooms are simple but offer virtually everything (from cable TVs to wireless Internet access and coffeemakers); some even have stunning harbor views. Throw in two inexpensive restaurants, a health club, and laundry facilities, and you have more than enough to satisfy budget-minded vacationers who don't want to sacrifice location or convenience. See p. 101.
- **Best Health Club:** Most of Hong Kong's deluxe hotels boast state-of-the-art health clubs. But what I like most about the health club at the **Hotel InterContinental Hong Kong,** 18 Salisbury Rd., Tsim Sha Tsui (ⓒ **800/327-0200**), is that it's open 24 hours a day, so you can work out when it fits your schedule. There's also an outdoor, filled-to-the-brim horizonless Jacuzzi that gives the illusion of flowing into the harbor, and a state-of-the-art spa that observes architectural rules for feng shui and specializes in jet-lag relief, cellulite, and Oriental treatments. And to top it off, this hotel even offers free tai chi and yoga classes for its guests. See p. 79.
- **Best Hotel Pool:** The **Grand Hyatt,** 1 Harbour Rd., Wan Chai (ⓒ **800/233-1234**), and **Renaissance Harbour View Hotel Hong Kong,** 1 Harbour Rd., Wan Chai (ⓒ **800/228-9290**), share one of Hong Kong's largest outdoor pools, surrounded by a lush, landscaped garden and with views of the harbor. In addition, the Grand Hyatt's spa also has a 50m lap pool. See p. 82 and 90.
- **Best Spa:** Spas are big business in Hong Kong, with many of the city's top hotels now offering a myriad of spa treatments. The Spa at **Four Seasons Hotel Hong Kong,** 8 Finance St., Central (ⓒ **852/3196 8333**), exceeds the rest with treatments that begin with hydrotherapy, including a Finnish sauna, an amethyst crystal steam room with mother-of-pearl covered seating, a fountain that rains crushed ice flakes, and hot tubs, and continue at one of 18 treatment rooms. For the ultimate splurge, spring for one of the VIP suites, where after your massage you'll retire to your own jet bath overlooking the harbor. As far as I'm concerned, it doesn't get any better than this. See p. 80.
- **Best Views:** Most of Hong Kong's deluxe hotels boast harbor views, making this category the toughest. However, in my opinion, the best harbor views are from the Kowloon side, where you can feast your eyes not only on the boats plying the water but also on Hong Kong Island with its stunning architecture, Victoria Peak, and, at night, the shimmering of neon lights and laser-light extravaganza of Hong Kong's nightly Symphony of Lights. And no Tsim Sha Tsui hotel is as close to the water as the **Hotel InterContinental Hong Kong** (see p. 79), built right over the harbor; as many as 70% of its rooms command sweeping views of the water and

Where to Stay in Causeway Bay & Wan Chai

Alisan Guest House **9**
Empire Hotel **2**
The Excelsior **10**
Express by Holiday Inn **8**
Grand Hyatt Hong Kong **5**
Harbour View
  International House **4**
Jia **14**
Lanson Place Boutique
  Hotel & Residences **15**
Metropark Hotel **13**
Novotel Century Hong Kong **7**
The Park Lane **11**
Renaissance Harbour View
  Hotel Hong Kong **6**
Rosedale on the Park **12**
Wesley **1**
Wharney Hotel **3**

Information *i*
Post Office ⊠
Tramway

1/10 mile
100 meters

Victoria Harbour

Ferry to Tsim Sha Tsui

Hong Kong Convention & Exhibition Centre

Wan Chai Ferry Pier

Ferry to Hung Hom

Tunnel

Causeway Bay

CAUSEWAY BAY

WAN CHAI

Wan Chai Sports Ground

HAPPY VALLEY →

VICTORIA PARK

CAROLINE HILL

SOUTHORN PLAYGROUND

SHENZHEN
NEW TERRITORIES
Sai Kung Peninsula
KOWLOON
Hong Kong International Airport
Lantau Island
Hong Kong Island
area of detail
South China Sea
10 mi
10 km

boast floor-to-ceiling and wall-to-wall windows, making the most of one of the world's most breathtaking city views. See p. 79.

- **Best for Art Lovers:** The **Island Shangri-La Hong Kong,** Pacific Place, Central (© **800/565-5050**), is a gorgeous hotel with more than 700 Viennese chandeliers, lush Tai Ping carpets, flower arrangements, and more than 500 paintings and artworks. But the clincher is the 16-story-high Chinese painting in the hotel atrium, drawn by 40 artists from Beijing and believed to be the largest landscape painting in the world. See p. 88.

- **Best for Ex-Pat Wannabes:** Mid-Levels has long been a favorite residential area for ex-pats living and working in Hong Kong. **Bishop Lei International House,** 4 Robinson Rd., Mid-Levels (© **852/2868 0828**), is located about halfway up Victoria Peak, with great views from its smallish rooms. Nearby ethnic restaurants and neighborhood bars abound, but for a real taste of Mid-Levels living, travel the escalator that local residents use to get to and from their jobs in Central. See p. 94.

2 Selecting Accommodations

No one area in this compact city is really a more convenient location than any other. Public transportation is efficient and easy to use, and the attractions are spread throughout the city. However, most visitors do stay in Tsim Sha Tsui, on the Kowloon side, simply because that's where you'll find the greatest concentration of hotels, as well as shops and restaurants. Business travelers often prefer the Central District, while those who want to avoid the tourist crowds may like the hotels strung along the waterfront of Wan Chai and Causeway Bay. Yau Ma Tei and Mong Kok, situated on the Kowloon Peninsula north of Tsim Sha Tsui, are great places to stay if you want to be surrounded by Chinese stores and locals, with hardly a souvenir shop in sight. See "The Neighborhoods in Brief," beginning on p. 50, for more information on these neighborhoods.

The hotel prices listed in this book are the rack rates, which you might end up paying if you come during peak season (Chinese New Year, Mar–May, Oct/Nov). Otherwise, you can probably get a room for much, much less. It's *imperative,* therefore, to shop around and ask about special packages, upgrades, or promotional fares when making reservations, particularly in the off season. Although I've included toll-free numbers for the United States and Canada for many of the listings below, I also recommend contacting the hotels directly to inquire about rates and special deals, and checking websites for deals that might be offered only through the Internet. A check of the Grand Hyatt's website, for example, revealed special summer prices that were half its rack rates.

Generally speaking, the price of a room in Hong Kong depends upon its view and height rather than upon its size. Not surprisingly, the best and most expensive rooms are those with a sweeping view of Victoria Harbour, as well as those on the higher floors. Is a harbor view worth it? Emphatically, yes. Hong Kong's harbor, with watercraft activity ranging from cruise ships and barges to fishing boats and the Star Ferry, is one of the most fascinating in the world; the city's high-rises and mountains are icing on the cake. Waking in the morning and opening your curtains to this famous scene is a thrill. Hotels know it, which is why they charge an arm and a leg for the privilege. There are, however, a few moderately and inexpensively priced accommodations that offer harbor views, though these, too, represent their most expensive rooms.

Tips Ways to Save on Your Hotel Room

The **rack rate** is the maximum rate that a hotel charges for a room. Although a few deluxe hotels stick to their published rack rates year-round and most hotels charge rack rates during peak travel times in spring and autumn and during major fairs and conventions, you can probably strike a better bargain.

- **Ask about special rates or other discounts.** Always ask whether a room less expensive than the first one quoted is available. Hong Kong hotels usually have a variety of rates based on room amenities, views, and other factors. If the hotel won't budge on price, ask whether special privileges or amenities can be thrown in, such as free breakfast.

- **Dial direct.** When booking a room, compare the rates offered by the hotel's local line with that of the toll-free number. A hotel makes nothing on a room that stays empty, so the local hotel reservation desk may be willing to offer a special rate unavailable elsewhere.

- **Book online.** Many hotels offer Internet-only discounts on their own websites. Cheaper rates are also available through room suppliers on the Internet (see "Planning Your Trip Online," beginning on p. 27), so be sure to shop around.

- **Remember the law of supply and demand.** Avoid high-season stays whenever you can: Planning your vacation just a week before or after official peak season (generally spring and autumn) can mean big savings. Many hotels offer promotional fares throughout the summer. Business hotels may offer discounts over the weekend.

- **Look into group or long-stay discounts.** If you come as part of a large group, you should be able to negotiate a bargain rate, since the hotel can then guarantee occupancy in a number of rooms. Likewise, if you're planning a long stay (at least a week), you might qualify for a discount.

- **Avoid excess charges.** Find out whether your hotel imposes a surcharge on local and long-distance calls. A pay phone, however inconvenient, may save you money. And don't be tempted by the room's minibar offerings: Most hotels charge through the nose for water, soda, and snacks.

- **Consider a suite.** If you are traveling with your family or another couple, you can pack more people into a suite (which usually comes with a sofa bed), and thereby reduce your per-person rate. Remember that some places charge for extra guests.

- **If traveling with children, try to find a hotel that allows children to stay free** in their parent's room. There's an age limit (usually under 12 years of age in Hong Kong), there's sometimes a maximum of three people to a room, and children are usually free only if no extra bed is required.

- **Book an efficiency.** A room with a kitchenette allows you to shop for groceries and cook your own meals. This is a big money saver, especially for families on long stays.

In any case, don't be shy about asking what price categories are available and what the differences are among them. Keep in mind that the difference in price between a room facing inland and a room facing the harbor can be staggering, with various price categories in between. There are, for example, "partial" or "side" harbor views, which means you can glimpse the harbor looking sideways from your window or between tall buildings. Double rooms that range from HK$2,000 to HK$3,000 (US$260–US$390/£143–£214), for example, may include five different categories, beginning with a "standard" room on a lower floor facing inland and then increasing in cost to those on upper floors facing inland, those with side harbor views, those on lower floors facing the harbor, and, most expensive, "deluxe" rooms on higher floors with full harbor views. To save money, consider requesting the highest room available in the category you choose. If "standard" rooms, for example, run up to the 8th floor and deluxe rooms are on floors 9 to 20, you'll save money by asking for a standard room on floor 8. If you decide to spring for a full harbor view, be sure to ask for it when making your reservation, and request the highest floor available.

For moderately priced or inexpensive lodgings, few of which offer any kind of view at all, rates are usually based on height, decor, and sometimes size, and it's prudent to inquire whether there's a difference in price between twin and double rooms; some hotels charge more for two beds in a room (more sheets to wash, I guess).

In any case, the wide range of prices listed below for double/twin rooms in each of the listings reflects the various categories available. In moderately priced and inexpensive lodgings, single rates are also usually available, but more expensive hotels often charge the same for double or single occupancy.

All of Hong Kong's expensive hotels, most of the moderately priced hotels, and a few of the inexpensive hotels are members of the Hong Kong Hotels Association (HKHA; www.hkha.com.hk), though not every hotel named in this chapter is. The advantage of staying at a member hotel is that if you have a complaint, you can lodge it directly with the Hong Kong Tourism Board. Furthermore, the HKHA maintains a counter at Hong Kong International Airport where you can reserve a room at one of its member hotels at no extra charge.

The hotels in this chapter are arranged first by price and then by geographical location. The categories are based on rates for a double room (excluding tax and service) as follows: **Very Expensive,** HK$3,500 (US$454/£250) and up; **Expensive,** HK$2,100 to HK$3,500 (US$273–US$454/£150–£250); **Moderate,** HK$1,200 to HK$2,000 (US$156–US$260/£86–£143); and **Inexpensive,** less than HK$1,200 (US$156/£86).

Keep in mind that prices given in this book are for room rates only—a 10% service charge and 3% government tax will be added to your final bill. Since a 13% increase can really add up, be sure to take it into account when choosing your hotel.

3 Very Expensive

Hong Kong's top hotels are among the best in the world, with unparalleled service, state-of-the-art business, health-club, and often spa facilities, guest rooms equipped with just about everything you can imagine, some of the city's best restaurants, and usually views of famous Victoria Harbour. They also offer the convenience of a concierge or guest-relations staff, on hand to help with everything from theater tickets to restaurant and tour reservations. Among other extras are turndown service, 24-hour room service, welcoming tea brought to your room shortly after your arrival, free newspaper delivered to your room, and many in-room conveniences and amenities, including voice mail, high-speed (broadband) or wireless Internet access, and bedside controls that regulate everything from do-not-disturb lights to the opening of the curtains (it's great to wake up in the morning and have the city appear before you with a mere push of a button). Many also offer executive floors, a "hotel-within-a-hotel" concept catering primarily to business executives with such added services as express check-in and checkout; use of a private executive lounge serving complimentary breakfasts, snacks, and drinks; free services that may include complimentary pressing service or free use of the business center; and an executive-floor concierge or attendant who can take care of such details as restaurant reservations or transportation arrangements.

KOWLOON
Hotel InterContinental Hong Kong ☆☆☆   Whereas The Peninsula, across the street, is the grande old dame of Hong Kong's hotels, the InterContinental is like its youthful, contemporary cousin. Taking over an existing property in 2001 and undergoing a slow but steady renovation that has stamped this flagship with its own identity, the InterContinental exudes a relaxed, informal atmosphere despite its stylish digs, with almost half its guests hailing from North America. It also boasts what may well be the best views of Victoria Harbour and Hong Kong Island from Tsim Sha Tsui. In fact, you can't get much closer to the water than this: Built in 1980 of polished rose granite and rising 17 stories, the hotel is located right on the water's edge. Its unfussy lobby, with a soaring glass facade and unobstructed views of harbor activity, is one of Hong Kong's best venues for afternoon tea or evening cocktails.

Great views are also trademarks of its guest rooms, 70% of which command sweeping views of the harbor with floor-to-ceiling and wall-to-wall windows (the remaining—and less expensive but larger—rooms face the outdoor swimming pool and landscaped sun terrace). Recently renovated, rooms come with 37-inch LCD TVs, iPod docking stations, air purification systems, and spacious bathrooms (each fitted in Italian marble with a sunken bathtub, separate shower, and adjoining walk-in closets). Rather than the executive-level floors common in most hotels, any guest can use the private lounge by paying HK$700 (US$91/£50) extra per room per night, entitling them to free breakfast, evening cocktails, use of computers hooked to the Internet, and other perks. Other notable hotel features are its high-rated restaurants; a state-of-the-art spa renowned for its jet-lag, anti-cellulite, and Oriental healing treatments; harbor views from outdoor whirlpools and the pool's sun terrace; free tai chi and yoga classes for hotel guests; and wireless broadband that enables guests to access the Internet even from poolside.

18 Salisbury Rd., Tsim Sha Tsui, Kowloon, Hong Kong. ✆ 800/327-0200 in the U.S. and Canada, or 852/2721 1211. Fax 852/2739 4546. www.hongkong-ic.intercontinental.com. 495 units. HK$3,900–HK$5,400 (US$506–US$701/£279–£386) single or double; HK$700 (US$91/£50) extra for Club lounge; from HK$8,000 (US$1,039/£571) suite. Children under 12 stay free in parent's room. AE, DC, MC, V. MTR: Tsim Sha Tsui. **Amenities:** 5 restaurants (French, Cantonese, contemporary Japanese, steaks, Continental); bar; lounge; outdoor pool; whirlpools overlooking Victoria Harbour; fitness room (open 24 hr.); spa; concierge; limousine service; business center; upscale shopping arcade; 24-hr. room service; massage; babysitting; same-day laundry service/dry cleaning; house doctor. *In room:* A/C, satellite TV w/keyboard for Internet access and on-demand pay movies, wireless Internet access, minibar, coffeemaker, hair dryer, safe, bathroom scale, complimentary welcoming tea, fruit, and bottled water.

CENTRAL DISTRICT
In addition to the recommendations here, consider the **Mandarin Oriental,** 5 Connaught Rd. (✆ **800/526-6566** in the U.S. and Canada, or 852/2522 0111; www.mandarinoriental.com), which reopened in late 2006 after a total top-to-bottom

renovation. One of Hong Kong's landmark hotels, it has preserved some of its much-beloved restaurants and bars, but rooms are now larger, starting at HK$3,600 (US$468/£257) for a single or double.

Four Seasons Hotel Hong Kong ✹✹✹   This newcomer is the most talked-about hotel of the moment, with rooms to die for, a luxurious spa, and one of the hottest restaurants in town. Opened in 2005 and just a stone's throw from the Central Ferry Piers, it also provides easy access to ifc mall, Hong Kong Station (with direct access to the airport), and the MTR subway, all without having to step outside. Rising 45 stories, it's a cool urban oasis, buffered from the city's inherent bustle and providing a polished service that rises above even Hong Kong's legendary pampering. Although its light-infused lobby is too low to provide views, its outdoor lap and infinity pools and whirlpool have great harbor views, and an executive lounge on the top floor, which any guest can use by paying a daily supplement, boasts fantastic views and even an outside deck. With 18 treatment rooms, its spa is among the largest of any hotel in Hong Kong, as well as one of the coolest: Who wouldn't love lounging, après massage, in a private jet bath with harbor views? If you want to snag a table in the French restaurant Caprice, book early.

Rooms, measuring 45 sq. m (484 sq. ft.) and featuring floor-to-ceiling windows overlooking either the city or harbor (harbor rooms, of course, cost more), are either contemporary Western with muted colors or a modern take on traditional Chinese design, the latter with gold-lacquered ceiling, red furniture, and mother-of-pearl inlay on the bathroom floor. All feature 42-inch plasma TVs, focused bedside reading lights, and spacious marbled bathrooms with two sinks, shower stalls and deep soaking tubs, from which you can operate a small, mounted LCD TV via remote. In short, with its seamless service and top-grade facilities, there's no mistaking that this is a Four Seasons, and until a new glam hotel comes along (and this being Hong Kong, one most assuredly will), it's at the top of the pack.

8 Finance St., Central, Hong Kong. © 800/819-5053 in the U.S. and Canada, or 852/3196 8888. Fax 852/3196 8899. www.fourseasons.com/hongkong. 399 units. HK$3,800–HK$4,200 (US$494–US$545/£271–£300) single or double; extra HK$700 (US$91/£50) single or HK$900 (US$117/£64) double for executive lounge; from HK$5,500 (US$714/£393) suite. AE, DC, MC, V. MTR: Central. **Amenities:** 2 restaurants (Cantonese, French); bar; lounge; 2 outdoor heated pools with whirlpool, open year-round; health club (open 24 hr.); spa; sauna; concierge; tour desk; limousine service; business center (open 24 hr); connected to shopping arcade; salon; 24-hr. room service; babysitting; same-day laundry service/dry cleaning. *In room:* A/C, satellite TV w/keyboard for Internet access and on-demand pay movies, wireless Internet access, minibar, coffeemaker, hair dryer, safe, DVD/CD players, bathroom scale, complimentary welcoming tea, fruit, and bottled water.

Landmark Mandarin Oriental ✹✹✹   Another Central newcomer, this small hotel eschews the boutique label because it doesn't scrimp on size, with rooms that flaunt both space and strikingly contemporary decor. Located atop the Landmark shopping complex and popular with designers who have shops there, it exudes a laid-back, refined atmosphere, with lobby seating grouped in a library setting and a stylish bar attracting a well-heeled crowd. Other diversions are limited to a 14-room spa with

---

Fun Fact **You've Got to Be Kidding!**

The Chinnery, a bar in the original Mandarin Oriental hotel with more than 100 single-malt whiskeys, remained off-limits to women until, incredibly enough, 1990.

a Zen-like atmosphere and workout rooms for yoga and Pilates, as well as a chic restaurant serving innovative European cuisine. Though the Lan Kwai Fong nightlife district is within staggering distance, it's hard to imagine guests who can afford to stay here taking advantage of it.

Rather, the big focus is on state-of-the-art guest rooms, which measure 42 or 56 sq. m (450 or 600 sq. ft.) and are priced accordingly, and huge windows. Both feature wall-mounted 32-inch HDTVs (with more than 40 hi-def programs in addition to cable), safes with electric outlets to recharge laptops, plug-in speakers for iPod/MP3 players, high-tech phones that include hands-free speakerphones and display text messages, walk-in closets, duvet-covered beds with 400-thread-count sheets, yoga mats, and fresh flowers providing splashes of color. But it's the stunning, glass-walled bathrooms, which take up about a third of the room's space, that take the cake. Big enough to live in, they have two separate vanities and dual sinks, shower stall, another TV, and a huge, round tub (in the larger rooms, the tub measures 7 ft. across). Unfortunately, surrounding buildings can make guests feel like they're living in a fish bowl. One unwitting guest closed the sheers immediately upon check-in but forgot to close the block-out drapes later when taking her nighttime bath, discovering her faux pas only the next morning. Needless to say, there are no views from this hotel, though the same may not be said, perhaps, for office workers across the street.

15 Queen's Rd. Central, the Landmark, Central, Hong Kong. © 800/526-6566 in the U.S. and Canada, or 852/2132 0188. Fax 852/2132 0199. www.mandarinoriental.com. 113 units. HK$4,000–HK$5,400 (US$519–US$701/£285–£385) single or double; from HK$8,800 (US$1,142/£628) suite. AE, DC, MC, V. MTR: Central. **Amenities:** Restaurant (European); bar; indoor pool; health club; spa; sauna; concierge; limousine service; shopping arcade; 24-hr. room service; babysitting; same-day laundry/dry cleaning service. *In room:* A/C, cable HDTV w/keyboard for Internet access and on-demand pay movies, DVD player, wireless Internet access, minibar, hair dryer, safe, bathroom scale, complimentary tea, fruit, and bottled water.

The Ritz-Carlton ★★★ (Kids)   Opened in 1993, The Ritz-Carlton occupies a smart-looking 25-story building in the heart of the Central District not far from the waterfront. It follows the Ritz-Carlton tradition of excellent service and fine dining and has an extensive collection of 18th- and 19th-century artwork and antiques. Its lobby is subdued and intimate, resembling more closely a wealthy person's home than a public place, with the reception desk tucked away in an alcove. All in all, the hotel, with its hushed, home-away-from-home atmosphere, is a far cry from the crowds at Hong Kong's more plebeian megahotels. Even the restaurants seem discreetly hidden, most without views so as to discourage outside traffic. If you revel in personalized service—from butler-drawn baths to personal shoppers—this is the place for you. And who could resist a chocolate facial at its health club?

The low-key atmosphere prevails upstairs as well; since there are only 10 to 12 rooms on each floor, it seems more like an upscale apartment complex than a hotel, which obviously appeals to its overwhelmingly business clientele, many of whom are long-staying guests. Yet the hotel doesn't overlook its wee guests either, installing safety devices such as electric outlet plugs for families with preschoolers. The rooms are rather neutral in tone with an understated elegance, with half facing the harbor and offering great views; even those that face inland provide a nice view of the pool, lush Chater Garden, skyscrapers, and The Peak. Marble bathrooms feature two sinks and separate toilet areas; flowers are a nice touch. Ritz-Carlton fans, take note: A second property, opening in 2009 above Kowloon Station, will undoubtedly raise the bar in hotel luxury, giving other first-class hotels in this tight market a run for their money.

3 Connaught Rd., Central, Hong Kong. ℂ **800/241-3333** in the U.S. and Canada, or 852/2877 6666. Fax 852/2877 6778. www.ritzcarlton.com. 216 units. HK$3,600–HK$4,100 (US$468–US$532/£257–£293) single or double; HK$4,300–HK$4,800 (US$558–US$623/£307–£343) Ritz-Carlton Club executive floor; from HK$7,000 (US$909/£500) suite. Children under 13 stay free in parent's room (maximum 3 persons per room). AE, DC, MC, V. MTR: Central. **Amenities:** 5 restaurants (Italian, Cantonese, Shanghainese, Japanese, Continental); lounge; heated outdoor pool; health club; Jacuzzi; sauna; concierge; limousine service; business center; 24-hr. room service; massage (including in-room); babysitting; same-day laundry service/dry cleaning; executive-level rooms. *In room:* A/C, cable/satellite TV w/pay movies on demand, high-speed dataport, minibar, coffeemaker, hair dryer, iron/ironing board, safe, bathroom scale, complimentary welcome tea, fruit, bottled water, and shoeshine.

CAUSEWAY BAY & WAN CHAI

Grand Hyatt Hong Kong 𝕬𝕬𝕬 *Kids*   Walking into the lobby of the Hyatt International's Asian flagship hotel is like walking into the Bavarian castle of a modern-day King Ludwig, a lobby so palatial in design that the word "understatement" has certainly never crossed its threshold. Decorated to resemble the salon of a 1930s Art Deco luxury ocean liner, it literally flaunts space, with huge black granite columns, massive flower arrangements, palm trees, bubbling fountains, and furniture and statuettes reminiscent of that era. It's not the kind of place you want to be seen on a bad hair day.

Located on the waterfront adjacent to the Convention Centre and only a 5-minute walk from the Wan Chai Star Ferry pier that delivers passengers to Tsim Sha Tsui, it offers smart-looking, contemporary rooms, soothingly decorated to ease stress and invite relaxation. Some 75% of the rooms provide a full harbor view, while the rest have a view of the free-form pool (Hong Kong's largest outdoor hotel pool) and garden with partial glimpses of the harbor. Pluses are the specially made beds with Egyptian cotton sheets, sliding clothes rack in the closet, cordless keyboards to access the Internet through an interactive TV, coffee-table books, and marble bathrooms complete with 18-karat-gold fixtures and separate bathtub and shower areas. For extra pampering, travelers can choose to stay at Plateau, a residential spa with 14 guest rooms in addition to nine treatment rooms, where guests can enjoy a massage, manicure, and a soak in an infinity bathtub without leaving the privacy of their room (doubles here start at HK$5,500/US$714/£393, including breakfast). They should, however, venture at least as far as the spa's sauna, which boasts a view of the harbor. I also like the hotel's restaurants, including the Grill, a poolside, landscaped restaurant offering sumptuous buffet spreads and grilled specialties year-round (weather permitting).

1 Harbour Rd., Wan Chai, Hong Kong. ℂ **800/233-1234** in the U.S. and Canada, or 852/2588 1234. Fax 852/2802 0677. www.hongkong.grand.hyatt.com. 549 units. HK$4,500–HK$6,000 (US$584–US$779/£321–£429) single; HK$4,750–HK$6,250 (US$617–US$811/£339–£446) double; from HK$5,700 (US$740/£407) Grand Club executive-floor double; from HK$8,000 (US$1,039/£571) suite. Children under 12 stay free in parent's room (maximum 3 persons per room). AE, DC, MC, V. MTR: Wan Chai. **Amenities:** 5 restaurants (Italian, Cantonese, Continental, Japanese, grilled food); lounge; champagne bar; club with live music; huge outdoor heated pool (shared with adjacent Renaissance Harbour View Hotel and open year-round); children's splash pool and playground; golf-driving range; 2 outdoor tennis courts; 2 squash courts; health club; spa w/50m outdoor heated pool and sauna; jogging track; concierge; tour desk; limousine service; business center; salon; 24-hr. room service; babysitting; same-day laundry service/dry cleaning; executive-level rooms; free shuttle to Central, Causeway Bay, and Admiralty. *In room:* A/C, satellite TV w/cordless keyboard for Internet access and on-demand pay movies, fax, wireless Internet access, minibar, coffeemaker, hair dryer, safe, bathroom scale, complimentary fruit and bottled water.

4 Expensive

A few hotels in this category offer almost as much as Hong Kong's very expensive hotels, including some of my favorites. Only a handful have great views of Victoria

Kids Family-Friendly Hotels

BP International House (p. 98) This inexpensive hotel offers "Family Rooms" with bunk beds that sleep four for HK$1,340 (US$174/£96). Parents will appreciate the convenience of a laundry room. But best of all is the adjacent Kowloon Park, with its indoor and outdoor public swimming pools, children's playground, lake with flamingos and other birds, and plenty of romping space for active bodies.

Grand Hyatt/Renaissance Harbour View (p. 82 and 90) These two hotels share one of Hong Kong's largest outdoor swimming pools, as well as a splash pool for smaller children and a playground. Both hotels also offer babysitting.

The Ritz-Carlton (p. 81) For toddlers used to only the best, this first-class hotel ensures their safety by installing precautionary devices upon check-in, including electrical-outlet plugs, water temperature controls and tub spout covers, locking lids for waste baskets, night lights, and more. And just in case, parents receive a first-aid kit with Band-Aids, diaper rash ointment, and other items.

The Salisbury YMCA (p. 101) The overwhelming choice for families in terms of price, facilities, and location (just a short walk to both the Star Ferry and the MTR), this Salisbury Road establishment offers large suites suitable for families, an inexpensive cafeteria serving buffet meals, two indoor swimming pools (including a children's pool), an indoor climbing wall, and a bookstore with a children's corner where tots can try out games and books before parents fork over the cash. Babysitting is also available.

Harbour. In this category, you can expect a guest-relations/concierge desk, 24-hour room service, health clubs, business centers, same-day laundry service, and comfortable rooms with hair dryers, cable or satellite TVs with in-room movies, voice mail, Internet access, and coffee/tea-making facilities. Many also have executive floors for business travelers.

KOWLOON

Holiday Inn Golden Mile Named after the "golden mile of shopping" on Nathan Road, this Holiday Inn, built in 1975 but renovated many times over from top to bottom, has a great location right in the heart of bustling Tsim Sha Tsui, about a 6-minute walk from the Star Ferry. The MTR is right across the street, too. Maybe that's why it's popular with tour groups, mainly from North America and China, which can make the lobby rather crowded, noisy, and bothersome. Rooms, decorated in Ming blue or Oriental red with Chinese-influenced accents on everything from the drapes to the TV cabinets, impart a warm, cozy feeling and are fairly large for Tsim Sha Tsui, featuring either a king-size bed or two double beds. Although rooms boast floor-to-ceiling windows, views are blocked by adjacent buildings; those facing the unsightly Chungking Mansion are glazed (believe me, it's better this way). Those facing Mody Road are brighter but noisier; try to get a room on a high floor. All in all, this is a functional hotel in a convenient location.

50 Nathan Rd., Tsim Sha Tsui, Kowloon, Hong Kong. (C) 800/465-4329 in the U.S. and Canada, or 852/2369 3111. Fax 852/2369 8016. www.holiday-inn.com/hongkong-gldn. 585 units. HK$2,100–HK$2,950 (US$273–US$383/£150–£211) single; HK$2,650–HK$2,950 (US$344–US$383/£189–£211) single or double; HK$3,050–HK$3,150 (US$396–US$409/£217–£225) Executive Club single or double; from HK$5,800 (US$753/£414) suite. Up to 2 children under 19 stay free in parent's room. AE, DC, MC, V. MTR: Tsim Sha Tsui. **Amenities:** 4 restaurants (modern European, international buffet, Cantonese, German); bar; heated rooftop pool open year-round; health club; sauna; concierge; tour desk; limousine service; business center; shopping arcade; salon; 24-hr. room service; massage; babysitting; same-day laundry service/dry cleaning; executive-level rooms; house doctor. *In room:* A/C, satellite/cable TV w/pay movies, high-speed dataport, minibar, coffeemaker, hair dryer, iron/ironing board, safe, complimentary bottled water.

InterContinental Grand Stanford 👁👁   This older hotel has seen lots of renovations and upgrades that have lifted it from its previous mundane existence into one of Tsim Sha Tsui East's top hotels. It's located right on the waterfront, near the hover-ferry service to Central, and boasts a lively, high-ceilinged lobby with a cafe perfect for watching the never-ending stream of international guests. I also like the rooftop swimming pool, which is heated and open year-round and affords great city views. Rooms are more homey than most hotel accommodations, with such added details as trim work bordering the ceiling, large mirrors above TV consoles, good bedside lights, plants on desks, lit magnifying mirrors that reveal flaws you never knew you had, and good harbor views through floor-to-ceiling windows of half the rooms (because of a highway that runs alongside the harbor, be sure to request a room on a high floor). If you can't afford a full harbor view, "side harbor views" are almost as good, due to the hotel's undulating V-shaped facade; unfortunately, the windows of the least expensive rooms open rather unceremoniously onto a windowless wall. Probably the biggest drawback is the 10-minute walk to Tsim Sha Tsui, but it does offer hotel guests a free shuttle service to several locations in Tsim Sha Tsui every 30 to 45 minutes.

70 Mody Rd., Tsim Sha Tsui East, Kowloon, Hong Kong. (C) 800/327-0200 in the U.S. and Canada, or 852/2721 5161. Fax 852/2732 2233. www.hongkong.intercontinental.com. 578 units. HK$2,500–HK$3,600 (US$325–US$468/£179–£257) single or double; HK$3,000–HK$3,800 (US$390–US$494/£214–£271) Club floor; from HK$4,500 (US$584/£321) suite. Children under 12 stay free in parent's room. AE, DC, MC, V. MTR: Tsim Sha Tsui. **Amenities:** 4 restaurants (contemporary Australian, international, Cantonese, Italian); bar; lounge; outdoor heated pool; health club (open 24 hr.); spa; concierge; tour desk; limousine service; business center; salon; 24-hr. room service; massage (including in-room); babysitting; same-day laundry service/dry cleaning; executive-level rooms; doctor and dentist on call; free shuttle service to Tsim Sha Tsui. *In room:* A/C, satellite TV w/pay movies on demand and CD/DVD player, high-speed dataport, minibar, coffeemaker, hair dryer, safe, bathroom scale, complimentary bottled water.

Kowloon Shangri-La, Hong Kong 👁👁👁 *Finds*   The 21-story Kowloon Shangri-La, on the waterfront of Tsim Sha Tsui East, is a popular choice for business travelers, the majority of whom are American. The well-trained staff provides sterling service, which is probably one reason why repeat guests make up more than 40% of hotel occupancy. The two-story lobby is one of the most spacious in Hong Kong, with an expansive white Carrara marble floor, massive Viennese crystal chandeliers, a fountain, and Chinese landscape murals. The hotel, near the hover-ferry pier with service to Central and KCR with service to the New Territories and China, is a 5-minute walk from Tsim Sha Tsui (there's also free shuttle service every 45 min. to the Star Ferry). Wireless Internet access is available in public areas. Rooms, offering either harbor views or rather mundane "garden views" (a popular euphemism for windows that face inland), are large and luxuriously appointed, with ceiling-to-floor bay windows and either a king-size bed or two double beds. If you pay rack rates, additional benefits include free airport transfer, free laundry service and dry cleaning, free American or continental breakfast, free local telephone calls and Internet access, and a late 6pm checkout.

64 Mody Rd., Tsim Sha Tsui East, Kowloon, Hong Kong. © 866/565-5050 in the U.S., or 852/2721 2111. Fax 852/2723 8686. www.shangri-la.com. 700 units. HK$2,500–HK$3,650 (US$325–US$474/£179–£261) single; HK$2,700–HK$3,850 (US$350–US$500/£193–£275) double; HK$400 (US$52/£29) Horizon Club executive-floor supplement; from HK$4,300 (US$558/£307) suite. Children under 12 stay free in parent's room. AE, DC, MC, V. MTR: Tsim Sha Tsui. **Amenities:** 5 restaurants (Italian, Cantonese, Japanese, international buffet, deli); tapas bar; lounge; small indoor pool; health club; Jacuzzi; sauna; concierge; limousine service; business center (open 24 hr.); salon; 24-hr. room service; massage (including in-room); babysitting; same-day laundry service/dry cleaning; executive-level rooms; house doctor; free shuttle service to Tsim Sha Tsui. *In room:* A/C, satellite TV w/pay movies, high-speed dataport, minibar, coffeemaker, hair dryer, iron/ironing board, safe, complimentary welcoming tea, fruit, and shoeshine.

Langham Hotel 🦋🦋🦋   This 16-story hotel, an affiliate of the historic Langham Hotel in London and Hong Kong's only member of The Leading Hotels of the World (more than half the hotel guests are from North America and Europe), is located a couple of blocks inland from the harbor, just a few minutes' walk from the Star Ferry and the huge Harbour City shopping complex, giving it a very convenient location. Its lobby, bathed in warm gold tones, exudes a classic Italian atmosphere, with chandeliers, marble floor, a hand-painted dome ceiling, and glass art by American artist Dale Chihuly. Its restaurants, which include a renowned Cantonese venue, an American deli, and a fun seafood restaurant, are well respected among the locals. Wireless Internet access is available in the lobby, restaurants, and even beside the rooftop pool. Contemporary rooms are small but comfortable, with marble bathrooms sporting separate showers and tubs, gold-plated fixtures, and mist-free mirrors. Bedside control panels allow guests to adjust air-conditioning levels, select a TV or radio program, call up messages or the hotel bill on the television screen, and switch on a "Do Not Disturb" light that automatically disconnects the door chime. As an added safety precaution, staff keys are programmed for specific times only, thereby barring anyone from entering rooms after a shift ends, and a printer records all hotel employee use, indicating when each key was used, where, and by whom. Unfortunately, none of its rooms have harbor views, though some of the more expensive "City View" rooms have glimpses of the harbor between buildings.

8 Peking Rd., Tsim Sha Tsui, Kowloon, Hong Kong. © 800/223-6800 in the U.S. and Canada, or 852/2375 1133. Fax 852/2375 6611. www.langhamhotels.com. 495 units. HK$2,400–HK$2,800 (US$312–US$363/£171–£200) single or double; HK$3,400–HK$3,800 (US$442–US$493/£243–£271) Club executive-floor; from HK$6,000 (US$779/£429) suite. Children under 13 stay free in parent's room. AE, DC, MC, V. MTR: Tsim Sha Tsui. **Amenities:** 4 restaurants (Cantonese, seafood, international buffet, American deli); lounge; rooftop outdoor pool and Jacuzzi open year-round; health club (open 24 hr.); sauna; concierge; limousine service; business center (open 24 hr.); shopping arcade; 24-hr. room service; massage; babysitting; same-day laundry service/dry cleaning; executive-level rooms; doctor on call. *In room:* A/C, satellite TV w/pay movies, high-speed dataport, minibar, coffeemaker, hair dryer, iron/ironing board, safe, bathroom scale.

The Marco Polo Hongkong Hotel   The best (and most expensive) of three Marco Polo properties lining this street, this hotel, built in the 1960s but well maintained, is as close as you can get to the Star Ferry and is connected to the largest shopping complex in Asia, Harbour City. In fact, its lobby opens right into the Lane Crawford department store, making for an "only in Hong Kong" surreal experience. Guest rooms, decorated in bold color schemes, are far from luxurious but are quite large and are mostly so-called "Hollywood" twins (two twin beds pushed together) with a sitting area, large working desks, and walk-in closet. The lowest-price rooms face the small courtyard swimming pool and other guest rooms and can be quite dark, while the most expensive rooms boast unparalleled views of harbor activity, including the ocean liners that dock right next door as well as evening sunsets. Avoid rooms facing

Canton Road, as these can be somewhat noisy. Down the street are the **Marco Polo Gateway** (© 852/2113 0888) and the **Marco Polo Prince** (© 852/2113 1888), which are cheaper but also have fewer facilities. For my money, however, I'd rather stay at any of the other recommended hotels in this price category than the merely functional Marco Polo brands.

Harbour City, 3 Canton Rd., Tsim Sha Tsui, Kowloon, Hong Kong. © **800/448-8355** in the U.S., or 852/2113 0088. Fax 852/2113 0011. www.marcopolohotels.com. 664 units. HK$2,700–HK$3,500 (US$350–US$454/£193–£250) single; HK$2,800–HK$3,500 (US$363–US$455/£200–£250) double; HK$3,000–HK$4,000 (US$389–US$519/£214–£286) Continental Club executive-floor double; from HK$4,900 (US$636/£350) suite. 1 child under 14 can stay free in parent's room. AE, DC, MC, V. MTR: Tsim Sha Tsui. **Amenities:** 5 restaurants (Continental, Japanese, Chiu Chow, American, coffee shop); lounge; small heated outdoor pool (open year-round); exercise room; concierge; tour desk; limousine service; business center (open 24 hr.); shopping arcade; salon; 24-hr. room service; babysitting; same-day laundry service/dry cleaning; executive-level rooms; doctor on call. In room: A/C, cable TV w/pay movies on demand, high-speed dataport, minibar, coffeemaker, hair dryer, safe.

The Peninsula 🏆🏆🏆 *Value*   This is Hong Kong's most famous hotel, *the* place to stay if you are an incurable romantic and have a penchant for the historical. Built in 1928, it exudes elegance from its white-gloved doormen to one of the largest limousine fleets of Rolls-Royces in the world. Its lobby, reminiscent of a Parisian palace with high gilded ceilings, pillars, and palms, has long been Hong Kong's foremost spot for afternoon tea and people-watching. Its restaurants are also among the city's best, and service throughout the hotel is sterling. After The Peninsula lost its fabled view of the harbor following construction of the unsightly Space Museum on reclaimed land across the street, it remedied the problem in 1993 with a magnificent 32-story tower providing fantastic harbor views from guest rooms and its top-floor restaurant Felix, designed by Philippe Starck. For the culture-minded, The Peninsula offers classes on everything from tai chi and feng shui to cooking; for the travel-weary, a new spa focuses on the journey to rejuvenation with a soothing, minimalist design of natural woods, bamboo, candles, cascading water, a tiny moss garden set in rocks, and views of the harbor even from its sauna. Compared to the spate of newer, more expensive hotels, The Peninsula seems like a downright bargain. I absolutely love this place.

Spacious rooms (with a minimum of 42 sq. m/456 sq. ft.)—so wonderfully equipped that even jaded travelers are likely to be impressed—include a silent fax machine with a personalized phone number; headphones for both radio and TV; tightly focused bedside reading lights designed to keep sleeping partners happy; telephones and control panels on both sides of the gigantic beds; a display panel showing outdoor temperature and humidity; mood lighting; and a box in the closet where attendants can place your morning newspaper or take your dirty shoes for complimentary cleaning. Each huge bathroom is equipped with its own TV, hands-free phone (which automatically mutes the TV or radio and digitally filters the sound of running water), separate bathtub and shower stall, and two sinks, both with a magnifying mirror. It's worth the extra money to spring for a stunning harbor view in the tower if you can afford it, since views facing the back are a disappointment and those in the older part of the hotel are marred by the Space Museum. Both the Star Ferry and MTR are just a short walk away.

Salisbury Rd., Tsim Sha Tsui, Kowloon, Hong Kong. © **800/462-7899** in the U.S. and Canada, or 852/2920 2888. Fax 852/2722 4170. www.peninsula.com. 300 units. HK$2,900–HK$4,200 (US$377–US$545/£207–£300) single or double; from HK$4,600 (US$597/£329) suite. AE, DC, MC, V. MTR: Tsim Sha Tsui. **Amenities:** 6 restaurants (French, Pacific Rim crossover, Continental, Swiss, Cantonese, Japanese); 2 bars; lounge; gorgeous indoor pool w/sun terrace overlooking the harbor; health club; spa; concierge; limousine service; business center; designer-brand shopping arcade;

salon; 24-hr. room service; massage; babysitting; same-day laundry service/dry cleaning; in-house nurse; practice music room with grand piano. *In room:* A/C, cable/satellite TV w/CD/DVD player and free in-house movies, fax, free high-speed dataport, minibar, hair dryer, safe, bathroom scale, complimentary welcoming tea, fruit, and bottled water.

Royal Garden 🐛🐛 *Finds* A small hotel with a lot of architectural surprises, the Royal Garden has always been one of my favorites. It features a cool, sleek lobby and a 15-story inner atrium, a concept adapted from the traditional Chinese inner garden (and employed here long before it became standard of some U.S. chains). Plants hang down from balconies ringing the soaring space, glass-enclosed elevators glide up the wall, a piano sits on an island in the middle of a pool, and the sound of rushing water adds freshness and coolness to the atmosphere. A wonderful 25m-long (82-ft.) rooftop swimming pool is uncovered in summer, covered and heated in winter. Off the lobby is a very interesting martini bar, and its Italian restaurant, Sabatini, is one of Hong Kong's best. All in all, it's the kind of hotel that invites exploration. The rooms, the most expensive of which have partial harbor views between two buildings ("partial harbor view" means either that other buildings are obstructing part of your view or that your windows do not squarely face the water), are smartly decorated with a mix of colonial-style and modern furniture and feature mounted plasma TVs and a chilled, purified water tap in the bathroom. The least expensive rooms face the Regal Kowloon Hotel. Although a slight hike to the action of Tsim Sha Tsui, it's only a few minutes' walk to the hover-ferry pier with service to Central and the KCR railway station.

69 Mody Rd., Tsim Sha Tsui East, Kowloon, Hong Kong. ⓒ 800/448-8355 or 852/2721 5215. Fax 852/2369 9976. www.rghk.com.hk. 422 units. HK$2,300–HK$3,000 (US$299–US$389/£164–£214) single; HK$2,450–HK$3,150 (US$318–US$409/£175–£225) double; HK$3,500–HK$3,800 (US$454–US$493/£250–£271) Crown Club executive-floor double; from HK$4,150 (US$539/£296) suite. 1 child under 12 can stay free in parent's room. AE, DC, MC, V. MTR: Tsim Sha Tsui. **Amenities:** 6 restaurants (Italian, Cantonese, Pekingese, Japanese, Continental, international buffet); bar; lounge; heated rooftop outdoor/indoor pool and Jacuzzi; lighted outdoor tennis court; exercise room; spa; sauna; concierge; limousine service; business center; shopping arcade; 24-hr. room service; massage; babysitting; same-day laundry service/dry cleaning; executive-level rooms. *In room:* A/C, satellite TV w/pay movies on demand, high-speed dataport, minibar, coffeemaker, hair dryer, safe, free bottled water.

Sheraton Hong Kong Hotel & Towers 🐛🐛 The 30-some-year-old Sheraton has one of the most envied locations in Hong Kong—near the waterfront on the corner of Nathan Road and Salisbury Road—and is an easy walk to the subway and Star Ferry. In fact, it's such a choice spot that for years rumors buzzed that the Sheraton would close down to make way for a more lucrative office building. Instead, the Sheraton underwent massive renovations that upgraded its facilities and image (and increased its room rates). Its lobby, previously plagued by overcrowding from locals who used it as a convenient waiting place to meet friends, was moved to the second floor to discourage foot traffic and was updated with a sleek, contemporary look graced by Asian motifs and subdued lighting. A plus is the outdoor rooftop swimming pool, heated in winter, offering a spectacular view and more privacy than pools lower to the ground. Guest rooms are decorated in neutral brown, which seems to be the rage nowadays and range from those facing an inner courtyard (the cheapest) to those facing the harbor with great views even from bathrooms. In between are those that overlook surrounding Tsim Sha Tsui, some of which face Nathan Road and even provide sideways glimpses of the harbor. Still, located between The Peninsula and Inter-Continental, it plays second fiddle to both in terms of reputation, class—and, luckily, price. Americans account for one-third of the guests here.

20 Nathan Rd., Tsim Sha Tsui, Kowloon, Hong Kong. ⓒ 800/325-3535 in the U.S. and Canada, or 852/2369 1111. Fax 852/2739 8707. www.sheraton.com/hongkong. 780 units. HK$2,400–HK$3,200 (US$311–US$416/£171–£229)

single, HK$2,700–HK$3,400 (US$337–US$442/£193–£243) double; Tower executive-floor rooms HK$3,600–HK$4,400 (US$467–US$571/£257–£314) single, HK$3,800–HK$4,600 (US$493–US$597/£271–£329) double; from HK$4,800 (US$623/£343) suite. AE, DC, MC, V. MTR: Tsim Sha Tsui. **Amenities:** 5 restaurants (American, oysters/seafood, Japanese, Cantonese, international); bar; 2 lounges (including a Cuban cigar lounge); outdoor heated rooftop swimming pool and Jacuzzi; health club; spa; concierge; tour desk; limousine service; business center; shopping arcade; salon; 24-hr. room service; massage; babysitting; same-day laundry service/dry cleaning; executive-level rooms; house doctor. In room: A/C, satellite TV w/keyboard for Internet access and pay movies, high-speed dataport, minibar, coffeemaker, hair dryer, iron/ironing board, safe, bathroom scale.

CENTRAL DISTRICT

Conrad International Hong Kong ✦✦✦
The 61-story Conrad, built in 1990, is one of a trio of exclusive hotels perched on a hillside above Pacific Place, an upscale shopping center located about halfway between the Central District and Wan Chai. One of the conveniences of staying here is that Pacific Place abounds in very good restaurants, greatly expanding dining options without having to venture far. Hong Kong Park is also just steps away, and the MTR can be reached without venturing outside. The Conrad's facilities appeal to both businesspeople (who make up 70% of the hotel's clientele, the majority of whom are American or European) and well-heeled leisure travelers. Although the architecture is contemporary, the hotel's classic furnishings and Asian touches throughout soften the modern effect, giving it a cozy atmosphere with wood paneling, polished granite, and comfortable furniture. Large-size rooms, which start from the 40th floor, boast windows that extend the width of the room, offering views of either The Peak or the harbor (harbor-view rooms, of course, are better and cost more, though some so-called "city view" rooms offer a partial harbor view through buildings). Bathed in tones of gold and brown, with Chinese vases and Chinese armoires concealing TVs, rooms have spacious bathrooms with separate shower and bathtub facilities and two sinks. On a playful note, the bathrooms even feature a floating duck or other toy for a bit of fun in the bathroom, while a stuffed bear is placed on beds at turndown. In short, this is a great choice for business or pleasure.

Pacific Place, 88 Queensway, Central, Hong Kong. © 800/CONRADS in the U.S. and Canada, or 852/2521 3838. Fax 852/2521 3888. www.conradhotels.com. 513 units. HK$3,300–HK$4,100 (US$428–US$532/£236–£293) single or double; HK$4,300–HK$4,800 (US$558–US$623/£307–£343) executive floor; from HK$7,000 (US$909/£500) suite. Children under 18 stay free in parent's room (maximum 3 persons per room). AE, DC, MC, V. MTR: Admiralty. **Amenities:** 4 restaurants (Italian, Cantonese, French, international); bar; lounge; heated outdoor pool; state-of-the art health club; Jacuzzi; sauna; concierge; limousine service; business center; shopping arcade; 24-hr. room service; massage; babysitting; same-day laundry service/dry cleaning; executive-level rooms; house doctor. In room: A/C, cable/satellite TV w/pay movies on demand and CD/DVD players, high-speed dataport, minibar, coffeemaker, hair dryer, iron/ironing board, safe, bathroom scale, complimentary welcoming tea, fruit, bottled water, and shoeshine.

Island Shangri-La Hong Kong ✦✦✦ (Finds)
Hong Kong Island's tallest hotel (measured from sea level) offers the ultimate in extravagance and luxury, rivaling the grand hotels in Paris or London: It's one of my favorite hotels in the world. More than 700 Viennese chandeliers, lush Tai Ping carpets, artistic flower arrangements, and more than 500 paintings and artworks adorn the hotel. The 17-story atrium, which stretches from the 39th to the 56th floors, features a marvelous 16-story-high Chinese painting, drawn by 40 artists from Beijing and believed to be the largest landscape painting in the world. Also in the atrium are a private lounge open only to hotel guests and a two-story old-world–style library. Wireless service is available in public areas. The hotel itself is enhanced by the connecting Pacific Place shopping center, with its many options in dining; across the street is Hong Kong Park.

Upon arrival, guests are personally escorted to their rooms (all of which ring the 17-story atrium) by a guest-relations officer, who also explains the rooms' features.

Rooms, among the largest in Hong Kong at 41 sq. m (441 sq. ft.) or more, face either The Peak or spectacular Victoria Harbour and feature marble-topped desks, Chinese lacquerware TV cabinets, and silk bedspreads. Oversize bathrooms are equipped with two sinks and separate tub and shower areas (harbor-view rooms only), bidet, LCD TVs, and even jewelry boxes. Fresh flowers are another nice touch. Guests paying rack rates receive such additional services as free transportation from and to the airport, free laundry service and dry cleaning throughout their stay, complimentary American or continental breakfast, free local telephone calls and Internet access, and 6pm late checkout.

Pacific Place, Supreme Court Rd., Central, Hong Kong. ✆ **866/565-5050** in the U.S., or 852/2877 3838. Fax 852/2521 8742. www.shangri-la.com. 565 units. HK$3,000–HK$4,300 (US$389–US$558/£214–£307) single; HK$3,300–HK$4,700 (US$428–US$610/£236–£336) double; from HK$6,600 (US$857/£471) suite. Children under 12 stay free in parent's room. AE, DC, MC, V. MTR: Admiralty. **Amenities:** 6 restaurants (French, international, Cantonese, Japanese, deli); lounge; outdoor heated pool big enough for swimming laps; health club (open 24 hr.); spa; Jacuzzi; sauna; steam bath; concierge; tour desk; limousine service; business center (open 24 hr.); adjoining shopping arcade; salon; 24-hr. room service; massage; babysitting; same-day laundry service/dry cleaning; executive-level rooms; medical clinic; free shuttle to Queen's Pier in Central and Convention Centre. *In room:* A/C, satellite TV w/pay movies on demand, DVD players, fax/printer/scanner, high-speed dataport, minibar, coffeemaker, hair dryer, iron/ironing board, safe, bathroom scale, complimentary welcoming tea, bottled water, fruit.

JW Marriott Hotel ⊛⊛ The 27-story Marriott, which opened in 1989 as the first of three hotels at Pacific Place, is overshadowed by the more luxuriously appointed Conrad and Island Shangri-La (see above). Its lobby, while not as grandiose as others in this category, is nonetheless the only one of Pacific Place's hotels to offer views of the harbor from its lounge (though recent construction has robbed the lounge of its once-grandiose panorama). Wireless access is available in the hotel's public spaces. Rooms, though small, are all designed with right-angled "saw-toothed" windows to maximize views of the harbor or Peak and are outfitted with duvet-covered queen- or king-size beds with red-and-gold runners, large marbled bathrooms with separate tub and shower areas, and oversize desks. On the downside, rooms facing the harbor are subject to the slight din of traffic; since rates are the same, request a room on a high floor.

Pacific Place, 88 Queensway, Central, Hong Kong. ✆ **800/228-9290** in the U.S. and Canada, or 852/2810 8366. Fax 852/2845 0737. www.jwmarriotthk.com. 602 units. HK$3,400–HK$4,000 (US$441–US$519/£243–£286) single or double; HK$4,400 (US$571/£314) Executive Floor; from HK$8,600 (US$1,117/£614) suite. AE, DC, MC, V. MTR: Admiralty. **Amenities:** 3 restaurants (Cantonese, Californian/sushi, coffee shop); wine bar; lounge; outdoor heated pool open year-round; health club (open 24 hr.); Jacuzzi; sauna; steam room; concierge; limousine service; business center (open 24 hr.); shopping arcade; 24-hr. room service; massage; babysitting; same-day laundry service/dry cleaning; executive-level rooms; doctor on call. *In room:* A/C, satellite TV w/pay movies on demand, high-speed dataport, minibar, coffeemaker, hair dryer, iron/ironing board, safe, bathroom scale, complimentary welcoming tea, fruit, bottled water, and shoeshine.

CAUSEWAY BAY & WAN CHAI

The Excelsior ⊛ Located on the Causeway Bay waterfront, next to the World Trade Centre and near a lively shopping area, Hong Kong Island's largest hotel stands on the very first plot of land sold at auction when this outpost became a British colony in 1841. Although it belongs to the Mandarin Oriental group of hotels, it is more plebian than its sister properties in Central, with correspondingly lower prices. Built in 1973 and overshadowed by newer, grander hotels, it nonetheless enjoys a solid reputation and a high occupancy rate, including many tour groups, which translates into an overcrowded lobby that often buzzes with activity, sometimes making it difficult to get front-desk service or find an empty seat. The elevators are also crowded.

On the plus side, this is a good place to stay if you like to jog, since it's close to 20-hectare (50-acre) Victoria Park, Hong Kong's largest city park. In addition, the hotel offers free guided tours to the historic Noon Day Gun across the street, which fires every day at . . . well . . . noon. Its top-floor ToTT'S Asian Grill & Bar (p. 148) offers spectacular harbor views, outrageous decor, and great East-meets-West cuisine. Most rooms are the same small size with the same decor and tend to be crowded. Those that command panoramas of the harbor, with window-side sofas from which to soak in the views, are the most expensive and largest; slightly cheaper are those with side harbor views or views of the park, while the cheapest face inland toward the city. Wireless connections are available in all hotel public areas, including restaurants.

281 Gloucester Rd., Causeway Bay, Hong Kong. © 800/526-6566 in the U.S. and Canada, or 852/2894 8888. Fax 852/2895 6459. www.excelsiorhongkong.com. 884 units. HK$2,400–HK$3,200 (US$312–US$415/£171–£229) single or double; HK$3,200–HK$3,400 (US$415–US$441/£229–£243) Executive Floor; from HK$5,000 (US$649/£357) suite. AE, DC, MC, V. MTR: Causeway Bay. **Amenities:** 5 restaurants (Pacific Rim fusion, Cantonese, Italian, international buffet, coffee shop); bar; lounge; 2 indoor tennis courts; exercise room; sauna; steam room; concierge; tour desk; business center; salon; 24-hr. room service; babysitting; same-day laundry service/dry cleaning; executive-level rooms. *In room:* A/C, satellite TV w/pay movies on demand, high-speed dataport, minibar, coffeemaker, hair dryer, iron/ironing board, safe.

Renaissance Harbour View Hotel Hong Kong *Kids Value* This large, 43-story hotel sits beside the Convention and Exhibition Centre on the Wan Chai waterfront, separated from the Grand Hyatt (p. 82) by Hong Kong's largest outdoor hotel swimming pool and a garden with a playground, shared by the two hotels. Just a couple of minutes' walk from the Wan Chai Star Ferry that delivers passengers to Tsim Sha Tsui (but a longer hike to the nearest tram or MTR station), it provides some of the same facilities and advantages as the Hyatt, but at a lower price; obviously, it caters largely to those attending functions at the convention center, which can make it quite busy, as well as business travelers. Its expansive, white-marbled lobby is airy with views of the harbor, and more than 65% of the rooms also boast outstanding views of the water.

1 Harbour Rd., Wan Chai, Hong Kong. © 800/228-9290 in the U.S. and Canada, or 852/2802 8888. Fax 852/2802 8833. www.renaissancehotels.com/HKGHV. 862 units. HK$2,700–HK$3,300 (US$350–US$428/£193–£236) single or double; HK$3,300–HK$3,700 (US$428–US$480/£236–£264) Renaissance Club executive floor; from HK$4,000 (US$519/£286) suite. AE, DC, MC, V. MTR: Wan Chai. **Amenities:** 3 restaurants (Continental, Cantonese, coffee shop); lounge; dance club; huge outdoor pool; children's splash pool and playground; golf-driving range; 2 lighted outdoor tennis courts; health club; Jacuzzi; jogging trail; concierge; limousine service; business center; 24-hr. room service; babysitting; same-day laundry service/dry cleaning; executive-level rooms; house doctor. *In room:* A/C, cable TV w/pay movies on demand, fax, high-speed dataport, minibar, coffeemaker, hair dryer, safe.

5 Moderate

Since tour groups have long been a mainstay of tourism in Hong Kong, you're most likely to encounter them at the moderately (and inexpensively) priced hotels, which account for the majority of hotels in Hong Kong. And with increased tourism from mainland China filling rooms in this category, it's imperative to book early. As for rooms, they tend to be rather small compared to American hotel rooms, with generally unexciting views, but usually have such amenities as hair dryers, minibars or empty refrigerators you can stock yourself, and instant coffee, as well as room service, bellhops, nonsmoking floors, tour desks, and sometimes a swimming pool and/or fitness room. Since harbor views are usually not available, rates are generally based on height/floor number and decor and sometimes on size.

KOWLOON

Eaton Hotel ✸✸✸ *Finds*   This hotel has more class and more facilities than most other hotels in this group, making it one of my top picks. A handsome brick 21-story hotel, located above a shopping complex not far from the Temple Street Night Market, it features one of the longest hotel escalators I've seen; it takes guests straight up to the fourth-floor lobby, where a cheerful and efficient staff awaits your arrival. The lobby lounge (offering wireless Internet connection) is bright and cheerful, with a four-story glass-enclosed atrium that overlooks a garden terrace with a water cascade, where you can sit outside with drinks in nice weather. Other pluses are the small but nicely done rooftop pool with sunning terrace, live music nightly in the bar, free daily guided tours of the night market, and free Internet service in its Aroma Coffee Exchange cybercafe. Guest rooms are small but welcoming, with all the basic creature comforts. I especially like the innovatively designed (and highest-priced) deluxe rooms, with curved floor-to-ceiling windows giving views of a distant harbor.

380 Nathan Rd., Yau Ma Tei, Kowloon, Hong Kong. ⓒ **800/223-5652** in the U.S. and Canada, or 852/2782 1818. Fax 852/2782 5563. www.eaton-hotel.com. 460 units. HK$1,950–HK$2,150 (US$253–US$279/£139–£154) single or double; HK$2,470–HK$2,670 (US$356–US$347/£176–£190) executive room double. AE, DC, MC, V. MTR: Jordan. **Amenities:** 3 restaurants (Cantonese, Asian/Western, coffee shop); bar; lounge; small outdoor pool; exercise room; concierge; business center (open 24 hr.); shopping arcade; 24-hr. room service; babysitting; same-day laundry service/dry cleaning; executive-level rooms. *In room:* A/C, satellite TV w/pay movies on demand, high-speed dataport, minibar, coffeemaker, hair dryer, safe, free shoeshine.

Empire Hotel Kowloon   Opened in 2002, this is one of Kowloon's newest hotels, giving it a contemporary, upbeat edge over competitors. Rooms, occupying the 8th through 26th floors of a round, hollow, glass-sheathed tower, boast wall-to-wall and floor-to-ceiling windows, though only those above the 17th floor have distant harbor views. Glass-topped desks and bowl-shaped basins rise above ordinary hotel furnishings in more deluxe rooms, but the dim, bedside-reading lamps will ruin your eyes. Unlike most Hong Kong hotels, showers here greatly outnumber tubs. There's a pool, but it's at the bottom of the pit-like tower, rendering it grossly uninviting. Still, this hotel, popular with Japanese guests, is a welcome addition to Kowloon's medium-priced accommodations.

62 Kimberley Rd., Tsim Sha Tsui, Kowloon, Hong Kong. ⓒ **800/830-6144** in the U.S. and Canada, or 852/2685 3000. Fax 852/2685 3685. www.empirehotel.com.hk. 315 units. HK$1,600–HK$2,400 (US$208–US$312/£114–£171) single or double; from HK$3,000 (US$389/£214) suite. Children under 12 stay free in parent's room. AE, DC, MC, V. MTR: Tsim Sha Tsui. **Amenities:** 2 restaurants (Japanese, buffet); bar; outdoor pool; exercise room; sauna; limousine service; business center; room service 7am–10pm; babysitting; same-day laundry service/dry cleaning. *In room:* A/C, satellite TV w/pay movies, high-speed dataport, minibar, coffeemaker, hair dryer, safe.

Guangdong Hotel ✸   The Guangdong, owned by mainland Chinese and once plagued by Asian tour groups, has upgraded its look, its image, and its prices, with tour groups now accounting for only 5% of its business. It's located in the heart of Tsim Sha Tsui, about a 10-minute walk from the Star Ferry and only minutes from the Tsim Sha Tsui MTR station. Its lobby is spare but upbeat, with an illuminated glass wall behind the reception desk and Picasso-esque masks adorning one wall. Its rooms are very small but clean and pleasant enough, with room rates based primarily on floor level. None of the rooms here offer views; most face other buildings. If you want to be away from the din of traffic, splurge for a larger deluxe room on a higher floor. Better yet are executive-floor rooms, which reflect either Japanese or European influences in their design and decor.

18 Prat Ave., Tsim Sha Tsui, Kowloon, Hong Kong. © **852/3410 8888.** Fax 852/2721 1137. www.gdhhotels.com. 245 units. HK$1,280–HK$1,780 (US$166–US$231/£91–£127) single or double; HK$1,880–HK$1,980 (US$244–US$257/£134–£141) executive floor; from HK$2,380 (US$309/£170) suite. 2 children under 12 stay free in parent's room. AE, DC, MC, V. MTR: Tsim Sha Tsui. **Amenities:** 2 restaurants (Cantonese, coffee shop); small fitness room; limousine service; business center; room service 7:30am–10pm; massage; babysitting; same-day laundry service/dry cleaning; doctor on call. *In room:* A/C, satellite TV w/pay movies on demand, wireless Internet access, minibar, coffeemaker (but no coffee), hair dryer.

Kimberley Hotel   The 20-story Kimberley Hotel, on the northern edge of Tsim Sha Tsui, about a 15-minute walk from the Star Ferry, opened in 1991 and was long one of my favorites for its moderate prices, location, and facilities. However, it is now starting to show its age, a bit worn around the edges and with outdated decor. It's clearly time for a face-lift (at press time, some rooms had received new carpets and wallpaper). Still, it does a thriving business attracting both the tourist and business trade, including many Japanese and tour groups. Guest rooms, constructed with V-shaped windows that let in more sunlight and allow for more panoramic—though not scenic—views, are rather small and plain but come with all the basics. The most expensive rooms are on higher floors and are larger, but even these are rather small. The suites represent an especially good deal since they occupy the top two floors and are equipped with kitchenettes and a lounging/dining area, making them ideal for long-term guests and families.

28 Kimberley Rd., Tsim Sha Tsui, Kowloon, Hong Kong. © **800/876-5278** in the U.S., or 852/2723 3888. Fax 852/2723 1318. www.kimberleyhotel.com.hk. 546 units. HK$1,250–HK$1,950 (US$162–US$253/£89–£139) single; HK$1,350–HK$2,050 (US$175–US$266/£96–£146) double; from HK$2,300 (US$299/£164) suite. AE, DC, MC, V. MTR: Tsim Sha Tsui. **Amenities:** 3 restaurants (Cantonese, Japanese, coffee shop); lounge; golf cages; fitness room; spa; sauna; tour desk; business center; shopping arcade; salon; room service 6am–midnight; massage; babysitting; same-day laundry service/dry cleaning. *In room:* A/C, satellite TV w/pay movies, high-speed dataport, minibar, coffeemaker, hair dryer.

Kowloon Hotel   The Kowloon is a modern glass-walled structure right behind The Peninsula, giving it a great location just a few a few minutes' walk from the Star Ferry and MTR. The hotel has a very good pizzeria, and even though it has no recreational facilities of its own, guests can use the pool and health club at the YMCA cater-cornered to the hotel or at its sister Harbour Plaza Metropolis hotel (free shuttle available) at reduced fees. The downside of the hotel: rooms are minuscule and are plagued by traffic noise. Although they have V-shaped bay windows, allowing unobstructed views up and down the street, The Peninsula's tower has robbed harbor views from all but the most expensive rooms.

19–21 Nathan Rd., Tsim Sha Tsui, Kowloon, Hong Kong. © **800/223-5652** in the U.S., or 852/2929 2888. Fax 852/2739 9811. www.harbour-plaza.com/klnh. 736 units. HK$1,600–HK$2,700 (US$208–US$350/£114–£192) single; HK$1,700–HK$2,800 (US$221–US$363/£121–£200) double; HK$2,800–HK$3,600 (US$363–US$467/£200–£257) executive-floor double; from HK$4,000 (US$519/£286) suite. Children under 12 stay free in parent's room. AE, DC, MC, V. MTR: Tsim Sha Tsui. **Amenities:** 3 restaurants (Italian, Cantonese, international buffet); bar; access to nearby YMCA or sister hotel pool and health club (fee charged); tour desk; limousine service; business center; shopping arcade; salon; room service 6am–2am; babysitting; same-day laundry service/dry cleaning; executive-level rooms. *In room:* A/C, satellite TV w/pay movies, fax, wireless Internet access, minibar, coffeemaker, hair dryer, safe.

Miramar   Across from Kowloon Park, the Miramar is strategically located in the midst of a shopping area, including the Park Lane shopping arcade and Miramar Shopping Centre. An older hotel once known for its showy exterior and glitzy gold-colored decor, this 50-some-year-old property toned down its public areas during a major renovation some years back; the last trace of the Miramar's former flashy self can only be seen in its stained-glass windows in the lobby's atrium ceiling. Since it caters largely to Asian tour groups, a high percentage of its rooms are twins. All are quite roomy though rather standard, with some of the higher-floor deluxe rooms offering views of Kowloon Park.

118–130 Nathan Rd., Tsim Sha Tsui, Kowloon, Hong Kong. ⓒ 852/2368 1111. Fax 852/2369 1788. www.miramarhk. com. 525 units. HK$2,000–HK$2,700 (US$260–US$350/£143–£193) single or double; HK$3,300–HK$3,700 (US$428–US$480/£236–£264) Miramar Club executive floor; from HK$4,800 (US$623/£343) suite. Children under 12 stay free in parent's room. AE, DC, MC, V. MTR: Tsim Sha Tsui. **Amenities:** 5 restaurants (2 Cantonese, Sichuan, East-meets-West fusion, coffee shop); bar; indoor pool; exercise room; sauna; concierge; tour desk; limousine service; business center; shopping arcade; room service 6am–1am; massage; babysitting; same-day laundry service/dry cleaning; executive-level rooms. *In room:* A/C, satellite TV w/pay movies on demand and keyboard for Internet access, minibar, hair dryer, safe.

New World Renaissance Hotel   This hotel is tucked inside the New World Centre shopping complex, which contains more than 50 shops and boutiques. Modern in both decor and technology, this 20-some-year-old hotel nevertheless suggests an Asian atmosphere with its large flower arrangements and sleek black furniture, but I find the windowless lobby slightly claustrophobic. Furthermore, despite its prime location right on the waterfront near the InterContinental (p. 79), oddly enough, only one restaurant provides harbor views, and none of its rooms face the water. Rather, all rooms face Salisbury Road or the pool (which is quieter), with a few offering partial glimpses of the water. Otherwise, the rooms are comfortable enough, with modern Asian decor and all the usual amenities, including separate tub and shower areas in deluxe rooms.

22 Salisbury Rd., Tsim Sha Tsui, Kowloon, Hong Kong. ⓒ 800/228-9290 in the U.S. and Canada, or 852/2369 4111. Fax 852/2369 9387. www.renaissancehotels.com/hkgnw. 545 units. HK$2,000–HK$2,600 (US$260–US$337/£140–£186) single or double; HK$3,000 (US$390/£214) Renaissance Club executive floor; from HK$3,300 (US$429/£236) suite. AE, DC, MC, V. MTR: Tsim Sha Tsui. **Amenities:** 3 restaurants (Euro-Asian, Cantonese, coffee shop); lounge; outdoor pool; health club; limousine service; business center (open 24 hr.); shopping arcade; salon; 24-hr. room service; babysitting; same-day laundry service/dry cleaning; executive-level rooms. *In room:* A/C, cable TV w/pay movies, fax, high-speed dataport, minibar, coffeemaker, hair dryer, safe, free bottled water.

Pruton Prudential Hotel Ⓖ   This 1991 hotel, at the northern end of Tsim Sha Tsui, towers 17 stories above a six-level shopping complex and the MTR Jordan station, providing easy and direct access to the rest of Hong Kong. About a 20-minute walk from the Star Ferry and only minutes from the Temple Street Night Market, Jade Market, and a Tin Hau (Goddess of the Sea) temple, it offers smartly decorated rooms with sleek furniture, artwork, and Japanese moving panels framing the windows. The rates are based on height, with the cheapest rooms—none of them nonsmoking—on lower floors. If possible, avoid those facing the back and nondescript buildings. Deluxe rooms feature floor-to-ceiling bay windows and receive more sunshine. Although the hotel itself has only a coffee shop and a bar, there are several other restaurants within the shopping complex. Another plus is the 18m-long (59-ft.) rooftop pool.

222 Nathan Rd. (entrance on Tak Shing St.), Tsim Sha Tsui, Kowloon, Hong Kong. ⓒ 852/2311 8222. Fax 852/2311 4760. www.prudentialhotel.com. 431 units. HK$1,300–HK$2,050 (US$169–US$266/£93–£146) single or double; HK$2,500 (US$325/£179) Executive Club floor; from HK$3,100 (US$402/£221) suite. Children under 12 stay free in parent's room. AE, DC, MC, V. MTR: Jordan. **Amenities:** Restaurant (buffet/coffee shop); bar; outdoor pool; exercise room; tour desk; limousine service; business center (open 24 hr.); shopping arcade; salon; room service 6:30am–11pm; babysitting; same-day laundry service/dry cleaning; executive-level rooms. *In room:* A/C, satellite/cable TV w/pay movies, wireless high-speed dataport, minibar, coffeemaker, hair dryer, safe.

Ramada Hotel Kowloon   Popular with Asian business travelers, this no-nonsense, Chinese-owned hotel offers simple, clean rooms and not much else in terms of facilities or services. Even its so-called business center has only one computer. Its location on Chatham Road, across the street from the science and history museums, is not as convenient as other business hotels in this category, though it is within walking distance of the MTR (about 6 min.), Star Ferry (about 15 min.), hover ferry with service to Central (about 10 min.), and KCR station (5 min.). The cheapest rooms, devoid of character, are small and have glazed windows, while the highest-priced rooms face Chatham Road and have the best views but can be noisy. In short, there's nothing exciting about this hotel, but it will suffice if more desirable and convenient properties are full.

73–75 Chatham Rd. S., Tsim Sha Tsui, Kowloon, Hong Kong. © 800/468 3571 in the U.S., or 852/2311 1100. Fax 852/2311 6000. www.ramadahongkong.com. 205 units. HK$1,300–HK$2,050 (US$169–US$266/£93–£146) single or double; from HK$2,800 (US$364/£200) suite. 1 child under 12 stays free in parent's room. AE, DC, MC, V. MTR: Tsim Sha Tsui. **Amenities:** Coffee shop; bar; limousine service; tour desk; tiny business center; room service 7am–8pm; babysitting; laundry service/dry cleaning. *In room:* A/C, cable TV w/pay movies, wireless high-speed dataport, minibar, coffeemaker, hair dryer, safe.

Regal Kowloon Hotel ⑤   The 15-story Regal Kowloon offers more services and is more attractive than many hotels in its price range, with a lobby that blends East and West with reproduction 18th-century French antiques and Louis XV–style furniture standing alongside Chinese works of art. Guest rooms, all soundproof, are rather middle-of-the-road but perfectly adequate, with the exception of good bedside reading lights. The cheapest rooms face another building, provide no view whatsoever, and tend to be dark. The more expensive rooms face a garden; some even have a glimpse of the harbor between buildings. Business travelers may opt for Regal Class rooms, while Regal Club executive floors go a step further with added services and amenities (like LCD TVs and broadband in addition to wireless Internet access). The most moderately priced of several hotels in Tsim Sha Tsui East, it's only a minute's walk to the hover-ferry service to Central.

71 Mody Rd., Tsim Sha Tsui East, Kowloon, Hong Kong. © 800/457-4000 in the U.S., or 852/2722 1818. Fax 852/2369 6950. www.regalhotel.com. 600 units. HK$2,000–HK$2,800 (US$260–US$363/£143–£200) single or double; from HK$3,000 (US$389/£214) Regal Class; from HK$3,600 (US$467/£257) Regal Club; from HK$6,000 (US$779/£428) suite. Children under 12 can stay free in parent's room. AE, DC, MC, V. MTR: Tsim Sha Tsui. **Amenities:** 2 restaurants (American, coffee shop); bar; lounge; exercise room; tour desk; limousine service; business center; shopping arcade; salon; 24-hr. room service; babysitting; same-day laundry service/dry cleaning; executive-level rooms. *In room:* A/C, satellite TV w/pay movies, wireless Internet access, minibar, coffeemaker, hair dryer, safe.

MID-LEVELS

Bishop Lei International House ⑤⑤ *Finds*   If you want to pretend that you live in Hong Kong, in a residential area popular with expats and abounding in charming neighborhood restaurants and bars, this is the place for you. Located on the slope of Victoria Peak in the Mid-Levels, at the top of the Central–Mid-Levels Escalator that delivers residents to jobs in Central in the morning and then reverses to bring them back home again later in the day, it is not as convenient as other hotels, but it has its certain charm. In addition, the hotel makes up for its out-of-the-way location with free shuttle service to Central, Admiralty, and Wan Chai; a half-dozen city buses also stop outside its door. Opened in 1996 and managed by the Catholic Diocese of Hong Kong, it offers tiny standard single and double rooms (with even tinier bathrooms, most equipped with showers instead of tubs) that have large windows letting in lots of sunshine. Unfortunately, these face inland. If you can, spring for a more expensive room facing the harbor (all twins or suites). Since they're so high up, views are fantastic. In any case, in acknowledgment that rooms are small, there's a reading room for relaxation, the coffee shop has an outdoor terrace, and surprising for a hotel this size, it also has a small pool and exercise room. If the frenetic pace of Hong Kong sets you on edge, you'll find this a nice retreat. Long-term packages are available.

4 Robinson Rd., Mid-Levels, Hong Kong. © 852/2868 0828. Fax 852/2868 1551. www.bishopleihtl.com.hk. 203 units. HK$1,280 (US$166/£91) single; HK$1,480 (US$192/£106); HK$1,880–HK$2,080 (US$244–US$270/£134–£149) double; from HK$2,480 (US$322/£177) suite. 1 child under 12 can stay free in parent's room. AE, DC, MC, V. Bus: 3B, 12, 12M, 23, 23A, or 40 to Robinson Rd. **Amenities:** Coffee shop; small outdoor pool; small exercise room; business center; 24-hr. room service; babysitting; same-day laundry service/dry cleaning; free shuttle bus to Central. *In room:* A/C, cable TV, high-speed dataport, minibar, coffeemaker (but no coffee), hair dryer, safe.

CAUSEWAY BAY & WAN CHAI

Empire Hotel ☆ (Value) Nicely situated in the heart of Wan Chai and popular with midlevel business travelers for its convenience to Central and the convention center, this business hotel offers good value, with many of the same amenities, services, and facilities found at higher-priced hotels, including a rooftop outdoor swimming pool large enough for swimming laps. Narrow hallways, however, may prove a challenge to the claustrophobic, and rooms are so small that couples will fight over the lone luggage rack. None provide a view of the harbor from their bay windows. Still, they're comfortable and pleasant enough, with duvet-covered beds and wall-mounted LCD TVs (leaving mercifully more desk space).

33 Hennessy Rd., Wan Chai, Hong Kong. © 800/830-6144 in the U.S. and Canada, or 852/2866 9111. Fax 852/2861 3121. www.empirehotel.com.hk. 360 units. HK$1,480–HK$1,880 (US$192–US$244/£106–£134) single; HK$1,580–HK$1,980 (US$205–US$257/£113–£141) double; HK$2,380 (US$309/£170) executive-floor double; from HK$2,980 (US$387/£213) suite. Children under 12 stay free in parent's room. AE, DC, MC, V. MTR: Wan Chai. **Amenities:** 3 restaurants (Cantonese, steak, coffee shop); lounge; outdoor pool; exercise room; sauna; concierge; tour desk; limousine service; business center; room service 7am–11pm; massage; babysitting; same-day laundry service/dry cleaning; executive-level rooms. *In room:* A/C, cable TV w/pay movies, high-speed dataport, minibar, coffeemaker, safe.

Harbour View International House ☆ (Value) Opened in 1986, this YMCA occupies a prime spot on the Wan Chai waterfront, right next to the Hong Kong Arts Centre and not far from the convention center. Rooms, all twin or double beds, are rather stylish for a YMCA, attracting guests mostly from mainland China and North America. Best of all, more than half the rooms face the harbor with V-shaped windows, making this the cheapest place on Hong Kong Island with great views. Rooms that face inland are even cheaper.

4 Harbour Rd., Wan Chai, Hong Kong. © 852/2802 0111. Fax 852/2802 9063. www.harbour.ymca.org.hk. 320 units. HK$1,300–HK$1,950 (US$169–US$253/£93–£139) single or double. 1 child under 12 stays free in parent's room. AE, DC, MC, V. MTR: Wan Chai. **Amenities:** Restaurant (Chinese/Western); coffee shop; tour desk; room service 7am–11:30pm; babysitting; laundry service/dry cleaning. *In room:* A/C, cable TV, wireless Internet access, minibar, coffeemaker (but no coffee).

Jia ☆☆☆ (Finds) Travelers who are allergic to ugly hotel rooms will want to head straight to Hong Kong's hippest boutique hotel, opened in 2004 by a Singaporean 20-something entrepreneur and designed by Philippe Starck. From the moment guests step into the low-key lobby with its teak wood floors, white sheer curtains, and whimsical furniture and are greeted by staff in chic Shanghai Tang–designed uniforms, they know this is no ordinary place of abode. Stylish rooms (35 sq. m/380 sq. ft.), bathed in white and divided into living, dining, and working areas, feature kitchens and home theater units consisting of flat-panel TVs, DVD/CD players, and surround sound. One- and two-bedroom suites are also available. Guests enjoy free local telephone calls, free broadband Internet access, complimentary continental breakfast and cocktail hour, free access to a local gym, and access to both Kee, a private members' club, and the VIP area of Dragon-i (p. 231). I wouldn't be surprised if some people check in and never move out, especially with this incentive: Long-staying guests get a free massage.

1–5 Irving St., Causeway Bay, Hong Kong. ① 852/3196 9000. Fax 852/3196 9001. www.jiahongkong.com. 54 units. HK$1,800 (US$234/£129) single or double; from HK$2,600 (US$338/£186) suite. Monthly rates available. Rates include continental breakfast. AE, DC, MC, V. MTR: Causeway Bay. **Amenities:** 2 restaurants (Australian, Asian); bar; free access to nearby health club; sun deck; room service noon–10pm; massage, same-day laundry service/dry cleaning. *In room:* A/C, satellite/cable TV w/DVD/CD player, high-speed dataport, kitchen, hair dryer, iron/ironing board, safe.

Lanson Place Boutique Hotel & Residences ✦✦✦ *Value* Following close on Jia's

heels (and just down the street), this stylish boutique hotel caters to long-staying guests with upbeat, contemporary rooms, decorated in natural woods, chrome, and glass. Ranging in size from 35 to 55 sq. m (380–590 sq. ft.), with one-and two-bedroom residences also available, they come with fully stocked kitchenettes, home theater systems with large LCD TVs and DVD players (you can check out DVDs for free at reception), and mobile phones you can carry to breakfast or the gym. The best views are over Victoria Park, while the cheapest rooms face other buildings. Continental breakfast, wireless Internet connections, and use of computers in the small business center are all free. While in-house facilities are limited, this is a perfect home-away-from-home for weary road warriors, and the staff, who run operations from sit-down desks rather than the usual front desk, couldn't be nicer.

133 Leighton Rd., Causeway Bay, Hong Kong. ① 852/3477 6888. Fax 852/3477 6999. www.lansonplace.com. 194 units. HK$1,500–HK$3,200 (US$195–US$415/£107–£229) single or double; from HK$4,200 (US$545/£300) suite. Weekly/monthly rates available. Rates include continental breakfast. Children under 12 stay free in parent's room. AE, DC, MC, V. MTR: Causeway Bay. **Amenities:** Bar; small gym; limousine service; business center; massage; babysitting; coin-operated laundry; same-day laundry service/dry cleaning. *In room:* A/C, satellite TV w/DVD/CD player, wireless Internet access, kitchen, hair dryer, iron/ironing board, safe, bathroom scale, complimentary bottled water and small basket of groceries.

Metropark Hotel ✦✦ Although not as centrally located as my other picks in

Causeway Bay, this new hotel has some compelling advantages that put it near the top of the list (and in any case, the MTR and tram lines are just outside the door and the hotel provides a free shuttle bus to the shopping district in Causeway Bay). For one thing, it's cheerier and more colorful than most hotels, with a contemporary and fun design that extends through the lobby and into the rooms, the most expensive of which have great views over Victoria Park to the harbor (the cheapest rooms face another building). In addition, it has all the facilities most travelers need, including free broadband Internet service and a rooftop pool complete with great views. Unfortunately, bathrooms are small, with showers instead of tubs and limited counter space, but in-room vanities provide extra place to stow stuff. In short, this is a welcome addition to Causeway Bay, despite its unlikely location.

148 Tung Lo Wan Rd., Causeway Bay, Hong Kong. ① 800/223-5652 in the U.S. and Canada, or 852/2600 1000. Fax 852/2600 1111. www.metroparkhotel.com. 266 units. HK$900 (US$117/£64) single; HK$1,500–HK$1,800 (US$195–US$234/£107–£129) single/double; from HK$2,600 (US$338/£186) suite. Children under 12 stay free in parent's room. AE, DC, MC, V. MTR: Tin Hau. **Amenities:** Restaurant (coffee shop); bar; outdoor pool; exercise room; Jacuzzi; sauna; tour desk; business center; 24-hr. room service; same-day laundry service/dry cleaning; free shuttle to Wan Chai and Causeway Bay. *In room:* A/C, cable/satellite TV w/pay movies on demand, high-speed dataport, minibar, coffeemaker, hair dryer, safe.

Novotel Century Hong Kong   Opened in 1992, this gleaming white 23-story hotel is a 7-minute walk via covered walkway from the Hong Kong Convention and Exhibition Centre and the Wan Chai Star Ferry terminus with service to Tsim Sha Tsui and Hung Hom. Its airy, smart-looking two-story lobby has floor-to-ceiling windows overlooking a busy intersection and is plagued by the constant hum of traffic, but since there are very few seats available, you probably won't spend much time here anyway. Narrow corridors lead to minuscule rooms, which are mercifully equipped with double-paned windows as well as touch pads on phones for controlling lights, the TV, and other functions. A few of the most expensive doubles offer a partial harbor view between buildings, as do some of the rooms on the Royal Club executive floor, but standard rooms face other buildings. Probably the best thing about this hotel is its facilities, including a wading pool.

238 Jaffe Rd., Wan Chai, Hong Kong. © **800/221-4542** in the U.S. and Canada, or 852/2598 8888. Fax 852/2598 8866. www.accorhotels.com/asia. 511 units. HK$1,600–HK$1,900 (US$208–US$247/£114–£136) single; HK$1,700–HK$2,000 (US$221–US$260/£121–£143) double; HK$2,300 (US$299/£164) Royal Club executive-floor double; from HK$3,800 (US$494/£271) suite. AE, DC, MC, V. MTR: Wan Chai. **Amenities:** 3 restaurants (Shanghainese, Italian, coffee shop); 2 lounges; outdoor pool; wading pool; exercise room; sauna; tour desk; limousine service; business center; 24-hr. room service; babysitting; same-day laundry service/dry cleaning. *In room:* A/C, satellite TV w/pay movies, wireless Internet access, minibar, coffeemaker, hair dryer, safe.

The Park Lane ⚐   Although it's inland, I've always liked the location of this hotel— across from huge Victoria Park and close to many area restaurants, shops, and department stores. First opened in 1974 and attracting primarily business travelers, this 28-story hotel underwent a huge renovation a few years back that gave its lobby a more modern, brighter look and its deluxe guest rooms fun, contemporary furnishings like glass-topped desks and coffee tables and bowl-shaped glass sinks. Rooms vary in price according to floor level, decor, and view—the best are those facing Victoria Park (where you can watch people practicing tai chi in the morning), with the harbor beyond. Standard rooms, on the other hand, have uninspiring views and are rather ordinary. On the downside, the lobby gets a lot of street traffic from area shoppers, making it difficult to attract individual attention from the overworked staff. Be sure to book at least one meal at the top-floor Riva, with sweeping views of Victoria Park and the harbor. Its coffee shop runs 24 hours, a rarity in Hong Kong hotels.

310 Gloucester Rd., Causeway Bay, Hong Kong. © **800/457-4000** in the U.S. and Canada, or 852/2293 8888. Fax 852/2576 7853. www.parklane.com.hk. 803 units. HK$2,000–HK$3,100 (US$260–US$402/£143–£221) single or double; HK$3,300–HK$4,100 (US$429–US$532/£236–£293) Premier Club executive rooms; from HK$5,000 (US$649/£357) suite. Children under 12 stay free in parent's room (maximum 3 persons per room). AE, DC, MC, V. MTR: Causeway Bay. **Amenities:** 3 restaurants (Continental, international, American); bar; lounge; health club; Jacuzzi; sauna; concierge; tour desk; limousine service; business center; shopping arcade; salon; 24-hr. room service; massage; babysitting; same-day laundry service/dry cleaning; executive-level rooms; house doctor. *In room:* A/C, satellite/cable TV w/pay movies, high-speed dataport, minibar, coffeemaker, hair dryer, safe, complimentary bottled water.

Rosedale on the Park ⚐ *Finds*   Opened in 2001 and already overtaken by savvier, newer hotels on the Causeway Bay scene, this is still a solid choice for its targeted corporate accounts, for which it sweetens the deal with complimentary broadband Internet service in each room, cordless phones, in-house mobile phones that allow you to receive calls if you're out of your room (but inside the hotel), free drinks in the fridge upon check in, and a lounge with computers and Internet access. Only 13 rooms on each floor give it a more intimate atmosphere than the city's many huge hotels. Rooms are minuscule but have everything you need, though note that the least expensive "superior" rooms are on lower floors and face another building. Some rooms on the

31st-floor executive level have side views of the harbor (you have to be standing at the window to see it), but the best deal is the junior suites with microwaves and kitchen utensils, making them a good bet for long-staying guests.

8 Shelter St., Causeway Bay, Hong Kong. (C) **800/521-5200** in the U.S. and Canada, or 852/2127 8888. Fax 852/2127 3333. www.rosedale.com.hk. 274 units. HK$1,380–HK$1,880 (US$179–US$244/£99–£134) single or double; HK$2,080 (US$270/£149) executive room; from HK$2,380 (US$309/£170) suite. Weekly and monthly rates available. Children under 12 stay free in parent's room. AE, DC, MC, V. MTR: Causeway Bay. **Amenities:** 3 restaurants (2 Cantonese, Western); lounge; small fitness room; business center; 24-hr. room service; babysitting; same-day laundry service/dry cleaning; executive-level rooms. *In room:* A/C, satellite TV w/pay movies on demand, free high-speed dataport, microwave (not all rooms), fridge, coffeemaker, hair dryer, iron/ironing board, safe, complimentary soda, beer, and bottled water.

6 Inexpensive

Unfortunately, Hong Kong has more expensive hotels than it does budget accommodations. Hotels in this category generally offer small, functional rooms with a bathroom and air-conditioning but usually have few services or facilities. Always inquire whether there's a difference in price between rooms with twin beds and those with double beds. If possible, try to *see* a room before committing yourself, since some may be better than others in terms of traffic noise, view, condition, and size. For the most part, however, you shouldn't have any problems with the inexpensive hotels recommended here.

KOWLOON

Booth Lodge 𝕲𝕲 *Finds*   About a 30-minute walk to the Star Ferry, but close to the Jade Market, Temple Street Night Market, and Ladies' Market, and only a 2-minute walk from the Yau Ma Tei MTR station, Booth Lodge is located just off Nathan Road on the seventh floor of the Salvation Army building. It has a comfortable lobby and an adjacent coffee shop offering very reasonably priced lunch and dinner buffets with Chinese, Japanese, and Western selections, but best is the restaurant's outdoor brick terrace overlooking a wooded hillside, where buffet barbecues are held in peak season. Rooms, all twins or doubles and either standard rooms or larger deluxe rooms, are spotlessly clean. Some face the madness of Nathan Road, but those facing the hillside are quieter. If you're looking for inexpensive yet reliable lodging in a convenient location, this is a good bet. A bonus: Local telephone calls are free.

11 Wing Sing Lane, Yau Ma Tei, Kowloon, Hong Kong. (C) **852/2771 9266.** Fax 852/2385 1140. http://boothlodge. salvation.org.hk. 53 units. HK$620–HK$1,500 (US$81–US$195/£44–£107) single or double. Rates include buffet breakfast. AE, MC, V. MTR: Yau Ma Tei. **Amenities:** Coffee shop; tour desk; laundry service/dry cleaning. *In room:* A/C, satellite TV, fridge, hair dryer.

BP International House 𝕲 *Kids*   The word "House" in the name is misleading, since it is actually a 25-story hotel, with a spacious but utilitarian lobby catering mainly to tour groups, school excursions, and budget-conscious business travelers, which gives it a dormitory-like atmosphere. Built in 1993 at the north end of Kowloon Park, it's just a stone's throw from the park's indoor and outdoor public swimming pools and a short walk to a playground, making it good for families. The park's many paths also make it popular with joggers. Guest rooms, located on the 14th to 25th floors, are tiny but spotless, pleasant, and modern, with showers rather than tubs and fold-down vanity mirrors to create more space. Although located inland, some Corporate rooms on the top floors offer great views over Kowloon Park of the harbor, the Peak, and the Symphony of Lights nightly laser show, as well as such extras like minibars and hot-water kettles. There are also very simple "Family Rooms" equipped with bunk beds that sleep four for HK$1,350 (US$175/£96).

8 Austin Rd., Tsim Sha Tsui, Kowloon, Hong Kong. ✆ 800/223-5652 in the U.S. and Canada, or 852/2376 1111. Fax 852/2376 1333. www.bpih.com.hk. 529 units. HK$1,100 (US$143/£79) double; HK$1,400–HK$2,100 (US$180–US$270/£100–£150) Corporate room from HK$3,100 (US$403/£221) suite. Children under 12 stay free in parent's room. AE, DC, MC, V. MTR: Jordan. **Amenities:** Coffee shop; lounge; tour desk; babysitting; coin-op laundry; laundry service/dry cleaning; executive-level rooms. *In room:* A/C, satellite TV w/pay movies, wireless Internet access, fridge, safe.

Caritas Bianchi Lodge *(Value)*   Just down the street from Booth Lodge and also convenient to the jade and night markets and Yau Ma Tei MTR station, this hotel is not as homey as Booth Lodge and has as much personality as a college dormitory. However, most of the year it charges only two-thirds or less of the rack rates listed below, making it a bargain that can't be beat. Most of its very simple rooms, with large desks and closets, face toward the back of the hotel, offering a view of a wooded cliff and a small park, certainly a nicer vista than most hotels can boast. Try to get a room on a higher floor. This establishment, under management of the Roman Catholic Church's social welfare bureau and popular with long-staying guests for its monthly rates, is a good choice for single travelers, including women.

4 Cliff Rd., Yau Ma Tei, Kowloon, Hong Kong. ✆ 852/2388 1111. Fax 852/2770 6669. cblresv@bianchi-lodge.com. 90 units. HK$720 (US$94/£51) single; HK$820–HK$1,200 (US$107–US$156/£59–£86) double. Rates include buffet breakfast. Monthly rates available. AE, DC, MC, V. MTR: Yau Ma Tei. **Amenities:** Restaurant (Western/Chinese); tour desk; room service 7am–9pm; laundry service/dry cleaning. *In room:* A/C, satellite TV, minibar, coffeemaker (but no coffee), safe.

Dorsett Seaview Hotel   This 19-story brick hotel looks slightly out of place amid the hustle and bustle of this Chinese neighborhood, just a stone's throw from a famous Tin Hau (Goddess of the Sea) Temple and Temple Street's famous Night Market. Catering mainly to visitors from the mainland and Southeast Asia, it has a tiny lobby (often packed) and, best of all, a cocktail lounge on the top floor offering views of a harbor (not the famous Victoria Harbour, but a working harbor nonetheless). Narrow corridors lead to the smallest rooms I've seen in Hong Kong, so miniature that TVs are mounted to the wall to save space. It reminds me of a Japanese business hotel, functional and clean but so small you can almost reach out and touch all four walls. At any rate, since rooms lack the convenience of a desk or large closet space, there's virtually no place to unpack or put your luggage. It's basically just a place to rest your weary bones; as for those Night Market bargains you just purchased, you'll have to either stow them under your bed or sleep with them. Nevertheless, this hotel gets recommended for its superb, colorful location.

268 Shanghai St., Yau Ma Tei, Kowloon, Hong Kong. ✆ 852/2782 0882. Fax 852/2781 8800. www.dorsettseaview. com.hk. 268 units. HK$880–HK$1,480 (US$114–US$192/£63–£106) single or double; from HK$2,380 (US$309/£170) suite. AE, DC, MC, V. MTR: Yau Ma Tei. **Amenities:** Restaurant (Continental); lounge; tour desk; small business center; room service 7am–4pm; babysitting; same-day laundry service/dry cleaning; doctor on call. *In room:* A/C, satellite TV w/pay movies, minibar, coffeemaker, hair dryer.

Imperial Hotel   Location, location, location—that's the best thing this hotel has going for it. It's located right on Nathan Road between the Sheraton and Holiday Inn and near the MTR station. Otherwise, it doesn't offer much in terms of service, and its standard rooms are tiny and motel-like; some even have pink bathrooms. Its cheaper rooms face the back of Chungking Mansion, notorious for its cheap and often uninviting rooms, laundry strung everywhere, and garbage piled up below, apparently tossed unconcernedly from the windows above. You won't know this, however, as glazed windows now hide the formerly enlightening view. It's an improvement with a price: Rooms are now rather gloomy and claustrophobic and the cheapest are quite small. If you can, spring for a deluxe room that faces Nathan Road, although keep in mind that these rooms are subject to the noise of traffic; those on the top floors are high enough to offer glimpses of the harbor. Because of its cheap prices, this hotel attracts a mixed international clientele, many of whom look like they wish they were elsewhere. It is a rather grim place, but the location is ideal.

30–34 Nathan Rd., Tsim Sha Tsui, Kowloon, Hong Kong. © 800/44-UTELL in the U.S. and Canada, or 852/2366 2201. Fax 852/2311 2360. www.imperialhotel.com.hk. 225 units. HK$950–HK$1,700 (US$123–US$221/£68–£121) single; HK$1,100–HK$2,000 (US$143–US$260/£79–£143) double. 1 child under 12 can stay free in parent's room. AE, DC, MC, V. MTR: Tsim Sha Tsui. **Amenities:** Restaurant (Italian); Irish pub; tour desk; babysitting; same-day laundry service/dry cleaning. *In room:* A/C, cable TV w/pay movies on demand, wireless Internet access, minibar, coffeemaker (but no coffee), hair dryer.

Majestic Hotel 🍴
This brick hotel, located in the colorful Yau Ma Tei district, with its main entrance on Saigon Street, is just a few minutes' walk from the Jordan subway station and the Temple Street Night Market. Built in 1992, it rises above the Majestic Centre complex, which includes a shopping arcade and food court. The hotel offers good-size rooms, with a desk, sitting area, large windows (but unfortunately no exciting views), and tubs too small for a good soak. The cheapest rooms occupy the lower floors and face another building, while the most expensive rooms, on higher floors with city views, were recently spiffed up with a new color scheme of brown and beige and with sheeted duvets and bed runners replacing bedspreads.

348 Nathan Rd. (entrance on Saigon St.), Yau Ma Tei, Kowloon, Hong Kong. © 852/2781 1333. Fax 852/2781 1773. www.majestichotel.com.hk. 380 units. HK$950–HK$1,850 (US$123–US$240/£68–£132) single or double; from HK$3,000 (US$390/£214) suite. 1 child under 12 can stay free in parent's room. AE, DC, MC, V. MTR: Jordan. **Amenities:** Restaurant (international buffet); bar; small gym; tour desk; business center; shopping arcade; room service 6am–midnight; babysitting; same-day laundry service/dry cleaning; doctor on call. *In room:* A/C, satellite TV w/pay movies, wireless high-speed Internet access, minibar, coffeemaker, hair dryer, safe.

Nathan Hotel
Almost 40 years old, this hotel underwent such a massive recent overhaul, it's no longer the same place. Gone are the drab lobby, dark rooms, and featureless public spaces, replaced by contemporary furniture, artwork by a local artist, an inviting rooftop bar with outdoor seating, and a Starbucks. Remaining, luckily, is one of the property's best features—large rooms and bathrooms, dating from an era when land was less expensive. The hotel attracts business travelers mainly from mainland China and other Asian countries, though its location near the Temple Street Night Market and Jordan MTR station make it a good choice for leisure travelers as well. It's located north of Tsim Sha Tsui, about a 20-minute walk from the Star Ferry.

378 Nathan Rd. (main entrance on Pak Hoi St.) Yau Ma Tei, Kowloon, Hong Kong. © 852/2388 5141. Fax 852/2770 4262. www.nathanhotel.com. 191 units. HK$1,080–HK$1,480 (US$140–US$192/£77–£105) single/double. Children under 12 stay free in parent's room. AE, DC, MC, V. MTR: Jordan. **Amenities:** Restaurant (Cantonese); coffee shop; bar; exercise room; tour desk; limousine service; business center (open 24 hr.); room service 7:30am–10:30pm; babysitting; same-day laundry service/dry cleaning. *In room:* A/C, cable TV, high-speed dataport, minibar, coffeemaker, safe.

New Kings Hotel 🔸Value
This 30-year-old property could do with some updating. Still, its low rates (it usually offers discounts on its rack rates, so be sure to ask when making a reservation) and interesting location near the jade and night markets and a Tin Hau (Goddess of the Sea) temple make it recommendable. Otherwise, it doesn't have any facilities, its tiny rooms are rather plain and dark, and the tiled bathrooms lack counter space. There are only six rooms on each floor, a good thing since corridors are

barely wide enough for one person. Expect to wait for the hotel's one elevator. This is a good choice only for budget travelers on the go, since you probably wouldn't want to spend much time here anyway.

473 Nathan Rd. (entrance on Wing Sing Lane), Yau Ma Tei, Kowloon, Hong Kong. © **852/2780 1281.** Fax 852/2782 1833. kln@kingshotelhk.com. 72 units. HK$550–HK$600 (US$71–US$78/£39–£43) single; HK$650–HK$750 (US$85–US$98/£46–£54) twin. AE, MC, V. MTR: Yau Ma Tei. *In room:* A/C, TV, fridge, coffeemaker (but no coffee), safe.

The Salisbury YMCA ★★★ *Kids*

For decades, the overwhelming number-one choice among low-cost accommodations has been the YMCA on Salisbury Road, which has the good fortune of being right next to The Peninsula hotel near the waterfront, just a 2-minute walk from both the Star Ferry and Tsim Sha Tsui MTR subway station. Great for families are its inexpensive restaurants and sports facility boasting two indoor swimming pools (one a lap pool, the other a children's pool, both free for all hotel guests except those in dormitory) and a fitness gym, two squash courts, and indoor climbing wall (fees charged). A ground-floor bookstore has a children's corner, with games and books kids can try out free before buying. Although expensive for a YMCA, the location and facilities are worth the price (you can usually get rooms for less than the rates below); here you have Tsim Sha Tsui's cheapest rooms with harbor views, making it highly recommended.

There are 19 single rooms (none with harbor view) and more than 250 doubles and twins (the most expensive provide great harbor views), as well as suites with and without harbor views that are great for families. Although simple in decor, these carpeted rooms are on a par with those at more expensively priced hotels in terms of in-room amenities. For budget travelers, there are dormitory-style rooms, each with two bunk beds, individual reading lights, private bathroom, and lockers, available only to visitors who have been in Hong Kong fewer than 7 days. Needless to say, the Salisbury is so popular that you should make reservations in advance, especially in peak times.

Salisbury Rd., Tsim Sha Tsui, Kowloon, Hong Kong. © **800/537-8483** in the U.S. and Canada, or 852/2268 7000 (852/2268 7888 for reservations). Fax 852/2739 9315. www.ymcahk.org.hk. 368 units. HK$950 (US$123/£68) single; HK$1,050–HK$1,250 (US$136–US$162/£75–£89) double; from HK$1,600 (US$208/£114) suite. Dormitory bed HK$230 (US$30/£16). AE, DC, MC, V. MTR: Tsim Sha Tsui. **Amenities:** 2 restaurants (international buffet, international cafeteria); 2 indoor pools; exercise room; Jacuzzi; sauna; squash courts; badminton; climbing wall; tour desk; salon; room service 7am–10pm; babysitting; coin-op laundry; laundry service/dry cleaning; bookstore. *In room:* A/C, satellite/cable TV, wireless high-speed Internet access, minibar, coffeemaker, hair dryer, safe, complimentary fruit basket.

Shamrock Hotel

A pioneer member of HKHA and catering mainly to visitors from China, the Shamrock was built in the early 1950s and, despite lobby renovations that added marble floors and walls and artwork from Beijing, I don't think it's changed much since then. The most remarkable thing about this hotel is its lobby: Although tiny, the ceiling is covered with about a half-dozen small chandeliers. The guest rooms are unexciting, clean, simple, and small, though high ceilings (with small chandeliers) give the rooms something of a spacious feeling. Avoid the cheapest room without windows—Dracula might feel at home, but you might want to spring for some sunshine, though deluxe rooms facing Nathan Road are also noisier. It's about a 20-minute walk from the Star Ferry, just north of Kowloon Park and not far from the Temple Street Night Market.

223 Nathan Rd., Yau Ma Tei, Kowloon, Hong Kong. © **852/2735 2271.** Fax 852/2736 7354. www.shamrockhotel.com.hk. 158 units. HK$550–HK$1,250 (US$71–US$162/£39–£89) single; HK$750–HK$1,450 (US$97–US$188/£54–£104) double. AE, DC, MC, V. MTR: Jordan. **Amenities:** Restaurant (Western); limousine service; business center; babysitting; laundry service/dry cleaning. *In room:* A/C, satellite TV w/pay movies, high-speed dataport, minibar, coffeemaker (but no coffee), hair dryer, safe.

Stanford Hillview Hotel ⑯ *(Finds)*   This small, intimate hotel, built in 1991, is near the heart of Tsim Sha Tsui and yet it's a world away from it, located on top of a hill in the shade of some huge banyan trees, next to the Royal Observatory with its colonial building and greenery. Knutsford Terrace, an alley with trendy bars and restaurants, is just around the corner. Its lobby is quiet and subdued (quite a contrast to most Hong Kong hotels) and its staff is friendly and accommodating. Rooms are mostly twins, fairly basic and small. Best are deluxe accommodations on higher floors (ask for one that faces the Observatory), while the cheapest are very tiny economy rooms with a double bed (these are usually used by lone travelers but are available to two people if you insist). There's a kitchen for long-staying guests. All told, this is a very civilized place, but be prepared for the uphill hike to the hotel.

13–17 Observatory Rd., Tsim Sha Tsui, Kowloon, Hong Kong. ⓒ 852/2722 7822. Fax 852/2723 3718. www.stanford hillview.com. 163 units. HK$1,000–HK$1,680 (US$130–US$218/£71–£120) single or double. Long-term rates available. AE, DC, MC, V. MTR: Tsim Sha Tsui. **Amenities:** Restaurant (international buffet); lounge; outdoor golf-driving nets; small exercise room; business center; 24-hr. room service; babysitting; same-day laundry/dry cleaning. *In room:* A/C, cable TV w/pay movies, wireless Internet access, minibar, coffeemaker, hair dryer.

YMCA International House   Located just off Nathan Road, only a minute's walk from the Yau Ma Tei MTR station, this YMCA renovated its old building and added a 25-story tower a few years back, transforming itself into a smart-looking establishment that can rival many of the more expensively priced hotels in terms of facilities. However, located halfway up Kowloon Peninsula, far from the action of Tsim Sha Tsui, it plays second fiddle to The Salisbury YMCA in terms of convenience and views. The cheapest rooms occupy the older building, while the new tower rooms are similar in decor and comfort to modestly priced hotel rooms anywhere in the city and even boast wireless Internet access. Ask for a room on a top floor, where it's brighter and you can look out over the city. There are also dormitory rooms, for men only.

23 Waterloo Rd., Yau Ma Tei, Kowloon, Hong Kong. ⓒ 852/2771 9111. Fax 852/2388 5926; reservation fax 852/2771 5238. www.ymcaintlhousehk.org. 409 units. HK$880–HK$1,380 (US$114–US$179/£63–£99) single or twin; dormitory bed HK$300 (US$39/£21). Children under 12 stay free in parent's room. AE, DC, MC, V. MTR: Yau Ma Tei. **Amenities:** Restaurant (Western); lounge; indoor pool (free to Y guests); tennis and squash courts; fitness room (fee charged); sauna; tour desk; business center; babysitting; laundry service/dry cleaning. *In room:* A/C, cable TV, high-speed dataport, fridge, coffeemaker (but no coffee), hair dryer, safe.

CAUSEWAY BAY & WAN CHAI

Express by Holiday Inn ⑯ *(Value)*   Targeting business travelers in town for only a night or two, this is a bare-bones, do-it-yourself kind of place, with luggage carts instead of bellboys and even a designated ironing room. That said, it does offer a few perks, including free breakfast, free use of computers in its Internet Corner, free in-room Internet access, and free shuttle service to the convention center. It also houses a China Travel Service office, which can arrange visas, transportation, and package tours to China. Its rooms, all measuring 24 sq. m (258 sq. ft.) and priced the same (the range below reflects low to peak seasons), feature contemporary furnishings (including sofa beds), good reading lamps, showers instead of tubs, and bowl-shaped sinks. Since prices are the same, try to get one of the 15 rooms on the highest floors that have partial harbor views between buildings. It's located across from Times Square, but its entrance is not well marked. For travelers looking for convenience and affordability, this is a good choice.

33 Sharp St. East, Causeway Bay, Hong Kong. ⓒ 888/465-4329 in the U.S. and Canada, or 852/3558 6688. Fax 852/3558 6633. www.expressbyholidayinn.com.cn. 269 units. HK$650–HK$850 (US$84–US$110/£46–£61) single or

double. AE, DC, MC, V. MTR: Causeway Bay. **Amenities:** 5 restaurants (Shanghainese, Cantonese, steakhouse, pizzeria, coffee shop); business center; access to nearby fitness club (fee charged); laundry service/dry cleaning; free shuttle service to convention center. In room: A/C, satellite/cable TV w/pay movies on demand, free high-speed dataport, coffeemaker, safe, hair dryer.

Wesley   This simple business hotel opened in 1992 on the former site of the famous Soldiers' & Sailors' Home, a Hong Kong landmark for more than a century. Its small lobby is sparsely furnished, and facilities and services are limited—it reminds me of business hotels in Japan. All rooms are minuscule, with V-shaped bay windows and modern decor, including LCD TVs. Rates are based on bed configurations, floor level, and, to a small degree, room size: The cheaper rooms are on lower floors and are furnished with twin beds; the most expensive are slightly larger, with king-size beds, a small sitting area, and microwaves. Rooms facing the front of the hotel are noisier. The bathrooms are only large enough for one person, and the closets aren't tall enough to hang dresses. Even its "business center" is the size of a closet. Pluses: It's located on the tramline and is only a few minutes' walk from the Pacific Place shopping center.

22 Hennessy Rd., Wan Chai, Hong Kong. ⓒ 852/2866 6688. Fax 852/2866 6633. www.hanglung.com. 251 units. HK$800–HK$2,000 (US$104–US$260/£57–£143) single or double. Monthly rates available. AE, DC, MC, V. MTR: Admiralty or Wan Chai. **Amenities:** Restaurant (Cantonese); tour desk; limousine service; business center; babysitting; same-day laundry service/dry cleaning; doctor on call. In room: A/C, satellite TV, high-speed dataport, fridge, coffeemaker, hair dryer.

Wharney Guang Dong Hotel   Plagued by tour groups (mainly from mainland China), this China-owned business hotel underwent recent renovations that delivered a crisper, cleaner image and is now focusing on attracting a Western rather than Asian market. Conveniently located in the heart of Wan Chai, it offers small but adequate accommodations (none with views) divided into five categories of rooms, based on decor and floor level. Standard rooms are run-of-the-mill, while the best rooms are located on higher floors with an updated contemporary look, including beds with sheeted duvets and bed runners. Best of all are those on the executive floor, with wall-mounted LCD TVs, glass-walled bathrooms, and either Japanese- or Western-influenced decor.

57–73 Lockhart Rd., Wan Chai, Hong Kong. ⓒ 852/2861 1000. Fax 852/2529 5133. www.gdhhotels.com. 358 units. HK$1,000–HK$2,200 (US$130–US$286/£71–£157) single or double; HK$2,800 (US$363/£200) executive-floor room. 1 child under 12 can stay free in parent's room. AE, DC, MC, V. MTR: Wan Chai. **Amenities:** 2 restaurants (Japanese, Cantonese); bar; outdoor pool; exercise room; steam room; sauna; limousine service; business center; room service 6:30am–11pm; babysitting; same-day laundry service/dry cleaning; executive-level rooms. In room: A/C, cable TV w/pay movies, wireless Internet access, coffeemaker, hair dryer.

7 Rock-Bottom Accommodations (Guesthouses & Youth Hostels)

GUESTHOUSES

Hong Kong's cheapest accommodations aren't hotels and aren't recommended for visitors who expect cleanliness and comfort. Rather, these accommodations, usually called "guesthouses," attract a young backpacking crowd, many of whom are traveling through Asia and are interested only in a bed at the lowest price. They also attract laborers, mostly men from Asia, Africa, and the Middle East. At any rate, some guesthouses offer rooms with a private bathroom; others are nothing more than rooms filled with bunk beds. Of Hong Kong's rock-bottom establishments, none is more notorious than **Chungking Mansion,** an inspiration for the Wong Kar-Wai film *Chungking Express.* Although it occupies a prime spot at 40 Nathan Road, between the

Holiday Inn Golden Mile and the Sheraton in Tsim Sha Tsui, Chungking Mansion is easy to overlook; there's no big sign heralding its existence. In fact, its ground floor is one huge maze of inexpensive shops. But above all those shops are five towering concrete blocks, each served by its own tiny elevator and known collectively as Chungking Mansion. Inside are hundreds of little businesses, apartments, guesthouses, eateries, and sweatshops. Some of the guesthouses are passable; many are not.

I stayed at Chungking Mansion on my first trip to Hong Kong in 1983, living in a neon-colored cell furnished with two sagging beds, a night table, and closet. In the shared bathroom down the hall lived the biggest spider I have ever seen, a hairy thing that nevertheless behaved itself whenever I was there—it never moved an inch the whole time I took a shower, and when I returned each evening, it was always motionless in another part of the room. I figured that it survived only by being unobtrusive, and I wouldn't be surprised if its progeny is still there. I shared my room with another woman and we paid US$5 each.

Chungking Mansion has changed a lot since then. Whereas most guesthouses were once borderline squalor, today many have cleaned up their act in a bid for the tourists' dollars. Still, Chungking is not the kind of place you'd want to recommend to anyone uninitiated in the seamier side of travel. The views from many room windows are more insightful than some guests might like—the backside of the building and mountains of trash down below. Even worse are the ancient-looking elevators filled to capacity with human cargo; you might want to stick to the stairs. In any case, sometimes the elevators don't work at all, making it a long hike up the dozen flights of stairs to the top floors. But the most compelling argument for avoiding Chungking Mansion is one of safety: It could be a towering inferno waiting to happen. However, for some budget travelers, it's a viable alternative to Hong Kong's high-priced hotels. And you certainly can't beat it for location.

If you insist on staying here, see my review below. Chungking Mansion contains approximately 100 guesthouses, divided into five separate tower blocks, from A Block to E Block. For the less daring, A Block is the best, since its elevator is closest to the front entrance of the building. The other elevators are farther back in the shopping arcade, which can be a little disconcerting at night when the shops are all closed and the corridors are deserted. I recommend that you begin your search in Block A. I also recommend that you stay on lower floors. But no matter what the block, never leave any valuables in your room.

CHUNGKING MANSION
Chungking House   This is the best-known guesthouse in Chungking Mansion, due primarily to its location in A Block, with front desks and lobbies on both the fourth and fifth floors. Rooms are dreary, dark, and depressing, with wood paneling, worn carpets, and ancient tiled bathrooms (ask for a "deluxe" room facing Nathan Road; though noisier, they are brighter and thus a tad more cheerful). The staff tends to be unconcerned and gruff. Still, you might want to try this place first before tackling the elevator or stairs to check out the guesthouses on the upper floors.

A Block, 4th and 5th floors, Chungking Mansion, 40 Nathan Rd., Tsim Sha Tsui, Kowloon, Hong Kong. ℂ 852/2366 5362. Fax 852/2721 3570. chungkinghouse@yahoo.com.hk. 75 units. HK$150–HK$250 (US$19–US$32/£11–£18) single; HK$250–HK$350 (US$32–US$45/£18–£25) double/twin. No credit cards. MTR: Tsim Sha Tsui. *In room:* A/C, TV.

NON-CHUNGKING MANSION GUESTHOUSE
Alisan Guest House   If Chungking Mansion is your idea of a horror house, this guesthouse, on the other side of the harbor, just around the corner from The Excelsior

hotel (p. 89) and World Trade Centre, is a good alternative and has been in business since 1987. Located in a typical residential building, it's owned by English-speaking Tommy Hou, who spends about 15 minutes with each of his mostly Western guests to give advice on sightseeing in Hong Kong. Rooms, scattered on several floors, are small but clean. The best rooms are the triples located on the third floor. However, though these rooms face the harbor, they also look out onto a busy highway, making them slightly noisy due to traffic. Mr. Hou offers free tea, a communal microwave and fridge, and use of his office computer for those who wish to check their e-mail.

Flat A, 5th floor, Hoi To Court, 275 Gloucester Rd. (entrance on Cannon St.), Causeway, Hong Kong. (C) 852/2838 0762 or 852/2574 8066. Fax 852/2838 4351. http://home.hkstar.com/~alisangh. 21 units. HK$280–HK$350 (US$36–US$45/£20–£25) single; HK$320–HK$380 (US$42–US$49/£22–£27) double/twin; HK$400–HK$480 (US$52–US$62/£28–£34) triple. Rates 20% higher in peak season. No credit cards. MTR: Causeway Bay. *In room:* A/C, TV.

YOUTH HOSTELS AND DORMITORY BEDS

If you don't mind giving up your privacy, the best rock-bottom accommodations in town are the dormitory beds available at The Salisbury YMCA (p. 101) for HK$230 (US$30/£16), followed by those in the YMCA International House for HK$300 (US$39/£21). Otherwise, Hong Kong's cheapest accommodations are at hostels. There are seven youth hostels in Hong Kong, including its islands and territories, and they offer the cheapest rates around. However, most are not conveniently located— indeed, some require a ferry ride and/or a 45-minute hike from the nearest bus stop, as they are located in country parks.

If you don't have a youth hostel card, you can still stay at a youth hostel by paying an extra HK$30 (US$3.90/£2.10) per night. After 6 nights, nonmembers are eligible for member status and subsequently pay overnight charges at members' rates. It's cheaper for the long haul, however, to purchase YHA membership for HK$110 (US$14/£7.70), available at any youth hostel. Note that children under 5 are not allowed at Hong Kong's youth hostels. For more information, contact the **Hong Kong Youth Hostels Association** (© 852/2788 1638; www.yha.org.hk). Bookings can be made through the Internet, and credit cards are accepted.

The most conveniently located youth hostel is the 169-bed **Jockey Club Mt. Davis Youth Hostel,** on top of Mount Davis on Hong Kong Island (© 852/2817 5715), with great panoramic views. It charges HK$80 (US$10/£5.60) per night for a dormitory bed for those aged 18 and over. There are also a few private rooms, with a double costing HK$260 (US$34/£18). Facilities include a communal kitchen and coin-op laundry room. To reach it, take the Ma Mui Hall Shuttle Bus, which departs from the Macau Ferry Terminal (MTR: Sheung Wan) daily at 9:30am and 4:30, 7, 9, and 10:30pm. A taxi from Central costs approximately HK$60 to HK$70 (US$7.80–US$9.10/£4.20–£4.90). The hostel itself is open daily from 7am to 11pm.

There are six other youth hostels on some of the outlying islands and in the New Territories; most charge HK$50 (US$6.50/£3.50) for dormitory beds for those 18 and older. Check-in is from 4pm. There are kitchens and washing facilities, as well as campsites. Since these hostels are not easily accessible, they are recommended only for the adventurous traveler. Of these, the **Hong Kong Bank Foundation S.G. Davis Hostel,** on Lantau island about a 10-minute walk from the Po Lin Monastery with its giant Buddha (© 852/2985 5610), is the easiest to reach from the airport.

6

Where to Dine

Dining is one of *the* things to do in Hong Kong. Half the population dines in the city's 11,000 eateries every day. Not only is the food excellent, but the range of culinary possibilities is nothing short of staggering. Hong Kong also has what may well be the greatest concentration of Chinese restaurants in the world. In a few short days, you can take a culinary tour of virtually every major region of China, dining on Cantonese, Sichuan, Shanghainese, Pekingese, Chiu Chow, and other Chinese specialties. Some restaurants are huge, bustling, family affairs, countless others are mere holes in the wall, and a few of the trendiest are Shanghai chic, remakes of 1930s salons and opium dens or strikingly modern affairs with sweeping views of the city.

But dining in the SAR is by no means limited to Chinese restaurants. Although various national cuisines have long been popular, particularly French, Italian, Thai, and Indian, ethnic restaurants have literally exploded onto the culinary scene in the past couple decades, offering even greater diversity from tapas and tacos to sushi. Japanese food is especially popular among locals, and you'll find Japanese offerings on virtually every international buffet spread in Hong Kong, along with sushi delivered via conveyor belts in an ever-growing number of sushi bars.

I'm convinced that you can eat as well in Hong Kong as in any other city in the world. And no matter where you eat or how much you spend, it's sure to be an adventure of the senses. Little wonder, then, that a common greeting among Chinese in Hong Kong translates literally as "Have you eaten?" In Hong Kong, eating is the most important order of the day.

By far, Hong Kong's most well known, exclusive restaurants, both Chinese and Western, have long been located in the hotels. That's not surprising when you realize that first-class hotels are accustomed to catering to well-traveled visitors who demand high quality in service, cuisine, and decor.

In a welcome trend, however, enterprising, ambitious, and talented chefs have been opening establishments in ever-greater numbers, often in modest but imaginative surroundings or in swanky digs on top floors of high-rises. These include ethnic restaurants as well as eateries offering innovative dishes, with limited but intriguing menus. A cluster of these restaurants has even created a whole new dining enclave, located on the steep hill alongside the Central–Mid-Levels Escalator that connects Central with the Mid-Levels. Dubbed "SoHo" for the region "south of Hollywood Road," it has blossomed into an ever-growing dining and nightlife district, making it Hong Kong's most exciting addition to the culinary scene.

Other welcome trends are the inclusion of vegetarian and healthy foods on many menus, and the growing popularity of crossover, East-meets-West fusion cuisine, which capitalizes on ingredients and flavors from both sides of the Pacific Rim in the creation of innovative dishes.

The restaurants listed below are grouped first according to location (the

Where to Dine in Kowloon

Tips   Ways to Save on Your Hong Kong Meals

Wherever you decide to eat, remember that a 10% service charge will be added to your food-and-beverage bill (see "Fast Facts: Hong Kong" on p. 62 for more information on tipping in Hong Kong). There is no tax, however. You can save a few Hong Kong dollars when eating out by keeping the following tips in mind:

- **Eat your big meal at lunch.** Most Asian (excluding Chinese) and Western restaurants offer special fixed-price lunches that are much cheaper than evening meals; their menus often include an appetizer, main course, and side dishes. Don't neglect expensive restaurants just because you assume they're out of your price range. If you feel like splurging, lunch is the way to go. For example, you can eat lunch at Gaddi's (one of Hong Kong's most famous restaurants) for HK$388 (US$50/£28) per person, including a glass of wine (dinner would be at least double that).

- **Jump on the buffet bandwagon.** Buffet spreads are another great Hong Kong tradition. Almost all hotels offer buffets, often for breakfast, lunch, and dinner; independent restaurants are more likely to feature buffets at lunch. Some include a variety of both Asian and Continental dishes, a real bonus for lone diners who want to sample a variety of cuisines at a reasonable cost. If you have a hearty appetite, buffets are one of the best bargains in town.

- **Eat an early or late dinner to take advantage of special fixed-price meals.** A few restaurants offer early-bird or late-night specials. If you dine before 7pm at trendy Felix, for example, a three-course meal costs only HK$388 (US$50/£28) as opposed to the HK$800 (US$104/£57) usually spent for dinner a la carte.

- **If you want to imbibe, stick with beer.** Wine is especially expensive in Hong Kong. The estimated meal prices for the restaurants presented in this chapter do not include wine, since you could easily spend a fortune on drinks alone. To keep costs down, try the two most popular brands of beer: **San Miguel** (Filipino) and **Tsingtao** (Chinese). And speaking of beer, many bars and pubs mentioned in chapter 10, "Hong Kong After Dark," also serve food.

- **Go the dim sum route.** Dim sum, served mainly in Cantonese restaurants, is another way to economize on breakfast or lunch. Dim sum are usually served four to a basket or plate; three baskets are usually filling enough for me, which means I can have breakfast or lunch for less than HK$100 (US$13/£7).

most popular areas are Kowloon, the Central District, and Causeway Bay/Wan Chai) and then according to price. Those in the **Very Expensive** category ($$$$) will cost more than HK$700 (US$91/£50) for dinner without drinks (some restaurants average HK$1,000/US$130/£71 or more per person). In the **Expensive**

Where to Dine in the Central District

Tramway
Post Office

Victoria Harbour

to Kowloon

Area of map below

CENTRAL DISTRICT

Pacific Place

Star Ferry

IFC Mall

Four Seasons

Central

Harcourt Rd.

Admiralty

Tamar St.

Queensway

Island Shangri-La Hotel

Pacific Place

HONG KONG PARK

Cotton Tree Drive

Lambeth Walk

Murray Rd.

ADMIRALTY

Queen's Pier

City Hall

Club St.

CHATER GARDEN

Edinburgh Place

Jackson Rd.

Connaught Rd. Central

STATUE SQUARE

Chater Rd.

STATUE SQUARE

Des Voeux Rd. Central

Bank St.

Exchange Square

General Post Office

Hong Kong

CENTRAL DISTRICT

Ice House St.

Pedder St.

Queen's Rd. Central

Queen's Rd. Central

Central

Connaught Rd. Central

Douglas Lane

Duddell St.

Man Yee Lane

Pottinger St.

Li Yuen St.

Wyndham St.

Jade Garden Restaurant 18

Stanley St.

Wellington St.

Wo On Lane

D'Aguilar St.

Queen Victoria St.

Jubilee St.

Graham St.

Cochrane St.

Lyndhurst Terrace

Wyndham St.

1/10 mile

100 meters

0

0

Avenue Restaurant & Bar 22
BB's Bistro 3
California Pizza Kitchen 9
City Chiuchow 31
Dan Ryan's Chicago Grill 9
El Cid Spanish Restaurant 4, 9
Fat Angelo's 21
Felix 26
Fook Lam Moon 7
Gaddi's 26
Gaylord 16
Genki Sushi 2, 31

Golden Island Bird's Nest Chiu Chau Restaurant 18
The Greenery 32
Happy Garden Noodles & Congee Kitchen 10
Harbour Side 29
Hutong 12
Jade Garden Restaurant 18
Jimmy's Kitchen 15
Koh-I-Noor 20
Main Street Deli 11
Nomads 6

Peking Garden 18
The Pizzeria 25
PizzaExpress 13
Ruth's Chris Steak House 33
Sabatini 32
The Salisbury 17
Shang Palace 35
Sorabol 5
Spaghetti House 1, 14, 24, 27
The Spice Market 8
SPOON by Alain Ducasse 29
Spring Deer Restaurant 30

STEAK HOUSE winebar + grill 29
Super Star Seafood Restaurant 19
T'ang Court 11
Tsui Hang Village Restaurant 5
Tutto Bene 3
Unkai 28
Woodlands 34
Wu Kong 23
Yan Toh Heen 29

109

category ($$$), dinners average HK$450 to HK$700 (US$58–US$91/£32–£50). **Moderate** restaurants ($$) serve dinners ranging from HK$200 to HK$450 (US$26–US$58/£14–£32), while **Inexpensive** restaurants ($) offer meals for less than HK$200 (US$26/£14). Keep in mind, however, that these guidelines are approximations only.

I should add that Chinese restaurants often have very long menus, sometimes listing more than 100 dishes. The most expensive dishes will invariably be such delicacies as bird's nest (bird's nest is a real nest, created by glutinous secretions of small swifts or swallows to build their nests), shark's fin, or abalone, for which the sky's the limit. In specifying price ranges for "main courses" under each Chinese establishment below, therefore, I excluded these delicacies as well as inexpensive rice and noodle dishes. In most cases, "main courses" refers to meat and vegetable combinations. Remember, since the price range is large, you can eat cheaply even at moderately priced restaurants by choosing wisely. Remember, too, that in Chinese restaurants it's customary to order one main dish for each diner, plus one extra to share.

The usual lunch hour in the SAR is from 1 to 2pm, when thousands of office workers pour into the city's more popular restaurants. Try to eat before or after the lunch rush hour, especially in Central, unless you plan on an expensive restaurant and have a reservation.

Unless stated otherwise, the open hours given below are exactly that—the hours a restaurant remains physically open but not necessarily the hours it serves food. The last orders are almost always taken at least a half-hour before closing. Restaurants that are open for lunch from noon to 3pm, for example, will probably stop taking orders at 2:30pm. To avoid disappointment, call beforehand to make a reservation or arrive well ahead of closing time.

As for dress codes, unless otherwise stated, many upper-end restaurants have done away with the jacket-and-tie requirement. Rather, "smart casual" or business casual is nowadays appropriate for most of the fancier places, meaning that men should wear long-sleeved shirts and that jeans, sport shoes, and flip-flops are inappropriate.

Finally, in addition to the restaurant recommendations below, there's HKTB's *A Guide to Quality Restaurants,* a hefty booklet listing restaurants that adhere to stringent guidelines designed to help visitors find restaurants they can trust.

1 Best Dining Bets

I'm convinced Hong Kong has some of the best restaurants in the world—which makes it extremely difficult to choose the best of the best. Nevertheless, the following are my personal favorites.

- **Best Spot for a Romantic Dinner:** With views of Hong Kong's fabled harbor, live piano music, French cuisine, and one of Hong Kong's best wine lists, **Petrus,** Island Shangri-La Hotel, Supreme Court Road, Central (© **852/2820 8590**), sets the mood for a special evening à deux. You'll want to linger for some time here, savoring the Mediterranean-influenced food, the castle-like ambience, the view, and each other. See p. 136.
- **Best Spot for a Business Lunch: Nicholini's,** in the Conrad Hotel, Pacific Place, Central (© **852/2521 3838,** ext. 8210), serves what some claim is the best Italian food in town, including weekday fixed-price lunches that are dependably good yet won't blow your expense account. Its atmosphere is both highbrow and relaxed, giving it a winning combination for clinching those business deals. See p. 136.

Where to Dine in Causeway Bay & Wan Chai

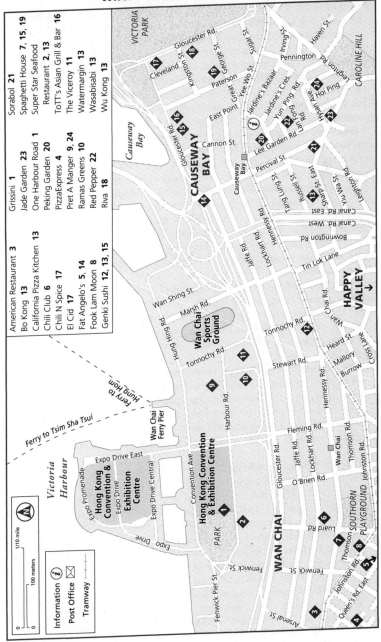

American Restaurant **3**
Bo Kong **13**
California Pizza Kitchen **13**
Chili Club **6**
Chili N Spice **17**
El Cid **17**
Fat Angelo's **5, 14**
Fook Lam Moon **8**
Genki Sushi **12, 13, 15**

Grissini **1**
Jade Garden **23**
One Harbour Road **1**
Peking Garden **20**
PizzaExpress **4**
Pret A Manger **9, 24**
Ramas Greens **10**
Red Pepper **22**
Riva **18**

Sorabol **21**
Spaghetti House **7, 15, 19**
Super Star Seafood
Restaurant **2, 13**
ToTT's Asian Grill & Bar **16**
The Viceroy **11**
Watermargin **13**
Wasabisabi **13**
Wu Kong **13**

- **Best Spot for a Celebration:** An elegant, colonial-age setting, attentive service, dependably good French haute cuisine, an extensive wine list, and a long history make **Gaddi's** at The Peninsula hotel, Salisbury Road, Tsim Sha Tsui (℗ **852/2315 3171**), a natural for a splurge or special celebration. See p. 121.
- **Best Decor:** The avant-garde **Felix,** in The Peninsula hotel, Salisbury Road, Tsim Sha Tsui (℗ **852/2315 3188**), was designed by Philippe Starck. In addition to providing Hong Kong's most unusual, innovative setting, the restaurant offers stunning views, one of the world's smallest discos, and slightly exhibitionist bathrooms. Wear your trendiest duds—you, too, will be part of the display. See p. 123.
- **Best View:** In a town famous for its views, you might as well go to the very top, where the curved facade of **Cafe Deco,** Peak Galleria, Victoria Peak (℗ **852/2849 5111**), offers Hong Kong's best panorama, along with live jazz in the evening and moderately priced—though occasionally mediocre—international cuisine. Reserve a harbor-view window seat a couple of weeks in advance; what you're really paying for here is the unparalleled view. See p. 152.
- **Best Wine List:** Not only does **SPOON by Alain Ducasse,** Hotel InterContinental Hong Kong, Salisbury Road, Tsim Sha Tsui (℗ **852/2721 1211**), offer great harbor views, excellent contemporary French cuisine, and impeccable service, but it also boasts a selection of 3,000 bottles of wine, on display at the restaurant's entrance. See p. 121.
- **Best Newcomer:** Everyone is talking about **Caprice,** ensconced in the sleek Four Seasons Hotel Hong Kong, 8 Finance St., Central (℗ **852/3196 8888**), but only those lucky enough to snag a reservation get to enjoy the innovative French cuisine by master chef Vincent Thiery, the restaurant's elegant mix of contemporary and Art Nouveau decor, and its harbor views. Take your cue, and book early. See p. 135.
- **Best Chinese Hot Spot:** Make reservations early for **Hutong,** on the 28th floor of an office building at 1 Peking Road, Tsim Sha Tsui (℗ **852/3428 8342**). This place is as hip as a Chinese restaurant can be, with fantastic views over Hong Kong, a darkened interior with splashes of red lighting, and innovative northern Chinese cuisine. Dining here will want to make you live forever, if only to see what can possibly top this; this being Hong Kong, something eventually will. See p. 156.
- **Best Dim Sum Experience:** The quaint ceiling fans, spittoons, and wooden booths evoke a 1930s ambience at **Luk Yu Tea House,** 24–26 Stanley St., Central (℗ **852/2523 5464**). First opened in 1933, it's one of Hong Kong's oldest restaurants, famous for its dim sum and filled daily with regular customers. It's hard to find an empty seat here but worth the effort. See p. 158.
- **Best Vegetarian:** With its informal atmosphere, wood furnishings, and healthfoods store, **Life,** 10 Shelley St. in SoHo (℗ **852/2810 9777**), is a lifesaver for those in search of organic, vegetarian fare, including salads, quiche, noodle and pasta dishes, daily specials, and power drinks. See p. 145.
- **Best Buffet Spread:** Lots of hotels offer buffets, but none can match the sheer extravagance and chic atmosphere of **café TOO,** Island Shangri-La Hotel, Supreme Court Road, Central (℗ **852/2820 8571**). Overlooking the greenery of Hong Kong Park and sporting a hip, contemporary look, it features open kitchens and seven "stations" of food presentations spread throughout the restaurant, eliminating the assembly-line atmosphere inherent in most buffet restaurants. The danger? The temptation to try every delectable dish on display. See p. 139.

- **Best Outdoor Dining:** Atop Victoria Peak, away from the constant drone of Hong Kong's traffic, is the delightful **Peak Lookout,** 121 Peak Rd., Victoria Peak (*© 852/2849 1000*), which serves international cuisine. From an outdoor terrace surrounded by lush foliage, you can actually hear the birds sing. Some tables provide views of Hong Kong Island's southern coast. Musicians entertain nightly with oldies but goldies. See p. 152.

- **Best Place to Chill Out:** If the stress of travel and the noise and crowds of Hong Kong have pushed you to the breaking point, take the free shuttle boat to Aberdeen's Jumbo Kingdom floating restaurant, where **Top Deck, at the Jumbo** (*© 852/2553 3331*) offers great seafood, live jazz Wednesday evenings, and alfresco dining with views of surrounding Aberdeen. See p. 154.

- **Best Afternoon Tea:** For that most British institution, no place is more famous than the golden-age and unparalleled **Peninsula Hotel Lobby,** Salisbury Road, Tsim Sha Tsui (*© 852/2920 2888*), where you can nibble on delicate finger sandwiches and scones, watch the parade of people, and listen to live classical music being played from an upstairs balcony. See p. 159.

- **Best Sunday Brunch:** You'll be spoiled forever—or at least for the rest of the day—if you begin Sunday morning at **The Verandah,** 109 Repulse Bay Rd., Repulse Bay (*© 852/2812 2722*), complete with a three-piece band. Wonderfully reminiscent of the colonial era, it features Hong Kong's most famous Sunday spread, with main courses like eggs Benedict from a menu, a carving of the day, pasta cooked to order, sushi, dim sum, and more. If ever there were a place that inspired champagne for breakfast, this is it. See p. 152.

2 A Taste of Hong Kong

MEALS & DINING CUSTOMS

Traditionally speaking, Chinese restaurants tend to be noisy and crowded affairs, the patrons much more interested in food than in decor. They range from simple diners where the only adornment is likely to be Formica-topped tables, to very elaborate affairs with Chinese lanterns, splashes of red and gold, and painted screens. In the 1980s, a new kind of Chinese restaurant exploded onto the scene: trendy, chic, and minimalist, many in Art Deco style, and catering to Hong Kong's young and upwardly mobile.

In any case, Chinese restaurants are places for social gatherings; since Hong Kong apartments are usually too small to entertain friends and family, the whole gang simply heads for their favorite restaurant.

The Chinese usually dine in large groups; the more, the merrier. The basic rule is to order one dish per person, plus one extra dish or a soup, with all dishes placed in the center of the table and shared by everyone. The more people in your party, therefore, the more dishes are ordered and the more fun you'll have. Dishes usually come in two or three different sizes, so ask your waiter which size is sufficient for your group.

You shouldn't have any problem ordering, since many Chinese restaurants have English menus. If you want to be correct about it, though, a well-balanced meal should contain the five basic tastes of Chinese cuisine—acid, hot, bitter, sweet, and salty. The texture should vary as well, ranging from crisp and tender to dry and saucy. The proper order is to begin with a cold dish, followed by dishes of fish or seafood, meat (pork, beef, or poultry), vegetables, soup, and noodles or rice. Some dishes are steamed, while others may be fried, boiled, or roasted. Many of the dishes are accompanied by sauces, the most common being soy sauce, chile sauce, and hot mustard.

Because most Chinese restaurants cater to groups and Chinese food is best enjoyed if there are a variety of dishes, lone diners are at a distinct disadvantage when it comes to Chinese cuisine. A few restaurants make life easier by offering fixed-price meals, but they're usually for parties of two people or more. An alternative is to dine at hotel buffets that offer Chinese and international dishes.

At any rate, at a Chinese restaurant, the beginning of your meal is heralded by a round of hot towels, a wonderful custom you'll soon grow addicted to and wish would be adopted by restaurants in your home country. Your eating utensils, of course, will be chopsticks, which have been around for 3,000 years and are perfect for picking up bite-size morsels. If you're eating rice, pick up the bowl and scoop the rice directly into your mouth with your chopsticks.

Keep in mind, however, that there are several superstitions associated with chopsticks. If, for example, you find an uneven pair at your table setting, it means you are going to miss a boat, plane, or train. Dropping chopsticks means you will have bad luck; laying them across each other is also considered a bad omen, except in dim sum restaurants where your waiter may cross them to show that your bill has been settled. You can do the same to signal the waiter that you've finished your meal and wish to pay the bill. When dining in a group, avoid ordering seven dishes, since seven dishes are considered food for ghosts, not humans.

As for dining etiquette, it's considered perfectly acceptable to slurp soup, since this indicates an appreciation of the food and also helps cool the soup so it doesn't burn the tongue. Toothpicks are also acceptable for use at the table during and after meals; they can even be used to spear foods too slippery or elusive for chopsticks, such as button mushrooms and jellyfish slices. As in most Asian countries, good manners call for covering your mouth with one hand while you dislodge food particles from your teeth.

A final custom you may see in Chinese restaurants is that of finger tapping: Customers often tap three fingers on the table as a sign of thanks to the person pouring the tea.

THE CUISINE

Chinese cooking has evolved over the course of several thousand years, dictated often by a population too numerous to feed. The prospect of famine meant that nothing should be wasted, and the scarcity of fuel meant that food should be cooked as economically as possible; thus, it was chopped into small pieces and quickly stir-fried. Food needed to be as fresh as possible to avoid spoiling. Among the many regional Chinese cuisines, the most common ones found in Hong Kong are from Canton, Beijing (or Peking), Shanghai, Sichuan, and Chiu Chow (Swatow).

Of course, there are many other dishes and styles of cuisine besides those outlined below. It's said that the Chinese will eat anything that swims, flies, or crawls; although that may not be entirely true, if you're adventurous enough, you may want to try such delicacies as snake soup, pig's brain, bird's-nest soup (derived from the saliva of swallows), Shanghai freshwater hairy crabs (available only in autumn), tiny rice birds that are roasted and eaten whole, or eel heads simmered with Chinese herbs. One of the more common—albeit strange—items found on most Chinese menus is *bèche-de-mer*, which translates as sea cucumber but which is actually nothing more than a sea slug.

Words of warning: According to government authorities, you're safe eating anywhere in the SAR, except when it comes to hawkers (food carts), as many of these are unlicensed. In addition, don't eat local oysters—there have been too many instances of oyster poisoning. Eat oysters only if they're imported from, say, Australia. The good restaurants will clearly stipulate on the menu that their oysters are imported. Some expats, warning of cholera, also steer clear of local shellfish and fish caught from local waters. Nowadays, restaurants catering largely to tourists offer fresh seafood caught outside Hong Kong's waters.

Hong Kong was also ravaged by several outbreaks of avian flu beginning in 1997 (6 out of 18 people infected in 1997 died), resulting in mass poultry cullings. Vigilance by local authorities has prevented any recent outbreaks in the SAR, and importation from mainland China ceases during outbreaks there. I still eat chicken in Hong Kong, but whether you choose to is up to you.

Watch your reaction to monosodium glutamate (MSG), which is used to enhance the flavor in Chinese cooking. Some people react strongly to this salt, reporting bouts of nausea, headaches, and a bloated feeling. Fortunately, an awareness of the detrimental side effects of MSG has long prompted most Chinese upper- and medium-range restaurants, especially those in hotels, to stop using it altogether. However, fast Chinese food is likely to be full of MSG, as are dishes prepared using products imported from China, where MSG is used as a matter of course.

CANTONESE FOOD

The majority of Chinese restaurants in Hong Kong are Cantonese; this is not surprising since most Hong Kong Chinese are originally from Canton Province (now called Guangdong). It's also the most common style of Chinese cooking around the world and probably the one with which you're most familiar. Among Chinese, Cantonese cuisine is considered the finest, and many Chinese emperors employed Cantonese chefs in their kitchens.

Cantonese food, which is noted for fast cooking at high temperatures (usually either steamed or stir-fried), is known for its fresh, delicate flavors. Little oil and few spices are used so that the natural flavors of the various ingredients prevail, and the Cantonese are sticklers for freshness (traditionalists may shop twice a day at the market). If you're concerned about cholesterol, Cantonese food is preferable. On the other hand, those with active taste buds may find it rather bland.

Since the Cantonese eat so much seafood, your best choice in a Cantonese restaurant is fish. I love steamed whole fish prepared with fresh ginger and spring onions, but equally good are slices of garoupa (a local fish), pomfret, red mullet, sole, and bream. It's considered bad luck to turn a fish over on your plate (it represents a boat capsizing), so the proper thing to do is to eat the top part of the fish, lift the bone in the air and then extract the bottom layer of meat with your chopsticks. Other popular seafood choices include shrimp and prawns, abalone, squid, scallops, crab, and sea cucumber. Shark's-fin soup is an expensive delicacy.

Other Cantonese specialties include roast goose, duck, and pigeon; pan-fried lemon chicken; stir-fried minced quail and bamboo shoots rolled in lettuce and eaten with the fingers; *congee* (thick rice porridge); crabmeat; sweet corn soup; and sweet-and-sour pork.

Another popular Cantonese dish is *dim sum*, which means "light snack" but whose Chinese characters literally translate as "to touch the heart." Dating back to the 10th century, dim sum is eaten for breakfast and lunch and with afternoon tea; in Hong Kong it is especially popular for Sunday family outings. It consists primarily of finely chopped meat, seafood, and vegetables wrapped in thin dough and then either steamed, fried, boiled, or braised. Dim sum can range from steamed dumplings to meatballs, fried spring rolls, and spareribs.

Many Cantonese restaurants offer dim sum from about 7:30am until 4pm, traditionally served from trolleys wheeled between the tables but nowadays more likely to be offered from a written menu. There are nearly 100 different kinds of dim sum, but some of my favorites are *shiu mai* (steamed minced pork dumplings), *har gau* (steamed shrimp dumplings), *cha siu bau* (barbecued pork buns), *au yuk* (steamed minced beef balls), *fun gwor* (steamed rice-flour dumplings filled with pork, shrimp, and bamboo shoots), and *tsuen guen* (deep-fried spring rolls filled with shredded pork, chicken, mushrooms, bamboo shoots, and bean sprouts). A serving of dim sum usually consists of two to four pieces on a plate and averages about HK$20 to HK$30 (US$2.60–US$3.90/£1.40–£2.15) per plate. Your bill is calculated at the end of the meal by the number of plates on your table or by a card stamped each time you order a dish.

Since I can usually manage only three dishes, dim sum is one of the cheapest meals I eat in Hong Kong and is also the best when I'm dining alone. I often have it for breakfast with lots of tea (the actual term is *yum cha,* traditionally meant as an early breakfast of dim sum and Chinese tea). But it's more than just the price that draws me to traditional dim sum restaurants—they are noisy, chaotic, and the perfect place to read a newspaper or gossip. No one should go to Hong Kong without visiting a dim sum restaurant at least once.

For a light snack or late-night meal, try *congee,* which is a rice porridge popular for breakfast and usually topped with a meat, fish, or vegetable. Many of Hong Kong's countless, cheapest restaurants specialize in *congee,* as well as noodles in soup, the most famous of which is probably *wun tun meen,* noodle soup with shrimp dumplings.

PEKINGESE FOOD

Many Pekingese dishes originated in the imperial courts of the emperors and empresses and were served at elaborate banquets. This theatrical flamboyance is still evident today in the making of Pekingese noodles and the smashing of the clay around "beggar's chicken." Because of its northern source, the food of Peking (or Beijing) tends to be rather substantial (to keep the body warm), and it is richer than Cantonese food. Liberal amounts of peppers, garlic, ginger, leeks, and coriander are used. Noodles and dumplings are more common than rice, and roasting is the preferred method of cooking.

Most famous among Peking-style dishes is Peking duck (or Beijing duck), but unfortunately, a minimum of six persons is usually required for this elaborate dish. The most prized part is the crisp skin, which comes from air-drying the bird and then coating it with a mixture of syrup and soy sauce before roasting. It's served by wrapping the crisp skin and meat in thin pancakes together with spring onion, radish, and sweet plum sauce.

Another popular dish prepared with fanfare is beggar's chicken: A whole chicken is stuffed with mushrooms, pickled Chinese cabbage, herbs, and onions, wrapped in lotus leaves, sealed in clay, and then baked all day. The guest of honor usually breaks open the hard clay with a mallet, revealing a tender feast more fit for a king than a beggar.

For do-it-yourself dining, try the Mongolian hot pot, where diners gather around a common pot in a scene reminiscent of campfires on the Mongolian steppes. One version calls for wafer-thin slices of meat, usually mutton, to be dipped in a clear stock and then eaten with a spicy sauce. Another variety calls for a sizzling griddle, over which thin-sliced meat, cabbage, bean sprouts, onions, and other vegetables are barbecued in a matter of seconds.

SHANGHAINESE FOOD

A big, bustling city, Shanghai incorporates the food of several surrounding regions and cities, making it the most diverse cuisine in China. Because of the cold winters in Shanghai, its food is heavier, richer, sweeter, and oilier than Cantonese or Pekingese food, seasoned with sugar, soy sauce, and Shaoxing wine. In addition, because of hot summers, which can spoil food quickly, specialties include pickled or preserved vegetables, fish, shrimp, and mushrooms. Some dishes are rather heavy on the garlic, and portions tend to be enormous. The dishes are often stewed, braised, or fried.

The most popular Shanghainese delicacy in Hong Kong is freshwater hairy crab (a crab with long, hairy-looking legs), flown in from Shanghai in autumn, steamed, and eaten with the hands. Other Shanghainese dishes include "yellow fish" (usually marinated in wine lees), braised eel with huge chunks of garlic, "drunken chicken" (chicken marinated in Chinese wine), sautéed shrimp in spicy tomato sauce over crispy rice, and sautéed shredded beef and green pepper. As for the famous hundred-year-old egg, it's actually only several months old, with a limey, pickled-ginger taste. Breads, noodles, and dumplings are favored over rice in this region's cuisine.

SICHUAN FOOD

This is my favorite Chinese cuisine, because it's the spiciest, hottest, and most fiery style of cooking. The fact that its spiciness recalls Thailand, India, and Malaysia is no coincidence, since this huge province shares a border with Burma and Tibet.

The culprit is the Sichuan chile, fried to release its explosiveness. Seasoning also includes chile-bean paste, peppercorns, garlic, ginger, coriander, and other spices. Foods are simmered and smoked rather than stir-fried. The most famous Sichuan dish is smoked duck, which is seasoned with peppercorns, ginger, cinnamon, orange peel, and coriander; marinated in rice wine; then steamed; and then smoked over a charcoal fire of camphor wood and tea leaves.

Other specialties include pan-fried prawns in spicy sauce, sour-and-peppery soup, sautéed diced chicken in chile-bean sauce, and dry-fried spicy string beans. Most Sichuan menus indicate which dishes are spicy.

CHIU CHOW FOOD

Chiu Chow refers to the people, dialect, and food of the Swatow area in southeastern Canton. Chiu Chow chefs pride themselves on their talents for vegetable carvings—those incredible birds, flowers, and other adornments that are a part of every Chiu Chow banquet.

Influenced by Cantonese cooking, Chiu Chow food is rich in protein, light, and tasty. Seafood, ducks, and geese are favorites, while sauces, often sweet and using tangerine or sweet beans for flavor, are liberally applied. A meal begins with a cup of *kwun yum* tea, popularly called Iron Buddha and probably the world's strongest and most bitter tea. It's supposed to cleanse the system and stimulate the taste buds. Drink some of this stuff and you'll be humming for hours.

Two very expensive Chiu Chow delicacies are shark's fin and bird's nests. Other common menu items include steamed lobster, deep-fried shrimp balls, sautéed slices of whelk, fried goose blood, goose doused in soy sauce, stuffed eel wrapped in pickled cabbage, and crispy fried *chuenjew* leaves, which literally melt in the mouth. While not greasy, the food does favor strong, earthy tastes.

DRINKS

Tea is often provided regardless of whether you ask for it, usually at a small charge. Grown in China for more than 2,000 years, tea is believed to help clear the palate and aid digestion. There are three main types: green or unfermented tea; black *bo lay* fermented tea (the most popular in Hong Kong); and *oolong,* or semifermented tea. These three teas can be further subdivided into a wide variety of specific types, with taste varying according to the region, climate, and soil. At any rate, if you want more tea at a restaurant, simply cock the lid of the teapot half open and someone will come around to refill it. Afterward, tap three fingers on the table as a sign of thanks.

If you want something a bit stronger than tea, there are **Chinese wines.** Although there are Chinese red and white wines made from grapes, most Chinese wines aren't really wines in the Western sense of the word. Rather, they are spirits distilled from rice, millet, and other grains, as well as from herbs and flowers. Popular Chinese wines include *siu hing,* a mild rice wine that resembles a medium-dry sherry, which goes well with all kinds of Chinese food, and is best served warm; *go leung* and *mao toi,* fiery drinks made from millet with a 70% alcohol content; and *ng ka pay,* a sweet herbal wine favored for its medicinal properties, especially against rheumatism. These wines can be cheap or expensive, depending on what you order, and remember that Chinese rarely drink outside of bars.

As for **beer,** there's Tsingtao from mainland China, first brewed years ago by Germans and made from sparkling mineral water. San Miguel is also very popular. One thing to keep in mind, however, is that excess drinking is frowned upon by the Chinese, who often don't drink anything stronger than tea in restaurants. In fact, one waiter told me that Westerners spend much more in restaurants than Chinese simply because Westerners drink alcoholic beverages.

3 Restaurants by Cuisine

AMERICAN

Al's Diner (Central, $, p. 145)

California Pizza Kitchen (Kowloon, Mong Kok, Causeway Bay, $, p. 151)

Dan Ryan's Chicago Grill ✿ (Central, Kowloon, $$, p. 126)

The Flying Pan (Central, $, p. 146)

Main Street Deli ✿✿ (Kowloon, $, p. 133)

Ruth's Chris Steak House ✿✿ (Kowloon, Central, $$$, p. 124)

ASIAN

Nomads ✿ (Kowloon, $, p. 134)

The Spice Market (Kowloon, $$, p. 129)

CANTONESE

Fook Lam Moon ✿✿✿ (Kowloon, Wan Chai, $$$, p. 156)

Happy Garden Noodles & Congee Kitchen (Kowloon, $, p. 133)

Jade Garden Restaurant (Kowloon, Causeway Bay, $$, p. 156)

Jumbo Kingdom ✿ (Aberdeen, $$, p. 154)

Luk Yu Tea House ✿✿✿ (Central, $$, p. 158)

One Harbour Road ✿✿ (Wan Chai, $$$, p. 147)

Shang Palace ✿✿ (Kowloon, $$$, p. 157)

The Square ✿ (Central, $$, p. 158)

Super Star Seafood Restaurant ✿ (Kowloon, Central, Wan Chai, Causeway Bay, $$, p. 130)

T'ang Courturant ✿✿ (Kowloon, $$$, p. 157)

Tsui Hang Village Restaurant (Kowloon, Central, $$, p. 157)

Yan Toh Heen 🦀🦀🦀 (Kowloon, $$$, p. 158)

Yung Kee 🦀🦀 (Central, $$, p. 144)

Zen Chinese 🦀🦀 (Central, $$, p. 144)

CHIU CHOW

City Chiuchow Restaurant (Kowloon, $$, p. 156)

Golden Island Bird's Nest Chiu Chau Restaurant (Kowloon, $$, p. 127)

CONTINENTAL

Avenue Restaurant & Bar 🦀🦀 (Kowloon, $$, p. 126)

Jimmy's Kitchen 🦀 (Kowloon, Central, $$, p. 141)

M at the Fringe 🦀🦀🦀 (Central, $$$, p. 138)

Post 97 🦀 (Central, $$, p. 142)

Riva 🦀🦀 (Causeway Bay, $$$, p. 147)

Sammy's Kitchen (Western District, $, p. 155)

The Verandah 🦀🦀🦀 (Repulse Bay, $$$, p. 152)

DIM SUM

See "Dim Sum," on p. 155

FRENCH

BB's Bistro (Kowloon, $$, p. 126)

Cafe des Artistes 🦀🦀 (Central, $$$, p. 137)

Caprice 🦀🦀🦀 (Central, $$$$, p. 135)

Gaddi's 🦀🦀🦀 (Kowloon, $$$$, p. 121)

Le Parisien 🦀 (Central, $$, p. 141)

Le Tire Bouchon 🦀🦀 (Central, $$, p. 141)

Petrus 🦀🦀🦀 (Central, $$$$, p. 136)

SPOON by Alain Ducasse 🦀🦀🦀 (Kowloon, $$$, p. 121)

FUSION

Felix 🦀🦀🦀 (Kowloon, $$$, p. 123)

ToTT'S Asian Grill & Bar 🦀🦀🦀 (Causeway Bay, $$$, p. 148)

HUNANESE

Hunan Garden 🦀🦀 (Central, $$$, p. 138)

INDIAN

Gaylord 🦀🦀 (Kowloon, $$, p. 127)

Koh-I-Noor 🦀 (Kowloon, Central, $, p. 133)

The Viceroy 🦀🦀 (Wan Chai, $$, p. 149)

Woodlands (Kowloon, $, p. 135)

INTERNATIONAL

Cafe Deco 🦀 (Victoria Peak, $$, p. 152)

café TOO 🦀🦀🦀 (Central, $$, p. 139)

The Greenery (Kowloon, $$, p. 128)

Harbour Side 🦀🦀 (Kowloon, $$$, p. 124)

Lucy's 🦀 (Stanley, $$, p. 153)

Ramas Greens 🦀🦀 (Wan Chai, $$, p. 148)

The Peak Lookout 🦀🦀 (Victoria Peak, $$, p. 152)

The Salisbury (Kowloon, $, p. 134)

Top Deck, at the Jumbo 🦀🦀🦀 (Aberdeen, $$, p. 154)

ToTT'S Asian Grill & Bar 🦀🦀🦀 (Causeway Bay, $$$, p. 148)

ITALIAN

Baci 🦀🦀 (Central, $$$, p. 137)

Fat Angelo's (Kowloon, Central, Wan Chai, Causeway Bay, $, p. 132)

Gaia Ristorante 🦀 (Central, $$$, p. 137)

Grappa's 🦀 (Central, $$, p. 140)

Grissini 🦀🦀🦀 (Wan Chai, $$$$, p. 147)

Isola 🦀🦀 (Central, $$$, p. 138)

Nicholini's 🦀🦀🦀 (Central, $$$$, p. 136)

The Pizzeria 🦀🦀 (Kowloon, $$, p. 129)

Sabatini 🦀🦀🦀 (Kowloon, $$$, p. 124)

Spaghetti House (Kowloon, Yau Ma Tei, Mong Kok, Central, Wan Chai, Causeway Bay, $, p. 134)

Tutto Bene ✿ (Kowloon, $$, p. 131)
Va Bene ✿✿ (Central, $$$, p. 139)

JAPANESE
Genki Sushi (Kowloon, Central, Wan
  Chai, Causeway Bay, $, p. 132)
Hanagushi (Central, $$, p. 140)
Tokio Joe ✿ (Central, $$, p. 143)
Unkai ✿✿ (Kowloon, $$$$, p. 122)
Wasabisabi ✿✿ (Causeway Bay, $$,
  p. 149)

KOREAN
Sorabol ✿ (Kowloon, Causeway Bay,
  $, p. 151)

MEXICAN
¡Caramba! (Central, $, p. 145)

NORTHERN CHINESE
Hutong ✿✿✿ (Kowloon, $$, p. 156)
Watermargin ✿✿ (Causeway Bay, $$,
  p. 150)

PEKINGESE
American Restaurant (Wan Chai, $,
  p. 150)
Peking Garden ✿ (Kowloon, Central,
  Causeway Bay, $$, p. 129)
Spring Deer Restaurant ✿ (Kowloon,
  $$, p. 130)

PIZZA
Baci Pizza ✿ (Central, $, p. 145)
California Pizza Kitchen (Kowloon,
  Mong Kok, Causeway Bay, $,
  p. 151)
PizzaExpress (Kowloon, Central, Wan
  Chai, $, p. 146)
The Pizzeria ✿✿ (Kowloon, $$,
  p. 129)
Spaghetti House (Kowloon, Yau Ma
  Tei, Mong Kok, Central, Wan
  Chai, Causeway Bay, $, p. 134)

SANDWICHES
Main Street Deli ✿✿ (Kowloon, $,
  p. 133)
Pret A Manger (Central, Wan Chai,
  Causeway Bay, $, p. 146)

SEAFOOD
Dot Cod Seafood Restaurant &
  Oyster Bar (Central, $$, p. 140)
Harbour Side ✿✿ (Kowloon, $$$,
  p. 124)
Super Star Seafood Restaurant ✿
  (Kowloon, Central, Wan Chai,
  Causeway Bay, $$, p. 130)
Top Deck, at the Jumbo ✿✿✿
  (Aberdeen, $$, p. 154)

SHANGHAINESE
Shanghai Garden (Central, $$, p. 142)
Wu Kong ✿✿ (Kowloon, Causeway
  Bay, $$, p. 131)

SICHUAN
Red Pepper ✿✿ (Causeway Bay, $$,
  p. 149)
Sichuan Garden ✿ (Central, $$,
  p. 143)

SPANISH/TAPAS
El Cid Spanish Restaurant ✿
  (Kowloon, Causeway Bay, Stanley,
  $$, p. 127)

STEAKS
Ruth's Chris Steak House ✿✿
  (Kowloon, Central, $$$, p. 124)
STEAK HOUSE winebar + grill ✿✿✿
  (Kowloon, $$$$, p. 122)

THAI
Chili Club (Wan Chai, $, p. 151)
Chilli N Spice ✿ (Stanley, Causeway
  Bay, $, p. 153)
Thai Lemongrass ✿✿ (Central, $$,
  p. 143)

VEGETARIAN
Bo Kong ✿ (Causeway Bay, $, p. 150)
Life ✿ (Central, $, p. 145)
Woodlands (Kowloon, $, p. 135)

VIETNAMESE
Chilli N Spice ✿ (Stanley, Causeway
  Bay, $, p. 153)
Indochine 1929 ✿✿ (Central, $$,
  p. 141)

THE TRAVELOCITY GUARANTEE

...THAT SAYS EVERYTHING YOU BOOK WILL BE RIGHT, OR WE'LL WORK WITH OUR TRAVEL PARTNERS TO MAKE IT RIGHT, RIGHT AWAY.

*To drive home the point,
we're going to use the word "right" in every single sentence.*

Let's get right to it. Right to the meat! Only Travelocity guarantees everything about your booking will be right, or we'll work with our travel partners to make it right, right away. Right on!

Here's a picture taken smack dab right in the middle of Antigua, where the Guarantee also covers you.

The Guarantee covers all but one of the items pictured to the right.

Now, you may be thinking, "Yeah, right, I'm so sure." That's OK; you have the right to remain skeptical. That is until we mention help is always right around the corner. Call us right off the bat, knowing our customer service reps are there for you 24/7. Righting wrongs. Left and right.

For example, what if the ocean view you booked actually looks out at a downright ugly parking lot? You'd be right to call – we're there for you. And no one in their right mind would be pleased to learn the rental car place has closed and left them stranded. Call Travelocity and we'll help get you back on the right track.

Now if you're guessing there are some things we can't control, like the weather, well you're right. But we can help you with most things – to get all the details in righting,* visit travelocity.com/guarantee.

*Sorry, spelling things right is one of the few things not covered under the Guarantee.

travelocity
You'll never roam alone.

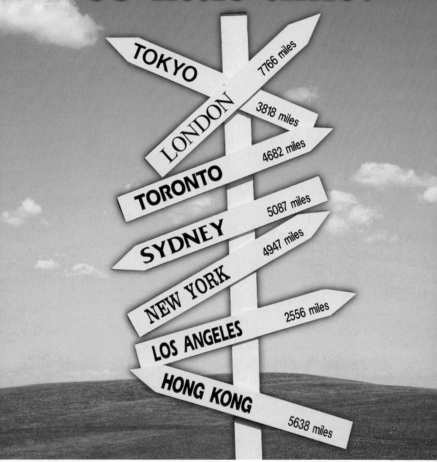

4 Kowloon

VERY EXPENSIVE

Gaddi's ✹✹✹ FRENCH   Opened in 1953 and named after a former general manager of The Peninsula, Gaddi's was once considered the best European restaurant in Hong Kong. Although that reputation has long been challenged by the birth of many other superb restaurants, the service is still excellent, the waiters are professional, and the food—classically French but with inventive, European influences—is always beyond reproof. Gaddi's is still a legend in Asia, the epitome of old Hong Kong. Its atmosphere, intended to evoke the hotel's original 1928 neoclassical architecture, is that of an elegant European dining room blended with the best of Asia, with crystal-and-silver chandeliers from Paris, Tai Ping carpet, and a Chinese coromandel screen dating from 1670. As for the food, it's French haute cuisine at its finest, with a changing menu that reflects the seasons in France and utilizes the highest-quality products imported from various countries. Examples of past dishes are roasted milk-fed lamb rack in herb crust with olive jus, and turbot poached on the bone in milk infused with cloves with a black truffle cappuccino. The wine cellar is among the best and largest in Hong Kong, with a collection of rare vintages—but who could blame you if you get carried away and splurge on champagne? There's live, discreet music at night and a small dance floor.

In The Peninsula hotel, Salisbury Rd., Tsim Sha Tsui. ℰ 852/2315 3171. www.peninsula.com. Reservations recommended at lunch, required at dinner. Jacket required for men at dinner. Main courses HK$420–HK$520 (US$55–US$68/£30–£37); fixed-price lunch HK$388 (US$50/£28); fixed-price dinner HK$1,188–HK$1,688 (US$154–US$219/£85–£120). AE, DC, MC, V. Daily noon–3pm and 7–11pm. MTR: Tsim Sha Tsui.

SPOON by Alain Ducasse ✹✹✹ FRENCH   Dinner at this sophisticated, seductive venue is more than just a meal—it's an experience. From the moment you walk past the restaurant's "wine cellar," with approximately 3,000 bottles of both New and Old World selections on display, you know that this is a place of superlatives. The focal point of the dining room is the ceiling, where 550 hand-blown Murano glass spoons are lined up like a landing strip, directing one's attention to the open kitchen and to the stunning harbor view just beyond the massive windows. The restaurant is

---

⌒Moments Dining Behind the Scenes

If you've ever wondered what a kitchen is like during the hustle and bustle of meal times, you'll have your chance to experience it firsthand by participating in Gaddi's Chef Table at The Peninsula hotel. Seating only four (with a minimum of two persons), it offers a fascinating front-row view of Gaddi's kitchen action, a tour of The Peninsula's massive kitchens, and includes three-course lunches for HK$688 (US$89/£49) or five-course and 10-course dinners for HK$1,488 and HK$2,088 (US$193/£106 and US$271/£149) per person. For Chinese food enthusiasts, a similar dining experience is offered by The Peninsula's Spring Moon Chef's Table. For reservations, contact The Peninsula at ℰ 852/2920 2888 or by e-mail at dining.pen@peninsula.com. On the other side of the harbor, Caprice, in the Four Seasons Hotel Hong Kong (ℰ 852/3196 8888), also has a Chef's Table for up to eight diners, with a minimum dinner charge of HK$12,000 (US$1,558/£857) for the group.

---

so low and close to the water that dining here is almost like being on a junk—albeit a very luxurious one.

The menu, featuring the contemporary cuisine inspired by chef and restaurateur Alain Ducasse, gives diners the freedom to mix and match food and cooking styles by selecting an entree (the steak is among the best I've had), its sauce, and accompanying vegetables. You might, therefore, pair Chilean sea bass with pistachio and macadamia with a coconut/lemon-grass condiment, served with a baby spinach bamboo salad. Or, your entire group may opt for the Sexy Spoon, a special tasting menu costing HK$750 (US$97/£54) per person for six courses or HK$950 (US$123/£68) for eight courses. For bargain hunters, the Sexy Sunset Menu, available from 6 to 7pm and again from 10 to 11pm, gives an appetizer, a choice of starter and entree, dessert, and a glass of champagne, for HK$450 (US$58/£32).

In the Hotel InterContinental Hong Kong, Salisbury Rd., Tsim Sha Tsui. © 852/2721 1211, ext. 2323. www.hong kong-ic.intercontinental.com. Reservations required. Main courses HK$235–HK$495 (US$31–US$64/£17–£35). AE, DC, MC, V. Daily 6pm–midnight. MTR: Tsim Sha Tsui.

STEAK HOUSE winebar + grill ����� STEAKS   Not only is the food great, but dining here is fun! Start your meal with a trip through one of Hong Kong's most extensive salad bars, featuring 24 different vegetables, six homemade salad dressings, and 11 condiments. Follow it with a filet mignon, Australian Wagyu beef, a New York strip, or other meat imported from around the world, cooked on Hong Kong's only charcoal grill. You then get to choose your gourmet steak knife (10 different options, from Japan, France, Germany, and other parts of the globe), your mustard (from a dozen homemade varieties), sauce (eight different kinds), and salt (from a selection of rock salts from around the world). There's no view here, but to be truthful I barely noticed, since I was so absorbed in making my many selections, including—need I add?—wine from the cellar's 3,000 choices.

In the Hotel InterContinental Hong Kong, Salisbury Rd., Tsim Sha Tsui. © 852/2721 1211, ext. 2323. www.hong kong-ic.intercontinental.com. Reservations required. Main courses HK$290–HK$980 (US$38–US$127/£21–£70); Sun brunch HK$488 (US$63/£35). AE, DC, MC, V. Sun noon–3pm; daily 6pm–midnight. MTR: Tsim Sha Tsui.

Unkai ��� JAPANESE   The Hong Kong branch of a well-known group of restaurants in Japan, Unkai might well be the best Japanese restaurant in town. With chefs from Osaka (known for its food), it caters to discerning Japanese, who make up a large proportion of the Sheraton's guests, with a variety of authentic dishes. True to Japanese form, the elegance of the restaurant is subtly understated, an aesthetic that is also carried into the food presentation. Foremost, of course, are the *kaiseki* courses, artfully arranged dishes that change according to the season. There's also tempura (meat and vegetables coated in batter and then deep-fried), *teppanyaki* (grilled foods), and sushi counters. Since ordering a la carte can be expensive and bewildering due to the many choices, order a fixed-price meal (called a "course" on the menu) or come for lunch, when you have a choice of several fixed-price meals, including sushi, tempura, and teppanyaki courses and an *obento* lunch box. The *obento* is especially charming, a small lacquered chest with dishes of food in each of the drawers.

In the Sheraton Hong Kong Hotel and Towers. 20 Nathan Rd., Tsim Sha Tsui. © 852/2369 1111, ext. 2. www.sheraton. com/hongkong. Reservations recommended. *Kaiseki* fixed-price meals HK$500–HK$795 (US$65–US$103/ £36–£57); *teppanyaki* fixed-price meals HK$820–HK$990 (US$106–US$129/£59–£71); fixed-price lunch HK$145–HK$350 (US$19–US$45/£10–£25). AE, DC, MC, V. Daily noon–2:30pm and 6:30–10:30pm. MTR: Tsim Sha Tsui.

EXPENSIVE

Felix ★★★ *Value* FUSION Located on the top floor of The Peninsula's tower addition, this strikingly avant-garde restaurant comes as something of a shock in the otherwise staid and traditionally conservative hotel. But what else can you expect from a restaurant designed by Philippe Starck? Your first hint that Felix is not your ordinary dining experience begins with the elevator's wavy walls, which suggest a voyage to the world beyond, and continues inside the restaurant with its huge aluminum wall and two glass facades that curve seductively to reveal stunning views of Kowloon on one side and Hong Kong Island on the other. Two eye-catching zinc cylinders vaguely resemble gigantic snails and contain a cocoon-cozy wine bar and what may be one of the world's tiniest discos, complete with a heat-sensitive floor that illuminates dancers' movements. Atop one of the cocoons is the American Bar, with expansive views and signature cocktails.

The dining area itself is rather—what can I say—stark, and even the view from the windows tends to take second place in this self-conscious, people-watching setting (you, however, should reserve a window seat on the harbor side). The food, featuring Pacific Rim ingredients brought together in East-meets-West combinations, rarely disappoints. You might start with lobster, prawn and scallop potstickers, followed by the hibachi-grilled Saikyo-miso salmon or the Mongolian-style barbecued rack of lamb. Bargain hunters can save bundles by dining early (before 7pm) and opting for the early-bird, three-course fixed-price dinner for HK$388 (US$50/£28) including a glass of wine. You can also come just for a drink, though note that the dress is smart casual (no flip-flops or shorts allowed).

In The Peninsula hotel, Salisbury Rd., Tsim Sha Tsui. ℂ 852/2315 3188. www.peninsula.com. Reservations required. Main courses HK$225–HK$350 (US$29–US$45/£16–£25). AE, DC, MC, V. Daily 6pm–2am (last order 10:30pm). MTR: Tsim Sha Tsui.

Fook Lam Moon ★★★ CANTONESE Upon entering this restaurant (look for the shrine to the kitchen god at the entrance), you immediately feel as if you've stepped back a couple of decades to a Hong Kong that has all but vanished. The decor is outdated and, unless you're a regular, the waiters are indifferent. Yet for almost 50 years this has remained *the* place to go for exotic dishes, including shark's fin, bird's nest, and abalone, served in a variety of ways, as well as more down-to-earth dishes such as fried crispy chicken and pan-fried lobster bars. Shark's fin, however, is the obvious number-one choice, with 12 different renditions listed on the menu. If you feel like splurging, prices for a bowl of shark's fin with crabmeat or shredded chicken begin at HK$350 (US$45/£25). If you are not careful, you could end up spending a small fortune (if you go for the exotic dishes, count on at least HK$1,000/US$130/£71 per person), but whatever you order, it's apt to be memorable. Indeed, some Hong Kong old-timers swear this restaurant serves the best Cantonese food in the world, and it's a favorite of local movers and shakers. Unlike many Chinese restaurants, this establishment provides both small (for two to four diners) and large tables.

There's another branch in Wan Chai at 35–45 Johnston Rd. (ℂ **852/2866 0663;** MTR: Wan Chai), with the same hours.

53–59 Kimberley Rd., Tsim Sha Tsui. ℂ **852/2366 0286.** www.fooklammoon-grp.com. Reservations recommended for dinner. Main dishes HK$100–HK$240 (US$13–US$31/£7–£17). AE, DC, MC, V. Daily 11:30am–2:30pm and 6–11:30pm. MTR: Tsim Sha Tsui.

Harbour Side ☆☆ INTERNATIONAL/SEAFOOD   This is the InterContinental's all-day "casual" restaurant, but if you go for the very tempting international seafood buffet—and who can resist?—you'll pay a pretty penny for the privilege of chowing down on fish, shrimp, sushi, and other seafood, along with pastas, pizzas, and salads. Included in the dining experience are views of people strolling along the waterfront Avenue of Stars promenade and chefs bustling about in an open kitchen. You can, however, dine more cheaply in this bright and airy informal dining hall by ordering a la carte, with selections ranging from burgers and sandwiches to steaks and Chinese and Japanese dishes.

In the Hotel InterContinental Hong Kong, Salisbury Rd., Tsim Sha Tsui. © 852/2721 1211, ext. 2323. www.hong kong-ic.intercontinental.com. Main courses HK$155–HK$390 (US$20–US$51/£11–£28); dinner buffet HK$458 (US$59/£33) Mon–Thurs, HK$488 (US$63/£35) Fri–Sun; lunch buffet HK$228 (US$30/£16) Mon–Thurs, HK$248 (US$32/£18) Fri–Sat; Sun Champagne brunch HK$518 (US$67/£37). AE, DC, MC, V. Daily 6am–midnight. MTR: Tsim Sha Tsui.

Ruth's Chris Steak House ☆☆ STEAKS/AMERICAN   Craving a big, juicy steak? This well-known American chain fits the bill with its U.S. prime Midwestern beef, available in cuts of filet, rib-eye, strip, porterhouse, T-bone, and veal in various sizes, broiled to exact specifications and served sizzling. Other entrees include tuna, chicken, lamb chops, and lobster; side dishes, which cost extra, range from mashed potatoes with roasted garlic to fresh sautéed spinach and Caesar salad. Less expensive fare for lunch includes sandwiches in addition to steak.

There's another branch in the Lippo Centre, 89 Queensway, Central (© **852/2522 9090;** MTR: Admiralty), open the same hours.

Empire Centre (opposite Regal Kowloon Hotel), 68 Mody Rd., Tsim Sha Tsui East. © 852/2366 6000. www.ruths chris.com. Reservations recommended for dinner. Main courses HK$240–HK$550 (US$31–US$71/£17–£39); fixed-price dinner HK$520–HK$750 (US$68–US$97/£37–£54); fixed-price lunch HK$140–HK$220 (US$18–US$29/£10–£16). AE, DC, MC, V. Daily noon–3pm and 5:30–11pm. MTR: Tsim Sha Tsui.

Sabatini ☆☆☆ _Finds_ ITALIAN   In 1954, three Sabatini brothers opened their first restaurant in Rome; their success led them to open branches in Japan and, in 1992, Hong Kong. The dining hall is rustic and cozy yet refined, with a terra-cotta tile floor, wooden ceiling, and traditional Roman murals, giving it a more casual and relaxed ambience than most hotel Italian restaurants in the same price range. Its menu is a faithful replica of the original Roman fare (along with chef specialties), with liberal doses of olive oil, garlic, and peppers and featuring such popular dishes as Dover sole with Prosecco, green and black olives, and herbed lemon butter, and veal with morel sauce. The pasta is all handmade, and the antipasti buffet is so delicious it's tempting to fill up just on its selections, but don't forget to leave room for the tiramisu. The list of mostly Italian wines is seemingly endless. Evenings feature guitar music; lunch is popular for its reasonable fixed-price menus. The service is cheerful and polished.

In the Royal Garden hotel, 69 Mody Rd., Tsim Sha Tsui East. © 852/2733 2000. www.rghk.com.hk. Reservations required. Main courses HK$278–HK$408 (US$36–US$53/£20–£29); fixed-price lunch Mon–Sat HK$125–HK$148 (US$16–US$19/£8.90–£11); Sun and holiday buffet HK$388 (US$50/£28). AE, DC, MC, V. Daily noon–2:30pm and 6–11pm. MTR: Tsim Sha Tsui.

Shang Palace ☆☆ CANTONESE   While many Chinese restaurants have ditched traditional red and gold for a more contemporary look, this remains one of Hong Kong's most traditionally and elaborately decorated restaurants, with walls of carved red lacquerware and Chinese lanterns hanging from the ceiling. All in all, it fits every expectation of how an "authentic" Chinese restaurant should look. If your experience of Chinese food is limited to chop suey, this is a comfortable and memorable place to go, though you also can't go wrong if you're a Chinese-food connoisseur. The dinner menu, which changes with the seasons, is quite extensive, with an emphasis on seafood but also serving chicken, duck, pigeon, beef, and pork, Cantonese-style. Consider starting with shark's-fin soup, followed by pan-fried scallops with minced shrimp in black-bean sauce or the deep-fried crispy chicken. If cost is no object, you might consider bird's nest with bamboo fungus, which runs HK$438 (US$57/£31) or more. Otherwise, expect to spend about HK$500 (US$65/£36) per person for a royal feast. Lunch is more economical and always includes a dozen or more varieties of dim sum.

In the Shangri-La Hotel, 64 Mody Rd., Tsim Tsui East. *852/2733 8754*. www.shangri-la.com. Reservations recommended. Main dishes HK$125–HK$290 (US$16–US$38/£8.90–£21). AE, DC, MC, V. Mon–Sat noon–3pm; Sun and holidays 10:30am–3pm; daily 6:30–11pm. MTR: Tsim Sha Tsui.

T'ang Court ❀❀ CANTONESE   Jackie Chan and a host of other celebrities have dined here, testament to this restaurant's award-winning cuisine famous for its original take on classic Cantonese fare. Named after the T'ang Dynasty, often characterized as the Golden Age in Chinese history, this hotel restaurant is richly decorated in burgundy and gold, with velvet curtains, contemporary sculptures, and generously spaced tables. Faced with an extensive menu of interesting choices, you might opt for one of the signature dishes like stir-fried lobster with spring onion, red onion and shallots, or baked blue-point oysters with port wine. If the sky's the limit, you can also dine on bird's nest and abalone, but on the other end of the spectrum are the fixed-price meals (good for lone diners) and the dim sum lunch.

In the Langham Hotel, 8 Peking Rd., Tsim Sha Tsui. *852/2375 1133*, ext. 2250. www.langhamhotels.com. Reservations recommended. Main dishes HK$120–HK$280 (US$16–US$36/£8.55–£20); fixed-price meal HK$350 (US$45/£25); dim sum lunch HK$208 (US$27/£15). AE, DC, MC, V. Mon–Sat noon–3pm; Sun and holidays 11am–3pm; daily 6–11pm. MTR: Tsim Sha Tsui.

Yan Toh Heen ❀❀❀ CANTONESE   With a name that translates loosely as an "elegant dining establishment to enjoy the beautiful view," this great restaurant envelopes diners in a sophisticated, hushed environment, with large windows treating diners to a view of famous Victoria Harbour. The decor emphasizes the beauty of stark simplicity, with bonsai trees and flower arrangements that change with the lunar calendar; the restaurant is famous for its beautiful jade table settings (each setting is valued at approximately HK$8,000/US$1,039/£571!). Dishes are traditional Cantonese, as well as imaginative creations that border on Chinese nouvelle cuisine. The menu changes with each lunar month but always includes seafood, the restaurant's signature barbecued suckling pig, Peking duck, and sautéed prawns with XO chile sauce, seasonal vegetables, and a wide selection of desserts. The restaurant is also known for its dim sum. Since most diners follow the Chinese custom of ordering several dishes and then sharing, the average dinner bill without wine here is HK$1,000 (US$130/£71) for two.

In the InterContinental Hong Kong, 18 Salisbury Rd., Tsim Sha Tsui. *852/2721 1211*. www.hongkong-ic. intercontinental.com. Reservations recommended (request a window seat). Main dishes HK$155–HK$320 (US$20–US$42/£11–£23); fixed-price lunch HK$168–HK$388 (US$22–US$50/£12–£28). AE, DC, MC, V. Daily noon–2:30pm and 6–11pm. MTR: Tsim Sha Tsui.

MODERATE

In addition to the choices here, a good standby for Continental cuisine is the Tsim Sha Tsui branch of **Jimmy's Kitchen,** covered in the Central dining section (p. 141).

Avenue Restaurant & Bar *★★* *Value* CONTINENTAL   The contemporary, upscale setting of this airy restaurant with its murals and abstract artwork, white-washed walls, palm trees, and greenhouselike dining area, together with its menu of modern European food and excellent service, could easily mislead one into thinking that this trendy establishment is much more expensive than it is, making it a very good value. It also overlooks Nathan Road, giving an unparalleled view of Hong Kong's bustling street life. Though known for its seafood and grilled steaks, along with monthly promotionals, the restaurant offers an extensive selection tailored to various budgets and tastes. You might wish to start with an appetizer like tian of crab and avocado with lemon mayonnaise, followed by sautéed sole with spinach, new potatoes, poached egg, and grain mustard sauce. For dessert, try the chocolate soufflé or the crème brûlée. For lunch, only fixed-price meals are available.

In the Holiday Inn Golden Mile, 50 Nathan Rd., Tsim Sha Tsui. ✆ 852/2315 1118. www.goldenmile-hk.holiday-inn. com. Reservations recommended weekend evenings. Main courses HK$165–HK$288 (US$21–US$37/£12–£21); fixed-price lunch HK$198–HK$228 (US$26–US$30/£14–£16); fixed-price dinner HK$438 (US$57/£31). AE, DC, MC, V. Mon–Sat noon–2:30pm and 6:30–10:30pm (last order). MTR: Tsim Sha Tsui.

BB's Bistro FRENCH   This is a good choice for casual dining on Knutsford Terrace, a tucked-away pedestrian lane lined with bars and restaurants at the north end of Tsim Sha Tsui. You can choose to sit outside and watch the human parade, or settle in the simple, dark restaurant at one of the booths or tables. A guitarist serenades in the evening. The cuisine ranges from classic French recipes to more interesting creations, including roasted black cod with fennel and star anise, coq au vin, and bouillabaisse. The cheerful service is a bit slow but not deliberately so, making this a good bet only when you won't be ruffled by a languorous—or should we say French?—and carefree dinner. Lunchtime is faster and more economical.

13–13a Knutsford Terrace, Tsim Sha Tsui. ✆ 852/2316 2212. www.mhihk.com. Reservations recommended. Main courses HK$168–HK$218 (US$22–US$28/£12–£16); fixed-price lunch HK$78–HK$98 (US$10–US$13/£5.55–£7). AE, DC, MC, V. Mon–Sat noon–1am. MTR: Tsim Sha Tsui.

City Chiuchow Restaurant CHIU CHOW   A longtime favorite for Chiu Chow food, this spacious restaurant overlooks gardens leading down to a major promenade in Tsim Sha Tsui East. Seating 500, it features a big tank with fish swimming about, soon to end up on the chopping block. Famous dishes here include Chiu Chow shark's-fin soup, much thicker and stronger tasting than the Cantonese version; double-boiled shark's-fin-and-chicken soup, not as strong but equally popular; sliced soy goose; fried chicken with a black spicy sauce; and seafood dishes, including lobster. I particularly recommend the cold sliced lobster in a special honey sauce—it's not on the menu but it's available year-round. Dim sum is also served. And don't forget to try the Iron Buddha tea, a specialty of Chiuchow's, a tea that is so strong it will knock your socks off—and may keep you awake all night.

East Ocean Centre, 98 Granville Rd., Tsim Sha Tsui East. ✆ 852/2723 6226. Main dishes HK$60–HK$130 (US$7.80–US$17/£4.30–£9.30). AE, DC, MC, V. Daily 11am–11pm. MTR: Tsim Sha Tsui.

Dan Ryan's Chicago Grill *★* *Kids* AMERICAN   Located in the huge Ocean Terminal complex at its southernmost end, where cruise ships dock, this casual restaurant serves real American food, with portions big enough to satisfy a hungry cowboy. The decor is Anywhere, USA, but with a difference—since it's located right by the Star Ferry, the Chicago Grill offers views of the famous harbor from a few select seats. The lunch menu is substantial, including such classic American favorites as buffalo chicken wings, potato skins, nachos, New England clam chowder, barbecued ribs, steaks, spaghetti, lasagna, chili, great hamburgers (a hit with kids), and large deli sandwiches. There are also daily lunch specials, available Monday through Friday, beginning at HK$70 (US$9.10/£5). The dinner menu is confined mainly to barbecued steaks, chops, fish, and pasta. Admittedly, most dishes here are a bit pricey, but if you're hungering for the real thing, you might consider it a lifesaver. You can also come just for a drink at its bar, and there are English-language newspapers for customer perusal.

There's another Dan Ryan's at Pacific Place in Admiralty, 88 Queensway (© 852/ 2845 4600; MTR: Admiralty), open Monday through Friday from 11am to midnight, Saturday from 9am to 2am, and Sunday from 9am to midnight.

200 Ocean Terminal, Harbour City, Tsim Sha Tsui. © 852/2735 6111. www.windy-city.com.hk/dans. Main courses HK$60–HK$250 (US$7.80–US$32/£4.30–£18) before 6pm, HK$92–HK$470 (US$12–US$61/£6.55–£34) after 6pm. AE, DC, MC, V. Mon–Fri 11am–midnight; Sat–Sun 10am–midnight. MTR: Tsim Sha Tsui.

El Cid Spanish Restaurant ⭐ Value SPANISH/TAPAS This cheerful restaurant

was one of the first to open on Knutsford Terrace, a narrow lane lined with bars and restaurants on the northern edge of Tsim Sha Tsui. Although the menu runs the gamut from classic paellas to grilled Chilean sea bass with tomato and roast bell-pepper salsa, probably the best thing to do is select from the several dozen tapas on the menu, which can make for wonderful nibbling or out-and-out feasts. Choices include grilled prawns, lamb kabobs, and spinach and cheese in filo pastry.

There are other El Cid branches at Shop G315 Harbour City, Tsim Sha Tsui (© 852/2721 2181; MTR: Tsim Sha Tsui), open daily noon to 11pm; 9–11 Cleveland St., Causeway Bay (© 852/2576 8650; MTR: Causeway Bay), open daily noon to 11:30pm; and Shop 102 in the historic Murray House (with great sea views from its delightful terrace), Stanley Plaza, Stanley (© 852/2899 0858), open Monday through Friday from noon to midnight and Saturday and Sunday from 11am to 11pm.

12 and 14 Knutsford Terrace, Tsim Sha Tsui. © 852/2312 1898. www.kingparrot.com. Main courses HK$145–HK$380 (US$19–US$49/£10–£27); tapas HK$40–HK$70 (US$5.20–US$9.10/£2.85–£5). AE, DC, MC, V. Daily noon–2:30pm and 6pm–midnight. MTR: Tsim Sha Tsui.

Gaylord ⭐⭐ Value INDIAN This long-established, first-floor restaurant in the

heart of Tsim Sha Tsui is classy and comfortable, with private booths and overstuffed sofas. It's popular for its authentic North Indian classics, including tandoori, lamb curry cooked in North Indian spices and herbs, chicken cooked in hot fiery vindaloo curry, prawns cooked with green pepper and spices, and fish with potatoes and tomatoes. There are a dozen vegetarian dishes, and the lunchtime buffet, served every day until 2:30pm except Sundays and public holidays, is a winner. There are also fixed-price dinners, along with a dinner buffet available until 9:30pm for only HK$138 (US$18/£9.85).

23–25 Ashley Rd., Tsim Sha Tsui. © 852/2376 1001. Main dishes HK$88–HK$168 (US$11–US$22/£6.30–£12); lunch buffet HK$88 (US$11/£6.30); fixed-price dinner HK$160–HK$210 (US$21–US$27/£11–£15). AE, DC, MC, V. Daily noon–3pm and 6–11pm. MTR: Tsim Sha Tsui.

Golden Island Bird's Nest Chiu Chau Restaurant CHIU CHOW This Chiu

Chow restaurant is conveniently located right in front of the Star Ferry terminus. As the prices below indicate, you can eat quite cheaply here if you order only one dish per person, but you'll pay more if you choose the house specialty—bird's nest, prepared 14 different ways and available as a soup, entree, and even dessert. This was Hong Kong's first restaurant to offer bird's nest as a specialty; although the prices for this dish have risen dramatically over the years, here it costs around HK$380 (US$49/£27)—expensive, but less than what you'd pay elsewhere. Anyway, I would suggest that you try at least one of the bird's-nest dishes, along with such Chiu Chow preparations as oyster omelets, prawn balls, or roast soy goose, topping it all off with a thimble-size cup of Chiu Chow tea, which is believed to aid in digestion.

Star House (2nd floor), 3 Salisbury Rd., Tsim Sha Tsui. (C) 852/2736 6228. Main dishes HK$60–HK$150 (US$7.80–US$20/£4.30–£11). AE, DC, MC, V. Mon–Sat 11:30am–3pm; Sun and holidays 11am–3pm; daily 5:30–11:30pm. MTR: Tsim Sha Tsui.

The Greenery INTERNATIONAL   If you're looking for a quick, filling feast in Tsim Sha Tsui East, look no further than the lunch or dinner buffets offered in this popular, airy restaurant, located in the hotel's 15-story atrium. The sounds of piano music, a waterfall, and multitudes of hungry diners make eating a rather noisy affair, but the food is good and varied, ranging from Chinese and Japanese to Western fare, from salads and vegetables to ribs and fish, and an efficient staff keeps water glasses filled and used plates whisked away.

In the Royal Garden Hotel, 69 Mody Rd., Tsim Sha Tsui East. (C) 852/2721 5215. www.rghk.com.hk. Lunch buffet HK$160 (US$21/£11); dinner buffet HK$308 (US$40/£22) Mon–Thurs, HK$328 (US$43/£23) Fri–Sun. AE, DC, MC, V. Daily noon–2:30pm and 6:30–9:30pm. MTR: Tsim Sha Tsui.

Hutong ★★★ *Finds* NORTHERN CHINESE   A hutong is an ancient alley or lane, common in Beijing's courtyard neighborhoods. This stunning restaurant, however, is about as far from a real hutong as one can get, since it's located on the 28th floor of a strikingly modern high-rise. Still, the restaurant is to be commended for its down-to-earth yet dramatic setting, with red lanterns providing the only splash of color against a dark, muted interior and with fantastic views of Hong Kong. Indeed, everything about this place is a class act. The cuisine, which is northern Chinese in origin but uses new ingredients and combinations to create its own trademark dishes, is so enticing it's hard to know what to recommend. I love the drunken raw crab (an appetizer marinated 3 days in Chinese wine), the crispy deboned lamb ribs, and crispy soft-shelled crab with Sichuan red chile. Even the pig throat with scallions and cilantro is a whole lot better than it sounds, especially when you wash it down with chilled lychee wine with a touch of soda. In short, Hutong raises the bar in chic Chinese restaurants, winning hands down in cuisine, presentation, atmosphere, view, and service. Note that there's a minimum charge of HK$300 (US$39/£21) per person for dinner. A set lunch for two people, costing HK$238 (US$31/£17) per person, is available weekdays only.

1 Peking Rd. (28th floor), Tsim Sha Tsui. (C) 852/3428 8342. www.aqua.com.hk. Reservations required for dinner. Main dishes HK$120–HK$288 (US$16–US$37/£8.55–£21). AE, DC, MC, V. Daily noon–3pm and 6–11pm. MTR: Tsim Sha Tsui.

Jade Garden Restaurant CANTONESE   Jade Garden is part of a chain of restaurants owned by the Maxim's Group, a company that has long been wildly successful throughout Hong Kong and is popular with large Chinese families (other establishments in the group include Sichuan Garden, Shanghai Garden, Chiu Chow Garden, and Peking Garden; the latter one also has a branch in Star House). Jade Garden is the place to go if you don't know much about Chinese food, feel that you should try it, but still aren't very keen on the idea. A plus is the view of the harbor afforded by some of the window-side tables. Dim sum is available for lunch from an English menu. If you'd rather come for dinner, you might consider drunken shrimp boiled in Chinese rice wine, deep-fried boneless chicken with lemon sauce, stir-fried minced pigeon served with lettuce leaves, glazed pork loin, or, if you feel like splurging, barbecued Peking duck, which costs HK$290 (US$38/£21).

Jade Garden has another branch at 1 Hysan Ave., Causeway Bay (© **852/2577 9332**), open daily from 7:30am to midnight.

Star House (4th floor), 3 Salisbury Rd., Tsim Sha Tsui. © **852/2730 6888.** Main dishes HK$68–HK$168 (US$8.85–US$22/£4.85–£12). AE, DC, MC, V. Mon–Sat 11am–11:30pm; Sun and holidays 10am–11:30pm. MTR: Tsim Sha Tsui.

Peking Garden ✦ PEKINGESE   Another Maxim's Group of restaurants, Peking Garden specializes in Pekingese and northern Chinese dishes, including stir-fried Pekingese noodles with shredded pork, braised prawns in red-wine sauce, Hunan ham with lotus seed in honey sauce, and beggar's chicken for HK$320 (US$42/£23; order it 24 hr. in advance). Try to be here during its nightly presentation of handmade noodles at 8 or 8:30pm. It's located in the Star House right in front of the Star Ferry.

You'll find other branches in the first and second basements of Alexandra House, 6 Ice House St., Central (© **852/2526 6456;** MTR: Central); Shop 003 in Pacific Place, 88 Queensway in Central (© **852/2845 8452;** MTR: Admiralty); and Hennessy Centre, 500 Hennessy Rd., Causeway Bay (© **852/2577 7231;** MTR: Causeway Bay); all have the same open hours.

Star House (3rd floor), 3 Salisbury Rd., Tsim Sha Tsui. © **852/2735 8211.** Main dishes HK$86–HK$188 (US$11–US$24/£6.15–£13). AE, DC, MC, V. Mon–Sat 11:30am–3pm; Sun 11am–3pm; daily 5:30–11:30pm. MTR: Tsim Sha Tsui.

The Pizzeria ✦✦ *Value* PIZZA/ITALIAN   Located on the second floor of the Kowloon Hotel (just behind The Peninsula), this casual and bustling dining hall with large windows is one of my favorite places in Tsim Sha Tsui for a relaxed meal at good prices, especially when I want great pizza or pasta in a classy venue but don't feel like getting dressed up (you won't however, want to wear shorts; it's a white-tablecloth kind of place even at lunch). With an a la carte menu that changes often, it offers a dozen different combinations of pizza, as well as pasta dishes like herbed pasta with homemade Italian sausage, porcini mushrooms and pecorino cheese and main courses like roasted rack of lamb with mustard and herb crust on a pumpkin and potato purée with a lentil red-wine sauce. Save room for dessert—they're all delicious. For the budget-conscious, there's a fixed-price lunch Monday through Thursday. Incidentally, to reach The Pizzeria, you have to walk through the Window Café, which specializes in international buffets.

In the Kowloon Hotel, 19–21 Nathan Rd., Tsim Sha Tsui. © **852/2929 2888,** ext. 3322. www.thekowloonhotel.com. Reservations recommended. Pasta and pizza HK$128–HK$158 (US$17–US$21/£9.15–£11); main courses HK$188–HK$238 (US$24–US$31/£13–£17); fixed-price lunch HK$98 (US$13/£7) Mon–Fri, HK$210 (US$27/£15) Sat–Sun. AE, DC, MC, V. Daily noon–3pm and 6–11pm. MTR: Tsim Sha Tsui.

The Spice Market ASIAN   Accessible from both the Marco Polo Prince Hotel and the third floor of Harbour City shopping mall, this dark and cozy restaurant specializes in buffets offering diners a culinary adventure throughout Asia. There are Chinese noodles; Indian curries; Japanese sushi; and Chinese, Thai, Vietnamese, and Singaporean favorites. Included are steamed fish, satays, Mongolian stir-fried noodles, tandoori, congee, dim sum, soups, salads, appetizers, and desserts. True to its name, some of the foods are spicy, but others lack pizzazz, probably due to international palates unaccustomed to fiery cuisine. While none of the dishes are outstanding, most of them are good; with so many choices, you'll probably end up eating more than you should.

In the Marco Polo Prince Hotel, 23 Canton Rd., Tsim Sha Tsui. ℂ 852/2113 6046. www.marcopolohotels.com. Lunch buffet HK$138 (US$18/£9.85) Mon–Fri, HK$148 (US$19/£11) Sat–Sun and holidays; dinner buffet HK$265 (US$34/£19) Sun–Thurs, HK$285 (US$37/£20) Fri–Sat and holidays. AE, DC, MC, V. Daily noon–2:30pm and 6:30–10pm. MTR: Tsim Sha Tsui.

Spring Deer Restaurant 𝒢 *Finds* PEKINGESE A longtime favorite in Hong Kong, this 30-some-year-old restaurant offers excellent Pekingese food at reasonable prices. Spring Deer is cheerful and very accessible to foreigners, but don't expect anything fancy; in fact, your tablecloth may have holes in it, but it will be clean—and the long, brightly lit dining hall is usually packed with groups of loyal fans. This is one of the best places to come if you want to try its specialty—honey-glazed Peking duck, which costs HK$280 (US$36/£20) and is good for two to four persons. Since you'll probably have to wait 40 minutes for the duck if you order it during peak time (7:30–9:30pm), it's best to arrive either before or after the rush. Chicken dishes are also well liked, including the deep-fried chicken and walnuts in soy sauce, and the handmade noodles are excellent. Other recommendations include the hot-and-sour soup, freshwater shrimp, and stewed ham and cabbage. Most dishes come in small, medium, and large sizes; the small dishes are suitable for two people. Remember, you'll want to order one dish apiece, plus an additional one to share. Unfortunately, since Spring Deer is crowded with groups, the lone diner is apt to be neglected in the shuffle; it's best to come here only if there are at least two of you.

42 Mody Rd., Tsim Sha Tsui. ℂ 852/2366 4012. Reservations recommended. Small dishes HK$54–HK$90 (US$7–US$12/£3.85–£6.40). AE, MC, V. Daily 11:30am–3pm and 6–11pm. MTR: Tsim Sha Tsui.

Super Star Seafood Restaurant 𝒢 CANTONESE/SEAFOOD Walk past the tanks filled with fish, lobsters, prawns, and crabs up to this lively Cantonese restaurant on the first floor. It's very popular with local Chinese, many of whom consider it one of Hong Kong's top Cantonese restaurants. Its menu includes pictures of major dishes; as its name implies, the restaurant specializes in fresh seafood (though the menu does offer more than seafood). Recommended are the deep-fried stuffed crab claws, sliced sole with spice and chile, baked lobster with minced spinach, and fish in season. Prices for seafood vary with the season and depend on the size of the creature you desire. If you want a specific fish or something else in the tank, simply point, but be sure to ask the price first. Stone fish is popular with the Chinese and is the restaurant's specialty. It's a rather ugly fish, and poisonous to boot if not prepared correctly. If this is what you want, you'll have to wait an hour for it to cook. Dim sum, served until 5pm, starts at HK$12 (US$1.55/85p) per plate.

There are other branches: in Tsim Sha Tsui's Harbour City, 4th floor, 21 Canton Rd. (ℂ **852/2628 0336;** MTR: Tsim Sha Tsui); in Central at 19–27 Wyndham St. (ℂ **852/2628 0826;** MTR: Central); in Wan Chai on the first floor of the Shui On Centre, 8 Harbour Rd. (ℂ **852/2628 0989;** MTR: Wan Chai); and in Causeway Bay on the 10th floor of Times Square, 1 Matheson St. (ℂ **852/2628 0886;** MTR: Causeway Bay). Call for individual open hours.

83–97 Nathan Rd., Tsim Sha Tsui. ℂ 852/2366 0878. Main dishes HK$75–HK$170 (US$9.75–US$22/£5.35–£12). AE, DC, MC, V. Mon–Fri 10:30am–4:30pm; Sat–Sun 9:30am–4:30pm; daily 5–11pm. MTR: Tsim Sha Tsui.

Tsui Hang Village Restaurant CANTONESE Tsui Hang is named after the home village of Dr. Sun Yat-sen (a Chinese revolutionary leader and statesman who lived from 1866–1925). Located across the street from the Miramar Hotel on the ground floor of a sparkling shopping complex called Miramar Plaza, it's a bright, clean, and modern place with a white jade statue of the Goddess of Mercy at its entrance. This restaurant specializes in its own Cantonese original creations but also serves traditional, home-style Chinese cooking. Dishes you might want to try include braised superior shark's fin and chicken soup in casserole, deep-fried minced shrimp balls with crisp almond, sautéed minced pigeon with lettuce, barbecued Peking duck, deep-fried crispy chicken with green onion, or roast goose. Dim sum, served during lunch and afternoon teatime, Monday through Saturday from 11:30am to 5pm and Sunday from 10am to 5pm, is priced from HK$16 to HK$40 (US$2.10–US$5.20/£1.15–£2.85) per plate.

There's another Tsui Hang Village in Central on the second floor of the New World Tower, 16–18 Queen's Rd., Central (© **852/2524 2012;** MTR: Central), open Monday through Friday from 11am to 3pm and 5:30 to 11:30pm, Saturday from 11am to 11:30pm, and Sunday from 10am to 11:30pm.

Miramar Shopping Centre, 132–134 Nathan Rd., Tsim Sha Tsui. © **852/2376 2882.** www.miramar-group.com. Main dishes HK$78–HK$260 (US$10–US$34/£5.55–£19). AE, DC, MC, V. Mon–Sat 11:30am–11:30pm; Sun 10am–11:30pm. MTR: Tsim Sha Tsui.

Tutto Bene ☞ ITALIAN   Located on the northern edge of Tsim Sha Tsui, on a tiny narrow lane known for its bars and restaurants, this small but popular eatery is often packed. Tight indoor quarters prevent it from being even remotely romantic (unless you speak some obscure language, your neighbor is going to hear every word you say); try for one of the outdoor tables. Prices seem a bit high (about HK$400/US$52/£29 per person without drinks), but the imaginative Italian food, spiced with Asian ingredients, has clearly won over a faithful clientele. Start with the buffalo mozzarella with fresh tomatoes and basil dressing. The antipasto platter is so huge that two can share. For a main course, consider the breaded veal scaloppini fried in olive oil and topped with proscuitto and mozzarella or the grilled tiger prawns with shiitake mushrooms and Italian parsley butter. This is a good choice for Italian food if you wish to dine outside a hotel but don't mind paying hotel restaurant prices.

7 Knutsford Terrace, Tsim Sha Tsui. © **852/2316 2116.** www.mhihk.com. Reservations recommended. Pasta HK$128–HK$218 (US$17–US$28/£9.15–£16); main courses HK$198–HK$268 (US$26–US$35/£14–£19). AE, DC, MC, V. Daily noon–3pm and 6–10:30pm. MTR: Tsim Sha Tsui.

Wu Kong ☞☞ SHANGHAINESE   This basement restaurant, in the heart of Tsim Sha Tsui, just off Nathan Road, is often packed during mealtimes with locals who come for the good food at excellent prices. More upscale than many Shanghainese restaurants, with its stark-white walls and pond with goldfish in the foyer, it serves a variety of shark's fin dishes, as well as the usual sautéed fresh prawns, braised shredded eels, braised eggplant with hot garlic sauce, stuffed bean curd, and other dishes common to Shanghai. Other selections include cold pigeon in wine sauce (its signature appetizer), Peking duck, and crispy duck. If you've had your fill of the more readily available and popular Cantonese and Sichuan food and are ready to experiment with other types of Chinese cuisine, this is an excellent place to start.

There's another branch on the 13th floor of Food Forum, Times Square, 1 Matheson St., Causeway Bay (© **852/2506 1018;** MTR: Causeway Bay), open daily from 11:45am to 3pm and 6 to 11:30pm.

27 Nathan Rd. (entrance on Peking Rd.), Tsim Sha Tsui. © **852/2366 7244.** www.wukong.com.hk. Main dishes HK$50–HK$180 (US$6.50–US$23/£3.55–£13). AE, DC, MC, V. Daily 11:30am–11:15pm. MTR: Tsim Sha Tsui.

INEXPENSIVE

These restaurants have branches in Tsim Sha Tsui: **PizzaExpress** (p. 146), specializing in pizza, is described in the Central dining section. **Sorabol** (p. 151), a Korean restaurant, and **California Pizza Kitchen** (p. 151), with salads, pastas, and sandwiches in addition to pizza, are both described in the Wan Chai/Causeway Bay section.

Fat Angelo's *Value* ITALIAN   With its checkered tablecloths, black-and-white family photographs, and other decor reminiscent of a New World Italian restaurant from the first half of the 20th century, this chain offers good value with its hearty, American renditions of Italian food, including pastas ranging from traditional spaghetti marinara to fettuccine with salmon and main courses that include rosemary roasted chicken, grilled salmon with pesto, and eggplant Parmesan, all of which come with salad and homemade bread. All pastas and main dishes come in two sizes to accommodate the Chinese penchant for sharing, with small dishes large enough for two to share. If you're a lone diner, you can request a half portion of the small dish. In any case, the emphasis here is on quantity, not quality, though the food isn't bad. And they really pack 'em in; this place is bustling, loud, and slightly chaotic, making it sometimes hard to flag down your waitress. Still, all in all, this place is good for a fun outing with a group.

There are three branches on the other side of the harbor, at 49A–C Elgin St., Central (✆ **852/2973 6808;** MTR: Central); Wu Chung House, 213 Queen's Rd. East, Wan Chai (✆ **852/2126 7020;** MTR: Wan Chai); and in the Elizabeth House, 250 Gloucester Rd. in Causeway Bay (✆ **852/2574 6263;** MTR: Causeway Bay). All are open daily noon to midnight.

Basement, The Pinnacle, 8 Minden Ave., Tsim Sha Tsui. ✆ 852/2730 4788. www.fatangelos.com. Reservations recommended. Small pastas HK$88–HK$178 (US$11–US$23/£6.30–£13); small main courses HK$128–HK$218 (US$17–US$28/£9.15–£16). AE, DC, MC, V. Daily noon–midnight. MTR: Tsim Sha Tsui.

Genki Sushi JAPANESE   Taking advantage of Hong Kong's surge in popularity of everything Japanese, this simple and always-crowded establishment offers plates of sushi, which circle around the counter via a conveyor belt. Customers, seated at the counter, simply reach out and take whatever they want. The color-coded plates vary in price and include traditional selections such as tuna and shrimp sushi, along with more unusual combinations like corn sushi, crab salad sushi, and California handrolls (seaweed rolled around rice, crab, and avocado). During lunch and dinner, there's often a line of customers waiting at the door (when I don't want to wait, I go straight inside and order takeout to bring back to my hotel). While the food is too generic to pass in Japan, this place is as good as it gets for rock-bottom sushi prices in Hong Kong.

Other branches can be found in Shop G36 on the ground floor of Chuang's London Plaza, 219 Nathan Rd., Jordan (✆ **852/2736 0019;** MTR: Jordan); on the ground floor of the Far East Finance Centre, 16 Harcourt Rd., Central (✆ **852/2865 2933;** MTR: Admiralty); Shop B222 in the second basement of Times Square, 1 Matheson St., Causeway Bay (✆ **852/2506 9366;** MTR: Causeway Bay); Shop P211A, Podium 2, World Trade Centre, Causeway Bay (✆ **852/2890 2600;** MTR: Causeway Bay); and Shop A, on the ground floor of the CRE Building, 303 Hennessy Rd., Wan Chai (✆ **852/2802 7018;** MTR: Wan Chai); all with the same open hours given below.

Shops G7–9, East Ocean Centre, 98 Granville Rd., Tsim Sha Tsui East. ✆ 852/2722 6689. www.genkisushi.com.sg. Main dishes HK$9–HK$35 (US$1.15–US$4.55/65p–£2.50). AE, DC, MC, V. Daily 11:30am–11:30pm. MTR: Tsim Sha Tsui.

Happy Garden Noodles & Congee Kitchen *Value* CANTONESE If you've passed all those hole-in-the-wall Chinese restaurants, knowing that they're often much cheaper than establishments catering to tourists but hesitating to enter because no one speaks English, this is the place for you. Small, clean, bright (too bright) lighting, and with old-fashioned booth seating, a high ceiling, and lacquered stools, it has an English menu and specializes in noodle dishes and congee (a rice porridge traditionally eaten for breakfast or a late-night snack and usually flavored with meat, fish, or vegetables). Approximately 40 different kinds of congee are available as well as a wide variety of noodle dishes, from braised and stir-fried noodles to shrimp wonton noodles and noodles in soup with barbecued pork. Although congee may not sound exciting, it's actually one of my favorite snack foods and can be very satisfying. Located about a 4-minute walk from the Star Ferry, this restaurant is especially good for a quick and inexpensive meal after visiting neighborhood bars.

72 Canton Rd., Tsim Sha Tsui. ℂ 852/2377 2604. Main dishes HK$28–HK$85 (US$3.65–US$11/£2–£6.05). No credit cards. Daily 7am–1am. MTR: Tsim Sha Tsui.

Koh-I-Noor *Finds* INDIAN Don't let the dinginess of the Peninsula Apartments building deter you from trying this restaurant. Located up on the first floor, it's modern and clean, with spotless tablecloths and a pleasant pink color scheme. What's more, service is prompt and courteous and the food is great and reasonably priced; the specialties here are North Indian tandoori and fresh seafood. It takes its name from a renowned diamond mined in central India years ago. The restaurant is especially proud of its king prawns, but there are also chicken, lamb, and vegetable curries; my favorites include the samosas, crab with coconut, and the Gosht vindaloo—a spicy mix of lamb and potatoes. There's mashed eggplant with onions and tomatoes; *palak paneer* (Indian cottage cheese with spinach); garlic-flavored nan (Indian flat bread) or nan stuffed with cheese, potatoes, or other ingredients. All of it is good and recommendable.

There's also a branch on the other side of the harbor in the Lan Kwai Fong nightlife district, on the first floor of the California Entertainment Building, 34 D'Aguilar St., Central (ℂ **852/2877 9706;** MTR: Central), open Monday through Saturday from noon to 2:30pm and daily from 6 to 11pm.

Peninsula Apartments, 16C Mody Rd., Tsim Sha Tsui. ℂ 852/2368 3065. www.lankwaifong.com. Curries HK$65–HK$150 (US$8.45–US$19/£4.65–£11); tandoori HK$70–HK$125 (US$9.10–US$16/£5–£8.90); buffet lunch (Mon–Fri only) HK$48 (US$6.25/£3.40) for vegetarian, HK$68 (US$8.85/£4.85) with meat. AE, DC, MC, V. Daily 11:30am–2:30pm and 6–11:30pm. MTR: Tsim Sha Tsui.

Main Street Deli *Finds* AMERICAN/SANDWICHES Hong Kong's first traditional New York–style deli comes as close as you can get to the real thing—its chef trained at the 2nd Avenue Deli in the Big Apple and the authentic ingredients are flown in from New York. The tiled floor, open kitchen, deli case, strung sausages, and wood furniture add to the ambience, but the chandeliers left over from a previous restaurant seem woefully out of place. Still, serious deli lovers will find plenty to love, including latkes, matzo ball soup, salads, pizza, pasta, burgers, and a large selection of three-decker and hot deli sandwiches, including a Reuben, the restaurant's signature sandwich (if you're counting carbs, order the Naked Reuben, which comes without bread). This is a lifesaver for those in desperate need of comfort food. Portions are so generous that the restaurant has instituted the doggy bag, a previously unknown concept in Hong Kong. Don't forget to save room for the cheesecake.

In the Langham Hotel, 8 Peking Rd., Tsim Sha Tsui. © 852/2375 1133, ext. 7883. www.langhamhotels.com. Sandwiches and burgers HK$98–HK$138 (US$13–US$18/£7–£9.85). AE, DC, MC, V. Sun–Thurs 10am–10pm; Fri–Sat 10am–11pm. MTR: Tsim Sha Tsui.

Nomads ✦ *Finds* ASIAN   This very popular Mongolian restaurant allows diners to select their own raw ingredients for one-dish meals that are then stir-fried by short-order cooks. All-you-can-eat lunches and dinners give choices of vegetables, meats, seafood, sauces, noodles, rice, and spices, spread buffet-style along a counter together with salads and dessert. Sheepskin-draped chairs, rawhide lampshades, animal skins, and tribal weaponry hung on walls transport this restaurant straight into the Mongolia of our fantasies, making dining here not only cheap but fun as well.

55 Kimberley Rd., Tsim Sha Tsui. © 852/2722 0733. www.igors.com. Lunch buffet HK$58 (US$7.55/£4.15) Mon–Thurs, HK$68 (US$8.85/£4.85) Fri–Sat; dinner buffet HK$168 (US$22/£12). AE, DC, MC, V. Daily noon–2:30pm and 6:30–10:30pm. MTR: Tsim Sha Tsui.

The Salisbury *Value* INTERNATIONAL   One of the cheapest places for a filling meal in Tsim Sha Tsui is the YMCA's main restaurant, a bright and cheerful nonsmoking dining hall located on the fourth floor of the south tower. It serves both Western and Asian food, with an a la carte menu offering sandwiches, pasta, and Asian dishes. Best, however, are the lunch and dinner buffets. The lunch buffet includes a roast-beef wagon, as well as other meat dishes, soups, salads, and desserts, while the dinner buffet includes many more entrees plus one soda or beer. A rare plus for seniors: They get a discount off the lunch buffet. While the food won't win any culinary awards, there's enough variety that probably everyone can find something they like. And if the prices here are too high, there's a cheaper ground-floor cafeteria, the Mall Cafe, which offers sandwiches and daily specials.

In The Salisbury YMCA, 41 Salisbury Rd., Tsim Sha Tsui. © 852/2268 7818. www.ymcahk.org.hk. Lunch buffet HK$98 (US$13/£7); Sun brunch buffet HK$140 (US$18/£10); dinner buffet HK$198 (US$26/£14) Mon–Thurs, HK$218 (US$28/£16) Fri–Sun. AE, DC, MC, V. Mon–Sat noon–2:30pm; Sun 11:30am–2:30pm; daily 6:15–9:30pm. MTR: Tsim Sha Tsui.

Spaghetti House *Kids* PIZZA/ITALIAN   The Spaghetti House chain has a total of 24 branches throughout Hong Kong—and there will probably be more by the time you read this. They're popular with families, young Chinese couples on dates, and foreigners who have had their fill of Chinese food and crave something familiar but cheap. Spaghetti and pizza cooked American-style or with Asian ingredients are the specialties here, and the decor and atmosphere resemble those of an American pizza parlor. There are more than a half-dozen varieties of spaghetti with both Western and Asian toppings, as well as pizzas (in two sizes). Although the food is only average in quality, the quantity more than makes up for it; most orders can be taken out.

Branches include 57 Peking Rd. (© 852/2367 1683) and 38 Haiphong Rd., both in Tsim Sha Tsui (© 852/2376 1015; MTR: Tsim Sha Tsui); 221 Nathan Rd., Yau Ma Tei (© 852/2377 2005; MTR: Jordan); 594 Nathan Rd., Mong Kok (© 852/2388 4379; MTR: Mong Kok); Shop 2004 in the International Finance Centre above Hong Kong Station, Central (© 852/2147 5543); 68 Hennessy Rd., Wan Chai (© 852/2529 0901; MTR: Wan Chai); Shop 8, PJ Plaza, Paterson St., Causeway Bay (© 852/2895 2928; MTR: Causeway Bay); and Shop P113, World Trade Centre, Causeway Bay (© 852/2972 2143l; MTR: Causeway Bay). All Spaghetti Houses are open daily 11am to 11pm.

32 Nathan Rd., Tsim Sha Tsui. © 852/2721 6703. www.spaghettihouse.com. Individual-size pizza and pasta HK$52–HK$88 (US$6.75–US$11/£3.70–£6.30). AE, DC, MC, V. Daily 11am–11pm. MTR: Tsim Sha Tsui.

Woodlands 🄥ₐₗᵤₑ INDIAN/VEGETARIAN   The focus of this very simple dining room, open since 1981 and looking slightly out of place on the ground floor of the Mirror Tower building in Tsim Sha Tsui East, is clearly on the food—vegetarian dishes from southern India, along with some selections from northern India. Best are the thali fixed-price meals, served on a round metal plate commonly used in India and including Indian bread, rice, and tiny portions of various dishes. Strangely, although the restaurant specializes in food from southern India, I find the North Indian thali tastier than its southern counterpart. Alcoholic drinks are not served, but there are fruit juices, milkshakes, Indian teas, and *lassi* (a yogurt shake).

Mirror Tower, 61 Mody Rd., Tsim Sha Tsui East. ℭ 852/2369 3718. Main dishes HK$35–HK$48 (US$4.55–US$6.25/£2.50–£3.40); fixed-price thali meals HK$55–HK$70 (US$7.15–US$9.10/£3.90–£5). AE, DC, MC, V. Daily noon–3pm and 6:30–10:30pm (last order). MTR: Tsim Sha Tsui.

5 Central District

VERY EXPENSIVE

Caprice 🟊🟊🟊 FRENCH   Ensconced in the sleek Four Seasons Hotel Hong Kong, this is *the* restaurant of the moment, and deservedly so (need I add that reservations are a must?). Under the skilled guidance of chef Vincent Thiery, brought from Le Cinq in the Four Seasons George V Paris where he worked as sous-chef, Caprice garners high marks for its innovative take on French classics. The restaurant's gorgeous setting, with dramatic views of Victoria Harbour, echoes the contemporary/classic theme, with a glowing catwalk leading diners into the dining room, portraits of women that combine an Art Nouveau style with Chinese influences adorning one

---

⟮Kids⟯ Family-Friendly Restaurants

Al's Diner (p. 145)   This may be the perfect antidote for restless teenagers who are threatening mutiny if they don't see any "real food" soon. It's located in Central's nightlife district (which might perk your teenager's interest) and offers burgers, hot dogs, sandwiches, sundaes, ice-cream floats, and banana splits. The tableside jukeboxes are a good diversion, too, but make sure you come during the day or early evening, since the house specialty, vodka jelly shots, attracts a wild crowd at night that may provide a bit more excitement than you want for your teenager.

Dan Ryan's Chicago Grill (p. 126)   These two restaurant/bars serve the best burgers in town, as well as huge deli sandwiches. There are plenty of other American dishes as well, and the setting looks just like home.

Spaghetti House (p. 134)   Locations all over town and low prices make this family chain a winner. There are more than a half-dozen different kinds of spaghetti, as well as a wide range of pizza. Just like pizza parlors back home.

Top Deck, at the Jumbo (p. 154)   A short shuttle by boat through Aberdeen harbor should catch any child's attention, but this alfresco seafood restaurant on top of a huge floating restaurant follows through with a children's menu and a play corner, allowing parents to relax as they soak in the views and feast on everything from salmon and sushi to steaks and curries.

wall, an open kitchen, and shimmering, custom-made chandeliers. The knowledgeable staff is happy to make recommendations from the menu, orchestrated around the seasons and drawing inspiration from provincial influences throughout France. You might, for example, opt for the pan-sautéed scallops with black truffles, nest of capellini pasta, butternut squash and Parmesan cream, or perhaps the warm duck foie gras with Granny Smith compote, beet root, and dry sherry. If making a decision is too painful, there's a fixed-price tasting menu for HK$1,080 (US$140/£77) per person; or, for a ringside seat of the kitchen's activity, there's the Chef's Table, which seats up to eight people and has a minimum group charge of HK$8,000 (US$1,038/£571) for lunch and HK$12,000 (US$1,558/£857) for dinner.

In the Four Seasons Hotel Hong Kong, 8 Finance St., Central. © 852/3196 8888. www.fourseasons.com/hongkong. Reservations required. Main courses HK$330–HK$690 (US$43–US$90/£24–£49). AE, DC, MC, V. Daily noon–2:30pm and 6–10:30pm. MTR: Central.

Nicholini's ★★★ ITALIAN   Most of Hong Kong's Italian restaurants seem to fall into one of two categories—highbrow and sophisticated, or rustic and trattoria-like. This one is neither and yet both, combining elegance and lightheartedness in keeping with the Conrad Hotel's overall playful style. Dress is casual to smart casual (though no jeans or tennis shoes are allowed), and the dining room bathes patrons in soothing colors of celadon green, yellow, and plum rose. If you're a fan of Murano glass, be sure to check out the collection at the front of the restaurant. The cuisine here is northern Italian, combined with inventiveness—some claim it's the best Italian restaurant in Hong Kong. Entrees range from roasted sea bass with herbs to veal shank *osso buco* in a vegetable orange-flavored sauce served with saffron risotto. Pasta—like the favorite angel-hair pasta with Maine lobster, fresh tomato, and basil—is available as either a side dish or a main course. For dessert, the Chef's Special Dessert Sampler solves the dilemma for those who want it all. The wine list, mainly Italian but also with international selections, is extensive and the service is beyond reproach. Too bad this restaurant doesn't have a view.

In the Conrad Hotel, Pacific Place, 88 Queensway Rd., Central. © 852/2521 3838, ext. 8210. www.conradhotels.com. Reservations recommended. Main courses HK$295–HK$580 (US$38–US$75/£21–£41); fixed-price dinner HK$628–HK$688 (US$82–US$89/£45–£49); fixed-price lunch HK$248–HK$348 (US$32–US$45/£18–£25). AE, DC, MC, V. Mon–Fri noon–3pm; Sun 11am–3pm; daily 6:30–11pm. MTR: Central.

Petrus ★★★ (Finds) FRENCH   Simply put, the views from this 56th-floor restaurant are breathtaking. In fact, they are probably the best of any hotel restaurant on the Hong Kong side; the only place with a better view is atop Victoria Peak. If you can bear to take your eyes off the windows, you'll find the restaurant decorated like a French castle, with the obligatory crystal chandeliers, black marble and gilded columns, statues, thick draperies, Impressionist paintings, murals gracing dome-shaped ceilings, and a pianist playing softly in the background.

The cuisine emphasizes contemporary Mediterranean/French seasonal ingredients, spiced sparingly to complement the dishes' natural aroma and flavor. The menu changes often but has included such intriguing choices as gooseliver confit ravioli with black truffles or poached salmon with garlic, black olives, and artichokes. Probably the best way to sample the continuously new creations is with one of the fixed-price meals. As expected, the wine list—particularly bordeaux—is among the best in Hong Kong, if not the world. With the impressive blend of great views, refined ambience, excellent cuisine, tables spaced far enough apart for intimacy, and professional staff, this restaurant is a top choice for a splurge, romantic dinner, or special celebration.

In the Island Shangri-La (56th floor), Pacific Place, Supreme Court Rd., Central. © **852/2820 8590**. www.shangri-la. com. Reservations recommended. Jacket required. Main courses HK$350–HK$800 (US$45–US$104/£25–£57); fixed-price lunch HK$338–HK$388 (US$44–US$50/£24–£27); fixed-price dinner HK$980 (US$127/£70). AE, DC, MC, V. Daily noon–3pm and 6:30–11pm. MTR: Admiralty.

EXPENSIVE

In addition to the restaurants here, **Ruth's Chris Steak House,** reviewed in the Kowloon section above (p. 124), has a branch near Pacific Place.

Baci 👒👒 ITALIAN   On the second floor, above a less expensive pizzeria under the same ownership, this smart-looking restaurant with a crisp, white, minimalist interior boasts a friendly staff and authentic Italian cuisine. Ingredients are flown fresh from Italy, and the pasta is homemade. Recommended are the *osso buco* braised in Barbera d'Alba wine and served with saffron risotto or the pan-fried monk fish medallions wrapped in pancetta ham and served in a porcini mushroom sauce crowned by grilled shrimp. You can also order pizza, which comes with a crispy-thin and delicious crust. There's also a small bar, with windows that open to the madness of Lan Kwai Fong below.

1 Lan Kwai Fong (2nd floor), Central. © **852/2801 5885**. www.lankwaifong.com. Reservations recommended. Pizza HK$98–HK$145 (US$13–US$19/£7–£10); main courses HK$185–HK$398 (US$24–US$52/£13–£28); fixed-price lunch HK$150 (US$19/£11). AE, DC, MC, V. Mon–Sat noon–2:30pm; Mon–Thurs 7–11pm; Fri–Sat 7–11:30pm; Sun 6:30–10:30pm. MTR: Central.

Cafe des Artistes 👒👒 FRENCH   This upscale restaurant is in the heart of Lan Kwai Fong yet remains aloof, removed from the milling crowds by its subdued setting. Dining here imparts a feeling of being above it all, but the real draw is the cuisine from southern France, expertly rendered by the chef into classic culinary masterpieces. The duck foie gras is not to be missed; other recommended dishes include the cassoulet (a stew of duck leg, Toulouse sausage, bacon, and white beans), the grilled sea bass and scallops with a creamy sea-urchin sauce, and the flambé beef tenderloin and foie gras with a morel sauce and potato gratin. Be sure to save room for desserts like the restaurant's legendary hazelnut chocolate soufflé.

California Tower (ground floor), 30–32 D'Aguilar St., Central. © **852/2526 3880**. www.lankwaifong.com. Main courses HK$190–HK$225 (US$25–US$29/£14–£16); fixed-price lunch HK$165–HK$185 (US$21–US$24/£12–£13); fixed-price dinner HK$350 (US$45/£25). AE, DC, MC, V. Mon–Sat noon–2:30pm; Sun–Thurs 7–10:30pm; Fri–Sat 7–11pm. MTR: Central.

Gaia Ristorante 👒 *Finds* ITALIAN   If you can't beat 'em, join 'em. That's the way I feel about all the new construction encroaching on the quaint Western District. This restaurant, ensconced in the colossal Grand Millennium Plaza building on the border between the Central and Western districts, has won me over with a great terrace, surrounded by lush trees and bushes that create the illusion of dining in a park. The contemporary interior is also inviting, with glass windows overlooking the terrace and a blindingly red bar off to one side. Of course, none of this would matter if the food didn't hold up, which it does. It's hard to resist such temptations as the homemade pasta tossed in a sangiovese-marinated rabbit stew ragout; the seared tuna with black pepper, capers, Black Liguria olives, and oregano paste; or the chargrilled black angus beef. The wine list is heavy on Italian imports.

Grand Millennium Plaza (look for the advertising screen), 181 Queen's Rd. Central, Central. © **852/2167 8200**. www.gaiaristorante.com. Reservations necessary. Pizza and pasta HK$158–HK$218 (US$21–US$28/£11–£16); main dishes HK$228–HK$328 (US$30–US$43/£16–£23); fixed-price lunch HK$228 (US$30/£16). AE, DC, MC, V. Daily noon–3pm and 6:30–11pm. MTR: Sheung Wan.

Hunan Garden 🐟🐟 *Finds* HUNANESE   Although the chile-rich cuisine of Hunan province is quite popular in Taiwan, this has long been one of the few Hunan restaurants in Hong Kong. It's puzzling, because Hunanese food is very spicy, and one would think that with the booming popularity of Thai and Sichuan food in the SAR Hunanese food would eventually catch on. In any case, this restaurant does a thriving business, especially for lunch due to its location next to Hong Kong Station (terminus of the Airport Express Line) and ifc mall. It's a great restaurant, both in decor and food, and even has live Chinese classical music from 7 to 9pm nightly. It's decorated in hot pink and green, and the motif is clearly lotus (Hunan province is famous for its lotus). The dining area is spacious, with tables spread luxuriously far apart. But the real treat is the food. The chefs were trained in both Hunan province and Taiwan and they don't tone down the spiciness of their authentic dishes. Start your meal with one of the soups like the Hunan minced-chicken soup, a clear soup base with ginger and mousse of chicken, served piping hot in a length of bamboo. If you like hot-and-spicy foods, you'll love the braised bean curd with shredded pork and chile, developed by one of Hunan province's most famous chefs. Other recommended dishes include the honey-glazed Hunan ham served in pancakes and fried chicken with chile and garlic. As a special treat, try one of the Hunanese wines.

The Forum (3rd floor), Exchange Square, Central. ✆ 852/2868 2880. Reservations required, especially for lunch. Main dishes HK$72–HK$168 (US$9.35–US$22/£5.15–£12). AE, DC, MC, V. Daily 11:30am–3pm and 5:30–11:30pm. MTR: Central.

Isola 🐟🐟 *Finds* ITALIAN   This Central newcomer bills itself as Hong Kong's most stunning waterfront restaurant. While there are other waterfront properties, what sets this one apart is its extensive outdoor terrace with panoramic views over the harbor, along with a popular bar with views and a balcony. Even in inclement weather, the restaurant's crisp white interior with a glass facade is an inviting venue. But don't expect a quiet tête-à-tête, since this bustling place, with an open kitchen, does a roaring business. All the pasta is handmade, the large, stone-baked, thin-crust pizzas can be ordered with different ingredients on each half (making them good for two people to share), and all the meat and fish arrive fresh at the restaurant instead of frozen. Main dishes include the likes of oven-broiled black cod with lemon, capers, and parsley and roasted veal chop with sage mashed potatoes, asparagus, and mushroom sauce. Lunch is a good time for grazers, who can choose their meal entirely from the antipasto buffet (which costs HK$188/US$24/£13 weekdays and HK$198/US$26/£14 weekends) or add a main dish to create their own fixed-price meal.

Levels 3 & 4, ifc mall, Central. ✆ 852/2383 8765. www.isolabarandgrill.com. Reservations required. Pizza and pasta HK$128–HK$238 (US$17–US$31/£9.15–£17); main courses HK$198–HK$338 (US$26–US$44/£14–£24); fixed-price lunch HK$218 (US$28/£16) Mon–Fri, HK$258 (US$33/£18) Sat–Sun. AE, DC, MC, V. Daily noon–2:30pm; Sun–Thurs 6:30–11pm; Fri–Sat 6:30–11:30pm. MTR: Central.

M at the Fringe 🐟🐟🐟 *Finds* CONTINENTAL   For a memorable, unusual dining experience, head for this delightful restaurant, located on the upper floor of a former dairy farm building, which is also home of the Fringe Club's theater (p. 225). This has long been a local favorite, with a meal here a treat in more ways than one: The artsy furnishings are a feast for the eyes, while the food, influenced by cuisines along the Mediterranean, is to die for. The handwritten menu changes every 3 months but is always creative and always includes lamb and vegetarian selections. An example of the former is a salt-encased, slowly baked leg of lamb with mashed roots and roasted beet root. The lunch menu includes a list of starters, all priced at HK$78 (US$10/£5.55), and main dishes that cost HK$138 (US$18/£9.85). Whatever you choose, don't pass up the Pavlova for dessert. Note that this is actually a private club, but nonmembers can dine here by paying a HK$15 (US$1.95/£1.05) temporary membership fee.

2 Lower Albert Rd., Central. © 852/2877 4000. www.m-atthefringe.com. Reservations strongly recommended. Main courses HK$208–HK$256 (US$27–US$33/£15–£18). AE, MC, V. Mon–Fri noon–2:30pm; daily 7–10:30pm. MTR: Central.

Va Bene ★★ ITALIAN This stylish, upscale Italian restaurant, in the middle of Central's Lan Kwai Fong nightlife district, strives for elegant simplicity in both food and decor. The long, dimly lit dining room's most eye-catching features are a wine cellar that extends the length of one wall and a sky-blue ceiling etched with floating clouds. With consistently creative and excellent, mostly northern Italian food, it has been popular with Hong Kong's well-heeled expat community for more than a decade. Perhaps you'll want to start with wafer-thin carpaccio, followed by one of the homemade pastas (available in two sizes) like fresh pasta pockets filled with meat ragout in sage, butter, bacon, and black truffle. As a main course, you can choose from a number of veal, beef, and seafood dishes that utilize fresh ingredients cooked in a style to draw out natural flavors, including pan-fried John Dory (a white Australian fish) served with a lemon and caper sauce, or breast of chicken with gooseliver and braised endives. Good Italian wines, great desserts, and attentive service round out the meal.

17–22 Lan Kwai Fong., Central. © 852/2845 5577. www.vabeneristorante.com. Reservations required. Pasta HK$108–HK$198 (US$14–US$26/£7.70–£14); main courses HK$228–HK$348 (US$30–US$45/£16–£25); fixed-price lunch HK$198 (US$26/£14). AE, DC, MC, V. Mon–Fri noon–2:30pm; Sun–Thurs 6:30–11:30pm; Fri–Sat 6:30pm–midnight. MTR: Central.

MODERATE

Several moderately priced restaurants already covered in the Tsim Sha Tsui section have branches in Central: **Dan Ryan's Chicago Grill** (p. 126), located in Pacific Place and offering American classics; **Peking Garden** (p. 129), with two locations in Central and serving food from Beijing; **Super Star Seafood Restaurant** (p. 130), known for its Cantonese seafood and dim sum; and **Tsui Hang Village Restaurant** (p. 130), serving Cantonese fare.

café TOO ★★★ *Finds* INTERNATIONAL Leave it to the Island Shangri-La to take a common dining concept and turn it into a feasting extravaganza. Quite simply, this is the most interesting buffet I've seen in Hong Kong. Light and airy with windows overlooking the lush greenery of Hong Kong Park, contemporary decor, and a well-trained staff dressed in hip traditional Chinese jackets and vests, this restaurant features open kitchens and seven "stations" of food presentations spread throughout the room, thereby dispelling the assembly-line atmosphere of most buffets and giving it a theatrical touch. Browse the appetizer-and-salad table, a cold seafood counter with sushi, fresh oysters, crab, and other delights, a Chinese section with dim sum and main courses, Western hot entrees, noodles that are prepared to order and run the gamut from Chinese to Italian, and Asian dishes from Thai curries to Indian tandoori. But don't fill up, because the dessert table is the crowning glory. The wine list, too, is very impressive. Come here after shopping in Pacific Place or visiting the park's Museum of Tea Ware.

In the Island Shangri-La Hotel, Pacific Place, Supreme Court Rd., Central. © 852/2820 8571. www.shangri-la.com. Reservations recommended. Lunch buffet HK$258 (US$34/£18) Mon–Sat, HK$298 (US$37/£21) Sun and holidays; dinner buffet HK$358 (US$46/£26) Mon–Thurs, HK$388 (US$58/£28) Fri–Sun and holidays. AE, DC, MC, V. Mon–Fri noon–2:30pm; Sat–Sun noon–3pm; Mon–Thurs 6:30–10pm; Fri–Sun 6–11pm. MTR: Admiralty.

Dot Cod Seafood Restaurant & Oyster Bar *Value* SEAFOOD   The Hong Kong Cricket Club owns this basement restaurant (HKCC members get a 30% discount), its location chosen for nostalgic reasons: Until the 1960s, the club practiced in nearby Chater Garden. Decorated in a nautical theme and popular for power breakfasts and lunches (though tables placed too close together rule out secretive deals), it takes its name from the popular choice of cod in its menu but is also a play on the dot.com era. Service is prompt and polished. You might start with the prawn cocktail, followed by such signature dishes as the cod fish and chips or baked salmon in aluminum foil with black beans, chile, and garlic. Check the website for monthly specials like the "B.Y.O. Bottle" Monday and Tuesday evenings, when corkage fees are waived for bottles of wine you bring to the restaurant. Combine that with the fixed-price dinner for two (HK$550/US$71/£39), and you've got a bargain.

Prince's Building, 10 Chater (entrance on Statue Square), Central. 𝄐 852/2810 6988. www.dotcod.com. Reservations recommended. Main dishes HK$168–HK$268 (US$22–US$35/£12–£19). AE, DC, MC, V. Mon–Sat 7:30am–10:30pm (last order). MTR: Central.

Grappa's 𝄐 ITALIAN   If you like to eat pizza or pasta to the accompaniment of noise, commotion, and lots of people parading past, this is the place for you. Grappa's is decorated like a trattoria, but with big glass windows overlooking the shops of Pacific Place; you can't escape the fact that this place is not a sidewalk cafe but is in a mall. The open kitchen, while providing some diversion, adds to the noise. Still, this is certainly the best place for moderately priced Italian food anywhere in the area, even though it is strictly standard fare, because all the sauces, pasta, sausages, and desserts are made in the restaurant's own kitchen. Homemade bread, served with olive oil and fresh Parmesan, is brought swiftly to every table (and replenished if desired); it is so delicious that you may be tempted to eat your fill before the meal arrives, especially if the place is full and service is slow. The salads are good here, as are the dozen or so authentic Italian pizzas and the even larger selection of homemade pastas. The entrees lean toward the tried and true, from veal-shank stew in Barolo red-wine sauce to roasted lamb chops with rosemary. The Italian wines here are affordable.

Pacific Place, 88 Queensway, Central. 𝄐 852/2868 0086. www.elgrande.com.hk. Reservations recommended. Pizza and pasta HK$92–HK$160 (US$12–US$21/£6.55–£11); main courses HK$118–HK$280 (US$15–US$36/£8.40–£20); fixed-price lunch HK$155 (US$20/£11). AE, DC, MC, V. Daily 11:30am–10:30pm (last order). MTR: Admiralty.

Hanagushi JAPANESE   The only thing missing at this traditionally styled Japanese restaurant, with its gleaming woods, tansu chests, woodblock prints, and waitresses decked out in provincial Japanese clothing, are tatami mats. Unfortunately, the tables are so closely packed here that you'd think you were in a Tokyo subway. The restaurant specializes in yakitori, morsels of food barbecued on a stick, with 46 different kinds available and costing HK$25 to HK$80 (US$3.25–US$10/£1.75–£5.70) for a pair. My favorites include asparagus, chicken meatballs, green pepper with minced chicken, and gingko nuts. You can also order fixed-price meals of yakitori (including a vegetarian version), teppanyaki, tempura or sashimi. Grilled fish, *udon* noodles, and other typical Japanese fare are also available, along with a dozen different kinds of sake to wash it all down.

17–22 Lan Kwai Fong (1st floor), Central. 𝄐 852/2521 0868. www.lankwaifong.com. Main dishes HK$65–HK$195 (US$8.45–US$25/£4.60–£14); fixed-price meals HK$200–HK$280 (US$26–US$36/£14–£20). AE, DC, MC, V. Mon–Sat 11:30am–3pm and 6–11:30pm. MTR: Central.

Indochine 1929 🦀🦀 VIETNAMESE· Designed to resemble a breezy, 1920s veranda from Vietnam's French colonial era with its wooden shutters, ceiling fans, fringed lampshades, wicker chairs, and tropical plants, this Lan Kwai Fong eatery serves delicious Indochinese cuisine to a consciously trendy crowd. Start with the signature spring rolls stuffed with shrimp, pork, and herbs or the hot-and-sour fish soup. Other specialties are the fish prepared Hanoi-style, with dill, turmeric, rice vermicelli, and peanuts; the salt-and-pepper soft-shell crabs; and the beef tenderloin with tomato. If you've never had Vietnamese food, this restaurant with a knowledgeable staff and laid-back atmosphere should make you an instant convert.

California Tower (2nd floor), 30–32 D'Aguilar, Central. ⓒ 852/2869 7399. www.lankwaifong.com. Reservations recommended. Main dishes HK$125–HK$260 (US$16–US$34/£8.90–£19); fixed-price lunch HK$92–HK$152 (US$12–US$20/£6.55–£11). AE, DC, MC, V. Mon–Sat noon–2:30pm; daily 6:30–11pm. MTR: Central.

Jimmy's Kitchen 🦀 CONTINENTAL This restaurant opened in 1928, a replica of a similar American-owned restaurant in Shanghai. Now one of Hong Kong's oldest Western restaurants, Jimmy's Kitchen has had several homes before moving in the 1960s to its present site. Some of its waiters are descendants from the original staff. The atmosphere reminds me of an American steakhouse, with white tablecloths, dark-wood paneling, and elevator music, but it's a favorite with older foreigners living in Hong Kong and serves dependably good, unpretentious European food. The daily specials are written on a blackboard, and an extensive a la carte menu offers salads and soups, steaks, chicken, Indian curries, and a seafood selection that includes sole, scallops, and the local garoupa. It's also a good place for corned beef and cabbage, beef stroganoff, and hearty German fare, including Wiener schnitzel (breaded veal), pig's knuckle, and knackwurst sausage.

There's a branch at 29 Ashley Rd., Tsim Sha Tsui (ⓒ 852/2376 0327; MTR: Tsim Sha Tsui), open the same hours.

1 Wyndham St., Central. ⓒ 852/2526 5293. www.jimmys.com. Main courses HK$142–HK$265 (US$18–US$34/£10–£19); fixed-price meal HK$208–HK$248 (US$27–US$32/£15–£18). AE, DC, MC, V. Daily 11:30am–3pm and 6–11pm. MTR: Central.

Le Parisien 🦀 𝘝𝘢𝘭𝘶𝘦 FRENCH Outside of hotels, this is the only French restaurant with a view of the harbor, and its convenient location in the ifc mall next to Hong Kong Station makes it a popular venue for well-attired business professionals. The friendly staff delivers fixed-price lunches that provide a choice of main dish and accompaniments. Dinner entrees, with an emphasis on freshness and seasonal choices, can include the likes of pan-roasted codfish, mushroom ravioli and creamed beans with capers in a butter sauce; roasted spring chicken; or pan-fried Dover sole. Avoid the lunchtime crunch; otherwise, instead of gazing on dreamy views of ferries coming and going, you might be shunted to one of the tables placed out in the shopping mall.

Ifc mall, Shop 2076 (Level 2), Central. ⓒ 852/2805 5293. Reservations recommended. Main courses HK$190–HK$350 (US$25–US$45/£14–£25); fixed-price lunch HK$178–HK$240 (US$23–US$31/£12–£17). AE, DC, MC, V. Mon–Fri 11:30am–2:30pm; Sat 11:30am–3pm; daily 6–11pm. MTR: Central.

Le Tire Bouchon 🦀🦀 𝘍𝘪𝘯𝘥𝘴 FRENCH This dark, cozy bistro near the Central–Mid-Levels Escalator was first established in 1986 and claims to be Hong Kong's oldest independent restaurant with a French chef. It sports a Parisian, casual atmosphere and serves classic French food heavy on the sauces. You might wish to start with escargots with garlic and parsley butter, moving on to beef filet in port-wine and shallot sauce, fresh duck liver, or steak with black peppercorn sauce. Fatten up even more on any of the sumptuous desserts, and indulge in one of the 190-some bottles of French wines from the restaurant's climatically controlled cellar. You probably wouldn't want to eat like this every day, but you certainly won't regret it while you're here.

48 Graham St., Central. (✆) 852/2523 5459. www.hkdining.com. Reservations recommended. Main courses HK$160–HK$280 (US$21–US$36/£11–£20); fixed-price lunch HK$98–HK$118 (US$13–US$15/£7–£8.40). AE, DC, MC, V. Mon–Sat noon–2:30pm and 6:30–10:30pm. MTR: Central.

Luk Yu Tea House 🐠🐠🐠 CANTONESE   Luk Yu, first opened in 1933, is the most famous teahouse remaining in Hong Kong. In fact, unless you have a time machine, you can't get any closer to old Hong Kong than this wonderful Art Deco–era Cantonese restaurant, with its ceiling fans, spittoons, individual wooden booths for couples, marble tabletops, wood paneling, and stained-glass windows. It's also one of the best places to try a few Chinese teas, including *bo lai* (a fermented black tea, which is the most common tea in Hong Kong; also spelled bo lay), jasmine, *lung ching* (a green tea), and *sui sin* (narcissus or daffodil).

But Luk Yu is most famous for its dim sum, served from 7am to 5:30pm. The problem for foreigners, however, is that the place is always packed with regulars who have their own special places to sit, and the staff is sometimes surly to newcomers. In addition, if you come after 11am, dim sum is no longer served by trolley but from an English menu with pictures but no prices, which could end up being quite expensive unless you ask before ordering. If you want to come during the day (certainly when Luk Yu is most colorful), try to bring along a Chinese friend. Otherwise, consider coming for dinner when it's not nearly so hectic and there's an English menu listing more than 200 items, including all the Cantonese favorites, though you'll be surrounded mostly by tourists.

24–26 Stanley St., Central. (✆) 852/2523 5464. Main dishes HK$110–HK$280 (US$14–US$36/£7.85–£20); dim sum HK$25–HK$55 (US$3.25–US$7.15/£1.80–£3.90). MC, V. Daily 7am–10pm. MTR: Central.

Post 97 🐠 *Value* CONTINENTAL   This is one of the old-timers in Lan Kwai Fong, opened in 1982 (its name is a cheeky reference to the handover), but it's every bit as popular as it was before all the surrounding competition moved in. That proves it must be doing something right, which it is—down-to-earth good food, reasonable prices, cheerful staff, an inviting bar with daily happy hours, and a comfortable, laid-back atmosphere where diners feel at home. Catering to area businesspeople during the day and to night revelers in the evening, it offers an all-day menu that includes breakfast items like eggs Benedict (free coffee refills until 11:30am), salads (like the detox salad, good after a night of carousing), and lighter fare, adding more entrees for dinner such as beef tenderloin, grilled duck breast, and roasted Chilean sea bass. Fixed-price meals are an especially good deal, allowing you to choose from the regular menu.

9 Lan Kwai Fong, Central. (✆) 852/2186 1817. www.ninetysevengroup.com. Main dishes HK$90–HK$175 (US$12–US$23/£6.40–£13); fixed-price lunch HK$125 (US$16/£8.90); fixed-price dinner HK$197–HK$250 (US$26–US$32/£14–£18). AE, DC, MC, V. Sun–Thurs 9:30am–1am; Fri–Sat 9:30am–2am. MTR: Central.

Shanghai Garden SHANGHAINESE   This upscale restaurant (part of the Maxim's group of restaurants) does a good job in presentation and cuisine. Since Shanghai does not have its own cuisine, the dishes served here are from Peking, Nanking, Sichuan, Hangchow, and Wuxi, as well as a few from Shanghai. The menu is extensive, including bird's nest and chicken soup or shark's-fin soup, such cold dishes as sautéed eel, and such main courses as sautéed prawns, beggar's chicken (which costs HK$280/US$36/£20 and must be ordered in advance), sautéed beef with spring onion, braised pig with vegetables, fried noodles Shanghai-style, and Peking duck (HK$280/US$36/£20). This place, pleasantly and soothingly decorated, does a roaring business, especially for lunch, when it also serves dim sum.

Hutchinson House (1st floor), Murray Rd., Central. ℂ 852/2524 8181. Reservations recommended. Main dishes HK$68–HK$250 (US$8.85–US$32/£4.85–£18); dim sum HK$20–HK$48 (US$2.60–US$6.25/£1.40–£3.40). AE, DC, MC, V. Daily 11:30am–3pm and 5:30–11pm. MTR: Central.

Sichuan Garden ☻ SICHUAN   Another Maxim's restaurant, the Sichuan Garden is a brightly lit, informal eatery in the basement of the Pacific Place mall, right next to Peking Garden. What it lacks in decor, it makes up for with excellent food at reasonable prices. It's quite popular and almost always crowded, especially at lunch. The hot-and-spicy dishes are clearly marked on the 80-item menu to help the uninitiated, though those who love fiery food will find that dishes here are only mildly hot. Recommended are the hot-and-sour soup, fried prawns in chile sauce, shredded pork in hot garlic sauce, bean curd with minced beef in a pungent sauce, smoked duck, and pigeon smoked in camphor wood and tea leaves. I ordered the pigeon and found it quite good, but I was not prepared to have the head brought out as well.

Shop 004, Pacific Place, 88 Queensway, ℂ 852/2845 8433. Reservations recommended. Main dishes HK$80–HK$160 (US$10–US$21/£5.70–£11). AE, DC, MC, V. Mon–Sat 11:30am–3pm and 5:30–11:30pm; Sun and holidays 11am–3pm and 5:30–11:30pm. MTR: Admiralty.

The Square ☻ CANTONESE   Opened in 2000 to capture some of the increased traffic in this area due to Hong Kong Station next door, this smartly decorated restaurant features flowers on each table and cabinets filled with Chinese antiques. On weekday evenings, a trio performs live music of popular tunes. The menu includes both traditional dishes and original creations, with an emphasis on presentation. Recommended are the homemade crispy chicken, minced pigeon with lettuce leaves, and barbecue suckling pig with a sweet dipping sauce. Dim sum is also available for lunch on weekends and holidays, with only a limited number served on weekdays.

Exchange Square II, Central. ℂ 852/2525 1163. Reservations required for lunch, recommended for dinner. Main dishes HK$88–HK$238 (US$11–US$31/£6.30–£17); fixed-price lunch (Mon–Fri only) HK$208–HK$298 (US$27–US$37/£15–£21). AE, DC, MC, V. Daily 11am–3pm and 6–11pm. MTR: Central.

Thai Lemongrass ☻☻ THAI   Rattan furniture, fake banana trees, and statues of Buddha set the mood in this upscale Thai restaurant in Lan Kwai Fong. The menu, drawing from regional cuisines from throughout Thailand and prepared by Thai chefs, includes such favorites as soft-shell crab with chile and garlic on fried basil leaves, steamed fish, and chicken in green curry. Unlike most Thai restaurants in Hong Kong, which often serve a watered-down version of Thai food, this one serves the real thing.

30–32 D'Aguilar St., Central. ℂ 852/2905 1688. www.lankwaifong.com. Main dishes HK$118–HK$220 (US$15–US$29/£8.40–£16); fixed-price lunch HK$138 (US$13/£9.85). AE, DC, MC, V. Mon–Sat noon–2:30pm; Mon–Thurs 6:30–11pm; Fri–Sat 6:30–11:30pm; Sun and holidays 6–10:30pm. MTR: Central.

Tokio Joe ☻ JAPANESE   As its quirky name suggests, this is a hip sushi bar catering to Lan Kwai Fong's youthful nighttime revelers. Dimly lit even for lunch, it offers sushi (raw seafood on vinegared rice) and sashimi (raw seafood) a la carte, as well as combination platters, prepared by Chinese sushi chefs trained in Japan. A platter of assorted sashimi large enough for two people to share as an appetizer costs HK$490 (US$64/£35); sushi combinations run from HK$150 to HK$360 (US$20–US$47/£11–£26). Unique, however, are the California-style roll creations, like the deep-fried soft-shell crab with avocado, cucumber, crab roe, and mayonnaise, and original dishes like the rock shrimp salad. Probably the best deal is one of the set lunches, featuring sashimi, tempura, or a box lunch. As the menu states, this restaurant has a "slightly irreverent, innovative, and casual approach to the Japanese culinary experience." Luckily, it succeeds.

16 Lan Kwai Fong, Central. © 852/2525 1889. www.lankwaifong.com. Sushi a la carte HK$35–HK$65 (US$4.55–US$8.45/£2.50–£4.60); fixed-price lunch HK$120–HK$190 (US$16–US$25/£8.55–£14). AE, DC, MC, V. Mon–Sat noon–2:30pm; daily 6:30–11pm. MTR: Central.

Yung Kee 🏵🏵 CANTONESE   Popular for decades, Yung Kee started out in 1942 as a small shop selling roast goose, which did so well that it soon expanded into a very successful Cantonese enterprise. Through the years, it has won numerous food awards and is the only restaurant in Hong Kong ever to be included in *Fortune* magazine's top 15 restaurants of the world (although, it must be added, the award was back in 1968). Its specialty is still roast goose with plum sauce, cooked to perfection with tender meat on the inside and crispy skin on the outside; a half bird, enough for five or six people, costs HK$180 (US$23/£13), while a smaller portion for two people costs HK$100 (US$13/£7.15; note that goose is pulled from the menu any time there's an avian flu scare). Other specialties include thousand-year-old eggs and any of the fresh seafood. Set meals, for two or more people, start at HK$300 (US$39/£21) per person. Dining is on one of the upper three floors, but if all you want is a bowl of congee or takeout, join the office workers who pour in for a quick meal on the informal ground floor.

32–40 Wellington St., Central. © 852/2522 1624. www.yungkee.com.hk. Main dishes HK$78–HK$180 (US$10–US$23/£5.55–£13). AE, DC, MC, V. Daily 11am–11:30pm. MTR: Central.

Zen Chinese 🏵🏵 CANTONESE   Both its name and its appearance leave no doubt that this is no ordinary Cantonese restaurant. Indeed, it became an instant trendsetter when it opened in 1989, eschewing the traditional flashy decor favored by most Chinese restaurants in favor of an austere Zen Buddhist style, with an open dining hall that allowed customers to see and be seen. To offset the simplicity and starkness of the room, a succession of large glass bowls running the length of the restaurant are suspended from the ceiling, creating a never-ending cascade as water trickles from one red bowl to the next; some think the arrangement looks like a dragon.

As for the food, there is a wide variety of Cantonese specialties that border on the nouvelle. Try the shark's-fin soup with minced chicken, sautéed prawns with dried chile and walnuts, or sautéed crab in an earthen pot. Unlike those of most Chinese restaurants, the wine list is rather extensive, though alcohol will greatly add to your bill. With most dishes averaging HK$90 to HK$130 (US$12–US$17/£6.40–£9.30), you can easily dine here for less than HK$400 (US$52/£29) if you abstain. For lunch, you can eat even more cheaply, with dim sum available for HK$30 to HK$48 (US$3.90–US$6.25/£2.15–£3.40) a plate.

Shop 001, Pacific Place, 88 Queensway, Central. © 852/2845 4555. Reservations recommended. Main dishes HK$90–HK$180 (US$10–US$23/£6.40–£13). AE, DC, MC, V. Mon–Fri 11:30am–3pm; Sat 11:30am–5pm; Sun 10:30am–5pm; daily 5:30–11pm. MTR: Admiralty.

INEXPENSIVE

Several inexpensive restaurants reviewed in the previous Tsim Sha Tsui section have branches in Central: **Fat Angelo's** (p. 132) is renowned for its massive portions of American-style Italian food; **Genki Sushi** (p. 132) offers conveyor-belt sushi at low prices; **Koh-I-Noor** (p. 133) is recommended for Indian curries; and **Spaghetti House** (p. 134) is a popular family restaurant.

In addition, many restaurants in the moderate category above offer lunches that even the budget-conscious can afford. Be sure, too, to check the section on "Dim Sum," later in this chapter, and bars in the nightlife chapter.

Finally, another good place for a casual, inexpensive meal is the **Food Fare** food court in Pacific Place, 88 Queensway, in Central (take the MTR to Admiralty), where various counters offer Chinese, Thai, Korean, and Japanese food, as well as sandwiches and pasta, daily from 7:30am to 10pm.

Al's Diner *Kids* AMERICAN   This is one of the cheapest places for a late-night meal if you're carousing Central's nightlife district of Lan Kwai Fong. Although it may not win any culinary awards, this informal diner, decorated in 1950s Americana style with mini juke boxes at each of the booths, definitely hits the spot with burgers, hot dogs, sandwiches, chili, meatloaf, macaroni and cheese, milkshakes, and breakfast served anytime. With food like this, it's a good, inexpensive bet if you have children in tow. Be aware, however, that this place really packs 'em in during the late hours, when the place pulsates with a DJ, people eating Jell-O shots (Jell-O laced with vodka), and revelers dancing on the tables weekend nights.

39 D'Aguilar St., Central. © 852/2869 1869. www.lankwaifong.com. Main courses HK$70–HK$135 (US$9.10–US$18/£5–£9.65). AE, DC, MC, V. Daily 11:30am–12:30am (last order). MTR: Central.

Baci Pizza *Kids* PIZZA   This tiny, casual, welcoming pizzeria offers good durum or homemade pasta and various kinds of wafer-thin pizza, including a "four seasons" pizza with cheese, mushrooms, black olives, ham, and artichokes, and a pizza with four cheeses—Gorgonzola, Parmesan, mozzarella, and fontina.

1 Lan Kwai Fong (1st floor), Central. © 852/2840 0153. www.lankwaifong.com. Pizzas and pastas HK$90–HK$185 (US$12–US$24/£6.40–£13). AE, DC, MC, V. Mon–Sat noon–2:30pm; Mon–Thurs 7–11pm; Fri–Sat 7–11:30pm. MTR: Central.

¡Caramba! MEXICAN   Located in the heart of Hong Kong's popular SoHo dining-and-nightlife district and easily accessible via the Central–Mid-Levels Escalator, this very narrow Mexican restaurant opened in 1997 as one of the first on the street. Now there are many other ethnic restaurants here, including those serving Cuban, Greek, Italian, and French cuisine. ¡Caramba! offers hearty dishes of tacos, burritos, enchiladas, chimichangas, fajitas, and fresh fish of the day, all served with side dishes of black beans and rice. Of all the Mexican restaurants in Hong Kong, this is probably the best. Tables are too close together for intimate discussions, but after a few margaritas, who cares? On weekends and holidays, brunch is offered until 6pm for HK$99 (US$13/£7.15), including one drink. *¡Ay caramba!*

26–30 Elgin St., Central. © 852/2530 9963. www.caramba.com.hk. Reservations recommended. Platters with side dishes HK$110–HK$148 (US$14–US$19/£7.85–£11); Mon–Fri lunch buffet HK$68 (US$8.85/£4.85). AE, DC, MC, V. Mon–Sat noon–11:45pm; Sun 11am–11:45pm. MTR: Central.

Life *Finds* VEGETARIAN   Located beside the Central–Mid-Levels Escalator in SoHo, Life is a godsend to travelers seeking vegetarian and vegan alternatives, with dishes made from natural and organic ingredients and utilizing fresh vegetables, whole grains, nuts, seeds, soy products, legumes, and other healthy fare. For guests with dietary restrictions, it will also prepare dishes that are free of yeast, gluten, garlic, onion, or wheat. Occupying the second story above a health-foods store in a simple, down-to-earth venue, with rooftop dining available in the evening, it serves salads, samosas made with tofu and veggies, quiche, noodles, vegetable lasagna, and daily specials, along with juices, power and protein shakes, teas, and organic wine and beer. Fitting the restaurant's earth-friendly philosophy, it even uses biodegradable packaging and cleaning agents that don't harm either the environment or, well, life. Ten percent of its profits go to charities.

10 Shelley St., Central. (☎) 852/2810 9777. Main dishes HK$80–HK$110 (US$10–US$14/£5.70–£7.85). AE, MC, V. Daily 10am–midnight. MTR: Central.

The Flying Pan AMERICAN   Breakfast 24 hours a day is the forte of this homey, casual eatery, located a short uphill hike from Hollywood Road in the SoHo district. Everything from hearty omelets and eggs Benedict to Belgian waffles, cheese blintzes, and even British breakfasts comprised of two eggs, bacon, black pudding, and grilled tomato are available from the lengthy menu, all with side dishes and juice or bottomless cups of coffee. There's a branch at 81–85 Lockhart Rd., Wanchai (☎ **852/2528 9997**; MTR: Wan Chai), also open 24 hours.

9 Old Bailey St., Central. (☎) 852/2140 6333. Breakfast platters HK$45–HK$100 (US$5.85–US$13/£3.20–£7.15). No credit cards. Daily 24 hr. MTR: Central.

PizzaExpress PIZZA   This glass-walled eatery, on a busy intersection where Lynhurst Terrace, Cochrane, and Gage streets all converge (and in the shadow of the Central–Mid-Levels Escalator), is a noisy place for a meal, mainly because there's nothing to break up the acoustics. However, it does diners a favor by devoting the ground floor to nonsmokers and the upper floor to indulgers. The pizza is great, ranging from the ordinary (such as the American Pizza with pepperoni, mozzarella, jalapeno, and tomato) to the unusual (like the Peking Duck Pizza with duck, hoisin sauce, chile, spring onion, and mozzarella). It also offers pastas and salads.

There are branches in Tsim Sha Tsui at 35 Ashley Rd. (☎ **852/2317 7432**; MTR: Tsim Sha Tsui) and in Wan Chai at 10 Wing Fung St. (☎ **852/3528 0541**; MTR: Wan Chai).

21 Lyndhurst Terrace, Central (☎) 852/2850 7898. www.pizzaexpress.com.hk. Pizza HK$88–HK$116 (US$11–US$19/£6.30–£8.30). AE, MC, V. Daily noon–midnight. MTR: Central.

Pret A Manger SANDWICHES   Located in the ifc mall at Hong Kong Station, this London import has met with resounding success, providing ready-made soups, salads, juices, cakes, wraps, and sandwiches to busy office workers. All food is made fresh daily without the use of chemicals, additives, and preservatives. What doesn't sell by the end of the day is given away to charities. Sandwiches include familiars like BLTs and clubs, as well as more exotic offerings like Thai chicken and tandoori fish. Although it's mainly for takeout, there are a few tables for dining in.

Other branches are located in the Central MTR Station (☎ **852/2537 9230**); in the Admiralty MTR Station (☎ **852/2537 9230**); the Lippo Center, 89 Queensway, Central (☎ **852/2537 4200**; MTR: Admiralty); Harbour Centre, 25 Harbour Rd., Wan Chai (☎ **852/2877 3686**; MTR: Wan Chai); and AIA Plaza, 18 Hysan Ave., Causeway Bay (☎ **852/2808 4402**; MTR: Causeway Bay).

Shop 1003B, Level 1, ifc mall, 1 Harbour View St., Central. (☎) 852/2295 0405. www.pret.com. Sandwiches and wraps HK$12–HK$34 (US$1.55–US$4.40/85p–£2.40). No credit cards. Mon–Fri 7:30am–7:30pm; Sat 8am–8pm; Sun 8:30am–8pm. MTR: Central.

6 Causeway Bay & Wan Chai

VERY EXPENSIVE

Grissini ⟨⟨⟨ ITALIAN   This stylish, airy Italian restaurant echoes the palatial set-ting of the Grand Hyatt Hotel, with a tall ceiling, parquet floors, slick black furniture, and ceiling-to-floor windows offering a spectacular view of the harbor—day and night. Dining is on two levels, giving everyone a ringside seat. The changing menu, which offers some of the best Northern Italian fare in town, always includes the *antipasto misto,* a selection of appetizers. If you're really hungry, you might want to fol-low it with one of the pasta or risotto dishes, such as the black squid-ink pasta filled with celery root, Italian cod, and green olives, or the risotto with buffalo mozzarella and black truffle. Main dishes have included grilled lobster with bell peppers, capers, garlic, and oregano, and roasted lamb rack with mustard, tangerine, and honey along with escarole with a black olive and wine sauce. The wine cellar, with 1,000 bottles, is exclusively Italian. At lunch there is lighter fare and more choices of pasta and risotto, but whether for lunch or dinner, you can't go wrong dining here.

In the Grand Hyatt Hong Kong Hotel, 1 Harbour Rd., Wan Chai. Ⓒ 852/2584 7933. www.hongkong.grand.hyatt.com. Reservations recommended. Main courses HK$250–HK$480 (US$32–US$62/£18–£34); fixed-price dinner HK$700 (US$91/£50); fixed-price lunch (Mon–Fri only) HK$248 (US$32/£18); Sun brunch HK$410 (US$53/£29). AE, DC, MC, V. Daily noon–2:30pm and 7–11pm. MTR: Wan Chai.

EXPENSIVE

Fook Lam Moon (p. 156), famous for its exotic Cantonese fare and already covered in the Tsim Sha Tsui dining section above, also has a branch in Wan Chai.

One Harbour Road ⟨⟨ CANTONESE   For elegant Chinese dining in Wan Chai, head to the lobby of the Grand Hyatt Hotel, where a glass bubble elevator will deliver you directly to this eighth-floor restaurant. Designed to resemble the terrace of an ele-gant 1930s taipan mansion, it's bright and airy, with split-level dining offering views of the harbor. A profusion of plants, a large lotus pond, and the sound of running water give the illusion of outdoor dining; tables spread far apart provide privacy. The extensive menu offers straightforward, traditional Cantonese fare, with no nouvelle nuances or foreign influences. There's the usual shark's-fin specialties, abalone, bird's nest, Peking duck (order in advance), beggar's chicken (order in advance), and roast goose (which costs substantially more than the prices given below). Specialties include stir-fried prawns in spicy sauce, crispy chicken, and simmered garoupa with hot chile and vegetables. There are also fixed-price lunch and dinner menus, which, unfortu-nately for lone diners, require a minimum order for two people.

In the Grand Hyatt Hong Kong Hotel, 1 Harbour Rd., Wan Chai. Ⓒ 852/2584 7938. www.hongkong.grand.hyatt.com. Reservations recommended. Main dishes HK$150–HK$300 (US$19–US$39/£11–£21); fixed-price dinner HK$680 (US$88/£49); fixed-price lunch HK$350–HK$475 (US$45–US$62/£25–£34). AE, DC, MC, V. Daily noon–2:30pm and 6:30–10:30pm. MTR: Wan Chai.

Riva ⟨⟨ CONTINENTAL   Using its location high over Victoria Park to full advantage, this restaurant boasts a dark and subdued interior with sweeping views beyond the park to the harbor, making this a great choice for a romantic dinner. The menu is eclectic, with the Australian chef taking inspiration from southern Europe, blending it with Australian seafood and ingredients, and adding Asian touches. The results are surprising creations like pan-seared Australian beef filet with pear and black truffle served with a Madeira jus and mousseline potatoes. There are, however, also more traditional dishes like the roasted rack of lamb. Lunch features a buffet table for appetizers and desserts and choice of a main dish from a menu. While diners who prefer the tried and true will find enough on the menu to satisfy, this restaurant is especially recommended for those who like culinary adventures. In the evenings, there's live music in the adjoining Riva Lounge (the HK$150/US$19/£11 cover charge is waived for people who dine here).

In the Park Lane Hotel (27th floor), 310 Gloucester Rd., Causeway Bay. ℂ 852/2839 3327. www.parklane.com.hk. Reservations recommended. Main courses HK$248–HK$320 (US$32–US$42/£18–£23); fixed-price lunch HK$210 (US$27/£15); Sun brunch HK$268 (US$35/£19). AE, DC, MC, V. Daily noon–2:45pm and 6–10:45pm (last order). MTR: Causeway Bay.

ToTT'S Asian Grill & Bar 🐾🐾🐾 INTERNATIONAL/FUSION   This flashy restaurant seems to suffer from an identity crisis: gigantic Chinese paint brushes at the entrance and a blood-red interior with zebra-striped chairs. I don't know whether I'm in Africa or China until I look at the fabulous view from the restaurant's 34th-floor perch. This is Hong Kong at its most eclectic, funky self, and though the setting seems contrived, the restaurant itself is relaxed, fun, and highly recommended for its innovative and varied East-meets-West fusion cuisine. Come early for a drink in the restaurant's bar (happy hour Mon–Sat 5–8pm; Sun 6–8pm), or retire there after dinner for live music and dancing Monday through Saturday nights from 10pm.

A glass-enclosed kitchen reveals food being prepared in woks, over charcoal grills, and in tandoori ovens. The menu is diverse, with main courses ranging from cumin-roasted Australian rack of lamb with pickled eggplant, tomato confit, and spiced jus to bamboo smoked tenderloin of beef with cauliflower sauce and truffle fingerling potatoes. Grilled items, from Boston lobster to Angus filet mignon, come with a choice of a half-dozen interesting sauces, including yellow Thai curry and foie gras sauce. Sushi and sashimi, including ToTT's own creations, are also recommended. This place is a good choice for those who want dining and entertainment in one spot, as well as for those entertaining first-time visitors to Hong Kong. Sunday brunch, featuring unlimited sparkling wine or Moët & Chandon champagne, is so popular you should book at least 2 weeks in advance.

In the Excelsior Hotel, 281 Gloucester Rd., Causeway Bay. ℂ 852/2837 6786. www.excelsiorhongkong.com. Reservations recommended for dinner (request a window seat). Main courses HK$198–HK$338 (US$26–US$44/£14–£24); fixed-price lunch (Mon–Fri only) HK$198 (US$26/£14); Sun brunch HK$378–HK$488 (US$49–US$63/£27–£35). AE, DC, MC, V. Mon–Fri noon–3pm; Mon–Sat 6:30–11pm; Sun 11:30am–3pm and 6:30–10pm. MTR: Causeway Bay.

MODERATE

Several restaurants already covered in the Kowloon dining section, above, have branches in Wan Chai or Causeway Bay: **El Cid** (p. 127), excellent for tapas and Spanish cuisine; **Jade Garden** (p. 128), good for Cantonese food and dim sum; **Peking Garden** (p. 129), which serves Pekingese food; **Super Star Seafood Restaurant** (p. 130), serving Cantonese dishes, seafood, and dim sum; and **Wu Kong** (p. 131), which specializes in cuisine from Shanghai.

Ramas Greens 🐾🐾 INTERNATIONAL   There are so many fusion, East-meets-West restaurants in Hong Kong that it's hard to keep track. This one, open since 2002 and moving from Times Square to this lovely location in 2005, has proven its staying power by continuing to attract a trendy crowd, who lounge on sofas and comfy chairs on an open deck, one of many new open-air restaurants ringing the Sanlitun building in Wan Chai, not far from the convention center. The changing menu runs the gamut from pasta and grilled meats to seafood, sashimi, and Asian cuisine. You might, for example, select the roasted French duck leg with a port wine shallot reduction, served with a sun-dried tomato salad and sautéed new potatoes and vegetables, or the baked herb-crust-gratinated Chilean sea bass served with mashed potatoes and vegetables. Although there's a small indoor dining room, the terrace, good for people-watching, is clearly where the action is. There's a happy hour from 4 to 9pm daily.

The Sunlitun, 28 Harbour Rd., Wan Chai. ℂ 852/3101 0656. www.ramasgreens.com. Main dishes HK$148–HK$268 (US$19–US$35/£11–£19); fixed-price lunch HK$78–HK$188 (US$10–US$24/£5.55–£13). AE, DC, MC, V. Daily noon–midnight. MTR: Wan Chai.

Red Pepper ⭐⭐ SICHUAN
Open since 1970, the Red Pepper has a large following among the city's expatriates, many of whom seem to come so often that they know everyone in the place. It's a very relaxing, small restaurant, with a rather quaint decor of carved dragons on the ceiling and Chinese lanterns. Specialties include fried prawns with chile sauce on a sizzling platter, sour-pepper soup, fried garoupa with sweet-and-sour sauce, smoked duck marinated with oranges, and shredded chicken with hot garlic sauce and dry-fried string beans. Most dishes are available in two sizes, with the small dishes suitable for two people. The set lunch is written only in Chinese, so ask for a translation. Litchi tea is a good accompaniment.

7 Lan Fong Rd., Causeway Bay. ℂ 852/2577 3811. Reservations recommended, especially at dinner. Small dishes HK$90–HK$220 (US$12–US$29/£6.40–£16); fixed-price lunch HK$48–HK$68 (US$6.25–US$8.85/£3.40–£4.85). AE, DC, MC, V. Daily 11:30am–11:15pm (last order). MTR: Causeway Bay.

The Viceroy ⭐⭐ Finds INDIAN
Under the same management as the long-popular Gaylord in Tsim Sha Tsui, this contemporary restaurant has something its sister establishment doesn't—outdoor seating on a terrace with great views of the harbor, Wan Chai waterfront, and Kowloon. In the evening, the experience is almost magical, making it a good choice for a romantic dinner. On days when the weather doesn't cooperate (too cold, too hot, or rainy), indoor dining is a good second choice, with large windows offering the same views. Although the innovative menu changes often, tandoori dishes may range from lamb and prawns to lobster. In addition to curries and dishes like roast chicken in yogurt and spices, there are also a fair number of vegetarian dishes, from potatoes cooked with curry leaves to yellow lentils with spinach. The lunch buffet, offered weekdays only, is a steal.

Sun Hung Kai Centre (2nd floor), 30 Harbour Rd., Wan Chai. ℂ 852/2827 7777. www.harilela.com.hk. Main dishes HK$62–HK$148 (US$8.05–US$19/£4.40–£11); lunch buffet (Mon–Fri only) HK$108 (US$14/£7.70). AE, DC, MC, V. Daily noon–3pm and 6–11pm. MTR: Wan Chai.

Wasabisabi ⭐⭐ JAPANESE
This stunning restaurant looks like it was airlifted straight out of Tokyo, and like that huge metropolis, it's easy to get lost here. Luckily, staff is on hand to lead diners past the mirrors and corridors that make this place a confusing maze, to the dark and cozy dining room, where palm leaves and bare branches form a simple but memorable backdrop behind the sushi bar. The menu lists all the usual sashimi (raw seafood), sushi (raw seafood on vinegared rice), and temaki (handrolled sushi), from tuna and prawns to anago (sea eel), but there are also the Japanese chef's own creations like the avocado and smoked-eel temaki and the shredded crab wrapped in nori (seaweed) with crab paste. The extensive menu also offers grilled dishes (like grilled black cod marinated in a special miso paste from Kyoto), tempura, and rice and noodle dishes. The restaurant's bar, open until midnight weekdays and 2am on weekends, is a good, happening place for an after-dinner drink, but

you don't have to move to enjoy it: The restaurant's C-shaped sofas can swivel to face the bar.

Times Square (13th floor), 1 Matheson St., Causeway Bay. © 852/2506 0009. www.aqua.com.hk. Sushi (2 pieces) HK$50–HK$160 (US$6.50–US$21/£3.55–£11); main dishes HK$98–HK$178 (US$13–US$23/£7–£13). AE, DC, MC, V. Daily noon–3pm and 6pm–midnight. MTR: Causeway Bay.

Watermargin ★★ *Value* NORTHERN CHINESE Sister restaurant to hip Hutong in Kowloon but without the latter's stunning views and slightly higher prices, this restaurant resembles a traditional teahouse with its reproduction antique screens and chairs and hanging lanterns. Sheer silk curtains partition the dining area into intimate niches, and jazz plays softly in the background. Dishes, artfully presented, include such delectable starters as clams steeped in Chinese rosé wine and chile paste, and mustard spinach with fresh scallops topped with fish roe. Main dishes include sautéed prawns with spicy sauce, whole crispy chicken infused with Chinese tea, and roasted prime beef ribs. About half the dishes are spicy, showing influences from Sichuan province. If spicy foods are your thing, you won't want to pass up the diced chicken in a sea of Sichuan red peppers, which is served with a huge mound of red peppers and is so spicy it burned my lips. For a real treat, order a 10-year-old bottle of Shao Xing wine for HK$268 (US$35/£19).

Times Square (12th floor), 1 Matheson St., Causeway Bay. © 852/3102 0088. www.aqua.com.hk. Main dishes HK$90–HK$228 (US$13–US$30/£6.40–£16). AE, DC, MC, V. Daily noon–3pm and 6pm–midnight. MTR: Causeway Bay.

INEXPENSIVE

Fat Angelo's, Genki Sushi, and **Spaghetti House,** reviewed in the Tsim Sha Tsui section, all have branches in Wan Chai and/or Causeway Bay. See p. 132, 132, and 134, respectively. **PizzaExpress** and **Pret A Manger,** both described in the Central section, have branches here; see p. 146. **Chilli N Spice,** recommended below in Stanley for its Thai and Vietnamese fare, has a branch in Causeway Bay; see p. 153.

In addition to the recommendations below, be sure to go through the moderate section above for inexpensive buffet and fixed-price lunches; also see the "Dim Sum" section later in this chapter.

American Restaurant PEKINGESE Despite its name, the American Restaurant serves hearty Pekingese food and has been doing so since it opened right after World War II. Recently renovated and often filled with noisy, celebratory patrons, it has an English menu listing almost 200 dishes (the small-size dishes are good for two or three people), but the perennial favorites have always been barbecued Peking duck (HK$295/US$38/£21 and good for two or more people), beggar's chicken (which must be ordered a day in advance and costs HK$385/US$50/£28), sizzling prawns, and the sizzling beef hot plate. Otherwise, the staff is happy to make recommendations.

20 Lockhart Rd., Wan Chai. © 852/2527 1000 or 852/2527 7277. Small dishes HK$50–HK$154 (US$6.50–US$20/£3.55–£14). AE, DC, MC, V. Daily 11am–11pm (last order). MTR: Wan Chai.

Bo Kong ★ *Finds* VEGETARIAN A bit too bright for comfort but soothingly decorated, this pleasant restaurant, located in the Food Forum of Times Square with a dozen other restaurants and with branches in Canada, offers Chinese vegetarian fare that is so cleverly prepared, you'd swear it contained meat. There is braised vegetarian "shark's fin," vegetarian sashimi, an appetizer plate of "cold cuts" that looks like meat but isn't, deep-fried vegetarian "chicken," vegetarian "prawns" in taro nest, and vegetarian "ham" rolled with bean-curd skin. There are also noodle, rice, and congee dishes, and dim sum is served to 4pm. Neither smoking nor the consumption of alcohol is allowed here.

Times Square (12th floor), 1 Matheson St., Causeway Bay. ℂ 852/2506 3377. Main dishes HK$62–HK$98 (US$8.05–US$13/£4.40–£7). MC, V. Daily 11am–10:30pm. MTR: Causeway Bay.

California Pizza Kitchen PIZZA/AMERICAN   This Beverly Hills transplant is known for its gourmet pizzas with unusual toppings, some of which sound like pizza sandwiches. There's the pastrami Reuben with pastrami, Swiss and mozzarella cheeses, sauerkraut, and Thousand Island dressing; the Thai chicken with chicken marinated in a spicy peanut-ginger and sesame sauce, mozzarella, green onions, bean sprouts, julienne carrots, cilantro, and roasted peanuts; and the Peking duck with roasted duck breast, mozzarella, soy-glazed Shiitake mushrooms, crispy wontons, slivered green onions and ginger hoisin sauce. There are more than two dozen pizzas listed on the menu, and I'd like to try all of them. There are also pastas, salads, and sandwiches.

You'll find branches on the other side of the harbor in Shop 280 of Ocean Terminal, Harbour City, Tsim Sha Tsui (ℂ 852/3102 0375; MTR: Tsim Sha Tsui), open daily 11:30am to 11:30pm; and near Ladies' Market at 56 Dundas St., Mong Kok (ℂ 852/2374 0032; MTR: Mong Kok), open daily 11am to 11pm.

Times Square (13th floor), 1 Matheson St., Causeway Bay. ℂ 852/3102 9132. www.cpk.com. Pastas and pizzas HK$72–HK$108 (US$9.35–US$14/£5.15–£7.70). AE, DC, MC, V. Daily 11:30–2:30pm and 5:30–11pm. MTR: Causeway Bay.

Chili Club 𝒱𝒶𝓁𝓊𝑒 THAI   This simple upstairs restaurant wastes little money on decor, with the only nod to fine dining apparent in its white table cloths. But the seafood, curries, and noodles, which include all the Thai favorites, are as spicy as this national cuisine should be. What's more, the price is right, making this one of Hong Kong's best dining values. Try to get a seat near the window, where you can watch the action on the street below, and, if possible, avoid the lunchtime rush.

88 Lockhart Rd., Wan Chai. ℂ 852/2527 2872. Main dishes HK$52–HK$150 (US$6.75–US$19/£3.70–£11). AE, MC, V. Daily noon–3pm and 6–10:30pm. MTR: Wan Chai.

Sorabol 𝒦 KOREAN   This is the Hong Kong branch of a successful Korean chain. Popular with local Chinese and Koreans, it can be quite noisy and busy, but partitions between tables lend some privacy. My own personal favorites are the beef strips of *bulgogi* or the *kalbi* (beef strips marinated in a spicy sauce and then barbecued at your own grill). Barbecued fixed-price meals come with side dishes of kimchee (spicy cabbage) and vegetables. Another popular dish is the Mongolian hotpot with vegetables for HK$158 (US$20/£11). You'll do your own barbecuing at smokeless grills at your table, which can be great fun, somewhat like an indoor cookout. In any case, the army of knowledgeable staff keeps things running smoothly and is happy to help the novice barbecuer.

There's also a branch in Tsim Sha Tsui on the fourth floor of the Miramar Shopping Centre at 132 Nathan Rd. (ℂ 852/2375 2882), open the same hours.

Lee Theatre Plaza (17th floor), 99 Percival St. (across from Times Square), Causeway Bay. ℂ 852/2881 6823. www.sorabol.com.hk. Barbecued dishes HK$85–HK$215 (US$11–US$28/£6.05–£15); fixed-price meals for 2 persons HK$340–HK$520 (US$44–US$68/£24–£37); fixed-price lunches (Mon–Sat only) HK$55–HK$80 (US$7.15–US$10/£3.90–£5.70); Sun lunch buffet HK$98 (US$13/£7). AE, DC, MC, V. Daily 11am–11:30pm. MTR: Wan Chai.

7 Around Hong Kong Island

VICTORIA PEAK

MODERATE

Cafe Deco 𝒞 𝒦𝒾𝒹𝓈 INTERNATIONAL No expense was spared, it seems, in designing this chic, airy restaurant with its wood inlaid floor, authentic Art Deco trimmings (many imported from the U.S. and Europe), and open kitchen serving cuisines of China, Japan, Thailand, India, the U.S., and Italy. In the evening (except Sun), diners are treated to live jazz. All this is secondary, however, to the restaurant's real attraction—the best view in town of Hong Kong. That alone is reason enough for dining here, though some of the view has been stolen by the Peak Tower. To assure a ringside window seat, be sure to make reservations for the second floor at least 2 weeks in advance, emphasizing that you don't want your view obstructed by the Peak Tower, or opt for one of the outdoor tables, which are often easier to get. The food, designed to appeal to visitors from around the world, is as trendy as the restaurant, with an eclectic mix of international dishes and ingredients, including tandoori kabobs and dishes, Asian noodles, sushi, grilled steaks and chops, pizzas, create-your-own pastas, soups, and salads. The salads are generous enough for two to share (the house salad is exceptionally good), but main dishes occasionally fall short of expectations. I suppose what you're really paying for here is the view. There's a children's play corner, to keep the wee ones occupied.

Peak Galleria, Victoria Peak. 𝒞 852/2849 5111. www.cafedecogroup.com. Reservations recommended for dinner (request window seat with view). Pizzas and pastas HK$98–HK$148 (US$13–US$19/£7–£11); main courses HK$118–HK$278 (US$15–US$36/£8.40–£20); fixed-price lunch (Mon–Fri only) HK$178 (US$23/£13); Sun brunch HK$298 (US$39/£21). AE, DC, MC, V. Mon–Thurs 11:30am–11pm (last order); Fri 11:30am–11:30pm; Sat 9:30am–11:30pm; Sun 9:30am–11pm. Peak tram.

The Peak Lookout 𝒞𝒞 INTERNATIONAL Although it's on The Peak, located across the street from the Peak tram terminus, there are only limited views of the South China Sea from The Peak Lookout's terrace. And yet, it has long been a Hong Kong favorite. A former tram station, it's a delightful, rustic place for a meal, with exposed granite walls, tall timber-trussed ceiling, open fireplace, wooden floor, and a greenhouselike room that extends into the garden. You can also sit outdoors amid the lush growth where you can actually hear birds singing—one of the best outdoor dining opportunities in Hong Kong on a glorious day (be sure to request a table outdoors if that's what you want). Musicians entertain nightly with oldies but goldies. The menu is eclectic, offering soups (from minestrone to the classic Thai seafood soup Tom Yam Goong), sandwiches, and a combination of American, Chinese, Indian, Japanese, and Southeast Asian dishes, including tandoori chicken *tikka*, Thai noodles, sushi and sashimi, penne with prawns, grilled steaks and salmon, and curries like Thai green chicken curry with coconut milk.

121 Peak Rd., Victoria Peak. 𝒞 852/2849 1000. www.peaklookout.com.hk. Reservations required for dinner and all weekend meals. Main courses HK$128–HK$258 (US$17–US$33/£9.15–£18). AE, DC, MC, V. Mon–Thurs 10:30am–11:30pm; Fri 10:30am–1am; Sat 8:30am–1am; Sun 8:30am–11:30pm. Peak tram.

REPULSE BAY

EXPENSIVE

The Verandah 𝒞𝒞𝒞 𝐹𝒾𝓃𝒹𝓈 CONTINENTAL Unless you like beaches (there's a popular one here at Repulse Bay), this wonderful, veranda-like restaurant is the only reason to venture to this destination on Hong Kong Island's south side, though you do pass it by on your way to Stanley. A throwback to Hong Kong's colonial days in a setting reminiscent of an exclusive private club, it boasts a stylish yet relaxed atmosphere, with tall ceilings and whirling fans, starched tablecloths and flowers, and windows open wide toward manicured lawns and the sea. If you can, book a table more than a week in advance and arrive starving at its famous Sunday brunch, complete with a jazz band. Otherwise, from the regular menu, you might wish to start with The Verandah's famous Caesar salad (topped with a choice of grilled chicken breast, grilled prawns, or home-smoked salmon), followed by lobster bisque or wild mushroom ravioli. For a main course, you might choose a lobster dish or the filet of U.S. prime beef tenderloin with merlot-braised oxtail. There are also vegetarian dishes. In any case, with its excellent service, great food, and wonderful ambience, this is a very civilized place; you'll want to linger.

109 Repulse Bay Rd., Repulse Bay. ℂ 852/2292 2822. www.therepulsebay.com. Reservations required. Main courses HK$270–HK$290 (US$35–US$38/£19–£21); fixed-price lunch HK$228–HK$248 (US$30–US$32/£16–£18); Sun brunch HK$338 (US$44/£24). AE, DC, MC, V. Tues–Sat noon–2:30pm; Sun 11am–2:30pm; daily 6:30–10:30pm. Bus: 6, 6A, 6X, 260, or 973.

STANLEY

In addition to the restaurants described here, **El Cid** (p. 127), already described in the Tsim Sha Tsui section and located in the Murray House, offers a dreamy view of the sea from its outside terrace, a live band Tuesday through Sunday evenings, and an expansive menu of tapas and Spanish food.

MODERATE

Lucy's ⟨ᴋ⟩ (Finds) INTERNATIONAL   This tiny, cozy, casual restaurant, snuggled in the ground floor of an older building just off Stanley market (look for the stairs to the right of the Delifrance bakery), is a friendly neighborhood restaurant, attracting expats who live in Stanley rather than hordes of tourists (maybe because it lacks a view of the sea). Its limited menu, which always includes some vegetarian options, changes often to reflect what's available and in season, with past entrees ranging from sea bass with orange vinaigrette and artichoke, almond and herb couscous, to chargrilled beef filet with portobello mushrooms, sautéed potatoes, and a black-pepper brandy cream sauce. Most diners, however, opt for one of the daily specials, which are almost always right on, making sure to save room for the restaurant's famed desserts. Lunches feature lighter, less expensive fare, like spinach and feta cheese soufflé with roast tomato sauce.

64 Stanley Main St., Stanley. ℂ 852/2813 9055. Reservations required weekends. Main courses HK$170–HK$210 (US$22–US$27/£12–£15) AE, MC, V. Mon–Fri noon–3pm; Sat–Sun noon–4pm; Mon–Thurs 7–10pm; Fri–Sat 6:30–10pm; Sun 6:30–9:30pm. Bus: 6, 6A, 6X, 260, or 973.

INEXPENSIVE

Chilli N Spice ⟨ᴋ⟩ (Value) THAI/VIETNAMESE   Located in the historic Murray House, a massive, colonnaded stone structure built in Central in 1843, dismantled, and rebuilt here stone for stone, this restaurant boasts views of the sea from its outdoor terrace and serves mostly traditional Thai and Vietnamese food, as well as a few other popular Asian dishes. Entrees include Singaporean-style fried curry crab, prawns with lemon grass, and Hainese-style chicken. This is both a relaxing place to end a day of shopping and an affordable option, with most dinners costing around HK$200 (US$26/£14).

There's another branch at 13–15 Cleveland St., Causeway Bay (ℂ **852/2504 3930;** MTR: Causeway Bay), open daily noon to midnight.

Shop 101, Murray House, Stanley Plaza, Stanley. ℂ **852/2899 0147**. www.kingparrot.com. Main courses HK$55–HK$135 (US$7.15–US$18/£3.90–£9.65). AE, DC, MC, V. Daily noon–11pm. Bus: 6, 6A, 6X, 260, or 973.

ABERDEEN
MODERATE

Jumbo Kingdom ✿ CANTONESE   No doubt you've heard about Hong Kong's floating restaurant in Aberdeen, in operation for more than a quarter of a century and claiming to be the largest floating restaurant in the world. Although often included in Hong Kong's organized nighttime tours, the restaurant was steadily losing out to newer, more authentic, and more affordable restaurants, prompting it to reinvent itself in 2004 as the Jumbo Kingdom, a complex housing several dining venues and retail shops. At any rate, if you've always wanted to eat in a floating restaurant, simply take the bus to Aberdeen and then board one of the Jumbo Kingdom's own free shuttle boats, with departures every few minutes from the waterfront Aberdeen Promenade.

The restaurant, which underwent a complete overhaul that rid it of its opulent golds and reds and transformed it into a slick, contemporary venue, specializes in fresh seafood but also offers roasted goose, Peking duck (HK$320/US$42/£23), and changing seasonal dishes. Dim sum is available from an English menu (from trolleys on Sun and holidays) until 4pm—certainly the least expensive way to enjoy the floating restaurant experience. Dragon Court, a smaller, more formal dining hall, offers the same fare, with dim sum served only off a menu (you might be able to get a table here immediately on Sun, bypassing the first-come, first-served waiting list for the more popular—and more fun—main dining hall).

Aberdeen Harbour, Hong Kong Island. ℂ **852/2553 9111**. www.jumbo.com.hk. Main dishes HK$60–HK$450 (US$7.80–US$58/£4.30–£32); dim sum HK$17–HK$23 (US$2.20–US$3/£1.20–£1.65). Table charge HK$12 (US$1.55/85p) per person. AE, MC, V. Mon–Sat 11:30am–10:30pm; Sun 7am–10:30pm. Bus: 7 or 70 from Central, 72 or 77 from Causeway Bay, or 973 from Tsim Sha Tsui to Aberdeen, then the restaurant's free shuttle boat.

Top Deck, at the Jumbo ✿✿✿ 𝐾𝑖𝑑𝑠 INTERNATIONAL/SEAFOOD   I was excited to discover this 2005 addition to Jumbo Kingdom, since it will undoubtedly breathe new life into this decades-old tourist spot and attract a new round of international travelers, especially those not fond of dim sum breakfasts. Brought to you by the same folks who run Café Deco on the Peak, it boasts a great, open-air rooftop setting on the Jumbo Kingdom, with comfortable sofas and oversize chairs grouped under and around awnings and a flamboyantly ornate Chinese dining hall, where an open kitchen turns out mouthwatering seafood delights from around the world, as well as other dishes.

The menu is so extensive it's hard to know where to start. Thai, Japanese, and Indian appetizer platters solve part of the dilemma by providing a sampler of goodies from those countries, while the seafood mountain comes with lobster, oysters, mussels, Alaskan King crag legs, prawns, and other seafood, along with dipping sauces. There's also a wide choice of sushi, sashimi, and hand rolls (the top deck hand roll comes with prawns, yellowtail, avocado, leek, and sesame). For a main course, there's salmon, tiger king prawns, steak, and other choices from the grill, fish and lamb chops from a tandoori oven, Asian curries, pastas, pizzas, and sandwiches. For the little tykes, there's a children's menu and a children's play corner (the boat ride to the restaurant is a bonus). For those who feel cheated choosing only an item or two from the menu, there's a Sunday seafood brunch buffet to 4:30pm. And for those who simply want to chill out, there's an afternoon tea buffet from 3 to 5:30pm daily except Sunday (HK$168/US$22/£12) and live jazz Wednesday evenings from 7:30pm.

Jumbo Kingdom (rooftop), Aberdeen Harbour, Hong Kong Island. ℂ 852/2553 3331. www.cafedecogroup.com. Main dishes HK$108–HK$358 (US$14–US$46/£7.70–£26); Sun brunch HK$328 (US$43/£23). AE, DC, MC, V. Daily 11:30am–10:45pm (last order). Bus: 7 or 70 from Central, 72 or 77 from Causeway Bay, or 973 from Tsim Sha Tsui to Aberdeen, then Jumbo Kingdom's free shuttle boat.

WESTERN DISTRICT
INEXPENSIVE
Sammy's Kitchen CONTINENTAL   There are few choices for Western food in the Western District, making Sammy's Kitchen, recognizable by the sign in the shape of a cow outside its door, your best bet. A simple and unpretentious place that has changed little over the decades, it offers reasonably priced, rather mediocre meals, but the service is friendly and welcoming. Owner/chef Sammy Yip has been cooking professionally for more than 50 years (including stints at The Peninsula and Mandarin Oriental hotels) and opened this restaurant on his own in 1970. Sammy, whose children have joined him in the family business, speaks English well and is happy to see foreign visitors. There are actually two menus, based on two different concepts. One is cheaper and quicker, available all day and offering rather plain dishes like spring chicken, lamb chops, and noodle and fried rice dishes; they're priced from HK$55 to HK$100 (US$7.15–US$13/£3.90–£7.15). In the evening, another, more expensive menu is also available (with entrees ranging from HK$95/US$12/£6.75 to HK$280/US$36/£20), cooked by Sammy himself and served in the separate, more formal Grill Room. This menu includes fresh seafood, imported steaks, and such specialties as veal with Parmesan and Marsala, chicken with special pepper sauce flaming with cognac, filet mignon, and roasted Siberian rib of lamb with herbs. You can bring your own bottle of wine for a HK$70 (US$9.10/£5) corkage fee.

204–206 Queen's Rd. W., Sheung Wan. ℂ 852/2548 8400. Main courses HK$55–HK$280 (US$7.15–US$36/£3.90–£20); fixed-price dinner HK$180 (US$23/£13); fixed-price lunch HK$55–HK$110 (US$7.15–US$14/£3.90–£7.85). AE, DC, MC, V. Daily 7:30am–11:30pm. MTR: Sheung Wan.

8 Dim Sum

Everyone should try a dim sum meal at least once, as much for the atmosphere as for the food. It's eaten primarily for breakfast or lunch, or as an afternoon snack with tea. On weekends, restaurants offering dim sum (mostly Cantonese restaurants) are packed with local families. On weekdays, they're popular with shoppers and businesspeople. Prices are low and you order only as much as you want. On weekends, some restaurants bring out their trolleys, filled with steaming baskets and pushed throughout the restaurant, allowing you to choose what appeals to you. Otherwise, most restaurants nowadays offer dim sum from a menu, which may or may not be in English (hotel restaurants have English menus; otherwise, many Cantonese restaurants have at least one staff member who speaks English, or use the suggestions earlier in this chapter as a guide). In any case, in most restaurants that offer dim sum, one pays by the basket, and each basket usually contains two to four items of dim sum; the average price is about HK$20 to HK$30 (US$2.60–US$3.90/£1.40–£2.15). The prices given below, unless otherwise specified, are per basket; expect to spend HK$60 to HK$100 (US$7.80–US$13/£4.30–£7.15) per person for a light meal. You'll be charged extra for tea, usually around HK$10 (US$1.30/70p).

You'll find most of the restaurants below also described earlier in this chapter, so they obviously serve more than dim sum. However, since dim sum is such a special Chinese tradition, they are emphasized again below. You may also notice that a restaurant listed in this section may have a different number of stars than was given previously in an above listing. This is not a mistake: A restaurant that might be ho-hum in all-round meals can be a standout in dim sum.

However, since dim sum is fairly predictable, with the most common dishes covered in the cuisine section at the beginning of the chapter, I've only made specific food recommendations below when the dishes are different and/or are standouts from the usual choices. The open hours below are for serving times for dim sum.

KOWLOON

City Chiuchow Restaurant CHIU CHOW   Although it's a Chiu Chow restaurant, this place serves its own dim sum, which is not too surprising if you consider that Chiu Chow food has been greatly influenced by Cantonese food.

East Ocean Centre, 98 Granville Rd., Tsim Sha Tsui East. (© 852/2723 6226. Dim sum HK$17–HK$28 (US$2.20–US$3.60/£1.20–£2). AE, DC, MC, V. Daily 11am–4pm, for dim sum. MTR: Tsim Sha Tsui.

Fook Lam Moon ✹✹✹ CANTONESE   This is a Hong Kong old-timer, with an atmosphere that is reminiscent of an earlier era. There aren't any trolleys here, however. The English menu is limited, listing only the restaurant's top choices, including the highest-priced item—steamed shark's fin dumpling with superior soup. There's a branch at 35–45 Johnston Rd., Wan Chai (© 852/2866 0663), open the same hours with the same menu.

53–59 Kimberley Rd., Tsim Sha Tsui. (© 852/2366 0286. www.fooklammoon-grp.com. Dim sum HK$30–HK$80 (US$3.90–US$10/£2.15–£5.70). AE, DC, MC, V. Daily 11:30am–2:30pm, for dim sum. MTR: Tsim Sha Tsui.

Hutong ✹✹✹ CANTONESE   Great views of the harbor and creative dim sum are what you get at this hip venue. Expect the likes of steamed lamb dumpling instead of pork, with about five different kinds of dim sum that change monthly. You can also order dim sum combination platters with either 12 or 20 pieces of dim sum for HK$128 (US$17/£9.15) or HK$198 (US$26/£14) respectively. This place is pricey, but worth it.

1 Peking Rd. (28th floor), Tsim Sha Tsui. (© 852/3428 8342. www.aqua.com.hk. Dim sum HK$78–HK$98 (US$10–US$13/£5.55–£7). AE, DC, MC, V. Mon–Sat noon–3pm; Sun and holidays noon–3pm, for dim sum. MTR: Tsim Sha Tsui.

Jade Garden Chinese Restaurant CANTONESE   An easy place for the uninitiated, this Cantonese chain is tourist-friendly and conveniently situated across from the Star Ferry terminus. It offers views of Victoria Harbour and an extensive English menu for dim sum, along with noodle and rice dishes and desserts. There's a branch at 1 Hysan Ave., Causeway Bay (© 852/2577 9332), serving dim sum Monday through Friday from 11am to 2:30pm, Saturday 11am to 5pm, and Sunday 10am to 5pm.

Star House (4th floor), 3 Salisbury Rd., Tsim Sha Tsui. (© 852/2730 6888. Dim sum HK$17–HK$38 (US$2.20–US$4.95/£1.20–£2.70). AE, DC, MC, V. Mon–Sat 11am–5pm; Sun and holidays 10am–5pm, for dim sum. MTR: Tsim Sha Tsui.

Serenade Chinese Restaurant ✹ *Value* CANONTESE   This is my top choice for inexpensive dim sum with a view in Tsim Sha Tsui. Located up on the first floor of the Hong Kong Cultural Centre, next to the Star Ferry, it offers views of Victoria Harbour and a comprehensive dim sum menu (only desserts are served from trolleys), including "figurine" dim sum, like the steamed shrimp dumpling in the shape of a fish. On weekdays (excluding public holidays) from 8am to noon, dim sum prices are cheaper than those given below, and even cheaper still from 2 to 4:30pm. Bright and cheerful, it's more upmarket than some but more casual than hotel restaurants.

Hong Kong Cultural Centre (1st floor), Restaurant Block, Salisbury Rd., Tsim Sha Tsui. ℂ 852/2722 0932. Dim sum HK$16–HK$38 (US$2.10–US$4.95/£1.15–£2.70). AE, DC, MC, V. Daily 8am–4:30pm, for dim sum. MTR: Tsim Sha Tsui.

Shang Palace ★★ CANTONESE

One of Kowloon's most elaborate Chinese restaurants comes complete with red-lacquered walls and Chinese lanterns hanging from the ceiling. Its dim sum is among the best in town—a bit more expensive, but worth it. Choose your dim sum from the English menu, which changes every 2 weeks and always includes more than a dozen varieties.

In the Shangri-La Hotel, 64 Mody Rd., Tsim Sha Tsui East. ℂ 852/2733 8754. www.Shangri-la.com. Dim sum HK$30–HK$38 (US$3.90–US$4.95/£2.15–£2.70). AE, DC, MC, V. Mon–Sat noon–3pm; Sun and holidays 10:30am–3pm, for dim sum. MTR: Tsim Sha Tsui.

Spring Moon ★★★ CANTONESE

As you'd expect from a restaurant in the venerable Peninsula hotel, this is a very refined and civilized place for the humble dim sum, with an English menu that lists more than a dozen mouthwatering choices that change with the seasons. Many dim sum connoisseurs believe the dim sum served here is among the best in town, with past examples including Shanghai-style steamed pork dumplings with lobster; steamed eggplant dumplings with minced pork and XO chile sauce; and deep-fried chicken and curry crisps in Portuguese sauce. Spring Moon is also famous for its more than two dozen varieties of Chinese teas and even employs professionally trained tea masters. The restaurant is decorated in an Art Deco style reminiscent of how the restaurant would have looked in 1928, the year The Peninsula opened, with stained glass, wood paneling, and Frank Lloyd Wright–inspired highlights.

In The Peninsula hotel, Salisbury Rd., Tsim Sha Tsui. ℂ 852/2315 3160. www.peninsula.com. Dim sum HK$42 (US$5.45/£3). AE, DC, MC, V. Daily 11:30am–2:30pm, for dim sum. MTR: Tsim Sha Tsui.

Super Star Seafood Restaurant *Finds* CANTONESE/SEAFOOD

This lively and popular seafood restaurant, filled with locals, is one of Tsim Sha Tsui's best places for trying authentic dim sum in a typical Chinese setting. There's no English menu (and unfortunately, no more trolleys), so you'll just have to look at the pictures on the Chinese menu. There are many branches in Hong Kong (see p. 130 for locations).

83–97 Nathan Rd., Tsim Sha Tsui. ℂ 852/2366 0878. Dim sum HK$12–HK$38 (US$1.55–US$4.95/85p–£2.70). AE, DC, MC, V. Mon–Fri 10:30am–4:30pm; Sat–Sun 9:30am–4:30pm, for dim sum. MTR: Tsim Sha Tsui.

T'ang Courturant ★★ CANTONESE

This fancy restaurant offers its own interpretations of classic Cantonese dim sum and even offers a dim sum lunch.

In the Langham Hotel, 8 Peking Rd., Tsim Sha Tsui ℂ 852/2375 1133, ext. 2250. www.langhamhotels.com. Dim sum HK$33 (US$4.30/£2.35); dim sum lunch HK$208 (US$27/£15). AE, DC, MC, V. Mon–Sat noon–3pm; Sun 11am–3pm, for dim sum. MTR: Tsim Sha Tsui.

Tsui Hang Village Restaurant CANTONESE

Tsui Hang Village, a modern restaurant located in a shopping complex across from the Miramar Hotel, offers inexpensive plates of dim sum, including traditional choices like steamed shrimp dumplings or steamed barbecue pork buns and its own creations like deep-fried shrimp in mashed taro or baked mini oyster tarts. There's a branch across the harbor on the second floor of the New World Tower, 16–18 Queen's Rd., Central (ℂ 852/2524 2012; MTR: Central), serving dim sum Saturday from 11am to 5pm and Sunday and holidays from 10am to 5pm.

Miramar Plaza, 1 Kimberley Rd., Tsim Sha Tsui. ℂ 852/2376 2882. www.Miramar-group.com. Dim sum HK$16–HK$40 (US$2.10–US$5.20/£1.15–£2.85). AE, MC, V. Mon–Sat 11:30am–5pm; Sun and holidays 10am–5pm, for dim sum. MTR: Tsim Sha Tsui.

Yan Toh Heen ⟨⟨⟨ CANTONESE   One of Hong Kong's top Cantonese eateries, this elegant restaurant with large windows treats diners to views of the harbor. A daily changing menu lists about two dozen varieties of dim sum, but signature dishes usually on offer include steamed bean curd sheet rolls with shrimp and chives, and steamed shark's fin and bamboo pith fungus dumpling in soup.

In the InterContinental Hong Kong, 18 Salisbury Rd., Tsim Sha Tsui. ⓒ 852/2721 1211. www.hongkong-ic. intercontinental.com. Dim sum HK$32–HK$68 (US$4.15–US$8.85/£2.30–£4.85). AE, DC, MC, V. Daily noon–2:30pm for dim sum. MTR: Tsim Sha Tsui.

CENTRAL

Luk Yu Tea House ⟨⟨ *Finds* CANTONESE   The most authentic dim sum teahouse in Hong Kong is often so packed with regulars that mere tourists can't get a seat. Furthermore, trolleys with dim sum are pushed through the place only until 11am, after which there's an English menu with pictures but no prices (ask before ordering). Yet it's worth the effort to come here; try to bring along a Chinese friend to help you with your selections.

24–26 Stanley St., Central. ⓒ **852/2523 5464.** Dim sum HK$25–HK$55 (US$3.25–US$7.15/£1.80–£3.90). MC, V. Daily 7am–5:30pm for dim sum. MTR: Central.

Maxim's Palace *Value* CANTONESE   There's no better place for cheap dim sum than this enormously popular restaurant, located on the second floor of City Hall with good harbor views. It's a lively, noisy place, with dim sum still offered from trolleys, plus there's an English menu with photos and prices. It doesn't get much easier than this.

Low Block, City Hall, Connaught Rd. Central and Edinburgh Place. ⓒ **852/2526 9931.** Dim sum HK$20–HK$29 (US$2.60–US$3.75/£1.40–£2.05). AE, DC, MC, V. Daily Mon–Sat 11am–3pm; Sun and holidays 9am–3pm, for dim sum. MTR: Central.

The Square CANTONESE   This smartly decorated restaurant, next to Hong Kong Station and ifc mall, offers only a dozen or so dim sum choices on weekdays but a greatly expanded dim sum menu on weekends and holidays (reservations are a must). The restaurant is renowned for its steamed lobster dumplings and jumbo shrimp and asparagus spring rolls, but even the humble steamed barbecued pork buns here are among the best I've had.

Exchange Square II, Central. ⓒ **852/2525 1163.** Dim sum HK$17–HK$58 (US$2.20–US$7.55/£1.20–£4.15). AE, DC, MC, V. Daily 11am–3pm, for dim sum. MTR: Central.

Zen Chinese CANTONESE   Starkly modern and hip, this Cantonese restaurant offers dim sum daily from an English menu, with more varieties available on the weekend.

The Mall, Pacific Place, 88 Queensway, Central. ⓒ **852/2845 4555.** Dim sum HK$30–HK$48 (US$3.85–US$6.25/ £2.15–£3.40). AE, DC, MC, V. Mon–Fri 11:30am–3pm; Sat 11:30am–5pm; Sun 10:30am–5pm, for dim sum. MTR: Admiralty.

CAUSEWAY BAY

Bo Kong ⟨ *Value* VEGETARIAN   Although there are at least a few dim sum vegetarian offerings at most restaurants, this simple Chinese restaurant with an English menu offers a larger selection than most, including a steamed vegetarian barbecued "pork" bun, steamed spinach dumpling, and deep-fried bean curd rolls with vegetable.

Times Square (12th floor), 1 Matheson St., Causeway Bay. ⓒ **852/2506 3377.** Dim sum HK$10–HK$15 (US$1.30– US$1.95/70p–£1.05). AE, DC, MC, V. Daily 11am–4pm. MTR: Causeway Bay.

9 Afternoon Tea

Colonial days are over, but the tradition of afternoon tea lives on in many of Hong Kong's best hotels. These are two of my favorites for a civilized midafternoon snack.

Lobby Lounge 😊😊 TEAS/CAKES   The InterContinental takes the honors of having the most gorgeous lobby view—soaring windows provide an almost surreal panorama of Victoria Harbour and Hong Kong Island. On weekends, you're serenaded by classic musicians. Feast your eyes on the view as you sip tea and indulge in finger sandwiches, scones with Devonshire clotted cream and preserves, and even dim sum (like a mini spring roll and barbecued pork puff). There's also a dessert menu.

In the Hotel InterContinental Hong Kong, 18 Salisbury Rd., Tsim Sha Tsui. ⓒ 852/2721 1211. www.hongkong-ic.intercontinental.com. Fixed-price afternoon tea for 2 HK$320 (US$42/£22). AE, DC, MC, V. Daily 2:30–6pm. MTR: Tsim Sha Tsui.

Peninsula Hotel Lobby 😊😊😊 TEAS/CAKES   The ornate lobby of The Peninsula hotel, built in 1928, is the most famous lobby in Hong Kong. A popular place to see and be seen, the lobby features soaring columns topped with elaborate gilded ceilings and sculpted figures of gods and angels, palm trees, a Tai Ping carpet, and classically styled furniture. As late as the 1950s, the lobby was divided into east and west wings—one for the British and one for everyone else, including, as one pamphlet put it, women "seeking dalliance." The fixed-price tea includes finger sandwiches, French pastries, and scones with Devonshire clotted cream and strawberry preserve, and tea cake. Desserts are also available from an a la carte menu. No reservations are accepted, so you may have to wait for a table. A classical string quartet serenades you from an upstairs balcony.

In The Peninsula hotel, Salisbury Rd., Tsim Sha Tsui. ⓒ 852/2920 2888. www.peninsula.com. Fixed-price afternoon tea HK$238 (US$31/£17) for 1 person, HK$338 (US$44/£24) for 2. AE, DC, MC, V. Daily 2–7pm. MTR: Tsim Sha Tsui.

7

Exploring Hong Kong

Most people think of Hong Kong as, primarily, an exotic shopping destination. In the past decade, however, Hong Kong has revved up its sightseeing potential, opening new city parks and attractions and revamping older ones, expanding museums or developing new ones, and redesigning organized sightseeing tours to reflect the territory's changing demographics. On the other hand, if all you want to do is hike or lie on the beach, you can do that, too.

If you really want to do Hong Kong justice, plan on staying at least a week. However, since the city is so compact and its transportation is so efficient, you can see quite a bit of the city and its outlying islands in 3 to 5 days, especially if you're

on the go from dawn until past dusk. To get the most out of your time, it makes sense to divide the city into sections when planning your sightseeing. The information on museums, parks, markets, and other attractions, therefore, is subdivided in this chapter according to area, making it easier to coordinate sightseeing and dining plans.

For specific ideas on how to spend your days in Hong Kong, be sure to read my recommended itineraries in chapter 3. In addition, you might find it useful to read over the suggested walking tours in chapter 8, since they include stops at several of Hong Kong's top attractions. For sightseeing information on the New Territories and Outlying Islands, see chapter 11.

1 Hong Kong's Top Attractions

The four activities I would recommend to every visitor to the SAR are: Ride the Star Ferry across the harbor, take the Peak tram to the top of Victoria Peak, ride one of the rickety old trams on Hong Kong Island, and take a ferry to one of the outlying islands (see chapter 11, "Side Trips from Hong Kong," for information on the islands). Nothing can beat the thrill of these four experiences, or give you a better insight into the essence of Hong Kong and its people. What's more, they're all incredibly inexpensive.

HONG KONG FERRIES

The stars of the Hong Kong show, of course, are the Star Ferries, green-and-white vessels that have been carrying passengers back and forth between Kowloon and Hong Kong Island since 1898. At only HK$1.70 (US20¢/10p) for the regular, lower-deck fare, it's one of the cheapest—and yet most dramatic—5-minute rides in the world. The entire trip from loading pier to unloading pier takes about 7 minutes in all; there are approximately 400 crossings a day. (For tips on using the Star Ferry, see "Getting Around" in chapter 4, beginning on p. 53.)

Since a 5-minute ride isn't nearly enough time to soak up the ambience of Victoria Harbour, another great way to relax and view the skyline is on a ferry to an outlying island. While most of Hong Kong's 260 outlying islands are uninhabited, ferry trips to the most interesting ones are described in chapter 11. These ferries, which depart

Kowloon Attractions

Clock Tower **7**
Hong Kong Museum of Art **6**
Hong Kong Museum
of History **2**
Hong Kong Science Museum **3**
Hong Kong Space Museum **5**
Kowloon Park **4**
Star Ferry **8**
Yuen Po Street Bird Garden **1**

SHENZHEN

NEW
TERRITORIES

Sai Kung
Peninsula

Hong Kong
International
Airport

KOWLOON

Lantau
Island

Hong Kong
Island

area of
detail

South China Sea

0   10 mi
0   10 km

KOWLOON
PENINSULA

Tung Choi St.

Soy St.

Nathan Rd.

Chun Yi Lane

Yau Ma
Tei

Waterloo Rd.

KING'S
PARK

Shek Lung   St.

Man Ming Ln.

Li Lung
Ln.

Tung Kun St.

Wing Sing Ln.

Lee Tak St.

Public
Square Rd.

Cliff Rd.

Market St.

Canton

Man Cheong St.

Pak Hoi St.

Man Wai St.

Man Yuen St.

Saigon St.

Woosung St.

Man Ying St.

Ning Po St.

Man Wui St.

Nanking St.

Parkes St.

Nathan Rd.

Chi Wo St.

Wai Ching St.

Wylie Rd.

Gascoigne Rd.

Kowloon
Station

Bus
Terminal

Jordan Rd.

Tak Hing St.

Cox's Rd.

Jordan Path

Shanghai St.

Bow-
ring
St.

Pilkem St.

Temple St.

Tak Shing

Austin Rd.

Jordan

Hillwood Rd.

TSIM SHA
TSUI EAST

2

KOWLOON
PARK

Observatory Rd.

Science Museum Rd.

3

Kimberley Rd.

Ferry Service to
Macau & China

Granville Rd.

Nathan Rd.

Mody Rd.

China Ferry
Terminal

TSIM SHA
TSUI

4

Haiphong Rd.

Tsim Sha
Tsui

Prat Ave.

Hart Ave.

Hanoi Rd.

Chatham Rd. S.

Salisbury Rd.

Mody Rd.

HARBOUR CITY

Canton Rd.

Park Dr.

Kowloon Rd.

Lock Rd.

High Speed
Ferry to
Central

Peking Rd.

Middle Rd.

KCR East
Tsim Sha Tsui
Station

Ocean Terminal

Hankow Rd.

Salisbury Rd.

New World
Centre

Information **i**

Ferry - - -

i

Bus Terminal

5

6

8 **7** Tsim Sha Tsui Promenade

Kowloon Public Pier

Avenue of Stars

Tsim Sha Tsui Promenade

0   1/4 mi
0   0.25 km

Star Ferry
to Central

Star Ferry
to Wan Chai

Victoria Harbour

Central District Attractions

City Hall **2**
Flagstaff House Museum of Teaware **8**
Hong Kong Museum of Coastal Defence **5**
Hong Kong Museum of Medical Science **4**
Hong Kong Park **8**
The Hong Kong Planning and Infrastructure Exhibition Gallery **3**
Man Mo Temple **4**
Peak Tram Terminal **7**
Star Ferry **1**
Zoological & Botanical Gardens **6**

Tramway
Post Office

0   100 meters
0   1/10 mile

Attractions Elsewhere on Hong Kong Island

Aberdeen floating
   restaurant **3**
Hong Kong Museum
   of Coastal Defence **6**
Madame Tussaud's **2**
Ocean Park **4**
Stanley Market **5**
Victoria Park **1**
Victoria Peak **2**

from the Central Ferry Piers, are by far the cheapest way to see Hong Kong harbor, with most trips lasting less than an hour. Some even offer an outside deck, where you can watch Hong Kong float past. In fact, part of the fun in visiting an outlying island is the ferry ride there and back.

VICTORIA PEAK

At 392m (1,286 ft.), Victoria Peak is Hong Kong Island's tallest hill, which naturally makes it the best place for spectacular views of the city and surrounding areas (if possible, go on a crystal-clear day). It's always been one of Hong Kong's most exclusive places to live, since, in addition to the views, the peak is typically cooler than the sweltering city below. More than a century ago, the rich reached the peak after a 3-hour trip in sedan chairs, transported to the top by coolies. Then, in 1888, the **Peak Tram** began operations, cutting the journey from a grueling 3 hours to a mere 8 minutes. In 1989, the older, cast-iron green funicular cars with mahogany seats were replaced by new, modern cars imported from Switzerland, which increased the passenger load from 72 to 120 people.

The easiest way to reach the Peak Tram Station, located on Garden Road, is to take the no. 15C shuttle bus that operates between the tram terminal and the Star Ferry in Central. Shuttle buses cost HK$3.20 (US40¢/20p) and run every 10 to 20 minutes between 10am and 11:45pm. Otherwise, it's about a 10-minute walk from Central's MTR Station to the tram terminus on Garden Road. Alternatively, you can take Minibus no. 1 from City Hall in Central directly to the top of Victoria Peak, but then you'd miss the tram unless you opt to take it down.

As for the trams, they depart every 15 minutes between 7am and midnight. The tram climbs almost vertically for 8 minutes before reaching the top of the peak—don't worry, there's never been an accident in its entire 100-odd years of operation. One-way tickets for the Peak Tram cost HK$20 (US$2.60/£1.40) for adults, HK$7 (US90¢/50p) for seniors, and HK$6 (US80¢/40p) for children. Round-trip tickets cost HK$30 (US$3.90/£2.15), HK$14 (US$1.80/£1), and HK$9 (US$1.15/65p), respectively. Or, you can use an Octopus card.

Upon reaching The Peak, you'll find yourself at the very modern **Peak Tower** (© **852/2849 7654;** www.thepeak.com.hk), designed by British architect Terry Farrell, which looks like a Chinese cooking wok. Head straight for the rooftop viewing deck, where you'll be privileged to one of the world's most breathtaking 360-degree vistas, with sweeping panoramas of Hong Kong Island, the South China Sea, the skyscrapers of Central, boats plying Victoria Harbour, the ever-expanding construction on Kowloon peninsula, and the many hills of the New Territories undulating in the background.

After a multimillion-dollar makeover in 2006, Peak Tower is also home to Chinese, Western, and Japanese restaurants in a wide range of price categories, as well as a shopping arcade designed to evoke traditional Hong Kong street scenes. There's also **Madame Tussauds Hong Kong,** Level 3, Peak Tower, 128 Peak Rd., Victoria Peak

---

Tips **The Best Peek of The Peak**

For the best view when riding the Peak tram up to Victoria Peak, try to get a seat at the front, on the right side of the tram. From 1908 to 1949, the first two seats at the front were reserved—for the governor of Hong Kong.

(© **852/2849 6966;** www.madame-tussauds.com.hk), with more than 100 life-size wax figures of national heroes, politicians, historical figures, Olympic medalists, movie stars, and musicians. In addition to the usual figures—Marilyn Monroe, the Beatles, Winston Churchill, victims in a medieval torture chamber—there are also local heroes like Jackie Chan, Michelle Yeoh, and Bruce Lee. Be sure to bring your camera. It's open daily from 10am to 10pm and costs HK$115 (US$15/£8.20) weekdays and HK$120 (US$20/£8.55) weekends and holidays. Children and seniors pay HK$65 (US$8.45/ £4.65) and HK$70 (US$9.10/£5) respectively. Combination tickets for both the Peak Tram and Madame Tussauds are also available. You'll probably spend about 30 minutes here.

Across the street from Peak Tower is the **Peak Galleria,** a three-story complex with more shops, restaurants, an outdoor children's playground, and a viewing terrace.

But the best thing to do atop Victoria Peak is to take a walk. One of my favorite walks in all of Hong Kong is the hour-long circular hike on Lugard Road and Harlech Road, both located just a stone's throw from the Peak tram terminus (turn right out of the terminus; both streets converge at the Peak Lookout restaurant). Mainly a footpath overhung with banyan trees and passing lush vegetation, it snakes along the side of the cliff, offering great views of the Central District below, the harbor, Kowloon, and then Aberdeen and the outlying islands on the other side. Along the path are signboards identifying flora and fauna. You will also pass Victoria Peak mansions. At night, the lighted path offers one of the world's most romantic views (I don't recommend walking it alone, however). Don't miss it.

RIDING A TRAM

Just as the Star Ferry is the best way to see the harbor, the tram is the most colorful and cheapest way to see the northern end of Hong Kong Island, including the Central District, Western District, Wan Chai, and Causeway Bay. In fact, the tram is so much a part of Hong Kong life that it was chosen for Hong Kong's exhibit at the Vancouver 1986 Expo. Dating from 1904, the tramline follows what used to be the waterfront (before the days of land reclamation). Old, narrow, double-decker affairs, the trams cut through the heart of the city, from Kennedy Town in the west to Shau Kei Wan in the east. There's only one detour—off to Happy Valley—so it's impossible to get lost.

In any case, if you're in Central, you can board the tram on Des Voeux Road Central. Climb to the upper deck and try to get a seat in the front row. (For more information on the fare and how to ride the tram, see "Getting Around" in chapter 4, beginning on p. 53.) I especially like to ride the tram at night, when neon signs are ablaze and the streets buzz with activity.

2 Museums & Galleries

If you plan to visit all six of Hong Kong's main museums—the Hong Kong Museum of Art, Hong Kong Museum of History, Hong Kong Space Museum (but not the Space Theatre), Hong Kong Science Museum, Hong Kong Museum of Coastal Defence, and Hong Kong Heritage Museum (located in Sha Tin in the New Territories; see p. 239)—you can save money by purchasing the Museum Pass for HK$30 (US$3.90/£2.15) at any of the participating museums or Hong Kong Tourism Board Visitor Information and Services Centres. Note, however, that museum admissions are free on Wednesdays.

Keep in mind, too, that municipal museums are closed December 25 and 26, January 1, and the first 3 days of the Chinese New Year. Private museums are usually also closed on bank holidays.

IN KOWLOON

Hong Kong Museum of Art ★★★ *(Finds)*   Because of its convenient location on the Tsim Sha Tsui waterfront, just a 2-minute walk from the Star Ferry terminus, and its manageable size, this museum is the most worthwhile if your time is limited. I love popping in to see the special exhibits and the museum's vast collection of Chinese antiquities and fine art—shown on a rotating basis—that make this one of my top picks in Hong Kong. Feast your eyes on ceramics, bronzes, jade, cloisonné, lacquerware, bamboo carvings, and textiles, as well as paintings, wall hangings, scrolls, and calligraphy dating from the 16th century to the present. The works are arranged in five permanent galleries on three floors of exhibit space, plus two galleries devoted to changing exhibits. The Historical Pictures Gallery is especially insightful, with works in oils, watercolors, pencil drawings, and prints that provide a visual account of life in Hong Kong, Macau, and Guangzhou (Canton) in the late 18th and 19th centuries. Another gallery displays contemporary Hong Kong works by local artists. You'll want to spend at least an hour here, though art aficionados may want to devote more time by renting audio guides for HK$10 (US$1.30/70p). A bonus is the beautiful backdrop of Victoria Harbour.

Hong Kong Cultural Centre Complex, 10 Salisbury Rd., Tsim Sha Tsui. ℂ 852/2721 0116. http://hk.art.museum. Admission HK$10 (US$1.30/70p) adults, HK$5 (US65¢/35p) children, students, and seniors. Free admission Wed. Fri–Wed 10am–6pm. MTR: Tsim Sha Tsui (exit E).

Hong Kong Museum of History ★★★ *(Kids)*   If you visit only one museum in Hong Kong and you're prepared to spend at least 2 hours, this should be it. Make it one of your first priorities, so you'll have a better understanding of what you see during the rest of your trip. Opened in 2001, this is Hong Kong's ambitious attempt to chronicle its long and fascinating history, starting with the formation of its natural history and its beginnings as a Neolithic settlement and continuing through its development as a fishing village and subsequent transformation into a modern metropolis. Through displays that include dioramas, replicas of fishing boats, models, reconstructed traditional housing, furniture, clothing, and items from daily life, the museum introduces Hong Kong's ethnic groups and their traditional means of livelihood, customs, and beliefs. These include the Tanka, who lived their entire lives on boats, the Five Great Clans who settled in what is now the New Territories and built walled communities, and the Hakka, primarily rice farmers.

You can peer inside a fishing junk, see what Kowloon Walled City looked like before it became a park, see the backstage of a Chinese opera, read about the arrival of European traders and the Opium Wars, study a map showing land reclamation since the 1840s, and see how Hong Kong changed under Japanese occupation (surprisingly, the section on Japanese occupation is quite extensive, considering that it takes up less than 4 years of Hong Kong's history). There are 10 small movie theaters spread throughout depicting everything from Hong Kong's beginnings and the Opium Wars to its movie industry, though showings in English are limited. One of my favorite parts of the museum is a re-created street of old Hong Kong, complete with a Chinese herbal-medicine shop actually located in Central until 1980, and reconstructed here. There are also 19th- and early-20th-century photographs, poignantly showing how much

Hong Kong has changed through the decades. You can easily spend 2 hours here. Audio guides, providing commentaries on more than 100 exhibits, are available for HK$10 (US$1.30/70p).

100 Chatham Rd. S., Tsim Sha Tsui East. © **852/2724 9042**. http://hk.history.museum. Admission HK$10 (US$1.30/70p) adults, HK$5 (US65¢/35p) children and seniors. Free admission Wed. Mon and Wed–Sat 10am–6pm; Sun and holidays 10am–7pm. MTR: Tsim Sha Tsui (a 20-min. walk from exit B2). Bus: 5 or 5C from the Star Ferry bus terminus.

Hong Kong Science Museum *Kids* The mysteries of science and technology come to life here, with plenty of hands-on exhibits sure to appeal to children and adults alike. More than 500 exhibits cover four floors, with sections devoted to the life sciences; light, sound, and motion; meteorology and geography; electricity and magnetism; computers and robotics; construction; transportation and communication; occupational safety and health; energy efficiency; and food science and home technology. There is also an area specially designed for children ages 3 to 7. Visitors can play with different optical illusions, enter a rotating room to learn physics in a noninertial frame, "freeze" their shadows on a wall, pick up remote voices with a large parabolic disc, play with bubbles, navigate a flight over Hong Kong Island or Kowloon at night, watch the mechanisms of an eight-cylinder gasoline engine, and learn about herbs used in traditional Chinese medicine. There are exhibits designed to test a visitor's fitness, such as lung capacity, endurance, and blood pressure. There are more than 30 personal computers in the computer section, where guests can learn about computer software, including word processing for children and graphics production, and surf the Internet for free (unfortunately, only two computers are for the Internet). This is a great place to bring kids on a rainy or humid day, when you'll want spend about 3 hours here. However, since this museum isn't unique to Hong Kong, I think childless adults can better spend their time elsewhere.

2 Science Museum Rd., Tsim Sha Tsui East. © **852/2732 3232**. http://hk.science.museum. Admission HK$25 (US$3.25/ £1.80) adults, HK$13 (US$1.70/90p) children, students, and seniors. Free admission Wed. Mon–Wed and Fri 1–9pm; Sat–Sun and holidays 10am–9pm. MTR: Tsim Sha Tsui (a 15-min. walk from exit B2). Bus: 5 or 5C from the Star Ferry bus terminus.

Hong Kong Space Museum *Kids* Located in front of The Peninsula hotel on the Tsim Sha Tsui waterfront, the Space Museum is easy to spot with its white-domed planetarium. It's divided into two parts: the Exhibition Halls with their Hall of Space Science and the Hall of Astronomy, and the Stanley Ho Space Theatre. The Hall of

---

Fun Fact **Did You Know?**

- The 1,355m (4,446-ft.) Tsing Ma Bridge, the world's second-longest road/rail suspension bridge, which connects the new international airport with Kowloon, is 95m (312 ft.) longer than San Francisco's Golden Gate Bridge and can withstand typhoon wind speeds up to 300km (186 miles) per hour.
- Hong Kong boasts several of the world's longest escalators. The world's two longest covered outdoor escalator systems are the four-section, 221m (725-ft.) system at Ocean Park and the 780m (2,559-ft.) Central–Mid-Levels Escalator connecting Central to the Mid-Levels with a capacity of handling 210,600 passengers a day. The Hongkong Bank headquarters in Central boasts the two longest freely supported (no supporting walls along their lengths) escalators in the world.

Space Science explores the human journey into space, with exhibits on ancient astronomical history, science fiction, early rockets, manned space flights, and future space programs. There are also several interactive rides and exhibits (most with weight and height restrictions), including a ride on a virtual paraglider, a harness that holds occupants aloft with the same approximate gravity they'd experience walking on the moon, and a multi-axis chair developed for astronaut training that gives the sensation of tumbling through space. The Hall of Astronomy presents information on the solar system, solar science, the stars, and the universe. However, I find the museum, which opened in 1980, rather dated. Come only if you have kids and extra time on your hands, in which case you'll spend about an hour here.

The Stanley Ho Space Theatre presents mostly OMNIMAX screenings with a projection system that produces an almost 360-degree panorama, as well as sky shows with a Zeiss star projector that can project up to about 9,000 stars. Forty-minute to hour-long shows are presented several times daily. Only a few are narrated in English, but for the others, free headsets are available with simultaneous English translations. You can buy Space Theatre tickets in advance at the museum or at any URBTIX outlet. In addition, telephone reservations are accepted at ℃ **852/2734 9009** until 1 hour before the show commences.

Hong Kong Cultural Centre Complex, 10 Salisbury Rd., Tsim Sha Tsui. ℃ **852/2721 0226**. http://hk.space.museum. Admission to Exhibition Halls HK$10 (US$1.30/70p) adults, HK$5 (US65¢/35p) children, students, and seniors. Free admission on Wed. Space Theatre HK$24–HK$32 (US$3.10–US$4.15/£1.70–£2.30) adults, HK$12–HK$16 (US$1.55–US$2.10/85p–£1.15) children, students, and seniors. Mon and Wed–Fri 1–9pm; Sat–Sun and holidays 10am–9pm. MTR: Tsim Sha Tsui (exit E).

ON HONG KONG ISLAND

Flagstaff House Museum of Tea Ware 🕮🕮 *Finds*   Flagstaff House, located in Hong Kong Park, is the oldest colonial building in Hong Kong—the best place to go if you want to see typical Hong Kong architecture of 150 years ago. The house was completed in 1846 in Greek Revival style for the commander of the British forces. Now a museum devoted to the subject of tea culture in China, its collection includes about 600 pieces of tea ware ranging from earthenware to porcelain, primarily of Chinese origin, dating from the 7th century to the present day. However, only 150 or so pieces are on display at any one time, with exhibitions changed two or three times a year. I always find them fascinating, especially the exhibits describing the various kinds of tea and tea-making methods favored by the major dynasties. Don't miss the museum shop, which sells beautifully crafted teapots as well as teas. You can see everything here in about 30 minutes.

Hong Kong Park, 10 Cotton Tree Dr., Central. ℃ **852/2869 0690**. www.lcsd.gov.hk/hkma. Free admission. Wed–Mon 10am–5pm. MTR: Admiralty (exit C1); then follow the signs through Pacific Place to Island Shangri-La Hotel/Hong Kong Park via 2 escalators.

Hong Kong Museum of Coastal Defence   Located in Lei Yue Mun Fort, one of Hong Kong's oldest and best-preserved British coastal fortresses dating from the Victorian period, this museum explores 600 years of the territory's coastal defense. Exhibits begin with the Ming and Qing dynasties, when coastal defenses guarded southern China against the invasion of Japanese pirates and Western imperialists, and continue through the Opium Wars, Hong Kong's role as a major base for the British navy, the Japanese 1941 invasion, and the recent handover to the People's Liberation Army. On display are naval costumes, models of war junks, weaponry, photographs, and memorabilia. The fort itself, built by the British in 1887 to defend the eastern

Life on the Water in Aberdeen

Situated on the south side of Hong Kong Island, Aberdeen is nestled around a naturally protected harbor. Famous for its colorful floating seafood restaurant and boat people who live on junks in Aberdeen Harbour, the town has undergone massive changes in recent years. Originally a typhoon shelter and land base for seafarers, it used to be a charming fishing village and boat-building port, supported primarily by several thousand junks and boat people. Many of the boat people, however, have since been moved to massive housing projects, and the waterfront surrounding Aberdeen is now crowded with high-rises. At anchor are almost as many yachts as fishing boats and junks.

Still, Aberdeen continues to be popular with the tourist crowd because of its remaining boat population and floating restaurant. Women operating sampans will vie for your dollars to tour you around the harbor, which is definitely worth the price since it's about the only thing to do here and is the best way to see the junks. Although the boat population is shrinking, you'll pass huge boats that house extended families; you'll see men repairing fishing nets, women hanging out their laundry, dogs barking, children playing, and families eating. I find the ride rather voyeuristic but fascinating just the same. There was a time when a boat person could be born, live, marry, and die onboard, hardly ever setting foot on shore. Nowadays, many young people move ashore to seek more stable employment.

A 20-minute tour from a licensed operator will cost approximately HK$60 (US$7.80/£4.30) per person and is offered daily between 9am and 5:30pm from the Aberdeen Centre promenade. There are also old women with wide-brimmed straw hats who will try to persuade you to board their sampan, with the price open to bargaining and depending on the numbers of tourists around at the time. On one particularly slow day, for example, I was offered, and took, a sampan tour for HK$50 (US$6.50/£3.55), and I was the only one in the boat.

Other Aberdeen attractions include the largest floating restaurant in the world—Jumbo Kingdom, which offers both Cantonese restaurants and a rooftop seafood restaurant (see p. 154), with free shuttle service from the Aberdeen Centre promenade—and a temple built in 1851. The temple is dedicated to Tin Hau, protectress of fishing folk, and is located at the junction of Aberdeen Main Road and Aberdeen Reservoir Road. A short taxi ride away is the huge Ocean Park amusement park with its thrill rides and aquarium.

To get to Aberdeen, take bus no. 7 from the Central Ferry Piers; bus no. 70 from the Exchange Square Bus Terminal in the Central District; bus no. 72 or 77 from Causeway Bay; or bus no. 973 from Tsim Sha Tsui.

approaches to the harbor against possible attacks by Russia or France, retains its batteries, underground magazines, protective ditch, caponiers, and torpedo station. With its strategic location on the coast, it provides a panoramic view of the eastern approach to Victoria Harbour. You'll probably spend at least 1½ hours here.

175 Tung Hei Rd., Shau Kei Wan. (✆) 852/2569 1500. http://hk.coastaldefence.museum. Admission HK$10 (US$1.30/70p) adults, HK$5 (US65¢/35p) students, seniors, and children. Free admission Wed. Fri–Wed 10am–5pm. MTR: Shau Kei Wan (exit B2, then a 15-min. walk).

Hong Kong Museum of Medical Sciences ✦ *Finds*   This museum charts the historical development of medical science in Hong Kong. It's located in the century-old, Edwardian-style former Pathological Institute, which was founded to combat the colony's most horrific outbreak of bubonic plague. Back then, British patients were treated upstairs, while the Chinese were relegated to the basement rooms. Several rooms remain almost exactly as they were, including an autopsy room and a laboratory filled with old equipment, while others serve as exhibition rooms devoted to such areas as the development of dentistry and radiology (note the X-ray of the bound foot). But what makes the museum particularly fascinating is its unique comparison of traditional Chinese and Western medicine, and its funding of research into Chinese medicine. Included are displays on acupuncture and traditional Chinese herbs. You can spend up to an hour here.

2 Caine Lane, Mid-Levels. (✆) 852/2549 5123. www.hkmms.org.hk. Admission HK$10 (US$1.30/70p) adults, HK$5 (US65¢/35p) children, students, and seniors. Tues–Sat 10am–5pm; Sun and holidays 1–5pm. MTR: Central; then bus 26 from Des Voeux Rd. in front of Hongkong Bank headquarters to Man Mo Temple; walk up Ladder St. (a particularly grueling set of stairs) to Caine Lane. Or take Minibus 8 or 22 from in front of Central's Star Ferry to Ladder St. (pronounced Lau Tai Kai in Chinese).

The Hong Kong Planning and Infrastructure Exhibition Gallery ✦ *Finds*   Its name is dry and unpromising, but anyone who has witnessed the SAR's changes over the past few decades will find this museum fascinating—Hong Kong is a never-ending work in progress. Over the next few decades, the city will continue to develop its tourism, transportation, and urban infrastructure at what seems like breakneck speed. The purpose of this museum is to help visitors visualize those changes through interactive displays, sophisticated computer simulation, and high-tech models that project Hong Kong's new look 2, 10, and 20 years from now. West Kowloon, embraced by a huge canopy to be designed by Norman Foster, will become one of the city's foremost cultural and entertainment centers the site is completed around 2012 (though, it must be added, there is strong local opposition to the proposed project as well, with critics contending it doesn't adequately meet residents' needs). Future and current works include a pedestrian promenade on Hong Kong Island stretching along the waterfront from Central to Causeway Bay; enlarged cargo capacity at the airport; a new town where Kai Tak Airport once stood; a fourth tunnel under the harbor; a new bridge connecting the New Territories to China's Shekou (completed in 2006); and 100km (62 miles) of new highway. There are some fun exhibits, too, including a 3-D flight over Sha Tin in the New Territories, virtual "walks" of the Lung Yeuk Tau and Ping Shan Heritage Trails, and a photo booth that takes your picture with a selected Hong Kong backdrop (like the giant Buddha on Lantau island) and then lets you e-mail it to friends for free. The museum is located on the north side of City Hall and can be toured in about 30 minutes.

3 Edinburgh Place, Central. (✆) 852/3101 1242. www.info.gov.hk/infrastructuregallery. Free admission. Wed–Mon 10am–6pm. MTR: Central.

3 Temples

For information on Po Lin Monastery and its adjacent Giant Tian Tan Buddha, see the section on Lantau island in "The Outlying Islands" in chapter 11, beginning on p. 244.

Chi Lin Buddhist Nunnery   Just one subway stop away from Wong Tai Sin (see below) is the Chi Lin Buddhist Nunnery, founded in the 1930s to provide religious, cultural, educational, and elderly care services to the Hong Kong community. Reconstructed in the 1990s in the style of Tang dynasty monastic architecture (A.D. 618–907), the nunnery is a successful union of ancient building techniques and modern technology. Imported yellow cedar from Canada was carved in China by skilled artisans and craftsmen and then reconstructed here like pieces in a jigsaw puzzle; no nails were used, but rather a system of wooden doweling and brackets. The main hall was modeled after the Foguang Monastery in Shanxi Province, while the double-eaved Hall of Celestial Kings is designed after the 11th-century Phoenix Hall outside Kyoto, Japan. On nunnery grounds are a lotus pond, sculpted bushes and bonsai, and statues of the Goddess of Mercy, God of Medicine, and others. A better garden, however, awaits across the street, connected to the nunnery by a bridge and styled in imitation of famous gardens in Suzhou with ponds, a waterfall, a hexagonal-shaped pavilion, and a variety of trees and shrubbery. Otherwise, there isn't much to see; this stopover will appeal mostly to architects, East Asian scholars, and gardeners.

Chi Lin Rd., Diamond Hill. © 852/2354 1604. Free admission. Daily 9am–4:30pm. MTR: Diamond Hill (exit C2) and then a 15-min. walk.

Man Mo Temple ☆   Hong Kong Island's oldest and most important temple (Taoist) was built in the 1840s as one of the new colony's first traditional-style temples. It's named after its two principal deities: Man, the god of literature, who is dressed in red and holds a calligraphy brush; and Mo, the god of war, wearing a green robe and holding a sword. Ironically, Mo finds patronage in both the police force (shrines in his honor can be found in all Hong Kong police stations today) and the infamous triad secret societies. Two ornate sedan chairs, carved in 1862, were once used during festivals to carry the statues of the gods around the neighborhood. But what makes this evocative temple particularly memorable are the giant incense coils hanging from the ceiling, imparting a fragrant, smoky haze—these are purchased by patrons seeking fulfillment of their wishes, such as good health or a successful business deal, and may burn as long as 3 weeks. No flash photography is allowed inside the temple.

Hollywood Rd. and Ladder St., Western District. © 852/2803 2916. Free admission. Daily 8am–6pm. Bus: 26 from Des Voeux Rd. Central (in front of the Hongkong Bank headquarters) to the 2nd stop on Hollywood Rd., across from the temple. Or take the Mid-Levels Escalator to Hollywood Rd.

Wong Tai Sin ☆☆   Located six subway stops northeast of Yau Ma Tei in the far north end of Kowloon, Wong Tai Sin is Hong Kong's most popular Taoist temple and attracts worshippers of all three traditional Chinese religions: Taoism, Buddhism, and Confucianism. Although the temple itself is less than 100 years old, it adheres to traditional Chinese architectural principles with its red pillars, two-tiered golden roof, blue friezes, yellow latticework, and multicolored carvings. Its construction also displays the five elements dictated by geomancy, namely bronze (the pavilion), metal (the archives hall), wood, water (a fountain), fire (Yue Heung Shrine, dedicated to the Buddha of Lighting Lamp), and earth (an earthen wall). The very popular temple attracts those seeking information about their fortunes—from advice about business or horse racing to determining which day is most auspicious for a wedding. Most worshippers make use of a bamboo container holding numbered sticks. After lighting a joss stick and kneeling before the main altar, the worshipper gently shakes the container until one of the sticks falls out. The number corresponds to a certain fortune, which is then interpreted by one of the temple's many soothsayers.

You can wander around the temple grounds, where there are halls dedicated to the Buddhist Goddess of Mercy and to Confucius; the Good Wish Garden with ponds, an artificial waterfall, a replica of the famous Nine Dragons relief (the original is in Beijing's Imperial Palace), and circular, square, octagonal, and fan-shaped pavilions; and a clinic with both Western medical services and traditional Chinese herbal treatments. Wong Tai Sin takes its name, in fact, from a legendary shepherd who learned the art of healing. A visit to this temple, surrounded by vast, government housing estates, provides insight into Chinese religious practices and is well worth a stop despite its out-of-the-way location.

2 Chuk Yuen, Wong Tai Sin Estate. (ℭ 852/2327 8141. www.siksikyuen.org.hk. Free admission to temple, though donations of about HK$1 (US15¢/5p) are expected at the temple's entrance, with an additional HK$2 (US25¢/15p) donation at the Good Wish Garden. Temple daily 7am–5:30pm; garden daily 9am–4pm. MTR: Wong Tai Sin (exit B2) and then a 3-min. walk (follow the signs).

4 Parks & Gardens

IN KOWLOON

KOWLOON PARK *(Kids)*   Occupying the site of an old military encampment first established in the 1860s, Kowloon Park (ℭ **852/2724 3344;** www.lcsd.gov.hk/parks/hp) is Tsim Sha Tsui's largest recreational and sports facility, boasting an indoor heated Olympic-size swimming pool, three outdoor leisure pools linked by a series of waterfalls, an open-air sculpture garden featuring works by local and overseas sculptors, a Chinese garden, a fitness trail, an aviary, a maze formed by hedges, two children's playgrounds, and a bird lake with flamingos and other waterfowl. On Sundays from 2:30 to 4:30pm there are free Kung Fu demonstrations at the Kung Fu Corner.

Not far from the Tsim Sha Tsui MTR station (take the A1 exit for Kowloon Park), it's easily accessible from Nathan, Haiphong, and Austin roads and is open daily from 6am to midnight, with free admission. The swimming pools (ℭ **852/2724 4522**) are open daily from 6:30am to 9pm and charge HK$19 (US$2.45/£1.35) for adults and HK$9 (US$1.15/65p) for children.

KOWLOON WALLED CITY PARK *(Kids)* *(Finds)*   Hong Kong's newest park is perhaps its finest. Although it doesn't boast the attractions of the city's other parks, the Kowloon Walled City Park, on Tung Tau Tsuen Road (ℭ **852/2716 9962;** www.lcsd. gov.hk/parks/kwcp), was designed to re-create the style of a classical Southern Chinese garden and is the largest such garden outside China. Beautifully landscaped with man-made hills, ponds, streams, pines, boulders, bonsai, bamboo, and shrubs, it features winding paths through a Chinese zodiac sculpture garden, flower gardens, and pavilions.

Even more fascinating is the site's history, described through photographs in a former almshouse. More than 150 years ago, the site was on the seashore, making it perfect in 1847 for the construction of a Chinese fort to defend Kowloon after the British takeover of Hong Kong Island. After 1898, when the British took over the New Territories, the 500 soldiers occupying the fort were expelled. But China did not consider the site part of the leased territories, and for most of the next century, the Kowloon Walled City remained in sovereign limbo, ignored by British authorities. It developed a lifestyle of its own, with its own set of laws. An enclave of tenements and secret societies that flouted Hong Kong's building regulations and health standards, it served as a haven for squatters, refugees, criminals, prostitutes, and drug addicts. Densely packed and infested with rats, many parts of the warrenlike slum never saw the light of day.

Hong Kong police ventured inside only in pairs. Following a special Sino-British agreement and years of lengthy negotiations over new housing for Walled City residents, the enclave was demolished in 1994. In addition to the almshouse, a few other historic structures remain, including the Old South Gate entrance, wall foundations, and flagstone paths.

To reach the park, take the MTR to Lok Fu station (exit B) and then walk 15 minutes on Junction Road to Tung Tau Tsuen Road; or take bus no. 1 from the Star Ferry in Tsim Sha Tsui to the stop opposite the park. It's open daily from 6:30am to 11pm, and admission is free.

YUEN PO STREET BIRD GARDEN 🌟🌟🌟 While in Hong Kong, you may notice wooden bird cages hanging outside shops or from apartment balconies, or perhaps even see someone walking down the street with a cage. Birds are favorite pets in Chinese households, and the price of a bird is determined not by its plumage but by its singing talents. To see more of these prized songbirds, visit the fascinating Yuen Po Street Bird Garden (© **852/2302 1762;** www.lcsd.gov.hk/parks/ypsbg), Prince Edward Road West, which consists of a series of Chinese-style moon gates and courtyards lined with stalls selling songbirds, beautifully crafted wood and bamboo cages, live crickets and mealy worms, and tiny porcelain food bowls. Nothing, it seems, is too expensive for these tiny creatures. In addition to people buying and selling birds, there are also visitors just taking their birds for an outing. This garden is very Chinese and a lot of fun to see (*Note:* Because of concerns about avian flu, signs warning against touching bird droppings are posted at the garden, along with hand sanitizers.) Incidentally, next door is Flower Market Road, lined with flower shops, while on nearby Tung Choi Street is the Goldfish Market with exotic fish.

To reach the Bird Garden, open daily from 7am to 8pm, take the MTR to Prince Edward Road station (exit B1) and walk 10 minutes east on Prince Edward Road West, turning left at the railway onto Yuen Po Street. Or take bus no. 1 from the Star Ferry in Tsim Sha Tsui. Admission is free.

ON HONG KONG ISLAND

HONG KONG PARK 🌟🌟 *Kids* Opened in 1991 and stretching 8 hectares (20 acres) along Supreme Court Road and Cotton Tree Drive in Central, Hong Kong Park (© **852/2521 5041;** www.lcsd.gov.hk/parks/hkp) features a dancing fountain at its entrance; one of Southeast Asia's largest greenhouses with more than 2,000 rare plant species, including desert and tropical jungle varieties; an aviary housing 800 exotic birds in a tropical rainforest setting with an elevated walkway; various gardens; a children's playground; and a viewing platform reached by climbing 105 stairs. The most famous building on park grounds is the Flagstaff House Museum of Tea Ware (p. 168). Since the marriage registry is located on an edge of the park, the gardens are a favorite venue for wedding photographs, especially on weekends and auspicious days of the Chinese calendar.

The park is open daily from 6am to 11pm, the greenhouse and aviary are open daily 9am to 5pm, and the Museum of Tea Ware is open Wednesday through Monday from 10am to 5pm. Admission to all is free. To reach the park, take the MTR to Admiralty Station (exit C1), then follow the signs through Pacific Place and up the set of escalators.

VICTORIA PARK The 17-hectare (42-acre) Victoria Park (© **852/2882 4151;** www.lcsd.gov.hk/parks/vp) is Hong Kong Island's largest, located on Causeway and

Gloucester roads in Causeway Bay and serving as the green lungs of the city. Constructed on reclaimed land formerly used for a typhoon shelter, it has tennis and squash courts, a 50m (164-ft.) swimming pool, soccer fields, basketball courts, playgrounds, a roller skating rink, a jogging and fitness trail, and—my favorite—a pebble path for massaging the bottom of your feet. It is also popular in early morning for those practicing tai chi (shadow boxing), a disciplined physical routine of more than 200 individual movements, designed to exercise every muscle of the body and bring a sense of peace and balance to its practitioners. The Mid-Autumn Festival is held here, as well as a flower market a few days before Chinese New Year. The park is open 24 hours and is free. To reach it, take the MTR or tram to Causeway Bay.

ZOOLOGICAL & BOTANICAL GARDENS 🐦 *Kids*   Established in 1864, the Zoological and Botanical Gardens, Upper Albert Road, Central (© **852/2530 0154;** www.lcsd.gov.hk/parks/hkzbg), are spread on the slope of Victoria Peak, making it a popular respite for Hong Kong residents. Come here early, around 7am, and you'll see Chinese residents going through the slow motions of tai chi. In the gardens themselves, which retain some of their Victorian charm, flowers are almost always in bloom, from azaleas in the spring to wisteria and bauhinia in the summer and fall. More than 1,000 species of plants, most of them indigenous to tropical and subtropical regions and planted throughout the grounds, include Burmese rosewood trees, varieties of bamboo, Indian rubber trees, camphor trees, a variety of camellia, herbs, and the Hong Kong orchid. The small zoo houses 600 birds, 90 mammals, and 20 reptiles, including jaguars, orangutans, tamarins, kangaroos, flamingos, a Burmese python, Palawan peacocks, birds of paradise from Papua New Guinea, cranes, and Mandarin ducks. The zoo is well known for its success in breeding birds on the verge of extinction and for supplying zoos around the world with new stock.

If you're tired of Central and its traffic, this is a pleasant place to regain your perspective. There's also a children's playground. Admission is free. The eastern part of the park, called Fountain Terrace and containing most of the botanical gardens and the aviaries, is open daily from 6am to 10pm, while the western half, with its reptiles and mammals, is open daily from 6am to 7pm. To reach it, take the MTR to Central and then walk 15 minutes up Garden Road to the corner of Upper Albert Road. Or take bus no. 3B or 12 from Queen's Road Central in front of the HSBC bank building in Central.

5 Amusement Parks

Hong Kong Disneyland 🐦🐦 *Kids*   Opened in 2005 on Lantau Island, just a 10-minute ride from the airport, this Disney venture is Asia's second (the first is Tokyo Disneyland). Recreating many of the exact features of the original Disneyland in California but on a smaller scale, the 126-hectare (311-acre) theme park contains the usual four Disney themed lands—namely, Main Street U.S.A., Fantasyland, Adventureland, and Tomorrowland—along with such classic rides and attractions as Space Mountain, Buzz Lightyear Astro Blasters, Tarzan's Treehouse, and the Jungle River Cruise, as well as high-caliber performances and shows, parades, and an evening fireworks extravaganza. Unique to the park is the world's only Fantasy Gardens, where Disney characters hang out to meet their fans. Note that admission is higher during peak times, including weekends, public holidays, summer school vacation (July/Aug), and the so-called Golden Week holidays for mainlander Chinese (May and Oct). You can purchase tickets at the gate, in advance online, or at the Hong Kong Disneyland Ticket Express counter at Hong Kong Station in Central, open daily 9am to 9pm.

Lantau Island. (C) 852/1 830 830. www.hongkongdisneyland.com. Regular admission HK$295 (US$38/£21) adults, HK$170 (US$22/£12) seniors, HK$210 (US$27/£15) children. Peak admission HK$350 (US$45/£25), HK$200 (US$26/£14), and HK$250 (US$32/£18) respectively. Open hours vary; in summer, usually 10am–8pm daily. MTR: From the Tung Chung Line, transfer at Sunny Bay for the Disneyland Resort Line.

Ocean Park ✦✦✦ *Kids*   If you're a kid or a kid at heart, you'll love Ocean Park, a combination marine park and amusement center. Situated along a dramatic rocky coastline on the island's southern shore, the park is divided into two areas: a "lowland" and a "headland," connected by cable car and escalator. Because of the wide range of attractions, Ocean Park is interesting for children and adults alike. Facilities are first class, and Ocean Park is Asia's first accredited member of the American Zoo and Aquarium Association.

The lowland is subdivided into several areas and attractions. The most popular residents of Ocean Park are An An and Jia Jia, a pair of pandas presented as gifts from China. Aimed at youngsters are the Dinosaur Discovery Trail, with 17 lifelike models of dinosaurs (the tyrannosaurus may be too scary for toddlers), and Kids' World, with its kiddie rides, playgrounds, remote-control cars and boats, shows geared toward children, and shooting-games arcade. Educational tours are given at Dolphin University (only one tour a day in English, however), where the audience can watch the training of dolphins at close range. Film Fantasia is a 100-seat theater with hydraulically actuated seats that move in time to the fast-paced action on the screen, kind of like riding a roller coaster without actually going anywhere but visually much more stimulating (participants must be at least 1.2m/4 ft. tall). Much gentler are walks through the magical Butterfly House (shaped, interestingly enough, like a caterpillar) with hundreds of free-flying butterflies, and, my favorite, the Golden Pagoda set in a lush garden, with more varieties of goldfish than you ever imagined possible, most of them from China. The pompommed fish, for example, have large pompomlike growths on their heads, while the bubble eyes, with huge bubbles under their eyes, are too bizarre for words.

From the lowland, visitors board cable cars for a spectacular 8-minute ride over a hill to the headland, while being treated to great views of the coastline and the South China Sea along the way. The headland area, situated on a peninsula that juts into the sea, is also subdivided into several areas and attractions. The marine life section includes an artificial wave cove that is home to sea lions; an aquarium housing more than 1,000 jellyfish and complete with theatrical lighting, multimedia sound, and visual special effects; and a tank with more than 200 sharks and rays representing more than 30 species, viewed from an underwater tunnel. Ocean Theatre features shows by talented dolphins, sea lions, and a killer whale. But my favorite is the Atoll Reef, one of the world's largest aquariums, with 2,600 fish of 200 different species. The observation passageway circles the aquarium on four levels, enabling you to view the sea life—everything from giant octopi to schools of tropical fish—from various depths and from different angles. There are also thrill rides, including a Ferris wheel, a roller coaster that turns upside down three times, another roller coaster that follows a Wild West theme, and a rather wet ride on a "raging river." Other exhibits include a Japanese Garden; a 69m-high (226 ft.) Ocean Park Tower offering revolving, panoramic views of Aberdeen and outlying islands; and an aviary with more than 2,000 birds.

After touring the headland, you can take the long escalator down to the Tai Shue Wan Entrance, from which it's a short taxi ride to Aberdeen with its sampan rides and floating restaurant. At any rate, to do Ocean Park justice, plan on spending a minimum of 4 hours here.

Aberdeen, Hong Kong Island. ℂ 852/2552 0291. www.oceanpark.com.hk. Admission HK$185 (US$24/£13) adults, HK$93 (US$12/£6.65) children. Daily 10am–6pm. Bus: Ocean Park Citybus 629 from the Admiralty MTR station every 10 to 20 min.; you can buy round-trip tickets that include park admission. Or take 70 from Exchange Square in Central or 72 from Causeway Bay (get off at the 1st stop after the tunnel and then walk 20 min.).

6 Especially for Kids

Many of the aforementioned attractions will appeal to children. On the Kowloon side, the **Space Museum** (p. 167) is very much oriented to children, with buttons to push, telescopes to look through, and computer quizzes to test what they've learned, not to mention the films featured in the Stanley Ho Space Theatre. In the **Science Museum** (p. 167), approximately 70% of its 500-some displays are hands-on, and there's also a special play area for children between the ages of 3 and 7. Across the Plaza is the **Museum of History** (p. 166), with life-size replicas and models that bring the history of Hong Kong to life. And don't forget **Kowloon Park** (p. 172), right on Nathan Road, which has two playgrounds for children (including one with restored fortifications and cannon emplacements), a pond with flamingos and other waterfowl, an aviary, swimming pools, and lots of space to run.

On Hong Kong Island, the biggest draw for kids of all ages is **Ocean Park** (see above), which boasts a wide mix of things to do and see, including thrill rides; a shark aquarium; animal performances; life-size dinosaurs; and a children's section with kiddie rides, a playground, shows geared to children, and lots more. Of all the things unique to Hong Kong, this is probably the one kids will enjoy most. For free entertainment, visit the **Zoological and Botanical Gardens** (p. 174) with its jaguars, monkeys, birds, and other animals, and **Hong Kong Park** (p. 173) with its greenhouse, aviary, children's playground, and climbing tower. Older kids will like **Victoria Peak** (p. 164), where there are not only fantastic views but also Madame Tussauds with its wax replicas of movie stars, musicians, athletes, and historical figures.

The SAR's most famous attraction, however, is **Hong Kong Disneyland** on Lantau Island (p. 174), which duplicates the Disney experience with the usual rides, attractions, shows, and fireworks.

7 Organized Tours & Cultural Activities

Hong Kong offers lots of organized tours, so if you're pressed for time, this may be the best way to go. Most major hotels have a tour desk where you can make bookings for city tours. In addition, I heartily recommend participating in one or more of the Hong Kong Tourism Board's Meet the People cultural activities, which are free, 1-hour tours, classes, or lectures given by local specialists covering everything from Chinese antiques to tai chi (shadow boxing).

LAND TOURS

For general sightseeing, **Gray Line** offers a variety of tours, with bookings available through most Hong Kong hotels or by calling ℂ **852/2368 7111** or searching www.grayline.com.hk. The Deluxe Hong Kong Island Tour is a 5-hour trip offered both morning and afternoon and includes stops at Man Mo Temple, Victoria Peak,

Aberdeen, and Stanley. It costs HK$295 (US$38/£21) for adults and HK$190 (US$25/£14) for children.

Other Gray Line tours take in the Po Lin Monastery and Giant Buddha on Lantau island or the New Territories; there are also sunset cruises (for information about organized evening tours, see the "Night Tours" section of chapter 10, "Hong Kong After Dark," beginning on p. 234). Most useful, in my opinion, are Gray Line's tours to the New Territories, since they cover large areas that would be very difficult, if not impossible, to reach in 1 day on your own. The "Land Between Tour" is a 6½-hour excursion that enables visitors to see how much this once-rural region has changed in the past couple decades, with traditional villages now overshadowed by huge government housing estates that house half of Hong Kong's population. Passing satellite towns with high-rise apartment buildings, farms, and villages, the bus stops at a temple, a lookout point on Hong Kong's tallest mountain, a walled village, and a fishing village to see how fisher folk breed fish in submerged cages, and a Cantonese restaurant for lunch. The price of this tour, with departures daily, is HK$395 (US$51/£28) for adults and HK$345 (US$45/£25) for children and seniors.

Gray Line's "Heritage Tour" also takes in the New Territories but emphasizes Hong Kong's past rather than the present and makes stops at historic Chinese sites that even Hong Kong residents seldom see. It's a must for those who are interested in local historical architecture; it also gives insight into clan life in the New Territories long before the region became part of colonial Hong Kong. Lasting approximately 5 hours, tours make stops at Tai Fu Tai, a Chinese-style ornate mansion built in 1865 by a high-ranking official, fascinating for its insight into how the rich lived; Tang Chung Ling, an ancestral hall belonging to one of the Five Great Clans; Lo Wai, a walled village built by the Tang clan; and the Man Mo Temple in Tai Po. Tours depart every Monday, Wednesday, Friday, and Saturday (except public holidays), and cost HK$295 (US$38/£21) for adults and HK$245 (US$31/£18) for children and seniors.

Splendid Tours & Travel (© 852/2316 2151; www.splendidtours.com) also offers a general city tour, excursions to Lantau and the New Territories, night tours, and cruises, which can also be booked through Hong Kong hotels.

BOAT TOURS

Since so many of Hong Kong's attractions are on or near the water, a variety of boat tours are available, including those given by Gray Line and Splendid Tours & Travel (see above). One of the most popular is the 1-hour **Star Ferry's Harbour Tour** (© 852/2118 6201; www.starferry.com.hk/harbourtour), with boarding available at Tsim Sha Tsui, Central, Wan Chai, and Hung Hom ferry piers. Cost of the daily cruises, which have on-board commentary, is HK$40 (US$5.20/£2.85) for adults and HK$36 (US$4.65/£2.55) for children and seniors. One-hour Star Ferry evening cruises, which include refreshments and some with views of the nightly Symphony of Lights multimedia show, cost HK$85 (US$11/£6.05) and HK$76 (US$9.85/£5.40) respectively, while 2-hour cruises cost HK$120 (US$16/£8.55) and HK$108 (US$14/£7.70) respectively.

Watertours (© 852/2926 3868; www.watertours.com.hk), Hong Kong's largest tour operator of boat and junk cruises, offers a 2-hour cruise that includes a trip to a typhoon shelter and its junks and the firing of the Noon Day Gun in Causeway Bay (a holdover from colonial days that you can see if you're there, but don't go out of your way to see it) by Jardine Matheson & Co., Hong Kong's oldest trading company. The cost of this tour, which departs at 10:15am from the Kowloon public pier and

---

> ## *Tips* A Junk Cruise for Free
>
> The best cruise deal in town is aboard the *Duk Ling*, an authentic Chinese junk. Free 1-hour cruises, organized by the Hong Kong Tourism Board, are offered 2 days a week (at last check on Thurs and Sat). Registration is required; contact the HKTB at ℰ **852/2508 1234** or go to www.discoverhongkong.com for the latest schedule.

10:30am from Queen's Pier in Central and includes refreshments, is HK$220 (US$29/£16) for adults and HK$130 (US$17/£9.30) for children. Watertours also schedules more than a half-dozen other longer boat trips, including a combination water-and-land tour and sunset and evening cruises aboard colorful boats (for evening cruises, see the "Night Tours" section of chapter 10, "Hong Kong After Dark," beginning on p. 234). You can pick up a Watertours pamphlet at HKTB Visitor Information and Services Centres and in many hotels.

Hong Kong Dolphinwatch (ℰ **852/2984 1414;** www.hkdolphinwatch.com) offers 4-hour trips several mornings a week that include a bus ride to the new satellite town of Tung Chung followed by a luxury cruise to the natural habitat of the endangered Chinese pink dolphins (Indo-Pacific Humpback dolphins), which live off Lantau island within sight of power plants, factories, Tung Chung, and the airport. Advance booking is necessary, and the cost is HK$320 (US$42/£23) for adults and HK$160 (US$21/£11) for children.

SPECIAL-INTEREST TOURS

"MEET THE PEOPLE" *Moments* Through this unique program of free 1-hour tours, lectures, classes, and seminars, visitors can meet local specialists and gain in-depth knowledge of Hong Kong's traditions. Programs are updated and revised annually; past offerings have included such subjects as Chinese antiques, Cantonese opera, pearls, jade, feng shui (geomancy), Chinese tea, and tai chi, with something going on every day of the week. Reservations are not necessary. For details on what, when, and where, pick up a *Cultural Kaleidoscope* brochure at a HKTB Visitor Information and Services Centre or go to HKTB's website, www.discoverhongkong.com, and click on "Heritage" and then "Cultural Kaleidoscope."

"COME HORSE RACING" TOUR This tour, offered by both Gray Line and Splendid Tours (see "Land Tours," above), allows visitors to experience the excitement of the races, at either Happy Valley or Sha Tin, an excitement that grows proportionally according to how much you bet. Tours are only scheduled during the horse-racing season—September to mid-June—usually on Wednesday evenings and on Saturday and/or Sunday afternoons. The tour includes transportation; a pre-race international buffet; beer, wine, or soft drinks; personal entry badge to the luxurious Visitors' Box in the Hong Kong Jockey Club's Members' Enclosure; a HK$30 (US$3.90/£2.15) betting voucher; guide services; and even hints to help you place your bets. Tours cost HK$550 (US$71/£39), except during special races when they cost more. Tours are limited to tourists 18 years of age and older (be sure to bring your passport with you when booking and participating in this tour) whose stay in Hong Kong is no more than 21 days. Bookings can be made through the tour operators, hotel tour desks, or any HKTB Visitor and Information & Services Centres.

8 Outdoor Activities

Despite the fact that the SAR is densely populated, there's enough open space to pursue everything from golf to hiking to windsurfing. For the hardworking Chinese and expatriates, recreation and leisure are essential for relaxing and winding down. With that in mind, try to schedule your golfing, swimming, or hiking trips on weekdays unless you enjoy jostling elbows with the crowds.

GOLF

Golf courses can be crowded, so it's recommended you call clubs beforehand to check whether they're open and the available tee-off times. It's best to book a tee-time in advance. For more information on courses in Hong Kong, contact the Hong Kong Golf Association (📞 852/2504 8659; www.hkga.com).

The **Jockey Club Kau Sai Chau Public Golf Course** (📞 852/2791 3388; www.kscgolf.com), carved out of an island formerly used by the British army for shelling practice, offers great panoramic vistas and one of the world's finest public golfing facilities. There is one 18-hole course that charges HK$640 (US$84/£45) on weekdays and HK$940 (US$122/£67) on weekends. There's also a 9-hole course that costs HK$380 (US$49/£27) and HK$550 (US$71/£39), respectively. To reach it, take the MTR to Choi Hung and then board bus no. 92 or green minibus no. 1A to Sai Kung Bus Terminus, followed by the special "golfer's ferry" to Kau Sai Chau.

There are also private golf clubs that admit nonmembers on weekdays only. Most charge HK$1,400 (US$182/£100) for greens fees on 18-hole courses. The **Hong Kong Golf Club** (www.hkgolfclub.org) maintains three 18-hole courses in **Fanling** (📞 852/2670 1211) and a 9-hole course in **Deep Water Bay** (📞 852/2812 7070). No advance reservations are taken, so visitors should first check availability by phone and then arrive early. To reach Fanling, take the KCR railway to Sheung Shui, followed by a 3-minute taxi ride. To reach Deep Water Bay, take bus no. 260 or 262 from Exchange Square in Central.

The **Discovery Bay Golf Club,** on Lantau island (📞 852/2987 7273), has a beautiful 18-hole course developed by Robert Trent Jones, Jr., offering great views of Hong Kong and the harbor. To reach it, take the 20-minute ferry ride from Central to Discovery Bay, followed by a ride in a special shuttle bus. Another scenic 18-hole course and a 9-hole course, operated by the **Clearwater Bay Golf and Country Club** (📞 852/2335 3888; www.cwbgolf.org), is located in Sai Kung in the New Territories, on a picturesque headland overlooking the South China Sea. To reach it, take the KCR railway to Sheung Shui, and then take a taxi.

HIKING

With 23 country parks—amounting to more than 40% of Hong Kong's space—there are many trails of varying levels of difficulty throughout Hong Kong, including hiking trails, nature trails, and family trails. Serious hikers, for example, may want to consider the famous **MacLehose Trail** in the New Territories, which stretches about 100km (62 miles) through eight country parks, from the Sai Kung Peninsula in the east to Tuen Mun in the west. The strenuous **Lantau Trail** is a 70km (43-mile) circular trail on Lantau island that begins and ends at Mui Wo (also called Silvermine Bay), passing several popular scenic spots and campsites along the way and including a 2½-hour trek to the top of Lantau Peak. Both the MacLehose and Lantau trails are divided into smaller sections of varying difficulty, which means that you can tailor your hike to suit your own abilities and time constraints. I also like the short Heritage Trails in the New Territories which take in historic architectural gems along the way (see section 1 in chapter 11). Easier to reach is the 50km (31-mile) **Hong Kong Trail,** which spans Hong Kong Island's five country parks.

Hikers are advised not to hike alone and to check weather reports before departing; from May to October, irregular thunderstorms, typhoons, and heavy showers can cause flooding and landslides. The best hiking season is considered November through February. The Hong Kong Tourism Board has some trail maps and a hiking and wildlife guidebook called *Exploring Hong Kong's Countryside: A Visitor's Companion.* HKTB also lists recommended hikes on its website, www.discoverhongkong.com.

JOGGING

The best places to jog on Hong Kong Island without dodging traffic are **Victoria Park's jogging track** in Causeway Bay, **Harlech Road** on Victoria Peak, and **Bowen Road,** which stretches 2.5km (1½ miles) from Stubbs Road to Magazine Gap Road in the Mid-Levels and offers great views over the harbor. In addition, an inside track at the Happy Valley racecourse is open for runners when the horses aren't using the field. On the other side of the harbor, there's **Kowloon Park,** as well as the waterfront promenade along Tsim Sha Tsui and Tsim Sha Tsui East.

Remember that it can be quite hot and humid during the summer months, so try to jog in the early morning or in the evening.

SWIMMING

In addition to the many outdoor and indoor swimming pools at Hong Kong's hotels that are available for hotel guests, there are numerous public swimming pools, including those at **Kowloon Park** and **Victoria Park.** Prices are HK$19 (US$2.45/£1.35) for adults and HK$9 (US$1.15/65p) for children and seniors (you can also use your Octopus transportation card to gain admission). Avoid hot weekends, when the pools can become quite crowded.

There are also about 40 **beaches** in the SAR that are free for public use; most of them have lifeguards on duty April through October, changing rooms, and snack stands or restaurants. Even on Hong Kong Island itself you can find a number of beaches, including Big Wave Bay and Shek O on the east coast, and Stanley, Deep Water Bay, South Beach (popular with the gay crowd), and Repulse Bay on the southern coast. Repulse Bay, by far the most popular beach in Hong Kong, becomes unbelievably crowded on summer weekends.

There are prettier beaches on the outlying islands, including Hung Shing Ye and Lo So Shing on Lamma, Tung Wan on Cheung Chau, and Cheung Sha on Lantau. It is, however, advisable to check on water pollution before plunging in, especially on the islands. Furthermore, I wouldn't recommend the waters around Sai Kung Peninsula. There seem to be fatal shark attacks here every couple of years, due to fish migration, though most of the public beaches have shark nets and guards patrolling the water.

TAI CHI

Tai chi (shadow boxing) is an ancient Chinese regimen designed to balance body and soul and thereby release energy from within. By strengthening both the mind and the body through seemingly fluid, slow movements that mask the strength and control required to perform the balletlike exercise, tai chi fosters a sense of well-being and nurtures self-discipline. It also helps develop balance, improves muscle tone and breathing, and aids in digestion. In Hong Kong, both young and old practitioners gather every morning in downtown parks and open public spaces to perform tai chi. Visitors, too, can join complimentary 1-hour **lessons** in English, offered by the Hong Kong Tourism Board's Meet the People cultural program, every Monday, Wednesday, Thursday, and Friday at 8am. Simply show up at the Tsim Sha Tsui waterfront promenade near the Avenue of Stars, where you'll be led through the exercises by a tai chi master. Participants are advised to wear casual clothing and comfortable sport shoes with rubber soles. For information, contact the **Hong Kong Tourism Board** (© 852/ 2508 1234).

9 Spectator Sports

A popular sporting event is the **Seven-A-Side Rugby Tournament** (called the Sevens), held in March or April. During the cooler winter months, a number of marathons are held, of which the best known are the **Hongkong-Shenzhen Marathon** in February and the **China Coast Marathon** in March. There are also tennis tournaments, including the **Super Tennis Classic** and the **Marlboro Championship.** If you enjoy watching golf, the highlight of the year is the **Hong Kong Open Golf Championships,** held in December at the Hong Kong Golf Club in Fanling (the New Territories).

If you're here anytime from September to mid-June, join the rest of Hong Kong at the **horse races.** Horse racing got its start in the colony in Happy Valley more than 150 years ago, when British settlers introduced the sport, making the Happy Valley track the oldest racecourse in Asia outside China. There is also a newer, modern track in Sha Tin (the New Territories), which can accommodate 90,000 spectators.

Without a doubt, horse racing is by far the most popular sporting event in Hong Kong. It's not, perhaps, the sport itself that draws so much enthusiasm, but rather the fact that, aside from the local lottery, racing is the only legal form of gambling in Hong Kong. There are more than 100 off-course betting centers throughout Hong Kong. Winnings are tax-free.

Races are held Wednesday evenings and some Saturday and Sunday afternoons. Both tracks feature giant color screens that show close-ups of the race in progress, photographs of jockeys and trainers, and videos of previous races. It's fun and easy to get in on the betting action, and you don't have to bet much—the minimum wager of HK$10 (US$1.30/70p) per race is enough.

The lowest admission price is HK$10 (US$1.30/70p), which is for the general public and is standing-room only. If you want to watch from the more exclusive Hong Kong Jockey Club (www.hkjc.com) members' enclosure (there are stands here so you can sit down), are at least 18 years old, and are a bona-fide tourist, you can purchase a temporary member's badge for HK$100 (US$13/£7.70) on regular race days and HK$150 (US$19/£12) on rare special race days. It's available upon showing your passport at either the Badge Enquiry Office at the main entrance to the members' private enclosure (at either track) or at designated off-course betting centers, including those at 10–12 Stanley Street in Central and 4 Prat Ave. in Tsim Sha Tsui. Tickets are sold on a first-come, first-served basis.

To reach Happy Valley Racecourse, take the tram to Happy Valley or the MTR to Causeway Bay (take the Times Square exit and walk toward the Wong Nai Chung Rd.). To reach Sha Tin Racecourse, take the KCR railway to Racecourse Station.

On the other hand, an easy way to see the races is to take a guided tour to the tracks, described in "Organized Tours & Cultural Activities," earlier in this chapter. For information on current sporting events and future dates, contact the Hong Kong Tourism Board (© **852/2508 1234**).

Hong Kong Strolls

Surprisingly compact, Hong Kong is an easy city to explore on foot. If it weren't for the harbor, you could walk everywhere—Tsim Sha Tsui, Yau Ma Tei, the Central District, Wan Chai, and Causeway Bay. Walking affords a more intimate relationship with your surroundings, permits chance encounters with the unexpected, and lets you discover that vegetable market, temple, or shop you would have otherwise missed.

If, for example, you're in the Central District and want to have dinner in Causeway Bay, you can walk there in less than an hour, passing through colorful Wan Chai on the way. Causeway Bay is good for exploring, since it's full of little sidewalk markets, Japanese department stores, restaurants, and shops patronized by the locals. Another great place for walking is the Western District just west of Central, fascinating because it encompasses a wide spectrum of traditional Chinese shops, from chop makers to ginseng wholesalers. If you like panoramic views, nothing can beat the hour-long circular walk on Victoria Peak.

On the other side of the harbor, a walk up Nathan Road from the harbor to the Yau Ma Tei subway station takes less than 30 minutes, although you might want to browse in some of the shops and department stores along the way. And Yau Ma Tei itself is another good place for wandering about since it also offers insight into the Chinese way of life with its markets and traditional shops. For easy strolling with great views of the harbor, walk along the waterfront promenade that stretches from the Star Ferry all the way through Tsim Sha Tsui East.

What follows are three recommended strolls: one through the Central financial district, where a few colonial-era buildings are sprinkled in among the modern skyscrapers; another through the Western District, with its Chinese shops and antiques stores; the third along Nathan Road in Kowloon, from Tsim Sha Tsui to Mong Kok.

If you're interested in additional self-guided walks throughout Hong Kong, be sure to pick up the free HKTB pamphlet called *Hong Kong Walks,* which covers points of interest in Central, the Western District, Victoria Peak, Yau Ma Tei, Mong Kok, Sha Tin in the New Territories, and Cheung Chau, Lantau, and Lamma islands. For more information, contact the Hong Kong Tourism Board (© **852/2508 1234**).

In addition to the three walks here, I also cover a couple of walks in the New Territories: the Ping Shan and Lung Yeuk Tau heritage trails, which highlight village life and architecture. See chapter 11 for more information.

Start:	Statue Square, Chater Road, Central District.
Finish:	Pacific Place, 88 Queensway, Central.
Time:	About 2 hours; add 1 to 2 hours if you include Victoria Peak.
Best Times:	Weekdays, when shops and restaurants are in full swing.
Worst Times:	Tuesday, when the Flagstaff House Museum of Tea Ware is closed; Saturday afternoon, Sunday, and public holidays, when some stores and restaurants in the Central District are closed.

The birthplace of modern Hong Kong, the Central District used to be called "Victoria," after Queen Victoria. It boasted elegant colonial-style buildings with sweeping verandas and narrow streets filled with pigtailed men pulling rickshaws. That's hard to imagine nowadays. With Central's gleaming glass-and-steel skyscrapers, there's little left of its colonial beginnings. Still, this is the logical starting place for a tour of Hong Kong. The handful of historic buildings scattered among towering monoliths symbolize both the past and the future of this ever-changing city. Yet, surprisingly, Central has several city parks, good for relaxation and sightseeing. If you have time, you can also take a trip to Victoria Peak during this walk, from the tram terminus in Central.

Take the MTR to Central, where, between Connaught Road Central and Des Voeux Road Central, lies:

❶ Statue Square
Divided by Chater Road, this historic square once held a statue of Queen Victoria, which has since been moved to the park in Causeway Bay that bears her name. On weekends, Statue Square and surrounding Central become the domain of Filipino housemaids, nannies, and waitresses, thousands of whom work in the SAR and send most of what they earn back home to their families. On their day off, they meet friends here, sitting on blankets spread on the concrete and sharing food, photographs, letters from home, and laughter, infusing the staid business district with a certain vitality and festivity. At any rate, perhaps appropriately for a town that was established to make money, the only statue remaining in Statue Square today is of a banker, Sir Thomas Jackson, former manager of the Hongkong and Shanghai Bank. It's interesting to note that he stands facing the:

❷ Legislative Council Building
Formerly the Supreme Court and looking curiously out of place in modern Central, the Legislative Council Building was built in the early 1900s by architect Aston Webb, who later redesigned Buckingham Palace, and now houses Hong Kong's lawmaking body, popularly known as "Legco." With its local pink-and-gray granite, Ionic columns, and Chinese roof, this neoclassical structure is typical of late-Victorian colonial architecture and boasts a carved-stone figure above the main portico of the Goddess of Justice holding scales. The building has two flags, one with the red star emblem of China and the other with the bauhinia flower of Hong Kong.

On the other side of the Legco building, to the east, is:

❸ Chater Garden
This was the site of the Hong Kong Cricket Club until the 1960s. Today, this is the only spot of green in the very heart of Central and is popular with those who practice tai chi in the early morning and among office workers on lunch break.

Walking Tour 1: The Central District

1. Statue Square
2. Legislative Council Building
3. Chater Garden
4. Des Voeux Road Central
5. Bank of China Tower
6. Hongkong and Shanghai Banking Corporation Limited
7. Court of Final Appeal
8. St. John's Cathedral
9. Government House
10. Hong Kong Zoological and Botanical Gardens
11. Peak Tram Station
12. Hong Kong Park
13. Flagstaff House Museum Of Tea Ware
14. Pacific Place

Tramway
Post Office ⊠
Take a Break stop C

1/10 mile
100 meters

SHENZHEN

NEW TERRITORIES

KOWLOON

Hong Kong International Airport

Lantau Island

Hong Kong Island

Sai Kung Peninsula

South China Sea

area of detail

185

Running alongside the south edge of the garden is:

❹ Des Voeux Road Central

This road is easily recognizable by the tramlines snaking along it. What a contrast these quaint double-decker trams make when viewed against the high-rise banks on the other side of the street. Established in 1904 and now the city's oldest form of transportation, trams are the most colorful way to travel from the Western and Central districts to Causeway Bay, especially at night when Hong Kong is ablaze in neon. Des Voeux Road itself was constructed as part of an early-1800s land reclamation project; before that the waterfront was situated farther inland, at Queen's Road. Land reclamation has proceeded continuously throughout Hong Kong's history, slowly encroaching on the harbor itself. One Hong Kong resident I met joked that so much land was being reclaimed it wouldn't be long before you could walk across the harbor. With Central's most recent reclamation project—which extended the ferry piers for outlying islands far into the water—the joke no longer seems quite so funny.

TAKE A BREAK
The most convenient place for a meal in this area is **Dot Cod Seafood Restaurant & Oyster Bar** (p. 140), in the Prince's Building with an entrance right on Statue Square (℡ 852/ 2810 6988). It's owned by the Hong Kong Cricket Club but is open to anyone.

Across from Chater Garden, on the other side of Des Voeux Road Central, is the:

❺ Bank of China Tower

This tower rises like a glass finger pointing into the sky. Designed by I. M. Pei, this 70-story futuristic building, with its crisscross pattern reminiscent of bamboo, also observes the principles of feng shui, as do all modern structures in Hong Kong in an effort to maintain harmony with their natural environment. (Otherwise, disaster would surely strike—something no builder in Hong Kong wants to risk.)

The most conspicuous building on Des Voeux Road Central, however, is farther west (to the right if facing the banks). It's the headquarters for the:

❻ Hongkong and Shanghai Banking Corporation Limited

This company, at 1 Queen's Rd. Central, which generally shortens its name to HSBC, maintains offices around the world. Hong Kong's first city hall once stood on this site. The Hongkong Bank, located here since 1865, issued the colony's first bank notes in 1881. The present building, designed in the mid-1980s by renowned British architect Sir Norman Foster and reputedly one of the most expensive buildings in the world (almost US$1 billion), attracts visiting architects the world over for its innovative external structure, rather than a central core. It was constructed from prefabricated components manufactured all over the world; the glass, aluminum cladding, and flooring came from the United States. Internal walls are removable, allowing for office reconfiguration. Walk underneath the bank's open ground plaza for a look up into this unique structure, or, if you choose, take the world's longest freely supported escalator up to the first floor. Much care was given to the angle of these escalators, as well as to many other aspects of construction, in order not to disturb the spirits (see the "Feng Shui: Restoring a Balance with Nature" box on p. 301 for more information about this) who reside here (altogether there are 62 escalators in the building, more than in any other office building in the world). Note, too, the two bronze lions you see at the entrance, which have been "guarding" the bank since 1935. You can rub their paws for good luck.

If you walk through the Hongkong Bank's open, ground-floor plaza to the other side, you'll find yourself on Queen's Road Central, where on the opposite side of the street you should take the stone steps leading up to a pathway overhung with branches, known as Battery Path, where you should turn left. Straight ahead is a handsome brick building, the 150-year-old:

❼ Court of Final Appeal

This building, which houses Hong Kong's highest court, was formerly the French Mission Building. Just beyond it is the cream-and-white–colored, Gothic-style:

❽ St. John's Cathedral

Inaugurated in 1849 and thought to be the oldest Anglican church in the Far East, this church was used for Japanese social functions during the Japanese occupation. You can enter the small church and take a look inside. It underwent extensive renovations following World War II but still retains quaint tropical characteristics like the ceiling fans.

Behind the church is busy Garden Road, where you should turn right and walk uphill. After passing the U.S. Consulate, you'll come to Upper Albert Road, where you should turn right. You'll soon see, on your right, the:

❾ Government House

Completed in 1855, this building served as the official residence of 25 British governors until 1997. During the World War II Japanese occupation, it also served as the headquarters of Lieutenant General Isogai, who ordered some extensive building renovations, a curious mix of Asian and Western architecture, including ceramic tile roofs and a tower reminiscent of Shinto shrines. Since the 1997 handover, the grand, whitewashed edifice has been used for official functions.

Across the street, on the corner of Upper Albert Road and Garden Road, is a staircase leading to the main entrance of the:

❿ Hong Kong Zoological and Botanical Gardens

This is a wonderful oasis of plants and animals (p. 174) that was established in 1864. It still imparts a Victorian atmosphere with its wrought-iron bandstand and greenhouse. Entrance is free, and the grounds are not too extensive, so it's worth taking the time to wander through to see its tropical botanical gardens, trees and plants, aviaries and birds, reptiles, and mammals such as apes. It opens daily at 6am, with the eastern half closing at 7pm and the western part at 10pm.

Exiting the same way you came in, cross to the other side of Garden Road and walk downhill, taking a right after passing the modern St. John's Building. Here, to your right, is the:

⓫ Peak Tram Station

When this station opened in 1888, the travel time to the top of Victoria Peak was reduced from 3 hours (by sedan chair) to 8 minutes. Today the tram is the steepest funicular railway in the world, and the view from the peak is the best in Hong Kong. I suggest you visit the peak twice during your stay: during the day for the great panoramic view of the city, and again at night for its romantic atmosphere. There's also a great, 1-hour circular walk around the peak, as well as attractions for children. In all, you'll probably want to spend at least an hour or two on the Peak, so if time is limited or it's foggy, save it for another day.

On the other side of the tram station, on Cotton Tree Drive, is:

⓬ Hong Kong Park

Before opening as a park in 1991, this was once the grounds of Victoria Barracks, a housing area for soldiers. In the park is the pink Rawlinson House, formerly the private residence of the Deputy General and now serving as a marriage registry. If it's a weekend or an auspicious day in the Chinese calendar, you'll find many newlyweds posing for pictures in the park. You'll also find a greenhouse, a great aviary with 800 birds, and a playground. Signs will direct you to the park's most important building and Hong Kong's oldest surviving colonial-style structure, the:

⑬ Flagstaff House Museum of Tea Ware

Built in 1846, this museum (☎ **852/2869 0690;** see p. 168) houses a small collection of tea utensils, with descriptions of tea making through the various Chinese dynasties. It's open Wednesday through Monday from 10am to 5pm. Like everything else in the park, it's free. From here, walk past the fountain (a favorite backdrop for picture taking) to the escalators that will take you downhill to:

⑭ Pacific Place

This is a large complex filled with department stores, clothing boutiques, restaurants, and hotels. The nearest subway station from here is Admiralty Station, which you can reach without having to venture outside; just follow the signs via the air-conditioned walkway.

WINDING DOWN
There are many eating and drinking establishments in Pacific Place. **Dan Ryan's Chicago Grill** (☎ 852/ 2845 4600; see p. 126) is a casual bar and grill that remains open throughout the day for drinks, burgers, and other American favorites. **Zen Chinese** (☎ 852/2845 4555; see p. 144) is the ultimate in Chinese hip dining, with a Zen-like decor and specialties that border on Cantonese nouvelle. **Grappa's** (☎ 852/2868 0086; see p. 140) is a moderately priced trattoria with an open kitchen and good food. But for all-you-can eat dining, **café TOO** (p. 139), in the Island Shangri-La Hotel at Pacific Place (☎ 852/2820-8571, ext. 8571), is an upscale buffet restaurant offering views of Hong Kong Park's greenery and beautifully presented international lunches and dinners.

WALKING TOUR 2   **THE WESTERN DISTRICT**

Start:	Pedder Street, Central District.
Finish:	Lan Kwai Fong, Central.
Time:	About 4 to 5 hours.
Best Times:	Tuesday through Friday mornings, when markets are in full swing.
Worst Times:	Sunday, when some shops are closed; Monday, when the Museum of Medical Sciences is closed.

While the Central District seems to be Western in style with its banks, high-rises, and smart department stores, the Western District is very Chinese—a fascinating neighborhood of family-owned shops and businesses, with nary a tourist in sight. Traditional herbs, ginseng, antiques, preserved fish, name chops, coffins, funeral items, Hong Kong's oldest temple, and an interesting museum comparing traditional Chinese and Western medicine are just some of the things you'll see in my favorite area on Hong Kong Island.

Named after Lieutenant William Pedder, Hong Kong's first harbor master, Pedder Street connects two of Central's major thoroughfares: Des Voeux Road Central (with its tram tracks) and Queen's Road Central. It is most well known to visitors, however, for its shopping, including the not-to-be-missed (yet easily overlooked due to its modest size):

❶ Shanghai Tang

In the Pedder Building (☎ **852/2525 7333**), this small, chic shop (p. 212) is a

reproduction of a Shanghai clothing department store as it might have looked in the 1930s, with gleaming wooden and tiled floors, raised cashier cubicles, ceiling fans, and clerks wearing traditional Chinese clothing. This is a great place to shop for typical Chinese goods in mod colors, from lime-green cheongsams to stylish Chinese jackets, as well as funky home accessories and gifts.

South China Sea

Sai Kung
Peninsula

SHENZHEN

NEW
TERRITORIES

Hong Kong
International KOWLOON
Airport

Hong Kong
Island

area of
detail

Lantau
Island

10 km
0

10 mi
0

Victoria
Harbour

Pier 4

Pier 3

Outlying Districts
Services Pier

Pier 2

Pier Road

Pier 1

Macau Ferry Pier

Taxi Stand

Jackson Rd

Edinburgh
Place

Connaught Rd. Central

STATUE
SQUARE
Chater Rd.

STATUE
SQUARE

CENTRAL
DISTRICT

Ice House St.

General
Post Office

Airport Express
Hong Kong
Station

Exchange
Square

Bus
Terminal

Pedder St.

Connaught Rd. Central

Central

★ start
here

1
2
3

Connaught Rd. Central

Des Voeux Rd. Central

Chiu Lung St.

Theatre Lane

D'Aguilar St.

Lan Kwai Fong

Wyndham St.

4

Pottinger Rd.

Li Yuen St. E.

Li Yuen St. W.

Queen Victoria

The
Center

Jubilee St.

5

6

Queen's Rd. Central

Cochrane St.

Stanley St.

Wyndham St.

Lyndhurst
Terrace

25

Wing Kut St.

Gilman's
Bazaar

Wing Woo St.

Wellington St.

Graham St.

finish
here

SOHO

26 Hollywood Rd.

Central/Mid-Levels
Escalator

Shelley St.

Rumsey St.

WESTERN
DISTRICT

Aberdeen St.

Sheung
Wan

Man Wa Lane

8

Wing Lok St. East

Strand
East

Hillier St.

Staunton St.

24

Bonham
Strand West

Cleverly St.

9

Jervois St.

Rd. Central

Hollywood Rd.

23

Connaught Rd. Central

10

Morrison St.

11

Queen's

Lok Ku Rd.

Cat Street

20

21

Ladder St.

Wing Lok St. West

12

Queen's

19

18

BLAKE
GARDEN

Tai Ping Shan St.

22

Po Hing Fong

Caine
Rd.

Bonham Strand West

Possession St.

17

16

SHEUNG
WAN

13

Sutherland

Ko Shing St.

14

Queen's Rd. West

15

Take a Break stop
Tramway
Post Office

1/10 mile

100 meters

Just beside Shanghai Tang to the left is the main entrance to the:

❷ Pedder Building

At 12 Pedder St., this has been a shopping center since 1926. It is now famous for its dozens of small factory outlets and clothing boutiques; look for the elevator that services the first to seventh floors. Be aware, however, that just a handful of shops here are true factory outlets. The rest are simply taking advantage of the location to set up boutiques to sell their usual goods at regular prices; there are also some secondhand shops selling used designerwear. If you have the time, you might want to hunt for some bargains here. I usually take the elevator up to the sixth floor (there are no shops on the seventh floor) and then work my way down.

Across the street from the Pedder Building is the:

❸ Landmark

This high-end shopping complex has brand-name boutiques, including Gucci, Tiffany & Co., Louis Vuitton, and Manolo Blahnik.

Head west on Des Voeux Road Central (the one with the tram tracks); in about 2 minutes you will come to:

❹ Li Yuen Street East and Li Yuen Street West

These two parallel pedestrian lanes, which rise steeply to your left, are packed with stalls that sell clothing and accessories, including costume jewelry, Chinese jackets, handbags, belts, and even bras. If you see something you like, be sure to bargain for it. Walk up Li Yuen Street East, take a right, and then head back down Li Yuen Street West.

After walking down Li Yuen Street West, turn left onto Des Voeux Road Central and continue walking west, keeping your eyes peeled for the:

❺ Tak Wing Pawn Shop

Located at 72 Des Voeux Road Central, this is one of many pawn shops in Hong Kong, but it's easy to overlook them and walk on by. Unlike U.S. pawnshops which double as stores selling unclaimed personal belongings after a prescribed length of time, in Hong Kong pawnshops simply hold items in storage, selling them to another store if the owner is unable to pay. Hong Kong pawnshops, therefore, look like secretive affairs, with walls shielding customers from casual street observers.

Farther West on Des Voeux Road Central, you'll see the entrance to the:

❻ Central–Mid-Levels Escalator

Opened in 1994 as the world's longest covered escalator, it stretches 780m (2,600 ft.) from Central to the Mid-Levels on Victoria Peak. Contrary to its name, however, it is not one long continuous escalator but rather a series of escalators and moving sidewalks, with 29 entrances and exits. Designed to accommodate commuters who live in the Mid-Levels but work in Central and beyond, the escalators operate downhill from 6 to 10am and then reverse their direction and go uphill from 10:20am to midnight (after this time, you have to walk down the hill—there are stairs beside the escalators). If you travel its entire length, it takes about 20 minutes to go from one end to the other. Because of the foot traffic, the escalator has spawned a number of easily accessible new restaurants and bars, most in an area dubbed SoHo (more on this later).

Continue walking west on Des Voeux Road Central, past Jubilee Street with its Cyber Café at 12–13 Jubilee, and turn left onto:

❼ Wing Kut Street

This is another small lane with stalls that sell clothing, handbags, and other accessories for women. More interesting, however, are the small shops behind the stalls, which specialize in costume jewelry in a wide range of styles and prices. Some shops sell only wholesale, but others will sell to individual shoppers as well.

After walking through Wing Kut Street, take a right onto Queen's Road Central.

TAKE A BREAK
Located in the palatial-looking Grand Millennium Plaza, the upscale **Gaia Ristorante** (p. 137), 181 Queen's Road Central (✆ 852/2167 8200), has a wonderful garden terrace, a contemporary interior, and very good Italian fare for both lunch and dinner.

Queen's Road Central will soon curve off to the left, but you'll want to keep walking straight westward onto Bonham Strand. Soon, to your right, just after the Hongkong Bank and Treasure Lake Seafood Restaurant, you'll see an interesting street:

⑧ Man Wa Lane

Since the 1920s this street has been the home of one of China's oldest trades—"chop" or carved-seal making. Sadly, the recent construction of many high-rises makes the stalls look out of place. Made from stone, ivory, jade, clay, marble, bronze, porcelain, bamboo, wood, soapstone, and even plastic, these seals or stamps can be carved with a name and are used by the Chinese much like a written signature.

You can have your own chop made at one of the several booths here, with your name translated into Chinese characters. It takes about an hour for a chop to be completed, so you may want to stop by again later after you've finished your walk. Calligraphy brushes are also for sale, and you can even have business cards made here with both English and Chinese characters; orders for that take about a day. Most stalls are open Monday through Saturday from 10am to 6pm.

Back on Bonham Strand, continue west for 2 blocks. Just a few years ago, this area was known for its many snake shops, which did a roaring business from October to February. Now only a few remain, easily identifiable by cages of pythons, cobras, and banded kraits piled on the sidewalk, or by the wooden drawers lining the walls of the shop. Just past Mercer Street is Hillier Street (which is unmarked; it's the second street after Man Wa Lane, just past the corner fruit shop), where you should turn left for the:

⑨ Snake shop

You can recognize this open-fronted shop, at 13 Hillier, by the many drawers lining its wall. Eaten as protection against the winter cold, snakes are often served in soup. They are also favored for their gallbladders, which are mixed with Chinese wine as cures for rheumatism. Who knows, you might see a shopkeeper fill a customer's order by deftly grabbing a snake out of one of the drawers, extracting the gallbladder, and mixing it in yellow wine. The snake survives the operation, but who knows what other fate it awaits. The more poisonous the snake, so they say, the better the cure. The mixture is also believed to be an aphrodisiac.

Backtrack to Bonham Strand and turn left, where you'll pass medicinal shops selling dried organic products such as mushrooms and roots; a tea merchant's shop; and, on the corner of Morrison Street, a rattan shop with handmade wares spilling out onto the sidewalks and hanging from hooks outside the shop. It takes an apprentice 3 years to learn the skills necessary to become a master rattan maker; the rattan itself comes from a climbing vine found throughout Asia. As a sign of the times, the shop has branched into plastic housewares. Take a right here onto Morrison Street and walk to the end where, on the left, you'll find the handsome, redbrick:

⑩ Western Market

At 323 Des Voeux Rd., this market was built in 1906 and was used as a public market until 1988; it escaped demolition when the decision was made to renovate the imposing Edwardian/Victorian landmark into a bazaar for shops and artisans. On the ground floor are souvenir and gift shops that sell everything from Chinese seals to jade jewelry, with most shops open daily from 10am to 7pm. Up on the first floor, retailers sell bolts of colorful cloth, buttons, clasps, and other sewing accessories. On the top floor is The Grand Stage, noted for its afternoon ballroom dancing daily from 2:30 to 6pm. Stop for a peek at Chinese couples as they glide dreamily across the floor.

TAKE A BREAK
There are several places in Western Market for casual dining, including eateries offering sandwiches and desserts. The top floor **The Grand Stage** (© 852/2815 2311) offers dim sum for lunch until 2pm daily and Cantonese fare from 7pm to midnight. But if you're on a budget or like adventuresome dining, head to the **Cooked Food Centre** on the second floor of the Urban Council Sheung Wan Complex (described below), Bonham Strand, where the second floor has food stalls selling various noodle, vegetable, and other Chinese dishes. There are no English menus, since most of the patrons are neighborhood residents, vendors working inside the complex's market, or nearby blue-collar workers. It's open Monday through Saturday from 6am to an astonishing 2am.

From Western Market, backtrack on Morrison Street to Bonham Strand, where across the street you'll see the large:

⓫ Urban Council Sheung Wan Complex

One of Hong Kong's largest neighborhood markets, this complex, also called the Sheung Wan Civic Centre, open from 6am to 8pm, features fish and poultry on the ground floor, meats and vegetables on the first floor, and a large dining hall with stalls selling cheap, cooked meals on the second floor. Early morning is the best time to come, when women buy the day's food for their families and chefs purchase ingredients for their daily specials. Following the Chinese penchant for freshness, chickens are killed on the spot, boiled, and then thrown into machines that pluck them. Almost every part of every animal is for sale, including the liver, heart, and intestines (live chickens will be banned from Hong Kong's wet markets by 2009). Wicker baskets may contain the discarded horns and skulls of bulls, with even the brains carved out—this is not a stop for the fainthearted.

Exit the market building back onto Bonham Strand, turn left, and continue straight ahead on Wing Lok Street. This street is nicknamed:

⓬ Ginseng and Bird's Nest Street

Obviously, shops here specialize in ginseng and bird's nest, both valued for their aid in longevity, energy, and a fair complexion. The kings of trade in this wholesale trading area are clearly ginseng, with more than 30 varieties on offer. The most prized are the red ginseng from North Korea, white ginseng from North America, and a very rare ginseng that grows wild in the mountains of northeastern China. Red ginseng is supposed to aid male virility, while the white variety helps cure hangovers.

By the way, this area has long had an exotic atmosphere—150 years ago it buzzed with activity as merchants from Shanghai, Canton (Guangzhou), Fujian, and other Chinese provinces and cities set up shop here, selling products from their native regions.

At the end of Wing Lok Street, turn left on Des Voeux Road West. Along this road you'll see:

⓭ Shops selling preserved foods

Dried and salted fish, flattened squid, oysters, scallops, abalone, sea slugs, fish bladders, starfish, shrimp, and many other kinds of seafood have been dried and preserved for sale here. You can buy bird's nest here, as well as shark's fin, and in winter there's also pressed duck and Chinese sausages made from pork and liver.

Continue west on Des Voeux Road, keeping your eyes peeled for a Park'n'Shop convenience store and Princeton Tower apartments on your left, at 92 Des Voeux Rd. Just past it is Sutherland Street, where you should turn left. Almost immediately you will come to a somewhat larger street, Ko Shing Street. This street is nicknamed:

⓮ Herbal Medicine Street

for its many shops dealing in the herbal medicine trade. Based on the Asian concept of maintaining a healthy balance between the yin and yang forces in the body, the range of medicinal herbs is startling, including roots, twigs, bark, dried

Chinese Gods

There are many gods in the Chinese world, each with different functions and abilities. There are household gods such as the kitchen god, as well as patron gods of various occupations, and gods who protect worshippers through certain stages of their lives. There is an earth god, a goddess of pregnant women, 60 gods representing each year of the 60-year Chinese calendar, a god of riches popular with shopkeepers, and a scholar god whose favor is curried by students.

Most popular in Hong Kong is **Tin Hau,** goddess of the sea and protector of seafarers (in Macau she is known as **A-Ma**). As the patron goddess of fisher folk, Tin Hau is honored by fishing communities throughout Hong Kong; there are more than two dozen Tin Hau temples, including those at Yau Ma Tei, Causeway Bay, Stanley, and Cheung Chau. According to popular lore, Tin Hau is the deification of a real girl who lived in Fujian Province around A.D. 900 or 1000 and who saved some fishermen during a storm. Her birthday is celebrated annually with gaily-decorated junks and lion dances. Another popular goddess is **Kuan Yin** (called Kun Iam in Macau), the goddess of mercy, capable of delivering people from suffering or misery.

There are also several temples in Hong Kong devoted to **Man** (the god of literature and the patron of civil servants) and **Mo** (the god of war). Mo was a great warrior of the Han dynasty, deified not only for his integrity but his ability to protect from the misfortunes of war. Ironically, for this reason Mo is worshipped not only by soldiers and the Hong Kong police force but also by gang members of the underworld. Hong Kong's most famous Man Mo Temple is in the Western District on Hollywood Road.

One of the most popular gods in Hong Kong is **Wong Tai Sin,** believed to generously grant the wishes of his followers, cure sickness, and—best of all—dispense horse-racing tips. The Wong Tai Sin Temple, located in a district by the same name, is always crowded with worshippers, as well as fortunetellers, making this one of the most interesting temple destinations in Hong Kong.

leaves, seeds, pods, flowers, grasses, insects (such as discarded cicada shells), deer antlers, dried sea horses, dried fish bladders, snake gall bladders, and rhinoceros horns. The herbalist, after learning about the customer's symptoms (most will not likely speak English) and checking the pulses in both wrists, will prescribe an appropriate remedy, using perhaps a bit of bark here and a seed there, based on wisdom passed down over thousands of years. A typical prescription might include up to 20 ingredients, which are often boiled to produce a medicinal tea.

Return to Sutherland and continue heading south (toward the playground). A few years back, this neighborhood was renovated and the Li Sing Street Playground was built in its midst, displacing some of the narrow alleys favored by one of Hong Kong's oldest professions—street-side barbers. Once plentiful, street-side barbers are now going the way of the rickshaw, but just past the playground and basketball court, to the left, is the only makeshift barbershop remaining in this area. At the top of Sutherland Street, on busy Queen's Road West, I used to see an elderly woman who set up shop on the sidewalk, using only a couple of stools and a string. She used the string to pull out the facial hairs of her customers, an ancient method that some salons still perform. But like much of old Hong Kong, she and her sidewalk business have vanished.

TAKE A BREAK
There's no better place for Western food in this immediate vicinity than **Sammy's Kitchen** (p. 155), 204–206 Queen's Rd. W. (reached from Sutherland St. by turning right and walking about 2 min.; © 852/2548 8400). A landmark for more than 3 decades, it's owned by the gregarious and friendly Sammy Yip, who treats foreign guests like royalty. It's a good place for inexpensive lunchtime fare, an afternoon snack, a soda or ice-cream sundae, or, in the evenings, fresh seafood, steaks, chicken, and house-invented specialties.

At the top of Sutherland Street, cross Queen's Road West and turn left, heading east. Here you'll pass several open-fronted:

⓯ Funeral and incense shops

Note the paper replicas of household goods and other items (such as houses, cars, running shoes, handbags, and even computers) hanging from the shops' eaves and ceilings. These are sold to accompany the deceased into the afterlife.

After the funeral shops, follow the sidewalk up and down a small hill. Shortly thereafter you will see a road leading uphill to the right. It's the famous:

⓰ Hollywood Road

This long road, which runs all the way to Central, is a strange mixture of shops selling coffins, funeral items, furniture, and antiques. In fact, there are more antiques shops concentrated here along this rather long road than anywhere else in Hong Kong, and you'll find everything from woodblock prints and rosewood tables to Neolithic pots, Ming dynasty ceramic figures, silk carpets, snuff bottles, porcelain, and round-bellied smiling Buddhas. Built in 1844 to accommodate British troops stationed here, the road takes its name from the woods of holly that used to adorn the area.

First, however, before hitting all the stores just mentioned, to your left will be:

⓱ Hollywood Road Park

A pleasant garden oasis with a children's playground, a pond with goldfish, and Chinese pagodas, this park makes a nice stop for a few moments of relaxation before continuing.

Just past the playground, to your left, you'll soon pass a historic landmark:

⓲ Possession Street

There's no need to enter it, but you might be interested to know that it was here that the British first landed in 1841 and planted the Union Jack to claim the island for Britain. At the time, of course, this was part of the waterfront. One of the first antiques shops you'll come to is:

⓳ Dragon Culture

One of Hong Kong's largest and most respected shops, it's owned by Victor Choi, who has given lectures on Chinese antiques for the HKTB's Meet the People program. Browse his shop, at 231 Hollywood Rd. (© 852/2545 8098), for everything from Tang pottery to Ming porcelain. If you want to learn more about antiques, pick up Choi's book *Collecting Chinese Antiques in Hong Kong*, which answers frequently asked questions about antiques, including how to ship them home.

After Dragon Culture, turn left at Lok Ku Road and then right onto Upper Lascar Row, better known as:

⓴ Cat Street

For almost a century, Cat Street was famous for its antiques, which could be bought for a pittance; now, however, with the new antiques shops on Hollywood Road and the nearby Cat Street Galleries, Cat Street vendors offer a fantastic mix of curios and junk. Pleasantly dotted with potted palms, this pedestrian lane is worth a browse for jade, snuff bottles, watches, pictures, copper and brass kettles, old eyeglasses, bird cages, and odds and ends. You should bargain with the vendors who have laid their wares on the sidewalk; most of them do business Monday through Saturday from 11am to about 5pm. You can also bargain at the surrounding antiques shops, where prices are rather high to begin with. If you're not an expert, be wary of purchasing anything of value. During one of my visits, it seemed that every shop was offering fossilized "dinosaur eggs" for sale. How many can there be?

At the end of Cat Street, turn right and go up the stairs. Across the street you'll see unmistakable:

㉑ Ladder Street

This extremely steep flight of stairs was once a common sight on steep Hong Kong Island. Now, of course, Hong Kong Island has escalators and the Peak Tram, but you're going to find out exactly how steep and tiring these stairs are by taking them almost to the top before turning right and following the sign down the short flight of steps to the:

㉒ Hong Kong Museum of Medical Sciences

This museum (p. 170) is housed in a stately, 1905 Edwardian-style brick building, at 2 Caine Lane (© **852/2549 5123**), that once served as the Pathological Institute, founded to combat Hong Kong's worst outbreak of bubonic plague, which eventually claimed 20,000 lives. With most rooms left intact and devoted to various aspects of early medicine practiced in colonial Hong Kong, it is the only museum in the world to compare traditional Chinese and Western medicine. You'll see acupuncture needles, an

autopsy room, an X-ray of a bound foot (once considered a sign of beauty for Chinese women), Chinese medicinal herbs, and the Halvo Pelvic Distraction Apparatus, a Hong Kong invention for treating humped backs. Very fascinating. It's open Tuesday through Saturday from 10am to 5pm and Sunday from 1 to 5pm.

Head back down Ladder Street and turn right onto Hollywood Road, where you'll immediately see the:

㉓ Man Mo Temple

This is Hong Kong Island's oldest and most well-known temple. It was in this area that the movie *The World of Suzie Wong* was filmed. The temple, which dates back to the 1840s and is open daily from 8am to 6pm, is dedicated to two deities: the god of literature (Man) and the god of war (Mo). Mo finds patronage both with the police force (shrines in his honor can be found in all Hong Kong police stations) and members of the underworld. Two ornately carved sedan chairs, dating from the 1800s and kept in the temple, were once used to carry the statues of the gods around the neighborhood during festivals. From the ceiling hang huge incense coils, which burn as long as 3 weeks, purchased by patrons seeking the fulfillment of their wishes. In a room to the right of the main hall is a small souvenir shop and an English-speaking fortuneteller.

Return to Hollywood Road and turn right to continue walking toward its eastern end. Here you'll find more chic and upscale antiques shops, selling furniture, blue-and-white porcelain, and goods from other countries, including Korean chests and Japanese hibachi. One of my favorites is:

㉔ True Arts & Curios

Located at 89–91 Hollywood Rd. (© **852/ 2559 1485**), this is a tiny shop packed with all kinds of surprises, from antique children's pointed shoes to porcelain, jewelry, and snuff bottles. It also carries about 2,000 temple woodcarvings, most of which are about 100 years old and small enough to carry with you on the plane.

Farther down, at 47 Hollywood Rd., just before the Central–Mid-Levels Escalator, are a couple of ancient-looking hole-in-the-wall shops selling bric-a-brac, old photographs and postcards of Hong Kong (including portraits of women engaged in that ageless profession), snuff bottles, and other interesting stuff.

Walk under the elevated people-mover, and just a bit beyond, to the right, on Old Bailey and Hollywood Road, is the former:

🖎 Central Police Station

Originally built in 1864 and expanded in 1919 and 1925, this is one of Hong Kong's largest clusters of Victorian-era buildings, built in the classical style. Plans call for the building's renovation into a new heritage center by 2009.

Return to the Central–Mid-Levels Escalator. Here, on the steep lanes flanking the escalator and on narrow side alleys, is Hong Kong's newest nightlife and dining district:

🖎 SoHo

Though SoHo stands for "south of Hollywood," the popularity of this area has made it blossom into side streets on both sides of Hollywood Road. Most establishments are tiny affairs, serving a great variety of ethnic cuisines at reasonable prices.

If you wish to return to Central, walk downhill on Cochrane Street (which runs underneath the escalator) to Queen's Road Central, where you should turn right.

WINDING DOWN
Since establishments are opening up in SoHo literally overnight, I suggest you simply walk along Shelley and Elgin streets and their side streets until something catches your fancy. Otherwise, at 10 Shelley Street, is **Life** ((© 852/2810 9777), a vegetarian restaurant with a relaxed, casual atmosphere (p. 145). Uphill from Hollywood Road, on the corner of Shelley and Staunton streets, is **Staunton Bar & Cafe** ((© 852/2973 6611), one of the first venues to open in SoHo. For Mexican food, head up Shelley street to ¡**Caramba!** (p. 145), 26–30 Elgin St. ((© 852/2530 9963), in SoHo, reached by going uphill on Shelley Street and turning right on Elgin Street.

WALKING TOUR 3   KOWLOON

Start: Star Ferry Terminus, Tsim Sha Tsui.

Finish: Temple Street Night Market.

Time: About 5 hours.

Best Times: Sunday afternoon, when there are free Kung Fu performances in Kowloon Park and the Jade Market is likely to stay open as late as 6pm, allowing you to see nearby Temple Street Night Market as well.

Worst Time: Thursday, when the Hong Kong Museum of Art is closed.

A stroll up Nathan Road through Tsim Sha Tsui and Yau Ma Tei will take you through the heart of Kowloon, past its famous hotels, restaurants, and shops, and on to the fascinating Chinese shops and markets in Yau Ma Tei and Mong Kok. You do, however, have to make some decisions before embarking on this tour. The Jade Market generally closes around 4pm and the nearby Temple Street Night Market isn't in full swing until 7pm. Because the MTR is so efficient, you can easily return to the night market later in the evening. Alternatively, because more and more Temple Street vendors are setting up shop early, from about 4pm, you can hit both the Jade Market and Temple

SHENZHEN

NEW
TERRITORIES

Sai Kung
Peninsula

Hong Kong
International
Airport

KOWLOON

Lantau
Island

area of
detail

Hong Kong
Island

0   10 mi
0   10 km   South China Sea

1 Harbour City
2 Chinese Arts & Crafts
3 Clock Tower
4 Hong Kong Cultural Centre
5 Hong Kong Museum of Art
6 Tsim Sha Tsui Promenade
7 Peninsula hotel
8 Nathan Road
9 Kowloon Park
10 Yue Hwa Chinese Products
    Emporium
11 Woosung Street
12 Saigon Street
13 Pawnshop
14 Reclamation Street
15 Jade Market
16 Tin Hau Temple
17 Ladies' Market
18 Goldfish Market
19 Fa Yuen Market
20 Flower Market Road
21 Yuen Po Street Bird Garden

Tung Choi St.
Soy St.
Nathan Rd.
finish

KOWLOON
PENINSULA

Yau Ma
Tei

Chun Yi Lane

Waterloo Rd.

KING'S
PARK

Shek Lung St.
Man Ming Ln.
Tung Kun St.   Li Lung Ln.
Lee Tak St.   Wing Sing Ln.
Public Square St.
Cliff Rd.

Market St.
Temple Street
Night Market

Man Cheong St.
Man Wai St.
Man Yuen St.
Man Ying St.
Man Wui St.
Pak Hoi St.
Saigon St.
Ning Po St.
Nanking St.

Canton Rd.
Woosung St.
Parkes St.
Chi Wo St.
Nathan Rd.

Kowloon
Station

Bus
Terminal

Jordan Rd.

Shanghai St.
Temple Sta.
Bow-
ring
St.
Pilkem St.
Tak Hing St.
Cox's Rd.
Tak Shing
Jordan Path

Gascoigne Rd.

Jordan
Austin Rd.
Hillwood Rd.

KOWLOON
PARK

Nathan Rd.

Observatory Rd.
Science Museum Rd.

TSIM SHA
TSUI EAST

Ferry Service to
Macau & China

China Ferry
Terminal

HARBOUR CITY

TSIM SHA
TSUI

Kimberley Rd.
Granville Rd.

Haiphong Rd.
Park Dr.
Canton Rd.
Kowloon Rd.
Lock Rd.
Hankow Rd.
Tsim Sha
Tsui
Prat Ave.
Hart Ave.
Hanoi Rd.
Mody Rd.
Chatham Rd. S.
Mody Rd.

KCR East
Tsim Sha Tsui
Station

Salisbury Rd.

High Speed
Ferry to
Central

start here
Ocean Terminal
Bus Terminal
Peking Rd.
Middle Rd.
Salisbury Rd.
New World
Centre
Tsim Sha Tsui Promenade

Ferry — —
Information ⓘ
Take a Break stop

Star Ferry
to Central
Kowloon Public Pier
Star Ferry
to Wan Chai
Tsim Sha Tsui Promenade
Avenue of Stars
Victoria Harbour

0   1/4 mi
0   0.25 km

Street Night Market if you time your walk just right and don't mind walking through Temple Street when it's not at its liveliest. In any case, nearby Ladies' Market, which is open all day, is very similar to the Temple Street market. Another possibility is to walk this tour on Sunday, when the Jade Market stays open later because of increased crowds. Finally, because this walk is such a long one, you might wish to either break it up into a 2-day stroll or cover only part of it, concentrating on those sights that interest you the most. Whatever you choose, a logical tour of Tsim Sha Tsui begins with the Star Ferry since, for more than a century, it served as the only link with Hong Kong Island.

Within the Star Ferry terminus itself is a Hong Kong Tourism Board's Visitor Information & Services Centre, where you can pick up free pamphlets, brochures, and maps of Hong Kong. In front of the Star Ferry concourse is Kowloon's main bus terminal. Straight ahead to the left is Ocean Terminal, the port of call for cruise liners docking in Hong Kong. It's probably no accident that it is immediately adjacent to:

❶ Harbour City

This is Hong Kong's largest interconnected shopping mall and one of the largest shopping complexes in the world. Stretching more than .8km (½ mile) along Canton Road, it contains more than 700 shops. Enter it and you might not escape during this lifetime; better save shopping here for another day. Instead, for one-stop shopping for high-quality Chinese products and gifts, head to the large, nondescript building to the right of Ocean Terminal, Star House, which contains mostly offices but also some restaurants and shops, including:

❷ Chinese Arts & Crafts

Located on the ground floor of Star House, 3 Salisbury Rd. (© **852/2735 4061**), this two-story store is open daily from 10am to 9:30pm and is the most upscale emporium specializing in Chinese products, including embroidered tablecloths, jewelry, ceramics, furniture, carpets, arts and crafts, and beautifully tailored clothing. It's also one of the safest places to buy jade.

Cross the street in front of Chinese Arts & Crafts back toward the harbor, where in front of you is the hard-to-miss:

❸ Clock tower

Built in 1915, and now dwarfed by the buildings around it, this is the only structure remaining from Hong Kong's old train station, once the final stop for those traveling overland from London on the Orient Express. In 1975, the Kowloon-Canton Railway terminus moved to Hung Hom. Occupying the train station's former site is the modern, salmon-colored:

❹ Hong Kong Cultural Centre

Opened in 1989 as the city's largest arena for the performing arts, this saddle-shaped structure, in my opinion, is terribly misplaced. After all, why situate concert and theater halls that have no windows on waterfront property with one of the world's most stunning views? Still, the Cultural Centre does offer first-rate concerts of both Western and Chinese music, as well as free shows and events on Thursdays from 6 to 7pm and Saturdays from 2:30 to 4:30pm.

Enter the Cultural Centre's ground floor and stop at the Enquiries counter to pick up a brochure detailing concerts and free events (there are also public toilets here). Exit the other side, where to the east you will soon come upon one of my favorite museums in Hong Kong, the:

❺ Hong Kong Museum of Art

Located at 10 Salisbury Rd. (© **852/2721 0116**), this museum contains an excellent collection of Chinese porcelain, bronzes, jade, lacquerware, bamboo carvings, and paintings of old Hong Kong and Macau, as well as works by contemporary Hong

Kong artists. It even has windows overlooking the harbor. Don't miss it. The museum is open Friday through Wednesday from 10am to 6pm. See p. 166.

Circle around behind the art museum, to the:

❻ Tsim Sha Tsui Promenade

Hugging the shoreline all the way from the Star Ferry to Hung Hom, the promenade offers a great vantage point of the harbor with its boat traffic, Hong Kong Island, and The Peak. It's also a good place for a romantic stroll at night, when the dazzling lights of Hong Kong Island are ablaze across the harbor. Nightly from 8 to 8:18pm, Hong Kong stages its "Symphony of Lights," an impressive laser-and-light show projected from more than 30 buildings on both sides of the harbor. Just a couple of minutes' stroll along the waterfront will bring you to the promenade's Avenue of Stars, where embedded plaques and handprints and a few statues honor Hong Kong's most famous movie personalities, including Jackie Chan and Bruce Lee.

At the end of Avenue of Stars, turn left into the New World Centre, a shopping mall, and walk straight through to its front entrance, beyond which is a pedestrian subway.

> **TAKE A BREAK**
> Many visitors feel that their Hong Kong stay would not be complete without dropping by the lobby of **The Peninsula hotel** (✆ 852/2920 2888). Classical music serenades guests throughout the afternoon and evening, but the best time to stop by is between 2 and 7:30pm daily, when an English-style afternoon tea is served for HK$165 to HK$220 (US$21–US$29/£12–£16).
> Another great place for afternoon tea is the **Lobby Lounge** of the Hotel InterContinental, 18 Salisbury Rd. (✆ 852/2721 1211), which offers fantastic views of the harbor and Hong Kong Island, along with its delicate finger sandwiches and tea daily from 2:30 to 6pm. See the "Afternoon Tea" section of chapter 6, on p.159, for more information.

Follow signs through the pedestrian subway to Tsim Sha Tsui's most famous landmark, the venerable:

❼ Peninsula Hotel

Built in 1928 to serve guests disembarking at the old train station and guarded by one of the largest all-Rolls-Royce fleet in the world, The Peninsula is Hong Kong's grandest old hotel, with a new tower that offers great harbor views from its front-facing rooms and top-floor restaurant. Its lobby, reminiscent of a Parisian palace, with high gilded ceilings, pillars, and ferns, has long been a favorite spot for a cup of coffee and people-watching.

Walk to the busy road running alongside the east side of The Peninsula hotel:

❽ Nathan Road

This is Kowloon's most famous street. It is also one of Hong Kong's widest and runs almost 4km (2½ miles) straight up the spine of Kowloon all the way to Boundary Road, the official border of the New Territories. Nathan Road is named after Sir Matthew Nathan, who served as governor at the time the road was constructed. After it was completed, it was nicknamed "Nathan's Folly." After all, why build such a wide road, seemingly leading to nowhere? Kowloon had very few people back then and even less traffic. Now, of course, Nathan Road is known as the "golden mile of shopping" because of all the boutiques and shops that line both sides.

You'll pass jewelry stores, electronics shops, optical shops, clothing boutiques, and many other establishments as you head north on Nathan Road. The side streets are also good hunting grounds for inexpensive casual wear, at prices comparable to those of Stanley Market. You'll want to return here to explore this area at leisure; shops are open until 9pm or later. After about 10 minutes (assuming you don't stop to shop along the way), you'll see a mosque on your left, built in 1984 to replace an older mosque built in the late 19th century for Muslim Indian troops belonging to the British army. Today, there are about 70,000 Muslims in Hong Kong; the mosque is not open to the public.

Just past the mosque, take the first steps you see on the left, leading up to:

❾ Kowloon Park

A good place to bring children for a romp through playgrounds and open spaces, Kowloon Park also boasts a water garden, Chinese garden, sculpture garden (with Scotland's Sir Eduardo Paolozzi's bronze version of William Blake's *Concept of Newton*), aviary, woodland trail, maze made of foliage, and swimming pools. Best for visitors, however, are the free Kung Fu Chinese martial arts performances held every Sunday from 2:30 to 4:30pm featuring children and adult practitioners. Follow the signs to "Kung Fu Corner."

Walk through the park northward, past the indoor/outdoor public swimming pools, to Austin Road, where you should turn right until you hit Nathan Road again, where you should turn left. Be on the lookout to the left for:

❿ Yue Hwa Chinese Products Emporium

On the corner of Jordan Road at 301–309 Nathan Rd. (✆ **852/2384 0084**), this emporium caters primarily to the local Chinese with traditional Chinese products. Its goods from China include silk, porcelain, jade, clothing, furniture, medicinal herbs, and everyday household goods. Hours here are 10am to 10pm daily.

Yue Hwa marks the beginning of the Yau Ma Tei District. Its name translates roughly as "the place for growing sesame plants," but you won't see any such cultivation today. Rather, like the Western District on Hong Kong Island, Yau Ma Tei offers a look at traditional Chinese life, with shops that sell tea, chopping blocks, joss, bamboo steamers, baked goods, embroidery, herbs, and dried seafood.

Just past the Yue Hwa store, take the first left onto Nanking Street and the second right onto:

⓫ Woosung Street

Here you'll pass restaurants with live seafood in tanks and glazed ducks hanging from windows, an herbalist shop, a mah-jongg parlor, and other family-owned businesses. After 2 blocks (there's a 7-Eleven on the corner), take a left on:

⓬ Saigon Street

Here, on the left side of the street on the corner of Saigon and Temple streets, is a shop for herbal teas. Temple Street is the site of the famous Night Market, but if it's past 4pm, some vendors may have already set up shop (but more on that later).

A block farther along Saigon, on the corner of Saigon and Shanghai streets to the left, is a:

⓭ Pawnshop

It looks unremarkable from the outside, with only a door and then a wall blocking views of the inside from pedestrians walking past, but this is a Chinese pawnshop, where customers leave their valuables for a loan. Unlike U.S. pawnshops, which double as stores selling unclaimed belongings, Hong Kong pawnshops simply hold items in storage, selling them to another store if left unclaimed.

After walking 1 block farther east on Saigon, turn right onto:

⓮ Reclamation Street

This street, along with the nearby Yau Ma Tei Market, is an interesting stroll if you haven't yet visited a city market. You'll pass butcher shops and stores selling fish, fruits, and vegetables.

At the end of Reclamation Street, straight ahead past the elevated highway, is a small red building with "Welcome" written in many languages. It's the:

⓯ Jade Market

This fascinating covered market, in two separate structures, consists of some 400 stalls selling jade, pearls, and collectibles and is open from about 10am to approximately 4pm daily, though vendors stay open until 6pm or so if business warrants it (especially Sun). The jade on sale here comes in a bewildering range of quality. The highest quality should be cold to the touch and translucent, but it's possible to infuse jade with color so that inferior stones acquire the brightness and translucence associated with more expensive stones. Therefore, unless you know your jade, you're better off just coming here for a look or limiting your purchases to pendants or bangles that cost only a few dollars. The freshwater pearls are also good buys. Although the Chinese here used to bargain secretly by using hand signals concealed underneath a newspaper so that none of the onlookers would know the final price, it appears that calculators have gained more popularity these days.

From the Jade Market, go east 1 block to Shanghai Street, where you will soon see the:

⓰ Tin Hau Temple

Shaded by banyan trees, this is one of many temples in Hong Kong dedicated to Tin Hau, the Goddess of the Sea. This popular community temple has a park, usually filled with people playing mahjongg, and inner recesses filled with people asking favors or giving thanks. The temple has sections dating back more than a century. It also reveres deities of the city, the earth, and mercy. It's open daily from 8am to 6pm.

Depending on when you started this tour, at this point you may want to go back to your hotel room to rest and then take a taxi back to visit Yau Ma Tei's most famous attraction, the **Temple Street Night Market** (see the "Temple Street Night Market" box below). The market is in full swing after 7pm, though some vendors start setting up stalls at around 4pm.

TAKE A BREAK
Several hotels in the vicinity make pleasant stops for an early evening drink. In the **Nathan Hotel,** 378 Nathan Rd. (enter via Pak Hoi St; ☏ 852/2388 5141), there's the rooftop Bali Bar, open daily from 5pm to 2am and offering happy hour nightly to 9pm. Across the street, the **Eaton Hotel,** 380 Nathan Rd. (which you also enter via Pak Hoi St; ☏ 852/2782 1818), has a small cozy bar called **Planter's,** just off the hotel's lobby on the fourth floor. It offers happy hour nightly from 5 to 9pm, when you can also enjoy a snack buffet for HK$38 (US$4.95/£2.70). There's also live music here from 6pm. For a meal, in the basement of the Eaton Hotel is a Cantonese restaurant, **Yat Tung Heen Chinese Restaurant,** good for seafood and regional dishes. Near the Ladies' Market is a branch of **California Pizza Kitchen,** 56 Dundas St. (☏ 852/2374 0032), with soups, salads, and pastas in addition to pizza.

Otherwise, if it's early, you like markets, and you're still feeling energetic, walk north on Nathan Road about 10 minutes, taking a right on Dundas Street and then a left onto Tung Choi, home of the so-called:

⓱ Ladies' Market

This is where street vendors sell women's clothing and accessories, including handbags, Chinese jackets, sunglasses, watches, and shoes, as well as men's and children's clothing and toys at low prices, from about 12:30 to 10:30pm daily. Although this market used to be geared to local tastes (with smaller sizes), an increasing number of tourists have turned it into a thriving market rivaling Temple Street Night Market. The Ladies' Market, in the heart of Mong Kok, extends from Dundas Street north to Argyle Street.

Continuing farther north on Tung Choi (past Mong Kok Rd., which you'll have to cross at the crosswalk to the left) soon brings you to the:

⓲ Goldfish Market

You'll recognize the Goldfish Market from the shop after shop selling exotic

Temple Street Night Market

The Temple Street Night Market is named after the street on which it's located. This market, with some stalls open from 4pm but busiest from 7 to 10pm, is an entertaining place to spend an evening, with its countless stalls that sell clothing, watches, lighters, imitation designer handbags, sunglasses, sweaters, Chinese souvenirs, cassettes, and more. The name of the game is bargaining. There are also seafood stalls, where you can eat inexpensive meals of clams, shrimp, mussels, and crab. Be sure to follow Temple Street to its northern end past the overpass and around the carpark; in the vicinity of the Tin Hau Temple, you'll find palm readers, musicians, and street singers (who favor Cantonese operas and pop songs). Several of the palm readers speak English.

The market is famous for its *dai pai dong* (Cantonese for "big rows of food stalls") that specialize in seafood. Fifty years ago, *dai pai dong* is where most Hong Kong families dined on an evening out, and they were found almost everywhere. Now the government has moved most food stalls into covered markets. The *dai pai dong* at this market are among the few remaining that retain their original ambience. You'll find several under one roof at the Temple Street Food Store at the intersection of Temple Street and Public Square Street, where you can dine inexpensively on clams, shrimp, mussels, and crab, sitting at simple tables in the middle of the action.

fish as well as other pets; most are open daily from 10am to 9pm. Aquariums are considered to bring good luck and are excellent for feng shui.

Head 1 block east (right), and you'll find yourself on:

19 Fa Yuen Street

This is a local market with stalls selling more clothing, handbags, socks, watches, cheap toys, and fruit, at very inexpensive prices. There probably won't be another tourist in sight here and you may pick up some bargains to boot.

At the end of Fa Yuen Street, turn right to cross Prince Edward Road West at the pedestrian light, turn left onto Sai Yee Street, and then take the first right for:

20 Flower Market Road

Shop after open-fronted shop here sells orchids, roses, and other wonderfully aromatic flowers, at prices so inexpensive you'll wish you could take some home. More transportable but not nearly as appealing are the fake flowers also sold on this street. Shops are open daily from around 7am to 7pm.

At the end of the road is the:

21 Yuen Po Street Bird Garden

This is an attractive series of Chinese-style open courtyards lined with shops selling songbirds, intricately fashioned bird cages, live crickets, and tiny porcelain water bowls. Note, too, the men who bring their pet birds here for an outing. This place is very Chinese and makes for some great photographs. It's open daily from 7am until 8pm.

After exploring this area of Mong Kok, walk west back to Nathan Road for the Prince Edward MTR station.

Shopping

No doubt about it: One of the main reasons people come to Hong Kong is to shop. According to the Hong Kong Tourism Board (HKTB), visitors here spend more than 50% of their money on shopping. In fact, the Hong Kong Special Administrative Region (SAR) is such a popular shopping destination that many luxury cruise ships dock here longer than they do anywhere else on their tours. I doubt that there's ever been a visitor to Hong Kong who left empty-handed.

1 The Shopping Scene

BEST BUYS

Hong Kong is a duty-free port, which means that imported goods are not taxed in the SAR with the exception of only a few luxury goods like tobacco and alcohol. What's more, there is no sales tax in Hong Kong. Thus, you can buy some goods in the SAR at a cheaper price than in the country where they were made. It's less expensive, for example, to buy Japanese products such as designer clothing, cameras, electronic goods, and pearls in Hong Kong than in Japan itself. In fact, all my friends who live in Japan try to visit the SAR at least once or twice a year to buy their business clothes, cosmetics, and other accessories.

Although not as cheap as it once was, clothing is probably one of the best buys in Hong Kong, simply because of the sheer quantity and variety. If you've looked at the labels of clothes sold in your own hometown, you've probably noticed that many say MADE IN HONG KONG or MADE IN CHINA. While international designer garments and custom-made clothing are comparable to what you'd pay in high-end shops around the world, there are numerous cheaper options, including factory outlets, discount shops that sell season's end merchandise, street markets, and small stores where you can pick up inexpensive fashions for a song. But even when I end up paying about as much for an outfit as I would back home, I know I've purchased unique clothing in Hong Kong that's impossible to find in homogenized shopping malls.

Hong Kong is also a great place to shop for other Chinese products, including porcelain, tableware, jade, cloisonné, silk, handicrafts, hand-embroidery, Chinese herbs, Chinese traditional dresses and jackets, exotic teas from China's many provinces, antiques, and artwork. While Hong Kong prices are higher than what you'd pay in mainland China, the quality and quantity is quite good.

Other good buys include shoes, gold jewelry, furniture, carpets, leather goods, luggage (you'll probably need a new bag just to lug your purchases home), handbags, briefcases, cosmetics, and eyeglasses. Hong Kong is also one of the world's largest exporters of watches and toys. As for electronic goods and cameras, they are not the bargains they once were. Make sure, therefore, to check prices on goods at home

Tips **Caveat Emptor**

Hong Kong is a buyer-beware market. Name brands are sometimes fakes; that cheap jade you bought may actually be glass; and electronic goods may not work. To make things worse, the general practice is that goods are usually not returnable, and deposits paid are not refundable.

On a personal note, I decided to buy a digital Sony camcorder and checked approximately 10 electronics stores, where I received price quotes ranging from HK$3,500 to HK$12,000 (US$455–US$1,560/£250–£857) for the exact same model. When I returned to the cheapest stores and asked to see the camcorder, however, I was told it was suddenly "out of stock," but the salesmen said they would be happy to show me a similar model for a slightly higher price. The problem is that there are so *many* models—including many that never make it to Western markets—that it's difficult to know exactly what you're getting and what constitutes a fair price. In the end, I fell for the old bait-and-switch and bought a discontinued Sony camcorder at a higher price than what I would have paid for a newer model in the United States. I didn't do my homework *before* departing home (even checking the Sony website while in Hong Kong would have been a smart move), and I ended up paying for my mistake.

To be on the safe side, try to make your major purchases at HKTB member stores, which display the HKTB logo (a gold circle with black Chinese calligraphy in the middle and the words "Quality Tourism Services") on their storefronts. There are hundreds of member stores, all listed in a hefty directory called *A Guide to Quality Shops,* which you can get free from the HKTB and at www.discoverhongkong.com/qts. Both give the names, addresses, and phone numbers of shops that sell everything from audio-video equipment to jewelry, clothing, optical goods, antiques, and custom-made clothing. QTS-accredited shops must pass stringent assessments each year, are required to give accurate information on the products they sell, and should respond promptly to justified complaints. Of course, prices are often higher than at nonmember stores, but the payoff should be peace of mind and reassurance that you are paying a fair price. If you do have a complaint against a member store, make sure you have the receipt and then contact either the **Travel Industry Council of Hong Kong** (© 852/2807 0707) or the **Consumer Council Hotline** (© 852/2929 2222) In case of a serious dispute you can also call the **Hong Kong Police** (© 999) 24 hours a day.

before you come to the SAR so that you can accurately assess a bargain. The best deals are on recently discontinued models.

If you're interested in fake name-brand watches, handbags, or clothing to impress the folks back home, you've come to the right place. Although illegal, fake name-brand goods were still being sold at Hong Kong's night markets during my last visit by vendors who were ready to flee at the first sight of an official (even cheaper prices are offered for fake designer handbags and watches just across the border in mainland China; see chapter 11, "Side Trips from Hong Kong"). Of course, if Customs officials spot these fake goods in your bags when you return home, they'll be confiscated and you could be fined. Approximately half the fake goods seized by U.S. Customs agents come from mainland China.

WHEN TO SHOP

Because shopping is such big business in Hong Kong, most stores are open 7 days a week, closing only for 2 or 3 days during the Chinese New Year. Most stores open at 10am and remain open until 7:30pm in Central, 9pm or 10pm in Tsim Sha Tsui and Yau Ma Tei, and 9:30pm in Causeway Bay. Street markets are open every day.

The biggest and best seasonal sale takes place around the Chinese lunar new year, generally in February. All the major department stores as well as shops in many of the huge shopping complexes hold sales at this time, with prices discounted about 40%. There is also a summer sale, usually in June or July, as well as end-of-season sales in the early spring and early autumn.

GUARANTEES & RECEIPTS

It's always a good idea to obtain a receipt from the shopkeeper for your purchases, if for no other reason than as proof of value when going through Customs upon return-ing home. You'll also need a receipt if the product you've purchased is defective. A receipt should give a description of your purchase, including the brand name, model number, serial number, and price for electronic and photographic equipment; for jew-elry and gold watches, there should be a description of the precious stones and the metal content. If you're making a purchase using a credit card, you should also ask for the customer's copy of the credit card slip, and make sure "HK$" appears before the monetary total.

If you're interested in a camera, electronic goods, watch, or any other expensive product, be sure to inspect the product carefully and make sure its voltage is compat-ible with that of your home country. Before purchasing, make sure that all parts, pieces, and the warranty card of your purchase are included in the box. Ask the shop-keeper for a manufacturer's guarantee, which should include the name and/or symbol of the sole agent in the SAR, a description of the model and serial number, date of purchase, name and address of the shop where you bought it, and the shop's official chop or stamp. Different products and models of the same brand may carry different warranties—some valid worldwide, others only in Hong Kong. Worldwide guarantees (which is what you'll want) must carry the name and/or symbol of the sole agent in Hong Kong for the given product. Be aware of parallel imports, items brought into Hong Kong by someone other than the official import agent and which may be cheaper but offer a restricted guarantee and after-sale services. If you're in doubt, check with the rele-vant Hong Kong sole agent (information on sole agents for Sony, Rolex, and others can be obtained by calling the **Consumer Council Hotline** at ℂ **852/2929 2222**).

COMPARISON SHOPPING & BARGAINING

The cardinal rule of shopping in Hong Kong is to shop around. Unless you're plan-ning to buy antiques or art, you'll probably see the same items in many different shops on both sides of the harbor. If you've decided to buy a washable silk blouse for that favorite niece, for example, check a few stores to get an idea of quality, color, and style. With the exception of department stores and designer boutiques, you may be able to bargain for your purchase, though I've noticed that some shopkeepers are less willing to bargain than they once were. Still, at some of the smaller, family-owned stores, a good strategy is to ask what the "best" price might be. You should also ask for a discount if you're buying several items from the same store, and generally speaking, you can get a better price if you pay with cash rather than by credit card. How much you pay will depend on your bargaining skills and how many items you intend to purchase. Begin your comparison shopping as soon as you arrive in Hong Kong, so that you can get an idea of the differences in prices. As for street markets, you most certainly must bargain, though nowadays some vendors will just shake their heads and say their prices are fixed. If vendors are willing to bargain, sometimes just saying the item is too expensive and walking away will suddenly get you that "special price."

SHIPPING

Many stores, especially the larger ones, will pack and ship your purchases home for you. Since basic insurance usually insures only against loss, it's a good idea to buy an all-risk insurance for valuable or fragile goods, available at the store. However, since these policies can be expensive, find out whether using your credit card to make your purchase will provide automatic insurance.

In addition, all upper-bracket and most medium-range hotels offer a parcel-wrapping and mailing service. If you decide to ship your purchases home yourself, the easiest thing to do is to stop by the post office and buy ready-made boxes, which come with everything you need to ship goods home. Packages sent to the United States or Europe generally take 6 to 8 weeks by surface mail and 1 week by airmail. For major purchases, you can also buy postal insurance covering damage or loss in transit.

2 Great Shopping Areas

Hong Kong is so filled with shops, boutiques, street markets, department stores, and malls, it's hard to think of places where you *can't* shop. Still, there are specific hunting grounds for various products, as well as areas that have greater concentrations of shops than elsewhere.

Tsim Sha Tsui has the greatest concentration of shops in Hong Kong. Nathan Road, which runs through Kowloon for 4km (2½ miles) from the harbor to the border of the New Territories, is lined with stores selling clothing, jewelry, eyeglasses, cameras, electronic goods, crafts from China, shoes, handbags, luggage, watches, and more. There are also tailors, tattoo artists, and even shops that will carve your name into a wooden chop (a stamp used in place of a signature for official documents). Be sure to explore the side streets radiating off Nathan Road for shops specializing in washable silk and casual clothing and for export overruns of fun, youth-oriented fashions at modest prices. There are also department stores, Chinese emporiums, and shopping arcades, as well as several huge shopping malls. Harbour City, on Canton Road, for example, is gigantic. Farther north, in Yau Ma Tei, is Hong Kong's most famous outdoor market, the Temple Street Night Market, with vendors selling clothing, CDs, watches, toys, mobile phones, Chinese souvenirs, and accessories. The nearby Ladies' Market is also great for inexpensive clothing and accessories. There are also specialist markets in Yau Ma Tei and Mong Kok selling everything from clothing and flowers to goldfish, songbirds, and jade.

For upscale shopping, **Central** is where you'll find international designer labels. The Landmark, Prince's Building, Alexandra House, and Chater House boast designer boutiques selling jewelry, clothing, leather goods and more, with names ranging from Armani, Cartier, and Chanel to Gucci, Louis Vuitton, and Tiffany & Co. Pacific Place

Shopping in Tsim Sha Tsui

Chinese Arts and Crafts Ltd **5, 14**
Chinese Carpet Centre **18**
Fa Yuen Street Market **1**
Fortress **12**
Harbour City **12**
Jade Market **3**
Joyce **8**
Kaiser Estates **11**
Ladies' Market **2**
Lane Crawford **12**
Marks & Spencer **12**
New World Centre **18**
The Peninsula arcade **16**
Sam's Tailor **10**
Shanghai Tang **16, 19**
Sogo **17**
Star Computer City **13**
The Swank Shop **12**
Temple Street Night Market **6**
Toys 'R' Us **12**
Vivienne Tam **12, 16**
Wing On **4, 20**
Yue Hwa Chinese
   Products **7, 9, 14, 15**

is an upscale shopping mall selling everything from clothing to electronics; ifc mall sells high-end clothing and accessories. Hip Shanghai Tang is a good place to shop for upscale Chinese clothing and souvenirs, while Li Yuen Street East and West street markets offer cheaper Chinese jackets, watches, children's clothing, and accessories.

Another happy hunting ground is **Causeway Bay** on Hong Kong Island. In contrast to Tsim Sha Tsui, it caters more to locals than to tourists, and prices are often lower. In addition to small shops selling everything from shoes and clothing to Chinese herbs, there are a couple of Japanese department stores and a large shopping complex called Times Square specializing in clothing and housewares. Also check the area around Jardine's Crescent (p. 218), an open-air market with cheap clothing, food, and produce. For shoes, get on the tram and head for Happy Valley; on Leighton Road and Wong Nai Chung Road (near the racecourse), where there are rows of shoe and handbag shops.

One of my favorite places to shop for inexpensive fashions is **Stanley Market** on the southern end of Hong Kong Island, where vendors sell silk clothing and business and casual wear. In recent years, shops specializing in Chinese crafts and products have also opened in Stanley Market. Another great shopping destination on southern Hong Kong Island is **Ap Lei Chau** (an island connected to Aberdeen by bridge), where at Horizon Plaza you'll find discount outlets for pricey downtown clothing stores, as well as many antiques and furniture stores.

Antiques and curio lovers also head for **Hollywood Road** and **Cat Street** in the Western District on Hong Kong Island, where everything from snuff bottles to jade carvings and Ming vases is for sale. Chinese handicrafts, including porcelain, furniture, silk clothing, and embroidery, are sold in Chinese-product department stores and Chinese arts-and-crafts shops located on both sides of the harbor. Several deluxe hotels boast arcades housing designer boutiques, most notably The Peninsula and Regent.

3 Shopping A to Z

The stores listed below are just a few of the thousands upon thousands in the SAR. For more detailed listings, see the booklet *A Guide to Quality Shops,* which lists shops that are members of the HKTB, or check the website www.discoverhongkong. com/qts. You might also want to look at *Suzy Gershman's Born to Shop Hong Kong, Shanghai & Beijing.*

ANTIQUES & COLLECTIBLES

Several of the Chinese-product stores, listed under "Chinese Craft Emporiums" later in this chapter, also stock antiques, especially porcelain. Additionally, some hotel shopping arcades have shops specializing in antiques. Antiques buffs should also inquire at HKTB whether international auctioneers Christie's or Sotheby's are holding one of their regular sales for antiques in Hong Kong.

The most famous area for antiques and chinoiserie, however, is around **Hollywood Road** and **Cat Street,** both above the Central District on Hong Kong Island. This area gained fame in the 1950s following the 1949 revolution in China (which flooded the market with family possessions). Hollywood Road twists along for a little more than .8km (½ mile), with shops selling original and reproduction Qing and Ming dynasty Chinese furniture, original prints, scrolls, porcelain, clay figurines, silver, and rosewood and black-wood furniture, as well as fakes and curios. Near the western end is

Upper Lascar Row, popularly known as Cat Street, where sidewalk vendors sell snuff bottles, curios, and odds and ends, as well as reproductions. At the eastern end of Hollywood Road, near Pottinger Street, is a cluster of chic antiques shops displaying furniture and blue-and-white porcelain, including goods from neighboring Asian countries such as Korean chests and Japanese hibachi. If you're a real antiques collector, I suggest you simply walk through the dozens of shops on and around Hollywood Road. Most are open daily from 10am to 6pm.

Another good stamping ground is **Horizon Plaza,** 2 Lee Wing St., Ap Lei Chau, an island connected to Aberdeen by bridge. This huge warehouse has more than a dozen shops selling antiques (take bus no. M590 from Exchange Square in Central to Ap Lei Chau).

If you cannot tell the difference between originals and reproductions, you're better off shopping at one of the HKTB member stores, which display HKTB's gold circle and calligraphy logo. Be sure to ask whether an antique has been repaired or restored, as this can affect its value. If the piece is quite expensive, ask that it be tested. (The most important rule is to shop with reputable dealers when buying expensive pieces. And make sure that if the test turns out negative, the shop will pay for the test. As you can see, this process takes time, money, and effort.) Wood, for example, can be tested using carbon-14 dating, while ceramics can be tested with the Oxford Test. The authenticity of bronze, jade, glass, and stone can also be determined through testing. If you're purchasing anything more than 100 years old, request a Certificate of Antiquity detailing its age and origin, along with a receipt detailing your purchase. Although it's illegal to smuggle antiques out of mainland China, many smuggled items do in fact end up in Hong Kong, where it is legal to then sell, buy, and own them. Needless to say, this has caused friction between China and Hong Kong, especially when international auction houses have sold well-documented smuggled Chinese antiques.

Arch Angel Antiques ✦ Established in 1988 by an American and Dutch couple, this is one of Hollywood Road's largest shops for Asian antiques and art, including museum-quality ceramics, furniture, Ming dynasty figurines, terra-cotta animals, boxes, and collectibles. In addition to this three-story main shop, nearby galleries (which the owners will show you on request) showcase ancient ceramics, bronze Buddhas, terra-cotta figures, stone sculptures, and contemporary Vietnamese art. Every antique item for sale is accompanied by a detailed certificate of authenticity. The main shop is open daily from 9:30am to 6:30pm. 53–55 Hollywood Rd., Central. ℂ **852/2851 6848.** MTR: Central.

Cat Street Galleries   Cat Street Galleries, located between Hollywood Road and Cat Street, houses several individually owned booths of arts and crafts and expensive antiques from the various dynasties, making it a good place to begin an antiques shopping odyssey. It's open Monday through Friday from 11am to 6pm and Saturday from 10am to 6pm. 38 Lok Ku Rd., Central. ℂ **852/2543 1609.** MTR: Sheung Wan. Bus: 26 (from Des Voeux Rd. Central in front of the Hongkong Bank) to the 2nd stop on Hollywood Rd., at Man Mo Temple.

China Art ✦ This family-owned shop, which has the elegance of an art gallery with its mixed displays of furniture and art, is one of Hong Kong's best for restored antique Chinese furniture, including chairs, tables, folding screens, chests, and wardrobes, mostly from the Ming dynasty (1368–1644). Located across from the Central Police Station, it's open Monday through Saturday from 10am to 6pm and Sunday and holidays from 1 to 5pm. (An additional showroom warehouse, open only by appointment, is located in Cat Street Galleries; see above). 15 Hollywood Rd., Central. © 852/2542 0982. www.chinaart.com.hk. MTR: Central. Bus: 26 (from Des Voeux Rd. Central in front of the Hongkong Bank) to Hollywood Rd.

Dragon Culture ★★ *Finds*   All serious fans of Chinese antiques eventually end up here. One of the largest and most knowledgeable purveyors of antiques in Hong Kong, Victor Choi began collecting Chinese antiques in the 1970s, traveling throughout China from province to province and to all the major cities. He shares his expertise in three books: *Collecting Chinese Antiquities in Hong Kong* (a must for both the novice and the experienced buyer), *Horses for Eternity,* and *Antiquities through the Ages,* which you can purchase in his shop. Choi has also given lectures on Chinese antiques in the HKTB's Meet the People program. With another gallery in New York, he carries Neolithic pottery, three-color glazed pottery horses from the Tang dynasty, Ming porcelains, bronzes, jade, woodcarvings, snuff bottles, calligraphy, paintings, brush pots, stone carvings, and more, and also guarantees authenticity for all items he sells. According to Choi, prices for antiques are a fourth of what they'd fetch in New York. He's open Monday through Saturday from 10am to 6pm. 231 Hollywood Rd., Sheung Wan. © 852/2545 8098. www.dragonculture.com.hk. MTR: Sheung Wan. Bus: 26 (from Des Voeux Rd. Central in front of the Hongkong Bank) to the 2nd stop on Hollywood Rd., at Man Mo Temple.

Teresa Coleman Fine Arts   Established in 1982, this gallery is best known for its collection of antique embroidered costumes from the Chinese imperial court, with approximately 2,000 pieces dating from the Qing Dynasty (1644–1912). Complimenting the collection are costume accessories and ornaments, including fans and paintings created in China during the 18th and 19th centuries expressly for the Western export market. The shop also has a good collection of antique Oriental rugs from Tibet and China. It's open Monday through Saturday from 9:30am to 6pm. 79 Wyndham St., Central. © 852/2526 2450. www.teresacoleman.com. MTR: Central.

True Arts & Curios *Finds*   This tiny shop is so packed with antiques and curios that there's barely room for customers. Although everything from snuff bottles, porcelain, antique silver, earrings, hair pins, and children's shoes (impractical but darling, with curled toes) are stocked, the true finds here are some 2,000 intricate woodcarvings, pried from the doors and windows of dismantled temples and homes. You'll find them hanging from the ceiling and in bins, many of them dusty and grimy from years of neglect. The best ones are carved from a single piece of wood, masterpieces in workmanship and available at modest prices. It's open Monday through Saturday from 10:30am to 6:30pm and Sunday from 2 to 6pm. 89–91 Hollywood Rd., Central. © 852/2559 1485. MTR: Sheung Wan.

ART GALLERIES

Several Hong Kong art galleries specialize in contemporary art from mainland China and Hong Kong. These are two of the most well known.

Hanart TZ Gallery   This very tiny gallery (in the same building as American Express) has been exhibiting, promoting, and selling experimental art from mainland China, Hong Kong, and Taiwan since 1983. Its owner/curator, Chang Tsong-zung, has given lectures on the contemporary local art scene for HKTB's Meet the People program. Exhibition space is small, so be sure to ask for recent catalogs. It's open Monday through Saturday from 10am to 6:30pm. 202 Henley Building, 2nd floor, 5 Queen's Rd., Central. © 852/2526 9019. www.hanart.com. MTR: Central.

Schoeni Art Gallery ☞   This 5,000-square-foot gallery shows contemporary Chinese oil paintings by both up-and-coming and established artists. A smaller gallery at nearby 27 Hollywood Rd. (✆ **852/2542 3143**) specializes in contemporary works by European and Asian artists. Both are open Monday through Saturday from 10:30am to 6:30pm. 21–31 Old Bailey St., Central. ✆ **852/2869 8802**. www.schoeni.com.hk. MTR: Central.

CARPETS

Hong Kong is a good place to shop for Chinese, Indian, Persian, and other types of carpets and rugs. Additionally, the locally made Tai Ping carpets are famous the world over, produced with virgin wool imported from New Zealand.

For imported carpets from India and the Middle East, there are several shops along the **Hollywood Road** and **Wyndham Street** areas in Central. For hand-knotted wool or silk Chinese carpets, be sure to check out the Chinese craft emporiums (listed below).

The **Chinese Carpet Centre,** in Shop LO21 on the ground floor of the New World Centre at 18–24 Salisbury Rd., Sim Sha Tsui (✆ **852/2730 7230;** www.cccrugs.com. hk; MTR: Tsim Sha Tsui), stocks more than 100,000 Chinese carpets, mostly handmade of silk, wool, or cotton but also machine-made acrylic, from modern to classical designs.

For **Tai Ping** carpets, there's a conveniently located showroom in Shop 213 of the Prince's Building, 10 Chater Rd., Central (✆ **852/2736 1773;** www.taipingcarpets. com; MTR: Central). If you don't see what you like, you can have one custom-designed, specifying the color, thickness, and direction of the weave. It takes about 3 months to make a carpet; the company will ship it to you.

For one-stop shopping, head to **Horizon Plaza,** 2 Lee Wing St., Ap Lei Chau, warehouse of mostly furniture and accessory shops, including more than a dozen stores selling Persian, hand-knotted Oriental, and other rugs (bus: M590 from Exchange Square in Central to Ap Lei Chau, on the south side of Hong Kong Island, near Aberdeen).

CHINA (PORCELAIN)

Chinaware, a fine, translucent earthenware, was first brought from China to Europe by the Portuguese in the 16th century. Its name was subsequently shortened to "china," and Hong Kong remains one of the best places in the world to shop for both antique (mainly from the Manchu, or Qing, dynasty, 1644–1912) and contemporary Chinese porcelain. Traditional motifs include bamboo, flowers, dragons, carp, and cranes, which adorn everything from dinner plates to vases, lamps, and jars. Also popular is translucent porcelain with a rice grain design. And, of course, European and Japanese china is also available in Hong Kong, including Meissen, Wedgwood, and Noritake.

Probably the best place to begin looking for Chinese porcelain is at one of the Chinese-product stores, listed below under "Chinese Craft Emporiums." In addition, malls and shopping centers like Pacific Place in Admiralty, Times Square in Causeway Bay, and Harbour City in Tsim Sha Tsui also have porcelain shops (see "Megamalls & Shopping Centers," later in this chapter). Nowadays, contemporary china is generally both dishwasher- and microwave-safe.

Overjoy Porcelain Factory   With more than 400 stock designs, dinner services are the specialty here. You may also mix and match, or even create your very own design. Sets are usually commissioned for 6, 8, or 12 diners and take 4 to 6 weeks to complete. It's open Monday through Saturday from 10am to 6pm, but because it's in the New Territories, you'd be wise to call first. Or, visit its smaller shop on the first floor of Fleet Arcade, Fenwick Pier Lung King St., Wan Chai (🕾 **852/2511 2763;** MTR: Wan Chai), open the same hours. 1st floor, Block B of Kwai Hing Industrial Building, 10–18 Chun Pin St., Kwai Chung, New Territories. 🕾 **852/2487 0615.** MTR: Kwai Hing station; then take a taxi.

Wah Tung China Company 🕸   This is reputedly the largest company specializing in hand-painted antique porcelain reproductions, especially huge pieces like vases and garden stools. Its vast collection covers all Chinese artistic periods, including Song dynasty celadons, Canton Rose, Chinoiserie, Chinese Imari, and 17th- and 18th-century Chinese export porcelain. A second shop is located at 59 Hollywood Rd., Central (🕾 **852/2543 2823;** MTR: Central). Both shops are open Monday through Saturday from 10am to 7pm and Sunday and holidays from 11am to 7pm. 8 Queen's Rd. East, Central. 🕾 **852/2520 5933.** www.wahtungchina.com. MTR: Admiralty.

CHINESE CRAFT EMPORIUMS

In addition to the shops listed here, which specialize in traditional and contemporary arts, crafts, clothing, souvenirs, and gift items from China, there are several souvenir shops at Stanley Market (located in Stanley on the southern end of Hong Kong Island) that carry lacquered boxes, china, embroidered tablecloths, figurines, and other Chinese imports. You'll also find Chinese souvenirs at the Temple Street Night Market, described later in this chapter under "Markets."

Chinese Arts and Crafts Ltd 🕸🕸   In business for more than 40 years, this is the best upscale chain for Chinese arts and crafts and is one of the safest places to purchase jade. Prices are high, but so is the quality. You can also buy elegant silk dresses and blouses, beautiful Chinese jackets, arts and crafts, antiques, jewelry, watches, carpets, cloisonné, furs, Chinese herbs and medicine, rosewood furniture, chinaware, Chinese teas, and embroidered tablecloths or pillowcases here—in short, virtually all the upmarket items that China produces. It's a great place for gifts in all price ranges. The main shop, spread on two floors and located in Star House near the Star Ferry, is open daily from 10am to 9:30pm. Branches are conveniently located in the Nathan Hotel, 378 Nathan Rd., Yau Ma Tei (🕾 **852/2730 0061;** MTR: Jordan); Shop 230 in Pacific Place, 88 Queensway, Central (🕾 **852/2523 3933;** MTR: Admiralty); and in the China Resources Building, 26 Harbour Rd., Wan Chai (🕾 **852/2827 6667;** MTR: Wan Chai). 3 Salisbury Rd., Tsim Sha Tsui. 🕾 **852/2735 4061.** www.crcretail.com. MTR: Tsim Sha Tsui.

Shanghai Tang 🕸🕸🕸   You are stepping back into the Shanghai of the 1930s when you enter this small but upscale two-level store with its gleaming wooden and tiled floors, raised cashier cubicles, ceiling fans, and helpful clerks wearing classical Chinese jackets. This is Chinese chic at its best, with neatly stacked rows of updated versions of traditional Chinese clothing, ranging from cheongsams and silk pajamas to padded jackets, caps, and shoes—all in bright, contemporary colors and styles. If you're looking for a lime-green or shocking pink padded jacket, this is the place for you. There are even Shanghai tailors on hand to custom-make something for you. You will also find children's clothing and funky accessories and home furnishings, from silk-covered photo albums and beaded picture frames to funky clutch purses and silver chopsticks.

There are tiny branches in The Peninsula hotel (🕾 **852/2537 2888**) and Hotel InterContinental (🕾 **852/2721 1211**), both on Salisbury Road in Tsim Sha Tsui

(MTR: Tsim Sha Tsui), as well as Shop 237 in Pacific Place (© **852/2918 1505;** MTR: Admiralty) and both east and west halls of Hong Kong International Airport (© **852/2261 0606** and © **852/2261 0318** respectively), but the main shop has the largest selection. Its sign is hidden under the eaves of the Pedder Building, so you may have to search for it. It's open Monday through Saturday from 10am to 8pm and Sunday from 11am to 7pm. Pedder Building, 12 Pedder St., Central. © **852/2525 7333.** www.shanghai tang.com. MTR: Central.

Yue Hwa Chinese Products   Yue Hwa caters to a local clientele with both traditional Chinese and everyday products. The main shop in Yau Ma Tei stocks everything from household goods to clothing, shoes, jade jewelry, arts and crafts, china, linens, furniture, tea, foodstuff, medicinal herbs like dried sea horses, and even antlers. It was here that I bought some friends a gag wedding gift years ago—Chinese whiskey with preserved lizards in it, all for only HK$25 (US$3.25/£1.75)—definitely a bargain. The store is open daily from 10am to 10pm.

The branch stores specialize primarily in Chinese handicrafts and jewels, with convenient locations at Park Lane Shopper's Boulevard at 143–161 Nathan Rd., Tsim Sha Tsui (© **852/2739 3888;** MTR: Tsim Sha Tsui); basement of Mirador Mansion, 54–64 Nathan Rd., Tsim Sha Tsui (© **852/2368 9165;** MTR: Tsim Sha Tsui); 1 Kowloon Park Dr. and Peking Rd., Tsim Sha Tsui (© **852/2317 5333;** MTR: Tsim Sha Tsui); and 375–379 Hennessy Rd., Wan Chai (© **852/3162 8998;** MTR: Wan Chai). 301–309 Nathan Rd., Yau Ma Tei, Kowloon. © **852/2384 0084.** www.yuehwa.com. MTR: Jordan.

DEPARTMENT STORES

It will probably come as no surprise to learn that the SAR has a great many department stores. Wing On and Lane Crawford, two upmarket local chain department stores, offer a nice selection of clothing, accessories, and local and imported designer fashions, gift items, and cosmetics. Japanese department stores are also quite popular with the locals, with a couple located in Causeway Bay.

LOCAL DEPARTMENT STORES

Lane Crawford Ltd ✿   This upscale department store, founded in 1850, is a hometown favorite for its large clothing and accessory departments for the whole family and its home furnishings, including shoes, handbags, silver, crystal, and cosmetics. It has branches on both sides of the harbor and is similar to established chain stores in England and the United States.

This main store is open daily from 10am to 9pm. Other branches can be found at: Pacific Place, 88 Queensway, Central (© **852/2118 3668;** MTR: Admiralty); Times Square, 1 Matheson St., Causeway Bay (© **852/2118 3638;** MTR: Causeway Bay); and Shop 100, Ocean Terminal, Harbour City, 3 Canton Rd., Tsim Sha Tsui (© **852/ 2118 3428;** MTR: Tsim Sha Tsui). Bargain hunters should head to the Lane Crawford Warehouse, on the 25th floor of Horizon Plaza, 2 Lee Wing St., Ap Lei Chau (© **852/2118 3403**), where last-season's clothing and accessories are sold at deeply discounted prices. Podium 3, ifc mall, Central. © **852/2118 3388.** www.lanecrawford.com. MTR: Central.

Wing On   Founded in Shanghai more than a century ago and one of Hong Kong's oldest department stores, this main shop offers a wide selection of clothing, jewelry, accessories, and household items, with conveniently located branches at Wing On Kowloon Center across from the Nathan Hotel, 345 Nathan Rd., Yau Ma Tei (© **852/ 2710 6288;** MTR: Jordan) and at Wing On Plaza, 62 Mody Rd., in Tsim Sha Tsui

East (© **852/2196 1388;** MTR: Tsim Sha Tsui). The main branch is open daily from 10am to 7:30pm. 211 Des Voeux Rd., Sheung Wan. © 852/2852 1888. www.wingonet.com. MTR: Sheung Wan.

JAPANESE DEPARTMENT STORES

Mitsukoshi   Mitsukoshi is a long-established department store; it first opened as a kimono shop in Japan in the 1600s and is still one of Japan's most exclusive stores. Today it houses the boutiques of well-known designers of shoes, accessories, and clothing, with high prices to match; it also carries lingerie, cosmetics, household goods, and toys. It's open daily from 10:30am to 10pm. 500 Hennessy Rd., Causeway Bay. © 852/2576 5222. www.mitsukoshi.com.hk. MTR: Causeway Bay.

Seibu   One of the largest department-store chains in Japan (its Tokyo store is the third-largest department store in the world), this was Seibu's first store to open outside Japan. An upscale, sophisticated department store targeting Hong Kong's affluent yuppie population, it is the epitome of chic, from its Art Deco Italian furnishings to fashions from the world's top design houses. More than 65% of its merchandise is European, and 25% is from Japan. The Loft department carries well-designed housewares and gifts, while Seed is the place to go for the latest fashions. The food department in the basement is especially good, stocking many imported items that are not available elsewhere in Hong Kong; it's also a good choice in inexpensive dining, with various counters specializing in international fare. It's open Sunday through Wednesday from 10:30am to 8pm and Thursday through Saturday from 10:30am to 9pm. There's a small branch in the Windsor House, 311 Gloucester Rd., Causeway Bay (© **852/2890 0333;** MTR: Causeway Bay). Pacific Place, 88 Queensway, Central. © 852/ 2971 3888. MTR: Admiralty.

Sogo   Sogo is much larger and more egalitarian than the other Japanese department stores listed above; its goods are cheaper and its prices lower. Consequently, the 12-story store is often packed (particularly on Sun), filled with families shopping for clothing, toys, furniture, household goods, and electrical appliances. In the second basement is a large supermarket. There's a small, subterranean branch across the harbor, at 12 Salisbury Rd. in front of the InterContinental, Tsim Sha Tsui (© **852/3556 1212**). Both are open daily from 10am to 10pm. 555 Hennessy Rd., Causeway Bay. © 852/ 2833 8338. www.sogo.com.hk. MTR: Causeway Bay.

OTHER DEPARTMENT STORES

Marks & Spencer   Known in Britain for its great prices on clothing and affectionately nicknamed "Marks & Sparks," this import from the United Kingdom (but with smaller sizes) is open daily from 10am to 8pm. It also has a couple branches on the Hong Kong side, including Central Tower, 28 Queen's Rd. Central (© **852/2921 8323;** MTR: Central), and Times Square, 1 Matheson St., Causeway Bay (© **852/2923 7972;** MTR: Causeway Bay). Ocean Centre, Harbour City, Canton Rd., Tsim Sha Tsui. © 852/2926 3344. www.marksandspencer.com. MTR: Tsim Sha Tsui.

ELECTRONICS

Because there is no import duty or sales tax and because Hong Kong may offer the latest models months before they're available in other countries, shopping for electronic goods has long been a popular tourist pastime. However, prices have increased for electronic products in recent years, so if you're interested in buying a digital camera, camcorder, DVD or MP3 player, computer, mobile phone, or other electronic product, be sure to check prices at home before coming to Hong Kong to make sure that what you want to buy here is really a bargain. Then, head to Tsim Sha Tsui for the many shops along Nathan Road and surrounding streets specializing in electronics galore. Compare prices first, and to be on the safe side, shop only in stores that are members of HKTB and skip those that do not have price tags. Otherwise, you may end up buying a discontinued model at inflated prices (see "Caveat Emptor," p. 204). **Fortress** (www.fortress.com.hk) is a big-name chain with locations throughout Hong Kong, including major shopping malls and tourist areas. Convenient outlets are shop no. 333A, Harbour City (© **852/3101 9205;** MTR: Tsim Sha Tsui), and Melbourne Plaza, 33 Queen's Rd. Central (© **852/2121 1077;** MTR: Central).

For computers and software, try dedicated malls such as **Star Computer City,** located on the second floor of the Star House across from the Tsim Sha Tsui Star Ferry terminal at 3 Salisbury Rd., or the **In Square Computer Plaza,** located on the 10th and 11th floors of the Windsor House, 311 Gloucester Rd. in Causeway Bay. In any case, whatever you buy, be sure to inspect every piece of equipment before leaving the store (do not assume what's inside a box matches the picture on the outside and check to make sure instructions are in English), make sure equipment works and that its voltage is compatible with yours at home, and obtain warranties and receipts. For computers, look for complete packages that offer computer, printer, scanner, and software at competitive prices, and be sure that the loaded software is in English.

A fun place for adventuresome shoppers is **Apliu Street** (beside Cheung Sha Wan Station), which functions as a street market for secondhand electronic goods and a hodgepodge of junk, including fishing poles, pots and pans, and more. The market is open weekdays from about 11am to 8pm and weekends from 11am to 11pm. You need to know your goods here, and be sure to bargain fiercely. Don't neglect the many stores behind the vendors, either, selling new and used mobile phones, watches, batteries, and more.

FASHION

Ever since Hong Kong received a large influx of Shanghainese tailors following the revolution in China in 1949, Hong Kong has been a center for the fashion industry. Today, clothing remains one of Hong Kong's best buys, and many major international design houses have boutiques here; several have factories as well, either here or just across the border in Guangzhou (p. 256). There are also a number of Hong Kong designers to watch out for, including Vivienne Tam, Walter Ma, Lulu Cheung, and Barney Cheng.

For a wide range in prices, the department stores listed above are best for one-stop shopping for the entire family, as are Hong Kong's many malls and shopping centers. Otherwise, small, family-owned shops abound in both Tsim Sha Tsui and Stanley Market, offering casual wear, washable silk outfits, and other clothing at very affordable prices. Cheaper still are factory outlets and street markets (see below).

If you're looking for international designer brands and don't care about price, there are several arcades and shopping centers known for their brand names. The **Landmark,** located on Des Voeux Road Central in Central, is an ultrachic shopping complex boasting the highest concentration of international brand names in Hong Kong, including Gucci, Tiffany & Co., Polo/Ralph Lauren, Manolo Blahnik, Marc Jacobs, Michael Kors, Sonia Rykiel, Louis Vuitton, Lanvin, and Christian Dior, as well as British luxury import Harvey Nichols, restaurants, and other shops. The shops here are generally open daily from 10:30am to 7:30pm. Other nearby fashion centers known for their international designer boutiques (and linked to the Landmark via elevated walkways) include the **Prince's Building,** next to the Mandarin Hotel, with boutiques for a. testoni, Chanel, Cartier, and others; **Alexandra House** with outlets for Prada and Yves Saint Laurent among others; and **Chater House,** with several Armani shops that sell everything from household items to clothing and cosmetics. Across the harbor, **The Peninsula** hotel, on Salisbury Road in Tsim Sha Tsui, has concessions for Hermès, Louis Vuitton, Loewe, Chanel, Gucci, Dior, Shanghai Tang, Prada, and Manolo Blahnik, to name only a few of the 80-some shops.

For trendier designs catering to an upwardly mobile younger crowd, check out the **Joyce** chain ⟨, the first fashion house in Hong Kong, established in the 1970s by Joyce Ma to satisfy Hong Kong women's cravings for European designs. Today her stores carry clothing by Issey Miyake, John Galliano, Stella McCartney, Yohji Yamamoto, Rei Kawakubo (Comme des Garçons), and others on the cutting edge of fashion. You'll find Joyce shops at 18 Queen's Rd. Central, Central District (© **852/ 2810 1120;** MTR: Central); 334 Pacific Place, 88 Queensway, Central (© **852/2523 5944;** MTR: Admiralty); and Shop G106 in The Gateway, Canton Rd., Tsim Sha Tsui (© **852/2367 8128;** MTR: Tsim Sha Tsui). Bargain hunters in the know head to the Joyce Warehouse, located on the south end of Hong Kong Island near Aberdeen, on the 21st floor of Horizon Plaza, 2 Lee Wing St., Ap Lei Chau (© **852/ 2814 8313;** bus: M590 from Exchange Square in Central to Ap Lei Chau). You never know what you may find among the discounted, off-season designer wear, but discounts run 30% to 70% off the original prices (open daily 10am–7pm).

For clothing by local designers, shop for Barney Cheng's classy evening wear at The Swank, which carries designerwear, with outlets at shop 202 of Alexandra House, Central (© **852/2868 3804;** MTR: Central) and in the Gateway Arcade of Harbour City (© **852/2175 4118;** MTR: Tsim Sha Tsui). You'll find the Chinese chic designs with a Western twist by Vivienne Tam at Shop 209, Pacific Place, 88 Queensway, Central (© **852/2918 0238;** MTR: Admiralty); Shop 2095, ifc mall, 8 Finance St., Central (© **852/2868 9268;** MTR: Central); Shop 302, Times Square, Causeway Bay (© **852/2506 0098;** MTR: Causeway Bay); Shop G310, Harbour City, Tsim Sha Tsui (© **852/2117 0028;** MTR: Tsim Sha Tsui); and The Peninsula arcade (© **852/ 2721 1818;** MTR: Tsim Sha Tsui).

FACTORY OUTLETS   Savvy shoppers head for Hong Kong's factory outlets to buy at least some of their clothes. These outlets sell excess stock, overruns, and quality-control rejects; because these items have been made for the export market, the sizes are Western. Bargains include clothes made of silk, cashmere, cotton, linen, knitwear, and wool, and some outlets have men's and children's clothing as well. Some manufacturers even produce clothing for famous designer labels, though it's not unusual to find labels cut out. Unfortunately, outlets are scattered throughout the territory, though there are clusters in the Central District on Hong Kong Island and Hung Hom in Kowloon.

There are, however, a few caveats about shopping in factory outlets. For one thing, you never know in advance what will be on sale, and sometimes the selection is disappointing. Some outlets do not have fitting rooms, and it's important to carefully examine garments inside and out for tears and stains. What's more, some outlets are indistinguishable from upmarket boutiques, with prices to match. Unfortunately, it seems that some shops simply call themselves "factory outlets" because that's what tourists are looking for. Thus, unless you have lots of time, it may not be worth your while to go to the outlets in Hung Hom in search of a good deal. Several street markets—notably Ladies' Market in Mong Kok (see "Markets" below)—also serve as outlets for mainland factories.

On Hong Kong Island, the best-known building that houses factory-outlet showrooms is the **Pedder Building,** 12 Pedder St., Central. During my last visit, I counted more than 30 shops here located on five floors, but many of these shops are not factory outlets—they're simply regular boutiques with the same merchandise at the same prices found at their other branches. In addition, a new trend seems to be shops selling used designerwear, shoes, and handbags, making it good for bargains in last season's fashions. In any case, it's convenient to have so many shops in one building and it's fun to just poke around here.

On the Kowloon side, the largest concentration of factory outlets is in Hung Hom, clustered in a group of warehouse buildings called **Kaiser Estates** on Man Yue Street. Although the Kaiser Estates comprise huge concrete factory buildings, the outlet shops inside look just like ordinary shops. To reach the Kaiser Estates, take bus no. 5C from the Tsim Sha Tsui Star Ferry bus terminal to Ma Tau Wai Road (the third stop after the KCR Kowloon Railway Station).

For a list of factory outlets along with their addresses, telephone numbers, and types of clothing, pick up the typed sheet called "Clothing & Accessories" at HKTB offices. Most outlets are open from 10 or 11am to 7pm Monday through Friday, with shorter hours on Saturdays. Some are open Sunday as well.

JEWELRY

According to the HKTB, Hong Kong has more jewelry stores per square mile than any other city in the world. Gems are imported duty-free from all over the world, and Hong Kong is reputedly the world's fourth-largest trading center for diamonds. Gold jewelry, both imported and locally made, is required by law to carry a stamp stating the accurate gold content.

Jade, of course, remains the most popular item of jewelry for both visitors and Chinese. It's believed to protect wearers against illness and ward off bad luck. The two categories of jade are jadeite and nephrite. Jadeite (also called Burmese jade) is generally white to apple green in color, although it also comes in hues of brown, red, orange, yellow, and even lavender. It may be mottled, but the most expensive variety is a translucent emerald green. Nephrite, which is less expensive, is usually a dark green or off-white. In any case, true jade is so hard that supposedly even a knife leaves no scratch. Unless you know your jade, your best bet is to shop in one of the Chinese-product stores, listed earlier in this chapter under "Chinese Craft Emporiums." For less expensive pieces and souvenirs, visit the Jade Market, described below under "Markets."

Pearls, almost all of which are cultured, are also popular among shoppers in Hong Kong. There are both sea- and freshwater pearls, available in all shapes, sizes, colors, and lusters. For inexpensive strands, check the vendors at the Jade Market. There are also many shops along Nathan Road in Tsim Sha Tsui that retail pearls.

MARKETS

Markets offer the best deals in Hong Kong, though a lot depends on how well you can bargain. Be sure to scrutinize the items that interest you carefully, since you won't be able to return them. Check clothing for faults, tears, cuts, marks, and uneven seams and hemlines. Make sure electronic gadgets work; the cheap alarm clock I bought my son lasted only a week.

HONG KONG ISLAND

STANLEY 𝕮𝕮   Stanley Market, rather small and easily navigated, is probably the most popular and best-known market in Hong Kong. Located on the southern coast of Hong Kong Island on a small peninsula, it's a great place to buy inexpensive clothing, especially sportswear, cashmere sweaters, silk blouses and dresses, and even linen blazers and outfits suitable for work. Men's, women's, and children's clothing are available. During my last visit, shopkeepers were not keen about bargaining unless you're buying several pieces, no doubt because tourists come here by the busload. In fact, Stanley is not as cheap as it once was, and many shops have remodeled into chic boutiques. Still, you're bound to find at least something you're wild about, especially if you like cheap, fun fashions. The inventory changes continuously—one year it seems everyone is selling tie-dyed shirts, the next year it's linen suits, washable silk, Chinese traditional jackets, or Gore-Tex coats. I usually walk through the market first, taking note of things I like and which stores they're in, and then I compare prices as I walk through. Most stores carry the same products, so it pays to comparison-shop. In addition to clothing, there are also many souvenir shops selling Chinese paintings, embroidered linen, beaded purses, handicrafts, curios, and jewelry.

To reach Stanley, take bus no. 6, 6A, 6X, or 260 from Central's Exchange Square bus terminal (bus no. 260 also stops in front of Pacific Place) or Minibus no. 40 from Causeway Bay. The bus ride to Stanley takes approximately 30 minutes. From Kowloon, take bus no. 973 from Mody Road in Tsim Sha Tsui East or from Canton Road in Tsim Sha Tsui. The shops are open daily from 9:30 or 10am to about 6:30pm.

LI YUEN STREET EAST & WEST   These two streets are parallel pedestrian lanes in the heart of the Central District, very narrow, and often congested with human traffic. Stalls are packed with Chinese jackets, handbags, clothes, scarves, sweaters, toys, baby clothes, watches, makeup, umbrellas, needles and thread, knickknacks, and even brassieres. Don't neglect the open-fronted shops behind the stalls. Some of these are boutiques selling fashionable but cheap clothing as well as shoes, purses, and accessories. These two streets are located just a couple of minutes' walk from the Central MTR station, between Des Voeux Road Central and Queen's Road Central. Vendors are open daily from 10am to 7pm.

JARDINE'S CRESCENT   The open-air market that spreads along this narrow street in Causeway Bay is a traditional Chinese market for produce, household goods, cheap clothing, and accessories, including shoes, costume jewelry, handbags, hair accessories, children's clothing, and cosmetics. Though you may not find something worth taking home at this very local market, it's fun just to walk around. The nearest MTR station is Causeway Bay (take exit F), but you can also reach this area easily by tram. It's open daily from 11am to 8pm.

WANCHAI MARKET   This local market, centered on Spring Garden Lane and Wan Chai Road (between Johnston Rd., Tai Yuen St., and Queen's Rd. East), is very much a local market, attracting housewives with its wet markets and household goods, but also young office workers with its stalls selling clothing, shoes, and handbags originally meant for export at very competitive prices. It's located near the Wanchai MTR Station and is open daily from 7am to 7pm.

KOWLOON

JADE MARKET   Jade, believed by the Chinese to hold mystical powers and to protect its wearer, is available in all sizes, colors, and prices at the Jade Market, located at the junction of Kansu Street and Battery Street in two temporary, tentlike structures in the Yau Ma Tei District. The jade comes from Burma, China, Australia, and Taiwan. Unless you know your jade, you won't want to make any expensive purchases here, but the quality of jade sold here is great for bangles, pendants, earrings, and inexpensive gifts. This market is also recommended for pearls, especially inexpensive freshwater pearls from China. Otherwise, this market is fun just for its unique atmosphere.

The Jade Market is open daily from 10am to about 4pm (mornings are best), though vendors stay until 6pm on busy days like Sunday. It's located halfway between the Yau Ma Tei and Jordan MTR stations or is less than a 30-minute walk from the Star Ferry.

LADIES' MARKET ⟨⟨   If you want to shop at a market on the Kowloon side in the daytime, this very large market is your best bet. Stretching along Tung Choi Street (between Argyle and Dundas sts.) in Mong Kok, it serves as a lively market for inexpensive women's and children's fashions, shoes, socks, hosiery, jewelry, sunglasses, watches, handbags (including fake designer handbags), and other accessories. Some men's clothing is also sold. Although many of the products are geared more to local tastes and sizes, an increasing number of tourists has brought more fashionable clothing and T-shirts in larger sizes, and you may find some great bargains here. The atmosphere is fun and festive, especially at night. The nearest MTR station is Mong Kok. Vendors are open daily from about 12:30 to 10:30pm.

FA YUEN STREET MARKET   Located just a few minutes' walk north of Ladies' Market, north of Mong Kok Road, this street market is geared to local residents rather than tourists and offers clothing for women and children, as well as toys and produce. With laundry fluttering from the apartments above, this is a typical Mong Kok Street, full of character. The nearest MTR station is Prince Edward, and stalls are open from 9:30am to 8pm daily.

TEMPLE STREET NIGHT MARKET ⟨⟨⟨   Temple Street, in the Yau Ma Tei District of Kowloon, is a night market that comes to life when the sun goes down. It offers the usual products sold by street vendors, including T-shirts, jeans, menswear, watches, lighters, pens, sunglasses, jewelry, CDs, mobile phones, electronic gadgets, alarm clocks, luggage, Chinese souvenirs, and imitation designer watches and handbags. Bargain fiercely, and check the products carefully to make sure they're not faulty or poorly made. The night market is great entertainment, a must during your visit to Hong Kong, though the surge of shoppers can be overwhelming. If you follow the market north around the left side of the car park (the wares here get decidedly more racy—sex toys, and so on), you'll come to the Tin Hau Temple, to the right of which are fortunetellers and sometimes even street-side performers singing Chinese opera. Although some vendors begin setting up shop at 4pm, the Night Market is busiest from about 7pm until it closes at 10pm, and is located near the Jordan MTR station.

MEGAMALLS & SHOPPING CENTERS

Hong Kong boasts shopping complexes that are so huge I call them "megamalls." Aside from the more convenient ones listed below, other Hong Kong megamalls include **Festival Walk** (located above Kowloon Tong MTR Station), the **New Town**

Plaza in Sha Tin in the New Territories, and the **Taikoo Shing City Plaza,** located at the Taikoo MTR station on Hong Kong Island.

Harbour City ☜ This is the largest of the megamalls and certainly one of the largest in Asia. Conveniently located right next to the dock that disgorges passengers from cruise liners and just east of the Star Ferry, it stretches more than .8km (½ mile) along Canton Road and contains more than 700 outlets, with shops selling clothing, accessories, jewelry, cosmetics, antiques, electronic goods, furniture, housewares, toys, Asian arts and crafts, and much more. Harbour City is divided into four zones (designated different colors on the map of Harbour City): Ocean Terminal with its many shops relating to kids and sportswear; Ocean Centre, anchored by Marks & Spencer department store; the Hongkong Hotel Arcade, consisting mostly of the Lane Crawford department store and restaurants; and the Gateway Arcade at its northernmost end. To most people, however, Harbour City may seem like one huge mall and the zones won't mean anything to them, unless they're searching for a specific shop, since stores and restaurants often give their zone as their address. Some shops are closed on Sunday but otherwise the hours are about 10 or 11am to 8 or 9pm. Canton Rd., Tsim Sha Tsui. ☏ 852/2118 8601. www.harbourcity.com.hk. MTR: Tsim Sha Tsui.

ifc mall ☜☜ ifc mall is part of a massive redevelopment beside Hong Kong Station, terminus of the Airport Express. It's a smart-looking, three-level complex housing more than 200 high-end shops (like Lane Crawford, Prada, Versace, and Vivienne Tam) and restaurants, as well as a five-screen cinema and open-air terraces with views of the harbor. While not nearly as large as the other malls mentioned here, its location, just minutes from the Central Ferry Piers and practically on top of Hong Kong Station, is convenient, and its restaurants boast great views. Most shops are open daily from 10am to 8pm. 8 Finance St., Central. ☏ 852/2295 3308. www.ifc.com.hk. MTR: Central.

Pacific Place Pacific Place was the largest and most ambitious commercial project to hit Central when it opened more than 15 years ago; in fact, it shifted the city center toward the east. With the opening of Hong Kong Station and the new ifc mall to the west, Pacific Place is no longer the center of attention, but it still ranks as one of Hong Kong's swankiest malls. Besides three hotels, Pacific Place boasts approximately 200 retail stores and restaurants and two major department stores (Lane Crawford and Seibu). Most shops are open daily from about 10:30am to 8pm. 88 Queensway, Central. ☏ 852/2844 8988. www.pacificplace.com.hk. MTR: Admiralty.

Times Square This stylish center offers 16 floors of shopping and dining. In the basement are fast-food outlets and stores selling health and beauty products, while the next six floors offer clothing, shoes, handbags, jewelry, watches, and other accessories. Shops dealing in computers, electronics, and home appliances dominate the seventh and eight floors, while the ninth floor is the place to go for children's clothing and toys. Marks & Spencer and Lane Crawford department stores are also here, but one of Times Square's major draws is its Food Forum on the top four floors, home to more than a dozen top-grade restaurants. Most shops are open daily from 10am to 10pm. 1 Matheson St., Causeway Bay. ☏ 852/2118 8900. www.timessquare.com.hk. MTR: Causeway Bay.

TAILORS

The 24-hour suit is a thing of the past, but you can still have clothes custom-made here in a few days. Tailoring in Hong Kong really began in the 1950s, when tailor families from Shanghai fled China and set up shop in Hong Kong. Today, prices are no longer as low as they once were, but they're often about what you'd pay for a ready-made, top-quality garment back home; the difference, of course, is that a tailor-made garment should fit you perfectly. The standards of the better, established shops rival even those of London's Savile Row—at less than half the price.

Tailors in Hong Kong will make anything you want, from business suits and evening gowns to wedding dresses, leather jackets, and monogrammed shirts. Some stores will allow you to provide your own fabric, while others require that you buy theirs. Many tailors offer a wide range of cloth from which to choose, from cotton and linen to very fine wools, cashmere, and silk. Hong Kong tailors are excellent at copying fashions, even if all you have is a picture or drawing of what you want.

On average, you should allow 3 to 5 days to have a garment custom-made, with at least two or three fittings. Be specific about what you want, such as lining, tightness of fit, buttons, and length. If you aren't satisfied during the fittings, speak up. Alterations should be included in the original price (ask about this during your first negotiations). If, in the end, you still don't like the finished product, you don't have to accept it. However, you will forfeit the deposit you are required to pay before the tailor begins working, about 50% of the total cost.

With more than 2,500 tailoring establishments in Hong Kong, it shouldn't be any problem finding one. Some of the most famous are located in hotel shopping arcades and shopping complexes, but the more upscale the location, the higher the prices. Tsim Sha Tsui abounds in tailor shops; one of the most well known is **Sam's Tailor,** 94 Nathan Rd., Tsim Sha Tsui (© **852/2367 9432;** www.samstailor.com; MTR: Tsim Sha Tsui), whose clients have included former U.S. president Bill Clinton and designer Armani. In any case, your best bet is to deal only with shops that are members of the HKTB, listed in the booklet *A Guide to Quality Shops,* mentioned earlier in this chapter.

Once you've had something custom-made and your tailor has your measurements, you will more than likely be able to order additional clothing later, even after you've returned home.

TOYS

Even though Hong Kong is one of the world's leading exporters of toys, they seem to be in short supply in Hong Kong itself. There is, however, an abundance of cheap plastic toys from mainland China; I've done some of my best (cheapest) shopping at Hong Kong's many outdoor markets. In addition to the shop below, the ninth floor of Times Square (p. 220) in Causeway Bay and Ocean Terminal of Harbour City have clothing and toy stores geared toward children.

Toys 'R' Us   This is one of the largest, if not *the* largest, toy store in Hong Kong. A huge department store, it offers games, sporting goods, hobby goods, baby furniture, books, clothing, and, of course, toys galore, including toys from mainland China, Japan, and other Asian countries that never reach U.S. markets (where else could you find a children's play dim sum set?). It's open daily from 10am to 9pm. Shop 032, in Ocean Terminal, Harbour City, 5 Canton Rd., Tsim Sha Tsui. © **852/2730 9462.** www.toysrus.com.hk. MTR: Tsim Sha Tsui.

10

Hong Kong After Dark

Nightlife in Hong Kong seems pretty tame when compared with that in Tokyo or Bangkok. With the world of Suzie Wong in Wan Chai now a shadow of its former wicked self, Hong Kong today seems somewhat reserved and, perhaps to some minds, yawningly dull. For the upper crust who live here, exclusive clubs are popular for socializing and entertaining guests, while the vast majority of Chinese are likely to spend their free evenings at one of those huge lively restaurants.

Yet it would be wrong to assume that the SAR has nothing to offer in the way of nightlife—it's just that you probably won't get into any trouble enjoying yourself. To liven things up, Hong Kong stages several annual events, including the Hong Kong Arts Festival in February/March, and the Hong Kong International Film Festival in April. There are cultural activities and entertainment throughout the year, including theater productions, pop concerts, and Chinese opera and dance performances. In addition, there are plenty of that finest of British institutions—the pub—not to mention sophisticated cocktail lounges, discos, hostess clubs, and topless bars. There are even a couple of nightlife districts in the Central District: in the vicinity of Lan Kwai Fong Street and D'Aguilar Street, where a string of bars and restaurants have long added a spark to Hong Kong's financial district;

and SoHo, along the Central–Mid-Levels Escalator, with its ever-growing number of ethnic restaurants and bars. Business is so good, some predict a future merging of the two as more and more establishments set up shop. Wan Chai has also witnessed a revival with a spate of new bars, restaurants, and strip joints, while Knutsford Terrace, a small alley on the north end of Tsim Sha Tsui, is popular for its open-fronted bars and restaurants. You can party until dawn; indeed, some bars and discos don't take off until after midnight.

Remember that a 10% service charge will be added to your food/drinks bill. If you're watching your Hong Kong dollars, take advantage of happy hour, when many bars offer two drinks for the price of one or drinks at lower prices. (Actually, "happy hours" would be more appropriate, since the period is generally from 5–8pm and often even longer than that.) Furthermore, many pubs, bars, and lounges offer live entertainment, from jazz to Filipino combos (musicians and singers together performing all kinds of music genres), which you can enjoy simply for the price of a beer. There are also a variety of ways to enjoy yourself at night without spending money—for example, strolling along the Tsim Sha Tsui harbor waterfront or around Victoria Peak, or browsing at the Temple Street Night Market.

1 The Performing Arts

The busiest time of the year for the performing arts is the month-long **Hong Kong Arts Festival,** held every year in February and March. This international 3-week affair

⎛Tips Information, Please

To find out what's going on during your stay in the SAR, be sure to pick up *What's On—Hong Kong,* an HKTB leaflet published weekly that tells what's happening in theater, music, and the arts, including concerts and Chinese opera (you can also access it only at **www.discoverhongkong.com**). *HK Magazine,* distributed free at restaurants, bars, and other outlets around town and aimed at a young readership, is a weekly that lists what's going on at the city's theaters and other venues, including plays, concerts, the cinema, and events in Hong Kong's alternative scene. *Where Hong Kong, CityLife,* and *bc* are three other free magazines published monthly with nightlife information and special events.

features artists from around the world performing with orchestras, dance troupes, opera companies, and chamber ensembles. Appearing at past festivals, for example, were the Hong Kong Philharmonic Orchestra, the London Philharmonic, the Empire Brass from Boston, the Hong Kong Chinese Orchestra, the Stuttgart Ballet, the Paul Taylor Dance Company, and the Georgian State Dance Company from Russia. For information about the Hong Kong Arts Festival programs, tickets (which are priced from HK$60/US$7.80/£4.30 to HK$650/US$85/£46), and future dates, call ✆ **852/ 2824 2430** or visit www.hk.artsfestival.org.

To obtain tickets for the Hong Kong Arts Festival, as well as tickets throughout the year for classical-music performances (including the Hong Kong Philharmonic Orchestra and the Hong Kong Chinese Orchestra), Chinese opera, rock and pop concerts, theatrical productions, dance, and other major events, contact the **Urban Council Ticketing Office (URBTIX),** the ticketing system run by the government's Leisure and Cultural Service Department. There are convenient URBTIX outlets in City Hall, Low Block, 7 Edinburgh Place in Central, open daily from 10am to 9:30pm, and the Hong Kong Cultural Centre, 10 Salisbury Rd. in Tsim Sha Tsui, open daily from 10am to 9:30pm. Drop by one of the outlets, or reserve a ticket in advance by calling URBTIX at ✆ **852/2734 9009.** Tickets reserved by phone must be picked up within 3 days of the order. You can even book tickets before arriving in Hong Kong, either by calling the Credit Card Hotline at ✆ **852/2111 5999,** daily from 10am to 8pm Hong Kong time, or through the URBTIX website at www.urbtix.gov.hk. The Hong Kong Tourism Board's website, www.discoverhongkong.com, also offers e-ticketing.

Full-time students and senior citizens are often eligible for half-price tickets, so be sure to ask when making reservations.

PERFORMING ARTS COMPANIES
CHINESE OPERA

Chinese opera predates the first Western opera by about 600 years, although it wasn't until the 13th and 14th centuries that performances began to develop a structured operatic form, with rules of composition and fixed role characterization. Distinct regional styles also developed, and even today there are marked differences among the operas performed in, say, Peking, Canton, Shanghai, Fukien, Chiu Chow, and Sichuan.

Most popular in Hong Kong are Peking-style opera, with its spectacular costumes, elaborate makeup, and feats of acrobatics and swordsmanship; and the less flamboyant but more readily understood Cantonese-style opera. Plots usually dramatize legends and historical events and extol such virtues as loyalty, filial piety, and righteousness. Accompanied by seven or eight musicians, the performers sing in shrill, high-pitched falsetto, a sound Westerners sometimes do not initially appreciate. Although lyrics are in Chinese, body language helps translate the stories.

Another aspect of Chinese opera that surprises Westerners is its informality. No one minds if spectators arrive late or leave early; in fact, no one even minds if a spectator, upon spotting friends or relatives, makes his or her way through the auditorium for a chat.

For visitors, the easiest way to see a Chinese opera is during the **Hong Kong Arts Festival** (see above), held from about mid-February to early March each year. Alternatively, Cantonese opera is a common feature of important Chinese festivals, such as the birthday of Tin Hau or the annual Bun Festival on Cheung Chau island, when temporary bamboo theaters are erected.

Otherwise, Cantonese opera is performed fairly regularly at Town Halls in the New Territories, as well as in City Hall in Central and the Hong Kong Cultural Centre in Tsim Sha Tsui. However, Chinese opera is immensely popular in Hong Kong, so much so that tickets for these shows sell out well in advance, making it almost impossible for tourists to attend performances. If you're still determined to try, call URBTIX in advance of your arrival in Hong Kong, book online (see above), or, once in the SAR, contact the HKTB or check with one of the tourist publications for information on what's playing and then call or drop by URBTIX. Alternatively, the concierge of your hotel may be able to secure seats. Prices generally range from about HK$100 to HK$300 (US$13–US$39/£7.15–£21).

CLASSICAL MUSIC

Hong Kong Chinese Orchestra ✦✦ Established in 1977, the Hong Kong Chinese Orchestra is the world's largest professional Chinese-instrument orchestra. It features more than 80 full-time musicians who perform both traditional folk music and full-scale contemporary works, including commissioned pieces, in approximately 30 concerts annually. Musicians play a wide range of traditional and modern Chinese instruments (mainly stringed Chinese instruments, which are completely different from Western violins, cellos, and so on), as well as suitable Western instruments, combining them with Western orchestrations or Chinese music. Performing at the Hong Kong Cultural Centre, 10 Salisbury Rd., Tsim Sha Tsui (© 852/2734 2009); and City Hall, Edinburgh Place, Central District (© 852/2921 2840). www.hkco.org. Tickets HK$100–HK$200 (US$13–US$26/£7.15–£14). MTR: Tsim Sha Tsui for Cultural Centre or Central for City Hall.

Hong Kong Philharmonic Orchestra The Hong Kong Cultural Centre is the home of the city's largest (Western-style) orchestra: the Hong Kong Philharmonic,

---

Fun Fact **Did You Know?**

- The world's largest professional Chinese instrument orchestra is the Hong Kong Chinese Orchestra, which has more than 80 members playing traditional and modern Chinese musical instruments.
- Bboss (p. 235), in Tsim Sha Tsui East, is the world's largest Japanese-style hostess club, occupying 6503 sq. m (70,000 sq. ft.).

founded in 1975. It performs regularly from September to July and at other scheduled events throughout the year, such as providing live accompaniment to the Hong Kong Ballet. Its conductor is Edo de Waart; guest conductors and soloists appear during the concert season. In addition to Western classical pieces, its repertoire is enriched by works commissioned from Chinese composers. Performing at the Hong Kong Cultural Centre, 10 Salisbury Rd., Tsim Sha Tsui (© 852/2734 2009); and City Hall, Edinburgh Place, Central District (© 852/2921 2840). www.hkpo.com. Tickets HK$100–HK$250 (US$13–US$32/£7.15–£18). MTR: Tsim Sha Tsui for Cultural Centre or Central for City Hall.

DANCE

Both the **Hong Kong Ballet Company** and the **Hong Kong Dance Company** have extensive repertoires. The Hong Kong Ballet Company (© **852/2573 7398;** www. hkballet.com), founded in 1979, performs both classical works and modern pieces, usually at the Cultural Centre or the Hong Kong Academy for Performing Arts. The Hong Kong Dance Company (© **852/3103 1888;** www.hkdance.com) specializes in traditional Chinese dance and the development of Chinese dance in modern forms, with about five major productions each year.

THEATER

Most plays presented in the SAR are performed in Cantonese. Hong Kong's leading local troupes are the **Chung Ying Theatre Company,** a community ensemble that plays in a wide range of venues, from schools and seniors' homes to Hong Kong's main theaters, often performing works by local writers, and the **Hong Kong Repertory Theatre,** which performs original Chinese works. Both perform in Cantonese at various venues, including City Hall in Central and the Hong Kong Cultural Centre in Tsim Sha Tsui. Prices range from about HK$100 to HK$160 (US$13–US$21/£7.15–£11).

Otherwise, your best bet for English-language performances is at the **Fringe Club** ✿✿, 2 Lower Albert Rd., Central (© **852/2521 7251;** www.hkfringeclub.com; MTR: Central), a venue for experimental drama (in English and Cantonese), live music, comedy, art exhibitions, and other happenings, from mime to magic shows. The Fringe Club occupies a former dairy-farm depot built in 1813 and consists of two theaters, exhibition space, a restaurant, and a rooftop bar.

> ## Impressions
> *Hong Kong illuminated . . . is wonderful. Imagine a giant Monte Carlo with a hundred times as many lights!*
> —Alfred Viscount Northcliffe, *My Journey Round the World,* 1923

MAJOR CONCERT HALLS

City Hall   Located right beside the Star Ferry concourse, City Hall's Low Block has a 1,500-seat balconied concert hall, as well as a 470-seat theater used for plays and chamber music. Exhibitions are frequently held in the foyer, while the lobby has pamphlets of upcoming events. Connaught Rd. and Edinburgh Place, Central District. © **852/2921 2840.** www.cityhall.gov.hk. Box office daily 10am–9:30pm. MTR: Central.

Hong Kong Academy for Performing Arts   Located across the street from the Arts Centre, the academy is Hong Kong's institution for vocational training in the performing arts. It also features regular performances in theater and dance, by both local and international playwrights and choreographers. Its Theatre Block is composed of six venues, including the Lyric Theatre, Drama Theatre, Orchestral Hall, and

Recital Hall; there's also an open-air theater. 1 Gloucester Rd., Wan Chai. © **852/2584 8633.** www.hkapa.edu. MTR: Wan Chai.

Hong Kong Arts Centre   Built on Wan Chai's new waterfront of reclaimed land, the Arts Centre hosts the Hong Kong Arts Festival and other international presentations, as well as performances by Hong Kong's own amateur and professional companies. It offers a regular schedule of plays or dances, exhibition galleries, and showings of foreign films. There are three auditoriums: Shouson Theatre, McAulay Studio Theatre, and Lim Por Yen Film Theatre. 2 Harbour Rd., Wan Chai. © **852/2582 0200.** www.hkac. org.hk. Box office Mon–Fri 9am–6pm. MTR: Wan Chai.

Hong Kong Cultural Centre   Sandwiched in between the Space Museum and the Star Ferry concourse, the Hong Kong Cultural Centre is the territory's largest arena for the arts. Opened in 1989, this complex is a good bet for free music and events, including family shows on Saturday afternoon from 2:30 to 4:30pm that may include Chinese dance, a magic show, or music. Thursday Happy Hour, from 6 to 7pm, features Chinese classical music, Western music, puppetry, and other performances by local performance groups. Pick up a monthly leaflet of events at the Centre or call the number below for program inquiries.

Otherwise, the pride of the Cultural Centre is its 2,100-seat Concert Hall, home of the Hong Kong Philharmonic Orchestra. It features a 93-stop, 8,000-pipe Austrian Rieger organ—one of the world's largest. Two levels of seating surround the stage, which is set near the center of the oval hall. There are also two theaters, the Grand Theatre, used for musicals, large-scale drama, dance, film shows, and Chinese opera, and the smaller Studio Theatre, designed for experimental theater and dance. 10 Salisbury Rd., Tsim Sha Tsui. © **852/2734 2009.** www.hkculturalcentre.gov.hk. Box office daily 10am– 9:30pm. MTR: Tsim Sha Tsui.

2 The Club & Music Scene

LIVE MUSIC

Hong Kong does not have the kind of jazz-, rock-, or blues-club scene that many other cities do. On the other hand, live music is such a standard feature of many restaurants, hotel cocktail lounges, and bars, that it would be hard *not* to hear live music in the SAR. Although a few establishments levy a cover charge, most charge absolutely nothing.

Bars, lounges, and clubs offering live music include **Hard Rock Cafe, Lobby Lounge** (in the Hotel InterContinental Hong Kong), and **Ned Kelly's Last Stand,** all in Kowloon; the **Captain's Bar, The Cavern,** and **Insomnia** in Central; **Dusk til Dawn, Fenwick, JJ's,** and **The Wanch** in Wan Chai; and **ToTT's Asian Grill & Bar** in Causeway Bay.

Otherwise, the **Fringe Club,** 2 Lower Albert Rd., Central (© **852/2521 7251;** www.hkfringeclub.com; MTR: Central), Hong Kong's best-known venue for alternative events, offers live music most Fridays and Saturdays from 10:30pm at its Fringe Gallery, including jazz, funk, folk, and blues, as well as other musical programs other days of the week. The cover for most events is HK$80 (US$10/£5.70). Call for an updated listing, visit its website, or pick up the Fringe Club's monthly calendar.

DANCE CLUBS

With only a couple of exceptions, most nightclubs in Hong Kong are small, simple bars that metamorphose into miniature discos late at night or on weekends, as well as

Mad About Mah-jongg

You don't have to be in Hong Kong long before you hear it: the clackity-clack of mah-jongg, almost deafening if it's emanating from a large mah-jongg parlor. You can hear it at large restaurants (there are usually mah-jongg parlors in side rooms), at wedding celebrations, in the middle of the day, and long into the night. In a land where gambling is illegal except at the horse races, mah-jongg provides the opportunity for skillful gambling.

Although mah-jongg originated during the Sung dynasty almost 1,000 years ago, today's game is very different, more difficult, and played with amazing speed. Essentially, mah-jongg is played by four people, using tiles that resemble dominoes and bear Chinese characters and designs. Tiles are drawn and discarded (by slamming them on the table), until one player wins with a hand of four combinations of three tiles and a pair of matching tiles. But the real excitement comes with betting chips that each player receives and which are awarded to the winner based on his or her combination of winning tiles. Excitement is also heightened by the speed of the game—the faster tiles are slammed against the table and swooped up, the better. Technically, the mah-jongg game is over when a player runs out of chips, though it's not unusual to borrow chips to continue playing. There are lots of stories in Hong Kong of fortunes made and lost in a game of mah-jongg. Many hard-core players confess to an addiction.

trendy clubs that cater mostly to their in-crowd members but may occasionally allow nonmembers on slow nights (the best plan of action to get into a membership club is to dress smartly, come on a weeknight or early in the evening, and be nice to the door-man). Discos and dance clubs in Hong Kong generally charge more on weekend nights, but the admission price usually includes one or two free drinks. After that, beer and mixed drinks are often priced the same. Bars, whether with DJs or live music, rarely charge cover.

In addition to the clubs below, check "The Bar, Pub & Lounge Scene" section below for places that offer dancing. These include **Bahama Mama's** and **Delaney's** in Kowloon; **Al's Diner, California, Captain's Bar, The Cavern, Club 97, Curve, D'A-partment, Dragon-i, Insomnia,** and **Lux** in Central; **Joe Bananas** and **Klong** in Wan Chai; and **ToTT's Asian Grill & Bar** in Causeway Bay.

CENTRAL DISTRICT

C Club   With a seductive interior of velvet sofas and a curved bar, all bathed in red lighting, this basement club packs 'em in with what management calls "sexy house" music, including funk, R&B, soul, and Latino. If you come on a weekend, be pre-pared to join the queue of beautiful people lined up outside waiting to be let in, but at least you don't have to be a member. It's open Monday through Thursday from 6pm to 2am, Friday from 6pm to 4:30am, and Saturday from 9pm to 4:30am, with happy hour weekdays until 9pm. California Tower, 30–32 D'Aguilar, Lan Kwai Fong, Central. ℭ **852/2526 1139.** www.lankwaifong.com. No cover Mon–Thurs; cover HK$200 (US$26/£14) Fri–Sat, including 1 drink. MTR: Central.

Propaganda ✦✦✦   Hong Kong's longest-standing and most popular gay disco, Propaganda moved into upgraded quarters a few years back in the new SoHo nightlife district, with a discreet entrance in a back alley (it's a bit hard to find; look for the alley off Pottinger St.). Only about 5% of the people who come through the doors are straight, but everyone is welcome. Come late on a weekend if you want to see this alternative hot spot at its most crowded. It's open Tuesday through Thursday from 9pm to 3:30am, Friday and Saturday from 9pm to 5am. 1 Hollywood Rd., Central. ☏ 852/ 2868 1316. No cover Tues–Thurs; cover HK$120 (US$13/£8.55) Fri–Sat. MTR: Central.

CAUSEWAY BAY & WAN CHAI

Fenwick   Revelers hoping to score for the night make a point of hitting this huge basement dance club, where a live band plays techno, R&B, top hits, and oldies ranging from The Beatles to The Doors. Happy hour is from 5 to 10pm every day except Sunday, but at this time of night you're apt to find yourself alone, as this place doesn't fill up until the wee hours of the morning. It's open Sunday through Thursday from 5pm to 6am, Friday and Saturday from 5pm to 7am. 41 Lockhart Rd., Wan Chai.☏ 852/ 2861 1669. No cover, except for occasional special events, when it's HK$80 (US$10/£5.70). MTR: Wan Chai.

Tribeca   This hotel club is more egalitarian than most, since it's located near the convention center and attracts a mixed local crowd in addition to conventioneers and out-of-towners. It's divided into three different sections, including one with a small dance floor and raised platforms for exhibitionists. On Thursdays, ladies drink for free; Saturday features hip-hop and R&B; Sunday is salsa night. Happy hour is Monday through Wednesday from 6pm to midnight, and Thursday and Friday from 6 to 9pm. It's open Monday through Friday 6pm to 3am, Saturday 8pm to 4am, and Sunday 7pm to 3am. Renaissance Harbour View Hotel Hong Kong, 4th floor, 1 Harbour View, Wan Chai. ☏ 852/2836 3690. Cover HK$120–HK$200 (US$16–US$26/£8.55–£14) Mon–Sat, HK$90 (US$12/£6.40) Sun, including 1 drink. MTR: Wan Chai.

3 The Bar, Pub & Lounge Scene

KOWLOON

For concentrated nightlife in Tsim Sha Tsui, head to Knutsford Terrace, a narrow, alley-like pedestrian lane just north of Kimberley Road, where you'll find a row of open-fronted bars and restaurants, many with outdoor seating.

Aqua Spirit ✦✦✦   This glam venue is one of Hong Kong's hottest bars, due in no small part to its unbeatable location on the 30th floor of a Tsim Sha Tsui high-rise, where slanted, soaring windows give an incredible bird's-eye-view of the city. Circular booths shrouded behind strung beads, designer drinks, and a voyeur's dream location on an open mezzanine overlooking diners at the 29th-floor Aqua, which serves passable Italian and Japanese fare, make this one of Kowloon's most talked-about venues. Note that there's a minimum drink charge of HK$120 (US$16/£8.55), but since drinks are pricey, you won't have trouble meeting your quota. Entrance to both Aqua and Aqua Spirit is on the 29th floor. The bar is open Sunday through Thursday from 5pm to 2am, and Friday and Saturday from 5pm to 3am. 1 Peking Rd., Tsim Sha Tsui. ☏ 852/3427 2288. MTR: Tsim Sha Tsui.

Bahama Mama's   One of many bars lining Knutsford Terrace, this one is decorated in a kitschy Caribbean theme and offers a few tables outside from which to watch the passing parade, as well as a small dance floor. Happy hour is daily from 4 to 9pm (all day on Sun), as well as Monday through Thursday from midnight to 3am. Drink specialties include fruit cocktails, frozen margaritas, and tequila shots. It's open Monday through Thursday from 4pm to 3am, Friday and Saturday from 4pm to 4am, and Sunday from 4pm to 2am. 4–5 Knutsford Terrace, Tsim Sha Tsui. ℂ **852/2368 2121**. MTR: Tsim Sha Tsui.

Delaney's This very successful, upmarket Irish pub is decorated in old-world style with its old posters and photographs. Its convivial atmosphere gets an extra boost from a Tuesday quiz night with prizes for winners and from a DJ on Friday nights, both free of charge. The great selection of draft beers and whiskeys also doesn't hurt. Big soccer and rugby events are shown on a big screen. In addition to a set carvery lunch offered Sundays, it also has an a la carte menu listing Irish stew, beef and Guinness pie, corned beef and cabbage, and other Irish favorites. Happy hour is from 5 to 9pm daily; open hours are daily from 8am to 2:30am. There's another Delaney's in Wan Chai at 18 Luard Rd. (ℂ **852/2804 2880**). 71–77 Peking Rd., Tsim Sha Tsui. ℂ **852/2301 3980**. MTR: Tsim Sha Tsui.

Hard Rock Cafe You can come to this international chain for a burger, fish and chips, fajitas, or a steak, but you can also come for its nighttime ambience, when a DJ enlivens the scene daily from 7pm and a live band takes over every night except Mondays from 10pm. Best of all, there's no cover charge. It's open Sunday through Thursday from 11am to 1am, and Friday and Saturday from 11am to 3am. On the ground floor of the Silvercord Building, 30 Canton Rd., Tsim Sha Tsui. ℂ **852/2375 1323**. MTR: Tsim Sha Tsui.

Lobby Lounge ⭑⭑⭑ *Value* This comfortable cocktail lounge boasts gorgeous water-level views of Victoria Harbour and Hong Kong Island. You'll fall in love all over again (with Hong Kong, your companion, or both) as you take in one of the world's most famous views (this is a very civilized place for watching the nightly Symphony of Lights laser show), listen to a live band (6pm–midnight), and imbibe one of the bar's famous martinis or one of its signature Nine Dragons cocktails. Note that after 9pm, non-hotel guests are charged a HK$140 (US$18/£10) cover. It's open daily from 8am to 2am. In Hotel InterContinental Hong Kong, 18 Salisbury Rd., Tsim Sha Tsui. ℂ **852/ 2721 1211**. MTR: Tsim Sha Tsui.

Murphy's Seven TV screens beaming in sports also beams in the guys, making this Irish pub a lively place indeed during testosterone-high sporting events. Otherwise, it's a decent place for pub grub (potato skins, Irish oysters, steak and porter pie, corned beef and cabbage) or the weekend roast. It also has a few computers where you can check e-mail for HK$20 (US$2.60/£1.40) an hour. It's open daily from 9am to 2am, with happy hour every day from 5 to 8pm. 32 Nathan Rd., Tsim Sha Tsui. ℂ **852/2782 3344**. MTR: Tsim Sha Tsui.

Ned Kelly's Last Stand Named after one of down under's most famous outlaws, this is a lively Aussie saloon, with free live Dixieland jazz daily from 9:30pm to 1am and attracting a largely middle-aged crowd. It serves Australian chow, including juicy pork sausages with mashed potatoes and onion gravy; beef stew; fish and chips; Australian sirloin steak; Irish stew; hamburgers; and cottage pie (baked bowl of minced beef, onions, vegetables, and mashed potatoes). Happy hour is from 11:30am to 9pm. It's open daily from 11:30am to 2am. 11A Ashley Rd., Tsim Sha Tsui. ℂ **852/2376 0562**. MTR: Tsim Sha Tsui.

Sky Lounge This plush and comfortable lounge is on the top floor of the Sheraton, affording one of the best and most romantic views of the harbor and glittering

Hong Kong Island. Unless you're a hotel guest, from 8pm onward there's a minimum drink charge of HK$118 (US$15/£8.40) per person Sunday through Thursday, HK$138 (US$18/£9.85) Friday and Saturday. Or, come earlier for the afternoon tea buffet, available Saturday and Sunday from 2 to 6pm and weekdays from 4 to 6pm for HK$95 (US$12/£6.75). It's open Monday through Thursday from 4pm to 1am, Friday from 4pm to 2am, Saturday from 2pm to 2am, and Sunday from 2pm to 1am. In the Sheraton Hotel and Towers, 20 Nathan Rd., Tsim Sha Tsui. ℂ 852/2369 1111. MTR: Tsim Sha Tsui.

CENTRAL DISTRICT

Agave   Fans of Mexico's most famous spirit should make a point of visiting this showcase for tequila in Hong Kong (or its branch in Wan Chai at 93–107 Lockhart Rd.; ℂ **852/2866 3228**), with approximately 150 brands of 100% agave tequila on offer, as well as 30 different kinds of margaritas and a range of Mexican food from tacos and fajitas to burritos. An open-fronted, noisy bar in Lan Kwai Fong, it has a daily happy hour from 5 to 8:30pm. Open Sunday through Thursday from 4pm to 1:30am, and Friday and Saturday from 5pm to 3:30am. 33 D'Aguilar St., Central. ℂ 852/ 2521 2010. MTR: Central.

Al's Diner   Rather innocent-looking during the day, this hamburger joint transforms into one of Lan Kwai Fong's most extroverted party scenes on weekend nights, no doubt fueled by the house specialty—Jell-O shots (vodka-spiked Jell-O)—and music supplied by a DJ. A few shots, and you may find yourself joining the others dancing on the tables. Offering happy hour Monday through Friday from 4 to 8pm, it opens daily at 11:30am, closing at 1am Sunday to Wednesday, 2am on Thursday, and 4am Friday and Saturday. 39 D'Aguilar St., Central. ℂ 852/2869 1869. MTR: Central.

Bulldog's Bar & Grill   Live broadcasts of Australian, English, and American sporting events shown on four large screens make this one of Lan Kwai Fong's most successful newcomers, especially among American navy personnel, who are attracted by a large U.S. flag that's hung outside its doors whenever they're docked in town. Comfort food ranges from burgers and all-day breakfasts to fish and chips and shepherd's pie. Happy hour is from 5 to 8pm daily. Opening at 11:30am daily, it closes at 2am Sunday through Thursday and 4am Friday and Saturday. 17 Lan Kwai Fong, Central. ℂ 852/ 2523 3528. MTR: Central.

California 𝕬𝕬   Located in Central's nightlife district, this chic bar opened in 1983 and was long the place to see and be seen—the haunt of young nouveaux riches in search of a definition. Newer establishments have since encroached upon California's exalted position, but it remains a respected and sophisticated restaurant/bar, with silent TV screens showing music videos or sporting events almost everywhere you look. You might consider starting your night on the town here with dinner and drinks: The menu exalts Californian cuisine with a wide range of pastas, pizzas, sandwiches, and main courses like grilled salmon and T-bone steak, though hamburgers (the house specialty) remain hugely popular. A plus to coming early is happy hour from 5 to 9pm (6–9pm Sun), with two drinks for the price of one. On Friday and Saturday nights from 11pm to 4am, it becomes a happening disco, with hot DJs playing the latest hits. This place is usually packed, so be prepared for crowds. It's open Monday through Thursday from noon to midnight, Friday and Saturday from noon to 4am, and Sunday from 6pm to midnight. 24–26 Lan Kwai Fong St., Central. ℂ 852/2521 1345. MTR: Central.

Captain's Bar 𝕬   This refined bar is so popular with Hong Kong's professional crowd, especially at the end of the working day, that the Mandarin Oriental's recent overhaul left it virtually unchanged (to have done otherwise would have unleashed a torrent of protest from the bar's fiercely loyal fans). Well known for its expertly made martinis, its pints of beer served in aluminum and silver tankards, and its weekday roast beef lunches, it's a small, intimate place, with seating at the bar or on couches. Live music begins nightly at 9pm; there's even a small dance floor for those inclined to shuffle around. It's open Monday through Saturday from 11am to 2am and Sunday 11am to 1am. In the Mandarin Hotel, 5 Connaught Rd., Central. © 852/2522 0111. MTR: Central.

The Cavern ⊛   Located at the top end of Lan Kwai Fong, this classy live-music venue attracts a slightly older crowd with its casual-chic dress code, large outdoor seating area, and sexy interior bathed in red lights. The house Filipino band, silhouetted on stage, plays unplugged, easy-listening acoustics from 8 to 11pm (including very good imitations of The Beatles). Then, at 11pm, the tables are removed; the band switches to electric, turns up the volume, and plays everything from the Rolling Stones to Green Day; and The Cavern transforms into a dance club (admission of HK$100/US$13/£7.15, which includes one drink, is charged Fri and Sat from 11pm). It's open Sunday through Thursday from 5pm to 2am and Friday and Saturday from 5pm to 4am or later. Lan Kwai Fong Tower, Ground Floor, 55 D'Aguilar St., Central. © 852/ 2121 8969. MTR: Central.

Club 97 ⊛⊛   Opened more than 25 years ago and still one of Lan Kwai Fong's most revered nightlife establishments, this club underwent a transformation some years back that changed it from a disco to a sophisticated lounge, in recognition that its customers had grown up and were more prone to predinner cocktails or late-night drinks rather than dancing. There's still a small dance floor, but gone is the foreboding entrance that once turned away any but the in crowd. Rather, an open-fronted facade invites a mixed clientele of gays and straights. Weekly events to watch out for are Salsa Wednesdays, Thursday Ladies' Night with drink specials, the Friday gay happy hour complete with drag shows, and Sunday reggae night, which draws a huge crowd wishing to chill out before the workweek begins. In any event, this place is a must for any decent pub crawl through Lan Kwai Fong. It's open Monday through Thursday from 6pm to 2am (happy hour 6–9pm), Friday 6pm to 4am (happy hour 6–10pm), Saturday 8pm to 4am (happy hour 8–9pm), and Sunday 8pm to 3am (happy hour 8–9pm). 9 Lan Kwai Fong, Central. © 852/2810 9333. MTR: Central.

D'Apartment   This basement bar has a cute premise: Each room is decorated like a room in an apartment. You can lie on a bed in the bedroom and watch a TV screen, chat in the living room on sofas and armchairs, lounge on beanbag chairs in the playroom, or peruse the books in the library. All it lacks is the kitchen. Of course, once the resident DJ starts spinning tunes for the tiny dance floor and the crowds surge, some visitors may feel like they've time-traveled to their first college apartment. It's open Monday through Thursday from 6pm to 2am (happy hour 6–10pm), Friday from 6pm to 3am (happy hour 6–9pm), and Saturday from 7pm to 4am (happy hour 7–9pm). California Entertainment Building, 34–36 D'Aguilar, Central. © 852/2523 2002. MTR: Central.

Dragon-i   This is one of Hong Kong's most talked-about bars; the fact that it lures models with promises of free drinks is obviously good for business, since it also brings in those who like to ogle models. Its interior is bathed in red from the glow of lanterns, while the outdoor patio, decorated with huge bird cages, provides some relief from the crowds, especially when things start hopping from 11:30pm when a DJ stirs action on the dance floor. The bar's other incarnation is as a venue for lunch or dinner (its all-you-can-eat lunch for HK$128/US$17/£9.15, served Mon–Sat from noon–3pm, includes dim sum and sushi); happy hour is from 6 to 9pm. Located on a hill above Lan Kwai Fong, it's open evenings Monday, Tuesday, and Thursday from 6pm to 3am and Wednesday, Friday, and Saturday from 6pm to 5am, but you'll never get in on Wednesday, Friday, or Saturday unless you're a dead ringer for Uma Thurman. The Centurium, 60 Wyndham St., Central. ✆ 852/3110 1222. MTR: Central.

Finds ✿✿ Think Scandinavian ice cave and you're close to the cool, minimalist design of this hip restaurant/bar that takes its name from the five Nordic nations (Finland, Iceland, Norway, Denmark, and Sweden) represented on its mouthwatering menu, which includes fresh seafood (like filet of North Sea halibut), hearty soups, and "scapas" (Scandinavian tapas, ranging from smoked salmon pie to Finnish meatballs with crushed lingonberries). Wireless broadband service in the lounge, specialty vodkas, an outdoor terrace, and happy hour from 5 to 8pm Monday through Saturday make this a good place to chill, work, or party. A DJ gets things rolling Wednesday through Saturday nights from 10pm. It's open Monday and Tuesday from noon to 1am, Wednesday and Thursday from noon to 2am, Friday from noon to 3am, Saturday from 7pm to 3am, and Sunday noon to 6pm. It's located at the top end of Lan Kwai Fong, on the second floor of the new Lan Kwai Fong Tower. 55 D'Aguilar St., Central. ✆ 852/2522 9318. MTR: Central.

Insomnia One of Lan Kwai Fong's most popular bars, it's aptly named, since live music by a Filipino band doesn't get underway until 10:30pm and it's at its most packed in the wee hours of the morning, when there's no room to spare on the crowded dance floor. Happy hour is from 5 to 9pm. It's open daily from 8am to 6am, leaving insomniacs 2 hours with nowhere to go. 38–44 D'Aguilar St., Central. ✆ 852/2525 0957. MTR: Central.

Lux ✿ Although this classy venue in the heart of Lan Kwai Fong serves as both a restaurant and a bar, it seems most successful as a bar, especially on Friday and Saturday nights when it morphs into a dance club after midnight. Its contemporary, international food, however, is not to be overlooked, particularly if you're in the mood for thin-crust pizzas, huge salads, Wagyu beef pie, or tapas. Happy hour is Monday through Saturday from 6 to 9pm and Sunday from 11am to 9pm. It's open Monday through Friday from noon to 3pm for lunch, from 11am to 3pm Saturday and Sunday for brunch, and from 6 to 11pm daily for dinner, closing at 1am Sunday to Wednesday, at 2am Thursday, and at 3:30am Friday and Saturday. California Tower, 30–32 D'Aguilar St., Central. ✆ 852/2868 9538. MTR: Central.

Red Those in search of a drink outside Lan Kwai Fong should head to this hip bar on the fourth floor of ifc mall, which has the added bonus of an outdoor patio and panoramic views of Central's skyscrapers and Victoria Harbour. Popular with bankers and other working professionals from surrounding Central, it features healthy Californian cuisine (entrance, in fact, is through a health club), live jazz Thursday nights from 10pm, and a DJ Friday nights from 7pm. It's open Monday through Thursday 11:30am to midnight, Friday and Saturday from 11:30am to 3am, and Sunday from 11:30am to 10pm. ifc mall, 8 Finance St., Central. ✆ 852/8129 8882. MTR: Central.

Staunton's Bar & Café Located on the corner of Staunton and Shelley streets, beside the Central–Mid-Levels Escalator, this open-fronted bar was one of the first of many bars and restaurants that now give the SoHo district its unique, homey atmosphere. Above the open-fronted ground-floor bar (which boasts views of commuters going up the escalator) is a restaurant serving contemporary Mediterranean Italian fare. Happy hour is from 5 to 9pm daily (and again midnight–2am Mon–Thurs), with 25 wines on offer by the glass. It's open Monday through Friday 10am to 2am, and Saturday and Sunday from 8am to 2am. 10–12 Staunton St., Central. ✆ 852/2973 6611. MTR: Central.

CAUSEWAY BAY & WAN CHAI

Back in the 1950s and 1960s, Wan Chai was where the action was, buzzing with sailors fresh off their ships and soldiers on leave from Vietnam. It was a world of two-bit hotels, raunchy bars, narrow streets, and dark alleyways where men came to drink and brawl and spend money on women. Nowadays, most of Wan Chai has become respectable (and a bit boring)—an area full of new buildings, mushrooming high-rises, and Hong Kong's expansive convention center. There is a small pocket of depravity, however, concentrated mostly on Lockhart and Luard roads and consisting of bars catering to young revelers and shows of erotic female dancers.

In addition to the listings below, there are branches for Agave and Delaney's (see p. 230 and 229).

Dusk til Dawn ✪   This is one of my top picks for an evening out in Wan Chai. It attracts a mostly expat and Southeast Asian clientele, who come to take advantage of its 5-to-11pm daily happy hour, food and snack menu served until 5am, and nightly free live music starting at 10pm. Open Monday through Friday from noon to 6am, and Saturday and Sunday from 3pm to 6am. 76–84 Jaffe Rd., Wan Chai. ✆ 852/2528 4689. MTR: Wan Chai.

JJ's ✪   This slick hotel venue, located in the swank Grand Hyatt near the convention center, is a bit off the beaten track for bar hoppers. In fact, you'll want to dress up so you won't feel out of place sipping drinks in its diminutive martini bar or roomier, classy main bar, where you can also dine on yummy Thai food. The real action takes place in the music room, where a polished resident band performs a mix of jazz, funk, and soul beginning at 9:30pm. Happy hour is Monday through Friday from 5 to 7pm. It's open Monday through Saturday from 5pm, closing at 2am Monday through Thursday and at 4am Friday and Saturday. Grand Hyatt Hong Kong, 1 Harbour Rd., Wan Chai. ✆ 852/2588 1234. MTR: Wan Chai.

Joe Bananas   This has long been one of the most popular hangouts in Wan Chai, maybe because it's reportedly also one of Hong Kong's best pickup bars. It's also a very popular place for lunch. Called "JB's" by the locals, it sports a casual, inexplicable Egyptian-themed decor. A DJ starts spinning at 6pm, but it doesn't transform into a disco until 10pm. Wednesday is Ladies' Night, with free drinks for women from 10pm to 3am. Happy hour is from 11am to 6pm Monday through Friday and from 4 to 6pm Saturday and Sunday. It's open from 11am to 6am daily. 23 Luard Rd., Wan Chai. ✆ 852/2529 1811. MTR: Wan Chai.

Klong Bar & Grill ✪   Wishing to evoke steamy, sensual Bangkok, this new establishment takes its name from the many canals that lace Thailand's capital. Its open-fronted ground-floor bar and grill, with an open kitchen turning out delectable Thai barbecue, looks dark and slightly rough around the edges. Go upstairs, however, and it's a whole different place, very posh and upmarket, with well-dressed urbanites crowded around a huge U-shaped bar and lounging in the corner "opium den." Things do get crazy, however, especially when both professionals and amateurs are encouraged to hop on the bar and perform an exotic pole dance, which probably happens most on Wednesday nights when ladies are served free vodka. Still, it's a long cry from Bangkok's truly wild and steamy nightlife scene. A DJ hits the scene Tuesday through Sunday nights. With happy hour daily from 3 to 9pm, it's open daily from 11:30am until 3am or later. The Broadway, 54–62 Lockhart Rd., Wan Chai. ℂ **852/2217 8330.** MTR: Wan Chai.

Old China Hand   This is one of the old-timers in Wan Chai (since 1977), an informal British pub popular with older expats but welcoming to tourists as well with its open facade good for people-watching. In the tradition of the pub lunch, meals include steak-and-kidney pie, fish and chips, sandwiches, salads, chili con carne, and a fixed-price lunch priced at HK$49 (US$6.35/£3.50). Happy hour is daily from noon to 10pm and midnight to 2am, with even cheaper drinks on offer during "crazy hour" Monday through Friday from 5 to 6pm. There's live music Sundays from 4pm to midnight. It's open 24 hours on Friday and Saturday; the rest of the week it's open from 10am to 5am. 104 Lockhart Rd., Wan Chai. ℂ **852/2527 9174.** MTR: Wan Chai.

ToTT's Asian Grill & Bar 🐾🐾   This flashy bar and grill, with a blood-red interior and zebra-striped chairs, offers fabulous views of Victoria Harbour and Kowloon from its 34th-floor perch. There's live music and dancing Monday through Saturday nights from 10pm, with a minimum drink/snack charge of HK$168 (US$22/£12) on weekends only (there's no minimum charge for hotel guests or diners who eat here; see p. 148 for the restaurant's review). Happy hour is from 6 to 8pm. The bar is open Sunday through Thursday from 6pm to 1am and Friday and Saturday from 6pm to 2am. In the Excelsior Hotel, 281 Gloucester Rd., Causeway Bay. ℂ **852/2837 6786.** MTR: Causeway Bay.

The Wanch 🐾   Offering free live music nightly, this unpretentious bar is a good bet for Wan Chai bar hopping. Tuesdays feature an all-female Filipino band, Wednesday is jam night, and Sundays it's singalong music. Live music begins at 9pm Monday through Thursday, 10pm Friday and Saturday, and 3pm Sunday. Happy hour is generous: all day Monday, Tuesday through Thursday all day except 9pm to midnight, and Friday through Sunday all day except 9pm to 1am. Hours here are Monday through Saturday 11am to 2am and Sunday noon to 2am. 54 Jaffe Rd., Wan Chai. ℂ **852/2861 1621.** MTR: Wan Chai.

4 Only in Hong Kong

NIGHT TOURS

If you have only 1 or 2 nights in Hong Kong and you're uncomfortable roaming around on your own, I recommend an organized night tour. **Watertours,** an old Hong Kong company that specializes in boat tours, offers several evening cruises, including those that combine cruises with various land activities. The Aberdeen & Harbour Night Cruise, for example, includes a sunset cruise with unlimited drinks, dinner aboard the Jumbo Kingdom floating restaurant in Aberdeen, and a stop at a scenic overlook midway up Victoria Peak. This 4½-hour tour is offered nightly and costs HK$680 (US$88/£49), including dinner. There are also nightly cruises that coincide with the Symphony of Lights laser show. Watertours can be booked through most hotels or by calling ℂ **852/2926 3868** (www.watertours.com.hk). Other tour companies offering night tours (these two concentrate on land tours but also offer evening cruises) include **Gray Line** (ℂ **852/2368 7111;** www.grayline.com.hk), which also offers an open-top bus night tour, and **Splendid Tours & Travel** (ℂ **852/2316 2151;** www.splendidtours.com).

One of the World's Biggest Hostess Clubs

Bboss, a dazzling, 70,000-square-foot hostess club that can seat 3,000 people, was the largest Japanese-style nightclub in the world when it opened in 1984. Even larger ones have since opened in China, but this place is still so big that a full-size electric replica of an antique Rolls-Royce delivers customers along a "highway" to their seats.

There are three nightly stage shows, at 9:20, 10:15, and 11:10pm, complete with a rotating stage so that everyone gets a chance to ogle the scantily clad performers. There's also a 20-member band, a smaller combo band, and a dance floor. Couples are welcome, though single women are not allowed, as they would compete with the scores of hostesses who flatter and chat with male customers. Big spenders can even take hostesses away from the club for the evening (escort services are big business in Hong Kong, as a perusal of any local newspaper will show). In any case, how much you end up spending will be determined by how many drinks you consume, how long you entertain a hostess at your table (it costs HK$1,000/US$130/£71 for 2 hr. during the early evening hours and HK$1,200/US$156/£86 for 2 hr. at night, not including her drinks), and the time of day or night you visit. If you're not careful, you could spend a fortune here.

On the other hand, the place is so overdecorated in bows and the color pink, 1 hour may be all you can stand; in that case, come for one of the 30-minute shows (see times above), which costs HK$200 (US$26/£14) per person, including a soft drink. However, since these shows all happen after 9pm, you'll still need to spend the HK$520 (US$68/£37) minimum drink charge on top of the show charge. If you come before 9pm, the minimum drink charge is HK$460 (US$60/£33). You'll find Bboss in Tsim Sha Tsui East in the New Mandarin Plaza, 14 Science Museum Rd. (✆ **852/2369 2883**).

If you're in Hong Kong anytime from September to May on a Wednesday evening, you can go to the **horse races** in **Happy Valley** or **Sha Tin.** Although you can go on your own for as little as HK$10 (US$1.30/70p), you can also take an organized trip to the races offered by both Gray Line and Splendid Tours, which includes a meal, a seat in the Royal Jockey Club members' stand, and racing tips. (For more information, see p. 178.)

NIGHT STROLLS

One of the most beautiful and romantic sights in the world must be from **Victoria Peak** at night. The peak tram, which costs only HK$30 (US$3.90/£2.15) round-trip and runs daily until midnight, deposits passengers at the Peak Tower terminal. From the terminal, turn right, and then turn right again onto a pedestrian footpath. This path, which follows Lugard Road and Harlech Road, circles the peak, offering great views of glittering Hong Kong. Popular with both lovers and joggers, the path is lit at night and leads past expensive villas and primeval-looking jungles. Definitely the best stroll in Hong Kong, it takes about an hour.

On the other side of the harbor, there's a promenade along the **Tsim Sha Tsui waterfront,** which is popular among young Chinese couples. It stretches from the Star Ferry terminus all the way through Tsim Sha Tsui East, with very romantic views of a lit-up Hong Kong Island across the choppy waters. Best of all is the nightly "Symphony of Lights" from 8 to 8:18pm, when an impressive laser-and-light show is projected from more than 30 buildings on both sides of the harbor. The best vantage point: Avenue of Stars, where there's music and English narration Monday, Wednesday, and Friday nights (another favorite viewing spot is Bauhinia Square in front of the Convention Centre in Wan Chai).

The Tsim Sha Tsui waterfront is very safe at night, as it has lots of people. As for Victoria Peak, I have walked it alone several times at night, but to be honest, it's probably best with someone else.

NIGHT MARKETS

If you're looking for colorful atmosphere, head for the **Temple Street Night Market** (p. 219), near the Jordan MTR station in Kowloon. Extending for several blocks, it has stalls where clothing, accessories, toys, pens, watches, sunglasses, cassettes, household items, and much more are sold. Be sure to bargain fiercely if you decide to buy anything, and be sure to check the merchandise to make sure it isn't going to fall apart in 2 weeks. This is also a good place for an inexpensive meal at one of the *dai pai dong* (roadside food stalls), which specialize in seafood, including clams, shrimp, mussels, and crab.

But the most wonderful part of the market is its northern end, to the right, around the white parking area. There, near the Tin Hau temple, you'll find palm readers and fortunetellers, some of whom speak English, as well as street musicians and singers. You'll have to hunt for the tiny alleyway of musicians, where group after group has set up their own stages and are surrounded by an appreciative audience. Cantonese pop songs and operas are among the favorites, and when the musicians do an especially good job, they are rewarded with tips. Get there before 9pm to see the musicians. Otherwise, although some vendors set up shop as early as 4pm, the market is in full swing from about 7 to 10pm daily.

Farther north, near the Mong Kok MTR station, is the **Ladies' Market** (p. 219), which stretches along Tung Choi Street between Argyle and Dundas streets. It's a great place to shop for inexpensive women's, men's, and children's fashions and accessories, including watches, handbags, T-shirts, and other goods. It's not quite as touristy as the Temple Street Night Market, and the atmosphere is fun and festive. It's open daily from about 12:30 to 10:30pm.

11

Side Trips from Hong Kong

Mention Hong Kong and most people think of Hong Kong Island's Central District, Victoria Peak, the shops and neon of Tsim Sha Tsui, and the Star Ferry crossing Victoria Harbour. What they don't realize is that Hong Kong Island and Kowloon comprise only 10% of the entire territory—the New Territories and the outlying islands make up the other whopping 90%.

If you have a day or two to spare, or even just an afternoon, I suggest that you spend it on a trip outside the city in one of the SAR's rural areas. Escape the bustle and chaos of the city to one of the region's small villages in the countryside, especially on the islands, and you'll have the chance to glimpse an older and slower way of life, where traditions still reign supreme and where lifestyles have a rhythm all their own.

1 The New Territories

Before the 1980s, the New Territories were made up of peaceful countryside, with duck farms, fields, and old villages. No longer. A vast 1,008-sq.-km (389-sq.-mile) region that stretches from Kowloon to the border of mainland China, the New Territories have long been Hong Kong's answer to its growing population. Huge government housing projects mushroomed throughout the New Territories, especially in towns along the railway and subway lines. Once-sleepy villages became concrete jungles virtually overnight.

Close to one-half of Hong Kong's population—about 3.3 million people—lives in the New Territories, many in subsidized housing. The New Territories, therefore, are vitally important to the SAR's well-being and its future. For visitors to ignore the area completely would be shortsighted; many find the housing projects, in some suburbs stretching as far as the eye can see, nothing short of astounding. If, on the other hand, it's peace and quiet you're searching for, don't despair. The New Territories are so large and so mountainous that not all the land has been turned into housing, and the area still makes an interesting side trip; it's so different from the city itself that it's almost like visiting an entirely different country.

Traveling in the New Territories, you may notice women wearing wide-brimmed hats with a black fringe and pajama-like clothing; many of them have gold-capped teeth as well. These women are Hakka, as are most of the farmers of the New Territories. They keep to themselves, preserving their customs and dialect. During the Ming dynasty (1368–1644), some of the Hakka clans in the area built walls around their homes to protect themselves against roving bandits and invaders. A handful of these walled villages still exist today, along with ancestral halls and other ancient, traditional buildings. One of my favorite things to do in the New Territories is to walk one of two Heritage Trails, both of which highlight village life in the New Territories and take you past significant historic buildings and walled villages. Both trails are described in more detail later, but be sure to pick up HKTB's two pamphlets, the *Lung Yeuk Tau Heritage Trail* and the *Ping Shan Heritage Trail.* I also suggest that before visiting any walled village, try to see the Sam Tung Uk Museum in Tsuen Wan (also described later), since it will greatly enrich your visit to a lived-in walled village.

As for getting around the New Territories, the Kowloon-Canton Railway (KCR), divided into an East Rail, a West Rail, and two smaller lines, is the fastest and most convenient way to reach major destinations. Subway lines also serve some satellite towns in the New Territories. All KCR train stations have free maps in English of their immediate surroundings, complete with descriptions of buses that serve the area. Simply stop by the ticket or customer service counter at your destination and ask for the station's map. Other useful pamphlets, which you should pick up at a HKTB visitor center before heading to the New Territories, are the leaflet "Major Bus Routes in the New Territories," which tells you which bus to take, the fare, and the frequency of buses along the route; and the booklet *Discover Hong Kong by Rail,* which describes attractions at KCR stations and provides maps.

If your time is limited, a good tactic for seeing the New Territories is to leave the driving to someone else and opt for an organized tour. The "Land Between" Tour emphasizes both the rural side of Hong Kong and its urban development, enabling visitors to learn about the lifestyle, customs, and beliefs of the local people. It visits a temple, a traditional market in Tai Po, and a fishing village, passing through sprawling satellite towns on the way. The Heritage Tour, a must for architectural buffs, covers historic Chinese architectural sites spread throughout Kowloon and the New Territories, including a restored 18th-century walled village, a Man Mo temple, an ancestral hall, and Tai Fu Tai, a stately country mansion. It's impossible for the individual traveler to cover as much ground in a single day as is covered on one of these tours. For more information on these and other tours, see "Organized Tours & Cultural Activities" in chapter 7, beginning on p. 176.

SEEING THE NEW TERRITORIES BY KCR EAST RAIL

For years, every visitor to the New Territories took the train to the border for a look into forbidden and mysterious China. Now, of course, it's easy to get permission to enter China, and the border lookout has lost its appeal—the view was never very exciting anyway. Still, you might want to take the train up into the New Territories just for the experience, as well as for the interesting stops you can make on the way.

The KCR East Rail, in operation since 1910, is Hong Kong's primary north-south transportation link. Departing from East Tsim Sha Tsui Station on Kowloon's southern tip, the East Rail travels 47km (29 miles), including an offshoot line called the Ma On Shan Rail (an additional spur line, running from Sheung Shui to Lok Ma Chau, is scheduled for completion by the end of 2007). The East Rail travels through 11 stations along its main route, passing through such budding satellite towns as Sha Tin, University Station, Tai Po Market, and Fanling before reaching Sheung Shui—your last stop unless you have a visa to enter China. The entire trip from East Tsim Sha Tsui Station to Sheung Shui costs only HK$12.50 (US$1.60/90p) one-way for ordinary class and HK$25 (US$3.25/£1.80) for first class and takes just 38 minutes. Trains depart every 3 to 8 minutes.

I have arranged the towns below in the order in which you'll reach them when traveling north from Kowloon. The names of the towns are also the names of the KCR stations. Before departing, be sure you have the *Discover Hong Kong by Rail* booklet on hand, available free from any HKTB office.

CHE KUNG TEMPLE

Tai Wai, the first stop on the KCR after passing into the New Territories, was once a small village but has now been engulfed by Sha Tin, described below. Change trains here for the Ma On Shan Rail and go one stop to Che Kung Temple Station (ask for a map of the surrounding area at the station; in addition, *Hong Kong Walks,* a free brochure at HKTB, has a map and gives instructions on how to reach attractions in Sha Tin on foot). Take Exit B from Che Kung Temple, walk through the pedestrian tunnel, and then turn right for **Che Kung Temple,** 7 Che Kung Miu Rd. (© 852/ 2603 4049). This modern Taoist temple, built in 1993 on the site of a previous temple established more than 100 years ago, honors Che Kung, a general from the Sung dynasty (A.D. 960–1279) credited with suppressing a revolt in southern China, controlling floods, and safeguarding villagers from a plague. You'll find a giant statue of Che Kung inside, holding his sword, but the temple is popular with nearby residents mainly because of Che Kung's reputation for granting good fortune. Many visitors bring food offerings and burn incense to ask for blessings. There are also many fortunetellers on hand. Admission is free, and it's open daily from 7am to 6pm.

Just a 15-minute walk east of the temple, on the other side of Lion Rock Tunnel Road on Sha Kok Street, is **Tsang Tai Uk** (also called Shan Ha Wai, which means Walled Village at the Mountain Foot), a tiny, walled village built in the 1840s for members of the Tsang clan, who made their fortune as stonemasons. (Tsang Tai Uk translates as "Mr. Tsang's Big House"). With its high, thick walls, four parallel rows, two side columns of houses, and central courtyard with the ancestral halls (and a painting of the clan founder) in the middle, it's typical of Hakka settlements in Guangdong Province (formerly Canton Province) but unusual for Hong Kong. Although not as old nor as famous as other walled villages, Tsang Tai Uk is, in my opinion, more intriguing and interesting because it has been spared the intrusion of the modern apartments that now plague most villages (the new Ma On Shan Rail, however, passes right outside Tsang Tai Uk, destroying some of its former pastoral peacefulness). Still occupied by about 300 members of the Tsang clan, it looks like a vision of communal life from Hong Kong's not-so-distant past, with children playing in the grassy field out front, seniors sitting in doorways, and women drawing water from courtyard wells.

The recent addition of public toilets has made life easier, as most of the 99 apartments are without private facilities and residents formerly relied on chamber pots. Since Tsang Tai Uk is off the tourist pathway and serves as home to a number of families, visitors should be respectful of the inhabitants' privacy when visiting the compound. Tsang Tai Uk is about a 15-minute walk from Che Kung Temple (above). To reach it, return to Che Kung Miu Road, turn right, and at the pedestrian tunnels follow signs to Tsang Tai Uk. After exiting the last tunnel, you'll pass a tennis court to your left before seeing Tsan Tai Uk. Since getting there is confusing despite a few small signs, it's best is to have the concierge of your hotel write out the name in Chinese so you can show people for directions.

North, across the river from Che Kung Temple and Tsang Tai Uk (walk back to the pedestrian tunnels and follow signs to the museum, crossing Lion Bridge), is the **Hong Kong Heritage Museum** ✦✦, 1 Man Lam Rd. (© 852/2180 8188;

http://hk.heritage.museum), in my opinion the main reason for a visit to the area. Opened in 2001, it presents both the history and culture of the New Territories in a series of themed exhibitions. Foremost is the New Territories Heritage Hall, with displays relating to the customs, religions, and lifestyle of the early fishermen and settlers and how they have changed over the centuries. A barge loaded for market, an ancestral hall, traditional clothing, and other items are also on display. Particularly stunning are the models showing the growth of Sha Tin since the 1930s. I also like the Cantonese Opera Heritage Hall, a must for anyone wishing to gain insight into the history and characteristics of this unique form of entertainment, with musical instruments, elaborate costumes and headgear, and a typical backstage scene. The Chao Shao-an Gallery shows the works of Chao Shao-an (1905–98), a Hong Kong artist famous for his bird-and-flower paintings, while the T. T. Tsui Gallery of Chinese Art contains porcelains, bronzes, furniture, jade, and other works of Chinese art dating from the Neolithic period to the 20th century. For the kids, there's also a toy museum and the hands-on Children's Discovery Gallery, where they can practice being an archaeologist, wear traditional costumes, and learn about marshes. Allow at least 2 hours here. It's open Monday and Wednesday through Saturday from 10am to 6pm and Sunday and holidays from 10am to 7pm. Admission is HK$10 (US$1.30/70p) for adults and HK$5 (US65¢/35p) for children, students, and seniors. Admission is free on Wednesdays. It's located about halfway between Tai Wai and Sha Tin stations, about a 15-minute walk from each.

SHA TIN

This is Hong Kong's prime example of a budding satellite town, with a population around 640,000. Fewer than 13km (8 miles) north of Tsim Sha Tsui, it's also home to a modern **horse racetrack,** as well as a huge shopping mall called the **New Town Plaza** (✆ 852/2684 9175; www.newtownplaza.com.hk), located next to the Sha Tin KCR Station and featuring a frequent 10-minute performance by an illuminated, computer-controlled musical indoor fountain and Asia's first Snoopy's World outdoor playground. Shops here are open from 10am to 10pm daily.

Most interesting for the visitor here, however, is the **Monastery of 10,000 Buddhas** (✆ 852/2691 1067; www.10kbuddhas.org), located on a hill west of Sha Tin KCR station (take the left-hand exit from the station and follow the signs a couple minutes past Grand Central Plaza to the foot of the hill). It takes about a half-hour's energetic walk to reach the actual monastery; first you have to climb more than 400 twisting steps, flanked by gold-colored statues. The temple was established in the 1950s by a monk named Yuet Kai, who wrote 98 books on Buddhism. He's still at the temple—well, actually, his body is still there. He's been embalmed and covered in gold leaf and sits behind a glass case. In attendance are more Buddha images than you've probably ever seen gathered in one place. In fact, despite the monastery's name, there are almost 13,000 of the tiny statues lining the walls, and no two are exactly alike. Also on the grounds are a nine-story pink pagoda and a very simple vegetarian dining hall. The temple affords a good view of Sha Tin's high-rise housing estates and the surrounding mountains. Admission is free, and it's open daily from 9am to 6pm.

Where to Dine

The **Monastery of 10,000 Buddhas** has a very simple dining hall (✆ 852/2699 4144) serving vegetarian dishes from an English menu, sweet-and-sour garoupa (not real fish, of course), deep-fried taro "fish," fried bean curd, and other choices, with dishes costing HK$35 to HK$45 (US$4.55–US$5.85/£2.50–£3.20). No credit cards are accepted and it's open daily from 10am to 5pm.

Otherwise, the **New Town Plaza,** Sha Tin's massive shopping mall located beside the Sha Tin KCR station, is a good place for a snack or quick meal, with cafeterias, fast-food outlets, and restaurants serving both Western and Chinese fare. The largest restaurant here is **Maxim's Palace Chinese Restaurant** on the sixth floor (✆ **852/ 2693 6918**), open daily from 8am to 11:45pm and serving dim sum and Cantonese food, including barbecued Peking duck, roasted goose, deep-fried crispy chicken, and seafood. Otherwise, restaurants with branches here that were described in chapter 6 are the **Spaghetti House,** in Shop 153 of Phase I (✆ **852/2697 9009**), one in a chain of successful American-style spaghetti-and-pizza parlors (p. 134); **Genki Sushi,** Shop A197a, Phase III (✆ **852/2608 9322**), with conveyor-belt sushi (p. 132); and **Koh-I-Noor,** Shop A181, Phase III (✆ **852/2601 4696**), an Indian restaurant (p. 133).

TAI WO

Tai Wo, across the Lam Tsuen River, consists of housing estates built in the last few decades and is a part of the Tai Po satellite town. Another satellite town of the New Territories, Tai Po was first settled by Tanka boat people more than 1,000 years ago because of its strategic location on a river that flows into Tolo Harbour. Today, many Hakka farmers and residents—more than 300,000 of them—call it home. Yet it retains its rural atmosphere, especially the vicinity around its market. Just a short taxi ride or a 15-minute walk from the Tai Wo KCR station (ask for the *Tai Wo Station Street Map and Information* pamphlet at the station) is the small **Hong Kong Railway Museum,** 13 Shung Tak St. (✆ **852/2653 3455;** http://hk.heritage.museum). It occupies what was formerly the very tiny Tai Po Market railway station, built in 1913 in traditional Chinese style with ceramic figurines cresting its gabled roof. Besides the station's original waiting hall and ticket office, the museum displays a few model trains, historical photographs of Tai Po, a narrow-gauge steam locomotive, and some vintage railway coaches dating from the early 1900s; its main appeal is to railway buffs, who will probably want to spend about 15 minutes here. It is open (and free) Wednesday through Monday from 9am to 5pm.

From the museum's main entrance, walk downhill 1 block and turn left onto **Fu Shin Street,** a pedestrian lane that has been serving as Tai Po's market since 1892. It bustles with activity from 7am to 6pm as housewives shop here twice daily to secure the freshest produce, fish, dried herbs, and other ingredients for the day's meals. Booths also sell traditional cakes, bamboo steamers, and Hakka-style clothing, including the distinctive broad-brimmed hats with black fringe.

Near the end of Fu Shin Street is a small **Man Mo Temple,** built in 1892 to commemorate the founding of Tai Po's market. Dedicated to the Taoist gods of war and literature, it could accommodate overnight guests to the market in its ladder-accessible upper floor, while side halls were used by market administrators to settle disputes between merchants and to store records. Today it's a popular spot for older residents to gather and play mah-jongg or simply pass the time. As at the Man Mo Temple on Hong Kong Island (p. 171), huge incense coils suspended from the temple's ceiling are purchased by worshippers and burn for more than 2 weeks. Behind the temple is the Town Earthgod Shrine, where townspeople burn offerings for dead relatives. A nearby shop sells paper offerings in the shapes of cars, gold bars, clothing, and other luxury goods that might prove useful for the dead in their afterlife.

FANLING

A small farming settlement for several centuries, Fanling is now a huge satellite town with more than 350,000 inhabitants. There is, however, a traditional part of Fanling that preserves its rural atmosphere and is the raison d'etre of the **Lung Yeuk Tau Heritage Trail.** Many of the historic buildings along the trail are legacies of the Tang clan, the first and largest of the Five Great Clans to settle in the New Territories, back in the 12th century. Royal descendants of the eldest son of the princess of the Southern Song dynasty (1127–1279), they established five *wais* (walled villages) and six *tsuen* (villages) in the area around Luk Yeuk Tau, which takes its name from the nearby Mountain of the Leaping Dragon. The trail, which stretches about 2.25km (1.4 miles) and takes approximately 1 hour to complete, passes more than a dozen historic structures along the way, including four walled villages, a study hall, a Tin Hau temple, and one of Hong Kong's largest ancestral halls, built in 1525 to honor the founding Tang ancestor. It also passes vegetable plots, tended by Hakka women wearing traditional fringed hats. The Tangs of the area still practice traditional village customs, including the Tin Hau festival (usually in Apr). This is a great walk.

To reach the Lung Yeuk Tau Heritage Trail, take minibus no. 54K from the east exit of Fanling Station to Lo Wai walled village (it's not the beginning of the trail, but it gets most interesting from here onward). Near the end of the trail, at the San Wai walled village, take bus no. 56K back to Fanling Station. Be sure to pick up the free brochure *Lung Yeuk Tau Heritage Trail,* which contains a map and information on historic buildings, at one of the HKTB Visitor Information and Services Centres.

Where to Dine

The most memorable place to dine in Fanling is at **Fung Ying Seen Koon,** 66 Pak Wo Rd. (© **852/2669 9186**), Hong Kong's largest Taoist temple, established in 1929 by refugees fleeing Canton (Guangzhou) and recently renovated. It offers vegetarian food daily from 11am to 5pm in a simple dining room to the left of the main hall. Main dishes on the English menu, ranging in price from HK$40 to HK$65 (US$5.20–US$8.55/£2.85–£4.65), include hot and spicy bean curd and fried elm fungus with three kinds of mushroom. There are also set meals for two or more people, costing HK$105 (US$14/£7.50) for two and HK$150 (US$19/£11) for three. No credit cards are accepted. To reach Fung Ying Seen Koon, visible from Fanling Station, take the west exit and go through the pedestrian underpass.

SHEUNG SHUI

Once its own market town, Sheung Shui, the last stop before the China border, has been swallowed up in the budding satellite town that now spreads out from Fanling. Although much of Sheung Shui's charm has been lost due to the construction of modern buildings all around, it's still more peaceful than other old villages that are closer to the beaten path. Of all the historic, traditional Chinese buildings in the New Territories, few impress me as much as **Tai Fu Tai** , built in 1865 and the only Mandarin mansion restored and remaining in Hong Kong. It belonged to Man Chung-luen, the 21st generation of the Man clan (another of the Five Great Clans), a merchant and scholar who attained the highest grade in the Imperial Chinese Civil Service Examinations. Constructed of granite and bricks and adorned with colorful ceramic figurines, fine plaster moldings, woodcarvings, and murals, it is striking for its simplicity, a stark contrast to mansions built by Westerners of the gentry class of the same period. Constructed like a miniature fort, without windows but with an inner courtyard to let in light, it contains a main hall, side chambers, bedrooms, study, kitchen, servants' quarters, and lavatory. In the back of the main hall is a portrait of Man Chung-luen, flanked by pictures of his two wives and two sons. Not shown are his eight daughters. Remarkably, the mansion was occupied by members of the Man clan until the 1980s. Nearby is the **Man Lun Fung Ancestral Hall,** built to honor the 8th member of the Man clan. Both Tai Fu Tai and the ancestral hall are open free to the public Wednesday through Monday from 9am to 1pm and 2 to 5pm. To reach them, take bus no. 76K from Sheung Shui KCR station traveling in the direction of Yuen Long (West) about 30 minutes to San Tin (near the post office), followed by a 5-minute walk back along Castle Peak Road to the signposted entrance. Since it's a bit difficult and time-consuming to visit on your own, you might want to take Gray Line's guided Heritage Tour (see p. 177 in chapter 7), which takes in this site, as well as a few stops of the Lung Yeuk Tau Heritage Trail and the Man Mo Temple in Tai Po, described above.

WEST NEW TERRITORIES

If I were to choose only one quick destination in the New Territories, it would be Tsuen Wan with its excellent walled-village museum. It's easily reached by taking the MTR Tsuen Wan Line, which runs from Central through Tsim Sha Tsui and Kowloon, to the last stop. Tsuen Wan was a small market town just 100 years ago, with a population of about 3,000 Hakkas and a thriving incense powder–producing industry. Then, as the first designated satellite town of the New Territories, it grew to a population of more than 275,000 residents, living mostly in high-rise housing estates.

The main reason for visiting Tsuen Wan is its excellent **Sam Tung Uk Museum** ✺✺✺, 2 Kwu Uk Lane, Tsuen Wan (© **852/2411 2001;** http://hk.heritage.museum), located just a few minutes' walk from Tsuen Wan MTR station by taking exit E and then turning left. The museum is actually a restored Hakka walled village, built in the 18th century by members of the farming Chan clan. It consists of tiny lanes lined with tiny tile-roofed homes, four houses that have been restored to their original condition, an ancestral hall, two rows of side houses, an exhibition hall depicting Tsuen Wan's history, and an adjacent landscaped garden. The four windowless restored houses are furnished much as they would have been when occupied, with traditional Chinese furniture (including elegant black-wood furniture), and contain farm implements, kitchens, and lavatories. Although as many as 300 clan members once lived here, the village was abandoned in 1980. Today the museum is a tiny oasis in the midst of modern high-rise housing projects. The museum is open Wednesday through Monday from 9am to 5pm, and admission is free.

From the MTR Tsuen Wan Station, it's a 15-minute walk on Tai Ho Road to Tsuen Wan West Station, a stop on the KCR West Rail line (stop by the customer service counter at MTR Tsuen Wan Station to pick up the "Location Map," which shows the location of both stations). From Tsuen Wan West Station, take the West Rail four stops to Tin Shui Wai Station.

At Tin Shui Wai Station, take exit E for the **Ping Shan Heritage Trail,** the start of which is easy to spot by its ancient pagoda (be sure to pick up the free *Ping Shan Heritage Trail* brochure at HKTB). This wonderful walking trail is only 1km (.65 miles) long and takes less than 30 minutes to complete, yet it passes a wealth of traditional Chinese structures along the way, most relating to the powerful Tang clan, who settled the Ping Shan area in the 12th century. The Tsui Sing Lau Pagoda (open 9am–1pm and 2–5pm; closed on Tues) is the only ancient pagoda in Hong Kong, constructed more than 600 years ago to improve the area's feng shui and ward off evil spirits. A small flea market, held near the pagoda on weekends and holidays, sells toys, clothing, jewelry, and accessories.

Other highlights of the trail are a walled village, two temples, and a study hall built for members of the Tang clan studying for the Imperial Civil Service Examination. But the main attraction is the 700-year-old Tang Ancestral Hall (open daily 9am–1pm and 2–5pm), still used by the Tang clan for ancestral worship, ceremonies, and festivals. Admission to this and other structures along the trail is free.

If you have more time to spare, following the map on the *Ping Shan Heritage Trail* brochure, walk 5 minutes to the Hang Mei Light Rail Station, and take Route 761 to Wetland Park Station, from which it's a 5-minute walk to the new **Hong Kong Wetland Park,** Tin Shui Wai (© **852/3152 2666;** www.wetlandpark.com). This 61-hectare (150-acre) park was created to replace habitat lost when the Tin Shui Wai satellite town was constructed. Boardwalks and pathways lead past freshwater marshes, fish ponds, woodlands, grasslands, mudflats, and mangroves, which serve as habitats for 150 species of birds (including the winter habitat of the endangered Black-faced Spoonbill), as well as fish, reptiles, mammals, butterflies, and dragonflies. A visitor center, overlooking the wetland reserve, introduces the importance of wetlands, from tundras to tropical swamps, and includes audiovisual shows that zoom in from outer space on wetlands across the planet and take viewers to cultures from different eras and continents, from ancient Mesopotamia in 3,000 B.C. to New York in the 1920s. Hong Kong Wetland Park is open Wednesday through Monday from 10am to 5pm. Admission is HK$30 (US$3.90/£2.15) for adults and HK$15 (US$1.95/£1.05) for children, students, and seniors.

2 The Outlying Islands

There are some 260 outlying islands around Hong Kong, most of them barren and uninhabited. Because construction in the New Territories is booming and transportation to underpopulated areas there can be slow, the islands offer the best opportunity to see something of rural Chinese life. What's more, they're easy to reach—hop on a ferry in Central and then sit back and enjoy the view. Taking a ferry to an outlying island is the cheapest harbor cruise there is, making getting there part of the fun.

Three of the most accessible and popular islands are **Lantau, Cheung Chau,** and **Lamma.** Each offers something different: Lantau, which can also be reached by MTR and then cable car, is famous for its giant outdoor Buddha—one of Hong Kong's major attractions—and Po Lin Monastery with its vegetarian meals; Cheung Chau, with its beach, boat population, and thriving fishing community, is a popular destination for families and is the best choice for immersion into village life; and Lamma, known for its open-air seafood restaurants, hiking trail, and beaches, is best for getting away from it all.

Ferries to all three islands depart approximately every hour or two from Hong Kong Island's Central Ferry Piers, piers built out into the harbor on reclaimed land and home also of the Star Ferry. You can purchase your ticket at the piers just prior to departure or use the magnetic Octopus transportation card, but avoid going on Sunday when the ferries are packed with city folks on family outings. There are two kinds of ferries: ordinary ferries and quicker hover-ferry service (called "Fast Ferries"). The Fast Ferries to Lantau, Cheung Chau, and Lamma are used mostly by commuters; I personally prefer the slower, ordinary ferries because the view is better, especially if you're headed for Lantau or Cheung Chau. These have the bonus of deluxe class, which is on the upper deck and has an open deck out back—a great place to watch the harbor float past when the weather is nice. In addition, deluxe cabins are the only ones that are air-conditioned, a plus when humidity is at its peak. Note, however, that ferries to Lamma have no deluxe class or outside deck. In any case, you might wish to head out to an island via regular ferry and then return via Fast Ferry. Note that on Saturday afternoon and Sunday, there is additional infrequent ferry service from Tsim Sha Tsui's Star Ferry concourse to Lantau and Cheung Chau, but it may not offer deluxe class.

Tips The Best Seat on Ship

The best view aboard ferries to the outlying islands is on the left side of the boat, as Central, the Western District, and Hong Kong Island glide past in all their glory.

Fares to the islands are a bargain. On weekdays and on Saturday, tickets for ordinary ferries cost just HK$11 to HK$11.30 (US$1.40–US$1.45/75p–80p) for ordinary class and HK$18 (US$2.30/£1.30) for deluxe. Fares are slightly higher on Sunday and public holidays, though they're never very expensive: HK$14 to HK$17 (US$1.80–US$2.15/£1–£1.20) for ordinary class, depending on the destination, and HK$26 (US$3.35/£1.85) for a deluxe ticket. Fast Ferries average HK$22 (US$2.85/£1.55) Monday through Saturday and HK$32 (US$4.15/£2.30) on Sundays and holidays.

In any case, by ordinary ferry it takes only 35 minutes to reach Lamma, 55 minutes to reach Cheung Chau, and 50 minutes to reach Lantau. Fast Ferry reduces travel time to 20 minutes for Lamma, 30 minutes for Cheung Chau, and 40 for Lantau.

For information on ferry schedules and prices, drop by the Hong Kong Tourist Board for a free copy of timetables and prices. You can also obtain information on schedules to Cheung Chau and Lantau at ℂ 852/2131 8181 and www.nwff.com.hk; for Lamma, call ℂ 852/2815 6063 or visit www.hkkf.com.hk.

LANTAU

Inhabited since Neolithic times and twice the size of Hong Kong Island, Lantau is Hong Kong's largest island. But while Hong Kong Island has a population of 1.4 million, **Lantau** ✸✸✸ has only about 84,000. Much of its population growth has occurred only recently, first with the founding of Discovery Bay, a large, modern, and expensive settlement of condominiums popular with expats, then with Hong Kong's new airport (which brought with it the creation of a new satellite town at Tung Chung), and finally with the 2006 opening of Hong Kong Disneyland (p. 174). One of its biggest draws is the Giant Tian Tan Buddha, the largest seated outdoor Buddha in the world. Accessible also via MTR and then cable car, Lantau is by far the most popular of Hong Kong's outlying islands.

Yet much of Lantau remains mountainous and lush. Country parks make up more than half of the island, with 69km (43 miles) of marked hiking trails. Lantau is an island of high peaks, remote and isolated beaches, small villages, temples, and monasteries. To do the island justice, I suggest arriving by ordinary ferry, taking a bus to the Giant Buddha, and then returning to the city by cable car and subway. You should allow at least 5 hours for the entire trip.

Ordinary ferries, with both ordinary and deluxe class, depart from Central Ferry Pier no. 6 in Central approximately every 2 hours between 6:10am and 10:30pm and arrive about 50 minutes later at Silvermine Bay, known as *Mui Wo* in Chinese. There is also more frequent hover-ferry service from the same pier, which gets you there in about 40 minutes but doesn't provide panoramic views from an outside deck in deluxe class. In Mui Wo, as soon as you exit the ferry pier, you'll see a bus terminal with buses going to other parts of the island, with departures coinciding with the arrival of the ferries. For the Giant Buddha and Po Lin Monastery, take bus no. 2 bound for Ngong Ping (Po Lin Monastery). The exact bus fare of HK$16 (US$2.05/£1.15) Monday through Saturday and HK$25 (US$3.25/£1.80) on Sunday and public holidays is required, so come with lots of change or use the handy Octopus transportation card. The bus hurtles around hair-raising curves and up and down through lush country-side—not for the faint of heart. The duration of the ride from Silvermine Bay to Po Lin Monastery takes about 45 minutes, and I always enjoy every minute of it.

If you don't wish to ride the ferry, you can also reach Lantau by taking the Tung Chung MTR Line, which departs from Hong Kong Station in Central and travels to Tung Chung, the end terminus, in about 30 minutes. In Tung Chung, you can board a 17-passenger cable car that travels 5.7km (3½ miles) directly to Ngong Ping in about 25 minutes, with fantastic views of the surrounding countryside, the airport and South China Sea. The round-trip fare of the Ngong Ping Skyrail is HK$88 (US$11/£6.30) for adults and HK$45 (US$5.85/£3.20) for children; one-way fares are HK$58 and HK$28 (US$7.55/£4.15 and US$3.65/£2) respectively. Note that on "special days" (about 60 days, mostly on holidays and weekends in summer), prices are higher by HK$5 to HK$10 (US65¢–US$1.30/35p–70p). Otherwise, bus no. 23 also travels between Tung Chung and Ngong Ping in about 50 minutes; the fare is the same as from Mui Wo and the ride is no less hair-raising.

EXPLORING LANTAU

The most famous attractions on Lantau (in addition to Disneyland) are the **Giant Tian Tan Buddha** and **Po Lin Monastery,** both situated on the plateau of Ngong Ping at an elevation of 738m (2,421 ft.). The Buddha is so huge that you'll have your first glimpses of it en route. More than 30m (98 ft.) tall and weighing 250 tons, it was erected in 1993 as the world's largest seated outdoor bronze Buddha and can be seen as far away as Macau (or so it is claimed) on clear days. There are 260-some steps lead-ing up to the Buddha itself, but first you should stop at the ticket office at the bottom of the steps to purchase a meal ticket, since the other reason people come to Po Lin is to eat. The monastery is famous for its vegetarian lunches, served in a big dining hall (see "Where to Dine," below). Your meal ticket, which specifies the time for your communal meal, doubles as your admission ticket to a small museum inside the base of the statue, but there isn't much to see here. Rather, the best part is the view of the surrounding countryside from the statue's platform, which is free. The Giant Buddha is open daily from 10am to 6pm.

It's a couple minutes to the colorful Po Lin Monastery, largest and best known of the dozens of Buddhist monasteries on Lantau. Po Lin (which means "precious lotus") was first established more than 100 years ago by reclusive monks; the present build-ings date from 1921 and 1970. The ornate main temple houses three magnificent bronze statues of Buddha, representing the past, present, and future; it also has a brightly painted vermilion interior with dragons and other Chinese mythical figures on the ceiling. You'll probably want to spend about a half-hour wandering through the grounds here, but the best thing to do here is dine on vegetarian cuisine (see below).

As for other things to do on Ngong Ping, about a 15-minute walk away, at the foot of Lantau Peak, is the **Wisdom Path,** designed in a figure eight to symbolize infinity and marked by 38 wooden pillars, each bearing a portion of the centuries-old Heart Sutra in Chinese characters. If you're truly adventurous or energetic, you can continue the climb to the top of Lantau Peak, the second-tallest peak in Hong Kong (1,000m/3,281 ft.); plan on 3 hours for the hike up and back.

Next to the Ngong Ping Skyrail is the new **Ngong Ping Village** (© **852/2109 9898**), which contains souvenir shops, restaurants, and the Ngong Ping Tea House, where you can enjoy a cup of tea and cake along with demonstrations of traditional Chinese tea ceremonies. There are also two attractions: **Walking with Buddha,** a multimedia museum that describes the life of Siddhartha Gautama (who lived 2,500 years ago in Nepal and became Buddha), his path to enlightenment, the origin of Buddhism, and the religion's subsequent expansion around the world; and **Monkey's Tale Theatre,** which presents a computer-animated comical story with a moral twist about a selfish monkey who, with the help of the Monkey King, learns about greed, humility, friendship, and kindness. Admission to either is HK$35 (US$4.55/£2.50) for adults and HK$18 (US$2.35/£1.30) for children, while a combination ticket to both is HK$65 (US$8.45/£4.65) and HK$35 (US$4.55/£2.50) respectively. Tickets that bundle attractions with the Skyrail are also available. Ngong Ping Village is open Monday through Friday from 10am to 6pm, and Saturday and Sunday from 10am to 6:30pm.

From Po Lin, you can take the Skyrail to Tung Chung; or you can board buses that will take you back to Mui Wo (Silvermine Bay) or Tung Chung (I always check departure times upon arrival at Po Lin, so I don't have to sit around after a just-missed bus). Energetic travelers can even opt to hike down to Tung Chung in about 3 hours, along a route described in the free HKTB brochure *Hong Kong Walks.*

Where to Dine

Po Lin Monastery ★★ VEGETARIAN   Po Lin Monastery, offering fixed-price vegetarian meals, is the most famous place to eat on the island. Buy your lunch ticket from the counter at the base of the Giant Buddha or at the monastery itself; your ticket is for a specific time, at an assigned table. Two different meals of soup, vegetarian dishes, and rice are available: The ordinary HK$60 (US$7.80/£4.30) meal is served in an unadorned dining hall and the procedure is rather unceremonious, with huge dishes of vegetables, rice, and soup brought to communal tables. Grab a plastic bowl and chopsticks and help yourself. Packed with Chinese families, the dining hall here is certainly colorful. The HK$100 (US$13/£7.15) "Deluxe" meal is served in a smaller adjacent "VIP Room" and is popular mostly with foreign visitors. Meals here are served on china plates, and the food is a notch above the cheaper meal. Both, however, are good and plentiful. There's also a snack menu available at an open-air counter at the monastery; it consists of fried noodles and bean curd—skip it.

Ngong Ping. © **852/2985 5248.** Fixed-price lunch HK$60 or HK$100 (US$7.80/£4.30 or US$13/£7.15). No credit cards. Daily 11:30am–4:30pm.

CHEUNG CHAU

If you have only 3 or 4 hours to spare and don't want to worry about catching buses and finding your way around, Cheung Chau is your best bet. In fact, if I were forced to select only one island to show visiting friends on a limited time schedule, Cheung Chau would be it. Only 12km (7½ miles) from Hong Kong Island, it's a 55-minute ride by ordinary ferry from outlying-ferry pier no. 5 in Central, with ferries leaving approximately every hour and offering scenic harbor views from the outdoor deluxe-class deck. Even quicker are the fast ferries, also departing every hour and making the trip in 30 minutes (but these don't have outdoor decks). Despite its name (Cheung Chau means "Long Island"), Cheung Chau is a tiny, dumbbell-shaped island (only 2.5 sq. km/1 sq. mile), with more than 25,000 residents concentrated in a thriving fishing village. There are no cars on the island, making it a delightful place for walking around and exploring rural village life. The island is especially popular with Chinese families for its rental bicycles and beach (you might want to bring your bathing suit), but my favorite thing to do here is to walk the tiny, narrow lanes of Cheung Chau village. Be sure to pick up the free HKTB brochure *Hong Kong Walks,* which includes a stroll on Cheung Chau and a map.

Inhabited for at least 2,500 years by fisher folk and serving as a haven for smugglers and pirates until the 1920s, Cheung Chau still supports a small population of fishing families, with fishing and tourism being the island's main industries. The waterfront where the ferry lands, known as the Praya, buzzes with activity as vendors sell fish, lobster, and vegetables. The village itself is a fascinating warren of narrow alleyways, food stalls, open markets, and shops selling everything from medicinal herbs and incense to dried fish, rice, haircuts, and—a reflection of the island's tourist trade—sun hats, sunglasses, and beach toys.

EXPLORING CHEUNG CHAU

Although there seem to be fewer and fewer junks in Cheung Chau's harbor each time I visit, a small group of fishermen and their families still live on their junks here. I like this harbor more than Aberdeen because boats are moored right next to the waterfront, and I find it amazing how many families keep dogs aboard their boats (not to mention radar systems and computers). To see Cheung Chau village, begin with a stroll along the **Praya,** the waterfront promenade right in front of the ferry pier. It's a good place from which to observe the many junks and fishing boats in the harbor. To the right as you leave the ferry pier are several open-air restaurants (and, as a sign of the times, a McDonald's), as well as the unimaginative-looking Regional Council Cheung Chau Complex, which houses a library, post office, and city market (open daily 6am–8pm) with more than 200 stalls that sell everything from fresh seafood to vegetables.

On the opposite end of the Praya (to the left as you leave the ferry) are more waterfront restaurants, shops with bicycles to rent, and souvenir shops. After about a 3-minute walk, take a right at the playground onto Pak She Fourth, at the end of which is the **Pak Tai Temple** (open daily 7am–5pm), guarded by stone lions. Built in 1783, it's dedicated to the "Supreme Emperor of the Dark Heaven," long worshipped as a Taoist god of the sea. Inside is an iron sword measuring almost 1.5m (5 ft.) in length that was found by local fishermen and thought to be 1,000 years old, as well as a sedan that is used to carry the statue of Pak Tai around the village during festivals. Before the altar are also statues of two formidable generals, Thousand Miles Eye and Favourable Wind Ear, who together can hear and see anything. Beside the temple, on a shaded terrace, old villagers are almost always engaged in games of mah-jongg.

The most important festival here is the Bun Festival, held in late April or May. It originated a century ago following a terrible plague and is famous throughout Hong Kong. It features 15m-tall (50-ft.) towers of buns (yes, they're edible!), but the biggest attraction is the parade of children who "float" through the streets suspended by hidden wires and rods.

Cheung Chau

ATTRACTIONS ●
Kwan Kung Pavillion **7**
Pak Tai Temple **2**
Tung Wan Beach **3**
Cheung Chau Windsurfing Centre **6**
Kwun Yam Beach **8**

DINING ◆
Terrace Cafe **5**
Hometown Teahouse **4**
New Baccarat Seafood
    Restaurant **1**

Leaving the Pak Tai Temple, take a left onto Pak She Street, which later becomes San Hing Street. As you walk back to the center of the village, you'll pass open-fronted shops that sell incense, paper funeral objects such as cars (cremated with the deceased to accompany them to the next life), medicinal herbs, lotus-seed cakes, pungent shrimp paste, vegetables, jade, rattan, cheap toys, and souvenirs. You'll also pass people's homes with the living rooms that hold the family altar opening onto the street. This is the traditional Chinese home, with the family business and communal rooms on the ground floor and the bedrooms up above. All day long you can hear people playing mah-jongg.

At the end of San Hing Street, at a square, take a left to Tung Wan Road, which cuts across the thinnest part of the island from the Praya with its ferry to Tung Wan Beach. Here, just past the square, is a gnarled old banyan tree, which is considered to be the dwelling place of the spirit of health and fertility. At the end of Tung Wan Road is **Tung Wan Beach,** the most popular beach on the island, with lifeguards and shark nets. Nearby, past the playground and Warwick Hotel, is another, smaller public beach, **Kwun Yam Beach,** and the **Cheung Chau Windsurfing Centre** (✆ 852/2981 8316), with a pleasant outdoor cafe and rental windsurfing boards ranging from HK$90 to HK$150 (US$12–US$19/£6.40–£11), depending on the size, for 1 hour, as well as kayaks that rent for HK$60 (US$7.80/£4.30) per hour. Unfortunately, views from both beaches are marred by the sight of the Lamma power plant and Hong Kong Island's high-rises.

From Tung Wan Beach, it's only a few minutes' walk via Tung Wan Road back to the Praya and ferry pier.

WHERE TO DINE
Hometown Teahouse TEA/SUSHI   This is a quirky teahouse, a laid-back and pleasant island oasis on the village's main passageway between the Praya and Tung Wan Beach. It's owned and managed by a Japanese woman, Takahiko-san, and her artist husband. Only a few items—sushi rolls with crab or sausage and herbal teas like ganoderma tea (which is thought to boost energy levels)—are available at the "counter," which is nothing more than an open window of a small house. Most people order the sushi set, which comes with tea, sushi, and a cookie. The teahouse itself is an outdoor terrace with a few tables and chairs.

12 Tung Wan Rd. ✆ 852/2981 5038. Rolled sushi HK$9–HK$16 (US$1.15–US$2.10/65p–£1.15); sushi sets HK$20–HK$24 (US$2.60–US$3.10/£1.40–£1.70). No credit cards. Daily noon–midnight.

New Baccarat Seafood Restaurant ⸙ CANTONESE   On the Praya, the last of many open-air restaurants now crowding the waterfront but also one of the oldest (located near the Pak Tai Temple on the corner of Pak She St. beside a playground), this simple spot offers outdoor seating under a canopy with a view of the harbor. Owned by a fishing family and sporting tanks of live sea creatures, it specializes in fresh seafood, including crab, lobster, squid, scallop, prawn, shrimp, and various other fish. Try the steamed fresh fish, deep-fried crispy shrimp or squid with spiced salt, or—my favorite—the steamed fresh scallops with minced garlic. Alternatively, you can buy your own fresh seafood from one of the many vendors on the Praya and have it cooked here for HK$30 (US$3.90/£2.15).

9A Pak She Praya St. ✆ 852/2981 0606. Main dishes HK$45–HK$100 (US$5.85–US$13/£3.20–£7.15). No credit cards. Daily 11am–10:30pm. Turn left from the ferry and walk along the Praya about 4 min.

Terrace Cafe DIM SUM/NOODLES   The Warwick Hotel, located on the beach, is a good choice for a simple lunch of dim sum. Its enclosed terrace, with a good view of the beach, offers six choices of dim sum from 7am to 2:30pm, as well as a limited selection of noodle dishes and sandwiches from 11:30am to 5:30pm. Since choices are limited, come here only for a snack-size meal.

In the Warwick Hotel, Tung Wan Beach. ✆ 852/2981 0081. Dim sum HK$15 (US$1.95/£1.05). No credit cards. Daily 7am–5:30pm. Take Tung Wan Rd. to Tung Wan Beach, about a 7-min. walk from the ferry pier.

LAMMA
Lamma is the island to visit if you want to escape city life, do some pleasant hiking, swim, or dine alfresco on fresh seafood with views of a peaceful waterfront. The closest of the outlying islands, only 35 minutes by ordinary ferry and 20 minutes by fast ferry from Central Ferry Piers no. 4 in Central, Lamma is Hong Kong's third-largest

island, has a population of about 12,000, and is still largely undeveloped. There are no cars on the island, and a 1½-hour hiking trail connects Lamma's two main villages—Yung Shue Wan and Sok Kwu Wan—both served by ferries from Hong Kong Island. Yung Shue Wan, with a large and youthful foreign population, has a decidedly bohemian laid-back atmosphere, while much smaller Sok Kwu Wan is popular for its open-air seafood restaurants. If it's summer, don't forget to bring your bathing suit, since there are several beaches along the trails. You'd be smart, too, to buy bottled water from one of the many stores in either Sok Kwu Wan or Yung Shue Wan before setting out on the trail. In addition, try to avoid Sundays, when the trail is crowded with families, seniors walking dogs, and even bicycles. For a map of the island, pick up the free HKTB brochure *Hong Kong Walks*.

EXPLORING LAMMA

Although ferries from Central will deposit you at either Yung Shue Wan or Sok Kwu Wan, I personally prefer to land at Sok Kwu Wan for a light seafood meal, hike 20 minutes to a nearby beach, and then continue onward to Yung Shue Wan for drinks or dinner before heading back to Central. The advantage of this route is that ferry service is more frequent from Yung Shue Wan, which means you're not constricted to a time schedule. However, you might choose to hike the trail in reverse from my description below. If you do, remember that ferries to and from Sok Kwu Wan are less frequent, so you'll have to time your arrival and departure with precision (or, if you dine at Rainbow Seafood Restaurant, described below, you can take advantage of the restaurant's free shuttle boat to Central and Tsim Sha Tsui by making advance reservations). The hike between the two villages along a marked, concrete footpath takes about 1½ hours and is a true delight, with great views of the surrounding sea and, in the distance, even Ocean Park and Aberdeen on Hong Kong Island.

Tiny **Sok Kwu Wan** is famous for its open-air seafood restaurants and is a popular destination for those lucky enough to own pleasure boats. These restaurants are aligned along the small waterfront, extended over the water on stilts and shaded by canopies; they offer views of the harbor (and, unfortunately, of denuded hills belonging to a defunct cement factory across the harbor; there is talk of eventual landscaping, but only time will tell). All restaurants here have tanks of fresh seafood from which you can choose your own meal. Fresh seafood is available by the *catty* (one catty is about 1½ lb.). Prices for a catty vary each day, depending on supply and demand. One catty of prawns will cost approximately HK$150 to HK$175 (US$20–US$23/ £11–£13), with half a catty usually enough for two people. A catty of lobster will cost about HK$250 to HK$280 (US$33–US$36/£18–£20), though small lobsters for one person are available for about HK$100 to HK$120 (US$13–US$16/£7.15–£8.55). If you go all out, meals here will average about HK$250 (US$33/£18) a person.

Incidentally, as you dine, you'll notice Hong Kong's largest fleet of fish-breeding rafts in the harbor, some also supporting family homes. Also in the harbor is **Lamma Fisherfolk's Village** (① 852/2982 8585; www.fisherfolks.hk), which you might want to visit if you're looking for something to do or simply want to support a worthwhile local endeavor. Reached by shuttle from Sok Kwu Wan's public pier (the same pier where the ferry docks), the floating "village" consists of moorings, fish-breeding rafts, and displays relating to local fisher-folk culture, including fishing tools, implements used to craft traditional junks, model boats, clothing, and more. Most interesting is the authentic 60-year-old junk, which you can explore at leisure, peeking into the boat's tiny sleeping quarters, the kitchen with its wood-burning stove, and even the "outhouse" toilet. It's open daily from 10am to sunset. Admission, including the shuttle boat to and from the village, is HK$40 (US$5.20/£2.85) for adults and HK$30 (US$3.90/£2.15) for children and seniors.

Turning right of the public pier and walking past the many seafood restaurants of Sok Kwu Wan, you will soon come to a newly renovated Tin Hau temple on the edge of town, first founded more than 150 years ago. Tin Hau temples are common near the sea, since the goddess Tin Hau is believed to protect fishermen. Continue on the concrete path that hugs the harbor about 10 minutes to Lo So Shing School, where you should turn left. Soon you'll see the turnoff for **Lo So Shing Beach,** which you can reach in about 5 minutes (there are also public latrines along this path). Prettily situated in a small bay, this is the island's nicest and least crowded beach, offering changing rooms and lifeguards on duty April through October daily from 9am to 6pm.

Otherwise, continuing on the main pathway takes you through lush and verdant valleys and banana groves, with butterflies flitting across the path and roosters crowing from the distance, before ascending to a hillside pavilion overlooking the scandalous cement factory. From this point, the path climbs higher onto barren and windswept hills. About halfway along the trail, on the top of a peak, is a pagoda where you can take a rest and enjoy the view of the South China Sea. After that, the barren hills give way to valleys and trees and then **Hung Shing Yeh Beach,** which also has changing facilities, showers, toilets, and lifeguards on duty in the summer. If it's hot, it may be hard to resist joining the throngs of families and taking another dip in the water. Regrettably, however, the beach is overshadowed by an unsightly power station.

The hiking path resumes on the other side of the beach. In less than 20 minutes, you'll reach **Yung Shue Wan,** but it takes a while to walk past a new development before reaching Yung Shue Wan Main Street and the center of town. Yung Shue Wan, which translates as "Banyan Tree Bay," is Lamma's main town. It used to be small and undeveloped, with old houses and small garden plots, but new apartment buildings and shops have sprung up on its hillsides in the past couple decades, and the town is unfortunately blighted by that unsightly power station. What's more, small motorized wagons carrying building supplies zip around as if they can't get to construction sites soon enough. Compared to how the village looked in the early 1980s, I can barely recognize the place. Still, the village has a laid-back, tropical-island atmosphere, with a sizable population of expatriates drawn by low rents and the slow pace of life. With Yung Shue Wan's narrow streets, funky eateries, and shops selling Southeast Asian crafts, jewelry, and clothing, Hong Kong's bustling city life seems more than a short boat ride away.

WHERE TO DINE

Bookworm Café *Finds* VEGETARIAN   Lined with shelves of used books and serving as an informal resource and meeting center for Yung Shue Wan's expat residents, with occasional jam sessions, video nights, and other happenings, this casual restaurant is a great alternative to seafood. The interesting menu includes breakfasts, sandwiches, veggie and tofu burgers, spinach lasagna, and salads like the "veg-out" salad plate with roasted eggplant, avocado, feta cheese, and black olives on a bed of mixed greens and herbs with Lebanese bread. There are also various teas, fresh juices, and power shakes. Dining is either in a small, air-conditioned room or across the street on an open terrace.

79 Yung Shue Wan Main St., Yung Shue Wan. © **852/2982 4838.** Main dishes HK$40–HK$80 (US$5.20–US$10/ £2.85–£5.70). MC, V. Mon–Fri 10am–9pm; Sat and holidays 9am–10pm; Sun 9am–9pm.

Concerto Inn Garden Cafe *(Kids)* WESTERN/CHINESE/SNACKS Located right on Hung Shing Yeh Beach, about a 30-minute walk from the ferry pier in Yung Shue Wan, this clean, low-key establishment offers both accommodations and a pleasant cafe, with outdoor, covered seating beside a running fountain and views of the beach. Its menu is limited, but the restaurant makes a comfortable stop along the hiking trail for a hamburger, sandwich, spaghetti, rice and noodle dishes, ice cream, juice, or beer. A toddlers' play area in back makes for a good diversion for the little ones, especially on crowded days when service can be a bit slow.

Hung Shing Yeh Beach, Yung Shue Wan. © **852/2982 1668.** Main dishes HK$48–HK$57 (US$6.25–US$7.40/ £3.40–£4.05). AE, DC, MC, V. Daily 8am–10pm.

Man Fung Restaurant *&* CANTONESE/SEAFOOD If you start your hike at Sok Kwu Wan and end up hungry on this side of the island, this restaurant is my number-one choice for a hearty meal. Located just a minute's walk from the ferry pier, it offers pleasant outdoor seating right by the water with a view of the harbor and town. Specialties are its fresh seafood straight from the tank, including lobster served with a cheese sauce; fried prawns with garlic and butter; steamed crab with chile and prune sauce; and various other fish, scallop, and seafood dishes available at market price (inquire first before ordering). Otherwise, the menu lists pork, beef, chicken, and pigeon dishes, as well as vegetarian dishes such as deep-fried bean curd with chile, fried broccoli and baby corn with garlic, sweet-and-sour bean curd, and braised eggplant in a hot pot. There are also pitchers of Carlsberg draft beer as well as wine from France and Portugal.

5 Yung Shue Wan Main St., Yung Shue Wan. © **852/2982 0719.** Main dishes HK$55–HK$95 (US$7.15–US$12/ £3.90–£6.80). AE, MC, V. Daily 11am–10pm.

Rainbow Seafood Restaurant *&&* CANTONESE/SEAFOOD This is the largest open-air restaurant on Sok Kwu Wan's waterfront, easily recognizable by its whir of ceiling fans and red lanterns. Farther from the pier (and the defunct factory across the harbor) than many other restaurants, it therefore offers a better view of the harbor and boat rafts (don't confuse it with its smaller branch just beside the ferry pier, which does nevertheless have the added convenience of an air-conditioned bar). A nice touch is the water sprayed over its canopy to cool the restaurant on hot summer days. A member of the Hong Kong Tourist Board, it offers an English menu with photographs of its main dishes, including a variety of fresh seafood dishes, with prices for lobster, prawn, and fish clearly marked. Among its specialties are steamed garoupa, lobster available several ways (grilled lobster with a cheese sauce is most popular), and fried crab with ginger and scallions. There are two fixed-priced feasts for two persons or more, costing HK$320 and HK$380 (US$42/£23 and US$49/£27) per person. Incidentally, this restaurant also offers free ferry service to and from Queen's Pier in Central and Tsim Sha Tsui's public pier, with less frequent service from Aberdeen; be sure to call first and make a reservation (the schedule is posted on the restaurant's website).

17 1st St., Sok Kwu Wan waterfront. © **852/2982 8100.** www.rainbowrest.com.hk. Seafood dishes HK$60–HK$160 (US$7.80–US$21/£4.30–£11). AE, DC, MC, V. Daily 10am–10pm.

A LOCAL BAR

The Island Bar Located next to Man Fung Restaurant on the waterfront, just a minute's walk from the ferry pier, this is a longtime bar and local *gwailo* (foreign) hangout, popular with a mostly middle-aged crowd. Owned by expats living in Yung Shue Wan, it's a comfortable place to wait for the next ferry, play darts, and meet the locals. Happy hour is from 6 to 8pm daily.

6 Yung Shue Wan Main St., Yung Shue Wan. (✆) 852/2982 1376. Mon–Fri 6pm–2am; Sat–Sun and holidays noon–2am.

3 China

Hong Kong is a major gateway to China. Many first-time visitors to China join an organized tour for excursions to the mainland, though it's certainly easy enough to do on your own. Avid shoppers with a sense of adventure may want to make a day trip across the border to Shenzhen a priority, where fake designer watches and handbags are sold for a song. There are, however, two caveats for would-be shoppers: The cost of visas for some nationals, including Americans, is so high that it cancels out bargains on goods; and pirated goods are illegal in many countries, including the United States. Frankly, I've never understood the desire for fake goods, but I do love shopping for fun accessories, and there are plenty of non-designer purses, watches, and other goods as well.

ORGANIZED TOURS

Virtually all hotels in Hong Kong work with tour agencies that offer a variety of excursions to China, ranging from 1-day trips to Guangzhou or Shenzhen to 11-day trips that include Guangzhou, Beijing, and other major destinations. Most of these trips follow identical itineraries at similar prices. For example, I joined a 1-day guided tour of Shenzhen (Shekou) and Guangzhou. In Shenzhen, we were shown a small, musty museum containing three terra-cotta figures taken from the tomb of China's first emperor near the city of Xi'an; and in Guangzhou, a local market; an unenlightened zoo with cramped, littered cages and a couple of panda bears; Six Banyan Temple; and the outside of a concert hall built in 1931 as a memorial to Sun Yat-sen (on weekdays, tours also take in a local kindergarten). What I most enjoyed about the trip, offered by Splendid Tours for HK$1,230 (US$160/£88) per person, was the journey by hover ferry to Shenzhen, the bus trip to Guangzhou, and the trip back by KCR railway, as these provided good vistas of the surrounding countryside with its duck and fish farms, rice fields, banana groves, and simple living conditions. The so-called attractions, however, were not worth seeing. In my opinion, you (and your pocketbook) are better off making the journey on your own, since the attractions are dismal. On the other hand, the most compelling reasons for joining a group tour are to see more than you could accomplish in a limited time on your own, and to save money through the tour's group visa, which is cheaper than individuals applying for visas on their own.

Companies offering organized trips into China (including day trips to Shenzhen's largest shopping mall, described below) include **Splendid Tours** ((✆) **852/2316 2151;** www.splendidtours.com), **Gray Line Tours** ((✆) **852/2368 7111;** www.grayline.com. hk), and **China Travel Service** (see "Visas," below), the official travel agency of the People's Republic of China. Unsurprisingly, CTS offers the most extensive list of tours, with trips that include Beijing, Guilin, Shanghai, Xi'an, and other major cities. CTS's 11-day trip, for example, includes train and plane travel from Hong Kong to Guangzhou, Guilin, Beijing, Xian, and Shanghai before returning to Hong Kong. The cost of this trip runs HK$13,660 to HK$14,230 (US$1,774–US$1,848/£975–£1,016), depending on the season.

VISAS

If you join an organized tour, your visa for China will be taken care of by the tour agency. Tour prices include the price of tour group visas (which cost less than individual visas). You can book tours up to the day before departure if there's room, but most charge more if you book later than 11:30am the day before departure, since the company will have to apply for an individual rush visa rather than submitting your passport along with the others for a group visa.

If you wish to visit China on your own, you'll need to obtain a visa yourself. Your hotel or a travel agency may be able to arrange this for you. Having your hotel's concierge or tour desk do the work certainly saves time, but prices can be high. Travel agencies are cheaper, but you'll have to first apply and then return to pick up the visa. You can also save money by planning ahead, as rush orders for visas add to the price.

One of the most popular places to apply for a visa is at a **China Travel Service** (CTS; www.ctshk.com), the official travel agency of the People's Republic of China. There are several branches in Hong Kong, including 78 Connaught Rd. Central, Central District (✆ **852/2853 3533;** MTR: Central); 138 Hennessey Rd., Wan Chai (✆ **852/2832 3888;** MTR: Wan Chai); and 27–33 Nathan Rd., Tsim Sha Tsui (✆ **852/ 2315 7188;** MTR: Tsim Sha Tsui), which is the most convenient with the most convenient hours: It's open Monday through Friday from 9am to 7pm, Saturday from 9am to 5pm, and Sunday and holidays from 9am to 12:30pm and 2 to 5pm. Although there is a CTS also at the Lo Wu border crossing, residents of the United States and United Kingdom cannot obtain a visa here.

To fill out an application for your visa, you will need your passport (with an expiration date of not less than 6 months away) and one passport photograph (you can have your portrait taken here for HK$35/US$4.55/£2.50; otherwise, there's a portrait machine at the nearby YMCA Salisbury on Salisbury Rd., as well as one at the Tsim Sha Tsui MTR station). It's best to make your visa application at least 3 business days prior to departure; cost of a single-entry visa (valid for 30 days) is HK$210 (US$27/£15). However, if you're in a hurry, you can obtain a visa more quickly by paying more: For HK$360 (US$47/£26), your visa will be processed and available for pickup by 2pm the next day; for HK$480 (US$62/£34), visa applications made before noon will be available by 5:30pm the same day. The cost for a visa at CTS is better than most places (especially hotel tour desks). Note, however, that at the time of going to press, Americans applying for visas were required to pay higher prices for visas: HK$450 (US$58) for a single-entry visa; HK$650 and HK$850 (US$84 and US$110) for the expedited services. U.K residents pay HK$500, HK$700, and HK$900 (£36, £50, and £64) respectively. Australians and New Zealanders enjoy the regular, low visa prices. In any case, visa requirements and prices can change overnight; check www.ctshk.com or call for updated information.

SHENZHEN

If you're planning a 1-day trip to China, your destination will be either Shenzhen or Guangzhou (see below). **Shenzhen,** located across the Hong Kong–China border, was established in the 1980s as one of China's first Special Economic Zones. Today, this experiment with capitalism looks almost like Hong Kong with its million people, concrete high-rises, traffic, industries, and relative prosperity. In recent years, it has become a shopping mecca for day-trippers, who come for fake designer handbags, watches, and other goods at prices much cheaper than in Hong Kong. However, the

HK$450 (US$58) minimum Americans now pay for a single-entry visa makes shopping Shenzhen less of a bargain.

You can travel to Shenzhen via the KCR Kowloon-Canton railway, with trains departing Kowloon KCR Railway Station in Tsim Sha Tsui East every 3 to 8 minutes between 5:28am and 12:30am. The trip from Tsim Sha Tsui East to Lo Wu, the border crossing (open daily 6:30am–midnight), takes about 42 minutes and costs HK$37 (US$4.80/£2.65) for ordinary class and HK$73 (US$9.50/£5.20) for first class. Prices are slightly cheaper if you have an Octopus card, but if you're traveling first class, you'll have to swipe your card once again on the train platform at the First Class Processor located in front of the first-class compartment. The Lo Wu Border Control is one of the busiest border crossings in the world. Avoid traveling through it on weekends and holidays, if possible, when crowds of day-trippers can make the wait to cross over very long.

After going through Customs, you can walk across the border into Shenzhen. Just across the border is a huge shopping mall called Luohu Commercial City (also called Lo Wu Shopping Mall by tour agencies), with five floors of tiny shops selling a bewildering amount of inexpensively priced handbags, shoes, and watches; jewelry; clothing (including Chinese padded jackets); and bolts of cloth. As for imitation designer bags and pirated DVDs, Chinese officials have cracked down on counterfeit goods (half the fake goods seized by U.S. Customs agents come from China, which should give would-be purchasers pause as well). That is not to say that such goods are unavailable. When I agreed, at a shopkeeper's insistence, to look at imitation handbags, I was whisked to a concealed backroom closet with rows and rows of bags. In a tiny electronics shop, the owner closed all his doors and sent his assistant scurrying up a concealed hole in the drop ceiling to retrieve pirated DVDs (don't bother buying DVDs—most of the time they aren't fully copied or they don't work). I can't believe that police, who regularly patrol Luohu Commercial City, are clueless, but the game seems to satisfy everyone. There are also shops offering combination manicures and pedicures for as little as HK$30 (US$3.90/£2.15), but lack of hygienic conditions may discourage most tourists from giving them a whirl. In any case, bargaining is the name of the game, and since there are no ATMs around, be sure to bring plenty of HK dollars. You should also guard your belongings against pickpockets. Shops are open daily from 10am to 10pm.

As for tourist attractions, they're limited to Splendid China, a theme park with more than 80 miniatures of China's most historic buildings, sites, and scenic wonders, including the Great Wall and the Forbidden City; Window of the World, which re-creates famous buildings, monuments, and scenic spots from around the world, including the Taj Mahal, Eiffel Tower, and Grand Canyon; and China Folk Cultures Villages, which presents the art and cultures of China's various ethnic groups with life-size villages and people dressed in native dress. All three are clustered together about 13km (8 miles) west of the border crossing and are included in several 1-day tours offered by tour companies listed above. Most visitors to Shenzhen, however, come for the shopping.

FARTHER AFIELD

Farther afield is **Guangzhou (Canton),** capital of Guangdong Province with a population of 7.5 million. A commercial city, Guangzhou is famous for its markets, including Haizhu Square with vendors selling electronics, toys, and souvenirs at great prices.

Otherwise, the sights are confined to a Buddhist temple and the monuments and statues in the city's largest park, Yuexiu Yuan, that include a memorial to Sun Yat-sen. You can reach Guangzhou by KCR railway in about 2 hours from Hung Hom Station in Kowloon; cost of this trip is HK$230 (US$30/£16) for "premium" class, HK$190 (US$25/£14) for first class, and HK$180 (US$23/£13) for second class. At last check, through-train service to Guangzhou departed Hung Hom every hour or so from 7:30am to 7:15pm, with the trip taking less than 2 hours.

Be forewarned, however, that since tourist attractions in Shenzhen and Guangzhou are extremely limited, if you're really interested in a trip to China, you should plan on traveling to Shanghai, Beijing, and beyond. For more information on China, see *Frommer's China.*

12

Macau

Hanging from China's gigantic underbelly on its southeastern coast, Macau covers all of 28 sq. km (11 sq. miles). About 64km (40 miles) west of Hong Kong across the Pearl River Estuary, it served as Portugal's last holdout in Asia until 1999, when it was handed back to China. Portugal's other former Asian strongholds, Goa and Malacca, had long before been claimed by neighboring powers.

With its unique mixture of Portuguese and Chinese cultures, Macau makes an interesting day trip or overnight stay if you want to get away from the bustle of Hong Kong after a business trip or strenuous traveling itinerary. Although Macau's rising reputation as a gambling mecca—spurred by the grand openings of ever larger and grander casinos—is a major attraction for many, there are also beaches, fortresses, churches, temples, gardens, and excellent museums to explore. What's more, although prices have risen the past few years, Macau's hotels are still cheaper than their counterparts in Hong Kong (you can bask in luxury in Macau for a fraction of what you'd pay in the former British colony); and as a duty-free port, Macau has also become something of a shopping mecca. And finally, Macanese cuisine, unique to Macau and combining ingredients from former Portuguese trading ports from around the world, is both inexpensive and delicious, especially when accompanied with Portuguese wine. If you're looking for a vacation from your vacation, I heartily recommend Macau.

That being said, Macau is no longer off the tourist radar, with 18 million tourists crossing its borders in 2005, a huge increase compared with 7.4 million in 1999. More than 90% of visitors are from mainland China (which relaxed travel restrictions in 2003), Hong Kong, and Taiwan. While casinos were always a part of Macau's draw, especially for Hong Kong Chinese, deregulation of the gaming industry in 2002 paved the way to an explosion of ritzier, more conspicuous casinos, including big-name imports from the United States like The Venetian and MGM Grand. The former Portuguese territory's transformation into Asia's Las Vegas has played nicely with Macau's vigorous policy of land reclamation, which has more than doubled its size over the last few decades and added high-rises, superhighways, housing complexes, and huge entertainment and shopping complexes like Fisherman's Wharf. Hotel properties opening over the next few years include a Sheraton, Hyatt, Hilton, Four Seasons, and a Shangri-La.

In short, Macau bears almost no resemblance to the laid-back town I first laid eyes on in the 1980s. A sleepy backwater just two decades ago—when the local populace got from place to place unhurriedly by pedicab and the road from the ferry to downtown was a lonely stretch of potholes—Macau is changing so rapidly that old-timers are right when they complain that the place isn't what it used to be—it's *more* than it used to be, with land reclamation and new construction

Macau

ZHUHAI SHI (P.R.C.)

Camoes Museum and Gardens
Old Protestant Cemetery

Jai Alai Casino

Tourism Activities Centre

Senado Square

Casino

Fisherman's Wharf

Cybernetic Fountain

Praia Grande Bay

Kun Iam Statue

Third Macau-Taipa Bridge

Macau-Taipa Bridge

Outer Harbour

Av. do Conselheiro Borja
Lin Fung Miu Temple
Av. de Venceslau de Morais
Reservoir
Av. da Amizade
Av. do Infante D. Henrique
Avenida-Dr.-Sun-Yat-Sen
Macau-Taipa Bridge

PEOPLE'S REPUBLIC OF CHINA   **GUANGDONG PROVINCE**

Macau (Portugal)

Pearl River

Hong Kong

South China Sea

↑ Islands

Taipa & Colôane

TAIPA

COTAI

RECLAIMED LAND

RECLAIMED LAND

ZHUHAI SHI (P.R.C.)

Taipa-Colôane Causeway

Macau International Airport

COLÔANE

Church ✝
Post Office ✉

dramatically altering the city's skyline in just 20 short years, and there seems to be no end in sight. The small downtown, built in the era of pedicabs with its narrow lanes, is ill-equipped to deal with Macau's ever-increasing traffic. Indeed, city planners seem so intent on expansion, I fear that much of Macau's unique architectural legacy and charm will be lost in an ever-growing concrete jungle.

Still, there have been many positive developments. When I first came to Macau, its downtown was crumbling and neglected, and there were few attractions beyond its casinos and a couple of ruined forts and churches. In the 1990s, however, the small downtown underwent a major renovation, with the restoration of its main plaza and its Mediterranean-influenced, colonial-era buildings with their arched, shuttered windows. In 2005, Macau's historic center was declared a UNESCO World Heritage Site, with 25 temples, churches, mansions, squares, fortresses, and other buildings and monuments now restored or undergoing restoration.

The things that drew me to Macau in the first place—the unique blend of Chinese and Portuguese culture, architecture, and food—remain an irresistible draw. It's as though two Macaus exist: the sterile new developments and glitzy casinos on reclaimed land; and the old downtown of candy-colored colonial buildings, banyan trees, narrow hilly streets, and low-key neighborhood restaurants.

The only pedicabs driven today are after the tourists' dollar, but Macau still possesses a lifestyle that is way less frenetic than that of Hong Kong. In fact, compared to the former British colony, Macau is downright Lilliputian, and, with its mixture of Portuguese and Chinese elements, feels different from Hong Kong, different from China—different from anywhere else. Maybe it's the jumble of Chinese signs and stores mixed in with freshly painted colonial-style buildings, or the Buddhist and Taoist temples alongside Catholic churches. Maybe it's because people smile here more readily than they do in Hong Kong, seem more relaxed, and friendlier. It's an attractive mix—Portuguese flair blended with Chinese practicality. There's something for everyone here—beaches, churches, museums, attractions, nightlife, and, yes, casinos—all in a setting found nowhere else in the world.

1 Frommer's Favorite Macau Experiences

- **Following the Mosaic Pathway to St. Paul's Church:** From Largo do Senado, Macau's main, colonial-era square, follow one of the wavy-patterned mosaic tiled streets through the old city uphill to the ruins of St. Paul's Church (p. 281), Macau's most photographed facade.
- **Dining on Local Macanese and Portuguese Specialties:** African chicken, spicy prawns, sole, and codfish are just some of the culinary treats for the visitor to Macau, all available at very reasonable prices. Portuguese wine, the perfect accompaniment to both Macanese and Portuguese food, is also a bargain. See the "Where to Dine" section, later in this chapter, for more information.
- **Splurging for a Room at a Resort Hotel:** After the traffic and crowds of Hong Kong, there's nothing more relaxing than gazing at the sea from your hotel room, sunning at an outdoor pool surrounded by greenery, and feeling tension and aches melt away under the expert care of a masseuse. Macau has several resort hotels; see the "Where to Stay" section, later in this chapter, for more information.
- **Learning about Macau's History at the Museum of Macau:** Macau's history museum (p. 280) is a delight, built into the ruins of a fortress and highlighting

not only the history of Macau but also unique Macanese traditions, culture, architecture, and cuisine.

- **Visiting Lou Lim Iok Garden Early in the Morning:** Get to this Chinese garden (p. 284) early in the morning, when you're apt to see the locals going through the motions of tai chi, playing traditional Chinese music, and taking birds for walks in cages.

- **Strolling through Macau's Fisherman's Wharf:** This huge combination entertainment/shopping destination features restaurants, souvenir shops, a small amusement park, a man-made volcano, street performances, and more, nestled in a village-like setting along the waterfront.

- **Swimming on Colôane Island:** Two public beaches, Cheoc Van and Hac Sa (p. 286), feature lifeguards on duty, dining facilities, and public swimming pools. Afterward, retire for a drink or a Portuguese meal at Fernando's (p. 278), a beach shack on Hac Sa.

- **Observing the Chinese Gambling at the Ornate Floating Casino:** This moored boat (p. 287) is abuzz 24 hours a day with gambling fever. Drop by and observe the Chinese gambling, or try your luck with the slot machines on the upper deck.

- **Watching the Sun Set from Macau Tower:** This 220m-high (722-ft.) Space Needle wannabe (p. 280) looks out of place in tiny Macau, but you can't beat it for its views: 55km (34 miles) on clear days. Come for a drink in its lounge or dinner in its revolving restaurant. Or, for the truly daring, there are adventure tours *outside* the tower, including a climb up its mast.

- **People-Watching after Midnight:** After the sun goes down, Macau's nighttime revelers head to the Docks, a string of bars and discos with sidewalk seating. But the action doesn't really start hopping until after midnight.

2 Orientation

ENTRY REQUIREMENTS

Entry procedures into Macau are very simple. If you are American, Canadian, Australian, or New Zealander, you do not need a visa for Macau for stays of up to 30 days—all you need is your passport. Residents of the United Kingdom and Ireland can stay up to 90 days without a visa.

VISITOR INFORMATION

ON THE INTERNET   You can obtain information on Macau via the Internet by visiting the Macau Government Tourist Office's website at **www.macautourism. gov.mo**.

OVERSEAS   The **Macau Government Tourist Office (MGTO)** maintains the following tourist offices:

- **United States:** 501 5th Ave., Suite 1101, New York, NY 10017 (© **646/227-0690;** fax 646/366-8170; macau@myriadmarketing.com), and 1334 Parkview, Suite 300, Manhattan Beach, CA 90266 (© **866/OK-MACAU** or 310/545-3464; fax 310/545-4221; macau@myriadmarketing.com).

- **United Kingdom:** 11 Blades Court, 121 Deodar Rd., London SW15 2NU (© **20/8877-4501;** fax 20/8874-4219; macau@representationplus.co.uk).

- **Australia:** Level 17, Town Hall House, 456 Kent St., Sydney NSW 2000 (© **02/9264-1488;** fax 02/9267-7717; macau@worldtradetravel.com).

A Blending of Cultures

Macau (also called Macao) was born centuries before Hong Kong was even conceived. Portuguese ships first landed in southern China in 1513; in 1557, Portugal acquired Macau from China. Before long, Macau had achieved a virtual monopoly on trade among China, Japan, and Europe, making the city Portugal's most important trading center in Asia and the greatest port in the East in the early 1600s.

As the only Europeans engaged in trade in Asia, the Portuguese made a fortune acting as middlemen. Every spring, Portuguese ships laden with Indian goods and European crystal and wines sailed out of Goa, anchored in Malacca to trade for spices, stopped in Macau for silk brought down from China, and then traveled on to Nagasaki to trade the silk for silver, swords, and lacquerware. Using the monsoon winds, the ships returned to Macau to trade silver for more silk and porcelain, then sailed back to Goa where the exotic Asian goods were shipped to eager customers in Europe. The complete circuit from Goa and back took several years.

As Macau grew and prospered, it also served as an important base for the attempt to introduce Christianity to China and Japan, becoming a springboard for Jesuit missionaries to China and a refuge for Asian Christians, including Japanese Christians who faced persecution and death at home. Many Portuguese married local Chinese, creating a new community of Macanese (Eurasian) families with a blend of the two cultures. This blending is still evident today in Macanese cuisine and architecture, as well as in the population.

Needless to say, because of Macau's obvious prosperity, it attracted jealous attention from other European nations. Dutch invasions were repelled

• **New Zealand:** Level 5, Ballantyne House, 101 Customs St. E., P.O. Box 3779, Auckland (© **09/308-5206;** fax 09/308-5207; macau@aviationandtourism.co.nz).

IN HONG KONG   Your first stop for information about Macau should be as soon as you arrive in Hong Kong, at the Hong Kong International Airport. In the arrivals lobby, at A06, you'll find the **Macau Government Tourist Office (MGTO)** information counter (© **852/2769 7970**), open daily from 9am to 10pm (closed for lunch 1–1:30pm and dinner 6–6:30pm). Stop here for a wealth of printed material about hotels and sightseeing in Macau. In addition, there's another MGTO information bureau at Hong Kong's Macau Ferry Terminal, the departure pier for most jetfoils and other craft bound for Macau. You'll find it on the third-floor Departure Floor, in room 336 of the Shun Tak Centre, 200 Connaught Rd., in Central (© **852/2857 2287**). It's open daily from 9am to 1pm and 2:15 to 5:30pm. Be sure to pick up a map of Macau; the hefty *Macau Guide Book,* with useful information on attractions; the tourist tabloid *Macau Talk; Where,* a quarterly with information on cultural activities, sightseeing, shopping, and entertainment; and *What's On,* a leaflet with information on festivals, exhibitions, and events.

several times in the first decades of the 1600s. In response to the threat of invasion, the Portuguese built a series of forts; some still exist.

In the 1630s, Japan closed its doors to foreign trade, granting a limited admittance only to the Dutch. This was a great blow for Macau, but the coup de grace came in 1841 when the British established their own colony on Hong Kong Island, only 64km (40 miles) away. As Hong Kong's deep natural harbor attracted trading ships, Macau lost its importance as a base for trade and slowly sank into obscurity.

However, Macau gained a new foothold in the world of trade in the 1970s by producing electronics, clothing, toys, and other items for export. At the same time, tourism began to grow, and with the establishment of casinos, Macau attracted a large number of Chinese gamblers from Hong Kong. In 1995, Macau opened an airport, making the colony easily accessible for the first time in its history.

On December 20, 1999, Portugal's 442 years of rule came to an end, with Macau's transition to a Special Administrative Region of China. Like Hong Kong, Macau is permitted its own internal government and economic system for another 50 years. Today, 95% of Macau's 488,000 residents are Chinese (half of whom were born in China). There are about 2,500 Portuguese and an additional 20,000 Macanese, of mixed Chinese and Portuguese heritage. Tourism and gambling are the economic mainstays of the economy, with visitors from mainland China accounting for almost 60% of Macau's annual 18 million tourists.

IN MACAU   Once in Macau, you'll find a **MGTO** at the Macau Ferry Terminal, located just outside Customs and open daily from 9am to 10pm; there is also a MGTO at Macau International Airport, open for all incoming flights. For complete information, however, your best bet is the **main Macau Government Tourist Office,** Largo do Senado, located in the center of town on the main plaza just across from the water fountain; it's open daily from 9am to 6pm. Other tourist information offices are located at Fisherman's Wharf, open daily from 10am to 1pm and 2 to 6pm; at Guia Fort and Lighthouse, open daily from 9am to 1pm and 2:15 to 5:30pm; and the Border Gate (also called Barrier Gate and serving visitors from mainland China), open daily from 9:15am to 1pm and 2:30 to 6pm. For information by telephone, call the Tourist Hotline at © **853/28333000.**

GETTING THERE
BY BOAT   Located only 64km (40 miles) from Hong Kong across the mouth of the Pearl River, Macau is most easily accessible from Hong Kong by high-speed jetfoil, with most departures from the **Macau Ferry Terminal,** located just west of the Central District in the Shun Tak Centre, 200 Connaught Rd., on Hong Kong Island. Situated above the Sheung Wan MTR station, the Shun Tak Centre houses booking

offices for all forms of transportation to Macau, as well as the Macau Government Tourist Office (Room 336, on the same floor as boats departing for Macau). On the Kowloon side, limited service is available also from the China Ferry Terminal on Canton Road, Tsim Sha Tsui, where boats also depart for China. The nearest MTR station for this terminal is Tsim Sha Tsui.

The fastest, most convenient way to travel to Macau is via sleek jetfoils and catamarans, operated by **TurboJET** (© **852/2859 3333** in Hong Kong, **853/287907039** in Macau; www.turbojet.com.hk). The trip to Macau takes approximately 1 hour. Jetfoils depart from the Macau Ferry Terminal west of Central about every 15 to 30 minutes, 24 hours a day. One-way fares Monday through Friday are HK$243 (US$32/£17) for super class and HK$141 (US$18/£10) for economy class; fares on Saturday, Sunday, and holidays are HK$259 (US$34/£10) in super class and HK$153 (US$20/£11) in economy. Fares for night service (6:15pm–6am) are HK$274 (US$36/£20) and HK$175 (US$23/£13) respectively. Fares from Macau to Hong Kong are an additional HK$1 (13¢/7p), a reflection a higher departure tax, included in the price of the ticket. Seniors older than 60 and children younger than 12 receive a HK$15 (US$1.95/£1.05) discount. Fares from the China Ferry Terminal in Tsim Sha Tsui are slightly cheaper but departures are less frequent.

If you plan to travel on a weekend or holiday, it's wise to buy round-trip tickets well in advance. Tickets can be purchased at either the Macau Ferry Terminal on Hong Kong Island or the China Ferry Terminal in Kowloon, as well as at all China Travel Service branches in Hong Kong (p. 255) and at the TurboJET Service Counter at Sheung Wan MTR Station, Exit D. You can also book by credit card by calling © **852/2921 6688** in Hong Kong. All tickets are for a specific time and cannot be changed. If, however, you've purchased your ticket in advance and then decide you'd like to leave at an earlier time, head for the special queue for standby passengers available at both Shun Tak Centre and in Macau. There is often a good chance that you can get a seat, except during peak periods.

If you plan to spend only 1 or 2 nights in Macau, consider leaving most of your luggage at your Hong Kong hotel, at the Luggage Services Centre on the ground floor of Shun Tak Centre (Shop G02, near the taxi stand), or in computer-monitored lockers located at both the Hong Kong Island and Kowloon Macau ferry terminals. Then travel to Macau with only a small, hand-carried bag. Otherwise, you could end up paying an extra charge. Passengers traveling on a TurboJET are allowed one piece of luggage, not to exceed 20 kilograms (44 lb.). Additional baggage must be checked, with charges ranging from HK$20 to HK$40 (US$2.60–US$5.20/£1.40–£2.85) depending upon its weight. Baggage must be at the check-in counter, located just before Customs, 20 minutes before the jetfoil's departure. Obviously, your life will be easier if you leave heavy luggage in Hong Kong.

If you're arriving at Hong Kong International Airport and wish to travel directly to Macau, you can do so via TurboJET's **Sea Express** service (www.turbojetseaexpress. com.hk) without passing through Hong Kong Customs and immigration formalities (if you do pass through Customs, you will not be allowed to take the Sea Express). Upon exiting your arrival gate, look for the FERRY TRANSFER DESK signs, where you can purchase your Sea Express ticket and produce your baggage identification tag for baggage reclaim (your luggage will be retrieved from baggage claim by a TurboJET employee). You will then board a bus for a 7-minute shuttle to the SkyPier, take the TurboJET directly to Macau, and go through Customs there. Baggage is limited to 20 kilograms (44 lb.) in economy class and 30 kilograms (66 lb.) in super class, except for passengers from North America, who are allowed two pieces of baggage, with each piece not to exceed 32 kilograms (71 lb.). There are four sailings daily (at 11:50am and 3:30, 6:15, and 9:15pm; check-in is 1 hr. before sailings), with fares costing HK$180 (US$25/£13) for economy class and HK$280 (US$36/£20) for super class.

BY PLANE Macau's **International Airport** (© **853/28861111;** www.macau-airport.gov.mo) opened in November 1995, heralding the birth of Air Macau, the territory's fledgling carrier, followed in 2006 by two low-cost airlines, Viva Macau and Macau Asia Express. The airport is located on reclaimed land on Taipa Island and is conveniently connected to the peninsula by a bridge and bus service. The airport serves flights mainly from China, including Beijing and Shanghai, as well as from several other Asian cities, including Taipei, Singapore, Seoul, Tokyo, and Bangkok. Departure tax from Macau International Airport ($110 ptcs/US$14/£7.30) is included in ticket prices. Contact your travel agent or the Macau Government Tourist Office for more information.

ARRIVING IN MACAU

Passengers traveling by boat arrive at the Macau Ferry Terminal, located on the main peninsula. After going through Customs, stop by the Macau Government Tourist Office for a map and brochures, including the useful *Macau Guide Book*. In the arrivals hall there's also a counter for hotels operating shuttle buses. Most expensive and moderately priced hotels operate free shuttle services from the terminal, including Holiday Inn, Mandarin Oriental, Lisboa, Pousada de São Tiago, Westin Resort Macau, and Sintra. Otherwise, city bus nos. 3, 3A, and 10 travel from the terminal to Avenida Almeida Ribeiro, the main downtown street. The fare is $2.50 ptcs (US30¢/15p).

From the airport, there's an airport bus, AP1, which travels from the airport to the ferry terminal, Holiday Inn, Lisboa Hotel, and the Border Gate. The fare for this is $3.30 ptcs (US45¢/20p). A taxi from the airport to the Lisboa costs approximately $40 ptcs (US$5.20/£2.80).

MONEY

Even though the **pataca** (ptc; also sometimes referred to as MOP$) is Macau's official currency, you can use your Hong Kong dollars everywhere, even on buses and for taxis (though you are likely to receive change in patacas). The pataca is pegged to the Hong Kong dollar at the rate of $103.20 ptcs to HK$100; however, on the street and in hotels and shops, the Macau pataca and Hong Kong dollar are treated as having equal value. I suppose, therefore, that you could save a minuscule amount by exchanging your money for patacas (US$1 equals $8 ptcs; UK£1 equals 15 ptcs), but I rarely have done so and don't consider it worth the hassle for short stays in Macau. You may wish to exchange a small amount—say, HK$20 (US$2.55/£1.30), but keep in mind that the pataca is *not* accepted in Hong Kong.

In addition, most Macau hotels and their restaurants, as well as restaurants catering largely to tourists, list room rates and menu items in Hong Kong dollars. For the sake of simplicity, the hotel rates given below are quoted in HK$, but this could just as well read "patacas." Outside of hotels, restaurants are more likely to give prices in patacas, but sometimes they use HK$, too. Attractions, however, always use patacas. To mirror the most common pricing practices in Macau, I use HK$ for hotels and restaurants but patacas for attractions listed below. In case you need it, there's an ATM at the ferry terminal that accepts American Express, MasterCard, Visa, and cards operating on the Plus and Cirrus systems.

CITY LAYOUT

Macau comprises a small peninsula and Taipa and Colôane, two former islands that are now merged due to a massive land reclamation called COTAI and are linked to the mainland by bridges. The peninsula—referred to as Macau—is where you'll find the city of Macau, as well as the ferry terminal and most of its hotels, shops, and attractions. The ferry terminal is located on what is called the Outer Harbour, which faces Taipa and connects to the South China Sea. On the opposite side of the Peninsula is the Inner Harbour, which faces China. Although I used to love the Outer Harbour for its dreamy view of boats plying the Pearl River waterway and the tree-shaded Avenida da República, which ran along the waterfront, land reclamation, including new highways, high-rises, the Macau Tower, and Fisherman's Wharf, has rendered the Outer Harbour a horror zone. I'd advise fleeing this side of the peninsula as hastily as possible for downtown and the more colorful Inner Harbour. Walking along the Inner Harbour from Avenida Almeida Ribeiro to the Maritime Museum, you will see an unchanged Macau, with decaying buildings, small family businesses, street-side barbers, and, occasionally, fish laid out on sidewalks to dry. In the evening, however, you may want to return to the Outer Harbour, where Macau's nightlife district, called The Docks, spreads along the waterfront near the Statue of Kun Iam. Fisherman's Wharf, with its restaurants, shops, and other diversions, is also well worth a stroll.

Near the middle of the peninsula is Guia Hill, the highest natural point of Macau. Because of its strategic location, a fort was constructed atop the hill in the 1630s, followed in 1865 by a lighthouse, the first of its kind on the China coast. Also on the grounds of Guia Fort are a small chapel and a tourist information counter (open daily 9am–1pm and 2:15–5:30pm). A jogging path, complete with exercise stations, circles the top of the hill. Although there's not much to do on Guia Hill, it does provide a good overview of Macau. You can reach it by taking bus no. 9 to Flora Garden and then boarding what must be the world's shortest ropeway to the top of the hill.

Connecting the two harbors is Macau's main road, Avenida Almeida Ribeiro, remarkably with only one traffic light despite nightmarish traffic. About halfway down its length is the attractive Senado Square, Macau's main plaza. Lined with colonial-style buildings painted in hues of yellows and pinks, it is paved in a wave pattern of colored mosaic tiles, which lead from the square to the ruins of St. Paul's Church crowning the crest of a hill and to side streets good for shopping. On the other side of the square is Leal Senado, Macau's most outstanding example of Portuguese colonial architecture. Radiating from Avenida Almeida Ribeiro in all directions is old Macau, a fascinating warren of narrow streets, street markets, open-fronted family shops, and a cacophony of sounds, sights, and smells.

Taipa, closest to the mainland and connected by three bridges, has witnessed a construction boom over the past decades, with the addition of high-rise apartments and Macau's airport. In its midst is the picturesque Taipa Village with its many restaurants. Connected to Taipa by reclaimed land (called COTAI) is Colôane, largely undeveloped and the site of Macau's best beaches. Although Taipa and Colôane are still referred to as individual islands, in reality COTAI is so extensive (5.2 sq. km/more than 2 sq. miles) that the two are now just one fused island. COTAI is being developed as a resort and entertainment destination, with the Venetian Macao-Resort-Hotel as the biggest player. Once completed, which is still several years down the road, COTAI will

Car Races & Fireworks—The Heat Is On!

Of Macau's several annual events, none is as popular or draws as many enthusiasts as the Macau Grand Prix, held in mid- to late November, and the Macau International Fireworks Display Contest, held every Saturday in September.

The **Macau Grand Prix,** first staged in 1954, features races for motorcycles, production cars (international group A), and Formula Three racers, and attracts drivers from all over the world. Very similar to the famous circuit in Monaco, the 6.2km (3¾-mile) Guia Circuit, which winds through town near the ferry terminal and is lined with grandstands along the way, includes the winding roads of Guia Hill, hard corners around the waterfront, and the straightaway along the Outer Harbour. Champion drivers can complete a lap in as little as 2 minutes and 20 seconds. Tickets for stands during the 2 practice days cost HK$50 (US$6.50/£3.55), while race-day tickets range from HK$150 (US$19/£11) for standing room to HK$800 (US$104/£57) for the best seats. For ticket inquiries, call **853/287962268** or refer to www.macau.grand prix.gov.mo. Note, however, that ferry tickets and hotel accommodations in Macau are tight during the races.

Macau's other major competition, the **Macau International Fireworks Display Contest,** has a more universal appeal with its dazzling displays of fireworks spread over Saturday nights in September. Begun in 1989, it is now the world's biggest fireworks contest, with almost a dozen international teams competing. Displays last 20 minutes and are judged using criteria such as the height reached by the fireworks, the explosive bang and spread of each firework, color and variety, and the overall choreographic effect of each display. The best place to view the fireworks is along the waterfront near Macau Tower.

boast more than a half-dozen resorts, convention space, a new ferry terminal, a bridge linking it to mainland China, and a light rail that will whisk visitors to downtown Macau.

GETTING AROUND

Because the peninsula is only 8.9 sq. km (about 3½ sq. miles), you can walk to most of the major sights (be sure to get a free map from MGTO). If you get tired, you can always jump into one of the licensed metered **taxis,** all painted black and beige and quite inexpensive. To overcome the language barrier, MGTO has supplied most taxis with a destination guide listing most destinations in both English and Chinese. The charge is $11 ptcs (US$1.45/75p) at flag fall for the first 1.5km (1 mile), then $1 ptc (US15¢/7p) for each subsequent 180m (594 ft.). A taxi from the peninsula all the way to Hac Sa Beach on Colôane Island costs about $85 ptcs (US$11/£5.95). Luggage costs $3 ptcs (US40¢/20p) per piece, and there's a surcharge of $5 ptcs (US65¢/35p) if you go all the way to Colôane. There is no surcharge, however, for the return journey to Macau. To order a taxi by phone, call © **853/939939** or 853/28519519.

Public buses run daily from 7am to midnight, with fares costing $2.50 ptcs (US30¢/15p) for travel within the Macau peninsula, $3.30 ptcs (US45¢/20p) for travel to Taipa, and $4 ptcs to $5 ptcs (US50¢–US65¢/30p–35p) for travel to Colôane. Bus nos. 3, 3A, 10, and 10A travel from the ferry terminal past the Lisboa Hotel to the main street, Avenida Almeida Ribeiro, in the city center and then continue to the Inner Harbour. Buses going to Taipa and Colôane islands stop for passengers at the bus stop in front of the Hotel Lisboa, located on the mainland near the Macau-Taipa Bridge. Bus nos. 11, 22, 28A, 33, and 34, as well as the airport bus no. AP1, travel between Macau and Taipa; bus nos. 15, 21, 21A, 25, 26, and 26A connect Macau, Taipa, and Colôane. The MGTO has a free map with bus routes. For my hotel recommendations below, I provide a list of buses that travel only from the ferry terminal to each individual hotel, but for restaurants and attractions, I list all the buses from throughout the city that that travel to each destination.

There are also **pedicabs,** tricycles with seating for two passengers. Even as late as the early 1980s, this used to be one of the most common forms of transportation in Macau for the locals. But increased traffic and rising affluence have rendered pedicabs almost obsolete, and I suppose they will eventually vanish from the city scene much like the Hong Kong rickshaw. Today, pedicab drivers vie mostly for the tourist dollar, charging about $150 ptcs (US$20/£10) for an hour of sightseeing, but keep in mind that there are many hilly sights you can't see by pedicab. The most popular route is along the Praia Grande Bay around the tip of the peninsula, and back via Rue do Almirante Sérgio. Be sure to settle on the fare, the route, and the length of the journey before climbing in. You'll find them parked outside the ferry terminal and Lisboa Hotel.

FAST FACTS: Macau

American Express You'll find an American Express counter in the Hotel Lisboa, Avenida da Amizade (📞 853/28579898), open 24 hours for all those gamblers.

Area Code The international telephone country code for Macau is 853. From Hong Kong, dial **001/853** before the number. When dialing an international number from Macau, you must first dial **00**, followed by the country code. However, when calling Hong Kong from Macau, you need only dial the prefix **01**.

Currency Macau's currency is the *pataca*. Like the Hong Kong dollar, the pataca is identified by the "$" sign, sometimes also written "M$" or "MOP$." To avoid confusion, I have identified patacas by the shortened "ptcs." The pataca is composed of 100 *avos*. Coins come in 10, 20, and 50 avos and 1, 2, 5, and 10 patacas. Banknotes are issued for 10, 20, 50, 100, 500, and 1,000 patacas. The Macau pataca is pegged to the Hong Kong dollar (which is in turn pegged to the U.S. dollar) at a rate of $103.20 ptcs to HK$100; if you're going to be in Macau for only a short time, there's no need to change your money into patacas since Hong Kong dollars are readily accepted everywhere in Macau. Hotel rates, in fact, are generally quoted only in Hong Kong dollars. If you do exchange U.S. dollars or U.K. pounds (which you can do at banks, generally open weekdays from 9am to 5pm; at hotels; or an ATM at the ferry), you'll receive approximately $8 ptcs for each US$1, $15 ptcs for each £1.

Emergencies Dial 📞 **999** for medical emergencies and 📞 **110** or 112 for the police's special tourist hot line, all free calls. For the fire department, dial

© **853/28572222,** a toll call. However, if necessary you can call © **999** and the operator will transfer you to the police or fire departments.

Hospitals If you need to go to a hospital, contact the S. Januario Hospital, Estrada do Visconde de S. Januario (© **853/28313731**), or Kiang Wu Hospital, Estrada Coelho do Amaral (© **853/28371333**), both with 24-hour emergency service. For non-emergencies, Metro International, Av. Da Praia Grande, 405 (© **853/28355522**), has an English-speaking doctor.

Internet The Macau Museum of Art (p. 282) has a Media Library on the ground floor, with 37 computers you can use for free Tuesday through Sunday from 2 to 7pm. Otherwise, several public libraries offer free Internet facilities, including the Central Library of Macau, Av. conselheiro Ferreira da Almeida, 89 A–B (© **853/28567567**), open daily 2 to 8pm (closed holidays).

Language Both Portuguese and Chinese are official languages, with Cantonese the most widely spoken language. However, hotel and restaurant staffs usually understand English.

Mail Mailboxes are red in Macau. The main post office (© **853/28323666**), located in the city center on Largo do Senado, is open Monday through Friday from 9am to 6pm and Saturday from 9am to 1pm. It costs $5 ptcs (US65¢/35p) to send a postcard or letter weighing up to 10 grams via airmail to the United States. By the way, Macau is famous for its themed series of stamps, including the "Chinese Zodiac" and "Legends and Myths," which you can purchase at philately counters at all post offices.

Taxes Hong Kong levies a HK$19 (US$2.45/£1.35) tax for boat departures for Macau, while the Macau government levies a $20 ptcs (US$2.50/£1.30) departure tax, but note that the tax is already included in the price of the ticket. Hotels levy a 5% government tax and a 10% service charge on room rates. Restaurants also levy a 10% service charge, but government tax has been waived on the consumption of food and beverages.

Telephone For local calls made from public phone booths, it costs $1 ptc (US15¢/7p) for every 5 minutes. Telephones in Macau also offer international direct dialing, though in your hotel room you may have to go through the hotel operator. It costs $5.50 ptcs (US70¢/40p) for a 1-minute phone call to the United States during peak hours (Mon–Sat 6am–noon and 8pm–midnight) and $4.50 ptcs (US60¢/30p) on Sundays and off-peak hours. If you think you'll be making a lot of international telephone calls, purchase a prepaid phone card for $50, $100, or $150 ptcs (US$6.50/£3.50, US$13/£7, or US$19/£11) at **Edificio CTM,** Rua Pedro Coutinho, 25 (© **853/1000**), where you can also check whether your own mobile phone will work in Macau and buy a SIM card starting at $50 ptcs (US$6.25/£3.30). A vending machine at the ferry terminal also sells SIM cards for $50 ptcs. For international directory assistance, dial © **101;** for local directory inquiries, dial © **181.**

Water Macau's water is from China and is purified and chlorinated. However, distilled water is supplied in restaurants and hotel rooms.

3 Where to Stay

Most of Macau's hotels are located in the city of Macau on the peninsula, providing convenient access to most of Macau's sights. For a more relaxed getaway, however, there are a few hotels on the islands, mostly in a resort setting.

Of course, big spenders will have many new options in hotel accommodations over the next few years, beginning with the mega Venetian Macao-Resort-Hotel (www.venetianmacao.com), opening in COTAI in mid-2007 with 3,000 rooms, 30 restaurants, and more than 350 shops, all in a Venice-themed setting complete with canals and even gondolas. MGM Grand Macau, with both a hotel and casino, is slated to open in late 2007. Other hotel properties muscling in on the action over the next few years are Hilton, Four Seasons, Conrad, Shangri-La, Hyatt, and Sheraton. In all, the Macau government expects the current 11,000 rooms now available to increase by 39,000 new rooms over the next 10 years. For updated information on the rapidly changing hotel scene, contact the Macau Government Tourist Office.

In addition to the room rates given below (which are the same whether you pay in Hong Kong dollars or in patacas), there is a 10% hotel service charge and a 5% government tax. Except for some of the moderate and inexpensive hotels, most charge the same price for single or double occupancy. However, as in Hong Kong, the prices given below are rack rates; you should be able to bargain for a better rate, especially in the off season. If you plan on visiting Macau during Chinese New Year, Easter, summer holidays (July/Aug), the two major holidays for mainland Chinese (the so-called Golden Week following May 1 and in autumn for up to 10 days from Oct 1), or the Grand Prix in November, you should book well in advance. Weekends can also be quite busy. Otherwise, you shouldn't have any difficulty securing a room even on short notice, though if you have a specific hotel in mind it's always a good idea to reserve in advance. Because most of Macau's hotels have reservations facilities in Hong Kong, I've included the Hong Kong reservation telephone numbers when available. For more complete information about hotel restaurants, see "Where to Dine," starting on p. 106.

EXPENSIVE

Mandarin Oriental Macau ★★★ *Kids*   A companion hotel of the Mandarin Oriental in Hong Kong and the Oriental in Bangkok, this has long been one of Macau's most exclusive hotels, with room rates much lower than you'd pay in Hong Kong. Located about a 7-minute walk from the ferry terminal in the direction of downtown, it used to enjoy a rather isolated spot right on the Outer Harbour, but huge land reclamation projects (including Fisherman's Wharf) have robbed the hotel of waterfront views, not to mention peace and quiet. On the plus side, the hotel claimed a small portion of the new land for its state-of-the-art resort facility, which includes a free-form outdoor swimming pool (heated in winter and chilled in summer) landscaped against a waterfall; a water slide, pool, playground, and children's center for the kids; and a gorgeous spa offering various types of massage, body scrubs and wraps, facials, and more. As for the hotel, although its exterior is rather nondescript, if not downright ugly, the interior is beautifully designed and elegantly decorated throughout with imports from Portugal, including blue-and-white tiles, chandeliers, tapestries, and artwork. Guest rooms are decorated in Portuguese fabrics and natural teak. For families, a huge plus are the baby-care amenities provided free of charge on request, including diapers, wipes, and baby shampoo. The least expensive rooms face inland, while the best are those on the top four Mandarin executive floors with large balconies overlooking the resort.

Av. da Amizade, 956–1110, Macau. ℂ 800/526-6566 in the U.S. and Canada, 853/28567888, or 852/2881 1288 for reservations in Hong Kong. Fax 853/28594589. www.mandarinoriental.com/macau. 435 units. HK$2,000–HK$2,600 (US$260–US$337/£143–£186) single or double; HK$3,300–HK$3,900 (US$428–US$506/£236–£279) Mandarin floors; from HK$5,300 (US$688/£379) suite. AE, DC, MC, V. Free shuttle bus from ferry terminal or bus 10A or 10B from ferry terminal. **Amenities:** 4 restaurants (Italian, Cantonese, international, Thai); bar; 24-hr. casino; outdoor heated pool open year-round; kids' pool; 4 outdoor floodlit tennis courts; 2 indoor squash courts; playground; health club and spa; outdoor Jacuzzi; children's day-care center for ages 3–12; concierge; business center; shopping arcade; salon; 24-hr. room service; massage; babysitting; same-day laundry service/dry cleaning; executive-level rooms; doctor on call. *In room:* A/C, satellite TV w/pay movies, high-speed dataport, minibar, coffeemaker, hair dryer, safe.

Pousada de São Tiago 𝒦𝒦 *Finds*   Built around the ruins of the Portuguese Fortress da Barra, which dates from 1629, this charming inn on the tip of the peninsula is perfect for travelers who prefer romantic, atmospheric getaways over chain hotels. The entrance is dramatic: a flight of stone stairs leading through a cavelike tunnel that was once part of the fort, with water trickling in small rivulets on one side of the stairs. Once inside, guests are treated to the hospitality of a Portuguese inn, with ornately carved wooden bedroom furniture imported from Portugal and the use of stone, brick, and Portuguese blue tile throughout. Os Gatos, a terrace restaurant shaded by banyan trees, is a great place to while away an afternoon, as is the nearby outdoor swimming pool; and most of the rooms, all of which face the water, have balconies. Although lacking the recreational resort facilities or polished service of other hotels in this category, this place is a true find. No wonder it's a popular spot for local weddings. The Maritime Museum and A-Ma Temple are within easy walking distance; you can also walk to the city center in about a half-hour.

Av. da República, Fortaleza de São Tiago da Barra, Macau. ℂ 853/28378111, or 800/969 153 for reservations in Hong Kong. Fax 853/28552170. www.saotiago.com.mo. 24 units. HK$2,600–HK$3,200 (US$337–US$415/£186–£229) single or double; from HK$4,200 (US$545/£300) suite. Sun–Thurs discounts available. AE, DC, MC, V. Free shuttle bus (on request) or bus 28B from ferry terminal. **Amenities:** Restaurant (international); lounge; outdoor pool; room service 7:30am–11pm; babysitting; same-day laundry service/dry cleaning. *In room:* A/C, cable TV, minibar, hair dryer, bathroom scale.

Westin Resort Macau 𝒦𝒦𝒦 *Kids*   Opened in 1993, this is Macau's most stunning luxury resort hotel (though resorts slated to open in 2007 and beyond will surely eclipse it), complete with beautifully landscaped grounds, indoor and outdoor swimming pools, a health club with free yoga, aerobics, tai chi, and other exercise classes, excellent restaurants, and Macau's first golf course (accessed from the top floor of the resort). Located just a stone's throw from Hac Sa Beach on Colôane Island (with its popular Fernando's restaurant), it's a bit far from the center of town (about a 20-min. ride from the ferry pier on the hotel's complimentary shuttle bus, with departures every 30 min.), but the management is betting that most prospective guests are those who want to get away from it all. Families are catered to with a child-care center; Westin Kids' Club, which provides a multitude of activities for children; a wading pool; and a playground.

The hotel, Mediterranean in design and atmosphere, is spacious and airy, with a red terra-cotta tile roof and a comfortable lounge off the lobby that takes advantage of the idyllic setting by providing lots of windows that overlook the sea. Constructed in tiers to harmonize with the hillside overlooking Hac Sa Beach, each of the eight-storied hotel's very spacious, vibrantly colored rooms faces either the South China Sea or the beach (sea views are better) and features glass sliding doors opening onto—I love this—a huge 25-sq.-m (269-sq.-ft.) private terrace with plants and patio furniture (for real luxury, you can succumb to an outdoor Chinese-style massage here). For guests who like to stay in shape, there are WestinWORKOUT rooms with exercise equipment. Roomy bathrooms have everything from shaving/makeup mirrors to separate tubs and shower stalls. Room rates are based on altitude, with the highest floors costing more. If all the development on COTAI makes you cringe, this isolated resort is the place for you.

Estrada de Hac Sa, 1918, Colôane Island, Macau. © 800/228-3000 in the U.S. and Canada, 853/28871111, or 852/ 2803 2008 for reservations in Hong Kong. Fax 853/28871122. www.westin.com/macau. 208 units. HK$2,200–HK$2,700 (US$286–US$350/£157–£193) single or double; from HK$5,000 (US$649/£357) suite. Children under 19 stay free in parent's room. Spa, dining, and golf packages available. AE, DC, MC, V. Free shuttle bus from ferry terminal, airport, and Hotel Lisboa. **Amenities:** 3 restaurants (Cantonese, Japanese, international); bar; lounge; outdoor swimming pool open year-round; outdoor children's pool; indoor pool; 18-hole golf course; golf-driving range; minigolf course; 8 outdoor floodlit tennis courts; basketball court; croquet; jogging lanes, health club and spa; indoor and outdoor Jacuzzis; solarium; rental bikes; children's day-care center; Westin's Kids Club (ages 4–12) and playground; game room; small 24-hr. business center with free access to the Internet; 24-hr. room service; massage; babysitting; same-day laundry service/dry cleaning. In room: A/C, satellite TV w/pay movies, high-speed dataport, minibar, coffeemaker, hair dryer, iron/ironing board, safe.

MODERATE

Holiday Inn Macau   Opened in 1993 but recently renovated to give it a fresh look, this well-known chain is familiar to North American guests. It's situated in a rather drab area of high-rises between the ferry terminal and downtown, and, like most moderately priced Macau hotels, caters largely to gamblers and tour groups, especially since opening its own on-site casino. Rooms, all with two double beds or queen- or king-size beds and LCD TVs, are simple and unimaginative and are tiny compared to their U.S. counterparts. Steer clear of the standard rooms, which are on lower floors and face another building. Rather, splurge instead on a deluxe room, being sure to request a room on the 25th floor or higher facing the front, where you have a glimpse of the harbor far away (though ongoing construction could rob rooms of that perk). A plus is that the hotel is about a 10-minute walk from the main downtown area of Avenida de Almeida Ribeiro, and its casual coffee shop offers outdoor sidewalk seating, a rarity in this part of town.

Rua de Pequim, 82–86, Macau. © 800/465-4329 in the U.S. and Canada, 853/28783333, or 800/282 0244 in Hong Kong. Fax 853/28782321. www.macau.holiday-inn.com. 410 units. HK$1,200–HK$1,500 (US$156–US$194/£86–£107) single or double; HK$1,800 (US$234/£129) executive floor; from HK$3,500 (US$454/£250) suite. Children under 12 stay free in parent's room. AE, DC, MC, V. Free shuttle bus or 3, 3A, 10, 10A, 10B, 12, 28A, 32, or AP1 from the ferry terminal. **Amenities:** 2 restaurants (international/Macanese, Cantonese); coffee shop; bar; casino; small indoor pool; exercise room; sauna; steam room; spa; business center; 24-hr. room service; babysitting; same-day laundry service/dry cleaning; executive-level rooms. In room: A/C, satellite TV w/pay movies, wireless Internet access, minibar, coffeemaker, hair dryer, safe, free bottled water.

Hotel Lisboa 🕙 *Finds*   The Lisboa is in a class by itself. Built in 1969, it's a Chinese version of Las Vegas on acid: huge, flashy (check out the peacock-like decoration on its roof), and with a bewildering array of facilities that make it almost a city within a city. I always get lost in this hotel. Located near the water and one of the bridges to Taipa Island, it also has great feng shui, which may explain why its 24-hour casino is one of the most popular in Macau, especially among Hong Kong and mainland Chinese. There are also numerous restaurants (even the front-desk staff is unsure how many), shops, display cases of owner Stanley Ho's private art collection, and nighttime diversions, including, you might say, the countless women roaming the shopping complex's halls hoping for some short-term business from a lucky gambler. Ah, the Lisboa.

As for rooms, they're located in an older east wing and a tower that was completed in 1993 (a 40-story sister hotel, the Grand Lisboa, is opening across the street in late 2007). The tower, which added 14 floors, offers the best—and most expensive—harbor views, including rooms with traditional Chinese architecture and furniture that are a bit over-the-top. Otherwise, standard rooms have a few perks that make them recommendable, including Jacuzzi tubs, free local calls, and ornate decor. In short, this is the place to be if you want to be in the thick of it, though don't expect any personal time with the busy staff. I suspect some guests check in and never leave the premises. If they do, they'll find buses traveling to the outlying islands and other parts of Macau stopping right out the front door; downtown Macau is only a 5-minute walk away.

Av. de Lisboa, 2–4, Macau. (℃ 853/28377666, or 800/969 130 for reservations in Hong Kong. Fax 853/28567193. www.hotelisboa.com. 927 units. HK$1,650–HK$3,000 (US$214–US$389/£118–£214) single or double; from HK$3,800 (US$494/£271) suite. Children under 13 stay free in parent's room. AE, DC, MC, V. Free shuttle bus or bus 3, 3A, 10, 10A, 10B, 12, 28A, 28B, 28BX, 32, or AP1 from the ferry terminal. **Amenities:** 15 restaurants (some 24 hr.); bar; lounge; 24-hr. casino; outdoor heated pool; health club; shopping arcade; salon; 24-hr. room service; same-day laundry service/dry cleaning. *In room:* A/C, satellite TV w/free movies, free high-speed dataport; minibar w/free drinks, coffeemaker, hair dryer, safe.

Sintra   With the best central location of any of the moderately priced hotels, the Sintra, under the same management as Hotel Lisboa, enjoys a prime spot in the heart of Macau, within easy walking distance of Avenida de Almeida Ribeiro (Macau's main street), Largo do Senado, and the Hotel Lisboa with its 24-hour casino. Originally built in 1975 but completely overhauled in the mid-1990s, it looks good for its age and the staff is friendly. Standard rooms face another building but are large. Even roomier are the higher-priced rooms occupying higher floors, some with high-speed Internet connections; individual bookings (not through a travel agency) are often upgraded to one of these rooms if space is available. Of note for night owls is the hotel's one restaurant, open 24 hours.

Av. de D. João IV, Macau. (℃ 853/28710111, or 800/969 145 for reservations in Hong Kong. Fax 853/28567769. www.hotelsintra.com. 240 units. HK$1,160–HK$1,760 (US$151–US$228/£83–£126) single or double; HK$1,780–HK$2,080 (US$231–US$270/£127–£149) executive floor; from HK$2,360 (US$306/£169) suite. Children under 13 stay free in parent's room. AE, DC, MC, V. Free shuttle bus or bus 3, 3A, 10A, from the ferry terminal. **Amenities:** Restaurant (international/Cantonese); sauna (men only); business center; 24-hr. room service; same-day laundry service/dry cleaning; executive-level rooms. *In room:* A/C, satellite TV w/pay movies, minibar, hair dryer, safe, free distilled water.

INEXPENSIVE

East Asia Hotel   This is one of Macau's better choices for inexpensive accommodations in the heart of the city (I've seen some pretty grim hotels and guesthouses in this category), located near the Inner Harbour just off Avenida de Almeida Ribeiro in an area filled with local color and atmosphere. Some of that local color extends to a room just off the lobby where a bevy of beauties await phone calls or customers, which may admittedly be a bit too atmospheric for some (maybe that's why the hotel brochure promises that "your nights with us will be the most enjoyable"). Still, the 70-year-old hotel features a polite staff and large, perfectly fine rooms with clean, tiled bathrooms and complimentary Chinese tea. The least expensive rooms are windowless and a bit depressing. Best are rooms on higher floors offering good views, including some of the Inner Harbour.

Rua da Madeira, 1–A, Macau. © **853/922433,** or 852/2540 6333 for reservations in Hong Kong. Fax 853/922431. 98 units. HK$270–HK$370 (US$35–US$48/£19–£26) single; HK$400–HK$500 (US$52–US$65/£29–£36) twin. Weekday discounts available. MC, V. Bus: 3, 3A, 10, or 10A from the ferry terminal. **Amenities:** Restaurant (Chinese). *In room:* A/C, TV.

Hotel Guia ⚔ Located on the slope of Guia Hill, below the Guia Fort and Lighthouse and surrounded by traditional colonial architecture, this is one of Macau's more secluded inexpensively priced hotels. It's also one of the most welcoming, small and personable with a friendly staff and spotless rooms that range from those facing inland to those with little balconies facing the distant sea. By far the best are those with a view of Guia Lighthouse and the harbor in the background—request a room with a balcony on the highest (fifth) floor, where you also have a ringside view of the annual Grand Prix. Suites have high-speed Internet access and LCD TV screens. The only drawback to its quiet residential location is that it's a bit far from the action, but a free shuttle bus makes runs every half-hour or so to and from the ferry pier and the Hotel Lisboa. A nearby jogging path on Guia Hill makes this an ideal choice for joggers and walkers.

Estrada do Engenheiro Trigo, 1–5, Macau. © **853/28513888.** Fax 853/28559822. www.hotelguia-macau.com. 90 units. HK$880–HK$1,080 (US$114–US$140/£63–£77) single or double; from HK$1,680 (US$218/£120) suite. AE, DC, MC, V. Free shuttle bus or bus 28C from ferry terminal. **Amenities:** Restaurant (Chinese seafood); nightclub/disco; room service 7am–11pm; same-day laundry service/dry cleaning. *In room:* A/C, cable TV w/free movies, minibar, coffeemaker, hair dryer.

Hotel Ko Wah *Value* Despite its name, this is actually a guesthouse. There are many guesthouses around the Inner Harbour, Macau's oldest district, but most are of very low standards. This one, on picturesque Rua da Felicidade, is better than most, with a white-washed long corridor adorned with fake flowers and with rooms on either side. Some of the rooms have windows, others don't, but all have the basics including bathrooms. If all you're looking for is cheap accommodations in the heart of Macau's most colorful old town, this place fits the bill.

Rua da Felicidade, 3rd floor, Macau. © **853/28375599.** 27 units. HK$150 (US$19/£11) single; HK$180 (US$23/£13) double. No credit cards. Bus: 3, 3A, 10, or 10A from ferry terminal. *In room:* A/C, TV.

Pousada de Colôane ⚔⚔⚔ *Finds* This small, family-owned property, perched on a hill above Cheoc Van Beach with views of the sea, is a good place for couples and families in search of a reasonably priced isolated retreat. Opened in 1977 as Macau's first beach property, it's a relaxing, rather rustic place, with modestly furnished rooms, nothing fancy but all with Portuguese-style furnishings, Jacuzzi bathtubs, and balconies facing the sea and popular public beach. For some visitors it awakens memories of beachside vacations from childhood. There's an outdoor terrace where you can relax over drinks with views of the sunset, and the inn's Portuguese restaurant is especially popular for its Sunday lunch buffet offered during peak season. The main drawback is one of access, but buses to Macau pass by frequently; when arriving at the Macau ferry terminal, you're best off traveling to the hotel by taxi (fares average HK$80/US$10/£5.70).

Praia de Cheoc Van, Colôane Island, Macau. © **853/28882144.** Fax 853/28882251. www.hotelpcoloane.com.mo. 30 units. HK$750–HK$880 (US$97–US$114/£54–£63) single or double. Weekday discounts available. MC, V. Bus: 21A, 25, or 26A from Lisboa Hotel (tell the bus driver you want to get off at the hotel). **Amenities:** Restaurant (Portuguese); bar; outdoor pool; children's pool; babysitting; laundry service. *In room:* A/C, TV, minibar.

4 Where to Dine

As a former trading center for spices and a melting pot for Portuguese and Chinese cultures, it's little wonder that Macau developed its own very fine cuisine. The Portuguese settlers brought with them sweet potatoes, peanuts, and kidney beans from Brazil, piri-piri peppers from Africa, chiles from India, and codfish, coffee, and vegetables from Europe. In turn, the Chinese introduced rhubarb, celery, ginger, soy sauce, lychees, and other Asian foods. The result is Macanese cuisine. One of the most popular dishes is African chicken, grilled or baked with chiles and piri-piri peppers, but I also love *minchi,* a Macanese dish of minced beef prepared with fried potatoes, onion, and garlic. Other favorites include Portuguese chicken (chicken baked with potatoes, tomatoes, olive oil, curry, coconut, saffron, and black olives), *bacalhau* (codfish), Macau sole, *caldeirada* (seafood stew), spicy giant shrimp, baked quail and pigeon, curried crab, Portuguese sausage, and *feijoada* (a Brazilian stew of pork, black beans, cabbage, and spicy sausage). There are also restaurants specializing in traditional Portuguese cuisine, and, of course, countless Chinese restaurants. And don't forget Portuguese wine, inexpensive and a great bargain. Most famous is the *vinho verde,* a young wine served very cold that is refreshing on hot summer days.

Restaurants will add a 10% service charge to your bill, but as you'll discover, even the "expensive" restaurants in Macau would be a bargain in Hong Kong.

VERY EXPENSIVE

Robuchon a Galera ☆☆ FRENCH   This is by far Macau's most exclusive—and expensive—restaurant to date, with an elegant decor and a polished staff. Although it initially seemed odd back in 2001 when renowned French chef Joel Robuchon chose Macau to showcase his talents (he passed over Maxim's on New York's Times Square in favor of Macau), the subsequent explosion of resort casinos in this Asian boomtown now makes Robuchon's choice almost prophetic. In any case, Robuchon flies in four times a year to supervise the change of the seasonal menu, which in the past has included such offerings as pan-seared Wagyu beef with aromatics, potato confit and arugula salad, and lobster cocotte with sautéed girolles mushroom and green asparagus. While beautifully presented, main courses sometimes fall short and seem too highly priced for what they are. Appetizers, however, are wonderful; the cheese, dessert, and after-dinner drink trolleys are hard to pass up; and the wine list is probably the best in town. However, I recommend coming for the more reasonable lunch or spending your money elsewhere, unless, of course, you strike it big at the casino.

In the Hotel Lisboa, 3rd floor of Lisboa Tower, Av. da Amizade. ✆ 853/28377666. Reservations recommended. Main dishes HK$290–HK$650 (US$38–US$84/£21–£46); 11-course tasting menu HK$1,500 (US$195/£107); fixed-price lunch HK$288–HK$488 (US$37–US$63/£21–£35). AE, DC, MC, V. Daily noon–2:30pm and 6:30–10:30pm (last order). Bus: 3, 3A, 8, 8A, 9, 9A, 10, 10A, 10B, 11, 12, 21, 21A, 22, 23, 25, 26, 26A, 28A, 32, 33, or AP1.

EXPENSIVE

Camoes ☆ PORTUGUESE   Named after one of Portugal's most famous poets and a resident of Macau in the 1550s, Camoes occupies the upper floor of a "house" in Fisherman's Wharf. Simply designed, with a wooden floor, wood ceiling beams, candlelit tables, and a veranda good for drinks and people-watching, it offers authentic Portuguese food, as well as live music on weekend nights. You might wish to start with a seafood soup, presented in a bowl made of bread, followed by baked codfish in a white sauce, seafood casserole, suckling pig, or grilled monkfish and prawns. You're forgiven if, after dinner and a nighttime stroll of the Wharf's picturesque streets, you think you've somehow landed in Portugal.

Fisherman's Wharf, Lisboa 3. ⓒ **853/28728818.** Main courses HK$98–HK$198 (US$13–US$26/£7–£14). AE, MC, V. Daily 11:30am–11pm. Bus: 1A, 3, 3A, 8, 10, 10A, 10B, 12, 17, 23, 28A, 28B, 28BX, 28C, or 32.

Clube Militar de Macau 𝒦𝒦 *Finds* MACANESE/PORTUGUESE   This is certainly one of Macau's most atmospheric dining halls, located in the Macau Military Club, built in 1870 as a private cultural and recreation center for military officers. Painted a bright pink, this striking colonial building behind the Hotel Lisboa opened its restaurant to the public in 1995, offering nonmembers the chance to dine in style in its old-fashioned dining hall with its tall ceilings, whirring ceiling fans, arched windows, wood floor, and displays of antique Chinese dishware. As for the food, it's best to stick to the classics, such as roasted codfish with hot olive oil and garlic, roasted beef filet with Portuguese sauce, or African chicken. The lunch buffet is a downtown favorite, and the list of Portuguese wines is among the best in town.

Av. da Praia Grande, 795. ⓒ **853/28714009.** Reservations recommended for lunch. Main courses HK$99–HK$163 (US$13–US$21/£7.05–£12); fixed-price lunch or dinner HK$90–HK$99 (US$12–US$13/£6.40–£7.05); lunch buffet HK$90 (US$12/£6.40). AE, DC, MC, V. Daily noon–3pm and 7–11pm. Bus: 3, 3A, 8, 8A, 9, 9A, 10, 10A, 10B, 11, 12, 21, 21A, 22, 23, 25, 26, 26A, 28A, 32, 33, or AP1.

Os Gatos INTERNATIONAL   Located in the delightful Pousada de São Tiago Hotel (a romantic and intimate getaway), Os Gatos occupies a wonderful tree-shaded brick terrace that faces the Pearl River. It's a great place to stop for a meal, snack, or drink if you're visiting the nearby Maritime Museum or A-Ma Temple or if you simply want to while away an hour or two of a dreamy afternoon (for lightweights unaccustomed to alfresco dining, there's also a glass-enclosed, air-conditioned room, but for me the real pleasure of dining here is the terrace). The menu, however, is disappointingly basic, offering a limited selection of Mediterranean, Macanese, and Asian food, including baked bacalhau and seafood paella. Perhaps best is to come for the afternoon tea set served from 3 to 6pm, beginning at HK$90 (US$12/£6.40).

In the Pousada de São Tiago Hotel, Av. da República. ⓒ **853/28378111.** www.saotiago.com.mo. Main courses HK$88–HK$198 (US$11–US$26/£6.30–£14). AE, DC, MC, V. Daily 11am–11pm. Bus: 9 or 28B.

Restaurante Espaco Lisboa 𝒦𝒦 *Finds* PORTUGUESE   This is a tiny two-story restaurant, popular with the locals for its traditional, country-style Portuguese food. Located in a Chinese village house just off the main square in Colôane Village (Vila Colôane), just a few minutes' walk from the St. Francis Xavier Chapel, it offers so many great choices it's hard to know where to start. Fried codfish cakes, an assortment of Portuguese sausages, or the sautéed clams with garlic and coriander are a good launch to a feast here, followed, perhaps, by the traditional Portuguese cabbage soup. For the main course, which comes with side dishes, you might opt for the roast codfish served with potatoes and hot olive oil and garlic or the tenderloin steak Portuguese-style, fried with garlic and white wine and served with Portuguese honey ham, fried egg, and potatoes. And to top it all off? How about mango ice cream, served with cherry sauce *au flambé?* In nice weather, you may want to sit at one of the three tables outside on the tiny balcony, where you can look upon ancient tiled roofs and listen to the clicking of mah-jongg.

Rua das Gaivotas, 8, Colôane Village, Colôane Island. ⓒ **853/28882226.** Reservations recommended on weekends. Main courses HK$99–HK$198 (US$13–US$26/£7.05–£14). MC, V. Mon–Fri noon–3pm and 6:30–10pm; Sat–Sun noon–10:30pm. Bus: 15, 21A, 25, 26, or 26A.

360 Cafe INTERNATIONAL   This is Macau's most conspicuous restaurant, more than 219m (719 ft.) above reclaimed ground in the soaring Macau Tower. Opened in 2001, the tower contains an observation deck and lounge, with an admission of HK$70 (US$9.10/£5). Head instead to the tower's revolving restaurant, where for the price of a buffet meal you'll get an equally good view. It takes 1½ hours for a complete spin, giving you ample time to sample the various Southeast Asian, Chinese, Macanese, and Continental dishes as you soak in the view. Safety precautions make this Macau's only nonsmoking restaurant.

In the Macau Tower, Lago Sai Van. (✆ 853/9888660. www.macautower.com.mo. Reservations recommended weekends. Buffet lunch HK$158 (US$21/£11) weekdays, HK$168 (US$22/£12) weekends and holidays; buffet dinner HK$228 (US$30/£16) weekdays, HK$248 (US$32/£18) weekends and holidays. Daily 11:30am–3pm and 6:30–10pm. AE, DC, MC, V. Bus: 9A, 18, 21, 23, or 32.

MODERATE

A Lorcha 🍴 PORTUGUESE   Just a stone's throw from the Maritime Museum and A-Ma Temple, this is the best place to eat if you find yourself hungering for Portuguese food in this area. Look for its whitewashed walls, an architectural feature repeated in the interior of the tiny restaurant with its arched, low ceiling. Casual yet often filled with businesspeople, it offers *feijoada*, codfish in a cream sauce, chargrilled king prawns, clams prepared in garlic and olive oil, grilled lamb chops, baked minced beef potato pie, and other traditional dishes that are consistently good. Its name, by the way, refers to a type of Portuguese boat, which is appropriate for a colony founded by seafaring explorers.

Rua do Almirante Sérgio, 289. (✆ 853/28313193. Reservations recommended for lunch. Main courses HK$68–HK$138 (US$8.85–US$18/£4.85–£9.85). AE, DC, MC, V. Wed–Mon 12:30–3pm and 6:30–11pm. Bus: 1, 1A, 2, 5, 6, 7, 9, 10A, 11, 18, 21, 21A, 28B, or 34.

A Petisqueira PORTUGUESE   A small, unpretentious restaurant just off Taipa Village's main road, on the corner of Rua de S. João and Rua das Virtudes, it offers typical Portuguese fare, including codfish grilled, roasted, or boiled; grilled sole with lemon butter sauce; grilled king prawns; paella; fried tenderloin steak Portuguese-style; grilled sea bass; and curried crab. All grilled dishes are cooked over a charcoal grill. The fresh cheeses are especially recommended. Of course, everything tastes better with Portuguese wine.

Rua S. João, 15, Taipa Village, Taipa Island. (✆ 853/28825354. Main courses HK$85–HK$165 (US$11–US$21/£6.05–£12). MC, V. Mon–Fri noon–2:30pm; Sat–Sun and holidays noon–3pm; daily 7–10:15pm. Bus: 11, 15, 22, 28A, 30, 33, or 34.

Cozinha Pinocchio PORTUGUESE/MACANESE   Opened in 1977, Taipa Island's first Portuguese restaurant is still going strong, though some who have known it since its early days claim that the atmosphere became more staid when a roof was added to the original roofless two-story brick warehouse. Nevertheless, things are still hopping; people crowd its doors for specialties like curried crab, king prawns, charcoal-grilled sardines, fried codfish cakes, grilled spareribs, roast veal, roast quail, and Portuguese-style cooked fish. The wine list is extensive.

Rua do Sol, Taipa Village, Taipa Island. (✆ 853/28827128. Main courses HK$52–HK$160 (US$6.75–US$21/£3.70–£11). DC, MC, V. Daily noon–midnight. Bus: 11, 22, 28A, 30, 33, or 34.

Fat Siu Lau MACANESE   This is Macau's oldest restaurant (dating from 1903), but its three floors of dining have been renovated in upbeat modern Art Deco. Its exterior matches all the other storefronts on this renovated street—whitewashed walls and red shutters and doors—which used to serve as Macau's red-light district. Macanese cuisine is served here, including roast pigeon marinated according to a 100-year-old secret recipe; spicy African chicken; curried crab; garoupa stewed with tomatoes, bell pepper, onion, and potatoes; and grilled king prawns. A branch is located at the Docks nightlife district, Avenida Dr. Sun Yat-Sen (© **853/28722922**), open daily noon to 3pm and 6:30pm to midnight.

Rua da Felicidade, 64. © 853/28573580. www.fatsiulau.com.mo. Main courses HK$50–HK$142 (US$6.50–US$18/ £3.55–£10). AE, MC, V. Daily 11:30am–11:30pm. Bus: 3, 3A, 5, 6, 7, 8, 10, 11, 18, 19, 21, or 21A.

Fernando's *Finds* PORTUGUESE   For years, Fernando's was just another shack on Hac Sa Beach. Although outwardly there is nothing to distinguish it from the others (it's the brick one closest to the beach, below the vines), a pavilion was added out back, complete with ceiling fans and an adjacent open-air bar with outdoor seating, making it *the* place to dine on the beach and a destination in itself. Now everyone knows Fernando's, and even though there's no air-conditioning (that goes for the kitchen as well), it doesn't seem to deter the faithful who pilgrimage here, especially on weekends, when you'll probably have to wait for a table. Outspoken Fernando is usually on hand, holding court. The menu is strictly Portuguese and includes Portuguese chorizo, clams, crabs, mussels, codfish, *feijoada,* charcoal-grilled chicken, pork ribs, suckling pig, beef, and salads. The bread all comes from the restaurant's own bakery, and the vegetables are grown on the restaurant's own garden plot across the border in China. Only Portuguese wine is served, stocked on a shelf for customer perusal (there is no wine list). It's all very informal, and not for those who demand pristine conditions.

Praia de Hac Sa, 9, Colôane. © 853/28882264 or 853/28882531. Reservations not accepted. Main courses HK$66–HK$148 (US$8.55–US$19/£4.70–£11). No credit cards. Daily noon–9:30pm (last order). Bus: 15, 21A, 25, or 26A.

Galo *Finds* PORTUGUESE/MACANESE   A delightful, two-story house in Taipa Village has been converted into this informal and festively decorated restaurant specializing in local cuisines and unique creations of the talented owner/chef. *Galo* means rooster in Portuguese; look for the picture of the rooster outside the restaurant, just off the main pedestrian street. Its menu, which includes photographs of each dish, offers such house specialties as Macau crabs, prepared with a mixture of Shanghainese and Macanese ingredients, rather than curry. You might also want to try giant prawns, mussels, African chicken, Portuguese broad beans, or the mixed grill. In any case, be sure to start out with the *sopa da casa* (house soup), made from potatoes, red beans, onions, and vegetables simmered in broth from boiled beef and sausages. Delicious!

Rua dos Clérigos, 45, Taipa Village, Taipa Island. © 853/28827423 or 853/28827318. Main courses HK$45–HK$85 (US$5.85–US$11/£3.20–£6.05). MC, V. Mon–Fri 11am–3pm and 6:30–10:30pm; Sat–Sun 11:30am–10:30pm. Bus: 11, 22, 28A, 30, 34, or 35.

O Porto Interior *Value* MACANESE/PORTUGUESE   Located on the Inner Harbour not far from the Maritime Museum and A-Ma Temple, this comfortable, classy restaurant decorated in colonial style with woodwork carvings, a brick floor, and decorative bird cages offers surprisingly inexpensive fare, making it a good value. You might wish to start with grilled Portuguese sausage, spicy shrimp, or the seafood supreme soup, served inside a bread bowl. Main dishes range from Macau curry crab and Macanese garlic king prawns to African chicken, black pepper steak, and *minchi.*

Rua do Almirante Sérgio, 259B. ℃ 853/967770. Main courses HK$55–HK$120 (US$7.15–US$16/£3.90–£8.55). AE, DC, MC, V. Daily noon–11:30pm. Bus: 1, 1A, 2, 5, 6, 7, 9, 10A, 11, 18, 21, 21A, 28B, or 34.

Restaurante Litoral 𝖆𝖆 MACANESE   Exactly which restaurant serves the most "authentic" Macanese food in town is a hotly contested subject, but this attractive restaurant with its dark-gleaming woods, whitewashed walls, and stone floor can certainly lay claim to the title. All the traditional favorites are here, including curry crab, curry prawns, African chicken, *feijoada,* and *minchi,* but Portuguese specialties like codfish baked with potato and garlic, roast Portuguese sausage, and Portuguese green soup are not overlooked. Wash it all down with Portuguese wine or beer. It's located along the covered sidewalk not far from the Maritime Museum and A-Ma Temple.

Rua do Almirante Sérgio, 261A. ℃ 853/967878. Main courses HK$95–HK$180 (US$12–US$23/£6.75–£13). AE, MC, V. Daily noon–3pm and 6:30–10:30pm. Bus: 1, 1A, 2, 5, 6, 7, 9, 10, 10A, 11, 18, 21, 21A, 28B, or 34.

INEXPENSIVE

Antica Trattoria da Ise ITALIAN   This casual, upstairs restaurant, located near the Docks nightlife district, is always crowded. Simply decorated with cast-iron chandeliers, plants, and palm trees, it offers 18 different kinds of pizza and 30 pasta dishes, as well as main courses like baked salmon with lemon thyme and T-bone steak with garlic and lemon dressing.

Av. Sir Anders Ljungstedt, Edificio Vista Magnifica Court, no. 40–46. ℃ 853/28755102. Reservations recommended. Pizza HK$50–HK$75 (US$6.50–US$9.75/£3.55–£5.35); main dishes HK$65–HK$110 (US$8.45–US$14/£4.65–£7.85). AE, DC, MC, V. Daily noon–11pm. Closed 2nd Tues of every month. Bus: 1A, 8, 12, 17, 23, or AP1.

Caravela *(Finds* PORTUGUESE   This local Portuguese hangout serves as a bakery, cafe, restaurant, and informal gathering spot for friends, with both sidewalk seating and a small dining room. Professionals stop by for breakfast on their way to work, old men peruse newspapers over cups of Portuguese coffee, and office workers take advantage of the daily set meal for HK$65 (US$8.45/£4.65) which includes soup, choice of a main dish, and dessert. The menu itself is limited, offering a few dishes like chargrilled codfish and steak, but the bread is homemade, the pastries are irresistible (a typical Christmas dessert that resembles French toast is always on offer), and the atmosphere is a slice of Portugal in the heart of Asia. It's located in downtown Macau but is a bit hard to find, on a side street 1 block northeast off Avenida Do Infante D. Henrique, between Avenida Da Praia Grande and Avenida D Joao IV.

Mata e Oliveira, no. 7. ℃ 853/28712080. Main dishes HK$65–HK$90 (US$8.45–US$12/£4.65–£6.40). No credit cards. Mon–Sat 8am–8pm. Bus: 3, 3A, 8A, 10, 10A, 22, 21A, 26A, or 33.

Carlos PORTUGUESE   Just a block inland from the Docks nightlife district, this bare room with a tall ceiling offers no-nonsense, home-cooked Portuguese food at very reasonable prices, assuring it a faithful clientele. The menu is extensive and includes all the classics, but standouts include the shrimp in garlic sauce and the clams and pork stewed in white wine and herbs.

Rua Cidade de Braga. ℃ 853/28751838. Main dishes HK$55–HK$100 (US$7.15–US$13/£3.90–£7.15). No credit cards. Tues–Sun 11am–3pm and 6–11pm. Bus: 1A, 8, 12, or 23.

Nga Tim Cafe 𝖆 *(Finds* CANTONESE/MACANESE/PORTUGUESE   This lively, open-air, pavilion restaurant is on the tiny main square of Colôane Village, dominated by the charming Chapel of St. Francis Xavier. Its popularity with the locals on weekends and holidays lends it a festive, community-affair atmosphere; it's a great place for relaxing and people-watching. The food, which combines Chinese, Macanese, and Portuguese styles of cooking and ingredients, is in a category all its own, with many unique dishes not available anywhere else. Try the salt-and-pepper shrimp, baked chicken in a fresh coconut, grilled prawns with curry, or the barbecued spring chicken, accompanied by Portuguese wine or fresh fruit juice. This is a good place to rub elbows with the natives, and when the weather is perfect, there's no finer place in Macau.

Rua Caetano, 8, Colôane Village, Colôane Island. ℭ 853/28882086. Main courses HK$15–HK$98 (US$1.95–US$13/£1.05–£7). MC, V. Daily 11:30am–1am. Bus: 15, 21A, 25, 26, or 26A.

5 Exploring Macau
THE TOP ATTRACTIONS

Macau Tower *Overrated*   Does the world really need another tower? Local authorities apparently thought so, opening the Macau Tower Convention & Entertainment Centre in 2001. In addition to exhibition and convention space, it contains restaurants and shops, but the crowning glory is the 330m (1,083-ft.) tower, with an observatory about 219m (719 ft.) high—the equivalent of 61 stories. Since admission to the outdoor observation deck and indoor lounge is rather exorbitant by Macau standards, I personally think you are best off coming for a meal in the revolving **360 Cafe** (p. 277). However, thrill seekers take note: The indoor observation lounge has a glass-floored section that gives the illusion of standing on thin air. But real dare devils will want to tour the observation deck's *outside* ramparts with the safety of harnesses and ropes, which costs $198 ptcs (US$25/£13), half price for children and seniors. Other ways to have fun with Macau Tower: climbing the mast (a 2-hr. ordeal); climbing 32m (105 ft.) up the tower's concrete shaft on what may be the world's highest artificial climbing wall; bungee jumping 233m (764 ft.; listed in the Guinness World Records as the "highest commercial decelerator descent"); and more.

Lago Sai Van. ℭ 853/933339. www.macautower.com.mo. Admission to observatory $70 ptcs (US$8.75/£4.65) adults, $35 ptcs (US$4.40/£2.30) children and seniors. Daily 10am–9pm. Bus: 9A, 18, 21, 23, or 32.

Museum of Macau *★★★*   Located in the bowels of ancient Monte Fortress, this ambitious museum provides an excellent overview of Macau's history, local traditions, and arts and crafts. If you see only one museum in Macau, it should be this. Entrance is via an escalator located near St. Paul's Church. Arranged chronologically, the first floor depicts the beginnings of Macau and the arrival of Portuguese traders and Jesuit missionaries. Particularly interesting is the room comparing Chinese and European

---

Tips **Museum Mania**

If museums are your passion, save money by purchasing the Museums Pass, valid for 5 days and allowing entry to six museums, including the Grand Prix Museum, Wine Museum, Museum of Macau, Maritime Museum, and Macau Museum of Art. Passes, which cost $25 ptcs (US$3.10/£1.80) for adults and $12 ptcs (US$1.50/80p) for children and seniors, can be purchased at any of the museums. (The sixth museum is Lin Zexu Museum of Art, which is not as conveniently located and is not covered below; it centers on Lin Zexu, who was commissioned by Beijing in the 1830s to abolish the opium trade.)

civilizations at the time of their encounter in the 16th century, including descriptions of their different writing systems, philosophies, and religions. The second floor deals with the daily life and traditions of old Macau, including festivals, wedding ceremonies, and industries ranging from fishing to fireworks factories. Displays include paintings and photographs depicting Macau through the centuries, traditional games and toys, an explanation of Macanese cuisine and architecture, and a re-created street in Macau lined with colonial and Chinese facades and containing tea, pastry, and traditional Chinese pharmacy shops. The top floor, the only one aboveground, is of modern Macau and its plans for the future. From here you can exit to the wall ramparts of the fort, which was built by the Jesuits about the same time as St. Paul's and largely destroyed by the same fire. You'll want to spend at least an hour here.

Citadel of São Paulo do Monte (St. Paul Monte Fortress). ℓ 853/28357911. www.macaumuseum.gov.mo. Admission $15 ptcs (US$1.90/£1) adults, $8 ptcs (US$1/55p) seniors and children. Tues–Sun 10am–6pm. Located next to St. Paul's Church.

St. Paul's Church ☆☆   The most famous structure in Macau is the ruin of St. Paul's Church. Crowning the top of a hill in the center of the city and approached by a grand sweep of stairs, only its ornate facade and some excavated sites remain. It was designed by an Italian Jesuit and built in 1602 with the help of Japanese Christians who had fled persecution in Nagasaki. In 1835, during a typhoon, the church caught fire and burned to the ground, leaving only its now-famous facade. The facade is adorned with carvings and statues depicting Christianity in Asia, a rather intriguing mix of images: a Virgin Mary flanked by a peony (representing China) and a chrysanthemum (representing Japan), and a Chinese dragon, a Portuguese ship, and a demon. Beyond the facade is the excavated crypt, where in glass-fronted cases are the bones of 17th-century Christian martyrs from Japan and Vietnam. Here, too, is the tomb of Father Allesandro Valignano, founder of the Church of St. Paul and instrumental in establishing Christianity in Japan. Next to the crypt is the underground Museum of Sacred Art, which you can tour in about 20 minutes. It contains religious works of art produced in Macau from the 17th to 20th centuries. Included are very interesting 17th-century oil paintings by exiled Japanese Christian artists, crucifixes of filigree silver, carved wooden saints, and other sacred objects. To the left of the church's ruins are tiny Na Tcha Temple and a remnant of Macau's old city wall, which, along with St. Paul's Church, are among 25 historic structures protected as World Heritage Sites.

Rua de São Paulo. ℓ 853/28358444. Free admission. Grounds daily 24 hr.; museum daily 9am–6pm. Bus: 8A, 17, 18, 19, or 26. Or a 10-min. walk northwest of Senado Square (off Av. Almeida Ribeiro).

MORE MUSEUMS

Grand Prix Museum   One of two museums located in the Tourism Activities Centre (see the Wine Museum, below), a 10-minute walk from the Macau Ferry Terminal, the Grand Prix Museum opened in 1993 to celebrate the 40th anniversary of the Macau Grand Prix. Its display hall is filled mainly with cars and motorcycles that have competed in the race through the years. There are also simulator games, which cost $10 ptcs (US$1.25/60p) extra and give visitors the thrill of "experiencing" high speeds down a racetrack (participants must be at 150 centimeters/59 in.). Together with the Wine Museum (see below), you'll spend less than an hour here.

Centro de Actividades Turisticas Macau, Rua Luis Gonzaga Gomes. ℓ 853/287984108. Admission $10 ptcs (US$1.25/60p) adults, $5 ptcs (US60¢/35p) children 11–18, free for seniors and children younger than 11. Combination ticket to Grand Prix Museum and Wine Museum $20 ptcs (US$2.50/£1.20). Wed–Mon 10am–6pm. Bus: 1A, 3, 3A, 10, 10A, 10B, 12, 17, 23, 28A, 28B, 28C, 32, or AP1.

Macau Museum of Art 🏛️   Located in the Macau Cultural Centre on reclaimed land in the Outer Harbour, this small but interesting museum displays historical paintings, Chinese calligraphy, pottery, and works by contemporary local artists. Particularly fascinating are paintings by Western artists such as British painter George Chinnery and others, who painted scenes, people, and customs of Macau and Guangdong, including depictions of the port town as it looked long ago. Their works were often copied and then sold to visiting foreigners as souvenirs. Also impressive is the collection of Shiwan ceramic figurines. There are also temporary exhibitions. Depending upon your interest, you'll spend anywhere from 30 to 60 minutes here. Incidentally, on the ground floor is the Media Library, with computers you can use for free from 2 to 7pm.

Centro Cultural de Macau, Av. Xian Xing Hai (Novos Aterros do Porto Exterior/NAPE). ℂ **853/287919814**. www.art museum.gov.mo. Admission $5 ptcs (US60¢/35p) adults, $3 ptcs (US40¢/20p) students and children, free for seniors; free admission Sun. Tues–Sun 10am–7pm. Bus: 1A, 8, 12, 17, 23, or AP1.

Maritime Museum 🏛️ *Kids*   Macau's oldest museum, ideally situated on the waterfront of the Inner Harbour where visitors can observe barges and other boats passing by, does an excellent job of tracing the history of Macau's lifelong relationship with the sea. It's located at the tip of the peninsula, across from the Temple of A-Ma, in approximately the same spot where the Portuguese first landed. The museum begins with dioramas depicting the legend of A-Ma, protectress of seafarers and Macau's namesake, and continues with models of various boats, including trawlers, Chinese junks, Portuguese sailing boats, and even modern jetfoils. There are also life-size original boats on display, ranging from the sampan to an ornate festival boat. Various fishing methods are detailed, from trawling and gill netting to purse seining, as well as various voyages of discovery around the world. The museum also has nautical equipment, navigation instruments used by the Portuguese and Chinese, and—a hit with children—a small aquarium, with tanks of exotic fish and a collection of shells. You'll probably spend about an hour here.

Largo do Pagode da Barra, 1. ℂ **853/28595481**. www.museumaritimo.gov.mo. Admission $10 ptcs (US$1.25/65p) adults, $5 ptcs (US60¢/35p) children, free for seniors and children under 10. Sun half price. Wed–Mon 10am–5:30pm. Bus: 1, 1A, 2, 5, 6, 7, 9, 10, 10A, 11, 18, 21, 21A, 28B, or 34.

Pawnshop Museum   Located on Macau's main street not far from Senado Square, this historic building was once a traditional pawnshop. Today it serves as a museum outlining the pawnshop business in Macau. Unlike pawnshops in the West, this pawnshop held personal possessions for up to 3 years, safeguarded against fires, floods, and theft in a thick-walled tower. There isn't a lot to see here (you can tour the entire building in about 15 min.), so be sure to stop by the second-floor shop selling local souvenirs and stop for refreshment at the third-floor tearoom.

Clube Cultural, Av. Almeida Ribeiro, 396. ℂ **853/921811**. www.culturalclub.net. Admission $5 ptcs (US60¢/35p). Daily 10:30am–7pm. Closed 1st Mon of every month. Bus: 2, 5, 7, 8, 9, 9A, 12, 16, 22, or 25.

Wine Museum   Located in the same building as the Grand Prix Museum (see above), this is Asia's first museum dedicated to wine. Modeled like a wine cellar, it begins with a brief history of winemaking, starting with its discovery by Egyptians and Phoenicians in 6000 to 4000 B.C. and its spread from Greece through the rest of Europe, reaching Portugal around A.D. 1100. On display are wines (the oldest is an 1815 Madeira), wine presses, storage barrels, harvesting tools, and other winemaking equipment, as well as descriptions of every winegrowing region in Portugal. Wine production in

China is also presented. A museum highlight is the free wine tasting of red, white, or verde wine. Bottles of Portuguese wine can also be purchased.

Centro de Actividades Turisticas Macau, Rua Luis Gonzaga Gomes. (C) **853/287984188.** Admission $15 ptcs (US$1.90/£1) adults, $5 (US60¢/35p) children 11–18, free for seniors and children younger than 10. Combination ticket to Wine Museum and Grand Prix Museum $20 ptcs (US$2.50/£1.40) adults, $10 ptcs (US$1.25/65p) children. Wed–Mon 10am–6pm. Bus: 1A, 3, 3A, 10, 10A, 10B, 12, 17, 23, 28A, 28B, 28C, 32, or AP1.

TEMPLES

Temple of Kun Iam Tong (Temple of the Goddess of Mercy) 𝒜𝒜   Of the many temples in Macau, one of the most important is the Temple of Kun Iam Tong, founded in the 13th century. Its present buildings, with ornate porcelain figurines adorning its roofs, date from 1627. The most significant historical event that took place at this largest and wealthiest of Macau's Buddhist temples was the 1844 signing of the first treaty of trade and friendship between the United States and China; the round granite table where the treaty was signed is still here. The temple houses images of Buddha, representing the past, present, and future, as well as the goddess of mercy (Kun Iam) dressed in the costume of a Chinese bride. She is attended by 18 gold-lacquered figures lining the walls that represent the 18 wise men of China. Curiously enough, the figure on the left with bulging eyes and mustache is identified here as Marco Polo, who, having embraced Buddhism, came to be viewed as one of China's 18 wise men. Behind the temple is a landscaped Chinese garden; it has four banyan trees with intertwined branches, popularly known as the Lovers' Tree and considered symbols of marital fidelity. According to local legend, the trees grew from the burial site of two lovers who committed suicide when they were forbidden to marry. Although the original trees died, new ones have taken their place.

As you wander through the various buildings on the temple grounds, you will notice small funeral rooms with altars dedicated to the newly deceased, complete with photographs, offerings of fruit and other food, and paper money to assist the departed in the afterlife. You may even chance upon a funeral service, in which participants are dressed in white. Please show respect by being quiet, and refrain from taking photographs. It is also considered bad manners—not to mention bad luck—to take a picture of a monk without his permission. In any case, a visit to this temple is like going back in time; allow 20 minutes in this time capsule.

Av. do Coronel Mesquita. Free admission. Daily 7am–6pm. Bus: 12, 17, 18, 19, 22, or 23.

Temple of A-Ma 𝒜𝒜   Another important temple is situated at the bottom of Barra Hill at the entrance to the Inner Harbour, across from the Maritime Museum. It is Macau's oldest Chinese temple, with parts of it dating back more than 600 years. This temple is dedicated to A-Ma, goddess of seafarers. According to legend, a poor village girl sought free passage on a boat but was refused until a small fishing boat came along and took her onboard. Once the boat was at sea, a typhoon blew in, destroying all boats except hers. Upon landing at what is now Barra Hill, the young girl revealed herself as A-Ma, and the fishermen repaid their gratitude by building this temple on the spot where they came ashore. The temple was already here when the Portuguese arrived; they named their city A-Ma-Gao (Bay of A-Ma) after this temple, now shortened, of course, to Macau.

At the entrance is a large rock, with a picture of a traditional sailing junk engraved more than 400 years ago to commemorate the Chinese fishing boat that carried A-Ma to Macau. The temple, spreading along the steep slope of a hill with views of the water, has good feng shui. There are several shrines set in the rocky hillside, linked by winding paths through moon gates. The uppermost shrine honors Kun Iam, the Goddess of Mercy, and affords good views of the Inner Harbour. If you happen to be here on the 23rd day of the 3rd moon, you'll be treated to the A-Ma Festival (similar to the Tin Hau festival in Hong Kong), with its throngs of worshippers and Cantonese opera performed on a temporary stage. At the very least, your visit may coincide with an explosion of fireworks, traditionally set off to scare away evil spirits and now a popular demonstration for visiting tour groups.

Rua de S. Tiago da Barra. Free admission. Daily 6:30am–6pm. Bus: 1, 1A, 2, 5, 6, 7, 9, 10, 10A, 11, 18, 21, 21A, 28B, or 34.

A GARDEN

Lou Lim Iok Garden *(Finds)*   Macau's most flamboyant Chinese garden was built in the 19th century by a wealthy Chinese merchant and modeled after the famous gardens in Suzhou, China. Tiny, with narrow winding paths, bamboo groves, rock grottoes, a nine-turn zigzag bridge (believed to deter evil spirits), and ponds filled with carp, it's a nice escape from the city. If possible, come in the morning, when the garden is filled with Chinese doing tai chi exercises, musicians practicing traditional Chinese music, and bird lovers strolling with their birds in ornate wooden cages.

Estrada de Adolfo Loureiro. ℂ 853/28356622. Free admission. Daily 6am–6pm. Bus: 2, 5, 9, 9A, 12, 16, 22, 25, or 28C.

TAIPA & COLÔANE ISLANDS

Macau's two islands—Taipa and Colôane—are now joined together by COTAI, a massive land-reclamation development that will see the opening of the Venetian Macao-Resort-Hotel in 2007, followed by many more projects over the next 10 years. Luckily, much of Colôane remains Macau's undeveloped playground, a good place to get away from it all.

TAIPA

Closest to the mainland, Taipa was accessible only by ferry until 1974, when the Macau-Taipa Bridge was finally completed. Two additional bridges have led to increased development on Taipa, including unsightly new apartment blocks and booming suburbs that have pushed the population on this small, 6.5-sq.-km (2½-sq.-mile) island to 42,000. Still, Taipa is worth a visit for quaint Taipa Village with its popular restaurants and colonial architecture. Taipa is also home of the United Chinese Cemetery with its blend of Confucianist, Taoist, and Buddhist influences, a university, Macau Stadium, and the Macau Jockey Club for horse racing.

For history and architecture buffs, the first stop should be **Taipa Village** *ℱ*, a small traditional community of narrow lanes, alleys, squares, and two-story colonial buildings painted in hues of yellow, blue, and green. Although now almost completely engulfed by nearby housing projects, village life remains in full view here, with women sorting the day's vegetables on towels in the street, children playing, and workers carrying produce and goods in baskets balanced from poles on their shoulders. On or near Rua do Cunha, the picturesque pedestrian-only main street with its hanging baskets of flowers, are a number of fine, inexpensive restaurants, making dining reason enough to come (see "Where to Dine," earlier in this chapter).

But for sightseeing, the best place to visit is the **Casa Museu da Taipa (Taipa House Museum),** on Avenida da Praia (ℂ 853/28827088). It is one of five colonial-style buildings lining the street—homes that belonged to Macanese families in the

East Meets West

The Historic Centre of Macau, a World Heritage Site, celebrates more than 400 years of cultural exchange between the East and the West. Encompassing most of the historic old town, it ensures the preservation of both traditional Chinese architecture and the oldest western structures on Chinese soil, with forts, temples, churches, mansions, squares, a library, cemetery, and a garden among 25 protected sites. Two of the most famous attractions— A-Ma Temple and the ruins of St. Paul's—are described here, but for a complete list of protected structures and a map, stop by the Macau Government Tourist Office for its *Macau World Heritage* pamphlet. Among my favorites: the Moorish Barracks, Mandarin's House, Leal Senado Building, Senado Square, Lou Kau Mansion, the Protestant Cemetery, and Guia Fortress.

At the other end of the spectrum is another "town," the newly fabricated **Fisherman's Wharf** (© 853/282993300; www.fishermanswharf.com), which opened in 2004 on reclaimed land in the Outer Harbour, just a few minutes' walk from the ferry terminal. It's divided into three themed zones: Tang Dynasty, with architecture and décor typical of the era; East Meets West, a fairy-tale rendition of history, with a man-made "active" volcano, thrill rides for the little ones at Aladdin's Fort (open daily 10am–10pm, with rides costing $20–$40 ptcs/US$2.50–US$5/£1.35–£2.70), and a 2,000-seat Roman Amphitheatre for concerts and performances; and Legend Wharf, with replica European, North American, and South African historic architecture. Mostly, Fisherman's Wharf is an excuse to shop and eat, with plenty of upscale opportunities for both. With regularly scheduled street performances and other events, it makes for an interesting stroll.

---

early 1900s. Combining both European and Chinese design as a reflection of the families' Eurasian heritage, the Casa Museu has a dining and living room, study, kitchen, upstairs bedrooms, and large verandas that face banyan trees and what was formerly the sea (now reclaimed land), reflecting the fact that most entertaining in this small colonial outpost—a boat ride from Macau—took place at home. The home is filled with period furniture, paintings, art, and personal artifacts reflective of a dual heritage. The museum is open Tuesday through Sunday from 10am to 6pm, and admission is $5 ptcs (US60¢/35p). Other buildings on the banyan-shaded Praia open to the public contain displays relating to the history of Taipa and its inhabitants, and traditional regional costumes of Portugal. Next to the buildings, on a hill, is Our Lady of Carmel Church, built in the 19th century for the devout Macanese Catholics.

The easiest way to reach Taipa Village is to board one of the buses that stops in front of the Hotel Lisboa near the bridge on the mainland. Bus nos. 11, 15, 22, 28A, 30, 33, and 34 all go to Taipa Village.

COLÔANE

Farther away and connected to Taipa via a huge added strip of reclaimed land called COTAI, which has essentially made the two islands one, Colôane once served as a haven for pirates who preyed upon the rich trading ships passing by. The last pirate raid was as late as 1910, when bandits kidnapped 18 children and demanded ransom. Government forces eventually overpowered the pirates, freeing all the children. At any rate, Colôane today, measuring 7.8 sq. km (3 sq. miles) but with a population of only 4,000, is less developed than Taipa and is known for its beaches, pine trees, eight marked hiking trails, golf course, and traditional village. At its center, on Colôane Hill and visible from miles away, is a 20m (65-ft.) white marble statue of A-Ma. Two of the most popular **beaches** are Cheoc Van and Hac Sa (which means "black sand"). Both beaches have lifeguards on duty in the summer, restaurants, and nearby public swimming pools that are open until 10pm. To reach them, take bus no. 21A or 26A from Avenida de Almeida Ribeiro in the city center or from the Lisboa Hotel; bus no. 25 also runs from the Lisboa Hotel to both beaches. Bus no. 15 connects the beaches with Taipa Village.

Also on the coast is the laid-back, quaint community of **Colôane Village** ✿✿. Now that Taipa Village has suffered so much surrounding development, I find Colôane Village much more picturesque and a worthy destination if exploring the islands. Located on the southwestern tip of the island, it is so close to China that it almost seems like you can reach out and touch it. Boats headed to and from China pass through the narrow waterway. The social center of the village revolves around a small, tiled square, which is lined on two sides with cloistered cafes. In its center is a monument erected in 1928 to commemorate those who fought in the 1910 battle against the pirates. At its end is the small but sweet **Chapel of St. Francis Xavier,** built in 1928 and dedicated to Asia's most important and well-known Catholic missionary. The church, built in classic Portuguese style, would seem rather plain if it weren't for its exuberant Asian artwork. For a snack, head to **Lord Stow's Bakery,** Colôane Town Square (✆ **853/ 28882534**), serving what some contend are Macau's best Portuguese egg tarts, best when eaten fresh from the oven.

6 Gambling, Shopping & Nightlife

GAMBLING

The Chinese so love gambling that it's often said that if two flies are walking on the wall, the Chinese will bet on which one will walk faster. It's not surprising, therefore, that mainland and Hong Kong Chinese together with Taiwanese make up more than 90% of the 18 million annual visitors to Macau. Since the only legal gambling in Hong Kong is comprised of the horse races and mah-jongg, you can bet that most of the Chinese come to Macau to gamble, whether it's at the casinos or the tracks.

In 2002, a 40-year monopoly on gambling ended, paving the way to grander casinos and an upsurge in Las Vegas–style entertainment. All are open 24 hours. Some are fancy, others aren't, but none allow photographs to be taken, and shorts may not be worn. Admission is free, but some require you show a passport to enter.

Several hotels have casinos, including the **Mandarin Oriental, Holiday Inn,** and **Hotel Lisboa,** all of which offer blackjack, baccarat, roulette, Chinese games, and slot machines (known, appropriately enough, as "hungry tigers" in Chinese). After deregulation, several themed, Las Vegas–style casinos opened on Macau peninsula, including **Sands Macau,** a million-square-foot entertainment complex near the ferry terminal and Fisherman's Wharf (✆ **853/28883388;** www.sands.com.mo). The first foreign venture in Macau's gaming industry, Sands Macau boasts a 51-suite hotel, restaurants, spa, and Macau's largest casino floor, with more than 400 gaming tables and 921 slot machines—specifically designed for the Asian market. **Wynn Macau,** across from the Lisboa near the center of town on Avenida Da Amizade (© 853/ **28889966;** www.wynnmacau.com), has opened a 600-room hotel and casino as its first phase of development, with shops, restaurants, and other diversions slated to open in late 2007. **MGM Grand Macau,** also with a hotel and casino, will make its debut in late 2007.

But the biggest developments are taking shape on COTAI (the strip of reclaimed land between Taipa and Colôane), where the **Venetian Macao-Resort-Hotel** will open in mid-2007 with a 50,725-sq.-m (546,000-sq.-ft.) casino. It will serve as the anchor of seven resort hotels, meeting and convention space, shopping complexes, and more.

Otherwise, for a glimpse of gambling Chinese-style, it's fun to take a stroll through the ornately decorated **Macau Palace Floating Casino,** moored in the Outer Harbour not far from the Mandarin Oriental Hotel.

SHOPPING

A duty-free port, Macau has long been famous for its jewelry stores, especially those offering gold jewelry along Avenida Horta e Costa and Avenida de Almeida Ribeiro. Many Chinese consider buying gold as an investment. Market prices per tael (1.2 oz.) of gold are set daily. When buying gold or jewelry, always request a certificate of guarantee.

After gold, Portuguese wines are another good bargain, as are Chinese antiques and leather garments. In recent years, a number of fashionable clothing boutiques have also opened in the center of town, similar to what you'd find in Hong Kong. More colorful are the clothing stalls near Largo do Senado square, many of which sell overruns and seconds from Macau's many garment factories. You can also pick up Chinese jackets here cheaper than at markets in Hong Kong. Another colorful local shopping experience is the **Red Market,** located on the corner of Avenida Almirante Lacerda and Avenida Horta e Costa. Built in 1936 in Art Deco style, it houses a lively food market open daily from 7:30am to 7:30pm. A street market extends from the Red Market to Rotunda de Carlos Maia, a district popularly dubbed the Three Lamps District and a fun place to browse for cheap clothing. To reach the Red Market, take bus no. 1, 1A, 3, 4, 5, 8, 16, 17, 23, 25, 26, 26A, 32, 33, or 34 to Mercado Vermelho.

On the islands, there's a **weekly outdoor market** held Sundays from 11am to 8pm in Taipa Village, with booths selling traditional crafts, souvenirs, clothing, toys, and food. In Colôane Village, check out **Asian Artefacts,** 9 Rua dos Negociantes (© 853/ **28881022**), which sells restored antique furniture from North China, including trunks, chests, tables, chairs, and more, as well as handicrafts from Thailand, India, and other Asian countries. It's open from 10am to 7pm daily and can arrange shipping.

Macau, which didn't have one department store when I first visited in the 1980s, let alone boutiques or shopping malls, is on the verge of a shopping explosion, with most new developments tied to its gaming industry. The first large-scale addition to Macau's shopping and entertainment scene was **Fisherman's Wharf** (© 853/ **282993300;** www.fishermanswharf.com), which opened in 2004 just a few minutes' walk from the ferry terminal. It offers upscale shopping, as well as dining and entertainment. In mid-2007, the Venetian Macao-Resort-Hotel will open its **Grand Canal Shoppes** in COTAI, with 350 luxury shops and restaurants, the first of many retail complexes planned for this new destination.

NIGHTLIFE

For many years, Macau's only nighttime entertainment outside gambling centered on hotel bars and lounges. While these are still recommendable for a drink and live entertainment, one of the few benefits to have arisen from the otherwise hideously sterile reclaimed-land development on the Outer Harbour is **the Docks,** a string of sidewalk cafes and bars lining Avenida Dr. Sun Yat-sen near the Kun Iam Statue (some locals also refer to it as Lan Kwai Fong, after Hong Kong's famous nightlife district). It's a great place for a drink and watching the parade of people file past. True to Macau's Mediterranean roots, the action doesn't start until after 10pm and is at its most frenetic after 1am. For a suggestion, try **Moonwalker** (© 853/28751326), open daily from 4pm to 4am (to 5am Fri and Sat) and offering live music Wednesday through Monday nights from 10pm. A great place to watch the sun go down is **180 Lounge and Grill** in the Macau Tower (© 853/9888659), open daily from noon to 1am and with live music nightly 7:30 to 8:30 and 10 to 11pm.

Appendix:
Hong Kong in Depth

Although some people might erroneously believe that Hong Kong's history began after the British took control of the island in 1842, it actually began millennia before that. Stone, bronze, and iron artifacts indicate that Hong Kong Island has been inhabited for at least 6,000 years, and more than 100 Neolithic and Bronze Age sites have been identified throughout the territory, including a 5,000-year-old kiln unearthed on Lantau island, 4,000-year-old burial grounds, a 2,000-year-old brick tomb, and Neolithic rock carvings.

1 History 101

EARLY SETTLERS

Although the area now called Hong Kong became part of the Chinese empire some 2,200 years ago during the Han dynasty, it was not until after the 12th century that the area became widely settled. Foremost were settler families, known as the Five Great Clans, who built walled cities complete with moats and gatehouses to protect their homes against roving pirates; a few of these walled cities remain. First to arrive was the Tang clan, who built at least five walled villages and maintained imperial connections with Beijing for 800 years, until the end of the 19th century. The other four clans were the Hau, Pang, Liu, and Man. The clans were joined by the Tanka people, who lived their whole lives on boats anchored in sheltered bays throughout the territory, and by the Hoklos, another seafaring people who established coastal fishing villages. They were followed by the Hakka, primarily farmers who cultivated rice, pineapples, and tea. There were also garrison troops stationed at Tuen Mun and Tai Po (now major satellite towns in the New Territories) to guard pearls harvested from Tolo Harbour by Tanka divers, while forts to guard against invasion were constructed at Tung Chung and other coastal regions.

TEA & OPIUM

Hong Kong's modern history, however, begins a mere 160-some years ago, under conditions that were far less than honorable. During the 1800s, the British were extremely eager to obtain Chinese silk and tea. Tea had become the national drink, but the only place it was grown was China, from which it was being imported to England in huge quantities. The British tried to engage the Chinese in trade, but the Chinese were not interested in anything offered—only silver bullion would do. The Chinese also forbade the British to enter their kingdom, with the exception of a small trading depot in Canton.

But then the British hit upon a commodity that proved irresistible—opium. Grown in India and exported by the British East India Company, this powerful drug enslaved everyone from poor peasants to the nobility, and before long, China was being drained of silver, traded to support a drug habit. The Chinese emperor, fearful of the damage being wreaked on Chinese society and alarmed by his country's loss of silver, declared a ban on opium imports in the 1830s. The British simply ignored the ban, smuggling their illegal cargo up the Pearl River. In 1839, with opium now India's largest export, the Chinese confiscated the British opium stockpiles in Canton and destroyed them. The British responded by declaring war and then winning the struggle. As a result of this first Opium War, waged until 1842, China was forced to open new ports for trade, agree to an exorbitant cash indemnity for the loss of the destroyed opium, and cede Hong Kong Island in perpetuity to the British in a treaty China never recognized. Not only was this Treaty of Nanking demoralizing to the Chinese, it also ensured that their country would remain open to the curse of opium. And although opium was the cause of the war, it was never even mentioned in the Treaty of Nanking.

Following the second Opium War, waged from 1856 to 1858 as the British sought more trading ports and pushed for the legalization of the opium trade, the tip of Kowloon Peninsula and Stonecutters Island were added to the colony in 1860. In 1898, Britain decided it needed more land for defense and dictated a lease for the New Territories (where approximately 100,000 Chinese were living at the time), including more than 200 outlying islands, for 99 years, until 1997.

THE PROMISED LAND

When the British took control of Hong Kong Island in 1842, some 7,000 Chinese lived on the island in farming and fishing communities. Although Hong Kong had a deep and protected harbor, no one, including the Chinese, was much interested in the island itself, and many in the British government considered its acquisition an embarrassing mistake. No sooner had the island been settled than a typhoon tore through the settlement. Repairs were demolished only 5 days later by another tropical storm. Fever and fire followed, and the weather grew so oppressive and humid that the colony seemed to be enveloped in a giant steam bath.

Yet, while the number of headstones in the hillside cemetery multiplied, so did the number of the living, especially as word spread of the fortunes being made by traders who had established trading houses. By the turn of the 20th century, the number had swelled to 300,000. British families lived along the waterfront and called it Victoria (now the Central District), slowly moving up toward the cooler temperatures of Victoria Peak. The Chinese, barred from occupying The Peak and other European-only neighborhoods, resided in a shantytown farther west, now called the Western District. Conditions were so appalling that when the bubonic plague struck in 1894, it raged for almost 30 years, claiming more than 20,000 lives.

Hong Kong's growth in the 20th century was no less astonishing in terms of

Dateline

- **4,000–1,500 B.C.** Early settlers of Asian Mongoloid stock spread throughout South China, including Hong Kong, leaving behind Neolithic artifacts ranging from pottery and stone tools to burial grounds.
- **221 B.C.** Hong Kong becomes part of the Chinese empire with unification of China by the first emperor of Qin.

- **960–1500s** Pirates roam the seas around Hong Kong.
- **1514** Portuguese traders establish a base in southern China.
- **1839** The Chinese emperor attempts to abolish the opium trade and destroys the British opium stockpile; the Royal Navy retaliates by firing on Chinese war junks, starting the first Opium War.

- **1841** British naval Capt. Charles Elliot seizes Hong Kong Island and declares himself governor.
- **1842** The first Opium War ends in the Treaty of Nanking, ceding Hong Kong Island to Britain in perpetuity.
- **1846** Hong Kong's population is 24,000. First horse races held at Happy Valley.
- **1856** Chinese officials searching for pirates arrest

both trade and population. In 1900, approximately 11,000 ships pulled into Hong Kong harbor; just a decade later, the number had doubled. In 1911, the overthrow of the Manchu dynasty in China sent a flood of refugees into Hong Kong, followed, in 1938, by an additional 500,000 immigrants. Another mass influx of Chinese refugees arrived after the fall of Shanghai to the Communists in 1950. From this last wave of immigrants, including many Shanghai industrialists, emerged the beginnings of Hong Kong's now-famous textile industry. Throughout the 1950s, Hong Kong grew as a manufacturing and industrial center for electronics, watches, and other low-priced goods. By 1956, Hong Kong's population stood at 2.5 million.

CHANGE, UNREST & THE LAST OF THE BRITISH

As a British colony, Hong Kong was administered by a governor appointed by the queen. There were no free elections, and the Legislative Council, Hong Kong's main governing body, was also appointed. As 1997 drew nearer, marking the end of the 99-year lease on the New Territories, it soon became clear that China had no intention of renewing the lease or renegotiating a treaty it had never recognized in the first place.

Finally, after more than 20 rounds of talks and meetings, Britain's Prime Minister Margaret Thatcher signed the Sino-British Joint Declaration of 1984, agreeing to transfer all of Hong Kong to Chinese Communist rule on June 30, 1997. China declared Hong Kong a "Special Administrative Region," granting it special privileges under a "one country, two systems" policy that guaranteed Hong Kong's capitalist lifestyle and social system for at least 50 years after 1997. Under provisions set forth in the Sino-British Joint Declaration and in Hong Kong's constitution, the Basic Law, Hong Kong would remain largely self-governing, and its people would retain rights to their property, to freedom of speech, and to travel freely in and out of Hong Kong. Throughout the negotiations, however, Hong Kong's residents were never consulted.

Then came the events of June 1989 in Tiananmen Square, in which hundreds of students and demonstrators were attacked by Chinese authorities in a brutal move to quash the pro-democracy movement. China's response to the uprising sent shock waves through Hong Kong and led to rounds of angry protest.

Those who could emigrate did so, primarily to Australia, Canada, and the United States; at its height, more than 1,000 were emigrating each week. After all, nearly half of Hong Kong's Chinese

---

the crew of a British ship, prompting the second Opium War, which ends in 1858.

- **1857** A popular Chinese baker, Cheong Ah Lum, is accused of putting arsenic into his bread and poisoning nearly 300 Europeans in retaliation for the Opium Wars. He is acquitted but deported to China.

- **1860** Victorious in the second Opium War and seeking a foothold on the mainland, Britain forces China to cede Kowloon Peninsula and Stonecutters Island to the British in perpetuity in the First Convention of Peking. Population reaches 94,000.

- **1865** Hongkong and Shanghai Bank founded.

- **1888** The Victoria Peak tram is completed, reducing the journey to the peak from 3 hours to 8 minutes.

- **1898** With the signing of the Second Convention of Peking, the New Territories are leased to Britain for 99 years, for which Britain pays nothing.

- **1900** Hong Kong's population is 263,000.

- **1904** The street tramway system is constructed along the waterfront on Hong Kong Island.

continues

are refugees from the mainland, and as one Hong Kong Chinese told me, his family fled to escape Communist rule, so why should he stay after 1997? Approximately 90% of Hong Kong's Chinese, however, remained confident (or at least hopeful) that China realized it had more to gain by keeping Hong Kong as it was. In a move that angered Communist China, Hong Kong Chinese were granted more political autonomy during the last few years of the colony's existence than in all the preceding 150 years, including various democratic reforms such as elections for the Legislative Council. Some early emigrants began returning to Hong Kong, confident they could do better in their native country and willing to wait to see how life might change under the Chinese. In any case, now they had a safety net: foreign passports.

On June 30, 1997, the last British governor of Hong Kong, Chris Patten, sailed out of Hong Kong, and Tung Chee-hwa, appointed by Beijing, became the new chief executive of the Special Administrative Region (SAR). Mainland China celebrated the event as the end of more than 100 years of shame. On July 1, it dissolved Hong Kong's elected Legislative Council and replaced it with a handpicked Provisional Legislature until a new Legislative Council, with both elected and appointed members, could be formed.

THE DECADE AFTER THE HANDOVER

Hong Kong's first elections under Chinese rule, held in May 1998, allowed for one-third of the 60-member legislature to be elected by direct popular vote, with the Democrats—Hong Kong's largest party, led by the SAR's main opposition figure Martin Lee—winning the most seats (although full suffrage, with a fully elected legislature and chief executive, is declared a goal in the Basic Law, there is no timetable). Meanwhile, like the rest of Asia, Hong Kong was hit hard by economic recession, made worse by manufacturers moving across the Chinese border into Shenzhen to take advantage of cheaper land prices and cheaper wages. Approval ratings for Tung and other government officials plunged, especially after unemployment hit 4.5%, a 15-year high.

After the handover, the SAR began allowing 150 mainland Chinese to migrate to Hong Kong every day—more than 54,000 a year. In January 1999, Hong Kong's Court of Final Appeal ruled that the Basic Law also granted automatic Hong Kong residency to any mainland Chinese with one Hong Kong parent, even if that parent gained residency after the child was born. However, fearing unplanned population growth, with an estimated 1.6 million additional qualified immigrants potentially pouring in from

---

- **1910** The Kowloon Railway is completed, linking Hong Kong with China.
- **1911** The Manchu dynasty is overthrown by Sun Yat-sen's Nationalist revolution; refugees flood into Hong Kong.
- **1925** Hong Kong's first and only general strike; Nationalists and Communists join in a United Front, organizing anti-foreign strikes and boycotts in

China that spread to Hong Kong, paralyzing the economy.
- **1938** Japan seizes Canton; Hong Kong becomes an arms-smuggling route for the Nationalist forces, now under Chiang Kai-shek; 500,000 Chinese refugees flee into Hong Kong.
- **1941** Japanese forces occupy Hong Kong and begin deporting residents to the mainland to ease food and housing shortages.

- **1945** The British resume control of Hong Kong following World War II. Hong Kong's prewar population of 1.6 million now stands at 600,000.
- **1949** Mao declares the founding of the People's Republic; a subsequent flood of refugees to Hong Kong causes the Communist government to seal the Chinese–Hong Kong border.

the mainland, coupled with increased unemployment, Tung Chee-hwa asked Beijing to review the immigration ruling, a move interpreted by critics as a threat to the judicial independence of the SAR. China responded by overturning the immigration judgment issued by Hong Kong's highest court and providing a narrower interpretation of the Basic Law, thereby cutting the number of potential new immigrants over the next decade from 1.6 million to about 200,000. Only mainland children who were born *after* a parent received legal resident status were given a "right of abode." In January 2002, Hong Kong's Court of Final Appeal affirmed the Chinese government's reversal of its earlier ruling and ordered 7,300 "unlawful migrants" to leave the SAR by March 31. Only 3,000 complied; the remaining 4,300 were forcibly removed to the mainland by police.

But the biggest rift in Hong Kong–Beijing relations came in 2003, when an anti-subversion bill was introduced by Tung Chee-hwa's Beijing-backed administration. The measure, meant to outlaw subversion, sedition, treason, the theft of state secrets, and other crimes against the state, brought more than 500,000 protesters to Hong Kong's streets on July 1, 2003, making it the SAR's largest protest since the Tiananmen Square massacre. Opponents of the measure said it would erode political freedoms and curb free speech. Although Tung withdrew the bill, some critics contend he did so only after a key ally quit his Cabinet, leaving him with insufficient support to enact the law.

Another blow to Hong Kong democracy came in 2004, when Beijing ruled against a public election for Hong Kong's chief executive in 2007 and declared that there would be no universal suffrage for the Legislative Council election slated for 2008. Hong Kong's pro-democracy leaders responded that Hong Kong's autonomy had been violated, with the core principals of the Basic Law and the 1984 Sino-British Joint Declaration—that Hong Kong would be ruled by the people of Hong Kong—replaced by a Beijing dictatorship. In September 2004, elections for the 60-member Legislative Council allowed an increase in the number of elected members from 24 to 30.

But the biggest news to garner international attention was not Hong Kong's struggle for autonomy, but rather its role in the eruption of a mysterious, flu-like illness in the spring of 2003. Spreading from a Hong Kong hotel, severe acute respiratory syndrome (SARS) infected more than 8,000 people in 29 countries over the next few months, killing more than 700 of them. In Hong Kong, which together with China suffered the most, the illness sickened 1,775 people and

---

- **1950** Mass influx of refugees continues following the fall of Shanghai to the Communists. Population of Hong Kong reaches 2 million.
- **1953** Following a huge fire in a squatter camp, Hong Kong begins an ambitious public housing program to house its still-growing population of refugees.
- **1966** A fare increase on the Star Ferry prompts clashes

between Chinese and the police.
- **1967** The Cultural Revolution in China leads to pro-Communist riots in Hong Kong; 51 people are killed, and hundreds more are wounded or arrested in the fighting.
- **1972** First cross-harbor tunnel opens.
- **1979** Establishment of Hong Kong's Mass Transit Railway subway system. Hong Kong governor Sir Murray

MacLehose goes to Beijing for the first Sino-British discussions on the return of Hong Kong to Chinese rule.
- **1981** British Parliament downgrades Hong Kong passports to prevent an exodus of Hong Kong Chinese to the United Kingdom.
- **1984** China and Britain sign the Joint Declaration for the handover of Hong Kong to China in 1997.

continues

claimed almost 300 lives. Needless to say, SARS was a major blow to Hong Kong's economy, reducing the city to a tourist ghost town and costing the city $4 to $6 billion in retail trade and business. Unemployment hit 8.7%, the highest since the statistic was first recorded in 1981. To encourage tourism and boost the local economy, Hong Kong turned to action film star Jackie Chan as its international spokesperson.

In March 2005, Tung Chee-hwa, Hong Kong's only leader since the handover, unexpectedly announced his resignation, citing ill health and igniting rumors that Beijing had forced his exit in an effort to curb Hong Kong's growing discontent and resultant push for greater democracy. Donald Tsang, a career civil servant educated at Harvard, was chosen to finish out Tung's remaining 2 years of office. Backed by Beijing and enjoying growing popularity in Hong Kong, Tsang seems the likely winner in June 2007 when the 800-member Election Committee chooses the next chief executive for a 5-year term.

2 Hong Kong Today

Ever since the 1997 handover, foremost in almost every visitor's mind today is, "How much has Hong Kong changed?" To the casual observer, not much. In fact, if it hadn't dominated the news, I doubt the average tourist would even notice there'd *been* a handover. Entry formalities for most nationalities remain unchanged. English remains an official language, and the Hong Kong dollar, pegged to the U.S. dollar, remains legal tender. Scores of lanes, roads, and sites are still named after Hong Kong's former governors, Queen Victoria's statue still graces Victoria Park, and barristers and judges still don off-white wigs and gowns. In most hotels, restaurants, and shops that cater to tourists, it's business as usual.

There are, however, discernable differences. Most visible was the replacement of the Union Jack and colonial Hong Kong flag with China's starred flag and the new Hong Kong Special Administrative Region's flag emblazoned with the bauhinia flower. In addition, new coins bearing the bauhinia were minted (the old coins with the queen's head remain valid but are being snapped up by collectors) and new stamps were issued. The words "Royal" and "ER" (Elizabeth Regina) disappeared throughout Hong Kong, along with royal crests, crowns, and coats of arms. The police sport new badges.

Of course, the British population also noticeably declined after the handover

- **1989** Events at Tiananmen Square in Beijing send shock waves through Hong Kong. Some 80,000 demonstrators brave a typhoon in support of the pro-democracy uprising.
- **1992** Hong Kong governor Chris Patten announces new democratic reforms.
- **1995** Elections for the Legislative Council brings landslide victory for the Democrats; China announces

it will dissolve the legislature after the handover.
- **1997** Britain transfers Hong Kong to Communist China, ending 156 years of British rule, in an agreement that allows Hong Kong—now a Special Administrative Region (SAR)—to retain many of its freedoms for at least 50 years. Four thousand Chinese troops march in; Tung Chee-hwa becomes chief executive of the SAR. Hong Kong's first

outbreak of avian flu at the end of the year, killing six people, prompts the new government to order the slaughter of 1.3 million chickens.
- **1998** Hong Kong's first election under Chinese rule allows for one-third of the Legislative Council to be elected by popular vote; Democrats win the most seats. Hong Kong's new airport at Chep Lak Kok opens.

(dropping from more than 20,000 in 1998 to less than 14,000 by 2005), due primarily to the completion of large construction projects such as the new airport, the departure of the British military, and stricter regulations making it more difficult for casual workers to remain in the SAR. Although the number of U.K. residents was never huge (less than 2% before the handover), British presence loomed understandably larger when Hong Kong was a colony. Today the SAR seems increasingly more Chinese, with more in common with Shenzhen across the Chinese border than with its former colonizer. Of course, Hong Kong has more links now—financially and emotionally—with mainland China than it ever had in the past. Tourists from Europe, North America, and Japan are now outnumbered by visitors from mainland China, especially since the 2003 introduction of relaxed travel laws that exempted mainland Chinese of certain geographic areas (mostly wealthy areas like Shanghai, Beijing, and so on) from the requirement that they visit Hong Kong only in tour groups, thereby allowing them to travel to Hong Kong on their own. Today, mainland Chinese make up more than half of all visitor arrivals into Hong Kong.

Naturally, another question that looms large in the minds of visitors to Hong Kong is, "What about SARS and avian flu?" While no one can be certain that new outbreaks will never happen, Hong Kong is ready. The temperatures of all passengers passing through border controls—at the Hong Kong airport, the border checkpoint between Hong Kong and mainland China, and ferry terminals serving Macau and beyond—are thermally scanned for fever, and there are hand sanitizers throughout Hong Kong.

Perhaps most striking about Hong Kong since the handover is that it suffers from an identity crisis: What should be its role in a greater China? Long serving as the manufacturing liaison between China and the rest of the world, Hong Kong is now challenged by a dazzling, dynamic, confident Shanghai. Hong Kong manufacturers have moved across the border to Shenzhen to take advantage of lower production costs. Guangzhou threatens to take over Hong Kong's role as a transportation hub. Pollution, primarily from rapid industrial development in the Pearl River Delta, has reached an all-time high, threatening not only the health of its citizens but its status as a major tourist destination. All these issues—worsening pollution, the high cost of living in Hong Kong compared to China, and a growing tendency for foreign companies to base their workers on the mainland—have even led to a decline

- **1999** Hong Kong's Court of Final Appeal rules that according to its constitution, Hong Kong residency can be extended to any mainland Chinese with one Hong Kong parent; Tung Chee-hwa invites Beijing to review the immigration ruling, which is subsequently overturned.
- **2002** Hong Kong's highest court affirms the mainland's 1999 reversal of its earlier

ruling on migrants and orders 7,300 "unlawful migrants" back to the mainland. Only 3,000 comply, with the rest of the "abode seekers" forcibly removed, causing great public outcry.
- **2003** An outbreak in Hong Kong of severe acute respiratory syndrome (SARS) spreads around the globe, infecting more than 8,000 people and delivering a

shocking blow to Hong Kong's economy.
- **2005** Tung Chee-hwa resigns; Donald Tsang, educated at Harvard, is appointed to fill Tung's remaining 2 years in office as chief executive.

of foreign professionals living in Hong Kong, with 14% fewer Americans, Canadians, Britons, and Australians living in Hong Kong in 2005 compared to the year before.

But if you ask me, Hong Kong seems poised for a tourism renaissance, due in no small part to increased tourism from the mainland. Many new attractions have opened in the past couple years, and, for the first time in a decade, new first-class hotels have opened in the Central District. New restaurants are blossoming all over the city, and the nightlife scene has never been more robust. Many hotels, particularly those offering reasonable rates, are often full, due largely to individual tourism from the mainland and Hong Kong's reputation as a convention destination. The economy is on a rebound, and it seems increasingly clear that Hong Kong's future lies as a financial center, not as a low-cost manufacturing base it enjoyed in the past.

Still, no one can predict the future, as Hong Kong has always been a city in transformation. The Hong Kong I am writing about now is not the same city that existed just a few short years ago and is not the Hong Kong you'll probably experience when you go there. Changes occur at a dizzying pace here: Relatively new buildings are torn down to make way for even newer, shinier skyscrapers; whole neighborhoods are obliterated in the name of progress; reclaimed land is taken from an ever-shrinking harbor; and traditional villages are replaced with satellite towns. Hong Kong's city skyline has surged upward and outward so dramatically since my first visit in 1983, it sometimes seems like decades rather than a year must have elapsed each time I see it anew. Change is commonplace, and yet it's hard not to lament the loss of familiar things that suddenly vanish; it's harder still not to brood over what's likely to come.

But don't worry. If this is your first trip to Hong Kong, you're much more likely to notice its Chinese aspects than its Westernized appearance. Ducks hanging by their necks in restaurant windows, bamboo scaffolding, herbal-medicine shops, street-side markets, Chinese characters on huge neon signs, wooden fishing boats, shrines to the kitchen god, fortunetellers, temples, laundry fluttering from bamboo poles, dim sum trolleys, and the clicking of mah-jongg tiles all conspire to create an atmosphere that is overwhelmingly Chinese.

In short, Hong Kong is a place like no other, with an energy and irresistible draw that will surely captivate travelers for generations to come.

3 Life in Hong Kong

THE PEOPLE

With a population of approximately 6.8 million, Hong Kong is overwhelmingly Chinese—some 95% of its residents are Chinese, more than half of whom were born in Hong Kong. But the Chinese themselves are a diverse people and they hail from different parts of China. Most are Cantonese from southern China, the area just beyond Hong Kong's border—hence, Cantonese is the most widely spoken language of the region. Other Chinese include the Hakka, traditionally farmers whose women are easily recognizable by their hats with a black fringe, and the Tanka, the majority of Hong Kong's shrinking boat population. Hong Kong's many Chinese restaurants specializing in Cantonese, Sichuan, Chiu Chow, Pekingese, Shanghainese, and other regional foods are testaments of the city's diversity.

Since the handover, Hong Kong's newest arrivals are again from mainland China. Many Hong Kong Chinese look down on these newcomers as provincial, rude, and uneducated, and indeed, many of them now occupy the lowest rung on the economic ladder, accepting squalid living conditions in hopes of forging a better life, just as other Hong Kong Chinese did before them. There are also many young mainland Chinese wives in Hong Kong, since eligible Hong Kong bachelors often return to their parents' or ancestors' homeland in China in search of a bride. "Hong Kong girls are considered too materialistic," one Hong Kong resident told me, "and mainland Chinese will work harder." And, for those in mainland China, Hong Kong has long been the promised land.

Hong Kong, with a total land area of approximately 1,100 sq. km (425 sq. miles; about half the size of Rhode Island), is one of the most densely populated areas in the world. The best place to appreciate this is atop Victoria Peak, where you can feast your eyes on Hong Kong's famous harbor, and as far as the eye can see, mile upon mile of high-rise apartments. If Hong Kong were a vast plain, it would be as ugly as Tokyo. But it's saved by undulating mountain peaks, which cover virtually all of Hong Kong and provide dramatic background to the cityscape and coastal areas. Because of its dense population and limited land space, with more than 16,000 people per square mile, Hong Kong has long been saddled with acute housing deficiencies. Just a few decades ago, in an area called Mong Kok in northwestern Kowloon, there were an astounding 652,910 people per square mile. One house designed for 12 people had 459 living in it, including 104 people who shared one room and four people who lived on the roof.

After 1953, when a huge fire left more than 50,000 squatters homeless, Hong Kong pursued one of the world's most ambitious housing projects, with the aim of providing every Hong Kong family with a home of its own. By 1993, half of Hong Kong's population lived in government-subsidized public housing, a higher proportion than anywhere else in the world (today, that number stands at about 30%, as new housing is constructed by the private sector).

Most public housing is clustered in the New Territories, in a forest of high-rises that leaves foreign visitors aghast. Each apartment building is approximately 30 stories tall, containing about 1,000 apartments and 3,000 to 4,000 residents. Seven or eight apartment buildings comprise an estate, which is like a small town with its own name, shopping center, recreational and sports facilities, playgrounds, schools, and social services. A typical apartment is indescribably small by Western standards—approximately 250 square feet, with a single window. It consists of a combination living room/bedroom, a kitchen nook, and bathroom, and is typically shared by a couple with one or two children. According to government figures, every household in Hong Kong has at least one TV; many have one for each member of the household, even if the house consists of only one or two rooms. But as cramped, unimaginative, and sterile as these housing projects may seem, they're a vast improvement over the way much of the population used to live.

ARCHITECTURE

If you never ventured much beyond the waterfronts of Victoria Harbour, you might easily believe that Hong Kong is nothing more than chrome-and-glass skyscrapers, huge housing projects, shopping malls, and miles of glowing neon signs heralding countless open-fronted shops.

But Hong Kong was inhabited long before the British arrived, and some precolonial Chinese architecture still survives in the hinterlands. Several rural villages boast buildings and temples with fine woodcarving, and are examples of centuries-old Chinese craftsmanship. Especially fascinating are the walled villages in

Tips for the Business Traveler to Hong Kong

- **Bring plenty of business cards.** They are exchanged constantly, and you'll be highly suspect without them (if you run out, hotel business centers can arrange to have new ones printed within 24 hr.). When presenting your card, hold it out with both hands, turned so that the receiver can read it. Chinese names are written with the family name first, followed by the given name and then the middle name.
- **Use formal names for addressing business associates** unless told to do otherwise; you'll find that many Hong Kong Chinese used to dealing with foreigners have adopted a Western first name.
- **Shaking hands is appropriate** for greetings and introductions.
- **Business attire**—a suit and tie for men; blazers/jackets and skirts for women—is worn throughout the year, even in summer (though women can get away with just blouses in the summer).
- **Avoid the Chinese New Year,** as all of Hong Kong shuts down for at least 3 days; based on the lunar calendar, it falls between late January and mid-February.
- **Entertainment** is an integral part of conducting business in Hong Kong, whether it's a meal in which the host orders the food and serves his or her guests, an evening at the racetracks, or a round of golf.
- If an invitation is extended, it is understood that **the host will treat.** Do not insist on paying; this will only embarrass your host. Accept graciously, and promise to pick up the tab next time around.

the New Territories, a few of which are still inhabited, and one of which has been meticulously restored and turned into a museum of traditional lifestyles (see chapter 11). These villages were built from the 14th through the 17th centuries by clan families to protect themselves from roving bandits, invaders, and even wild tigers. A few of the clans' ancestral halls, homes, and mansions also survive. Also surviving are some of Hong Kong's temples, most famous of which is Man Mo, built in the 1840s and dedicated to the gods of literature and war (p. 171).

Some colonial architecture also remains. One of Hong Kong's most familiar landmarks is the clock tower next to the Star Ferry terminus at Tsim Sha Tsui; it is all that remains of the old railway station that once linked the colony with China and beyond. On the Hong Kong Island side, the former Supreme Court in Central features Greco-Victorian columns and Chinese wood beam eaves. Today it houses the Legislative Council chamber. Nearby, in Hong Kong Park, is the Flagstaff House, Hong Kong's oldest surviving colonial-style building and now home to a museum of tea ware (p. 168).

Construction in Hong Kong has been going on at such a frenzied pace that if you haven't been here in 20 years (or even 10), you probably won't recognize the skylines on both sides of the harbor. Among the most dramatic buildings are the extension of the Hong Kong Convention and Exhibition Centre on reclaimed land on the Wan Chai waterfront, boasting the world's largest plate-glass window and a three-tiered roof said to resemble a gull's wings in flight; the 78-story Central Plaza, located near the Wan Chai waterfront and boasting an Art Deco style with eye-catching nighttime lighting that changes color with each quarter-hour, thereby giving the time; and the Hongkong and Shanghai Bank, designed by British architect Norman Foster and featuring entire floors suspended from steel masts and a 48m-tall (160-ft.) sun scoop on the roof that uses 480 mirrors to reflect sunlight down into the bank's atrium and public plaza. Atop Victoria Peak is the Peak Tower, topped by a crescent-shaped bowl not unlike a wok. But Hong Kong's tallest building is the Two IFC (International Finance Centre) tower, standing 420m (1,378 ft.) high beside Hong Kong Station and the fourth-tallest building in the world.

Even though Hong Kong's structures are Western, they were built using bamboo scaffolding and constructed according to ancient Chinese beliefs, especially the 3,000-year-old Taoist principle of feng shui that allows humankind to live in peace with the environment and nature, ensuring good luck, prosperity, wealth, health, and happiness. Even today, most office and apartment buildings in Hong Kong have been laid out in accordance to feng shui principles (see the "Feng Shui: Restoring a Balance with Nature" box below).

CULTURAL LIFE

If you want to see Hong Kong's Chinese cultural life, simply step outside. Much of Hong Kong's drama is played in its streets, whether it's amateur Chinese opera singers at the famous Temple Street Night Market or a fortuneteller who has set up a chair and table at the side of the road or a Taoist temple. Virtually everything the Chinese consider vital still thrives in Hong Kong, including ancient religious beliefs, superstitions, wedding customs, and festivals.

The first sign that Hong Kong's cultural life is not confined to its stages and concert halls can be observed if you get up early and stroll through a city park,

where you'll see people practicing tai chi, which looks like dance in slow motion. Originally a martial art developed about 1,000 years ago, tai chi today is a form of exercise that restores harmony in the body through 200 individual movements designed to use every muscle in the body. Good places to observe the art include Kowloon Park in Tsim Sha Tsui as well as Victoria Park, Hong Kong Park, and the Zoological and Botanical Gardens on Hong Kong Island. If you wish, you can even partake in a free tai chi session held 4 mornings a week on the Tsim Sha Tsui waterfront (p. 181).

Hong Kong's many festivals are the most obvious expression of cultural life, most of which feature parades, dances, and observances of local customs. Lion dances, for example, may be performed to the accompaniment of drums, while in the evenings, there may be puppet shows or Chinese opera performances.

Of the various Chinese performing arts, Chinese opera is the most popular and widely loved. Dating back to the Mongol period, it has always appealed to both the ruling class and the masses. Virtue, corruption, violence, and lust are common themes, and performances feature elaborate costumes and makeup, haunting atonal orchestrations, and crashing cymbals. The actor-singers train for many years. The costumes signify specific stage personalities; yellow is reserved for emperors, while purple is the color worn by barbarians. Unlike Western performances, Chinese operas are noisy affairs, with families coming and going during long performances, chatting with friends, and eating.

In Hong Kong, you can also attend concerts of Western classical music, jazz, and pop, and performances of ballet, modern dance, and theater (see chapter 10).

CHINESE MEDICINE

For most minor ailments, many Chinese are more likely to pay a visit to their neighborhood medicine store than see a doctor. Most traditional medicine stores cater solely to the practice of Chinese herbal medicine, with some cures dating back 2,000 years. The medicinal stock, however, includes much more than roots and plants—take a look inside one of Hong Kong's many medicinal shops and you'll find a bewildering array of jars and drawers containing everything from ginseng and deer's horn to fossilized bones and animal teeth. Deer's horn is said to be effective against fever; bones, teeth, and seashells are used as tranquilizers and cures for insomnia. In prescribing treatment, herbalists take into account the patient's overall mental and physical well-being in the belief that disease and illness are caused by an imbalance in bodily forces. In contrast to Western medicine, treatment is often preventive rather than remedial. Visitors particularly interested in traditional Chinese medicine will want to visit the Hong Kong Museum of Medical Sciences (p. 170).

Acupuncture is also alive and well in Hong Kong, with approximately 400 acupuncturists offering their services. With a history that goes back 4,000 years, acupuncture is based on 365 pressure points, which in turn act upon certain organs; slender, stainless-steel needles are used, which vary in length from 1.3 to 25 centimeters (½–10 in.). Most acupuncturists also use moxa (dried mugwort), a slow-burning herb that applies gentle heat.

RELIGION, MYTH & FOLKLORE

Most Hong Kong Chinese worship both Buddhist and Taoist deities, something they do not find at all incongruous. They also worship their family ancestors. There are ancestral altars in homes, and certain days are set aside for visiting ancestral graves. Many temples have large tablet halls, where Hong Kong families can worship the memorialized photographs of their dead. There are about 360 temples scattered throughout Hong Kong; some embody a mixture of both Buddhist and Taoist principles.

While Buddhism is concerned with the afterlife, Taoism is a folk faith whose devotees believe in luck and in currying its favor. Fortunetellers, therefore, are usually found only at Taoist temples. Tao, essentially, is the way of the universe, the spirit of all things, and cannot be perceived. However, Taoist gods must be worshipped and Taoist spirits appeased. Most popular is Tin Hau, goddess of the sea and protectress of fishermen. Hong Kong has at least 24 temples that were erected in her honor. But each profession or trade has its own god—ironically, policemen and gangsters have the same one.

If you look for them, you'll find shrines dedicated to the earth god, Tou Ti, at the entrance to almost every store or restaurant in Hong Kong. They're usually below knee level, so that everyone pays homage upon entering and departing. Restaurants also have shrines dedicated to the kitchen god, Kwan Kung, to protect workers from knives and other sharp objects.

Although not a religion as such, another guiding principle in Chinese thought is Confucianism. Confucius, who lived in the 5th century B.C., devised a strict set of rules designed to create the perfect human being. Kindness, selflessness, obedience, and courtesy were preached, with carefully prescribed rules of how people should interact with one another. Since the masses were largely illiterate, Confucius communicated by means of easy-to-remember proverbs.

But despite the fact that many Hong Kong Chinese are both Buddhist and Taoist, they are not a particularly religious people in the Western sense of the word. There is no special day for worship, so devotees simply visit a temple whenever they want to pay their respects or feel the need for spiritual guidance. Otherwise, religion in Hong Kong plays a subtle role and is evident more in philosophy and action than in pious ceremony. To the

Feng Shui: Restoring a Balance with Nature

Feng shui, which translates literally as "wind water," is an ancient method of divination in which harmony is achieved with the spirits of nature. Virtually every Hong Kong Chinese believes that before a house or building can be erected, a tree chopped down, or a boulder moved, a geomancer must be called in to make certain that the spirits inhabiting the place aren't disturbed. The geomancer, who uses a compasslike device as an aid, determines the alignment of walls, doors, desks, and even beds, so as not to provoke the anger of the spirits residing there. He does this by achieving a balance among the eight elements of nature—heaven, earth, hills, wind, fire, thunder, rain, and ocean. Also considered are the spirits of yin (male-active) and yang (female-passive) forces that control our world.

Even non-Chinese-owned companies in Hong Kong comply with feng shui principles, if only to appease their Chinese employees. But it doesn't hurt to be safe; tales abound of ill luck befalling those working or living inside buildings that ignored the needs of resident spirits.

Since facing the water is considered excellent feng shui, when the Regent Hotel (now the InterContinental) was constructed, it incorporated a huge glass window overlooking the harbor. The next best thing, if you can't look out over water, is to bring the water inside, which is why many offices, shops, and restaurants have aquariums. Another way to deflect evil influences is to hang a small, eight-sided mirror outside your window. Other Chinese touches are incorporated into modern architecture—the Hongkong and Shanghai Bank, for example, is guarded by a pair of bronze lions, protecting its occupants.

If you wish to learn more about the principles of feng shui, see whether a lecture is being offered through the HKTB's Meet the People program (see chapter 7 for more details). Also note that feng shui, the transliteration used by the HKTB, is also transliterated as *fung shui.*

Chinese, religion is a way of life and thus affects everyday living.

Almost every home has a small shrine, where lighted joss sticks are thought to bring good luck. In New Year celebrations, door gods are placed on the front door for good luck, and all lights are switched on to discourage monster spirits. On New Year's Day, homes are not swept for fear of whisking away good luck. And during a full moon or major festival, housewives will often set fire to paper creations of homes, cars, or fake money to bring good luck.

But since no one can ever have too much good luck, superstitions abound in Hong Kong. Certain numbers, for example, have connotations. The most auspicious number is 8, because its pronunciation *(baht)* is similar to the word for wealth *(faht).* Likewise, the most inauspicious number is 4, since it sounds almost exactly like the Chinese word for death. Thirteen is also an unlucky number, so many Hong Kong buildings simply skip it in their floor-numbering scheme.

To be on the safe side, Hong Kong Chinese will also visit fortunetellers. Some read palms, while others study facial features, consult astrological birth charts, or let a little bird select a fortune card from a deck.

Index

See also Accommodations and Restaurant indexes, below.

THE NEW TRAVELOCITY GUARANTEE

EVERYTHING YOU BOOK WILL BE RIGHT, OR WE'LL WORK WITH OUR TRAVEL PARTNERS TO MAKE IT RIGHT, RIGHT AWAY.

*To drive home the point,
we're going to use the word "right" in every single sentence.*

Let's get right to it. Right to the meat! Only Travelocity guarantees everything about your booking will be right, or we'll work with our travel partners to make it right, right away. Right on!

Here's a picture taken smack dab right in the middle of Antigua, where the guarantee also covers you.

The guarantee covers all but one of the items pictured to the right.

For example, what if the ocean view you booked actually looks out at a downright ugly parking lot? You'd be right to call – we're there for you. And no one in their right mind would be pleased to learn the rental car place has closed and left them stranded. Call Travelocity and we'll help get you back on the right track.

Now, you may be thinking, "Yeah, right, I'm so sure." That's OK; you have the right to remain skeptical. That is until we mention help is always right around the corner. Call us right off the bat, knowing that our customer service reps are there for you 24/7. Righting wrongs. Left and right.

Now if you're guessing there are some things we can't control, like the weather, well you're right. But we can help you with most things – to get all the details in righting,* visit **travelocity.com/guarantee**.

*Sorry, spelling things right is one of the few things not covered under the guarantee.

I'd give my right arm for a guarantee like this, although I'm glad I don't have to.

travelocity
You'll never roam alone.